Vietnamese Tradition on Trial, 1920–1945

DAVID G. MARR

Vietnamese Tradition on Trial, 1920–1945

UNIVERSITY OF CALIFORNIA PRESS

Berkeley · Los Angeles · London

To my mother, father,
and grandmother

University of California Press
Berkeley and Los Angeles, California
University of California Press, Ltd.
London, England
© 1981 by
The Regents of the University of California
Printed in the United States of America

1   2   3   4   5   6   7   8   9

Library of Congress Cataloging in Publication Data

Marr, David G
  Vietnamese tradition on trial, 1920–1945.
  Bibliography: p.
  Includes index.
  1. Vietnamese—Intellectual life. 2. Intellectuals—
Vietnam. 3. Nationalism—Vietnam. 4. Vietnam—History
—1858–1945. I. Title.
DS556.8.M37   959.7′03   80-15802
ISBN 0-520-04180-1

CONTENTS

ABBREVIATIONS

AFIMA Association pour la Formation Intellectuel et Morale des Annamites

AOM Archives Nationales de France, Section Outre-Mer (Paris and Aix-en-Provence)

BEFEO *Bulletin de l'Ecole Française de l'Extrême Orient* (Hanoi)

BN Bibliothèque Nationale

CCP Chinese Communist Party

CMCD *Cach Mang Can Dai Viet-Nam*

DIRIP Direction de l'Instruction Publique

FLPH Foreign Languages Publishing House (Hanoi)

HT *Hop Tuyen Tho Van Viet-Nam*

ICP Indochinese Communist Party

INDOCHIN. Fonds Indochinois de la Bibliothèque Nationale (Paris)

LT *Luoc Truyen Cac Tac Gia Viet-Nam*

NCLS *Nghien Cuu Lich Su*

NF Noveau Fond

NP *Nam Phong Tap Chi*

PNTV *Phu Nu Tan Van*

SEAP Southeast Asia Program (Cornell University)

SLOTFOM Service de liaison avec les originaires des territoires de la France d'outre-mer

SPT *Su Phat Trien cua Tu Tuong o Viet-Nam tu The Ky XIX den Cach Mang Thang Tam*

TCVH *Tap Chi Van Hoc*

TCVT *Thuong Chi Van Tap*

PREFACE

As a U.S. Marine Corps intelligence officer in Vietnam in 1962–1963 I could not help but be struck by the ability of the National Liberation Front (more properly the National Front for the Liberation of South Vietnam) to conduct complex political and military operations amidst some of the most difficult conditions imaginable. Although scattered in a hundred different locations, hounded from air, sea, and ground, seemingly short on everything except tenacity, the NLF managed to avoid being fragmented and destroyed piecemeal. Moreover, by 1963 it was clear that the NLF was reaching the point where it could directly challenge and perhaps overcome the U.S.-supported regime headquartered in Saigon.

My attention was caught by one piece in this intelligence puzzle. We knew that the NLF had an extremely primitive communications system, yet we also observed that even the lowest units in the organization generally understood what was expected of them and tried to act accordingly. Then, too, there were times when all the NLF leaders in a specific village or district were killed, captured, or forced to flee to another area, yet 'anti-government' activity did not cease entirely. Indeed, after a period of several months or a year, such activity had a tendency to build up again. Links were reestablished with higher NLF echelons and the U.S.–Saigon apparatus was in a worse situation than before.

There were other times when I noticed that two NLF unit leaders miles from each other, facing identical new situations that could not await guidance from above, tended to react in essentially the same manner. They did not always make the right choice, but apparently they did share some vision, some approach to reality that was not dependent in the first instance on organizational hierarchy. Among other things, this suggested that those counter-insurgency specialists who planned to beat the NLF by pursuing a 'leopard-spot' strategy, i.e., isolating areas and attempting to promote contradictions within the enemy ranks, were doomed to fail. The NLF might still lose, but not because of a U.S.–Saigon policy of divide and rule.

In short, I began to suspect that there was enough ideological consensus among NLF members to enable local cadres to function for weeks or even months without specific orders from higher echelons. Moreover, when the local leadership was eliminated as the result of U.S.–Saigon actions, there often remained enough accord among followers to renew the movement in a fairly short period of time.

I left the Marine Corps in 1964 but remained interested in this question of ideology. How to proceed? I ruled out political science as an appropriate methodology within a year of starting graduate studies at the University of California, Berkeley. It was ridiculous to suppose, for example, that I could go into a Vietnamese village and conduct accurate surveys. Nor did I wish to get involved in interviewing prisoners. I tried content analysis, perusing current NLF and North Vietnamese leaflets, newspapers and pamphlets, but decided that the technique was superficial and that the sources were opaque on a number of key problems. In 1965 I interviewed a number of South Vietnamese urban intellectuals, but was surprised to discover how little they knew about modern Vietnamese anticolonialism or the development of Vietnamese communism.

So far as I could judge, that left history as the only alternative. There was no particular hurry in this quest, for after 1966 I no longer thought of Vietnamese communists as enemies to be outfoxed and overcome. Indeed, while conducting Ph.D. research in South Vietnam in 1967, I became convinced that the communists were going to win, largely because they were heirs to a strong national and anticolonial tradition. In 1971 I published *Vietnamese Anticolonialism, 1885–1925* (University of California Press). At that juncture, instead of writing a sequel, it seemed more meaningful to pool whatever knowledge I had acquired with others of like mind to try to convince fellow Americans that our actions in Southeast Asia were both disastrous and inhumane. To that end we founded the Indochina Resource Center. Although we could never expect to rival the huge information apparatus of the U.S. Executive branch, our endeavors were not without the occasional success. The last American ambassador to Saigon even gave the Indochina Research Center backhanded credit for 'losing' Vietnam. In all fairness, history should record that in 1975 it was the Vietnam People's Army—now possessing a sophisticated command and communications system—that settled the issue.

Coming to the Australian National University in 1975, I planned initially to research and write a second volume on Vietnamese anticolonialism. However, that idea was altered when I discovered how rich and varied were the original sources for the period 1920–1945. Almost 10,000 titles in Vietnamese had been deposited in the Bibliothèque Nationale (Paris) alone. Several hundred serials in Vietnamese and French were available at Versailles or could be ordered on microfilm. At least eighty individuals had published memoirs on their political, military and cultural activities up to the August 1945 Revolution. The Archives d'Outre-Mer (Paris and Aix-en-Provence) contained some clandestine Vietnamese publications, and others had been reprinted by scholarly journals in Hanoi. Although it was obviously not possible to read all these materials, I felt that none could be dismissed in advance as irrelevant.

What emerged most vividly from the original sources was the mood of experimentation, the profusion of exciting ideas, the informal interactions, the sharp disappointments, the painful reappraisals, and the eventual division of the intelligentsia along lines familiar to any student of later decades in Vietnam. While it might still be desirable for other scholars to draw up balance sheets as between colonialists and anticolonialists, nationalists and communists, traditionalists and modernists, it seemed to me more challenging and fruitful to try to convey this general intellectual milieu, this veritable explosion of curiosity and discourse followed by more focused testing and implementation.

The resulting book consists essentially of eight topical chapters, none of which was preordained when I began exploring the original sources. Admittedly, on the basis of my research into the previous generation of Vietnamese scholar-gentry, I was not too surprised to see that this generation of intellectuals continued to be concerned with the relation between ethics and politics, with the meaning of the past, and with problems of social harmony and social struggle. I also had a strong hunch that the problem of how to relate theory to practice, and vice versa, would be crucial to those intellectuals who by choice or circumstance became part of organized political movements. On the other hand, I was unprepared for the profusion of texts and articles on moral education. Nor had I realized the extent of discussion on language reform. And the intensity of the debate over the changing roles of Vietnamese women caught me quite unprepared.

At least three other topics were seen to be significant, but unfortunately not capable of detailed description or analysis in this book. Popular fiction exerted considerable influence in Vietnam during this period. However, after reading several score novels and short stories among the thousands available, I came to the conclusion that the study of fiction had methodological complications for which I was poorly prepared. The same could be said of religion and religious writings, except that here the problem was not so much methodological as one of mastering the highly specialized terminology. Finally, there was the important question of Vietnamese popular culture, both from the perspective of writers of the period 1920–1945, and as reflected in surviving oral literature. After some hesitation I chose to defer this subject to a planned third volume, dealing with Vietnamese peasant attitudes, Viet Minh mass mobilization campaigns, and the practice of people's war after 1945. Hopefully that book will suggest answers to two questions lingering at the end of this current endeavour: to what extent did elite concepts reach and motivate the Vietnamese peasantry; and to what degree were leaders forced to make certain accommodations with traditional mass attitudes in the interests of building an effective political and military movement?

Having identified eight intellectual topics for discussion, it was still necessary to set them in an adequate historical context and to arrange them in meaningful sequence. The introduction and chapter 1 are designed to meet the first need, although I would be the first to recognize my inadequate research grounding in such matters as the Vietnamese colonial economy, social classes, French administrative and police systems, and the relation of all this to the diverse financial and psychological demands of the *métropole*. Each subsequent chapter incorporates some historical background on the specific topic at hand, which I hope is enough for the general reader and not too much for the specialist. As for sequence, there is a rough progression in the book from earlier to later intellectual preoccupations, from conservative to radical political thought, and from ideas to action. I believe this reflects historical currents of the period, although I will not deny the role of hindsight as well.

On the other hand, some readers will feel that I devote inadequate attention to the Indochinese Communist Party and to Ho Chi Minh in particular. One answer would be to point to various monographs, biographies, and translations already available in Western languages on those topics. More fundamentally, however, I think that to concentrate solely on the winners risks misunderstanding why the losers lost. Losing, like winning, has its own creative process, its own historical momentum. To ignore the larger context, or to reduce everyone except communists to convenient stereotypes, ironically risks downgrading the historical achievements of both the ICP and Ho Chi Minh. Besides, the conviction has persisted throughout my research that the ability of the ICP twice to survive almost complete destruction, and then to spearhead a revolution, to establish a viable government, and to mount a thirty-year national resistance struggle, was not to be explained either by organizational history or by the brilliance of one man.

Among contemporary historians of Vietnam there has been a tendency to argue that Vietnamese success in defeating first the French and then the Americans was due primarily to traditional strengths, for example, relative ethnic and linguistic homogeneity, ancient civilization, and a proud record of struggle against northern invaders. Such factors were certainly important, as I also tried to demonstrate in my first book. Nevertheless, the cumulative effect of all these studies (in Vietnamese, English, and French) stressing the power of tradition has been to downgrade the historical significance of major transformations occurring during the colonial period in Vietnam (1859–1945). Why the continuity thesis has been so pervasive is an interesting question in itself. Presumably some historians have found in it a comfortable reaffirmation of their own conservative philosophy of life. Others have tended to confuse the wish to condemn imperialism morally with the more objective question of determining exactly what factors helped or hindered the imperialist and anti-imperialist causes. Among Vietnamese Marxists there has been the additional desire for historiography always to serve politics— both when employed as an analytical tool and when used as propaganda. What is striking, as we shall see later, is the way in which Vietnamese Marxist writers have emphasized historical change when analyzing colonial society or building a hardcore revolutionary following, but continuity when mobilizing a more diffuse national liberation movement. Where that leaves them, now that the liberation struggle is concluded and the job of building an advanced agro-industrial society has begun, is a question touched on in my conclusion.

Over the past eight years a great many people have helped in the creation of this book. Above all I would like to thank Christiane Rageau of the Bibliothèque Nationale, since without her special permission it would have been impossible to survey the Vietnamese collection methodically. During the earliest stages, in 1972, Pham Nhu Ho provided able assistance. Then and later, members of the Archives d'Outre-mer Staff in Paris and Aix-en-Provence were as accommodating as official guidelines would permit. The same proved true of librarians at the History Institute in Hanoi. Field work was made possible in 1971–1972 by a grant from the U.S. National Endowment for the Humanities (via the Cornell Southeast Asia Program), and in 1977–1978 by a grant from the Research School of Pacific Studies of the Australian National University.

Several early draft chapters were critiqued thoughtfully by Frederic Wakeman, Jr., Alexander Woodside, John Whitmore, Joseph Esherick, Jeffrey Barlow, and David Elliott. During later writing efforts I was especially grateful to David Chandler, Christine White, and Jennifer Brewster for their detailed remarks and suggestions. Others offered useful comments on particular sections, including Wang Gungwu, Daniel Hémery, Anthony Reid, Gail Kelly, Alfred McCoy, Michael Stenson, Craig Reynolds, William O'Malley, and John Spragens, Jr. In February 1978, three scholars at Vietnam's History Institute, Van Tao, Ngo Van Hoa, and Duong Kinh Quoc, read the first draft of the book and commented vigorously. Although I am sure they still take exception to some of my interpretations, I am happy to report that we have been able to sustain and expand the dialogue. Also in 1978, and again in April 1980, Tran Van Giau graciously discussed with me both the overriding intellectual issues and events in which he was personally involved. His remarks will keep me working far beyond the bounds of this book.

The administrative staff of the Department of Pacific and Southeast Asian History, Australian National University, managed to convert my endless handwritten sheets into clean typescript, for which Robyn Walker deserves notable credit. Philip Robyn helped edit the final manuscript. My wife Ai continued to create an environment uniquely conducive to the study of her country, while our children, Danny, Aileen, and Andy, kept us from thinking perpetually about the past. Our good friends, Do Quy Tan, Chris Jenkins, and Tran Khanh Tuyet, helped in ways too numerous to mention, hence being all the more appreciated.

Part of chapter 5, on "The Question of Women," appeared originally in the *Journal of Asian Studies*, vol. 35, no. 3 (May 1976), pp. 371–89, and is reprinted by permission. Chapter 6 is a revised version of my chapter contribution in Anthony Reid and David Marr, editors, *Perceptions of the Past in Southeast Asia* (Heinemann, 1979), and is reprinted by permission of the Asian Studies Association of Australia.

INTRODUCTION

In 1938 at least eighteen million Vietnamese were being kept in check by a mere 27,000 colonial troops. Yet a scant sixteen years later, colonial forces totalling 450,000 were unable to avoid tactical disaster at Dien Bien Phu and compulsory strategic evacuation south of the seventeenth parallel. Finally, in the years 1965–1975, various combinations of American, Republic of Vietnam, South Korean, and other allied armed forces totalling up to 1.2 million men were outfoxed, stalemated, and eventually vanquished by the National Liberation Front and the People's Army of Vietnam.

A host of explanations have been offered for this dramatic transformation in the capabilities of both sides. French and American generals have argued that massive attacks in the early stages of Vietnamese revolutionary activity could have nipped resistance in the bud. Possibly. Nevertheless, those same generals discovered that political and economic realities at home, first in Paris, then in Washington, ruled out such a Draconian solution. Other participants or observers have variously stressed the strength of primordial Vietnamese patriotism, the fury of any oppressed people lashing out at its oppressors, sophisticated communist organizing techniques, an increased Vietnamese capability to assimilate and employ modern technology, substantial international support, French and American ignorance of Vietnamese conditions, and the mass media explosion, which may have heightened revulsion in the "home" country.

None of these answers should be ignored by serious students of the struggle in Vietnam. Yet none really succeeds in explaining how, in a matter of a few years, hundreds of thousands of Vietnamese changed from seemingly docile French colonial subjects to experienced political cadres, pith-helmeted soldiers (bo-doi), literacy instructors, hygienists or soil technicians—all dedicated to driving out the foreigner and establishing an independent, strong, egalitarian nation. Patriotism and angry reactions to oppression may well have provided the emotional foundations, yet neither could tell Vietnamese how, when, or where to act. Organization and modern technology were certainly important, but to employ both effectively demanded some degree of conceptual transformation. Although international support was valuable, psychologically as well as materially, ultimately it was what the Vietnamese did with this backing that made the difference. As for weaknesses in enemy ranks, Vietnamese revolutionaries tried to comprehend and to exploit these wherever possible. However, they also learned from painful experience that simply to wait for enemy contradictions to manifest themselves was often to leave the initiative in the hands of others.

It is the thesis of this book that all such developments in the twentieth-century history of Vietnam must be understood within the context of fundamental changes in political and social consciousness among a significant segment of the Vietnamese populace in the period 1920–45. These changes, while not necessarily decisive, were at least one precondition for mass mobilization and successful people's war strategies from 1945 onward. To cite only one example, there was the growing conviction that one's life was not preordained, that one need not eat dirt forever, that one could join with others to force change. Victory would not occur in a blinding flash, as assumed by many earlier Vietnamese political and social movements. Yet victory was inevitable, the fruit of millions of Vietnamese perceiving their self-interests and uniting against the common enemy, foreign and domestic.

Such ideas were only the beginning of a new consciousness. What was to be the nature of that victory? Certainly it was not seen by most to be the transferring of a heavenly mandate from one ruler to another. Nor was it to be simply destruction of the colonial system. Often the objective was said to be transforming Vietnam into a "civilized" (van minh) nation. Although this concept meant different things to different people, it generally encompassed mastery over nature, a spirit of civic responsibility, full development of the individual's mental, physical, and moral faculties, and the ability of Vietnamese to stand proud among other peoples of the world.

These were not tasks to be accomplished overnight. Indeed, much time was spent in the early stages questioning Vietnamese capacities to do much of anything except obey fate, squabble incessantly, and scramble for petty personal gains. Beneath this severe self-criticism, even psychological flagellation, however, lurked the belief that people could change dramatically. Otherwise, why bother to publish hundreds of pamphlets and articles challenging readers to renovate themselves? At any rate, by the late 1920s both the mood of self-disparagement and the emphasis on moral rearmament were being replaced by the belief that history was moving in Vietnam's direction, and that social forces would accomplish what individual regeneration could not.

This new faith was badly shaken by the French colonial repression of 1929–32. It recovered in the Popular Front period of 1936–39. It suffered again in the Japanese-Vichy crackdowns of 1940–44. And then it burst forth as never before in the August 1945 Revolution. Through all these ups and downs a growing number of Vietnamese were learning to combine optimism and patience, moral suasion and social mobilization, theory and practice. The intelligentsia also rediscovered pride in Vietnamese culture—on a selective basis.

Without a variety of economic and social changes from precolonial to colonial times in Vietnam there would probably not have been major changes in consciousness, or, if such changes had occurred, they would have been limited to a much smaller group of people, perhaps "enlightened" members of the royal family, trusted mandarins, and a handful of foreign-language interpreters, merchants, and literate Catholics. To carry this speculation a bit further, such men might have employed their newly acquired knowledge to engineer and to justify a range of institutional reforms. They might even have ended up sharing power with small new military and business elites, as happened in Thailand. But, just as in Thailand, the depth and breadth of intellectual transformation would have been far less substantial.

Vietnam never had that choice. From the 1850s Vietnam was under severe military threat. It was dismembered in the 1860s and 1870s, then swallowed completely by the French in the 1880s. By 1897 all armed resistance had been quelled. During the next five years Governor General Paul Doumer laid down the foundations and framework which were to characterize Indochina (Cambodia and Laos included) for the next four decades. These included a centralized and rather top-heavy administration, an expanded and greatly reinforced tax and corvée system, continued growth of the primary export sector by means of large land grants (often disregarding prior ownership or occupancy), near-monopoly status for French finance capital and product imports, and the construction of an impressive if not always economically viable network of railroads, roads, and canals.[1]

Already before World War I three major changes were apparent in the lives of ordinary Vietnamese. First, the French had capacities to control and to coerce never dreamed of by previous rulers. For this reason less attention was devoted to the conciliatory political arts, to understanding local grievances, compromising, or sharing power with subordinates. It also meant that traditional village obligations to the ruler, in particular, taxes, corvée service, and military service, were no longer the subject of discreet negotiations, but could now be enforced with unprecedented efficiency. Nor was there still an open frontier beyond reach of the system, where aggrieved families could flee. It followed, too, that those Vietnamese who attached themselves to the new rulers and quickly grasped alien procedures could advance to positions of considerable wealth and self-esteem (but little real authority), without having to trouble themselves much about popular anger or any ethic of responsible government. In short, the French can be said to have strengthened some aspects of the traditional hierarchical structure to the detriment of the majority of Vietnamese, while allowing a new indigenous

1. Joseph Buttinger, *Vietnam: A Dragon Embattled*, vol. 1 (New York: Praeger, 1967), pp. 3–43; Martin Murray, *The Development of Capitalism in Colonial Indochina, 1870–1940* (Berkeley and Los Angeles: University of California Press, 1980).

minority to share in the returns as long as they remained obedient and necessarily insensitive to popular grievances.

Secondly, through a policy of granting large land concessions to French companies and Vietnamese collaborators, together with the introduction of French
concepts of private property and individual legal responsibility, the colonial government stimulated fundamental changes in village economic and social relations. Phrased most simply, there were now unprecedented pressures toward
concentrated wealth, land alienation, and the growth of a class of landless and
land-poor Vietnamese. For example, peasant families who had devoted one or
more generations to clearing, tilling, and improving land now found themselves
being evicted or converted into tenants, perhaps simply because they had not
learned the new administrative rules as quickly as others. Small proprietors, who
thought they had protected themselves legally, could still be outmaneuvered by
means of usurious loans, cadastral manipulations, seizure for back taxes, or simply the duplicity of corrupt local officials. To cry out for redress in such situations
was usually hopeless, and sometimes dangerous, since colonial retaliatory power
was normally at the disposal of any landlord or official who kept in the good
graces of his superiors.

As a corollary of this economic process, the corporate character of Vietnamese
villages was gradually eroded. Communal lands—traditionally the basis of village social welfare palliatives, as well as providing modest support for local temples, schools, and routine administrative tasks—now increasingly became the
private property of several well-placed families, or even came under the control
of non-village members. As disparities in wealth increased, the selection of village notables, the observance of village festivals, the organizing of weddings, funerals, ceremonies to honor returning scholars and the like, became ever more
the sources of contention and conspicuous consumption (both of which had always been present to some degree), and ever less the vital ritual reinforcements
of community self-consciousness and solidarity. Simultaneously, richer and poorer
members of clans and extended families drew further apart, the former mostly
interested in special status to reflect their new wealth, the latter trying to borrow
money cheaply and loosely according to outmoded lineage rationales. The ultimate breakdown of corporate ties often occurred, as one might expect, in those
areas where individuals amassed enough land to leave the villages entirely. Such
absentee landlords, particularly prevalent in south Vietnam, controlled the fates
of hundreds or thousands of local people without ever having to meet them face
to face, or, perhaps even more upsetting, showing up only at rent- or loan-collec-
tion times.

Finally, it may well be that the most important transformation of all had to do
with the penetration of a cash economy into even the most isolated hamlets of
Vietnam. While the implications of this change took several decades to become
apparent, there is no doubt that from the turn of the century (earlier in
Cochinchina) traditional multiple and personal forms of socio-economic interac-

tion were being replaced by the single, essentially impersonal commercial exchange system. Central taxes were the cutting edge in most cases, levied on individuals rather than corporate villages as before. While several Vietnamese dynasties had experimented with taxes in cash, particularly portions of the land tax, payment in kind had always remained dominant. Now the French ordered that both the entire land tax and the even more onerous head tax be paid in silver—not the copper, zinc, or paper money recognized for other transactions, but solid silver piasters, which peasants often had to acquire solely for this purpose at marked-up rates of exchange from the money lenders or landlords. Corvée obligations could also be rendered in cash, for those who had it. On top of these payments there were diverse indirect taxes (marketing, stamp, consumer goods, transit, entrepot, navigation, etc.) as well as the government-controlled salt and liquor monopolies—all being more rigorously enforced than any comparable taxes of precolonial days. Even if a peasant continued to think of himself as essentially a subsistence farmer, he was being drawn further into the money economy by the tax system.

The preeminent economic objective of the French was to develop a modern export sector. They focused particularly on rice and mining, then later rubber as well. Taxation, monopoly, and market mechanisms soon worked relentlessly against the interests of peasants whose output had previously met the more diverse needs of an autonomous economy, but who were now non-competitive in an imperial operation controlled from Paris. Vietnamese might still need to eat something other than rice, but there were now financial disincentives in many regions to specializing in non-rice production. The same process hit traditional artisans hard, indeed wiping them out entirely if their specialty happened to compete with French imports. Peasants who derived some off-season income from making handicrafts, tools, or other simple essentials also found such opportunities drying up. Rice was now king—not just any rice, but rice in quantities and qualities suitable for export, and sent through channels dominated by non-local interests. A modicum of capital and contacts with officialdom were the two essential ingredients to success. Those who failed became part of the cheap labor pool, another essential ingredient if any company or family wished to set up a new plantation or start a new mining project.

With the outbreak of war in Europe in 1914 investments terminated abruptly. Vietnamese were pressed to help defeat the "Huns." As many as 100,000 peasants and artisans were rounded up and shipped to France to serve in labor battalions, and provided a source of some worry to the colonial authorities when they returned. Meanwhile, in Vietnam during the war, people were strongly "encouraged" to buy war bonds, in effect yet another tax. Rice exports increased. Locally produced goods were allowed temporarily to substitute for normal French imports. Larger numbers of Vietnamese were permitted to enter the bottom rungs of the colonial bureaucracy, and a modest expansion of the public school system was ordered. With that special French penchant for idealistic overstatement, Governor-General Albert Sarraut spun all of these changes into a vision of Franco-Vietnamese collaboration, complete with references to Liberty, Equality, and Fraternity. France, he said, was ready to act as "elder brother" in transmitting the full benefits of modern civilization, and to consider the possibility of native self-rule at some unspecified point in the future. After Germany was defeated, the French Government conveniently ignored these grandiloquent promises. But for many educated Vietnamese the cat had been let out of the bag. If the French needed reminding, they would be the ones to do it. If that did not work, they would try pursuing the ideal of "civilization" on their own.

In 1922, as France itself was slowly managing to pull out of a postwar depression, the Ministry of Colonies organized a grand exposition in Marseilles to try to revitalize in people's minds the French "mission" overseas and to attract new investment capital. Looked at in terms of overall twentieth-century historical trends, France had been permanently weakened by the Great War. The French people were probably more divided than ever on the colonial question. Nevertheless, viewed from the perspective of the 1920s, the response to the Marseilles exposition and other forms of colonial propaganda was nothing short of spectacular. While thousands of ordinary French citizens amused themselves by tasting strange foreign dishes, ogling native dancers, and laughing at the clothing and manners of diverse oriental potentates, potential capital investors concentrated their attention on government promises of monopoly privileges, tax shelters, cheap labor, and solid social order.[2]

Close to three billion francs was invested in Indochina between 1924 and 1930, almost sixty per cent of the total since French arrival. Rubber cultivation, begun very modestly before the war, now was seen by investors as the new bonanza, some 700 million francs being advanced between 1925 and 1929.[3] To provide the physical labor, somewhere between 100,000 and 200,000 Vietnamese were deceived or dragooned into the "red earth" rubber-growing region of Cochinchina during the boom years of the 1920s. Conditions were abysmal, including endemic malaria, contaminated or insufficient food and water, long hours, the docking of wages, and vicious punishments. Consequently the turnover rate due to death, escape, and non-renewal of contracts was extraordinarily high, as indi-

2. For three different Vietnamese views of the Marseilles Exposition, especially the puppet king Khai Dinh's involvement, see Nguyen Ai Quoc, *Truyen Va Ky* (Hanoi, 1974), pp. 25–29, 61–65; Phan Chu Trinh, *That Dieu Thu* (Hue, 1958); and Pham Quynh, "Phap Du Hanh Trinh Nhat Ky," NP 63 (Sept. 1922), pp. 230–31, and NP 66 (Dec. 1922), pp. 433–37. The official French view is captured in *Réception de Sa Majesté Khai Dinh* (Paris, 1923).

3. Rubber plantations expanded from 15,000 to 100,000 hectares between 1920 and 1929. See Charles Robequain, *The Economic Development of French Indo-China* (London: Oxford Univ. Press, 1944), pp. 162–63. Pierre Brocheux, "Le prolétariat des plantations d'hévéas au Vietnam méridional: aspects sociaux et politiques (1927–1937)," *Le Mouvement Social* 90 (Jan.–Mar. 1975), pp. 55–86.

cated by the fact that the rubber plantation work force never exceeded 41,000 in any one year.[4]

Conditions were only slightly better for the miners, of whom there were at least 50,000 during peak years, mostly in the Hon Gay pits of north Vietnam. Here the formula for profit-making included dirt-cheap labor, company stores, 12- to 14-hour shifts, physical brutality, and the absence of safety precautions. Yet French economists still complained that it was "carelessness," "lack of conscientiousness," and "delicate constitution(s)" that caused Vietnamese miners to produce at only one-quarter the rate of their French or Japanese counterparts.[5] New coffee and tea plantations were established in the same way, and more land was cleared and drained so that more Vietnamese tenants and wage laborers could produce more rice for export. Significant expansion occurred in rice milling, distilling, sugar refining, and the production of cement, textiles, and timber. On top of this economic pyramid sat a handful of directors of prestigious French financial institutions. As of 1924, Paris and Saigon were linked by direct transoceanic cable for the first time. Direct airmail service soon followed. Indochina was now a classic colony, her economic fibers attuned to the demands of the "mother country" and the international marketplace.

With the advent of the Great Depression the bottom fell out of the rubber and rice markets. By early 1931 the Indochina economy was in serious trouble—landowners defaulting on bank loans, companies going into bankruptcy, *colons* banging on government doors demanding assistance, and uncounted thousands of Vietnamese tenants, agricultural laborers, plantation hands, miners, and factory workers thrown out of employment, roaming to and fro in search of survival.[6] Not until 1936 did the economy begin to pick up again. Then, a mere four years later, Nazi Germany occupied France, the Vichy-sympathizing authorities in Indochina subordinated themselves to the Japanese, and the economy underwent dislocation once again. By the winter of 1944/45, a tragic but quite predictable situation had developed, whereby hundreds of thousands of tons of rice remained in warehouses in the south (or was converted to alcohol to propel

4. It should be recognized that all rubber plantation labor figures were notoriously unreliable, since it was hardly in the interests of owners, managers, or overseers to expose the grisly mechanics of their operation. These estimates are based on information found in Robequain, *Economic Development*, pp. 56, 214–16; in Daniel Hémery, *Révolutionaires Vietnamiens et Pouvoir Colonial en Indochine* (Paris: Maspéro, 1975), p. 214; and in Ngo Vinh Long, *Before the Revolution: The Vietnamese Peasants under the French* (Cambridge, Mass.: MIT Press, 1973), pp. 113–14. For an autobiographical account of plantation working conditions, see Tran Tu Binh, *Phu Rieng Do*, 2nd printing (Hanoi, 1971).

5. Robequain, *Economic Development*, p. 76. The author also conveniently ignores mentioning machinery differentials in the three locations.

6. Pierre Brocheux, "Crise économique et société en Indochine française," *Revue Française d'Histoire d'Outre-mer* 232–33 (1976), pp. 655–67.

motor vehicles), while somewhere between one and two million Vietnamese people died of starvation in the north.

Looked at from the perspective of eighty years of French colonial activity, the only period when truly favourable conditions existed for full-scale capitalist economic exploitation of Indochina was from 1922 to 1929—a mere eight years. Economic fragility combined with administrative uncertainty underlay the entire colonial operation. No governor-general ever spent a term of more than five and one-half years in Indochina, and the average tenure was a scant two years and eight months.[7] Conservative politicians spoke grandly about colonial restoration while socialists talked vaguely of provisional tutelage.[8] Projects were begun and left uncompleted, or altered in such a way that profits survived but not the ameliorative social trimmings. This fundamental weakness of French colonialism, hardly sensed previously by even the most astute Vietnamese observers, was to become a subject of serious analysis among the new generation of intellectuals.

Vietnam has had three generations of intellectuals since 1900. Scholar-gentry or literati (si phu) intellectuals realized during the first decade of the twentieth century that Vietnam was being transformed whether it liked it or not. They tried desperately with whatever weapons, physical or mental, that came to hand to face up to altered conditions. By the end of World War I, however, it was obvious that they were unable to formulate either a penetrating new view of the world or a realistic program of action. Even the most sophisticated and experienced scholar-gentry members remained suspended between the Neo-Confucian classics, which they knew intimately but had come to doubt, and the ideas of Montesquieu, Rousseau, Smith, and Spencer, which they understood only vaguely but assumed to be essential to Vietnam's future. What they did manage to convey to the next generation, nevertheless, was a sense of historical crisis, a profound respect for knowledge, a commitment to action, and faith in the perfectability of humankind.

The intelligentsia (gioi tri thuc) that emerged during the 1920s faced many of the same problems as the scholar-gentry, but in yet another social and economic context and with very different intellectual equipment. While not divorced from the villages and the lives of the literati, small farmers, and handicraft workers, the intelligentsia was indubitably a product of the colonial system, just as were

7. The turnover was only slightly less disturbing at the next lower level of governors and residents-superior of the three regions (Buttinger, *Vietnam*, vol. 1, p. 63, and vol. 2, pp. 1215–22). This phenomenon was, of course, related to governmental instability in metropolitan France.

8. Daniel Hémery, "Aux origines des guerres d'indépendence vietnamiennes: pouvoir colonial et phénomène communiste en Indochine avant la Seconde Guerre Mondiale," *Le Mouvement Social* 101 (Oct.–Dec. 1977), pp. 3–35.

the big landlords, tenants, miners, and plantation laborers. Young intelligentsia graduating from French and Franco-Vietnamese schools in increasing numbers generally sought employment as clerks, interpreters, primary teachers, or journalists. As career aspirations exceeded colonial possibilities, there was considerable disenchantment and unrest. To assume a correlation between job frustration and anticolonial attitudes among the intelligentsia would be risky, however. There were well-employed Vietnamese who ended up opposing the French, just as there were thwarted journalists who joined the colonial police or signed on as overseers for landlords, mine supervisors, and plantation administrators.[9]

Unlike the scholar-gentry, the intelligentsia understood the Neo-Confucian classics only vaguely but were impatient to digest two millenia of European learning in a matter of a few years. The great advantage, and simultaneously the primary weakness, of these young men and women was that they stood unsteadily between two worlds and tried hard to envisage a third. Most of them had either grown up in villages or had meaningful rural kinship ties. Their parents still believed in ghosts, arranged marriages, and strict social harmony. However, in school, and increasingly through extracurricular means, they learned of cameras, germs, atoms, galaxies, free love, class struggle, and biological evolution. Many found the advice of their elders to ignore the obvious contradictions between old and new and to concentrate on passing examinations and securing a clerkship morally and intellectually repulsive. They wanted to look further, to explain the contradictions, and to fashion a new consciousness for themselves and for the Vietnamese people at large. Often they used the image of discovering a conceptual "lodestone" *(kim chi nam)* that would guide everyone to a brighter future. Although the enthusiasm, aggressive curiosity, and iconoclasm of the intelligentsia were themselves repulsive to many other Vietnamese, social and economic changes were so profound that the latter often felt impotent, incapable of reasserting authority. Youth seized the day.

This was only the beginning, however. One of the most difficult tasks facing the intelligentsia was to distinguish universal insights from the particularities of either European or Vietnamese experience. The traditional Vietnamese preference had been to draw a line between cultured East Asians and the many barbarian peoples, Europeans included, who did not comprehend the way of the universe and hence behaved improperly. Well into the twentieth century some Vietnamese continued to seek comfort in this model of reality, even while being forced to admit that "Eastern spirit" no longer had any claim to universality. At the other extreme, many early products of French colonial schools tended to

---

9. No systematic analysis has been done of the class backgrounds, education, and early political experiences of the several thousand intelligentsia and anticolonialists of this period for whom data are available.

assume that to be European was civilized and to be Asian barbarian. Yet those who tried simply to imitate Europeans found that they were neither accepted as such by French *colons* nor emulated by the mass of Vietnamese.

The spectacle of China disintegrating into warlordism, of Japan trying to outfox the Western imperialists at their own game, and of the Vietnamese "emperor" on annual salary from the French, made Neo-Confucianism look pathetic. Buddhism and Taoism were seen to be more attractive in such chaotic times, yet only a small minority of the intelligentsia went beyond general knowledge of these philosophies to firm, sustained adherence. On the other side of the world, the spectacle of Europe tearing itself to pieces in World War I undercut those Vietnamese who advocated radical Westernization. If Verdun and the Somme lay at the end of the path of assimilation, then better not try.

During the 1920s Vietnamese writers started to reach beyond the East-versus-West paradigm. They eagerly sought information from anywhere, in the hope that it would help to explain and resolve their own dilemmas. Of particular interest were social upheavals in China, postwar unrest in Europe, the ongoing revolution in Russia, and non-violent resistance in India. Increasingly writers became convinced that there was no qualitative distinction between Europeans and Vietnamese. A vast reservoir of knowledge and techniques was available to anyone in the world. It might often appear to bear a particular national stamp, but that was superficial, capable of being isolated and eliminated. In place of idealized philosophical and cultural systems, Vietnamese writers moved increasingly to historical process as a central explanation of reality. The key question then became one of assessing Vietnam's place in this universal process, and determining how to improve it.

In politics this same historical quest led many Vietnamese writers to conclude that it was not enough to simply exhort people to be patriotic, to unite, and to help save the country. Writers were now poignantly aware of other peoples in the world who presumably loved their homeland and their mother tongue as deeply as did the Vietnamese their own, who even possessed a similar tradition of resisting foreign domination, yet ultimately were completely vanquished and absorbed. Clearly some ethnic groups survived and others did not. Understanding why and how became a major preoccupation. Again, Vietnamese came to the conclusion that much knowledge in the world bore no moral stamp but was available to the evil as well as the good, to colonials and anticolonials, to reactionaries, conservatives, liberals, and radical revolutionaries alike.

The next step was to relate new knowledge and techniques to specific Vietnamese conditions. This proved to be more difficult. First of all, the intelligentsia had to learn a great deal about Vietnam, past and present, that was either unavailable in the colonial schools or had previously been considered irrelevant by young men and women trying first to understand the outside world. Nor was it easy for members of the intelligentsia to move around the country collecting information. The colonial authorities imposed physical restrictions. And a young intellectual in Western dress, speaking with a different accent and having no local relatives, might have to spend months simply gaining the confidence of a few people. When it came time to publish, writers discovered a curious fact about colonial censorship: the authorities were often more charitable toward the printing of esoteric foreign information and theories than they were toward independent data on the Vietnamese experience. Many an article was blanked out precisely at the point where it shifted from foreign generalities to Vietnamese colonial particulars.

Vietnamese intellectuals overseas took the lead in discussing specific political and social developments inside the colony. Ho Chi Minh was the most notable example, but he was followed by scores of other Vietnamese residing for one period of time or another in France, the Soviet Union, and China. While they obviously could not conduct on-the-spot investigations, they did talk intensively with overseas Vietnamese from other provinces and social backgrounds. Publishing was less of a problem than smuggling copies home. Ironically, while most writers in Saigon, Hanoi, or Hue were still grappling with universals, whether in history, philosophy, the social sciences, medicine, or mathematics, writers in Paris, Moscow or Canton were trying to analyze the Bank of Indochina, the conditions of Vietnamese peasants, miners, and plantation workers, or the causes of high infant mortality. Distance from events provided the perspective for sorting the momentous from the trivial, the politically relevant from the intellectually curious.

Eventually, however, this work would have to be carried on inside the country. In the late 1920s a few authors in Saigon and Hue were able to append a bit of specific Vietnamese data to otherwise general discussions of historical evolution, religion, nationalism, and imperialism. In the early 1930s novelists and short-story writers took the lead, describing the lives of Vietnamese functionaries, landlords, intellectuals, shopkeepers, and peasants according to conceptual and stylistic criteria that had not existed in the country several decades earlier. By the late 1930s they had been joined by critical essayists, and the emphasis increasingly was on the lives of poor peasants, tenants, proletarians, beggars, and prostitutes. Collectively these publications amounted to a penetrating indictment of both Vietnamese traditional society and the colonial system.

Preoccupation with the negative could prove self-defeating, however. By the early 1940s many discussions of current conditions were naturalistic caricatures rather than realistic exposés. Sensing an impasse, other writers shifted to selective revitalization of the Vietnamese past and to assertions of a bright future. Vietnam was now seen by even the most radical intelligentsia to possess a history to some degree unique, incapable of being understood simply by reference to universal laws. As might be expected, particular attention was given to military heroes, administrative innovators, and literary giants. Popular culture was mined for evidence of an underlying strength and wisdom among the Vietnamese masses transcending the historical dialectic.

These changes coincided with momentous political developments, including the collapse of the Popular Front (1939), the establishment of the Japanese-Vichy alliance (1940), and the formation of the Communist-led Viet Minh (1941). As a group, the Vietnamese intelligentsia was badly divided on how to respond to these events. Some saw the Japanese as liberators; others hoped for Vietnamese self-rule within a French Union; still others joined the Viet Minh and worked for an allied victory and international recognition of Vietnam's independence. Probably the only thing the intelligentsia shared by 1942-44 was a feeling that the urban milieu of office bureaus, elite societies, coffee shops, and amusement parlors was very constraining, perhaps unreal. The new focus was the Vietnamese village, whether for purposes of preserving its alleged communal character, for suggesting institutional reforms, or for convincing the peasants to seize control of their own destiny.

In 1944-45 members of the intelligentsia joined the Viet Minh by the thousands. Their skills as writers, speakers, teachers, and administrators proved extremely valuable, perhaps essential. They were also competent to ferret out information and to digest and distill it for broad political and military intelligence purposes. The same ability was put to use when learning how to utilize captured materiel, or when devising new equipment and techniques appropriate to primitive conditions. However, intelligentsia linking up with the Viet Minh soon discovered that they were regarded as neither the political nor the intellectual vanguard of society. Those roles were held by the Indochinese Communist Party. Although in 1944 most members of the ICP were probably still of intelligentsia background, the Party took its worker-peasant vision very seriously. The upheavals of 1945 provided a perfect opportunity to identify and enroll thousands of suitable members from these classes.

Members of the ICP, intellectuals or otherwise, had already learned through bitter experience that to will victory, or to analyze the road to victory, was not the same as to achieve victory. They had been forced into agonizing personal choices, endured considerable deprivation, tested a variety of concepts in practice, and tried to reformulate everything in terms meaningful to the majority of their unlettered (but not necessarily ignorant) countrymen. What they wanted from any intelligentsia recruit of 1945 was a willingness to accept group discipline, to concern himself more with means than with ends, and to help the Viet Minh to establish a common frame of reference between the elite and the masses, modernity and tradition, universal and particular. The era of the educated cadre, as distinct from the alienated explorer, had begun.

In the early 1920s Vietnam's young intelligentsia had had a talismanic approach to knowledge. It was to be their invincible weapon to gain independence, freedom, and "civilization." Twenty years later, however, many intelligentsia realized that new ideas might promote or impede change; they might produce unintended as well as intended and dysfunctional as well as functional consequences. Few ideas were inherently good or bad, and even fewer remained as originally conceived. To try to force the "right" ideas in the wrong historical conditions might prove disastrous, yet to wait for the right conditions might be equally dangerous. What was needed was a complex interweaving of ends and means, strategy and circumstance, conscious formulation and spontaneous action. It is this quest that gives our story significance beyond the period, beyond even Vietnam itself.

1. The Colonial Setting

The weather was mild, the trees verdant after the recent monsoons. In front of the Hanoi colonial court and prison buildings, beginning as early as 6:00 A.M., people gathered Monday, 23 November 1925, to watch the veteran revolutionary Phan Boi Chau (1867–1940) go on trial for his life.

For the first time the Vietnamese public was to be allowed to enter the courtroom to observe a trial before the French High Criminal Commission. Once the doors swung open it quickly became evident that there was not enough space; many people were directed to adjacent rooms and could only hope to catch brief snatches of the proceedings. The courtroom itself, the corridor, main entrance, and passageway to the jail were all lined with well-equipped gendarmes, Sûreté police, and soldiers.

At 7:30 A.M., escorted by two gendarmes, a wispy-bearded, bald, thin-faced gentleman made the passage from his cell to the seat in court for the accused. Phan Boi Chau had chosen to wear a simple but properly fitted Chinese-style tunic. As he waited, Phan's eyes scanned the audience intently, while his slender hands stroked his beard in the absentminded fashion of the Confucian literatus. He had not seen this many Vietnamese together in twenty years.

At 8:25 A.M. the court bell rang thrice, everyone stood, and in marched four French magistrates plus entourage to institute proceedings. For the rest of the day and into the evening the audience remained spellbound. Long-suppressed details on anticolonial events of the past forty years were brought forth. Basic colonial policy was the object of unprecedented public jousting. Most importantly, however, people were moved by the moral demeanor of the accused. There, in that single scholar, poet, essayist, political activist, and organizer—facing the full weight of French "justice"—they saw themselves, or what they might have been.

Initially the judges may have wanted to limit argument to eight criminal charges dealing with assassinations and conspiracy plots of the year 1913. Phan Boi Chau, however, repeatedly denied complicity in these episodes, devoting his remarks instead to the need for independence, democracy, and modern culture in Vietnam. With this the court recessed until afternoon and then came back with a long, precise indictment of Phan's entire life, beginning with his teenage admiration of royalist armed resistance figures and ending with his formation in

1912 of the democratic republican oriented Viet-Nam Quang Phuc Hoi (Vietnam Restoration Society). Basing their remarks on no less than three hundred police dossiers, the judges thus put on public record a story that almost all contemporary Vietnamese were aware of in only the most sparse, folklore-tinted form. Newspapers printed everything their reporters were able to copy down. Circulation figures doubled or tripled overnight.[1]

Although Phan Boi Chau retained his composure and refused to be bullied, the specific answers he and his two court-appointed French lawyers gave were not particularly consistent or even credible. On the one hand, they made attempts to defend distant actions, or at least place them in historical context: on the other, they requested that the court forgive and forget everything prior to 1917 and concentrate on Phan's publicly stated willingness since then to promote Franco-Vietnamese collaboration.[2]

Phan's lawyers had evidently convinced him that the best hope, both personally and in terms of larger political objectives, was to speak beyond the court to the new socialist governor-general, Alexandre Varenne. They clearly did not give him any inkling of the public outcry that had developed, not only in Vietnam, but in China and France as well, from the moment of his capture in Shanghai earlier that year. Having experienced twenty years of defeat and exile, the violent deaths of most of his comrades, polite rejection by many of his Japanese and Chinese friends, and, most recently, five months incommunicado in a French jail, Phan had no way of sensing, much less understanding, the new optimism and energy welling up among tens of thousands of Vietnamese.

---

1. In addition to the daily newspapers, several publishers quickly printed 5,000- and 10,000-copy editions in pamphlet form; see Thuc Nghiep Dan Bao, *Tap An Phan Boi Chau* [Phan Boi Chau Trial Proceedings] (Hanoi, 1925), and Trung Bac Tan Van, *Viec Phan Boi Chau tai Hoi Dong De Hinh* [The Phan Boi Chau Affair at the Criminal Court Session] (Hanoi, 1925). A 2,500-copy version, titled *Viec Phan Boi Chau* [The Phan Boi Chau Affair], followed in Saigon in early January 1926; it was compiled by two young journalists whom we will meet later, Tran Huy Lieu and Bui Cong Trung. There are various discrepancies in these three published accounts, due mostly, it would seem, to imperfect note-taking.

2. Phan Boi Chau's best-known essay on this subject was *Phap Viet De Hue Luan* [An Essay on Franco-Vietnamese Collaboration], written in China in 1917. Its basic premise was that Japan had superseded the Western powers as all Asia's most dangerous enemy. If the Vietnamese wanted to survive an inevitable onslaught from Japan, and if the French hoped to retain any benefits at all, the two would have to work out a new relationship based on mutual advantage rather than unilateral exploitation. Phan Boi Chau, *Phap Viet De Hue Chinh Kien Thu* [Some Views on Franco-Vietnamese Collaboration], 3rd edition (5,000 copies) (Hanoi, 1926). For further discussion of Phan Boi Chau's shift in position after 1917, see Tran Van Giau, *Su Phat Trien cua Tu Tuong o Viet Nam tu The Ky XIX den Cach Mang Thang Tam* [Development of Ideas in Vietnam from the Nineteenth Century to the August Revolution], vol. 2 (Hanoi, 1975), pp. 422–37 (hereinafter cited as SPT-2).

There were occasional sparks from the earlier Phan Boi Chau, nevertheless. Several times he patiently instructed everyone on important political nuances, for example, the difference between the old particularistic "loyalty" to a leader (*trung quan*) and the new "patriotism" (*ai quoc*) of modern nation-states. At one point he stated that he had originally shifted to violent overthrow of the French because peaceful "cultural" change had proven quite impossible. He had done this, he said, in full knowledge that there were only two possible outcomes: either he, Phan Boi Chau, would lose his head, or Vietnam would gain its independence. Toward the end of the proceedings, in a move almost surely designed to discredit him in the eyes of the spectators, and perhaps to bait him into making further damaging remarks, the chief judge accused him of having opposed the Protectorate simply because he had failed the metropolitan examinations of 1904. Phan responded heatedly, sometimes having to stop in mid-sentence to readjust his badly-fitting set of false teeth. His first anticolonial treatise had been written and circulated at court before the exams, he pointed out. Besides, given his previous top-ranking regional success and his far from dishonorable score of seven in the metropolitan exams, he could easily have obtained a mandarinal position if he had so wished. Indeed, he had chosen to leave his wife and children, the graves of his ancestors, and the shores of his country in exchange for a life of considerable danger and no financial recompense. The French could accuse him of almost anything, Phan said, but the charge of "seeking after wealth and official prestige" was completely untenable and could not go unanswered. This confrontation between French administrators with *de facto* power to dispense money and medals on the one hand and a single aging Confucian scholar with *de jure* legitimacy on the other probably moved the audience more deeply than any other moment in the trial. The chief judge had erred seriously in trying to advance into ethical competition, the rules of which Phan and the audience understood intimately, but which he, a foreigner, could only dimly perceive.

At 8:00 P.M. the indictments were read once again, and Phan Boi Chau was invited to make a final plea. His answer:

If the French government employs aircraft, cruisers, submarines, artillery, in short, brute force, to rule this country, according to the principle of the "big fish" swallowing the "small fish," then I am ready to die without a further word. On the other hand, if France brings civilization (*van minh*), justice, and law to develop better conditions for the peoples of Indochina, then truly I am innocent and should be released.[3]

The court adjourned briefly, and just before 9:00 P.M. returned to declare Phan Boi Chau guilty on almost all counts, sentencing him to life imprisonment at hard labor.

3. Thuc Nghiep Dan Bao, *Tap An Phan Boi Chau*, p. 23.

Phan Boi Chau in traditional Vietnamese garb. *Phap Viet De Hue* (Hanoi, 1926). Courtesy of the Bibliothèque Nationale (Paris).

During the next month an even greater popular effort was mounted to gain Phan's release. Hanoi newspapers led the way, including several of the moderate French-owned publications.[4] Vietnamese-language newspaper circulation figures shot up again, sometimes reaching 12,000 copies in the case of the most enterprising papers. The arch-conservative Pham Quynh (1892–1945) was stunned to see that newspaper circulation was not limited to "cultivated" Vietnamese; the "most humble" men, as well as some women, were also reading. He even overheard a rickshaw puller declare, "The French have condemned Phan because he is too patriotic." Pham Quynh himself felt that the French would have been much wiser to have left Phan Boi Chau in faraway China. Failing that, Pham Quynh called for Phan's release to avoid turning him into a martyr.[5] Around the country, groups of citizens drafted telegrams requesting a pardon and sent them to the governor-general. In an attempt to mobilize foreign support, someone sent copies of petitions and leaflets to the League of Nations, the International Tri-

4. One of the papers most active on behalf of Phan Boi Chau was the *Argus Indochinois*, edited by M. Clémenti; see, in particular, the issues of 5 and 12 Dec. 1925.

5. *Indochine Républicain* (Hanoi), 2 December 1925.

bunal at The Hague, the Chinese ambassador in Paris, and various French government bureaus and political organizations.

On 5 December 1925, the day Varenne arrived for the first time in Hanoi, hundreds of students organized peaceful demonstrations. Splitting up in discreet groups at key intersections along the route traveled by the governor-general's auto, they displayed banners in French, such as, "Long live the Socialist Varenne," "A Pardon for Phan Boi Chau," and "Down with Colonialism of the Cudgel." With a sharp eye for contemporary symbolism, they had painted the first and third slogans in socialist red and the second in mourning black. At one location a hundred market women sat down in the middle of the street, halting the governor-general's auto and allowing time for their leader, an elderly white-haired woman, to present a petition to the smiling, apparently relaxed Varenne. Later, young women studying at the School of Pedagogy were able to visit Mme. Varenne and give her a petition as well.

In late December, Varenne ordered what amounted to a conditional parole for Phan Boi Chau and immediately sent him to Hue. Phan soon discovered he was subject to constant surveillance and not allowed to form any organization or establish his own newspaper. In central Vietnam, students who had signed amnesty telegrams were harassed by their French principals. In Phan Boi Chau's native district of Nam Dan (Nghe An), local mandarins, after failing to get permission to jail Phan's entire family according to traditional principles of jurisprudence, apparently were still able to force his two sons to work as menials, one as a hospital ward sweeper and the other as an underling to the "boys" (servants) of the Vinh Hôtel. These tactics, when publicized throughout the country by newspapers and pamphlets, only increased sympathy for Phan and anger at the colonial administration.[6]

The overriding sentiments, however, were relief that Phan Boi Chau had avoided hard labor in prison and enthusiasm that so many Vietnamese could become concerned and mobilized over a political issue. As one prominent young commentator in Saigon affirmed, Vietnamese had finally joined together to try to protect one of their own. No longer would they be content to leave each ensnared individual to fend desperately for himself.[7] He could have added, if it were not already obvious, that the young Vietnamese intelligentsia were rapidly learning techniques of information gathering, proselytizing, organizing, and political struggle completely unknown to the generation of Phan Boi Chau.

On the evening of 24 March 1926, Phan Chu Trinh (1872–1926) lost his private struggle with tuberculosis and died in a Saigon hospital. Recently returned

6. Trung Bac Tan Van, *Viec Phan Boi Chau*, pp. 28–39; Thuc Nghiep Dan Bao, *Nhung Tin Tuc va Du Luan ve Ong Phan Boi Chau* [News and Public Opinion Concerning Phan Boi Chau] (Hanoi, 1926), pp. 1–8.

7. Tran Huy Lieu's summary remarks, in Trung Bac Tan Van, *Viec Phan Boi Chau*, p. 48.

An obviously suspicious Phan Boi Chau being urged by Governor-General Varenne to walk in the direction of "Franco-Vietnamese Collaboration." Le Cuong Phung, *Phan Boi Chau Ngay Nay* (Saigon, 1926). Courtesy of the Bibliothèque Nationale.

from a fourteen-year exile in France, and admired at least as much as Phan Boi Chau, Phan Chu Trinh had worked hard during his last months to encourage the new intelligentsia in the direction of cultural renaissance and non-violent political agitation.

A committee to organize a public funeral for Phan Chu Trinh was immediately organized, combining wealthy landlords and officials on the one hand and young intellectuals on the other. Copies of a proclamation naming 4 April as a day of national mourning were successfully transmitted to all parts of the country. The ceremonial form and political tone of the planned observances were spelled out in detail, following precedents set by Sun Yat-sen's funeral in China the previous year. Students should leave school; factories, shops, and stores should close down. A solemn public procession was to be organized in Saigon, and other localities were to be encouraged to organize their own more modest ceremonies.

Most importantly, there were not to be any quasi-royal trappings to the funeral nor extravagant expenditure and endless labor on a tomb. At the core would be explanation and enhancement of Phan Chu Trinh's life as a "morally upright patriot" (*chi si yeu nuoc*).

At exactly 6:00 A.M. on 4 April some 60,000 mourners in ranks of four, wearing black or white armbands depending on whether they were modern or traditional in their outlook, began the long procession from rue Pellerin in downtown Saigon to a suburban gravesite near the present Tan Son Nhut airport. Ahead of the casket were ten well-organized groups of students, workers, women, and members of the progressive Vietnam Youth Party, each holding aloft identification banners and brief poems extolling Phan Chu Trinh. Six prominent individuals escorted the horse-drawn hearse, followed by row upon row of general mourners, all observing the prohibition on loud conversation and smoking. Somber music was added by a small orchestra from the elite Taberd Catholic School. Several photographers moved parallel to the procession, taking pictures at major intersections. As the temperature rose, tea, lemonade, and mint gelatin were offered free to the mourners by people who had thought to set up small stands along the way.[8]

Nearly two hundred laudatory banners in Chinese, *nom* (demotic characters), and *quoc-ngu* (romanized script) dominated the gravesite. Some were carefully composed couplets contributed by well-known individuals, including Phan Boi Chau. The majority, however, seemed to come from groups of students, shopkeepers, artisans, workers, clerks, and monks. Words like "independence," "freedom," "bravery," "unity," and "descendant of Lac Hong" (a prehistoric Vietnamese kingdom) interlarded otherwise stilted or honorific phraseology. More than anything else, the fact that people in at least fifty different locations around the country had sent these praises to a departed hero made this a truly national funeral.[9]

While there were many emotional pledges to continue Phan Chu Trinh's lifework and perhaps even bring it to fruition, it is apparent that this meant different things to different participants. Students tended to emphasize Phan's commitment to raising popular consciousness; elderly traditionalists pointed to his rigorous self-discipline and denial of worldly pleasures; merchants stressed Phan's perception that competition was the overwhelming law of life, as well as

8. Tran Huy Lieu (Nam Kieu), *Tieu Su Ong Phan Chau Trinh* [Biography of Phan Chau Trinh] (Saigon, 1926), pp. 87–110.

9. Tran Huy Lieu, *Tieu Su Ong Phan Chau Trinh*, pp. 117–52. The national implications of the funeral are reflected in the distribution of commemorative banners: fifty-three banners were contributed by northern Vietnamese groups or individuals, forty-eight by southern Vietnamese, and forty-three by central Vietnamese; a further seventeen came from the Vietnamese community in Phnom Penh; and thirty-one cannot be identified by location.

his earlier willingness to get involved in promoting commercial enterprises; and bureaucrats fastened onto his support for Franco-Vietnamese collaboration. As it turned out, the two main gravesite orations exposed the central dichotomy. Bui Quang Chieu (1873–1945), leader of the bourgeois Constitutionalist Party, claimed that Phan's greatest legacy was to have originated the idea of "relying on the French and seeking progress." As if in reply, Huynh Thuc Khang (1876–1947), one of only three or four men who could be considered lifelong comrades of the deceased, chose to stress the need for Vietnamese self-sufficiency and solidarity, as well as Phan's essential optimism about life and human nature.[10] It was a harbinger of more general political cleavages soon to widen further and then to become unbridgeable after 1930.

At least sixteen other localities around Vietnam plus the Vietnamese community in Phnom Penh are also known to have organized funeral observances for Phan Chu Trinh. Generally these involved closing shops, wearing armbands, perhaps forming a procession, then coming together at a temple, theater, or open piece of land to conduct a ceremony. There was usually a simplified altar holding Phan Chu Trinh's picture, incense burners, and character banners but none of the customary offerings of food or other paraphernalia destined for the spirit world. Generally a local personality recited Phan's life story, some individuals pledged future actions appropriate to Phan's memory, there was a collection of modest amounts of money to send to Saigon to maintain the tomb, and then people disbanded, feeling that something meaningful had occurred. In southern Vietnam, local landlords and merchants tended to take the lead, although pupils, artisans, government clerks, and women also participated energetically. In the center and north, individual literati often headed the organizing committees, but it was groups of students and pupils who disseminated leaflets, visited shopowners to encourage them to shut down during the indicated hours, and drafted statements and pledges to present at the public ceremonies.

In some places principals punished or expelled pupils for these activities, or even for simply wearing a black armband in school. This produced a series of historically significant student strikes.[11] A number of expellees subsequently involved themselves full-time in local agitation or left the country to investigate more closely new political and intellectual currents.

---

10. Tran Huy Lieu, *Tieu Su Ong Phan Chau Trinh*, pp. 110–16. There were three other brief orations by: (a) the head of the funeral society that donated the land and promised to maintain the modest tomb; (b) a representative of the 1,000 or more Vietnamese laborers at the French Arsenal, a significant inclusion even though the speaker's remarks were open to diverse interpretations; and (c) a member of the local Chinese Kuomintang organization.

11. Tran Huy Lieu, *Tieu Su Ong Phan Chau Trinh*, pp. 155–200; *La Cloche Fêlée*, 22 and 29 Apr. 1926; Louis Roubaud, *Vietnam* (Paris, 1931), p. 67; and Nguyet Tu, *Chi Minh Khai* (Hanoi, 1976), pp. 22–23.

Assessing matters immediately afterward, one of the prime initiators, Tran Huy Lieu (1901–1969), seemed momentarily stunned by just how successful the "state funeral" (*quoc tang*) had been. "From prominent personalities to rickshaw pullers, from cities to rural marketplaces, people were deeply pained, their faces showed real sadness," he wrote. Yet there had also been pride, joy that Vietnamese knew how to honor one of their own. "Surely we can record 4 April as the day the citizens of Vietnam mourned a Vietnamese upholder of the righteous cause, Phan Chu Trinh." Then, backing away from the trap of complacency, Tran Huy Lieu focused on the transcendent need to complete Phan's work:

It is good to mourn Phan Chu Trinh by voice and by pen, but above all we must demonstrate our affection in the form of action. . . . One, ten, one hundred, a thousand, ten thousand, a hundred thousand people should combine all their love for Phan Chu Trinh into a democratic army to destroy the citadels of oppression and injustice. Surely that would cause Phan's spirit to smile and say, "Great! Wonderful!" . . . Among our countrymen, who is prepared to remember Phan Chu Trinh in this way?[12]

Social and Economic Structure

Although Tran Huy Lieu had grasped brilliantly the political significance of the events of 1925–1926, he and his intelligentsia peers still possessed only the vaguest understanding of the social and economic context within which they were operating. Over the next decade they moved to correct that deficiency. Realizing that the "citadels of oppression and injustice" would not come tumbling down simply as the result of mass demonstrations, no matter how well organized, nor be dissolved by spellbinding rhetoric, many intelligentsia shifted their attention to the analysis and testing of ideas concerning the society of which they themselves were only a small component. As it turned out, conditions prevailing during the Popular Front period (1936–39) and, in a very different way, during World War II presented at least the radical segment of the Vietnamese intelligentsia with a series of unparalleled opportunities to combine theory and practice.

To begin to appreciate those opportunities, it is necessary to understand the general outlines of colonial society during the interwar period. At the top were about 39,000 Europeans, half of them women and children classified as "without profession," and another one-quarter made up of army and navy personnel who generally stayed only a few years. The remaining 10,000 or so were divided among the government agencies, professions, trading firms, mining companies, plantations, industries, and banks.[13]

12. Tran Huy Lieu, *Tieu Su Ong Phan Chau Trinh*, pp. 115, 201–203.

13. An additional 3,100 Europeans lived in Cambodia and Laos. These and subsequent figures are from 1937, the first time a reasonably systematic general census was taken. Charles Robequain, *The Economic Development of French Indo-China* (London, 1944), pp. 21–31.

A comparison with British, American, and Dutch colonies in South and Southeast Asia reveals that the French continued to occupy a much higher percentage of middle- and low-level bureaucratic, entrepreneurial, and technical positions. In 1930, for example, Europeans still held twenty percent of all available government administrative and clerical positions in Indochina and managed to consume at least sixty percent of the general personnel budget.[14] French entrepreneurs monopolized the three major sectors of the non-subsistence economy: rice exporting, rubber production and mining. They also controlled most second-tier endeavors in coffee, tea, tobacco, timber, cement, distilling, and textiles. In 1938 the authorities decided to give serious attention to training indigenous technical cadres, but six years later, Vietnamese technicians were still outnumbered by Europeans.[15]

European property owners who resided in the colony for at least a decade tended to become politically aggressive. No governor-general could ride roughshod over their interests and remain effective. On the other hand, neither the *colons* nor the governors-general could seriously challenge the interests of the corporate directors in faraway Paris, Lyon, or Marseilles. It was the job of the Ministry of Colonies to try to resolve differences between these three parties when they occurred. Finally, beyond *colons*, governors-general, colonial-oriented corporations, and the Ministry of Colonies there existed more fundamental divisions within French society, for example, between domestic industry and overseas investment, urban and rural lobbies, political left and right, and anti-cleric and Catholic elements. The net effect of such metropolitan contradictions on a place like Indochina was to restrict considerably the developmental potential of capitalism—French, Chinese, or Vietnamese.[16]

The overall population of Vietnam (Tonkin, Annam, Cochinchina) was estimated in 1937 to be nineteen million;[17] 217,000 Chinese were listed, ranging from the wealthiest rice merchants to small town moneylenders and shopkeepers, poor dockworkers and sweatshop laborers. While the Chinese minority had its

14. Gouvernement Géneral de l'Indochine, *Annuaire Statistique de l'Indochine* (1931), vol. 3 (1930–31) Hanoi: Imprimerie d'Extrême-Orient, 1932, pp. 196–7, 203–220. Gouvernement Général de l'Indochine, *Annuaire Administratif de l'Indochine, 1931*, Hanoi: Imprimerie d'Extrême-Orient, 1931, contains rosters of government employees, including seniority and salary data.

15. Nguyen Khac Dam, *Nhung Thu Doan Boc Lot cua Tu Ban Phap o Viet Nam* [Exploitative Activities of French Capital in Vietnam] (Hanoi, 1958).

16. For a recent analysis of French colonial policy debates of the 1930s, see Daniel Hémery, "Aux origines des guerres d'indépendence vietnamiennes: pouvoir colonial et phénomène communiste en Indochine avant la Second Guerre Mondiale," *Le Mouvement Social* 10 (Oct.–Dec. 1977), pp. 3–35.

17. Due to imperfect census procedures and to conscious efforts by citizens to avoid being recorded, the population may well have been ten percent higher.

own legal status, political organizations, and social hierarchy, this did not mean that the Chinese were completely isolated from the Vietnamese majority or vice versa; on the contrary, there seems to have been a fair degree of interaction.[18] Another small but economically significant element was the 5,000 or more Indian moneylenders and brokers, almost all in Cochinchina. In the lower Mekong delta there remained no fewer than 326,000 Khmers, while 191,000 Vietnamese were listed as having settled as a minority in Cambodia. Along the Vietnamese borders with China, Laos, and Cambodia there lived at least 1.6 million people of diverse ethno-linguistic backgrounds.[19]

The remainder of the population was ethnic Vietnamese, probably eighteen million people in 1937, but certainly no less than the 16.7 million census figure. The Vietnamese population was estimated to be growing by at least 200,000 per year. Between ninety-three and ninety-five percent of all Vietnamese continued to live in the countryside. Nevertheless, as a result of structural changes alluded to in my introduction, rural patterns of social interaction were not at all the same as in the days before French arrival. From a society previously characterized by a preponderance of peasant proprietors, village self-government, and a limited number of royal estates, the trend was now toward commercial estates, increasingly concentrated landlord wealth and power, alienation of communal property, and growth in the numbers of tenants and agricultural laborers.[20] During the 1920s and 1930s the social ideal for most rural Vietnamese remained that of three generations under one roof, owning and tilling one's own land, sharing harvest tasks with one's neighbors, and being listened to respectfully in the village council. How many of them realized that reality was moving further and further from this ideal is an extremely difficult question to answer. The proportion certainly increased in the 1930s, and may have become preponderant in the 1940s.[21]

Reality in Vietnamese society of the 1920s and 1930s began with those land-

---

18. The Chinese minority may have been in a worse relative economic position in 1945 than it had been sixty-five years earlier in 1880. The French pushed into Chinese mining, banking, transport, and export-import spheres and worked persistently to subordinate the Indochinese economy to the metropole. Nguyen Khac Dam, *Nhung Thu Doan Boc Lot*, pp. 96–127, 163–65, 221–24.

19. Robequain, *Economic Development*, pp. 32–49. The main border groups would be of Thai, Nung, Meo, Muong, Malayo-Polynesian, and Mon-Khmer ethnolinguistic origins.

20. Ngo Vinh Long, *Before the Revolution: The Vietnamese Peasants Under the French* (Cambridge, Mass.: MIT Press, 1973), pp. 4–41.

21. Objective conditions and subjective perceptions thereof also differed from one region or province to another. Numerous Vietnamese intelligentsia accounts of rural conditions exist. For selected translations, see ibid., pp. 146–276. Assessing directly the attitudes of different rural strata is a more difficult job, one which no one has really attempted systematically, as far as I know. A theoretical model for such research is suggested in James C. Scott, *The Moral Economy of the Peasantry* (New Haven: Yale Univ. Press, 1976).

lords who were wealthy enough to spend the bulk of their time in the cities or provincial towns, conducting their rural business via a bevy of managers, clerks, and field supervisors. Perhaps as many as seven thousand Vietnamese families had attained this privileged position by the 1920s. Up to seventy-five percent of them lived in Saigon, as well as maintaining second villas in towns nearer to their Mekong delta estates. Another cluster of absentee landlords was located in Hanoi, and the remainder could be found in northern and central Vietnamese towns like Nam Dinh, Hai Duong, Thanh Hoa, and Hue.[22]

Absentee landlords combined with entrepreneurs and a few higher officials and magistrates to make up what was called the "indigenous bourgeoisie" (*tu san ban xu*). These three groups, totalling perhaps 10,500 families, or 0.5 percent of the Vietnamese population in 1937, tended to overlap substantially. Wealthy landlords understood the benefits of trying to obtain official positions for themselves or their sons. Merchants and officials often invested in rural land and made loans to peasants or tenants because of the very high rates of return. There is little doubt that rural land rents and interest payments constituted the largest proportion of total indigenous bourgeois income, with commercial profits and government salaries in second and third positions respectively.[23] Thus, although members of the Vietnamese bourgeoisie thought of themselves as urbanites, and tried to model themselves on their Parisian counterparts, complete with champagne and cheeses, fashionable furniture and clothing, dinner parties, mistresses (or concubines), government medals, and advisory council positions, most of them were still dependent on rural income. They naturally sought for their children "the best education that money could buy." However, given the sharply pyramidal character of the colonial school system, this was not always possible. Nor was there any certainty of employment commensurate with secondary or tertiary educational achievement.

As a result of the limitations imposed by the French colonial system, the Vietnamese bourgeoisie became highly proficient in certain matters, yet remained grossly deficient in others. Much energy, for example, was devoted to arranging

22. Exactly how to delineate Vietnamese social strata is a complicated and seldom discussed question. Here I am making the assumption that someone who owned fifty or more cultivated hectares in Cochinchina (5,500 families), or eighteen or more cultivated hectares in Tonkin (1,000) and Annam (500), was a wealthy and probably absentee landlord. Tonkin and Annam tended to have higher annual yields per hectare due to more intensive cultivation. Pierre Gourou, *L'Utilisation du Sol en Indochine* (Paris: Hartmann, 1940), pp. 229, 255; Yves Henry, *L'Economie Agricole de l'Indochine* (Hanoi, 1932), pp. 109, 145.

23. One study has suggested the term "official-landlord-capitalist-entrepreneur class" rather than "bourgeoisie" (Ngo Vinh Long and Nguyen Hoi Chan, *Vietnamese Women in Society and Revolution*, vol. 1: The French Colonial Period [Cambridge, 1974], p. 7); perhaps "landlord-entrepreneur-official" would be more accurate. At any rate, I have chosen to stick with the term "bourgeoisie" as understood at the time in Vietnam and explained here.

socially enhancing marriages for one's children, or to organizing elaborate charity functions to which members of the French community as well as one's Vietnamese peers could be invited. Some bourgeois Vietnamese did become quite knowledgeable on particular economic topics, most notably interest rates, the international market in agricultural commodities, and maritime shipping tariffs. As will be discussed later, a few others became proficient in medicine and law, and perhaps a larger number chose to patronize various artistic, literary, and publishing endeavors. Particularly striking, however, was the low regard which most members of the Vietnamese bourgeoisie had for practical political activities. Nor was much attention given to developing a coherent ideology of their own. Only when they saw a threat from communism did some of the members of the bourgeoisie try to remedy this situation. Not surprisingly, their efforts remained reactive, lacking in positive content, and generally premised on indefinite maintenance of the colonial status quo.

In a rather different position were the 55,000 or so smaller landlord families.[24] Generally they continued to live in their home villages and to conduct affairs with tenants and wage laborers without resort to intermediaries. Despite the commercial character of this relationship, most village landlords wanted to think of themselves as inheritors of the traditions of the local Confucian literati and the village notables; they tended to be staunch upholders of status hierarchy, traditional festivals, rites for village tutelary deities, patriarchal discipline, and various religious doctrines preaching harmony, human compassion, and rewards in the afterlife. Village landlords could also be quite nationalistic in their own way, dwelling proudly on ancient Vietnamese heroes, promoting the development of *quoc-ngu* literature, condemning Western-induced cultural alienation, and, on safe occasions at least, displaying rancor at the manner in which the French lorded it over the Vietnamese. Many poorer members of the village accepted the landlord's cultural pretensions and felt themselves lucky to be linked in a patron-client relationship, tilling "his" land, borrowing "his" money. Only from 1930 onward did the idea take hold that the landlord might have stolen the land and money from those who tilled the soil.

During the 1920s and 1930s there remained a significant stratum of middle-level farmers, perhaps 750,000 families, or close to thirty percent of the rural Vietnamese population. Basically they attempted to produce enough on their

24. Gourou, *L'Utilisation du Sol*, p. 273, and Henry, *L'Economie Agricole*, pp. 109, 145. I am categorizing "smaller landlords" or "village landlords" as owning 10–50 hectares in Cochinchina (28,000 families), 3.6–18 hectares in Tonkin (20,000), and 5–18 hectares in Annam (7,000). Actually, the percentage of income derived from land rents and loans or the number of hours per year put into properties of given sizes by tenants and hired laborers would provide a more accurate picture; unfortunately, however, I have been unable to locate any studies of sufficient scope to permit rural class estimates to be made according to those criteria.

own property to subsist, although they often hired a few hands to help at plant-ing or harvest times and in turn offered themselves for hire during slack periods of the year. Unlike village landlords, who might be wedded to the pomp and rhetoric of tradition, but who made their money by understanding colonial mar-ket forces, subsistence farmers tried very hard to preserve and revitalize certain precolonial village social and economic institutions. They favored the diffusion of decision-making, the restoration of viable village schools, and, above all, the pres-ervation of communal lands from private alienation.[25]

To avoid going into debt to landlords or moneylenders, subsistence farmers organized among themselves a variety of mutual credit associations. Of necessity, however, such associations were limited to trusted relatives, friends, and immedi-ate neighbors, with normally twelve to twenty-four participants.[26] Although the amount of shared capital was small, all were living on such precarious economic margins that the default of one or two partners could spell real trouble for all.[27] Several bad seasons in a row were enough to convert a subsistence farmer into a poor peasant or tenant, with little chance of reversing the sequence. During the late 1930s the Indochinese Communist Party endeavored to promote mutual aid associations among subsistence farmers. Some farmers were then recruited as Party members, and others joined the Viet Minh in the early 1940s. During the subsequent War of Resistance (1945–1954), subsistence farmer families may well have provided the largest proportion of Party cadres.

Well before 1945, however, hundreds of thousands of subsistence farmers al-ready had lost their land, or were hanging on to tiny scraps that were quite insufficient to maintain their dependants. Poor peasants, tenants, and agricultural laborers together made up nearly seventy percent of the rural Vietnamese popu-lation by the late 1930s.[28] Often a subsistence farmer began the downward spiral to tenancy as a result of some regional calamity, for example, a flood, drought, typhoon, insect plague, or disease epidemic. Another common cause was unfore-seen family expenses, for example, a serious illness, funeral, legal entanglement,

---

25. The communal land issue had important social and political implications, as some French and Vietnamese policy analysts learned late in the game. See Vu Van Hien, "La propriété com-munale au Tonkin" (Ph.D. thesis, University of Paris, 1939; a nineteen-page English synopsis of this thesis, titled "Communal Ricefields and Lands in North Vietnam," was distributed by the Yale University Southeast Asia Studies Center in 1950). For a schematic description of land uti-lization in precolonial villages, see John Adams and Nancy Hancock, "Land and Economy in Traditional Vietnam," *Journal of Southeast Asian Studies* (Sep. 1970), pp. 90–98.

26. Nguyen Van Vinh, "Savings and Mutual Lending Societies (*Ho*)," Yale University South-east Asia Studies mimeograph (1949); translated from a series appearing in *L'Annam Nouveau* (Hanoi), Feb.–Sept. 1931.

27. Vu Quoc Thuc, *L'Economie Communaliste du Viet Nam* (Hanoi, 1951), pp. 108–13.

28. The percentage may have been higher, depending on where one draws the line between subsistence farmers and poor peasants. Very generally, those families possessing less than one hec-tare would probably have had to rent some additional land or hire themselves out as agricultural

accident, or loss of livestock. None of these perils was new, of course. What made them considerably more maleficent, however, was the relentless market mechanism. If one's crop was lost, a loan would probably be needed to obtain seed for the next crop, not to mention interim nourishment. If one's water buffalo died, it was necessary to borrow another from someone more fortunate, generally on commercial terms, not merely by promising to return the favor later. Indeed, even relatives were increasingly reluctant to loan simply on the basis of social reciprocity.

Beyond all this there were taxes to be paid in cash, and cash was also needed to purchase a number of essential commodities that were neither produced locally nor available by means of barter (salt, fish sauce, soap, matches, cloth, kerosene, farm implements, cooking utensils). Assuming that a subsistence farmer possessed a surplus after a good harvest, he still had a much more difficult time than the landlords in keeping track of price fluctuations, and he was seldom able to store his grain to await a better market. In short, rice was increasingly being produced and circulated for its commercial value and less and less for its food value—a trend inherently favorable to the landlords and inevitably causing an increase in landless and land-poor Vietnamese.

Landlords were normally quite eager to loan money, grain, or buffalo to subsistence farmers, knowing that this was an easy, profitable, and safe way to use capital. If a debtor defaulted, as happened fairly often, he could be converted into a full or partial tenant. For the same reasons, a tenant was often treated harshly or ejected if he did not borrow from his landlord. Maintaining a tenant in a relationship of permanent indebtedness was the most efficient method of extracting maximum labor at minimum cost, as both sides knew how ruthlessly the colonial police tracked down and punished absconders.

In the event of partial or total loss of land, a rural family (or in the first instance one or two young adult members) had the option of departing for the mines, plantations, factories, or government public works projects. Since working conditions were uniformly bad in such places, there was a tendency to gravitate back to one's home village if at all possible. There were also seasonal movements from country to town and back again. During the 1920s alone it seems likely that at least 600,000 men and women spent several years as non-rural wage la-

---

laborers. If they were involved in handicraft production, in small trading, or had family members working seasonally in the "modern" sector (factories, mines, plantations), then less land would suffice (Gourou, *L'Utilisation du Sol*, pp. 229, 255, 272–73, 282, and idem, *Les Paysans du Delta Tonkinois* [Paris: Editions d'Art et d'Histoire, 1936], p. 376). The most recent discussion of these and related questions is contained in Ngo Vinh Long, "Peasant Revolutionary Struggles in Vietnam in the 1930s" (Ph.D. thesis, Harvard University, 1978), pp. 99–350; see also Pham Cao Duong, *Thuc Trang cua gioi Nong Dan Viet-Nam duoi thoi Phap Thuoc* [True Status of the Vietnamese Peasantry under French Rule] (Saigon, 1966), pp. 102–24, 171–202.

borers.[29] Those who stayed on longer became increasingly class-conscious, organized, and capable of mounting strikes for both economic and political objectives. Although probably never more than two percent of the population at any given point, this proletariat in the proper sense of the term had a significance far beyond what numbers can indicate. Workers were more or less detached from traditional mechanisms of social control (father, family elders, village notables). They were physically located in positions of most economic and psychological concern to the French. And they rapidly demonstrated an ability to influence certain other elements of the population along new lines as well.

In the long run the proletariat, like the intelligentsia, was more important as a tiny but energetic core group and catalytic factor than as a foundation upon which to build a revolution. One French economist was close to the mark when he argued in 1939 that the considerable turnover in labor supply, although delaying formation of a distinct, self-conscious working class and postponing "establishment of a strict line of demarcation between the wage earner and the peasant," still had the effect of extending "the new way of life to a rather large portion of the population."[30] To be more precise, this was the "new way of life" as experienced and explained by people on the bottom of the modern economic heap, not by the native bourgeoisie. Vietnam's subsistence farmers, poor peasants, and agricultural laborers were thus exposed more persistently to proletarian political formulations than to those of the bourgeoisie—a factor of no little significance in the unfolding of rural events from 1930 onward.[31]

Between the French *colons* and the Vietnamese bourgeoisie on one side, and the proletariat (and quasi-proletariat) on the other, stood a volatile component made up of shopkeepers, small traders, artisans, clerks, managers, interpreters, primary school teachers, journalists, and technicians. From very scattered evi-

---

29. I base this figure on the following estimates: (a) 221,000 officially registered miners and plantation and factory workers in French companies in 1929; (b) probably another 50,000 family members or friends who quietly shared the official employee cards because of high illness rates and the exhausting twelve- or thirteen-hour work days; (c) 50,000 coolies employed on big public works projects; and (d) a minimum 100 percent turnover rate in eight years. To this figure one might add perhaps 200,000 unattached coolies, rickshaw pullers, itinerant handymen, servants, and beggars, all more or less on the fringes of the working class but likely to follow its leadership in times of crisis. In social terms one might also include the unknown numbers of family members who went along with the primary wage earners and thus shared in the new ethos. On the other hand, one would have to subtract workers who died and, from the point of view of unified political potential, workers of Chinese nationality.

30. Robequain, *Economic Development*, p. 82. He might have added that the proletariat's disseminator role was heightened by the firing and return to rural localities of at least 100,000 workers during the Depression.

31. Ngo Van Hoa and Duong Kinh Quoc, *Giai Cap Cong Nhan Viet Nam Nhung Nam Truoc Khi Thanh Lap Dang* [The Vietnamese Working Class in the Years Before Formation of the Party] (Hanoi, 1978).

dence it seems that this petit bourgeois stratum accounted for about half of the urban Vietnamese population, or 550,000 people in 1937.[32] They tended to be avid joiners of organizations, felt the psychological degradations of foreign rule more directly than others, tried hard to obtain modern schooling for their children, and probably provided the bulk of subscribers to *quoc-ngu* newspapers and journals. Although dependent on salaries, commissions or small shop profits, some petit bourgeois families retained tiny plots of land in their ancestral villages, and almost all visited "home" (*que huong*) periodically. Unlike the proletariat, however, they had neither a coherent political vision nor much consciousness of themselves as a separate economic stratum. All they shared with each other, and with anyone else who would listen, was a feeling that the colonial system was failing to meet their needs.

It was the petit bourgeoisie who probably contributed the largest numbers to a group that will concern us greatly—the "new intelligentsia" (*gioi tri thuc moi*). However, other social categories were well represented in the new intelligentsia too. These included some progeny of absentee landlords who had come to believe there was more to life than counting money or obtaining French citizenship, some sons and daughters of disgruntled literati, and a small but growing number of individuals from subsistence farming and poor peasant backgrounds. During the 1930s a few young working-class men and women also came to be regarded as of the intelligentsia. The social composition of the Vietnamese intelligentsia was further complicated by the fact that many members chose to deny their class backgrounds and tried to assert a new identity based on job category, ideological affiliation, or creative achievements. This was most notable among those children of literati, landlords, or subsistence farmers, who subsequently declared themselves to be "proletarianized" (*vo san hoa*). However, some children of poor peasant or working-class origins were equally eager to move in the reverse direction. A few managed to do this by dint of intellectual brilliance.

To be part of the new intelligentsia during the 1920s and 1930s was not primarily a matter of class origins, wealth, or social status, however; it was rather a state of mind. In the first instance it meant that an individual had committed himself to thinking, talking, reading, and writing about change. Some intellectuals endorsed changes that had occurred since colonization; others denounced them. Some demanded radical action, others advised extreme caution. All agreed, however, that Vietnam was profoundly different from when the French had arrived, that there could be no return to the past, and that critical, informed discussion of future political, socio-economic, and cultural changes was essential to the survival and development of the nation. Combined with these concerns

---

32. Although some members of the petit bourgeoisie spent considerable time in rural areas as primary teachers, clerks, or land managers, they still thought of themselves as "urban" and made every effort to find future positions in the towns and cities.

was the feeling that the older generation of Vietnamese leaders were either too hidebound or too fainthearted to be able to take the necessary initiatives.

As with the earlier Confucian literati, or the French-speaking collaborator generation, some analysts might wish to identify the new intelligentsia simply as those Vietnamese people of the 1920s and 1930s who worked with their minds rather than their hands. This would virtually eliminate the usefulness of the term. It would also differ from what people meant at the time. First of all, there were clearly members of the Vietnamese elite who "worked with their minds" on problems of land purchase, loans, concessions, commerce, administration, and judicial affairs, yet were not considered by their peers to be members of the intelligentsia. On the other side of the coin, there were some individuals who made their living primarily by means of petty commerce or even manual labor, yet were included in the intelligentsia because of their valued, albeit far less remunerative, artistic, journalistic, or verbal activities.

In the last analysis, what probably served to define the Vietnamese intelligentsia, other than the previously mentioned preoccupation with change, was its propensity to form small, informal study groups, to publish prolifically, and to enjoy reasoning with each other on a wide spectrum of topics. In the mid-1920s there may have been 5,000 Vietnamese, mostly young, mostly possessing three to ten years of formal education, taking active intelligentsia roles. By the end of the 1930s the figure had probably doubled to 10,000. During those fifteen years, too, intellectual leadership shifted perceptibly away from progeny of landlord and literati families and toward individuals who, by personal choice or social origins, had no convenient place to which they might retreat in the event of serious setback. When the colonial authorities cracked down on a particular study group, newspaper, or publishing endeavor, these members often had to make decisions of major personal consequence.

By 1939 the Vietnamese intelligentsia was older, poorer, wiser, and harder. The authorities had demonstrated repeatedly that they could accommodate only technical competence, not critical thought. By dint of the ruthless logic inherent in any autocratic system, members of the intelligentsia were forced in one of three directions: they could accept the French rules of public behavior, they could retreat to quiet aestheticism, or they could engage in dangerous illegal activities. During the early 1940s the intelligentsia fragmented more or less along those lines. While intellectuals continued to play significant historical roles, it was not as members of a coherent fraternity of the mind, but as units subsumed to particular social classes and political organizations. The era of the Vietnamese intelligentsia was over.

Language and Literacy

Besides the above schematic model of society, something needs to be said about language, literacy, education, and publishing in colonial Vietnam. Among all the countries of Southeast Asia, Vietnam probably enjoyed the most favorable conditions for meaningful intellectual activity.

Although many members of the intelligentsia were slow to appreciate it, the seventeen or eighteen million ethnic Vietnamese were extremely fortunate to possess a single spoken language. At least eighty-five percent of the population inhabiting what the French called Tonkin, Annam, and Cochinchina spoke the same language with only minor dialectal variations.[33] While there were admittedly different tone stresses, variations in vowel pronunciations, and alternative words for particular plants, culinary items, or work tools, Vietnamese of various regions of the country had little difficulty communicating when the occasion arose.[34]

Vietnam initially was in a much less fortunate position as regards writing systems. At the turn of the century it was possible to argue persuasively in favor of Chinese characters, *nom* (demotic characters), French, or *quoc-ngu* (romanized script). One might also argue for some combination of the four (see Chap. 4). However, by the 1920s the choice was narrowing down to French or *quoc-ngu*. By 1945 almost everyone was focusing on enrichment and dissemination of *quoc-ngu*. Vietnamese also proceeded to incorporate into their spoken vocabulary thousands of coined *quoc-ngu* words. To meet new historical demands, the syntax of both written and spoken Vietnamese changed considerably. Somewhere in this period the colonial authorities lost control of language strategy. All of these language developments were crucial to Vietnamese who preached cultural renaissance or political independence. They eventually were to prove quite important to the entire population.

The roots of Vietnamese fascination with writing and literacy go back many centuries, not only for the elite, but also for the poorest and least educated.[35] The sacred and aesthetic connotations of calligraphy served to bolster one of the central socializing activities of the country: individual memorization of large chunks of Chinese literature leading to competition in periodic civil examinations. In the nineteenth century perhaps an average of 4,000 scholars attempted the regional examinations held every three years.[36] This implied a core group of at least

33. The only countries in Asia with higher primary language percentages are Korea (100%) and Japan (99%). Thailand and Cambodia are in approximately the same percentile group as Vietnam; at the other end of the spectrum are countries like Nepal, Indonesia, Malaysia, India, and the Philippines, which have no majority languages. Joshua A. Fishman, comp., *Language Problems of Developing Nations* (New York: John Wiley and Sons, 1968), pp. 95–96.

34. The degree of difficulty involved in Vietnamese cross-regional communication may be compared with someone from the Bronx trying to be understood in Alabama.

35. One prominent Western scholar goes so far as to argue that "Vietnam is and always has been one of the most intensely literary civilizations on the face of the planet." Alexander Woodside, *Community and Revolution in Modern Vietnam* (Boston: Houghton Mifflin, 1976), p. 2.

36. Alexander Woodside, *Vietnam and the Chinese Model: A Comparative Study of Nguyen and Ch'ing Civil Government in the First Half of the Nineteenth Century* (Cambridge, Mass.:

20,000 accomplished literati. A second group, perhaps two or three times that size, while not skilled enough to attempt the regional examinations, was still able to read official proclamations, texts on family morality, and certain collections of poetry, folklore, and social satire. Finally, it seems reasonable to assume that up to twenty-five percent of Vietnamese over fifteen years of age were able to decipher several hundred Chinese and *nom* characters—enough to help them examine family and village records, check basic private contracts, or appreciate local ceremonies.

Applying those same rough gradations of literacy to Vietnamese of the colonial period, it is doubtful that there was any improvement. Sophisticated knowledge of Chinese probably decreased only very gradually until the first decade of the twentieth century. However, the literati were finding their skills to be of less and less social utility. After World War I, if they wished to exert any influence beyond their own villages it was necessary for them to learn French. Many literati were unable to master this entirely new language and literature. The decline was more apparent in the second and third categories of literacy. Unlike the literati, who had access to an institution for conversion to French and *quoc-ngu* if they chose to use it, most other Vietnamese found themselves caught between colonial efforts (1919–1927) to close down remaining village-level Sino-Vietnamese schools and the simultaneous reluctance of the authorities to subsidize alternatives. Landlords were generally disinterested, since they could afford to send their children beyond the village for schooling. Subsistence farmers, who wanted local schools more than any other social stratum, were less and less able to pay for them. Landless and land-deficient members of the village could seldom spare their children from daily work tasks, much less contribute money to help pay for a teacher and school supplies. As a result village-financed *quoc-ngu* schools teetered between pathetic irregularity and outright collapse.

It seems unlikely that in the mid-1920s more than five percent of the Vietnamese population, or about 750,000 people, could read a newspaper, proclamation, or letter in any language. After the mid-1920s official school enrollments did edge upwards. Equally important was the growing tendency of unschooled young men and women to learn to read and write *quoc-ngu* on their own initiative, perhaps with assistance from family members, party comrades, or small intelligentsia groups conducting free night classes. By 1939 functional ("newspaper") literacy may have grown to ten percent of the current population, or 1.8 million people. Literacy continued to expand during World War II, providing a solid foundation for truly national literacy campaigns from 1945 onward.

Harvard Univ. Press, 1971), pp. 194–223. The 4,000 estimate is mine, based on various figures mentioned by Woodside. Numbers may have increased in later years. For example, one source mentions an average of 6,000 candidates in the 1876 and 1879 Hanoi regional examinations alone (Maurice Durand and P. Huard, *Connaissance du Vietnam* [Hanoi Ecole Française d'Extrême-Orient, 1954], p. 84).

Education

Half in admiration, half in exasperation, French officials often remarked on persistent Vietnamese requests to upgrade formal education. Meanwhile, to many Vietnamese it appeared that the authorities had designed colonial schools in order to discourage serious learning. Almost ninety percent of all children who entered grade one between 1920 and 1938 were destined not to get beyond the third grade. This was partly due to obvious constraints on poor families, partly a problem of walking distance from home to school in many rural areas, but also a function of the stiff examinations imposed on children wishing to advance to higher levels. Thus, fourth-year pupils constituted perhaps six percent of total enrollments, while less than .3 percent were to be found in the seventh year. From 1920 to 1938 the total enrollment increased by 128 percent, from about 126,000 to about 287,500; yet at no point were even ten percent of school-age children actually going to school.[37]

Despite the short duration of schooling and the limited enrollment—perhaps 1.2 million children between 1920 and 1938—there can be no doubting the profound impact of the educational experience on those involved. Children who underwent a mere one year of formal education were still confronted with a host of strange phenomena: the tri-color; the French school inspector; the self-consciously urban Vietnamese instructor; and the introductory classes in geography, French history, math, hygiene, and general science. At this elementary level (grades 1–3) pupils were expected to learn how to read and write *quoc ngu*, and were usually given some French language instruction as well. Many individuals compelled to drop out of elementary school after a year or two discovered subsequently that they had somehow assimilated enough basic *quoc ngu* reading skills to consolidate literacy with the aid of friends and of manuals published specifically for the informal learner.

The key to understanding such individual achievements, quite extraordinary when compared with elementary pupils in most other countries, probably lies with the young Vietnamese instructors.[38] Often their extracurricular contacts with pupils proved to be of equal importance to classroom exercises. Many of these young men and women were profoundly disenchanted with tradition and disturbed by colonial practices, and they impatiently searched for alternatives. They conveyed both anguish and excitement to pupils, and it was also not un-

37. Gail P. Kelly, "Franco-Vietnamese Schools, 1918–1938" (Ph.D. dissertation, University of Wisconsin, 1974), tables 1 and 4.

38. The government by 1938–39 employed 6,550 Vietnamese instructors and auxiliary instructors for grades 1–6. Ten percent were women. DIRIP, "Rapport sur le fonctionnement de la Direction de l'Instruction Publique pendant l'année scolaire 1938–39," AOM NF carton 259, dossier 2226.

Three generations of school teachers in Soc Trang province, south Vietnam. The eldest is wearing traditional literati garb; the man to his right is dressed in a manner favored by colonial functionaries of the early twentieth century; and the man to his left represents the new intelligentsia of the late 1920s. Gouvernement Général de l'Indochine, *La Cochinchine Scolaire* (Hanoi, 1931).

common for them to come into sharp conflict with local officials or parents, which placed pupils in the difficult position of choosing between authority figures.[39]

Students who persisted to grades 4–6, or what was called primary-level education, faced different but no less challenging problems. Often the school was much too far from home to walk back and forth, necessitating boarding arrangements with relatives or family friends. At this level, one was expected to master French; however, the Vietnamese instructors were often barely competent in French themselves, and to make matters worse, the French language curriculum seemed designed to accomplish three conflicting objectives at once: to impart French cultural and behavioral norms, to reinforce Vietnamese traditionalist morality, and to teach students how to read basic instructions and talk properly to their colonial masters.[40]

---

39. For an example of cautious support for teachers in this situation, see Nguyen Gy, *Long Nguyen Vong cua Quoc Dan Viet Nam* (Hanoi: Moderne, 1933), pp. 5–6. The opposite viewpoint is stated in *Nien Lich Thong Thu* [Calendar-Almanac] (Hanoi, 1932), p. 204.

40. Kelly, "Franco-Vietnamese Schools," chapter 3, contains an excellent discussion of French language instruction in the primary (and to a lesser extent elementary) grades.

Elementary class taking place in the Duong Xa village communal hall, Bac Ninh province, north Vietnam. Gouvernement Général de l'Indochine, *Le Tonkin Scolaire* (Hanoi, 1931).

In 1929 there were 32,646 public school students in the primary (4–6) grades. A decade later enrollments had just about doubled. All in all, perhaps 130,000 Vietnamese experienced primary schooling between 1920 and 1939.[41] These were the young men and women who often became local functionaries, scribes, and village school instructors. Or, if they chose to leave their home districts, they might find employment as clerks, shopkeepers, or petty brokers in the towns and cities. They tended to be eager recipients of periodicals, tracts, and leaflets. If they went a step further and became focal points for local discussion of contemporary issues, they were clearly on the fringes of the intelligentsia. During the Depression many young people in this primary education category lost their jobs, yet were extremely reluctant to accept parental maintenance or to take up manual occupations. They remained frustrated, poor, and volatile.

The next level, that of upper primary education (grades 7–10), furnished the bulk of the Vietnamese educated elite. In 1920 upper primary enrollments totalled 2,430; by 1938 they had increased to only 4,552. In the period between the two world wars perhaps 20,000 young men and women studied at the upper

41. Ibid., table 4. The figure 130,000 is extrapolated from partial statistics and assumes a repeat rate of at least ten percent.

An elementary class in geometry, Tan An province, south Vietnam. Gouvernement
Général de l'Indochine, *La Cochinchine Scolaire* (Hanoi, 1931).

primary level.[42] Considerably less than half ever became active enough publicly
to be regarded as members of the intelligentsia. The rest simply left school, accepted arranged marriages, and fitted quietly into the existing system—the men
accepting desk jobs, the women obeying their in-laws and bearing children.

Formal education beyond year ten was the privilege of the tiniest minority. In
1923 only eighty-three Vietnamese were enrolled in public secondary schools
(years 11-13). In 1929 the figure was 121, and in 1939 it was still only 465.
Perhaps an equal number made it to the secondary level in private French *lycées*
in the colony. Yet, given the structure of colonial society, even those Vietnamese
who could afford secondary schooling and who had developed the necessary
French language skills must have wondered if it was worthwhile. Most upper
primary graduates were already twenty or twenty-one years old.[43] French nationals tended to get the best jobs, even though their academic credentials were
often inferior. In short, the upper primary certificate probably already sufficed

42. Ibid., table 1. Again I am extrapolating from partial statistics, in this case assuming a
twenty percent repeat rate.

43. Students generally entered school at age seven or eight, repeated perhaps two grades, and
took another year along the way to prepare for examinations. Private school students were often
several years younger, having worked with French from the beginning.

"Practical Work" at the Institute of Agriculture, University of Hanoi. Note the French instructor and the immaculate clothing of the students. Gouvernement Général de l'Indochine, *Le Service de l'Instruction Publique en Indochine en 1930* (Hanoi, 1930).

for those Vietnamese who were job-oriented. For those who sought something more, there was the unsettling realization that it was not likely to be found in the colonial secondary curriculum.

The French also established a University of Indochina, better known as the University of Hanoi. For most of its lifetime the University provided a mishmash of advanced secondary, technical, and vocational schooling. By 1937, however, admission qualifications had been stiffened, the curriculum reinforced, and the teaching staff improved. Including French, Chinese, and Cambodian nationals as well as Vietnamese, the student body totalled 631 in that year. During World War II, being cut off from educated French from the *métropole*, the colonial authorities increased native university enrollments and gave the graduates better jobs. In 1944 there were 1,109 Vietnamese students at the university: 681 from the north, 216 from the center, and 212 from the south.[44]

44. This was out of a total of 1,528. The School of Law had 594 students; Medicine and Pharmacy, 343; Sciences, 275; Fine Arts, 118; Public Works, 84; Agriculture, 63; and Veterinary Sciences, 29. (Twelve students are somehow unaccounted for.) "Tableau statistique de l'enseignement en Indochine" (1946[?]), AOM NF 1323. The same source indicates that non-French public secondary enrollment in 1944 was 687, and that non-French secondary enrollment at the lycées totalled 1,329.

A prime reason for the French government's upgrading the University of Indochina in the 1930s was its conclusion that too many young Vietnamese students had already travelled to the *métropole* and learned the wrong things. From before World War I some absentee landlords in Cochinchina had been able to send children to *lycées* in Toulouse, Aix-en-Provence, and Bordeaux. The numbers swelled in the mid-1920s when French families in Indochina pressured the authorities to segregate and then slowly to eliminate Vietnamese students attending colonial French *lycées*. Governor-General Varenne proved quite willing to liberalize procedures for those Vietnamese students wishing to travel to France. However, his successor, Pierre Pasquier, worked hard to stem the flow.[45] Besides being of more conservative temperament, Pasquier was aware that an increasing number of young Vietnamese were leaving the colony for political as much as scholastic reasons. Particularly after the student strikes of 1926–1927 the atmosphere in many colonial schools was stifling. "Liberation" overseas was one solution. Even if unable to enroll properly in a metropolitan school, it was enough for Vietnamese to experience the excitement of the Left Bank in Paris. Others headed in the direction of Canton and classes initiated by Ho Chi Minh. However, violent termination of the Kuomintang–Chinese Communist Party alliance after April 1927 made this an increasingly dangerous option.

According to a count by the Sûreté, there were 1,556 Vietnamese students in France in early 1930. Although scattered in nine locations around the country, students were increasingly choosing to concentrate in Paris.[46] A significant minority was already very much involved in left-wing activities, including participating in diverse French organizations, meeting with Vietnamese sailors stopping off in Marseilles, Le Havre, or Bordeaux, and smuggling printed materials back to Vietnam. In May 1930 more than a hundred Vietnamese students and workers demonstrated in front of the Elysée Palace in protest against the sweeping colonial repression that had followed the abortive Viet Nam Quoc Dan Dang (Vietnam Nationalist Party) uprising in February. Forty-seven demonstrators were arrested, nineteen of whom were eventually deported to Saigon, where they took leading roles in Marxist proselytizing efforts of the 1930s.[47] Following the 1930 confrontation, the French government was more successful in reducing the number of students in the *métropole*. It was aided by the Depression, which

45. Pierre Pasquier, *Circulaire aux familles au sujet de l'envoi des étudiants indochinois en France* (Hanoi: Le Van Tan, 1930).

46. Daniel Hémery, "Du patriotisme au marxisme: l'immigration vietnamienne en France de 1926 à 1930," *Le Mouvement Social* (Paris) 90, Jan.–Mar. 1975, pp. 22–23. Another official report indicated that 438 students had returned to Indochina between 1928 and 1930.

47. For an authoritative study of the overt political activities of these "returned students," see Daniel Hémery, *Révolutionnaires Vietnamiens et Pouvoir Colonial en Indochine* (Paris: Maspéro, 1975).

hit some landlord families hard enough to force them to bring their children home. Thenceforth French policy was to keep Vietnamese students in the colony.[48]

By the mid-1930s a number of private schools owned and operated entirely by Vietnamese were in existence. The prototype had been established in Saigon by a prominent Cochinchina landlord, Nguyen Phan Long. Thang Long Lycée in Hanoi boasted radical teachers like Vo Nguyen Giap and Dang Thai Mai. One of the most interesting experiments in private education occurred in Hue, where Vietnamese teachers rather than a wealthy patron took the initiative in re-organizing an existing institution and then inviting a former political prisoner, Ton Quang Phiet (1900–73), to become principal of Thuan Hoa School. The emphasis was on experienced instructors providing a reasonably comprehensive and stable learning experience up to grade ten, rather than offering a vehicle for examination cramming, as was the case with many other private schools. For every twenty-eight fee-paying students, the equivalent of two full scholarships were offered. Surprisingly, the French resident superior allowed the experiment to proceed, even though he must have been aware of ongoing leftist tendencies among the staff of Thuan Hoa School.[49]

Besides the public and private colonial schools there were a number of formally approved educational societies (*hoc hoi*) that attracted elite Vietnamese participation. The Tonkin Mutual Instruction Society, founded in 1892 by interpreters and school teachers of French, boasted regular public lectures in French, private courses, a thrice-yearly *Bulletin*, and sixteen affiliated committees in the northern provinces. In 1924 the Society's courses attracted over three hundred pupils, some of whom were striving to be admitted to the Collège du Protectorate or the Ecole Normale, while others were simply trying to pass examinations leading to the primary school certificate.[50] During 1929 the Society sponsored bimonthly lectures on French and Vietnamese literature, Vietnamese history, local ritual and village organization, science, and Japanese history and geography.[51]

48. There were some notable exceptions, particularly in tertiary degree studies. The following individuals, among others, completed tertiary work in France in the 1930s: Hoang Xuan Han, Pham Duy Khiem, Nguyen Manh Tuong, Nguyen Van Huyen, Hoang Thi Nga, Doan Khac Thinh, Ngo Dinh Nhu, and Buu Hoi. "Etat des Indochinois diplômes, 1936–1945," AOM NF 1193.

49. Institution Thuan Hoa, *Hoc Sinh Nghi He* [Student Summer Vacation] (Hue, 1937). Ton Quang Phiet was at the time a clandestine member of the Indochinese Communist Party. Another prominent participant was Dao Duy Anh, editor, writer, and lexicographer (see chapters 6 and 8).

50. AOM NF 2232. Provincial committees of the Société d'Enseignement Mutuel du Tonkin were reported to be particularly active in Nam Dinh, Haiphong, and Thai Binh. However, eight committees were chastised for failing to submit annual reports. The society's 1924 financial statement listed total assets of 13,194 piasters: in bank savings, in general income, and in colonial subsidies.

51. DIRIP, *Les oeuvres complémentaires de l'Ecole en Indochine* (Hanoi, 1929).

A more exclusive northern Vietnam organization, the Society for the Protection of French Studies, appears to have concentrated increasingly on the awarding of private scholarships.[52] Perhaps the most interesting group, however, was the Society for the Support of Public Schools in Nam Dinh province. Created in 1923 at the initiative of the local French inspector of schools, the Nam Dinh Society sponsored activities as diverse as French cinema shows, Vietnamese cultural exhibits, and modern sporting competitions. However, its particular strength appears to have been to translate French books into *quoc-ngu*, to publish them locally as a "Bibliothèque Annamite de Vulgarisation," and then to transport copies from village to village in the manner of mobile libraries.[53] Similar if less industrious groups functioned in the provinces of central and southern Vietnam.[54] Individual secondary schools and *lycées* often sported alumni associations as well.

What was the relationship between education and social class origins in colonial Vietnam? No detailed studies have been done, but the situation appears to have differed strikingly according to school levels. At the elementary level (years 1–3) class representation was reasonably broad. Indeed, the extent to which some poor peasants and agricultural laborers would go to ensure that at least one of their children (usually the eldest son) obtained a year or two of basic instruction was mute testimony to their high regard for formalized knowledge. Nevertheless, rural elementary schools were probably dominated numerically by children from middle and rich peasant backgrounds. Urban elementary schools were filled mostly with children from petit bourgeois families, although some working-class children also attended. Meanwhile, the children of absentee landlords, higher officials, and rich merchants were generally able to avoid the public elementary schools entirely, relying either on private tutors or going straight to the French-language *collèges* and *lycées*.

Class background became relatively more important at the primary (years 4–6) level. Private tutoring was often necessary for children to be able to pass the French language section of the entrance examinations. Children from outlying villages might well have to board with relatives or family friends living closer to the primary school, often located at the canton or district center. Then, too, poor children who somehow managed to pass both the intellectual and the financial

---

52. *Phap Hoc Bao Tro Hoi* [Society for the Protection of French Studies] (Hanoi, 1930). Ironically, the society was not able to hold its normal annual meeting in 1930 because of a nighttime government curfew. At an extraordinary daytime meeting, the chairman, Do Dinh Thuat, used the occasion to support ongoing colonial repression of nationalist and communist activists.

53. R. Michel, *La Société de Patronage des Ecoles Publiques de Nam Dinh* (Nam Dinh, 1927). Support seems to have come from parents and alumni of the local schools.

54. Société d'enseignement mutuel de l'Annam, *Statuts* (Hue, 1929); Société pour l'amélioration morale, intellectuelle et physique des indigènes de Cochinchine, *Statuts* (Saigon, 1927).

hurdles might still have to be withdrawn from school in the event of family misfortunes, for example, crop failure, loan default, unemployment, or illness.

There were only eleven cities and towns in Vietnam where upper primary education (years 7–10) could be obtained: Hanoi, Haiphong, Lang Son, Nam Dinh, Thanh Hoa, Vinh, Hue, Qui Nhon, Saigon, My Tho, and Can Tho. Poor peasant families generally found that the cost of sustaining a young man or woman at one of those places was hopelessly beyond their reach. Subsistence farmers might try to enable a particularly bright individual to enroll as a calculated risk, in the hope that he or she would bring subsequent reward to the family. Petit bourgeois families probably enjoyed considerably more success in placing children in upper primary schools than either their population numbers or average incomes would indicate. Most of them lived in the above cities or towns, spoke some French, regarded post-primary education as the best way to improve family status, and were reasonably familiar with the intricacies of preparing for and taking entrance examinations. In the end, however, it was almost certainly the children of landlord and urban bourgeois families who constituted the largest proportion of upper primary enrollments. If a son or daughter of a wealthy family failed the public school examinations it was still possible to keep them moving ahead at the private schools, or, until 1930, to send them to France. The same was true at the secondary level (years 11–13).

Enough lower-class children appear to have made it to the post-primary level, however, to warrant further explanation. In the first instance, at both public and private institutions there were a few scholarships set aside for bright children from poor families. Secondly, it was not uncommon for a wealthy uncle or more distant relation to underwrite the education of a particularly intelligent boy, naturally assuming that the favor would be repaid later. Thirdly, a wealthy but unrelated family might sponsor the schooling of a boy on the understanding that he would subsequently marry an eligible daughter. This was particularly likely to happen if sons of the wealthy family showed little or no academic promise even after extensive tutoring. Fourthly, there were cases of French or Vietnamese officials operating as private patrons of promising students.[55] And, finally, a few teenage boys simply left home and tried to fend for themselves scholastically. Some had the nerve to stow away on ships to France, to obtain entry to a *collège* or *lycée*, and to live hand-to-mouth for as long as their luck held out.[56] Such bright upstarts from the lower classes seem to have played inordinately signif-

---

55. This was apparently the case, for example, with Nguyen Van Tao (b.1908), who became one of the most important ICP leaders in Cochinchina during the 1930s. He is said to have been helped to go to study in France by a Vietnamese official in his home district of Go Den. Ho Huu Tuong, *41 Nam Lam Bao* (Saigon: Tri Dang, 1972), p. 23.

56. Ibid., pp. 10–45, has numerous anecdotes about the precarious yet exciting existence of Vietnamese students in France, 1927–31.

icant roles in the political and intellectual life of Vietnam after 1925. It was a time when the right combination of intelligence, audacity, and luck could thrust a young Vietnamese of unremarkable social origins into prominence. Also, youths of more favored circumstances often relied on such individuals to help explain the conditions and attitudes of the vast majority of less privileged Vietnamese. They probably would not go so far as to invite lower-class friends home to the family villa, yet that did not preclude cooperation in school activities, publishing ventures, and political organizations. Together they took part in actions that risked school suspension, being barred from any further education, exclusion from government jobs, police surveillance, arrest, and above all the anguish and despair of their parents. French colonial administrators had assumed that the beneficiaries of an elite education would settle down, take a seat quietly in some bureau, and perhaps dabble in the arts and sciences as cultured bourgeois Frenchmen so often did. Many Vietnamese families made the same assumption. However, enough upper primary and secondary school students violated these rules to make a sharp impression on the political and intellectual history of the period.

Publishing

Besides formal schooling, one other colonial innovation helped give cohesion and purpose to Vietnamese intellectual activities: the printing press. Without access to modern printing techniques, intellectuals would have been forced to limit their written communications mainly to hand-copied manuscripts or leaflets printed by means of crude wood or gelatin blocks. As it was, members of the new intelligentsia often gained access to printing presses while still in school. Those who took their mission seriously continued after graduation—or expulsion—to live the life of ideas via the printed page, becoming journalists, creative writers, editors, publishers, and booksellers. As might be expected, a suspicious colonial government subjected all this activity to a range of controls and harassments, which in turn led some intellectuals to drop or downgrade overt publishing in favor of more clandestine operations. From September 1939 to March 1945 the colonial authorities exercised such tight supervision of publishing that covert printing and distribution came to the fore. However, public journalism and publishing had developed far enough in the 1920s and 1930s to present the ICP and the Viet Minh with considerable mass communications potential when they seized power in August 1945. Although they subsequently had to withdraw from most cities and towns, some of the equipment and not a few of the printers, editors, and writers went with them.

The first modern printing press had been brought in by French commanders almost on the heels of their troops, and French-language bulletins were printed in Saigon as early as 1861. An official *quoc-ngu* monthly, the four page *Gia Dinh*

Bao, began appearing in 1865.[57] Colonial government printing operations extended to Hanoi in 1883. There too, in 1892, François Henri Schneider, close friend of the governor-general, started what was soon to be the largest private printing and publishing operation in Indochina. About a decade later, Vietnamese literati of modernizing, anticolonial inclinations also gained access to several publishing businesses. However, their printed articles and poems were one cause for the French to tighten controls, jail some participants, and drive others overseas. From about 1909 the Sûreté was able to choke off almost all bulk imports of materials printed overseas by Vietnamese emigrés, which left the field to the French and a small group of collaborators until at least 1920. During those years, and especially in the period 1914–1918, F. H. Schneider, the entrepreneur, Governor-General A. Sarraut, the journalist-turned-politician, and L. Marty, the chief of the Sûreté (fluent in Vietnamese and Chinese), experimented enthusiastically with "colonization by means of books."[58]

While top-level French were confidently giving lessons in publishing as a vehicle for promoting elite consensus, small clusters of French *colons* were demonstrating the use of newspapers to excoriate each other or to condemn specific government policies or individuals. *La Tribune Indigène*, published in Saigon from August 1917 by a group of up-and-coming Vietnamese bourgeoisie, can be seen as the first serious effort to follow the *colons'* example and employ a newspaper as a political and economic weapon.

Only six years later, however, all of these groups were upstaged by Nguyen An Ninh (1900–43), a brash young law graduate who had observed journalism at the font, Paris, and who was equipped to use even the smallest loophole in French jurisprudence in order to continue printing unmuzzled. His newspaper, *La Cloche Fêlée*, begun in December 1923, was only the first in a string of saucy, incisive periodicals to capture the imaginations of the French-reading intelligentsia and lead them in the direction of modern media advocacy. Nguyen An Ninh not only wrote and edited most of *La Cloche Fêlée* but scandalized older intellectuals by hawking his own papers on the street as well. Aspiring journalists from northern and central Vietnam were soon rushing to Saigon to emulate and expand his efforts. For perhaps a decade Saigon took the lead in publishing activity. After that, although Saigon remained important for its trenchant French-

57. The two Vietnamese most closely identified with the late nineteenth-century colonial publishing efforts are Truong Vinh Ky (1837–98) and Huynh Tinh Cua (1834–1907). See Milton Osborne, *The French Presence in Cochin China and Cambodia: Rule and Response (1859–1905)* (Ithaca: Cornell Univ. Press, 1969), pp. 89–100, 134–37, 166–71.

58. Huynh Van Tong, *Lich Su Bao Chi Viet Nam to Khoi Thuy den 1930* (Saigon, 1973), pp. 49–122. This is a revised version of the author's unpublished Thèse de doctorat de IIIe cycle, "Histoire de la press vietnamienne des origines à 1930," 2 vols. (Paris: University of Paris, 1971).

language press, and was not without significant *quoc ngu* periodicals, Hanoi regained the initiative in Vietnamese-language publishing.

Wherever one chose to publish, the problems were formidable. First it was necessary to pull together a small group of writers and editors prepared to work long hours for very little pay. Then, too, unless one of the group had a rich father or uncle, some other propertied Vietnamese willing to advance a bit of capital or secure a loan would need to be found. The law required that every periodical have a French citizen accept responsibility as *gérant*, or director. While this individual might be found among the few Vietnamese granted French citizenship, it was also possible to locate a sympathetic French businessman or professional who would lend his name to the endeavor.

No sooner did a newspaper or journal get started than it was faced with serious editorial choices. If it avoided controversy, readers might well drift elsewhere. If it began discussing issues critically, then it was quickly suppressed, perhaps to pop up a month or two later with a different title and different legal and financial guarantors. From 1926, however, the government occasionally went beyond the mere issuing of closure notices and proceeded to jail participants, ransack offices, harass patrons, or scare printing houses into rejecting job orders. Fearing that such harsh tactics might later be used against them, too, conservative French *colons* sometimes joined Vietnamese in protesting. In Cochinchina, alleged offenders were often released, providing that more serious criminal charges had not been set forth simultaneously, and providing that the police could be prevailed upon to bring cases to court. In Tonkin and Annam, publishing laws and legal practices were generally more stringent.[59]

For all the intellectual stimulation and political excitement of French-language journalism, the maximum circulation for any one French newspaper was probably 3,500 copies. Average circulation was perhaps only 1,200.[60] Admittedly, it was fairly common for copies to pass from hand to hand, and for individuals competent in French to sight-translate or interpret articles into Vietnamese for eager listeners, thus causing information to be more widely disseminated.

Nevertheless, the circulation of French-language newspapers was far lower than that of the Vietnamese papers, and the disparity increased with time. One

59. The rapid turnover of periodicals is reflected in statistics for the year 1934 in Indochina: in Tonkin, among a total of 187 titles (as of 1 Jan. 1935), there were 37 new and 28 discontinued titles (turnover rate of 31%); and in the greater Saigon area, there were 31 new and 17 discontinued titles out of a total of 117 (turnover rate of 41%) (*La Patrie Annamite* [Hanoi], 108 [3 Aug. 1935]).

60. The most influential French-language paper of all, *La Lutte* (Saigon), claimed a circulation of 3,000 in 1937. *Jeune Annam* (Saigon), during an earlier highpoint of French journalism in 1926, claimed 2,500. The more conservative editors of *La Tribune Indochinoise* (Saigon) managed 2,500 in 1926 and 1,000 in 1938. *Dépêche d'Indochine* (Saigon) asserted 3,500 and *Avenir du Tonkin* (Hanoi) 2,500 in 1938.

Saigon *quoc ngu* newspaper of the mid-1920s, *Trung Lap Bao* (Neutral News), regularly printed 15,000 copies per day. One of the reasons this particular paper prospered was reflected in its title, which implied objective reporting. In reality it was controlled by a group of *colons*, and the editors relied heavily on translations of official French news briefs.[61] Lacking anywhere near the financial and technical resources of *Trung Lap Bao*, several *quoc ngu* papers owned and operated by Vietnamese still managed to sustain circulations of around 10,000 copies each. Occasionally they took risks with their investments or their jobs and criticized particular government policies as well as the economic maneuvers of the *colons*.[62] Perhaps most impressive of all, *Phu Nu Tan Van* (Women's News), a thirty-four-page weekly journal of no little intellectual and social significance, was somehow able to sustain an average circulation of 8,500 copies from May 1929 to late 1931. Subsequently the effects of the Depression reduced this to 5,000 (the average for the period October 1931 to July 1932) and then 2,500 until it was suppressed by the authorities in December 1934.[63] During the Popular Front period (1936–1939), nine of the most popular *quoc ngu* periodicals had a combined circulation of 80,000 copies, whereas seven of the best known French-language titles could muster a combined total circulation of only 11,700.[64]

Quoc-ngu publications were effective for reasons other than impressive circulation figures. They could be appreciated by individuals of more diverse class background than the French publications. Regional distribution was likely to be wider. Illiterate audiences could listen to articles being read to them directly, without translation. And finally, *quoc-ngu* journalism provided some of the most important ingredients for strengthening both written and spoken Vietnamese. Although Vietnam already possessed an established tradition of secular literature and a differentiated group of writers, scribes, and scholars, the profusion of *quoc ngu* publications provided an effective link with the spoken language, served to

61. *Trung Lap Bao* was allegedly sold in 1926 for the incredible price of three million piasters. Huynh Van Tong, *Lich Su Bao Chi Viet Nam*, pp. 223–27. The name was supposed to be a translation of *l'Impartial*, the French-language newspaper published by the same business interests, but it had a slightly different connotation in Vietnamese.

62. Papers with circulations in the range of 10,000 copies included *Dong Phap Thoi Bao* (1923–27), *Than Chung* (1929–30), and *Dien Tin* (?–1939) in Saigon and *Thuc Nghiep Dan Bao* (1920–33) and *Dong Phap* (?–1939) in Hanoi. Most of the hundreds of *quoc ngu* as well as French newspapers and journals of this period are available for reading at the Bibliothèque Nationale (Versailles collection). Positive microfilms can be obtained from the Association pour la Conservation et la Reproduction Photographique de la Presse (Paris).

63. *Phu Nu Tan Van* (Saigon) was organized by a group of Vietnamese merchants and professionals, but editorial policy was strongly influenced by a variety of young intellectuals (see chapter 5).

64. Daniel Hémery, "Journalisme révolutionnaire et système de la presse au Vietnam dans les Années 1930," *Les Cahiers du Cursa* 8 (1978), p. 63.

stimulate popular interest in learning how to read, and offered a new model of the writer as mass media publicist. Ancient and modern preoccupations thus combined to propel Vietnamese publishing to a level unprecedented in the rest of Southeast Asia.[65]

Precisely because *quoc-ngu* publications were potentially more subversive than French-language publications, the colonial authorities tended to censor them more rigorously. Editors often had to carry their copy back and forth to the censor's bureau, trying to negotiate compromises in wording. Even so, blank spaces could be seen sprinkled through the more sensitive articles. Postal authorities had a tendency to "lose" controversial publications, and village officials occasionally punished individuals severely for possessing quite legal printed materials.[66]

As with French publications, if a *quoc-ngu* newspaper was forced to shut down, the owners might seek new editors and writers, or vice versa. Application would then be made to start again under a new title. Six months or more might go by, however, before approval or denial was given. Censorship guidelines changed abruptly, and were never the same in the three different administrative regions.[67] Ironically, all of this maneuvering probably served to encourage more sophisticated powers of written communication, Vietnamese participants hoping to accomplish by nuance what was prohibited overtly.[68] If writers and editors kept alert, patient, and mobile it was often possible to outfox the system.[69]

Broadly speaking, a particular team of editors, writers, and financial supporters had four tactical options when starting a periodical. They could employ the paper to the narrow political and economic advantage of a specific individual or small group. For example, some papers were initiated simply to take advantage of a single event, perhaps an election, or the anticipated allocation of a new colonial monopoly. Secondly, they could strike a posture of "loyal opposition" as a way to extract small concessions from the authorities, to defuse more serious criti-

---

65. In this respect, Vietnam had more in common with Japan, China, Korea, India, and the Arab states than with the other countries of Southeast Asia. See Herbert Passin, "Writer and Journalist in the Transitional Society," in Fishman, comp., *Language Problems*, pp. 443–45.

66. *Tin Tuc* (Hanoi), 23 (3 Aug. 1938). There were also more routine problems of slow rural delivery, stamp taxes, and subscription payments (Huynh Van Tong, *Lich Su Bao Chi Viet Nam*, p. 199).

67. For a detailed complaint to the authorities by Huynh Thuc Khang (1876–1947), editor of *Tieng Dan* [Voice of the People], the most important and longest-lasting (1927–43) central Vietnam paper, see his letter of Sept. 10, 1931, to the resident-superior of Annam (AOM NF 54, dossier 633).

68. Admittedly, a reader today is sometimes led to wonder, however, if some of the shorthand innuendoes aimed at circumventing the censor were not also lost on most of the reading audience.

69. For a breezy, sometimes disingenuous memoir of journalistic activities during this period, see Ho Huu Tuong, *41 Nam Lam Bao*, pp. 46–130. See also Tran Huy Lieu, *Mat Tran Dan Chu Dong Duong* [The Indochina Democratic Front] (Hanoi, 1960).

cism, or perhaps to accomplish both objectives simultaneously.[70] Thirdly, they could formulate an essentially antagonistic position but then release it in dribs and drabs, hoping the censors would not anticipate the drift and close the paper down prematurely. This technique was used in the 1930s in a number of papers, including some controlled by the Indochinese Communist Party. And, finally, they could mount a full-blown anticolonial barrage, with the clear expectation of being terminated the next day, the next month, or the next year, depending on political circumstances. Often this tactic involved elaborate precautions in printing and widespread distribution of copies before the censor was able to read the edition.[71]

Readers of both the French and *quoc-ngu* press became increasingly familiar with the political and economic interests of various publishers and editors. People were aware that the French authorities quietly subsidized some groups,[72] kept a wary eye on others, and were openly hostile toward still others. They followed the careers of particular writers from one paper to another, seeing whether personal outlook changed or not. In short, keeping track of developments in the periodical press was an education in itself, and a pursuit that literate Vietnamese found quite stimulating and fruitful.

Of equal significance to periodicals were *quoc-ngu* books and pamphlets. In the period 1923–44 a total of about 10,000 titles were published, covering a very wide range of topics.[73] Until 1937 there was a fairly steady increase in the num-

---

70. The best examples of this approach were *La Tribune Indigène* in the period 1922–25 and its successor, *La Tribune Indochinoise*, in the period 1926–29. After 1929 *La Tribune Indochinoise* became the increasingly strident voice of wealthy Cochinchinese who supported the colonial status quo.

71. For example, in May 1927 the team publishing *Phap Viet Nhut Gia* [Franco-Vietnamese United Family] carefully prepared the abrupt demise of their weekly journal by printing an issue sharply attacking "Franco-Vietnamese Harmony," the Bank of Indochina, and colonial suppression of democratic rights. While a copy was en route to the censor, the other copies, totalling almost 10,000, were distributed throughout Saigon. The police were able to confiscate only a limited number. The journal's license was rescinded and the manager jailed. See Tran Huy Lieu, Van Tao, and Nguyen Cong Binh, *Cach Mang Can Dai Viet Nam* [Vietnam's Modern Revolution], vol. 4 (Hanoi, 1958), pp. 107 (hereinafter CMCD-4).

72. In 1918, for example, F. H. Schneider received 4,500 piasters to supply the governor-general regularly with 600 copies of *Trung Bac Tan Van* and 250 copies of *Luc Tinh Tan Van*. The governor-general also doled out 500 piasters per month to *Nam Phong* (see chapter 4). (AOM [Aix] R 19.133 and 19.140.) The 1931 Indochina budget allocated 796,650 piasters to support selected periodicals in both the colony and the *métropole*. Vietnamese publications receiving subsidies included *Nam Phong* (9,000 piasters), *Trung Bac Tan Van* and *Hoc Bao* (12,000), and *Luc Tinh Tan Van* (1,600). (Nguyen Khac Dam, *Nhung Thu Doan Boc Lot* [Hanoi, 1958], p. 60, citing Budget général, *Compte Administratif*, Exercise 1931, p. 743.)

73. Mme Christiane Rageau, curator of the Vietnamese-language collection at the Bibliothèque Nationale (Paris), has identified 9,050 titles in the period 1923–42. Some titles are admittedly second or third editions of essentially the same publication. On the other hand, it is clear that

ber of titles published (except for 1931–33, when colonial repression sharply cut overt intellectual activity in northern and central Vietnam). After 1937, however, the number of titles declined. For the two years 1938–1939 this was probably due both to the intelligentsia's preoccupation with reaching a broader, politically energized public quickly via newspapers, leaflets, and unauthorized pamphlets, and to the increasing preference for novels and short-story collections printed under one cover rather than serialized in "penny fiction" fashion. From September 1939 to March 1945 the colonial authorities were stricter than ever in censorship. Paper and ink became increasingly scarce, and a higher proportion of the intelligentsia was involved in clandestine activities.[74]

Since throughout the period 1925–45 the established publishing companies tended to focus on books with clearly defined markets and bland political content (e.g., school texts, religious tracts, almanacs), new or provocative authors often had to push their own wares from beginning to end. It was fairly common practice for an individual author or a small group of intellectuals to approach a printing house with a manuscript, agree on a printing cost, pay about thirty percent in advance, obtain censorship clearance, and then handle most of the publicity and distribution as well. Those who could not afford the thirty percent down payment signed a contract with the printing house to receive minimal royalties.[75] Another approach was to locate a newspaper or journal to serialize a particular novel, short story, or topical essay, and then, if response was favorable, to arrange republication in book form. Bookstores in all the major towns received bulk shipments on consignment, then relied on a string of students and petty entrepreneurs to carry titles around and sell them at a further profit. Some writers tried to circumvent these mark-ups by offering a series of books by means of postal subscription.[76] While all such activity may have kept authors from being dependent on the bigger publishing firms, it also involved financial risk and considerable distraction from more creative pursuits.

---

some titles never reached the colonial Dépôt Légal or were subsequently lost. There are also a number of clandestine pamphlets and periodicals that do not appear in this collection. The same is true of most Vietnamese periodicals printed in France.

74. During this period the number of French-language titles increased sharply to accommodate the local French community shut off from the *métropole*. Some of the 1943–44 *quoc-ngu* publications are on such coarse paper that reading is difficult.

75. Trinh Dinh Du, "Ve Van De Soan Sach" [On the Question of Preparing Books], PNTV 67 (28 Aug. 1930), pp. 3–5.

76. Editors, "Lam Sach, In Sach, Ban Sach" [Preparing, Printing, and Selling Books], PNTV 52 (15 May 1930), pp. 11–12; see also PNTV 60 (10 July 1930), PNTV 160 (21 July 1932), and PNTV 166 (1 Sept. 1932). To my knowledge, there is as yet no detailed study of the publishing business in Indochina, particularly with regard to questions of financing, censorship, printing, distribution, style, and technique. Huynh Van Tong, *Lich Su Bao Chi Viet Nam*, has occasional remarks but focuses mostly on individual participants, periodicals, and content.

Most books and pamphlets were printed in editions of 1,000–2,000 copies. However, in the case of well-known authors, printing houses were prepared to share the risk in runs of 3,000–5,000. Given the limited size of the readership and the far from cheap prices, this was quite impressive. In a different category entirely were the various colonial-approved textbooks for elementary and primary instruction. These might easily reach 50,000 copies per edition, and were presumably a source of considerable profit to publishers, printers, and authors alike.[77] Altogether we can estimate that no less than fifteen million bound publications were printed in Vietnam in the two decades or so prior to the August 1945 Revolution.[78] This amounted to perhaps eight or nine books per literate individual during that period.[79]

Modern novels and short-story collections, two genres that had come to Vietnam only in the early 1920s, accounted for twenty-four percent of all bound *quoc-ngu* publications between 1923 and 1942.[80] Another six percent were theatrical reprints or dramatic presentations, particularly of the new *cai luong* (reform opera), which originated in the south and swept the country in the 1930s. Traditional literature, folktales, poetry, and popular humor constituted another nineteen percent of all titles. From the point of view of form, or mode of presentation, it might thus appear that almost half the titles published were designed simply for recreational reading. In terms of content, however, a good proportion of the fiction, drama, and poetry was written with quite serious social, political, and cultural objectives in mind.

Religious publications, including tracts, prayer books, ritual chants, and catechisms, constituted twenty percent of all titles. This proportion remained fairly steady from one year to the next, reflecting the continuing influence of various non-intelligentsia intellectuals (e.g., priests, monks, local adepts, fraternal society leaders). However, Catholic titles declined, whereas Buddhist publications and those of the new syncretic Cao Dai religion grew vigorously. Small publishing outlets also existed for believers in Confucianism, Taoism, and Protestantism, as well as fortune-telling, trance communication, and other occult phenomena.

77. Texts enjoying the imprimatur of the Education Bureau were purchased by the government and distributed via the public schools. The government also actively promoted these titles to other potential buyers. Authors whose textbooks lacked the imprimatur could still encourage individual schools to stock copies—assuming, of course, that they had gained the approval of the censorate (Trinh Dinh Du, "Ve Van De Soan Sach," p. 4).

78. This calculation is based on an estimated average printing run of 1,500 copies for a total of 10,000 titles. Also, it is worth noting that the government recorded publication of 7,911,507 school textbooks alone for the period 1924–39. (DIRIP, "Rapport sur le fonctionnement," p. 35.)

79. This assumes five to ten percent literacy levels and normal mortality among the reading public.

80. I would like to thank Mme Rageau for sharing with me her statistical breakdown of the 9,050 titles mentioned previously (see fn. 73).

Nineteen percent of all titles appearing in the period from 1923 to 1942 may be grouped together roughly under the rubric of "functional" publications. These included school texts, morality primers, practical ("how-to-do-it") manuals, medical guides, and almanacs and calendars. Within this group there was a dramatic increase over time in the numbers of titles directed towards people not able to attend formal classes. This probably reflected increasing disenchantment with the school system, but also growing adult literacy and the growing ability of authors to deal with more diverse subject matter. There were still extremely few publications of a highly technical nature, however. Numbers of titles authorized for colonial school use narrowed perceptibly, presumably reflecting more rigorous government regulation of curriculum structure and content.

Rather surprisingly, government edicts and administrative explanations accounted for only 1.6 percent of all *quoc-ngu* titles. This reveals the degree to which the authorities still relied on French for official dissemination, as well as their continuing tendency to assume that ordinary Vietnamese, even if literate in *quoc-ngu*, were disinterested in affairs of state.

The remaining titles, about 10.5 percent of the total, can be grouped together under the important—if vague—category of modernizing essays and translations. While it is obvious that the reading public was not inclined to focus primarily on dry analytical essays or monographs, the variety of subject matter encompassed by this category is still extraordinary. Topics ranged from outwardly detached discourses on political economy, law, philosophy, and linguistics to concrete analyses of Vietnamese history, contemporary literary criticism, current affairs, and political and social prescriptions for the country's future. There was a gradual shift from unassimilated translations to analyses geared to specific Vietnamese conditions. The colonial censor remained very much a factor in the way authors chose to handle particular subjects. Quantitatively, as one might expect, modernizing essays and translations increased modestly during the relatively liberal Varenne administration (1923–1928), dropped off during the repression of 1929–1933, blossomed dramatically during the Popular Front period, and practically disappeared during World War II. Partly because Vietnamese writers were becoming increasingly tired of adjusting their serious essays to the whims of the colonial censor, however, such materials came more and more to be printed and circulated outside the law.[81] Certainly, intellectual exchange was far from terminated during the years 1940–1944.

The trial of Phan Boi Chau and the funeral of Phan Chu Trinh which opened this chapter can now be seen in a broader historical context. It was a time of profound economic and social change. New groups were being formed, old rela-

81. As early as March 1931, a French abridgment of Karl Marx's *Das Kapital* was being cleverly disguised within a book of logarithm tables (AOM [Aix] F50. P. Arnoux, letter dated 19 March 1931).

tionships were breaking down. A new educational system was enrolling more than one hundred thousand Vietnamese children each year, most of them not destined to continue for long, yet none of them left untouched by the experience. The modern printing press brought individuals of diverse localities and backgrounds into intellectual contact with each other. *Quoc-ngu* blossomed as a medium of written communication.

In 1925, neither an old literatus like Phan Boi Chau nor a member of the new intelligentsia like Tran Huy Lieu could really understand the significance of the developments. Each, in his own way, sensed that Vietnam was at a historical crossroads. Tran Huy Lieu was much better equipped to turn vague impressions into organized knowledge, and had the advantage of youth. He shared with Phan Boi Chau the conviction that knowledge was only meaningful if it served to direct behavior. Later, in jail, he learned the value of concrete experience in altering intellectual outlook. Ultimately, it was this growing interaction between theory and practice that made the intelligentsia significant; ironically, it also led to their demise as a group, a fact few if any of them could have anticipated in 1925.

2. Morality Instruction

Once upon a time there lived a Vietnamese mandarin. A very difficult case was brought before him for adjudication. After pondering the situation at great length, he decided that the accused had been framed, and released him. Overjoyed, the man tried to present the mandarin with a gift. Outraged, the mandarin put the man in jail for one year. Some time later, the mandarin was ordered to a new post. As was his preference, he travelled on foot, with only one student and one satchel of belongings. Having walked a few miles, he noticed he was being followed by the thoroughly chastened man who earlier had been jailed and was now free. The man begged the mandarin's permission to be his lifelong retainer, but was quietly refused. The man then offered an ornate umbrella, made by his own hands, he said, to shade the mandarin in his journeys. At this, the mandarin cut off the lower part of the umbrella, which was embellished in gold, accepted the upper part, and proceeded on his way.

This story, recounted at slightly greater length in a 1923 journal,[1] tells us a lot about orthodox Vietnamese ideals, from the stern sense of official rectitude to the simple lifestyle, yet also the subtle willingness to compromise when there seems to be good intent. More importantly, the 1923 author was set on contrasting this past ideal with current practice. According to him, Vietnamese in the colonial bureaucracy sent subordinates hustling to arrange the biggest gift possible before they took any action. Worse yet, they had the effrontery to label this as "proper ceremony" (*le nghia*), to claim that they were preserving the traditional relationship between official and subject, and to say proudly that they remained untouched by the current disease of "freedom and equality" (*tu do binh dang*). Meanwhile many young Western-influenced students who talked loudly of freedom and equality and condemned obscurantism became just as selfish as the older officials once they had degrees in hand.

A great many Vietnamese of the 1920s shared this author's anguished assessment without necessarily agreeing with his prescription, which amounted to a

---

1. An Khe, "Quoc Tuy va Van Minh" [The National Essence and Civilization], NP 78 (Dec. 1932), pp. 453–58. The story was said to refer to a mandarin of central Vietnam during the reign of Tu Duc (r. 1847–83).

simple return to orthodox ethical principles—the alleged "national essence" (*quoc tuy*) of Vietnam. They also sensed that the problem went far beyond the Confucian-educated officials or the new Western-educated functionaries. One of the results of this perception was an unprecedented outpouring of books and pamphlets designed to uplift the reader morally, as well as a spate of more introspective essays on ethical choices facing Vietnamese in the twentieth century (discussed in the next chapter). Clearly, people shared a certain malaise. And, unlike some rarified concepts we will encounter later, morality seemed to bring in a lot of opinions from more ordinary literate Vietnamese, as reflected, for example, in the large number of unsolicited manuscripts and letters to the editor received by newspapers and journals.

At least four reasons can be suggested for this preoccupation with ethical questions. First of all, the changes described in the previous chapter had indeed provoked serious questions in the minds of many Vietnamese. The clash between old and new, East and West, collaborator and anticolonial, rich and poor, urban and rural, was tangible, and people had no certainty about what they should do in these circumstances. As one provincial literatus plaintively expressed, he was somehow prepared to accept the fact that the twentieth century was the age of electricity and chemistry, of momentous struggle and competition, but he was deeply troubled to discover that most people could not tell him what they were struggling *for*.[2]

Secondly, and only outwardly in contradiction to the first, ethics was an area in which just about all Vietnamese still felt themselves competent to pass judgment on what was good behaviour and what was bad. In fact, the moral categories and symbols of Confucianism were so entrenched in the language, poetry, and social life of the Vietnamese that they could hardly not make daily judgments. As time went on, however, it became apparent that Confucianism was losing its hold and that new moral alternatives were available.

Thirdly, ethics also held a special fascination for the French. Many Frenchmen honestly wanted to communicate their moral ideals to the colonized people, and some Vietnamese were eager to listen. At a different level, French administrators, pedagogues, and missionaries, increasingly worried about signs of native unrest, looked to moral instruction as one solution. Metropolitan textbooks on *morale* were imported and used in colonial schools. Translations were included in the Vietnamese-language curriculum. Vietnamese were soon writing their own morality texts and seeking the lucrative government imprimatur. Often, books turned down for official use were able to pass the censor and be sold commercially. The French concern for morality undoubtedly served to reinforce and to legitimize Vietnamese predispositions. But idealism, whether of French or Confucian derivation, proved highly volatile in a repressive colonial environment.

2. Nguyen Duy Tinh, comp., *Dong Phuong Ly Tuong* [Eastern Ideals] (Nam Dinh, 1931), p. 4.

A Vietnamese literatus teaching Chinese characters. Gouvernement Général de l'Indochine, *Le Tonkin Scolaire* (Hanoi, 1931).

Finally, we should not lose sight of the fact that for Vietnamese participants it was the young, the new generation, their own sons and daughters, nieces and nephews, who were meant to be the targets and beneficiaries of most of this moral concern. A lot of older people were of the opinion that it was not in their power to solve Vietnam's problems, that only the young could do it. Yet, paradoxically, the elders wanted to make certain that the next generation operated from essentially the same moral assumptions as did they.

None of this is unique to Vietnam. The promotion of 'good' conduct and discouragement of 'bad' is as natural for animals who stay with their young as feeding and protecting. Among animals living in permanent groups, practical instruction in acceptable behavior serves additionally to strengthen the social system and to reduce psychological tensions. It has been left to human beings, however, to go another crucial step and develop elaborate transcendental

The education mandarin of Ha Dong province, north Vietnam. Gouvernement Général de l'Indochine, *Le Service de l'Instruction Publique en Indochine en 1930* (Hanoi, 1930).

explanations for the way we educate our young, mete out justice, and select or perpetuate group leadership. In so doing, we both reinforce the status quo and create a perpetual threat to it, since reality seldom matches the ideal. Indeed, without that persistent feeling of what *ought to be* as distinct from what *is*, humankind might still be depending on accident for advancement.

In Vietnam during the 1920s, at least, there can be no denying the centrality of this moral quest. After 1930 there was a perceptible shift toward discussion of appropriate means to achieve favored objectives, and toward the valuation of concrete experience as distinct from endless hypothesizing. Still, ideals remained an intensely debated subject, and young Vietnamese continued to be bombarded with moral prescriptions both in and out of school. More importantly, ideals tended to change, even while many of the categories and symbols remained the same. Ho Chi Minh understood all this as well as anyone in Vietnam, even though he was out of the country for three decades prior to 1941. In particular, his ability to weld together revolutionary aspirations and selected traditional morality, often employing language that only a few years before had been the forte either of the Neo-Confucian literati or of the French-educated schoolteachers, surely represents one of the pillars upon which Ho Chi Minh's political accomplishments were built.

The New-Confucian Legacy

During the nineteenth century, Sung Neo-Confucianism dominated the thinking of Vietnamese monarchs, mandarins, and local scholars alike.[3] More precisely, it was normally via the writings of Chu Hsi (1130–1200) that Vietnamese approached the Confucian Four Books and Five Classics. The heart of this Confucian doctrine lay in the cultivation of virtuous conduct. Socially this was expressed in the five relationships (*ngu luan*): ruler-subject, father-son, husband-wife, elder brother-younger brother and friend-friend. Only the last held any egalitarian possibilities, the others being inherently vertical and unequal. By far the most important were the ruler-subject and father-son relationships, each patterned to some degree on the other. Personal loyalty (*trung*) of subject to ruler was the essence of one, filial piety (*hieu*) the essence of the other. Each concept was surrounded with an elaborate exegesis and historical case law. Nevertheless, a king, a father, or an elder brother was supposed to rule primarily by example, by cultivating and projecting the inner quality of virtue (*duc*), not by promulgating an outer system of laws and institutions (*phap*).

Ethical cement for this structure was supplied by a set of cardinal virtues, the number eventually stabilizing at five: "benevolence" (*nhan*), "righteousness" (*nghia*), "ritual" (*le*), "knowledge" (*tri*), and "sincerity" (*tin*).[4] "Benevolence" was clearly the most important, occasioning intricate debate and refinement among Chinese writers over two millenia. For Vietnamese of the nineteenth century, however, benevolence seems to have taken on qualities of abstract, even mystical goodness, often limited to the king alone. By contrast, "righteousness" had much more concrete implications, which even the most lowly subject was expected to understand. Righteousness meant doing what was correct rather than what was of immediate personal gain, of accepting one's obligations within the system—in short, of practising self-denial for the greater good. "Ritual" meant careful attention to social forms, to decorum, as well as intricate ceremonies directed toward Heaven, the ancestors, local deities, and assorted wandering spirits. "Knowledge" emphasized the judging of human character in order to maximize other ethical traits; it was never an end in itself, nor did it focus on nature. "Sincerity" meant the cultivation of trust, the elimination of scheming and suspicion between ruler and subject, father and son, and so on; it seems to have been the least discussed of the cardinal virtues.

---

3. Confucianism also exerted strong influence on the broader Vietnamese populace, although exactly how and to what degree remains a subject of debate. For interesting examples of Confucian morality combined with general folk wisdom, see Ninh Viet Giao, comp., *Hat Phuong Vai* [Cloth-Weaving Songs] (Hanoi, 1961).

4. The famous Vietnamese poet Nguyen Dinh Chieu (1822–88) styled these "the five treasures in the forest of classical learning [*nho*] that must be cherished." *Tho Van Nguyen Dinh Chieu* [Poetry and Prose of Nguyen Dinh Chieu] (Hanoi, 1971), pp. 234–35.

The ideal product of this code was the *quan-tu* (in Chinese, *chün-tzu*), the superior man, princely man, or gentleman. Such individuals were masters of the appropriate rituals and scholarly flourishes, yet at the same time were said to personify the fundamental goodness or perfectability of man. Their lodestar was the *Dao* (in Chinese, *Tao*), the Way, an immutable norm nevertheless subject to many different interpretations. Whatever the interpretation, the problem for the superior man was not to change with the times but to seek out the Way amidst the many diversions, the temporal vicissitudes of life. When there was order in the world, the Way was not a matter of much argument, being left to the ruler and his immediate learned advisors. In times of upheaval and fratricide, however, each scholar who took the quest for the *Dao* seriously was under some degree of ethical compulsion to assess the situation for himself and take appropriate action.

Confucian social formulas and moral strictures had become a state religion in China long before their doctrinal transferal to Vietnam. Perhaps most interesting was the influence of Tung Chung-shu (ca. 179—ca. 104 B.C.), who incorporated the cyclical *yin-yang* concept from the *Book of Changes* into the divination principles of the five elements (wood, fire, earth, metal and water). By means of this ingenious codification, Heaven and humanity were linked together by an abundance of omens, often comprehensible only to those who had fully mastered the subject. Subsequent Confucian diviners put themselves at the service of rulers, who insisted on maintaining a tight monopoly on actual communication with Heaven, and whose moral (or immoral) conduct was presumed to influence heavenly phenomena.

Nineteenth-century Vietnamese rulers were deep believers in this system. For example, Minh Mang (r. 1820–41) was convinced that some personal lapse in morality had caused the drought and plague which greeted his accession to the throne. When a court mandarin tried to absolve him from blame by referring to reports of the plague having come from the West, Minh Mang rejected this notion with impeccable logic, saying that "If I had not been lacking in virtue, how could disaster get in from overseas?"[5] Tu Duc (r. 1847–83), faced with more profound cataclysms, repeatedly 'punished' himself by writing sharply self-critical poetry, by reducing the number of dishes at the royal dinner table, or by desisting from regal hunting expeditions for several weeks. In this way the sincere desire of the monarch to alleviate the growing dangers facing Vietnam was focused ever more intensely on the search for omens and the subsequent personal rituals of blame or exaltation rather than on serious, sustained investigation of military, economic, and political causes. As for the Western enemies, because

5. Quoted in Tran Van Giau, *Su Phat Trien cua Tu Tuong o Viet-Nam tu The Ky XIX* [The Development of Ideas in Vietnam from the Nineteenth Century to the August Revolution] (hereinafter SPT), vol. 1 (Hanoi, 1973), p. 132.

their thinking ignored the *yin-yang* duality and the five elements, Tu Duc declared it out of tune with nature's unifying principle (*ly*) and thus undeserving of any respect.[6]

As the royal court lost round after round to the encroaching French, Vietnamese literati became increasingly upset and inclined to make their own judgments (remaining, however, entirely within the Neo-Confucian framework). Debate became intense, and eventually went beyond boundaries acceptable to any monarch. Employing impeccable classical references, popular scholar-poets like Nguyen Dinh Chieu (1822–88) and Phan Van Tri (1830–1910) expounded the idea that men, all men, have the potentiality of changing first themselves and then external reality. Significantly, Nguyen Dinh Chieu used Catholicism as his foil, arguing that Confucianism was the close, comprehensible, patriotic "Way of Man" (*Dao Nguoi*), versus the other-worldly, determinist, and traitorous "Way of Heaven/God" (*Dao Troi*).[7]

French occupation and "pacification" of Vietnam, essentially complete by 1900, had the important philosophical effect of stripping Confucianism of most of its sacral and universalistic claims among the scholar-gentry. If the Vietnamese king was to remain a creature of the French, whence the ethical linkage between ruler and Heaven? If evil barbarians could subjugate good believers in the *Dao*, then there was something profoundly wrong, either with the world or with the previous way of looking at it. Those who judged the world to be wrong tended to withdraw into themselves or their families, perhaps retaining a small circle of pupils and friends of like mind. Their moral example and their vivid poetical indictments of contemporary conditions undoubtedly moved the next generation, but their lack of program and their inability or refusal to provide broader leadership made them increasingly anachronistic.[8]

Those scholar-gentry who decided that the world had to be looked at in a different light had little appreciation of how fundamental a revision might ensue. Partly this was because they relied on recent Chinese (and, to a lesser extent, Japanese) publications which had already filtered Western concepts into familiar classical terminology. Nevertheless, the syncretic, utopian writings of K'ang Yu-wei (1858–1927) and the iconoclasm of Liang Ch'i-ch'ao (1873–1929) provided enough of a stimulus to both thought and action to insure that tendencies toward

6. Ibid., pp. 134–44, 150–53.

7. *Tho Van Nguyen Dinh Chieu*, pp. 234–35; see also Nguyen Cong Khai, "Nguyen Dinh Chieu: *Duong Tu Ha Mau*" [The Tale of Duong Tu and Ha Mau, by Nguyen Dinh Chieu] (Ph.D. thesis, Univ. of Saigon, 1973).

8. Two important examples of this tendency are the poets Nguyen Khuyen (1835–1909) and Tran Te Xuong (better known as Tu Xuong) (1870–1907). See Vu Dinh Liem et al., eds., *Hop Tuyen Tho Van Viet-Nam* [Collection of Vietnamese Poetry and Prose] (hereinafter HT), vol. 4 (Hanoi, 1963), pp. 319–41, 345–65; and LT-1, pp. 475–76.

aestheticism or eremitism never gained in popularity among the Vietnamese educated elite.[9] The next step for many was to consult older Chinese writings outside the comfortable Neo-Confucian canon, to include Lao-tzu, Chuang-tzu, Motzu, the Legalists, and some of the Ming and Ch'ing philosophers and textual critics. Buddhism, long regarded by Vietnamese literati as heresy yet still quite influential among Vietnamese peasants, was given the benefit of a new look. Others were stimulated to track down the same Western philosophers that had excited attention in Japan and China, especially Montesquieu, Rousseau, and Herbert Spencer.

Sometime in the second decade of the twentieth century, however, most of these eager, inquiring Vietnamese literati came to realize that the study of Western philosophy still left them in a mental quagmire. For some this was rationalized into a defense of collaboration, in short, the need for an extended period of French tutelage before Vietnamese could hope to sort things out properly. Others adopted an essentially passive "all things according to the times" (tuy thoi) outlook. Still others retreated to a narrow interpretation of the Confucian classics centered on the five social relationships. More than anything else they seemed to share a fear that their private moral quandaries, if written large across Vietnamese society, would produce chaos and fratricide. This was not merely a selfish fear, although that played a part. Almost all had come to accept the Social Darwinian image of "survival of the fittest," at least as it applied to the rise and fall of nations and ethnic groups. To their minds, chaos and fratricide among Vietnamese was a sure route to extermination, which reinforcement of traditional ethical norms, however, adumbrated, might help to prevent.

The Ethics of Collaboration

The other key ingredient in the moral instruction of the 1920s was an intense colonial campaign to convince Vietnamese that French rule was not only inevitable but just and beneficial as well. And, beyond listening to this colonial propaganda, Vietnamese had to demonstrate in a hundred ways, large and small, that they accepted the colonial status quo. For ordinary peasants this ranged from paying increased taxes at every turn to scurrying out of the way as a French automobile roared down a country road. For the minority that went to school it was necessary to go further, to endorse the system in front of many others. Children had to write essays glorifying French occupation and defending the local police and collaborator officials for maintaining peace and order. They had to address French individuals with particular respect and refer to France as the "Motherland" (Mau Quoc). No pupil could expect to get beyond primary school without extolling the French in answers to examination questions. Post-primary

---

9. For an account of discussions and actions growing in part out of Vietnamese literati contact with Chinese reformist publications, see Marr, *Vietnamese Anticolonialism*, pp. 98–211.

education was also impossible without favorable "moral" recommendations from persons trusted by the French. No one could take up a salaried position, travel from region to region, publish a newspaper, or form an organization without further loyalty checks. In short, being a member of the Vietnamese intelligentsia in the 1920s and 1930s demanded some concessions, willing or unwilling, to the foreign-inspired and foreign-directed system. Either that or enter into an illegal clandestine existence, which only a minority of the minority did until the 1940s.

Precisely because every educated Vietnamese had to face this problem of foreign domination in his daily life, however, a subtle gradation process emerged. Some attitudes or actions were considered evidence of enthusiastic collaboration; others reflected passive endorsement, grudging acceptance, or simply an attempt to do the minimum necessary to avoid retribution. What was "enthusiastic," "passive," or "grudging" in the 1920s might well have altered in the 1930s, and certainly had changed by 1944-45. Another common response was to attack colonialism in the privacy of one's home or among one's closest friends, but to remain meek and outwardly trustworthy in one's public life. This could lead to considerable psychological tension, however, especially when sons and daughters grew up to question such a bifurcated existence, or when a friend asked for some favor that involved overt commitment.[10]

From the point of view of the French, having established the basic economic and administrative frameworks before World War I, another important task was to build up Vietnamese support, to make Vietnamese feel they were a part of this grand colonial endeavour. Previous visions of mass conversion having mostly gone by the boards, attention tended to focus on building a sympathetic, reasonably competent native elite. The French now appreciated that this elite would have to have moral as well as material reasons for active participation. From Albert Sarraut's second governor-generalship (1917-19) onward, a considerable amount of time and energy was expended by French administrators trying to perfect a formula to increase the numbers of enthusiastic collaborators while simultaneously neutralizing the ambivalent component and isolating or eliminating the inevitable malcontents. This formula was never found, not least of all because the French promised "benefits of civilization" that could not possibly be realized in a colonial context.

Viewed from the perspective of enthusiastic Vietnamese collaborators, it was even more imperative that moral justifications be developed, first to improve their own self-respect, secondly to convince other educated Vietnamese to join them, and not least of all to generate more respect among the public at large. As

10. These observations are based on numerous discussions with South Vietnamese intellectuals in the 1960s. The older ones tended to focus on such ethical tensions in the 1930s and 1940s, whereas the younger ones were preoccupied with the same immediate dilemma in relation to the Americans.

one ranking collaborator theoretician explained, a simple tightening of discipline by those on top, without equivalent improvement in the "talent and virtue" (*tai duc*) of the elite, would only make people below more likely to perceive rules of hierarchy and order as being "improper and insufferable." [11]

The result of this combined French and collaborator Vietnamese concern was a proliferation of moral arguments defending France's seizure of Vietnam, supporting France's contemporary 'mission,' and painting a future glowing with harmony and fruitful cooperation. (While the subject of collaboration will come up again, here I am raising it only in the moral context.) Up until the mid-1920s, perhaps the most convenient moral defense of collaboration was to present France as father to the Vietnamese son, or as teacher to pupil. [12] The French father/teacher had the responsibilities of protecting and patiently instructing, while the Vietnamese son/pupil responded with filial piety, gratitude, and diligent attention. Exactly why the more obvious relationship, that of ruler-subject (*vua-toi*), was not taken as the primary model is unclear. Perhaps it was simply because there remained a Vietnamese king (no matter how weak), and residual monarchists who were also colonial collaborators would be hard put to explain 'loyalty' (*trung*) to two different masters. At any rate, the father/teacher image was more intimate, and probably closer to the way French idealists wanted themselves to be seen

The main weakness, which even a seven- or eight-year-old Vietnamese pupil could ascertain, was that French colonialists seldom acted like traditional fathers or teachers. There was also the problem of no blood ties, and the embarrassing question of how long it might take the Vietnamese 'child' to reach adulthood and the capacity for self-assertion. When collaborator moralists protested that critics were taking the traditional language too literally, they simply exposed themselves to further ridicule, since the very strength of the five Confucian relationships lay with their particularity and the comfortable knowledge that certain patterns of behavior were fixed.

As with all propaganda, there was also the constant danger of gross overstatement and consequent devaluation; this definitely happened during World War I. Thus, after claiming that "Heaven has created the people of Great France [*Dai Phap*] to carry out their magnificent calling in Indochina," the monthly journal *Nam Phong* [Southern Ethos], argued that the Vietnamese must first contribute labor and money to the French Motherland so that she could eliminate the "barbarian Huns" from Europe. Such messages were often accompanied by poems affirming Vietnamese faithfulness in the most gushing imagery imaginable. At one point, Governor-General Albert Sarraut was equated with the Meiji Em-

---

11. Tran Trong Kim, *Nho Giao* [Confucianism], vol. 1, pp. xiv–xv.

12. Metropolitan textbooks often used the imagery of French *mother* and Vietnamese son, an example of cultural confusion that was soon filtered out in *quoc-ngu* texts.

peror. And Sarraut himself joined the chorus by exhorting Vietnamese to buy more French war bonds so that in the future they could hang up the certificates as part of the family ancestral altar.[13] Literary effusion was not unknown in the earlier Sino-Vietnamese relationship, but never had it reached this extreme.

At the same time, perhaps partly because France was seen to need the help of Vietnamese in World War I, a feeling seemed to grow, particularly among propertied Vietnamese collaborators, that more should be forthcoming from the father/teacher than didacticism and paper certificates amidst the ancestral incense. For example, when Sarraut reestablished the tiny University of Hanoi the rumor quickly spread that education compatible with tertiary metropolitan standards would be provided. Clearly called upon by the authorities to scotch this misconception, *Nam Phong* argued that it was inconceivable that Vietnamese colonial education could reach a level equal to the French. "You are asking for something that can never possibly happen," *Nam Phong* told the unnamed aspirants bluntly.[14]

Nevertheless, a utilitarian view of the quasi-familial explanations of collaboration was gaining ground. When a Vietnamese court figure published a language primer in 1915, for example, the majority of lessons were based on the conventional five relationships and five virtues. He also chose, however, to tackle the new concept of 'freedom' (*tu do*). The quality of freedom, he said, was dependent on becoming strong, wealthy and learned. Since Great France was showing Vietnam the way, the more Vietnamese who followed the French, the more Vietnam would acquire these attributes.[15] Simple enough. But this was not how a child was meant to look upon a father or a teacher. There was an element of calculation here, and hence of qualified as distinct from absolute loyalty.

The key Vietnamese words in these qualified commitments were generally *ich* or *loi*, each meaning advantage, usefulness, or profit, and each conveying in Confucian moral terms a certain odor of personal gratification—in short, of selfishness. Soon, government-commissioned schoolbooks were using these same rationales. A third-year text, for example, after giving passing mention to the "quietude" and spirit of "harmony" that had prevailed since French occupation,

13. Tuyet Huy, "Bai Ky Ngay Ky Niem Quan Toan Quyen Sarraut den Hanoi" [Remembering the Day that Governor-General Sarraut Arrived in Hanoi], NP 1 (July 1917), pp. 52-53; idem, "Luan Thuyet: Mot Nen Minh Tri" [On the Concept of a Meiji Era], NP 7 (Jan. 1918), pp. 1-6; and idem, "Dong Bao Ta Nen Mua Ve Quoc Trai" [Our Countrymen Should Buy National Savings Bonds], NP 15 (Sept. 1918), pp. 181-90. Poems and further equations of Vietnamese honor with buying war bonds are found in NP 16 (Oct. 1918). Just after the Armistice, the authorities announced that 176.5 million francs had been raised in Indochina from the sale of war bonds, 57 percent of the total for 1918. (NP 17 [Nov. 1918] p. 310.)

14. "Luan Thuyet: Truong Dai Hoc" [On the Concept of a University], NP 3 (Sept. 1917). pp. 150-51.

15. Ung Trinh, *Quoc Ngu Van Luan* [Essays in the National Script], Hanoi, 1915.

then focused most of its attention on the alleged practical, material benefits of colonial rule. At the end, pupils were told to write an essay on a Western-trained physician coming to their village to treat the ill.[16] This must have been an exercise in total imagination for most children, since very few doctors or nurses were available, and fewer still came to the villages. A visit of the tax collector would have been more apposite, but harder to explain in any utilitarian framework.

No Vietnamese could read the proliferation of lessons and texts dealing with the Franco-Vietnamese relationship without realizing that the classic Confucian dichotomy of "righteousness/profit" (*nghia/loi*) was being subjected to considerable stress, even being rankly violated. Thus, in 1932, when the Great Depression was driving hundreds of thousands of Vietnamese into despair and beggarhood, a morality primer still tried to convince children that "France is treating us better than our own fathers and mothers could!" The title of the lesson: "We must be thankful to the State."[17] In contrast, another primer of the same period led off with the assertion that "Franco-Vietnamese collaboration is the road to a paradise of advantages."[18] One well-known classical moralist, Nguyen Ba Hoc (1857–1921), had tried to resolve the obvious contradiction by employing father/son imagery for the inner spirit of the colonial relationship and utilitarianism for matters of outer implementation. However, his own continuing disquiet was revealed in his conclusion:

It is wrong for people to say that mere competition for food and pleasure constitutes reformist development. Not only does that attitude retard the advance of civilization, it also demonstrates a lack of proper gratitude to the Protectorate.[19]

Another possibility was simply to ride roughshod over the traditional dichotomy. When the French floated the fifth Indochina bond issue in 1920, for example, *Nam Phong* specifically called upon Vietnamese to buy for reasons of both "righteousness" and "profit." It was a righteous act to assist France in rebuilding after suffering heavily at the hands of the Germans. Besides, it showed gratitude for the "precious Western civilization" that France had brought and taught to Vietnamese. On the other hand, it was a profitable act, because French bonds were a much more solid investment than loans by the day or month to one's compatriots. True, the interest was lower, but readers were assured that the prin-

16. Tran Trong Kim, Nguyen Van Ngoc, Dang Dinh Phuc, Do Than, *Quoc Van Giao Khoa Thu* [Textbook on National Literature], 4th printing, (Hanoi[?], 1930), lesson 9. The same attention to French doctors showed up in French-language instruction.

17. Bui Van Banh, *Chung Quanh Gia Dinh: Luan Ly So Luan* [Around the Family: Elementary Morality] (Saigon, 1932).

18. Nguyen Dinh Hong, *So Hoc Luan Ly Tiep Vinh* [A Further Aid for Elementary Moral Instruction] (Hanoi, 1934).

19. Nam Dinh Hoc Gioi Bao Tro Hoi, *Tan Quoc Van* [New National Literature] (Nam Dinh, 1925), lesson 51.

cipal would double or triple in value as the franc gained in strength in relation to the piaster. Fathers were told to instruct children to buy bonds, wives to encourage husbands, friends to go together to the bank. Not only would individuals reap a windfall and display great righteousness, but the world would see that "The Vietnamese people have a heart that upholds righteousness, that values loyalty; they know how to take advantage of opportunities too." The following ditty concluded the exhortation:

> The sea has become quiet,
> The waves are translucent,
> We shall buy lots of government bonds,
> To help our teacher Great France
> Improve the country in beauty.[20]

With such a tendency toward obfuscation and overstatement, collaborator moralists presented a large target indeed for anyone with the nerve to attack them publicly. One of the most trenchant barrages was mounted by a classically educated gentleman, Tran Huu Do (?-1939), born in the lower Mekong Delta province of Go Cong and making his living in part from prescription of traditional medicines. Tran Huu Do argued that the ultimate objective of the French and their native lackeys was to make the Vietnamese people feel that national independence was no longer necessary or even desirable.[21] They were quite patient and methodical in trying to erode and eventually destroy the Vietnamese spirit, he said. First they tried to get hold of children at an early age and to train them away from their natural inclinations, such as intellectual curiosity, individual initiative, and identification with their own ethnic group. The model was one of horses, monkeys and lions in the circus, which if taken at infancy and subjected to an artificial regimen, could be induced to act quite contrary to their natural selves. In line with this concept, Tran Huu Do pointed out the sharper restrictions that had recently been placed on young Vietnamese travelling to France for higher studies, the government obviously being worried they would learn the wrong things. Then, too, students receiving scholarships were obliged to serve seven years with the government, an experience that might break even the most determined patriot. In short, the result was often akin to those generations of Chinese women with tightly bound feet. Even if the bandages were unwound in adulthood, deformed feet could never walk naturally again.

The second coherent policy of the French, Tran Huu Do asserted, was to cultivate a desire among their colonial subjects for colorful medals, ranks, and titles. If

20. "Quoc Trai lan thu Nam" [Fifth Series of National Savings Bonds], NP 32 (Feb. 1920), pp. 185-86.

21. Tran Huu Do, *To Co Mat Quyen Tu Do* [The Causes of Our Loss of Freedom] (Saigon, 1926), pp. 24-33.

subjects had the outward panoply of power, perhaps they would not feel so bad about lacking the real thing. Money might also enter the equation, in the same way that dogs performing tricks will receive snacks, or geisha girls satisfying customers will obtain trinkets. Competition among subjects for these petty favors was encouraged, sharpening cleavages and promoting a pecking-order mentality. Those who entered this trap tended also to be the ones who aped French fads and fashions. Here Tran Huu Do recounted firsthand an incident in which a particular French official developed a taste for a certain very ordinary type of banana for dessert. Soon all of his Vietnamese subordinates were seeking out and eating the same kind of banana, praising it to the skies, and sneering at those around them who did not know a "civilized" dessert when they saw one.

Reinforcing the above policies, in Tran Huu Do's opinion, was the French system of indirect rule. Without docile Vietnamese mandarins and village elders to execute their every instruction, the French would have had a difficult time maintaining control, especially since they still lacked intimate knowledge of the customs and language of the country. In the West, according to the author, bureaucrats thought of themselves as servants of the people, but in Vietnam bureaucrats were ravenous instruments of foreign dictatorship. Yet, Tran Huu Do added ironically, the French treated these local native officials much as they would mere machines in their own country, each part replaceable if it failed to function properly. At the wheel of the Indochinese automobile was the governor-general, viewing thousands of spineless officials like rubber tires, spark plugs, and piston rings.[22]

Finally, Tran Huu Do explained, for those Vietnamese who for one reason or another refused to respond properly to indoctrination, petty enticements, and machine-like commands, there was brute force. Yet, as Mencius had said long ago, there would always be times of revolt. Dictators could never rest comfortably in their own beds. The French could respond to unrest by tightening the judicial, police and military controls even further. But a master who locked up his slaves would not get much productive labor out of them. Nor would he see them helping out much in the event of attack by a third party. Besides, an army organized for internal suppression would not be very effective when called upon to defend the borders.[23]

Actually, by the late 1920s even many formerly enthusiastic Vietnamese col-

22. There is a hint here, it might be added, of the traditional Confucian protest against emperors who treat literati as mere tools.
23. In this passage Tran Huu Do foretold the French dilemma of the following decade, as Japanese armies moved into South China, seized Hainan, and even arranged for poorly-trained Thai divisions to threaten Indochina from the west. Faced with the choice of either distributing arms to the Vietnamese populace for joint antifascist resistance or giving in to the Japanese and perhaps salvaging some colonial privileges, the French readily chose the latter.

laborators were prepared to concede that France was not fulfilling the positive moral roles ascribed to it. The father/teacher was neglecting his duties. The architect of a paradise-on-earth was apparently preparing one place for himself and another for the rest. Coincidental with this awareness, as we shall see, was a more general movement of intelligentsia self-assertion, of willingness to take modernizing initiatives with, without, or, if necessary, against the French. As if sensing the profound risks involved in this line of reasoning, some elite Vietnamese gathered together hastily under the cautious banner of "education first, politics later." This had the transitory merit of permitting flamboyant rhetoric about the need for change while actually prescribing little more than self-improvement and the formation of more study societies. Thus, Cao Chanh, after a rousing denunciation of slavish attitudes and a glowing portrait of Japan as example of what self-respect could accomplish, proceeded merely to recommend his own pamphlet as the first step in an extended "movement of national education."[24] Nguyen Van Vinh (1882-1936), one of the most prominent older pro-French intellectuals, cautioned his countrymen to figure out precisely where they wanted to go and how they would get there before actually embarking on the voyage.[25] Both authors would have joined a third writer, Phan Dinh Long, in arguing that any strategy employing violence was absolutely unacceptable.[26]

Educated Vietnamese over forty years of age were intimately aware that more forthright, coherent proposals for 'national education' had been advanced in 1905-1908. A private movement had been organized, only to be smashed by the colonial administration.[27] During World War I, Governor-General Sarraut and his gifted head of Indochina intelligence and security operations, Louis Marty, encouraged a similar endeavour aimed at defusing radical and anticolonial feelings. *Nam Phong* was permitted to hint that France might eventually grant self-governing status if the Vietnamese proved to be good and faithful students.[28] Another ripple of excitement accompanied the 1925 arrival of the Socialist Governor-General Alexandre Varenne only to fade within a year. With the trau-

24. Cao Chanh, *Phuong Cham Cuu Quoc: Dan Dao va Dan Quyen* [Lodestar for National Salvation: Democracy and People's Rights] (Saigon, 1926).

25. Tan Nam Tu (Nguyen Van Vinh), *Thuc Tinh Dong Bao* [Awakening Sentiment of Countrymen] (Saigon, 1926).

26. Phan Dinh Long, *Cay Kim Chi Nam* [The Compass Needle] (Saigon, 1928), p. 14. This affirmation did not prevent the author from being jailed from 1930 to 1933.

27. Marr, *Vietnamese Anticolonialism*, pp. 159-84, 195-211.

28. Pham Quynh, "May Nhoi Noi Dau" [Some Opening Remarks], NP 1 (July 1917), pp. 1-7. Colonial archives reveal that the exact phrasing of this hypothetical reference to self-government was prepared by Louis Marty and cleared with Sarraut in advance of publication. It was designed as a safety valve for "existing nationalist sentiments" (Marty report to Sarraut, 22 April 1917). Even so, the resident-superior of Tonkin registered his opinion that talk of this kind, even if theoretical, was still dangerous (Res. Sup. Le Gallen, letter to Sarraut, 19 Sept. 1917). (Both documents are in the former Archives Centrales de l'Indochine, Hanoi.)

matic events of 1929-31 it became obvious to the majority of the Vietnamese intelligentsia that drastic alteration of the political system would have to precede substantive educational development, not the reverse.

Nevertheless, Pham Quynh and other continuing collaborators had little choice but to offer up yet again their prescriptions of moral-educational-cultural renaissance. Culture (*van hoa*) was the foundation of the nation, Pham Quynh wrote in 1930, the "roots" that had to be tended before the "branches" could become fresh and strong. Besides, political action was too dangerous, "especially if tried too fast."[29] A new twist was provided in the 1932–33 campaign to project the young Emperor Bao Dai as a moral exemplar, a model of East-West harmony, a Vietnamese appropriately "dyed with the new but never forgetting the old." Assisted by Pham Quynh as relevant court minister, Bao Dai was expected to lead a campaign of "national people's education" (*quoc dan giao duc*). Ruler-subject imagery and court ceremony were refurbished, patriotism was re-equated with monarchism, and Bao Dai was given the restoration potential of the Japanese Meiji Emperor. Proponents were careful to point out, however, that ultimate authority remained in the hands of the French.[30] By the mid-1930s most participants, including Bao Dai himself, had lost enthusiasm for the project.

In the early 1940s morality primers were still trying to combine florid images of Vietnamese pushing themselves forward and "struggling enthusiastically" (*phan dau*), with stern warnings that these actions could only be attempted according to the material and intellectual level of society and depending on historical circumstances.[31] A curious new element was provided by Vietnamese morality lessons devoted specifically to Marshal Pétain, head of the Vichy regime, and to the exact way of saluting the tricolor before start of school each day.[32] On St. Mary's Cathedral in downtown Saigon could be seen a huge portrait of the Marshal with the caption, "A single chief: Petain. A single duty: to obey. A single motto: to serve."[33] The Vichy slogan of "Work-Family-Fatherland" was splashed on walls and hoisted on banners, since, in the opinion of the current Governor-General, Admiral Decoux, it "corresponded marvelously with the deep-seated and traditional aspirations of the [Vietnamese] masses, and tallied with Confucian morality."[34]

From 1930 onward, whatever the moral pretensions of the French, collaborator

29. Thuong Chi (Pham Quynh), "Doc Sach co Cam" [Reading a Book Sympathetically], NP 149 (Apr. 1930), p. 308. This is a review of Tran Trong Kim's book, *Nho Giao*.

30. Nguyen Gy, *Long Nguyen Vong cua Quoc Dan Viet-Nam* (Hanoi, 1933), pp. 11–24; *Sach Choi Xuan Nam Quy Dau* [Amusement for Spring 1933] (n.p., 1933), pp. 5–14. Pham Quynh made various proposals for educational reform in 1932–34 (see AOM NF 2226).

31. Vu Nhu Lan, *Tu Than Luan Ly* [Self-Cultivation Morality] (Nam Dinh, 1941), p. 28.

32. DIRIP, *Van Quoc Ngu* [Learning the National Script] (1942), lessons 65 and 66.

33. *Indochine* (Hanoi) 71 (8 Jan. 1942), p. 8.

34. Amiral Decoux, *A la Barre de l'Indochine* (Paris, 1949), p. 360.

Vietnamese were increasingly pessimistic about the future and increasingly ready to support any system that seemed to insure their physical security. Partly they were shocked by violent peasant upheavals and repeated workers' strikes. Perhaps even more upsetting was the readiness of young educated Vietnamese to disobey parents and to ignore teachers on matters large and small. There were ever more plaintive comments about the "virus of moral decline,"[35] about the breakdown of alleged quasi-familial ties between landowners and tenants.[36] Yet collaborators seemed to have reached a moral impasse. Pham Quynh, for example, even while denouncing contemporary "anarchy of spirit" and "Disorder in the heart," admitted wistfully that "Le Sage de K'iu-fou [Confucius] paraît loin, bien loins dans l'espace et le temps."[37] To make matters worse, wealthy Vietnamese were still largely excluded from the social life of the French community. Sometimes *colons* were downright nasty: when one called a Vietnamese physician an "imbecile" in public, the physician responded, and another Frenchman tried to punish him on the spot by twisting his ears.[38] The Depression also served to demonstrate how tenuous, even ephemeral, were economic gains among the Vietnamese bourgeoisie. In short, lacking moral legitimacy, and existing in very fragile social and economic circumstances, the claim to future political leadership of Vietnam's collaborator elite seemed to lose much of its significance.

In 1944, a small incident occurred which tells us a lot about moral relationships of the time. A Vietnamese communist leader was captured, brought before the collaborator mandarin of Bac Ninh province, and treated to a fatherly lecture on the abysmally low level of popular consciousness and the consequent need to concentrate on educational and cultural activities before any thought was given to serious political mobilization. "The people only know how to struggle over a bit of sweet rice and meat," the mandarin commented wryly, adding "The slightest smell of these delicacies and they'll start a lawsuit." Then, to the undoubted surprise of the mandarin, the prisoner interrupted, commenting that educated people appeared to be more lost than uneducated ones. "Do you want to be educated and a slave?" the prisoner cried angrily, at which point the mandarin is said to have broken off the encounter and ordered the communist to jail.[39] What makes the episode even more interesting is that the mandarin had permitted his own family and servants to gather round to listen to the instruction,

35. *La Tribune Indochinoise*, 13 Mar. 1935.

36. Ibid., 27 Apr. 1938.

37. Pham Quynh, "Réflexions sur Confucius et la Confucéisme," NP (French Supplement) 148 (Mar. 1930), p. 17.

38. This incident created a stir among educated Vietnamese in November 1934. PNTV 267 (22 Nov. 1934), p. 4.

39. Van Tien Dung, "Nuoc Song Hong len rat cao nhung de van vung" [The Red River Has Risen but the Dikes Are Holding], *Rung Yen The* [The Yen The Forest] (Hanoi, 1962), pp. 126-27.

and that the prisoner obviously risked harsher treatment in the interests of countering a collaborator in front of his own dependents. Three decades later, this same communist, Van Tien Dung (b. 1917), was commander-in-chief of the offensive that ended the Vietnam War.

Morality Texts

Having stressed the importance attached to moral instruction by the French as well as their Vietnamese collaborators, it would seem to follow that textbooks published in the colony would maintain a coherent moral posture. Yet a survey of several hundred *quoc-ngu* morality and language instruction books reveals conflicting visions of good and evil, of the meaning of life, and of the relationship between man and nature. One textbook serves to contradict another, and separate lessons within a single book provide starkly different prescriptions for ethical behavior. While such a muddle must have mystified many a young Vietnamese reader, it may also have been a stimulus to seek answers outside approved channels. For some readers, confusion may have been the first step to creative thinking.

Perhaps it is worth suggesting first, however, some of the reasons why even morality textbooks subject to close colonial scrutiny failed to project a consistent message. First of all, at home in Paris, or even in the tighter colonial communities of Saigon and Hanoi, French men and women often disagreed among themselves on what constituted the ultimate in French morality and moral experience. Secondly, assuming they reached a consensus, there remained the question of how much of the metropolitan essence ought to be transplanted to a colonial environment, part of the larger and never resolved dispute over strategies of "assimilation" and "association." Thirdly, colonial administrators were never able to entirely seal out foreign ideas that they knew to be detrimental to colonial interests, including quite a few coming from France itself. On the other hand, there was the problem of the French not being able to identify some ideas as potentially disruptive when they saw them—and some they even taught to young Vietnamese themselves. Finally, and probably most important, Vietnam was hardly a moral wasteland ready to be injected with new seed and cultivated at will according to the gardening metaphor still current among many Western colonialists of the early twentieth century. Vietnamese had their own particular passion for moral questions, operating from different traditions entirely. Even some of the faithful collaborators discussed above spent a fair amount of their time formulating ethical ideals separate from the question of whether the French were in Vietnam legitimately or not.

Quantitatively, my preliminary survey of the Bibliothèque Nationale (Paris) collection turned up 142 *quoc-ngu* morality texts (narrowly defined), which is to say, books and booklets prepared either for use in classroom morality instruction[40] or designed for reading at home, where it was assumed the family would continue to play a major role in conveying and enforcing moral values.[41] Notations on the covers of most of these publications point to a minimum of 1.7 million copies being printed in the two decades or so prior to 1945.[42] To the morality primers one would add at least 370 manuals for the beginning study of quoc-ngu, since almost all of these mixed in a strong element of basic morality with their ABCs and sound sequences.[43] Then, too, there were no less than sixty-seven elementary literature textbooks, usually organized in brief lessons for copying, memorization, and recitation, which also emphasized moral prescriptions of one kind or another. Many of the 288 history texts, historical dramatizations, biographies, and traditional Vietnamese literary works discussed in Chapter 6 had overt moral statements as well. There were also more than thirty examination preparation or cram texts, which attempted to combine morality, language, literature, history, and perhaps a bit of hygiene and natural science.[44] It was not unusual for morality or language primers to go through five, ten, or even twenty editions or reprintings. A text authorized for use in the regular colonial curriculum might enjoy 50,000–60,000 copies per printing, while the others had to be content with about 2,000 copies and reprintings according to popularity.

It is possible to delineate four general categories of morality instruction during the thirty years preceding the August 1945 Revolution: (a) that based in large part on late nineteenth-century French metropolitan school primers; (b) disseminations of the Catholic Church; (c) reformulations and modifications of nineteenth-century Vietnamese moral teachings; and (d) a type of citizen's education or civics program appearing after 1938 as the result of reforms in the French school curriculum.

In reality, these types were not exactly isolated. Thus, even though a French

40. Dr. Gail Kelly has identified at least twelve quoc-ngu texts that were approved by the colonial Office of Public Instruction for use in the morality syllabus between 1919 and 1938. There were also about the same number of approved morality texts in the French language for that period (personal correspondence, 20 Sept. 1977).

41. This figure does not count some 35 texts aimed specifically at girls and young women, a subject taken up in chapter 5.

42. This is probably a conservative figure. Between 1925 and 1930, admittedly years of intense printing activity, the Office of Public Instruction reported publication of 900,000 approved morality texts in quoc-ngu (Indochine Française, Les manuels scolaires et les publications pédagogiques de la Direction Générale de l'Instruction Publique [Hanoi, 1931], p. 23).

43. Approved quoc-ngu language primers printed between 1925 and 1930 totalled 980,000 (ibid.).

44. In this cursory survey of the Bibliothèque Nationale collection it was necessary to count separate editions of the same publication separately, since I did not have the time to cross-check and to cross-index all individual publications; nor did I try to systematically contrast approved school texts with the much larger number of texts lacking the imprimatur but having clearance from the censor.

metropolitan primer might rely heavily on culturally specific material, for example an animal fable from La Fontaine, or the story of the Dutch boy who kept his finger in the dike, the act of translation into Vietnamese and the reading of such accounts by a Vietnamese child often altered the original message. Catholic priests had been acutely aware of this cultural problem since their arrival several centuries earlier. Their publications of this period, however, reveal a conscious effort to reinforce selected Confucian concepts and to attack all free-thinking and materialist ideas coming from the West. By the same token, Vietnamese traditionalists, whether of Confucian, Buddhist, Taoist, or eclectic persuasions, were reacting to a particular array of difficulties arising in a French colony of the twentieth century. Finally, civics texts of the late colonial period seem to have represented recognition, at least among some, that all three of the other approaches were failing to achieve adequate results.

French Primers in Vietnamese

Although content was to vary considerably, most twentieth-century Vietnamese moralists owed a great deal to French forms. Primary schools in metropolitan France had continued to stress formal moral instruction long after the outward separation of church and state. Many French colonial administrators and pedagogues were content to bring standard metropolitan texts and curriculum outlines to Indochina and to have them translated into Vietnamese with only occasional modifications or additions.[45] Not surprisingly, therefore, some *quoc-ngu* morality primers presented those precepts which a comfortable French bourgeois gentleman would want children of the French petit bourgeois, peasant, and proletarian classes to understand and obey.[46] Besides the obvious lessons on respecting one's parents and teachers, not lying or cheating, and keeping clean, quiet, and sober, there were forcefully worded essays on the obligation of everyone to work hard, save money (but not be avaricious), respect the authorities, and pay all taxes. Children were told that a wage laborer who failed to work to full capacity was in effect stealing money from his boss (quite in contrast to the quasi-familial emphasis of most traditionalist texts). A merchant was to be considered a public thief if he jacked up prices, advertised deceptively, or sold faulty goods (a moral problem beneath the dignity of traditionalist discussion). Indi-

45. A 1918 list of approved texts for Franco-Vietnamese schools includes twenty-four morality primers, fifteen in the French language and nine in Vietnamese (there is also one Laotian text). Most Vietnamese textbooks appear to be translations or reformulations from the French. An exception is Nguyen Trai, *Gia Huan Ca* [Family Training Ode], n.p., n.d. *Journal Officiel de l'Indochine Française*, vol. 30, no. 37 (8 May 1918), p. 842.

46. See, for example Nguyen Van Nhan and Phan Dinh Giap, *Au Hoc Tu Than Luan Ly Giao Khoa* [Children's Self-Cultivation Morality Text], 3rd edition (Hanoi, 1920). The authors dedicated the book to C. Mus, director of the Collège de Protectorat (Hanoi) and also, incidentally, father of the well-known scholar, Paul Mus.

viduals who beat animals were also condemned, both because donkeys, cows, and chickens had feelings, and because severe treatment might hinder an animal's ability to provide labor or meat for the owners. More than one Vietnamese child must have wondered about this special consideration for animals, when his own parents and elder siblings were hardly treated better by the local landlord, plantation overseer, or mine supervisor.

Until perhaps 1920 in Vietnam there was a naive assimilationist air to most French-based morality texts. It was simply assumed that the maxims of Voltaire, Chateaubriand, Thierry, and Michelet, as well as Cicero, St. Augustine, Jonathan Swift, and Benjamin Franklin, would all serve to motivate Vietnamese children in the same way they presumably motivated French children. Pedagogues seemed unaware that certain metropolitan ideas could provide a jolt to Vietnamese readers in a colonial setting. Thus, one book had a delightful tale about a boy trying to lure a bird into a gilded cage, the bird preferring a less secure existence on its own. The lesson's title was, "There is nothing more precious than freedom," a phrase that, with the added goal of "independence," became the most famous words ever written by Ho Chi Minh.[47] Another potentially provocative story was titled, "Power comes from uniting [*sum hop*] with each other."

Glorification of French history and French heroes was another routine theme in metropolitan primers that had possibly disruptive effects in colonial Vietnam. For example, a book of apparent translations titled *Great France Public Spirits* had originally been designed to overawe readers with its host of stirring anecdotes and appropriate moral tag-lines. It might also have had the effect, however, of stimulating Vietnamese to reassess their own history and to reemphasize their own heroes, with results quite different from what must have been wished by the French lieutenant governor of Cochinchina who lent his name to the book's preface.[48] Textbooks with rousing, even joyous accounts of French seizure, pacification, and "development" of Vietnam were also quite common in this period, often compiled by collaborator mandarins as a form of merit-making.[49] World War I saw this type of propaganda take on a strident character. Perhaps the ultimate was a text titled *Liberators of the Human Race*, with an unprecedented color cover composed of the French tricolor and pictures of Poincaré, George V, Albert I (of Belgium), and Czar Nicolas. Inside there were passionate essays

47. Nguyen Quang Oanh and Nguyen Dinh Que, *So Hoc Doc Ban* [Elementary Reader], 10th printing (Hanoi, 1915).

48. Le Van Thom, *Dai Phap Cong Than* [Great France Public Spirits] (Saigon, 1907).

49. See, for example, Hoang Thai Xuyen, *Guong Su Nam* [Paragons from Vietnamese History] (Hanoi, 1910). Captain Jules Roux, who played a curious and possibly important role in the colonial politics of this period, went to the trouble of translating this work into French, presumably to demonstrate Vietnamese loyalty to a metropolitan audience.

about Joffre, Foch, and the Grand Duke Nicolas, climaxed, however, by a paean to the French 75-mm cannon.[50]

Young Vietnamese inducted into the colonial army received moral instruction too. A bilingual manual on military spirit issued in 1914 included lessons on upholding one's honor, respecting the tricolor ("protect it to the last man"), unit camaraderie, obeying orders, and personal heroism.[51] Also included were stories of Vietnamese soldiers who upheld these values, most particularly individuals who had risked death to rescue their French commanders. This was the French version of Neo-Confucian unconditional loyalty and righteousness. One cannot help but wonder, however, if the French officers who conceived the book were bolstering their own image of themselves as much as they were trying to motivate new Vietnamese recruits.

In the climactic section of this military morality manual the French fell into the same righteousness/profit trap as the collaborator Vietnamese discussed earlier. After a ringing justification of French sovereignty over Indochina and a warning that jealous foreigners and selfish anticolonial Vietnamese "bandits" still had to be dealt with forcefully, there followed the clear promise that Vietnamese, working together with their French overlords, could learn the mysteries of the modern world and become wealthy. Vietnam was backward, the argument went, because of earlier Chinese exploitation, domestic disorder, and the nineteenth-century refusal to communicate or trade with the foreign powers. Now, however, Great France was in charge and was getting things done. The people of Great France were famous for their ability to tell good from evil, for their attention to method and for their courage and personal initiative. Soon, Vietnamese too would be able to climb into airplanes and fly above the ricefields and ponds, like the magnificent Vietnamese dragon of yore. There would be wonderful development in peace and prosperity, provided that Vietnamese knew how to be "grateful to the Government" (biet on Nha Nuoc).[52]

By the mid-1920s more and more French administrators seem to have developed doubts about the efficacy of simply translating French texts and throwing in references to Vietnamese dragons to demonstrate their cultural sensitivity. True, French colonial pedagogues continued to assert the absolute superiority of French morality, or sometimes the universality of moral standards, often amounting to the same thing in descriptive terms. Either way, the Vietnamese were still said to

50. Ho Dac Khai, Les Libérateurs de la Race Humaine (Hanoi, 1915) (both French and quoc-ngu sections).

51. Le Livre du Soldat Annamite (Nam Binh Tu Tri) (Hanoi, 1914) (collateral French and Vietnamese renditions).

52. Ibid., pp. 125–35. At one point (p. 133) the authors promised that Tonkin, whence most of the soldiers came, would achieve at least a tenfold increase in income.

score badly, being unclean, lazy, wasteful, and fatalistic, gambling and lying too much, and refusing to plan for the future.[53] The French having already been around as masters for some decades, however, the question must have arisen as to whether or not the colonial schools were using the right tools to correct these alleged character deficiencies. Besides, the volatile nature of some Western ideas was worrying an increasing number of Frenchmen charged with maintaining order and balancing financial ledgers.

It is in this light, I think, that a new series of government-commissioned and approved primers by a small group of Vietnamese pedagogues and officials should be viewed.[54] First appearing in 1925, these school texts were clearly modeled on French metropolitan materials, but crafted for particular colonial purposes by Vietnamese who also happened to be involved in efforts to enrich *quoc-ngu* literature as an alternative to both French and Chinese (see Chapter 4).

In these new texts, even though the broad outline of family, school, and individual moral conduct was still derived from French primers—as were many of the lessons, for that matter (wear your clothes properly, help the young, the poor, the elderly, and those in danger, do not steal candy . . .)—the manner of expression in Vietnamese was much smoother, and the authors had a more concrete idea of what they wanted to accomplish locally. Thus, second-year pupils were shown a drawing of a Vietnamese mandarin coming to settle village business, followed by a lesson text arguing that a country was like a house, because both required leaders. "If no one obeys the mandarin's orders," the lesson concluded pointedly, "how can political stability [*tri yen*] be maintained in the country?" The next lesson had a picture and story of village elders going to present their respects (and gifts) to the prefect mandarin on the first day of the lunar New Year (*Tet*). Perhaps the most interesting twist, however, was to take the required

---

53. For a good account of the 1920s French pedagogical attitudes on Vietnamese morality and moral instruction, see Kelly, "Franco-Vietnamese Schools," chapter 4, pp. 2–17. Curriculum is discussed perceptively in idem, "Colonial Schools in Vietnam: Policy and Practice," *Proceedings of the Second Annual Meeting of the French Colonial Historical Society* (March 1977), pp. 105–14.

54. There were separate morality primers for each of the first three grades, all authored by Tran Trong Kim, Nguyen Van Ngoc, Dang Dinh Phuc, and Do Than, all titled *Luan Ly Giao Khoa Thu* [Textbook on Ethics] (subtitled according to grade), and all published in Hanoi by the Direction de l'Instruction Publique en Indochine (DIRIP). The same was true of the basic reading-writing-memorization-recitation primers, each titled *Quoc Van Giao Khoa Thu* [Textbook on National Literature]. Tran Trong Kim and Dang Dinh Phuc also authored a DIRIP text on history and geography for third-year pupils, *Su Ky Dia Du Giao Khoa Thu*, 1st edition (Hanoi, 1927[?]). The four also jointly authored a third-year practical science manual, *Cach Tri Giao Khoa Thu*, 1st edition (Hanoi, 1927). By 1933 the morality and elementary literature texts had all gone through at least six printings of 15,000–70,000 copies each, with occasional modifications in content. The latest edition I have been able to locate is a 13th printing of the third-year morality primer, issued in 1941.

topic of "respecting manual labor," and then to focus on the Vietnamese king, as well as the village elders down the line, who *ritually* planted the first rice at the beginning of each year.[55]

More subtle elements were added to third-year instruction. In the school conduct section, for example, an analytical distinction was made between being merely learned and being properly educated. To be more precise, a bright, knowledgeable pupil who lacked moral integrity might well grow up to be a bandit, be captured, and suffer punishment. In the section on personal conduct, detailed attention was given to the proposition that a healthy body promotes a healthy mind. Opium addiction and alcoholism were attacked, even though the sale of these products constituted major, perhaps essential sources of colonial revenue. Liquor was labeled "a form of poison," which weakened not only the individual but the entire race. A lesson on hygiene tried briefly to explain the scientific linkage to preventive medicine, and pupils were advised to go to a pharmacist rather than a priest or medium if they wanted to get well. For the required topic of "self-sacrifice," pupils were not given a Western story but rather an account of one of Le Loi's (fifteenth century) subordinates, who had chosen to dress in his master's clothing and die at the hands of the encircling Ming troops, thus enabling Le Loi to escape and eventually emerge victorious. The concluding section of this third-year morality textbook involved a description of local administration and customs in the five regions of Indochina, as well as model writing forms for borrowing, selling, preparing one's last will and testament, and petitioning for a reduction in rent.[56]

Related Curricular Offerings

Three other subjects in the formal primary school curriculum had profound future significance: general science, hygiene, and physical education. Although each was given only minor status and was presented in rather desultory fashion, there is evidence that they made an impression on pupils sufficient to cause many to study independently, write articles for newspapers and journals, and form relevant organizations to proselytize further. At some point this eager identification with modern science, medicine, and physical fitness became a potential threat to the colonial system. A few French *colons* sensed this from the beginning. Most French administrators, however, wanted to share with the Vietnamese elite their pride in Descartes, Pascal, Lavoisier, Pasteur, and Curie.

Primary science lessons were generally limited to memorizing parts of the

55. Tran Trong Kim et al., *Luan Ly Giao Khoa Thu* (2nd grade), 3rd printing (Hanoi, 1928), lessons 58, 60, and 61.

56. Tran Trong Kim et al., *Luan Ly Giao Khoa Thu* (3rd grade), 6th printing (Hanoi, 1933). The last section appears to have been appended at some point after the original 1925 edition, reflecting the fact that most pupils would never go beyond the third grade.

human body, names of plants and animals, rock and soil types, weather patterns, and geological features. As such, they differed little from traditional texts of natural classification. In fact, the latter had the advantage of often being couched in poetry. Explanations of why things had developed in certain ways, or how they functioned, were almost non-existent in both cases. The only serious attempt at explanation in one colonial school text, for example, was devoted to the disadvantages of slash-and-burn agriculture and detailed instructions on forms that had to be filled out before any trees could be felled in the forest.[57]

Hygiene instruction was even less imaginative, generally involving long peremptory lists of terms having to do with washing, brushing teeth, wearing clean clothes, etc., an enumeration of contagious and congenital diseases, and some basic anatomy.[58] Almost no attempt was made to explain the germ theory or endemic diseases. Physical education, which seemed designed mainly to provide a change of pace in the school routine, consisted of ten or twenty minutes of exercise next to one's desk, some outdoor marching or games, and an occasional soccer match for the older boys.[59]

If the schools were not prepared to do more, young Vietnamese would do it themselves. Manuals specifically designed for use at home were published; these explained the origins and uses of lightning and electricity, explosives, and kerosene, described how to grow and process one's own chocolate, coffee and tea, identified particular insect pests and told how to counter them.[60] Newspapers and journals aimed at a general audience regularly included thoughtful yet simply worded articles on science, hygiene, medicine, and physical education. For example, *Phu Nu Tan Van* [Women's News], which appeared weekly from 1929 to 1934, had concise presentations ranging from scientific subjects as broad as the origins of the universe or the relationship between brain functions and human intelligence to such practical topics as how to build your own wet-cell battery

57. Tran Trong Kim et al., *Cach Tri Giao Khoa Thu* (3rd grade) (Hanoi, 1927), sec. 8. A total of 390,000 approved general science texts were printed between 1925 and 1930 for second- and third-year *quoc-ngu* instruction.

58. Tran Van Thong, *Cach Tri Ve Sinh* [Practical Science and Hygiene], 2nd edition (Hanoi, 1911). Dr. L. Collin, *Ve Sinh Yeu Luoc* [Essentials of Hygiene] (Hue, 1925). Dr. Guillemet, *Ve Sinh Giao Khoa Thu* [Textbook on Hygiene] (1st and 2nd grades), 7th printing (Hanoi, 1933); 480,000 approved hygiene texts were printed in the period 1925-30 for first- and second-year *quoc-ngu* instruction.

59. Kelly, "Franco-Vietnamese Schools," chap. 4, pp. 32-33. It may well be that general primary instruction possessed an equally unimaginative tenor in metropolitan French schools of the same period. This has yet to be investigated in depth, and in any event is tangential to my topic.

60. Le Van Kinh, *Khoa Hoc Tung Dam* [Science Notes] (Saigon, 1934); To Van Duc, *Than Luon* [The Eel's Body] (Hanoi, 1940); and T. C., *Cach Tri Pho Thong* [Popular Practical Science] (Hanoi, 1944). The latter was published by the Northern Vietnam Buddhist Association and was written largely in verse.

and thereby avoid dependence on foreign imports.[61] It also took pains to condemn at every opportunity astrology, reliance on mediums, and other superstitions. Like most other Vietnamese periodicals, *Phu Nu Tan Van* was deeply concerned about the high incidence of tuberculosis, infant mortality, and venereal disease in the colony. These problems, as well as the need to build physical fitness, were explicitly linked to the question of Vietnamese ethnic survival and future social and political strength.

The moral implications were considerable. A son or daughter bringing home strange new ideas about living things that could not be seen, yet which caused people to die, was bound to test the authority of parents, local leaders, and scholar-gentry figures. The findings of modern astronomy, geology, biology, and physics must have exerted a corrosive effect on Neo-Confucianism's ethical interaction between Heaven and man, 'doctrine of the mean' (*trung dung*), and nonprogressive cyclical view of history. And what happened to the *yin-yang* duality, the five elements, ancestor worship, ghosts, mediums, soothsayers, and geomancers? Much of this will concern us later. At this point, however, we can speculate that a large proportion of the complaints from Vietnamese elders of this period about the lack of respect shown them by young people was traceable not to willful disobedience but rather to this growing clash of received knowledge about the world and man's role in it. What had begun as bland French morality instruction quickly took on controversial implications in a Vietnamese colonial context. The French, perhaps more than any other colonizing power, wanted to be custodians of the moral order as well as the social order. However, their efforts undermined both.[62]

Healthy Bodies and Healthy Minds

Even more obvious was the new attraction of young Vietnamese to energetic sports, self-defense, hiking, and scout jamborees. Actually, the Neo-Confucian model of pallid, frail students cloistered for years over classical texts had never been fully accepted, and was subject to frontal attack from 1905 onward. Nevertheless, one prominent literatus was still arguing in 1919 that thoughtful, reflective individuals were almost always physically weak, while strong individuals seldom took time to study. If pupils wanted to engage in a sport, he advised them

61. PNTV, 17 (22 Aug. 1929), 18 (29 Aug. 1929), 62 (24 July 1930), 66 (21 Aug. 1930), and 75 (23 Oct. 1930).

62. French administrators allowed, even encouraged Vietnamese collaborators to publish articles on the most recent scientific discoveries, for example, neurology, radioactivity, atomic particles, rocket research, and relativity theory. See NP 36 (June 1920), 38 (Aug. 1920), 42 (Dec. 1920), 48 (June 1921), and 76 (Oct. 1923); see chap. 8 for further discussion of the "knowledge explosion."

to restrict it to non-study days, lest they be too fatigued to concentrate on books.[63] Ignoring such advice, youths developed their proficiency in soccer, swimming, weight-lifting, judo, Western-style boxing and, above all, traditional martial arts exercises (vo).[64] There were exercise manuals for women to use in the privacy of their homes, as well as ones for fathers to employ in training their children.[65]

In a sense, the growing Vietnamese interest in Lord Baden-Powell and the scouting movement summarizes the moral significance of this new linkage of healthy bodies and healthy minds. The first scout troop was apparently formed in Hanoi in September, 1930, with Saigon, Hue and other towns following suit soon after.[66] There is little doubt that the colonial authorities encouraged scouting as an adjunct to school moral instruction and as a likely diversion from more serious political involvements. The young Emperor Bao Dai was often linked with scouting projects. Scout leaders of conservative persuasion went to great lengths to create a traditionalist atmosphere in their organizations, complete with sub-unit "lineages" named after the five Confucian virtues, and Chinese characters for loyalty and filial piety on the walls; and the leader was addressed as "mister first notable" rather than director or scoutmaster. In 1935, Indochinese Communist Party leaders even blamed their recent lack of success in recruiting youths on the "scouting ideology." [67]

Nonetheless, some Vietnamese scout leaders saw their mission as much more than a bolstering of traditional morality and social hierarchy. One manual, for example, pointedly argued that scouting was quite different from current school routines, in that the emphasis was on action, expansiveness, happiness, freedom, adventure, and practice.[68] Also new, and seen to be new, was scouting's emphasis of physical labor, body-building, competition, and adherence to precise time schedules. Scout units were allowed to be named after heroic historical figures,

63. Nguyen Ba Hoc, "Loi Khuyen Hoc Tro" [Encouraging Words to Pupils], NP 24 (June 1919).

64. Without being systematic, I counted at least 45 books and pamphlets on these sports published during the period 1929–43, of which perhaps one-third were explanations, with diagrams, of the martial arts.

65. Nguyen An, *The Thao Phai Dep* [Exercises for the Fair Sex] (Hanoi, 1940); Nguyen An, *Choi ma Tap* [Practicing while playing] (Hanoi, 1943).

66. Hong Nhan, "Che Do Dong Tu Quan" [The Scouting System], NP 153 (Aug. 1930); PNTV 157 (2 July 1932), 166 (1 Sept. 1932), 170 (29 Sept. 1932); *Sao Mai* (Vinh), 6 (23 Feb. 1934), 9 (16 Mar. 1934), 21 (8 June 1934), 47 (7 Dec. 1934), 49 (21 Dec. 1934).

67. Alexander Woodside, *Community and Revolution in Modern Vietnam* (Boston, 1976), pp. 149–51. See also idem, "Development of Social Organizations in Vietnamese Cities in the Late Colonial Period," *Pacific Affairs*, vol. XLIV, no. 1 (Spring 1971), p. 59.

68. Ba To, trans. and comp., *Doan Huong Dao (Les Scouts)* (Hanoi, 1930).

A Boy Scout troop exercising in Hanoi. Gouvernement Général de l'Indochine, *Le Comité Central d'Instruction physique et de préparation militaire de l'Indochine* (Hanoi, 1931).

ancient myth symbols, and famous geographical locations.[69] Hikes and bicycle excursions to historic landmarks became a favorite activity among young urban Vietnamese, quickly extending well beyond the scouting movement itself.[70] Proposals were advanced for a separate Girl Scout organization, and by 1936 it seems that some units had come into existence.[71]

69. In Hanoi in 1934, for example, the cub packs were named "Nang Son" and "Trung Rong" (both part of Vietnamese creation myths); the scout troops were "Hung Vuong," "Hoan Kiem," "Lang Bac," "Hong Bang," and "Gia Long"; and the explorer units were "Lam Son" and "Luc Dau Giang" *(Muon Tro Nen Huong Dao Sinh* [So You Want to Become a Scout] [Hanoi, 1934]). Further discussion of historical heroes and symbolism can be found in chapter 6.

70. A journal published by the communist-led Doan Thanh Nien Dan Chu (Democratic Youth Group) in the Popular Front period, for example, warmly supported the "bicycle movement" that had developed in the years 1936–38. Young women were to be especially congratulated for preferring bicycle trips to sitting at home reading romantic novels, the journal said. Three months later, however, they felt it necessary to condemn certain elements for trying to use long bike rides as a cover for "hedonist, sexual, or other depraved purposes." See *The Gioi* [World] (Hanoi), 1 Oct. 1938 and 15 Jan. 1939.

71. PNTV 186 (9 Feb. 1933); *Luat Huong Dao* [Scout Laws] (Sadec, 1936).

As all former scouts in the English-speaking world will recall, "A Scout is Trustworthy, Loyal, Helpful, Friendly, Courteous, Kind, Obedient, Cheerful, Thrifty, Brave, Clean and Reverent." In the Vietnamese version there were some interesting cultural nuances. "Trustworthy" was rendered as 'truthful, direct of speech.' "Friendly" was placed within the elder/younger brother language hierarchy. For some unknown reason, "kind" became 'kind to animals.' "Brave" was omitted entirely, presumably in deference to the colonial authorities, although personal courage and daring were upheld elsewhere in Vietnamese scout literature. "Reverent" was also left out, perhaps a victim of cross-cultural sensitivities about the Christian God, or the broader problem of exactly whom or what a Vietnamese scout was to regard as most sacred.[72] The problem was approached a bit differently in one rendition of the Scout Oath:

On my honor I promise before God [this part according to religion] to do everything possible to revere the Fatherland, help one and all, and obey the Scout Laws.[73]

Catholic Instruction and the Origins of Anti-Communism in Vietnam

Partly because of long-standing sectarian disputes in metropolitan France, which echoed occasionally in the colonies, and partly because Catholic missionaries had tried to immerse themselves in Vietnamese society long before Indochina was a glimmer in anyone's eye, the Catholic Church had its own set approach to moral questions in twentieth-century Vietnam. On the one hand, the Church had gradually come to link its own theology with Confucian morality. Many Catholic moral lessons for Vietnamese would be entirely at home in Confucian primers focusing on the five relationships. Catholic texts even chose to uphold the increasingly anachronistic ruler-subject (vua-toi) relationship, something of an historical irony, since in the nineteenth century priests and followers had been killed, tortured, and otherwise persecuted, largely because they pledged themselves to a God and a Roman Pope above and beyond the Vietnamese king and concept of loyalty (trung). Catholic writers had also become quite adept at using Vietnamese folk maxims, traditional literary forms, and choice epigrams from the Chinese classics. One Catholic text was entirely devoted to the Confucian theme, "First study ritual, then study literature," concentrating particularly on proper traditional speaking etiquette. There were entire sections on speaking to

---

72. Doan Huong Dao, *Chuong Trinh Ngay Hoi* [Jamboree Program], Saigon, 11 Dec. 1932. *Muon Tro Nen Huong Dao Sinh.*

73. *Muon Tro Nen Huong Dao Sinh.* The term used for "God," *Duc Thuong De,* literally meaning "higher emperor," was different from the Catholic *Duc Chua Troi,* or "heavenly Lord." It was most commonly used in connection with popular Taoism, for example, the "Jade Emperor" (*Ngoc Hoang Thuong De*). As for "Fatherland" (*To Quoc*), another publication, *Luat Huong Dao,* preferred "loyal" (*trung thanh*) to "reverent" (*tho*).

one's superiors and inferiors.[74] Perusing these primers, one wonders whether the ordinary Vietnamese Catholic's conception of religion was much different from the traditional Way, or the idea of "God" different from 'Heaven/Sun.' The language terms, *Dao* and *Troi*, remained identical. Probably the bishops had come to consider this a philosophical convenience.

On the other hand, the Catholic Church in Vietnam had certain concerns that set it apart from everyone else. Priests were constantly reminding followers of nineteenth-century martyrdoms, while non-Catholics never forgot the way the Church had mobilized thousands of faithful to serve in colonial units and to provide badly needed supplies to the French invaders. In terms of religious practices, baptism, confession, and holy water were the butt of many a non-Catholic joke or anecdote.[75] The Church remained acutely aware of its minority status (about ten percent of the population), and saw any sign of social or political unrest as a direct threat to its existence.

Catholic children were fed a different moral diet from an early age, despite the Confucian components. Thus, one text included lessons detailing differences in Catholic and non-Catholic education, concluding with an explanation of how the two sides might be able to live together peacefully.[76] Other texts focused on converting the heathen and "praying for those who rule us, so that they and our entire homeland will return to the religion of God. . . ."[77] Unlike pupils in government schools, who were told that not washing would cause other people to scorn them, Catholic children were given a story about a heavenly angel who had shunned an unclean boy.[78] Catholic pupils were also given sharp warnings against polygamy, child marriages, and divorce, the two former practices also coming under increasing fire from non-Catholic Vietnamese intellectuals, while the latter was slowly becoming accepted as a right of wives as well as husbands. Perhaps most interesting, given the preferences of the majority of Vietnamese, was the Catholic teaching that it was absolutely wrong to believe that moral instruction could be separated from religious faith, specifically, faith in God the Creator and the existence of an afterlife.[79]

---

74. Simon Chinh, *Con Nit Hoc Noi* [Children Learning How to Speak], 7th printing (Qui Nhon, 1924). (Qui Nhon was the location of the Church printing establishment.)

75. To cite only one example, Vietnamese women in jail joked about cleaning menstrual flow as a form of "washing away sins" (*rua toi*)—the same term as Christian baptism. Ngo Vinh Long, *Vietnamese Women in Society and Revolution*, vol. 1, p. 188.

76. Vu Dang Khoa, *Luan Ly Tan Ca* [New Code of Ethics] (Hanoi, 1930).

77. *Cua Toi Tap Doc Chu Quoc Ngu* [My Book to Practice Reading the National Script], 3rd printing (Qui Nhon, 1930). See also Pierre Luc, *Au Hoc Truong Thanh Than* [Children Studying to Be Mature] (Qui Nhon, 1930).

78. Tran Trong Kim et al., *Luan Ly Giao Khoa Thu* (2nd grade), p. 18; and *Cua Toi Tap Doc Chu Quoc Ngu*, lesson 9.

79. Vu Dang Khoa, *Luan Ly Tan Ca*, sec. 8.

In November, 1929, after a meeting of the Tonkin Church hierarchy, the apostolic vicar of Hanoi wrote to the resident superior proposing the establishment of government-subsidized parochial schools (*écoles confessionnelles*) in both Catholic and "Buddhist" areas.[80] The main reason given was growing unrest in the villages, and the main cause for this unrest was said to be the existing government schools. A large number of Vietnamese instructors were reported not to be responding properly to the "confidence with which they had been honored" by the colonial authorities, but were in fact "propagandists of subversive ideas." The apostolic vicar specifically indicted the "spirit of independence" and the "revolt against the family" as subversive, and predicted they would bring disorder to the country if not quelled by means of the local confessional schools.

How the resident superior responded is not known, but no such ambitious project was ever undertaken. Nevertheless, some Catholic priests became ever more insistent that only full-scale conversion could save colonial society from a terminal case of moral degeneration. One prominent Vietnamese priest listed the following grave symptoms: youngsters not listening to teachers, wives not fulfilling duties for husbands, servants disobeying masters, workers striking whenever they wished, and the spread of murder, free love, revolution, and Communism. The growth of materialism had to be blocked by Catholic idealism, and "free thought" countered by acceptance of the authority of the Pope on all spiritual matters.[81] The Catholic weekly *Vi Chua* [For the Lord], published in Hue in the 1930s, mounted bitter attacks against "atheistic" Buddhism, positivism, utilitarianism, and egalitarianism. Sometimes it seemed as if *Vi Chua* was opposed to every thought since Galileo, as when it claimed that God had created the entire universe, from the stars to the smallest flowers and birds, specifically for the use of man. The tone of its argument is exemplified by the following assault on the idea of equality:

If everyone and everything were entirely equal, just imagine what the world would be like! What would happen to class discipline? And how about that rock you stepped on or that dirt clod you kicked? Surely they would have a right to ask why they are not human like you, or at least why they should not be a precious jewel treasured and fondled by all.[82]

Of course, time had not stood still since the Counter-Reformation, and the Catholic Church in Vietnam was not unmindful of this. Communism was an

---

80. Letter dated 12 Nov. 1929 from M. Gendreau, Vicariat Apostolique de Hanoi, to resident-superior. AOM Indochine, carton 326, dossier 2637.

81. J. M. Thich, *Van De Luan Ly Ngay Nay* [Today's Ethics Questions] (Qui Nhon, 1930). The preface to Vu Dang Khoa, *Luan Ly Tan Ca*, also states a prime fear that morals were being destroyed by such ideas as "freedom" (*tu do*) and "equality" (*binh dang*).

82. *Vi Chua* (Hue), 19 Feb. 1937, as quoted in Tran Van Giau, SPT-2, pp. 405-10.

absolute obsession, and the Church mounted an anti-Communist crusade before there was any Indochinese Communist Party, indeed before more than a handful of Vietnamese had had the opportunity to study any basic Marxist-Leninist texts. More importantly, the Church in Vietnam chose to equate Communism with *any* attempt to transform the established order. In fact, with neat teleological reasoning, a 1927 booklet titled *The Question of Communism* made all social and intellectual changes of the previous three hundred years responsible for the contemporary Communist threat.[83] At the core of the argument was belief in man's original sin. Short of putting everyone in a Catholic monastery and forcing them to be perfect, the author of this booklet asserted, human beings would always covet the money, land, and labor of others. Therefore, talk of rectifying inequalities was extremely dangerous, since the *"lower orders"* (*ha luu*) of society would take this as license to slack off, gabble about politics, disobey legitimate authority, and pillage the houses of the rich and fight among themselves for the spoils. Russia was cited as current proof of this thesis, the author lacing his account with unsubstantiated figures on Orthodox clergy killed, orphanages disbanded, mass starvation, and teenage girls violated because they had to go to the new coeducational schools. Even worse, the Communists were trying to export their brand of chaos to other countries. There followed a stunningly distorted yet significant view of recent events in China:

If you want to know the outcome of Communism, simply look at China. Over the past fifteen years Communism has been responsible for overturning the monarchy, establishing democracy, fomenting civil war, and pushing the populace ever further into the mud. Liang Ch'i-ch'ao and K'ang Yu-wei are the Engels and Marx of China. Sun Yat-sen is the Lenin, with his concept of people's livelihood in the same category as the Soviet proletariat.[84]

Bringing matters home to Vietnam, the author of *The Question of Communism* pointed to increasingly loose talk of "freedom and equality," to strikes in the factories and schools, and to Nguyen Ai Quoc (Ho Chi Minh) establishing a cadre training program in Canton. Again there was resort to sweeping generalization:

The evil of Communism is to take current affairs, political questions, problems meant for the governing agencies, and discuss them with ordinary citizens and children who still do not know how to examine them properly. Communists also exploit the greedy, cruel instincts of the lower classes and employ violent, barbarian means to reach their objectives quickly.[85]

83. J. M. Thich, *Van De Cong San* [The Question of Communism] (Qui Nhon, 1927).
84. Ibid., pp. 29–30.
85. Ibid., p. 33.

One way to deal with this problem in colonial Vietnam, the author suggested, was to eliminate political content from the school curriculum entirely, replacing it with more moral instruction and practical occupational training. Most Vietnamese intellectuals had reason to believe that this was already the basic policy, but presumably the author was alluding to ideas still slipping in via French secular texts. The prime antidote to Communism in Vietnam, however, was to be the rapid expansion of the Catholic Church—after all, had not history demonstrated that in times of trouble, "Only one nation, the Christian nation, only one official, the Pope, only one organization, the worldwide Catholic Church, was able to maintain discipline and stand firm forever."[86]

With the outbreak of peasant disorders in 1930–1931, sparked by Vietnamese Communists (see Chapter 9), colonial authorities took a leaf from the Catholic book and distributed anti-Communist materials of the most flamboyant character imaginable. A set of twelve leaflets prepared at this time tells us little about Vietnamese Communism but a great deal about colonial assumptions concerning contemporary Vietnamese society.[87] First there was an idyllic montage of a school, train, marketplace, hospital (with bearded French doctor in charge), and farm. Whereas most Vietnamese peasant families in reality were lucky to have one buffalo, the farmer in the latter scene was blessed with four. Several leaflets then pictured Communists destroying all this, with particular attention to the schools. In a throwback to ancient Confucian indictments of Ch'in Shih Huang-ti, Communists were shown burning piles of books, pulling the teacher by the beard and beating him mercilessly, all the while yelling, "Education is our enemy!" Another pair of leaflets provided images of good and bad pupils. The former prayed at the family altar, scored high in the government examinations and returned home in triumph, shaded by a parasol, bowed to by villagers, and causing his parents to run towards him with undisguised happiness. The caption began, "This person does not involve himself in political matters, but rather devotes all year round to his studies." As for the bad pupil, he was kicked out of class by the teacher, left the village, but then returned later (wearing a hammer-and-sickle armband) to organize a band of ruffians, swear at his parents, and beat up the village elders.[88]

86. Ibid., p. 36.

87. AOM Indochine, carton 198, dossier 1472. For intellectuals, the authorities arranged translation and publication (12,000 copies) of the anticommunist polemic *Moscou sans Voiles*, by J. Douillet (*Mat Na Cong San* [Communism Unmasked] [Hanoi, 1931]).

88. Two leaflet variations on the "bad pupil" theme were: an unruly youngster being lured by a knife-wielding, extra-village cadre, the captain warning that such pupils must be kept under surveillance, especially as to the company they keep; and a sobbing, remorseful young communist excluded from the *Tet* family gathering because he has allegedly renounced his family and ancestors.

好 學 生 之 陽 鄉

"A good pupil returns to his village." The colonial image of how a young man, having benefitted from outside education yet maintaining traditional customs, is received at home. Courtesy of Archives Nationales de France.

By far the most complicated, yet morally revealing leaflet featured two large trees, one a splendid, bird-filled Vietnamese banyan, the other a dried-up Russian elm, some birds still on the branches but a lot of them dead on the ground. The Vietnamese tree had seven roots, prominently numbered and identified: "kings and princes of past and present," "filial piety," "Buddhism," "virtuous morality," "ancestor worship," "Confucianism," and "spirits and sages." Then, in addition, there were three hardwood posts propping up the corner branches of the tree, two of them labeled "brought from France" and one indigenous. A Russian in bearskin cap was urging on several Vietnamese Communists as they tried to chop down these posts, but a number of broken axes indicated they were not having much success. This message was supplemented by leaflets showing a huge Communist spider spreading its legs across Indochina (the caption calling for immediate extermination of Communists), and one of a sage walking in the forest and speaking to his companion:

See that gang of monkeys over there? It's just like the Communists. No religion, no mandarins, no education, common finances, common parents, wives and children. Those monkeys are truly Communistic!

Equal division of property was attacked in yet another leaflet, a grossly Westernized Communist cadre being told by a peasant that he had no money, no buffalo, and was not about to share the only thing he did possess, which was a small plot of land containing his ancestors' graves and meant to be passed on to his children and children's children. Apparently something the Communists said was potentially enticing, however. A final leaflet pictured a beautiful girl, labeled

共 產 學 生 之 歸 鄉

此 學 生 共 產 及 歸 鄉 掉 手 大 擺 揚 徒 之 言 相 其 兄 及 老 親 迤 之

Người học trò cộng-sản về làng

Người này bị cộng-sản đồ dành, tình một lại không tốt, bị thấy đuổi không cho học nữa. Khi về làng này cầm bó đuốc, làm đầu cho bọn du côn, gặp cha mẹ hồ con thì chưởi mắng, gặp thêm bảo chức sắc thì đánh đập

"Communist pupils return to their village." One of twelve leaflets prepared by colonial officials to counter the uprising of 1930–31. Courtesy of Archives Nationales de France.

"Communism," dancing in front of an obviously enchanted mandarin or village elder. In one ear a Vietnamese intellectual was telling the gentleman how well the girl sang, while in the other ear a traditionally garbed individual was whispering the double entendre, "You'd best not feel her, she's got the red sickness."

Traditionalist Reformulations

Faced with a proliferation of publications based on French secular and Catholic teachings, many scholars raised on Chinese and *nom* texts felt the need to reassert a "unique" Vietnamese morality for young people. Provided the authors included at least one lesson praising French colonial rule, the authorities permitted such materials to be distributed for use at home and, it would seem, for supplementary reading in the schools. Indeed, as social problems appeared to multiply in the colony, some officials actively supported these private traditionalist endeavours. For authors there was also the financial incentive, particularly since the government was making it steadily more difficult for literati to earn an income by formal teaching. One well-known scholar-poet, Tan Da (1888–1939), wrote two primers that together sold at least 67,000 copies in the years 1920–35.[89] A few others were able to be reprinted several times, 2,000–5,000 copies

---

89. Tan Da (Nguyen Khac Hieu), *Len Sau* [Reaching Six], 6th printing (Hanoi, 1925), a work written in verse, like the traditional *Three-Character Classic (Tam Tu Kinh*; in Chinese, *San-tzu Ching)*. Idem, *Len Tam* [Reaching Eight], 5th printing (Hanoi, 1926), also written in verse. Tan Da was excerpted quite often by authors of morality or language compilations. Just before his death in 1939, Tan Da suggested that he owed as much to Epicurean and Romantic philosophers as to Confucianism. (Truong Tuu, *Uong Ruou voi Tan Da* [Drinking with Tan Da] [Hanoi, 1939]).

per printing. On the whole, however, traditional moralists of the 1920s and 1930s could not expect to make a living from textbooks.

A small number of these texts were attempts to return directly to the Neo-Confucian classics. Thus, the previously mentioned scholar who complained that Vietnamese did not know what they were struggling for, gave as his answer two hundred passages from the classics, carefully translated and annotated in *quoc-ngu*.[90] His efforts rated a letter of endorsement from the French Resident Superior of Tonkin, which the author proudly reproduced at the head of his text. Interestingly enough, this type of fundamentalism may have been more common in Cochinchina, where Chinese characters had been pushed into the shadows earlier, and where the government curriculum was most Westernized, than in Tonkin and Annam, where candidates were still taking the civil examinations in Chinese until 1915–18.[91] Normally a key Chinese character was placed at the top of each lesson, a bit of sacral veneer to hide the fact that much was lost when translating into *quoc-ngu*.[92] Authors tried very hard to give readers a taste of the old Confucian or Mencian magic, yet their disquiet could be measured by the number of times they warned against paying too much attention to Western studies, thus "losing one's roots" (*mat goc*).[93]

Another minority approach was to return to the past eclectically, bring in Buddhist and Taoist teachings as well as the more common Confucian prescriptions. Thus, the Northern Vietnam Three-Religions Association (Bac Ky Tam Giao Hoi) published a morality primer upholding karma, compassion, non-action, and esoteric enlightenment together with the routine five relationships. A final section repeated Confucian justifications for some people being masters and others servants, each with carefully defined roles and obligations. Only slavery was declared no longer legitimate.[94] A 1933 Saigon primer threatened children with Buddhist Hell if they did not respect their parents.[95]

It was the new Cao Dai Church, however, which revived the three-religion

90. Nguyen Duy Tinh, comp., *Dong Phuong Ly Tuong*.

91. See, for example, Nguyen Dinh, *Ngu Luan Minh Canh* [Elucidating the Five Relationships], 7th printing (Saigon, 1928); Nguyen Ky Sat, *Au Hoc Tam Nguyen* [Children Studying Spiritual Aspirations] (Saigon, 1928; Dang Le Nghi, comp., *Sach Day Hoc Noi Chu* [Learning Proper Speech], 2nd printing (Saigon, 1931); Nguyen Ky Sat and Phan Van Cuong, *Sach Day Hoc Noi Chu Annam* [Learning Proper Annamese Speech] (Saigon, 1931).

92. As early as 1886 one French administrator worried that suppression of Chinese-language instruction was equivalent to supression of morality teaching, since the two were done simultaneously with identical texts. (A. Landes, "Notes sur le Quoc-Ngu," *Bulletin de la Société des Etudes Indochinoises*, 1-1886, p. 6)

93. In addition to texts cited in fn. 91, see Nguyen Van Ban (Ngo Dam), *A Dong Luan Ly* [East Asian Ethics] (Hanoi, 1933).

94. Bac Ky Tam Giao Hoi, *Luan Ly Yeu Luoc* [Essentials of Ethics] (Nam Dinh, 1937).

95. Tran Cong Thang, *Bao Hieu Phu Mau* [Instructions on Filial Piety] (Saigon, 1933). A much more subtle Buddhist-Confucian approach is taken in *Dao Duc Pho Thong* [Popular Morals]

concept most successfully. Cao Dai leaders also borrowed from Christianity, from spiritism of both ancient Vietnamese and contemporary European derivation, and even from the popular *Tale of Three Kingdoms*, for panache.[96] In matters of day-to-day human interaction, nevertheless, Confucianism took precedence. The only obvious divergence was the Cao Dai stress on an all-knowing and immortal arbiter, the Jade Emperor.[97] Cao Dai apostles were more effective than anyone else in breathing new life into traditional hierarchical relations, a prime reason why southern Vietnamese landlords found it so convenient to join, and to urge their tenants to do likewise.[98]

However, for most writers trained in Confucianism, it was not Buddhism or Taoism that demanded attention but modern science and modern nationalism. Although they wanted to return to the traditional basics, they were astute enough to realize that this could not be accomplished by having young people memorize arid *quoc-ngu* translations of the classics or mouth crudely eclectic "three-religion" formulations. Since these writers were also convinced that existing government morality texts were too foreign, the challenge was to create primers that were neither antiquarian nor alien, but refreshing, indigenous and dynamic. Few were able to advance very far, yet their writings did provide an important if unwitting link to post-1941 Viet Minh efforts to combine traditional and revolutionary morality.

Nguyen Van Ngoc (1890-1942), one of the authors of the previously discussed government-commissioned primers, felt the need to prepare his own separate collection of 176 poems for children, considerably more subtle and enticing in both style and content. While many of the same moral instructions were there (e.g., study assiduously, keep clean, respect your parents and teachers, work hard), they were generally phrased in the more familiar and thus less obtrusive Confucian terminology. Then, too, there were poetic evocations of minding the water buffalo, transplanting rice, listening to a distant pagoda bell, going fishing with one's elder brother, enjoying the Mid-Autumn and *Tet* festivals—none of which had managed to find a place in the officially initiated morality texts. A lesson on "Countrymen" was in the warm, intimate spirit of Phan Boi Chau two decades earlier, albeit stripped of any anticolonial call to action. On "The Land of our Ancestors," Nguyen Van Ngoc concluded:

> Many homes make up a village,
> Many villages form a country.

(Hanoi, 1943), which is in verse; 10,000 copies of this work were printed and apparently distributed without charge by a local organization.

96. Tran Van Giau, SPT-2, pp. 188-229; Jayne S. Werner, "The Cao Dai: The Politics of a Vietnamese Syncretic Religious Movement" (Ph.D. dissertation, Cornell University, 1976), pp. 29-76.

97. Dai Dao Tam Ky Pho Do, *Luan Ly So Giai* [Ethics Briefly Explained] (Dakao-Saigon, 1928).

98. Werner, "The Cao Dai," pp. 77-121.

Our country's name is Viet Nam.
To be citizens, you children must remember that.
Love your country, respect it,
Help make it famous, wealthy and strong,
Able to stand equal with others.[99]

Other authors risked even more pointed language. For example, amidst routine poetic messages about diligent study, filial piety, and avoiding gambling, Duong Tu Quan (1901–69) included lessons on group solidarity, the dangers of being timid, the value of travelling to distant places to learn new things, the need for every citizen to read modern newspapers, and the historically proven necessity of Vietnamese sacrificing for their country. At the end of the lesson on patriotic sacrifice, pupils were asked, "Does human life in conditions of servitude result in a dishonorable attitude of existence for its own sake? What is your personal opinion on this?"[100] It is hard to imagine some pupils not being stunned by the implications of those questions. Nguyen Cong Hoan (1903–77), after necessarily praising the French Protectorate, which had "come from afar," argued the following in direct apposition:

People of one country
Must love one another.
We are not distant,
But of the same ancestry.
We must understand,
The nation is a house,
Our House,
And we are of the nation.[101]

This corporate message was sometimes conveyed to pupils rather brutally, as the following passage demonstrates:

Vietnam! Vietnam! Living in this long, splendid land, anyone who doesn't love one another must be some sort of rubbish! *And anyone who betrays another should have his corpse divided up and thrown to the dogs and pigs to eat!*[102]

Luong Van Can (1854–1929), two decades earlier principal of the seminal Dong Kinh Nghia Thuc School, thence exiled to Cambodia, now living out his last days as a distinguished scholar-merchant in Hanoi, had his own way of in-

99. Nguyen Van Ngoc, *Nhi Dong Lac Vien* [Kindergarten] (Hanoi, 1929), lesson 144.

100. Duong Tu Quan, *Van Van Bach Tuyen* [A Literature Compendium], 2nd edition (Hanoi, 1927). There were eight more printings between 1929 and 1953.

101. Nguyen Cong Hoan, *Van Chu Viet Nam* [Learning Vietnamese Words] (Hai Duong, 1929). At the time a teacher in Hai Duong province, ten years later Nguyen Cong Hoan had become famous for his realist novels and short stories.

102. *Van Xua Nay Va Sach Tap Doc* [Literature Past and Present, and Practice Lessons] (Saigon, 1926), p. 46 (emphasis in original). The use of the term "Viet-Nam" rather than "An-Nam" often carried anticolonial implications.

structing children. His general format was taken from recent Chinese pedogogical discussions, with separate parts for "physical education" (*the duc*), "moral education" (*duc duc*), and "intellectual education" (*tri duc*). Anecdotes and poems on Vietnamese and Chinese historical personalities were used to make specific points. Not being able to write what he felt about the French, Luong Van Can simply ignored them, even to the extent of inferring that the Nguyen monarchs were still independent. Probably his most interesting lesson was on "The Government" (*Nha Nuoc*), again avoiding reference to the colonial administration and concluding with an important reversal of the ancient *Ta Hsüeh* sequence,[103] to the effect that Vietnamese pupils had to love their country (*Nuoc*) before they could love their homes (*Nha*).[104] Luong Van Can has retained a favorable image among Vietnamese writers, including those of Marxist-Leninist persuasion. There is even an illustrated story of his life for children of the Socialist Republic of Vietnam.[105]

Of equal if not greater importance to any patriotic affirmations, however, was the extraordinarily quick acceptance by most traditionalist writers of the Social Darwinian image of "survival of the fittest"(see Chapter 7). While they must have felt very uneasy about the moral implications of sharp human conflict, since it violated a previous fundamental assumption that *goodness* produced success, they did treat it as current reality and conveyed it to young readers. Social Darwinism led in turn to respect for scientific knowledge, or at least for those components that promised to be immediately useful for survival. Thus, in their morality and language primers, traditionalists readily incorporated lessons on personal hygiene, sanitation, physical exercise, agricultural improvements, the development and significance of the steam engine, and even, occasionally, some basic astronomy, physics, or chemistry. Although it is apparent from reading these lessons that the traditionalists were mostly cribbing bits and pieces from one book or another, without any firsthand knowledge, their unquestioned ability to put whatever they did understand into catchy Vietnamese rhymes or colloquial speech certainly improved the chances of pupils' remembering it (in contrast to the French-modeled texts discussed earlier). On the other hand, knowledge of modern trappings could divert readers from comprehension of underlying causes. Thus, one author wrote an ode to French houses, with their high ceilings,

---

103. The *Ta Hsüeh* sequence was usually simplified in Vietnamese morality texts to *tu than, te gia, tri quoc, binh thien ha* (self-cultivation, family regulation, state order, universal peace).

104. Luong Van Can (On Nhu), *Au Hoc Tung Dam* [Children's Study Notes] (Hanoi, 1925, republished in 1928). Luong Van Can also published an annotated translation of Confucian dialogues on filial piety: *Hieu Kinh* [Classic of Filial Piety] (Hanoi, 1929).

105. Hoai Van and Mai Long, *Ong Thay Yeu Nuoc* [A Patriotic Teacher] (Hanoi, 1974), written in verse. The fact that Luong Van Can's son Luong Ngoc Quyen died in 1917 while leading an uprising against the French is a contributing factor.

bathroom, lamps, and fans, and then proceeded to condemn Vietnamese houses for lacking all these things and thus being unhygienic and hopelessly outmoded.[106] He made no attempt to explain bacteria.

Traditionalists tended to come together with secular French and Catholic moralists in defense of social hierarchy. Practically everyone seemed to agree that it was inevitable that some Vietnamese would be rich and some poor. How to treat one's domestic servants was worth at least one lesson in almost all morality primers. A 1919 text claimed that the poor were best able to endure sickness.[107] Under the heading of "Helping the Poor," a book republished at least four times in the late 1920s counseled, "If you don't have some money to give the poor, at least say something nice."[108] Since some young readers came from poorer families there was likely to be moral advice for servants too. Thus, one primer, after asserting that all must do their jobs on earth correctly, instructed servants that they must work hard enough to deserve their keep, always lower their heads when passing in front of the master, and always use deferential language when spoken to (thua, bam, da). "Even though you meet up with an intensely evil master," the author went on, "You must accept it and not complain, talk back, or be pig-headed."[109] On the other hand, a servant lucky enough to have a kind master would be treated like a member of the family. Then, reverting to general moral principles, the author cited a Western maxim to the effect that "Poverty is a Virtue," testing one's true mettle. Others were to take this to mean that the poor shall inherit the earth.

Civics' Texts

By the late 1930s most Vietnamese intellectuals could agree that modern patriotism was more than family morality written large. Well-ordered families presided over by self-improving fathers did not necessarily produce citizens of a nation. What, then, was the key to developing public consciousness? Increasingly, writers looked to the fostering of direct, perceived linkages between each individual and society. As the Vietnamese came to understand that they possessed precise, legally enforceable rights and responsibilities as citizens, they would participate more energetically in building and defending their country.

There were problems with this formula, most obviously de facto control of the state by the French. As it happened, the advent of the leftist Popular Front government in France in 1936 temporarily deferred this question. A loose coalition of left and center Vietnamese groups developed in response. Among other things,

---

106. Nguyen Van Hung, *Dong Au Tu Tri* [First-Year Self-Edification] (Hanoi, 1930[?]).

107. Ung Trinh, *Quoc Ngu Van Luan*.

108. Vu Dinh Long, *Quoc Van Doc Ban* [National Literature Reader], 3rd printing (Hanoi, 1928).

109. Bui Van Canh, *Chung Quanh Gia Dinh*.

it disseminated the idea that any citizen with a grievance or demand should be able to present it to French Popular Front representatives and expect it to be seriously considered, if not always accepted in toto. The public response to this idea was broadly enthusiastic, probably surprising many of the initiators, and certainly shocking the local French *colons*. Upon seeing ten thousand Vietnamese march down the street in ranks, yell predetermined slogans, and obey detailed instructions from cadres, colonial administrators had reason to be upset by the quality of opposition as well as the quantity. The quasi-familial model of Vietnamese moral and political conduct was changing before their eyes.

In January, 1938, following reforms made in metropolitan schools, the governor-general ordered colonial primary schools to add a course on "citizen's education" (*cong dan giao duc*) to the second-, third-, and fourth-year curriculums. Soon several Vietnamese pedagogues had published relevant textbooks. It is not clear how many schools actually used these books as replacements for or supplements to the previously discussed government-commissioned morality texts, especially when only two years later the Vichy-appointed authorities reverted to a more traditionalist posture. Nevertheless, these civics texts do tell us something about attitudes of the day and form a clear prelude to the more radical citizen's education activities of the Viet Minh Front only a few years later.

Because of the abrupt shift in doctrine, one textbook author felt he had to provide teachers with a six-page conceptual justification and pedagogical guide,[110] in which he argued that the old Confucian five relationships had inhibited development of impersonal social ties, and that this in turn helped to account for the failure of many contemporary Vietnamese organizations to live up to their lofty objectives. Perceiving how much actual social change was afoot, yet also observing the apparent indifference of ordinary Vietnamese toward public affairs, many individuals became discouraged, and others behaved rashly. What was needed, he concluded, was general comprehension of the functional interrelationship in modern nations between the individual and the whole:

> Society is a mechanism, and each citizen is a component of that mechanism. If you want it to operate successfully, the entire mechanism must transmit power to the appropriate components, while each component simultaneously contributes its strength to the total mechanism. A single component breaking down will cause the mechanism to malfunction or lose rhythm. And if that occurs, no component is able to remain firm.[111]

Understanding this symbiosis, each Vietnamese citizen could ascertain his proper place, that is to say, the point where personal advantage (*ich loi*) and honor (*danh du*) coincided, and then be able to project himself with the right "public spirit"

---

110. Nguyen Khoa Toan, *Cong Dan Giao Duc* [Citizen's Education] (Hue, 1938). The author was a functionary in the royal "Ministry of Education." His teacher's guide can be contrasted with the earlier *Chuong Trinh Ba Lap Bac So Hoc Yeu Luoc Ban Xu* (Hue, 1936).

111. Nguyen Khoa Toan, *Cong Dan Giao Duc*, p. iii.

(*cong tam*). Since public spirit was a learned characteristic, not a natural or emotional predisposition (here the author would have been disputed by other writers), some individuals took longer than others to achieve it, and some would always have more of it than their compatriots.

In order to implement his theories, the author offered teachers and pupils twenty-six concise lessons. Not one of them dealt with personal, family, or school morality. This was not uncharacteristic. Another civics text, for use in Tonkin rather than Annam, had only about ten percent devoted to these subjects over a three-year course.[112] A third author mixed a few such lessons in the fifty percent of his total content that focused on village life and organization.[113] Clearly, all three authors saw village activities as crucial to the formation of a young citizen's consciousness, devoting between one-quarter and three-fifths of their texts to that level alone. For most readers, however, the more novel sections would be those depicting administrative echelons beyond the village (canton, district, prefecture, province, governor-general), which accounted for between one-fifth and two-fifths of instruction in these three texts. Two authors devoted about one-sixth of their books to sample paperwork, for example, petitioning to kill one's own buffalo, filing legal complaints, selling land, or borrowing money. One author used ten pages to explain various colonial electoral procedures, which only served to demonstrate in detail the unrepresentative and strictly advisory nature of the institutions in question.[114]

Each author had lessons on Vietnamese cultural traditions, although the tone was half-hearted and openly manipulative. Thus, two authors using similar language, marched through the following startling—if logically obtuse—sequence for their young readers: (1) traditions are permanent and can never be entirely extinguished; (2) ancestor worship, arranged marriages, securing a male heir, and non-remarriage of widows are examples of Vietnamese tradition; (3) actually, some of these customs are not entirely appropriate for today, but they *were* meaningful in the past; (4) they can be "slightly modified"; (5) however, to propose their elimination is to threaten the Vietnamese "national essence" (*quoc tuy*) and to jeopardize the social order—in short, to be wildly "destructive" (*pha hoai*); and (6) as the popular maxim puts it, "When the paper is torn and tattered, you must protect its edges."[115]

By contrast, discussions of current colonial administrative procedures were competent and matter-of-fact, offering readers what amounted to a manual for

112. Ha Mai Anh, *Cong Dan Giao Duc* (Nam Dinh, 1938). Approved for use in colonial schools.

113. Two texts in sequence: Bui Huy Hue, *Cong Dan Tu Tri (Lop Du Bi)* [Citizen's Self-Edification (2nd Grade)], 2nd printing (Hanoi, 1940), and idem, *Cong Dan Tu Tri (Lop So Dang)* [Citizen's Self-Edification (3rd Grade)] (Hanoi, 1939). At least the first text was approved for use in colonial schools.

114. Bui Huy Hue, *Cong Dan Tu Tri (Lop So Dang)*, pp. 79–88.

115. Ibid., p. 47; Ha Mai Anh, *Cong Dan Giao Duc*, p. 52.

getting along within the system.[116] There were detailed explanations of direct and indirect taxes, police functions of provincial military posts, and the intricate French and native judicial hierarchies. French residents were accurately described as controlling all activities within their provincial domains, while Vietnamese mandarins were merely "helpers." Readers were warned against initiating lawsuits, as they could be frustrating, time-consuming, and expensive; it was better to seek reconciliation out of court.[117] Perhaps most interesting, pupils were given exact instructions on how to enter a government office. They were to be quiet and respectful, to ask for directions rather than wander from one room to another, and, above all, to wait their turn rather than push and shove for first attention. Once in front of the proper official they were to state their business immediately instead of trying to engage in pleasantries, avoid being too self-demeaning, but also avoid being "too free" in manner. One text warned that insolence toward officials was a criminal offense, further emphasizing the point by including a woodblock drawing of several citizens bowing respectfully to two Vietnamese functionaries—the latter backed up by a tough-looking policeman just in case.[118] As if to milk tradition to its last drop, the lesson concluded with the popular maxim: "When you eat the fruit, remember who planted the tree." Previously this had been used to defend ancestor worship and respect for the past generally. Now it was employed on behalf of those who "carry out the mandate (*menh lenh*) of the Government."

Civics texts of the late 1930s had one grave deficiency in comparison with earlier morality texts: they did not tell pupils *why*. At best, only one-tenth of lesson content dealt with general concepts, for example, respecting public property because it "belonged to everyone," or paying taxes faithfully because otherwise someone else would have to pay more. The rest was names, definitions, descriptions, and functional delineations. Even the study questions for pupils to answer were remarkably arid, requiring mere regurgitation of terminology.[119] Perhaps the authors really believed that learning *how* the machine operated was

116. One author in fact suggested that his text could also serve as an administrative guide for village and canton functionaries. (Nguyen Khoa Toan, *Cong Dan Giao Duc*, p. vi.)

117. One common French complaint was the growing number of Vietnamese legal disputes. At least two causes can be suggested: a minority had come to realize that the law was a weapon they could use to personal advantage if they had the necessary contacts and resources; and there was a perceptible increase in the number of "conflict situations" during the colonial period, which family and village mechanisms of reconciliation were progressively less able to solve.

118. Bui Huy Hue, *Cong Dan Tu Tri (Lop So Dang)*, p. 27. This text also has pointed drawings of a citizen reaching into his pocket to pay his annual land tax (p. 23), and one of a very young, plainly dressed Vietnamese before the bar of a court composed of three heavily robed justices, two of them definitely French (p. 16).

119. I found only one truly substantive question among hundreds: the author asking pupils if the new seven-tiered head tax promulgated in February 1938 was "equitable" (*cong binh*) or not. (Ha Mai Anh, *Cong Dan Giao Duc*, p. 43.)

the key to pursuading each individual to play his role more energetically; perhaps they sensed that any serious presentation of organic political theory raised as many new problems for the existing system as it answered. In either case, the inner rationale for young Vietnamese developing public spirit within the colonial framework was largely ignored.

Nevertheless, there had been a break with the past. Civics texts operated from very different premises compared to the earlier personal-family-study morality primers. This became apparent when the Vichy French authorities tried to reverse field and to restore familial and quasi-familial rationales. The tone of Vichy booklets was a mixture of musty romanticism and martial zeal. Thus, a 1942 school primer devoted about one-quarter of its study lessons to idealizing the Vietnamese village and the life of the Vietnamese peasant.[120] Pupils were urged to "return to the ricefields and learn to love the smaller skills," in line with the teachings of Marshal Pétain. The Marshal himself was painted in distinctly Confucian terms, complete with stress on his venerable years and allegedly snow-white beard. On the other hand, the lesson on raising the tricolor before morning classes was a bundle of military force and precision, including correct formation time (7:50 A.M.), loud commands from the teacher, three beats of the drum, hats off, and a post-ceremony march into the classroom, with all "determined to devote every bit of energy to studying so that rapid progress can be made."[121]

In 1942 a poetry contest was held on the topic of "Franco-Vietnamese Renaissance." Eleven contributors were rated worthy of publication for their sharp attacks on freedom, equality, and individualism. The remainder were chastised for not understanding the purpose of the exercise well enough.[122] Meanwhile, the Japanese distributed propaganda of a similar character and even sponsored some alternative religious organizations, youth groups, and sporting activities. The Vichy authorities responded by stepping up their own efforts at moral proselytizing and social mobilization among the Vietnamese. Young people joined these wartime organizations by the thousands, undoubtedly learning something about how effectively to channel and release energy for themselves, even as they chanted slogans, flexed muscles, and kept neat and clean ostensibly for the Vichy government or the Japanese Co-Prosperity Sphere.

By late 1944, however, it was the Communist led Viet-Minh Front that was exciting the most attention among politically alert Vietnamese. As we shall discuss later, the Viet-Minh appeal was both extraordinarily simple, as symbolized,

---

120. DIRIP, *Van Quoc Ngu (Nam Ky)* [National-Script Reader: Cochinchina] (Saigon[?], 1942). The remaining three-quarters was divided about equally among personal habits, family relationships, and study discipline.

121. Ibid., pp. 114–16.

122. Viet Bao, *Phap Viet Phuc Hung Ca* [Ode to Franco-Vietnamese Renaissance] (Hanoi[?], 1942). Originally serialized in the newspaper *Viet Bao*.

for example, by the slogan "Independence and Freedom," and highly complex, with different explanations and prescriptions being directed to a wide variety of potential adherents. The belief was spreading that power belonged to the people (*dan*), and that only some sort of mass initiative could bring success over enemies both foreign and domestic. In the spring of 1945, while the Japanese-approved Prime Minister, Tran Trong Kim, labored to put together a cabinet of diploma'd professionals, selected his vice-premier because of age, and designed his flag according to the *Book of Changes*, groups of Vietnamese citizens at the neighborhood, village, and district levels were simply bypassing constituted authority and starting to take authority into their own hands.[123] This process was given final impetus by the mid-August 1945 Viet Minh call for a general uprising, under a red flag with yellow star that reflected modern revolutionary symbolism. Mass initiatives were legitimized by the 2 September 1945 Declaration of Independence, complete with appropriate quotes from the American Declaration of 1776 and from the 1791 French Declaration on the Rights of Man and the Citizen.[124]

Within weeks of these momentous events a Viet-Minh affiliate was publishing a booklet entitled *The Rights and Responsibilities of Being a Citizen*.[125] Like the colonial civics texts of the late 1930s, it contained an abundance of terminology and structure to absorb. Unlike the previous authors, however, Viet-Minh writers went to considerable lengths to explain the concepts behind the framework. Thus, two pages on "personal freedom" defined this as the right to live peacefully, to be protected from harassment, to own property, and to send letters without having them opened by the authorities. Unless a citizen had committed treason, stolen, or otherwise broken the law, no one had the right to imprison him. Arraignment was necessary within twenty-four hours, or else suspects were to be released. Somewhat briefer descriptions were provided for the "political freedoms" of speech, publication, organization, assembly, belief, and travel. Under "equal rights," primary attention was given to eliminating judicial discrimination:

All are equal before the law, whether they be cabinet minister or ploughman, boss or laborer, rich or poor. A cabinet minister who breaks the law will be punished exactly as any other citizen.[126]

All systems of restricted suffrage were also repudiated, specific mention being made of those based on wealth or educational status and those excluding women or certain degraded castes.

123. Tran Trong Kim, *Mot Con Gio Bui* [A Puff of Dust] (Saigon, 1969), pp. 51–61, 82–94.

124. Bernard Fall, *Ho Chi Minh on Revolution* (New York: Praeger, 1967), pp. 139–43.

125. Hoi Van Hoa Cuu Quoc, *Quyen Va Bon Phan Lam Dan* [Rights and Responsibilities of the Citizen] (Hanoi, 1945) (10,000 copies).

126. Ibid., p. 21.

According to this Viet-Minh booklet, the most important citizen's right (and responsibility) was the vote. As new masters of the country, citizens could contrast their role to olden days, when the people served the king, or to colonial days, when Vietnamese were enslaved to the French. On the other hand, "democracy" did not mean that citizens could do whatever they wished. There was still government. Here the Viet-Minh authors tried to be as concrete as possible, not only defining such things as direct representation, secret ballots, and powers of referendum, initiative, and recall, but also pointing out the dangers if any one of these procedures was missing, and then providing examples of positive implementation at the village level.[127] Thus, they argued, the vote gave alert citizens the power to eject traitors and reactionary local gentry from village administrative bodies, and the power to prevent them from infiltrating any newly elected committees. Or, if citizens were dissatisfied with policies but not personnel, they could start a popular initiative and, providing they obtained a majority of signatures, force the village committee to obey their will. What would happen if "traitors" or "reactionaries" used the village voting system to their advantage was not discussed.

Perhaps the answer was implicit in the concluding section on "responsibilities of citizenship." The Constitution had to be respected because it was the highest law of the land. Laws had to be obeyed because they were enacted by legitimate representatives of the citizenry. Most importantly, the Fatherland (To Quoc) had to be defended, since without a country there could no longer be "rights to life" for the citizens. The provisional constitution specified that all men reaching age twenty had to join the army. With French units even at that moment attacking in the south, it would be necessary to struggle further for independence. Hence the ominous qualification:

> While we are struggling it is not possible to enjoy all the rights to freedom, democracy, and equality. As long as aggressor forces (quan giac) have not been completely eliminated the people cannot sit quietly and appreciate peace.[128]

Even the most pessimistic Viet-Minh writer probably had no inkling that at least another thirty years of terrible conflict would ensue before that proviso could begin to be reconsidered.

In the meantime, however, the Viet-Minh was also quite capable of drawing selectively from other traditions: Neo-Confucian, Marxist-Leninist, Catholic, or Buddhist. Ho Chi Minh, for example, had long insisted that a revolutionary cadre

---

127. Much the same message was conveyed in far less technical fashion by another booklet describing voting day in a fictional village. The atmosphere was festive, like Tet, but the ritual involved getting out the vote, secret balloting, public observation of the vote-tallying, and joyful announcement of the results. (Binh Dan Hoc Vu, Ngay Hoi Lon [A Great Festival Day] (Hanoi[?], Dec. 1945).

128. Quyen Va Bon Phan Lam Dan, p. 24.

must set the highest conceivable example. Upon returning to Vietnam in 1941 he consistently tried to project certain personality traits, such as simplicity, punctuality, physical fitness, cleanliness, direct speech, and personal intimacy. Not only did these characteristics influence his immediate Party associates profoundly, but they served as models for several generations of cadres and, eventually, were incorporated by DRVN pedagogues in primary school texts. Later in life, half seriously, half in jest, he advised young Vietnamese *not* to emulate two of his practices: smoking cigarettes and never marrying. In reality, only the former was ever seen as a vice. The latter added greatly to Ho Chi Minh's status as a selfless revolutionary who "took the entire people as his family."

Of course there was more to Ho Chi Minh than idealized virtue. He was a master of clandestine operations, a skilled analyst of international affairs, a shrewd judge of lieutenants, a patient designer of political consensus. Particularly from September 1945 onward, however, Ho Chi Minh knew that his most important role was that of charismatic leader—the personification of Vietnam's new, independent national identity. What made him unique was his ability to project both a mundane and a transcendental character, to cause people to identify with him both because of what they were as well as what they ought to be. All of this was summarized in their reference to him as "Uncle Ho" (*Bac Ho*), an indication of both familiarity and respect.

During the Resistance War against the French (1945–54) a handbook titled *Let's Change our Methods of Work* was used to train Party cadres. It listed benevolence or humaneness (*nhan*) as the highest revolutionary virtue, yet provided a new interpretation of this most hoary of Confucian values:

> The virtue of humaneness consists of loving deeply and of wholeheartedly assisting one's comrades and compatriots. That is why the cadre who displays this virtue wages a resolute struggle against all those who would harm the Party and people. That is why he will not hesitate to be the first to endure hardship and the last to enjoy happiness. That is why he will not covet wealth and honor, nor fear hardship and suffering, nor be afraid to fight those in power. Those who want nothing are afraid of nothing and will always succeed in doing the right thing.[129]

Here was a statement of idealism in the stern, priestly tradition of many countries, not simply Vietnam. Without question it motivated tens of thousands of Vietnamese to improve themselves. Nevertheless, it was not enough to engineer a revolution and a protracted anti-imperialist war. For that, much more would be needed than self-cultivation and moral rectitude.

---

129. As quoted in Nguyen Khac Vien, *Tradition and Revolution in Vietnam*, (Berkeley: Indochina Resource Center, 1974), p. 48.

3. Ethics and Politics

In October 1929, *Phu Nu Tan Van* [Women's News] printed a letter from a wealthy Vietnamese landowner. Some thirty years earlier, it seems, this enterprising individual had pulled together a large sum of money to purchase the position of canton chief, his plan being to recoup rapidly by means of corruption and by arranging to marry into a wealthy family. When income proved a bit slow, he managed to create problems where none had existed before, for example, inciting one family to take action against another, or searching local land records to uncover discrepancies. Each case yielded cover-up bribes or pay-offs to resolve the problem "officially." Gradually he was able to build up his own landholdings by inside purchase of concessions and by forcing disadvantaged owners to sell cheaply. One hundred hectares of his paddy fields were cultivated at little or no personal cost simply by coercing peasants and tenants to do extra work. However, he had recently been outfoxed in a particularly flagrant attempt to bilk another rich family, as a result losing a great deal of money, the position of canton chief, and the opportunity to bribe his way into the higher office of district magistrate. Then, too, he was increasingly shocked by the dissolute behavior of his children. His son ran around with prostitutes, gambled recklessly, and smoked opium, while his daughter was said to be "unlucky in love," drifting from one man to another. The landowner had thought over this sorry turn of events and decided that it must be due to the previous lack of virtue of both himself and his grasping wife.[1]

At about the same time, a teenage peasant named Chanh Thi was arguing bitterly with his mother, wandering the countryside fruitlessly in search of employment, and rejecting his family's efforts to marry him to the spinster daughter of a local landlord.[2] Although he had passed the examination certifying ability to continue schooling beyond the third grade, Chanh Thi had since given up hope of obtaining the necessary funds. He asked himself searching questions: "Why

---

1. PNTV 25 (17 Oct. 1929), pp. 21–22.
2. Chanh Thi, "Roi Ba Duoc Vao Dang" [Then Your Father Joined the Party], *Len Duong Thang Loi* [Road to Victory] (Hanoi, 1960), pp. 7–18. The author felt the need in 1959 to explain to his children what life in colonial times had been like.

are some people rich and others poor?" "Where does the collected rice and money go?" "What sort of 'virtue' (*duc*) could have created this society?" By going to an adjacent village he was able to read a newspaper published in Hue, and it was thus that he learned of the 1930 uprisings in Nghe An and Ha Tinh provinces. What confused him at first was the paper's repeated references to the "Protectorate" and the "Royal Government" putting down "Communist bandits." Pondering the situation carefully, he concluded that the "bandits" had to be Vietnamese peasants like himself. This problem resolved, he wanted to become a "Communist." Having no idea how to contact an authentic representative, Chanh Thi simply moved to form a group among the village poor. When a recruit asked if being a Communist meant that each would receive at least three piasters per month, Chanh Thi responded:

> What kind of Communist receives a salary? Being a Communist means urging each other to chop off French heads, chop off landlords' heads, and divide property for the poor and thus for ourselves.[3]

Although Chanh Thi's group was not able to do any of these things for the moment, they did try minor acts of sabotage against the landlords, and they refused to passively endure further corporal punishment or verbal insults. Quickly the word spread that there was a bunch of hardheads who spoke their minds and did not whore, drink, or gamble; they had to be up to something. Some Confucian literati referred to the entire village as a place where traditional proprieties were being broken, the "rich not acting like rich, poor not acting like poor." Their verbal outrage was counterbalanced, however, by the favorable comments circulating among the poor majority of the district. Finally a Communist Party cadre did arrive, using a lot of terminology Chanh Thi failed to understand. However, the cadre did give pointers on how to oppose taxes, corvée, and maldistribution of communal lands. This, plus the knowledge of the uprisings in Nghe An and Ha Tinh, was enough to raise Chanh Thi's enthusiasm to join. After enrollment he learned that being a Communist involved a great deal of pain and tribulation, including, in his case, three prison terms. Nevertheless, to abandon the Party meant returning to a life of "no family and no land" (*vong gia that tho*), and this Chanh Thi refused to do.

These two vignettes, although obviously different in particulars, serve to point up some of the ethical dilemmas facing Vietnamese in the 1920s and 1930s. It was a time when the masks of ritual and institution were partly stripped away, when very few rules had prima facie justification. The landlord, having found no formula that could both justify unbridled material competition and return his children to a state of grace, was clearly looking for some meaningful reaffir-

3. Ibid, p. 14.

mation of Confucian ethics. The peasant had reason to be more alienated than the landlord, and this was reflected not only in the depth of his ethical questioning but in his readiness to take dangerous action.

Intellectuals of this period who called for simple faith in the old ethical formulas were often hooted down or, worse yet, ignored completely. Ideas had to be worked out and argued, not assumed. This gave considerable influence to innovators, not only members of the radical intelligentsia but creative conservatives as well. Most Vietamese still wanted to believe that evil conduct brought retribution, and that individual insight carried with it the obligation to stand up for right and oppose wrong. However, trying to agree on what was evil, how to achieve individual insight, or when and where to act on that knowledge were matters of intense debate.

Much of traditional Vietnamese ethics was summarized in the Confucian *Ta Hsüeh* formula, wherein knowledge and self-cultivation led to proper family regulation, which induced state order, which promoted universal peace. Among other things it should be apparent that the *Ta Hsüeh* formula tended to make political theory a sub-category of ethics. By contrast, most Western ideological formulations of the nineteenth and early twentieth centuries operated on the premise that those on top were either rich because they ruled or ruled because they were rich. Either way, ethics took a subordinate position. Young Vietnamese encountering this difference were often both shocked and excited. Thus Thach Lan, writing a pungent two-page essay in Paris for publication at home, pointed out how the ancient sages had glorified humaneness and righteousness while demeaning self-interest or profit (*loi*). Now, however, economics had to replace morality, or at least the latter had to serve the former. Throughout the world, he argued "every action, every problem, every conflict, every advance" was wrapped up in the struggle for survival. In reality, the Vietnamese were not ethically superior to others; they had not protected their interests against the Chinese or wiped out the Cham with morality. Yet, when the time had come to fight to avoid European colonization, a lot of energy was dissipated in pompous moralizing. Today, Thach Lan concluded, "That unnatural attitude continues to make us stubborn and confused, able neither to rise to the status of heavenly immortals nor to turn ourselves into men and women as strong as others."[4] Seldom was the Vietnamese intellectual's sense of being caught between two philosophical systems described more poignantly.

Many traditional Vietnamese proponents of ethical self-cultivation had not practiced what they preached; yet they became politically powerful, just as some Western individuals were neither rich nor rulers yet managed to exercise consid-

4. Thach Lan, "Luan Ly va Kinh Te" [Morality and Economics], PNTV 36 (9 Jan. 1930), pp. 5–6.

erable moral or intellectual influence. In Vietnam, peasants had summarized their skepticism concerning the dominant ideology with the phrase, "Win and you're called Emperor, lose and you're a bandit." Folk maxims and anecdotes about rapacious mandarins and useless scholars abounded. On the subject of conventional education they remarked wryly that the real objectives seemed to be "learning to eat properly, learning to say things correctly, learning to wrap up things one has to say, and learning to open up things that others have wrapped up."[5] Nevertheless, because Vietnamese peasants lacked an alternative system, most of their spicy observations were criticisms of those who deviated from Confucian ethical ideals rather than attacks on the ideals themselves. Indeed, in times of political decay or social chaos it was in the villages, particularly among the small peasant proprietors, that a skilled leader upholding true benevolence and righteousness could find the most eager supporters.

Given the preoccupation with ethical norms, it follows that Confucianists often spent more time delineating personal attitudes toward a given situation than in analyzing the situation itself. In politics this often led them to be more interested in motives than in results.[6] In historiography it was necessary that all major actors, indeed entire political groups, be labeled either "legitimate" (chinh) or "illegitimate" (nguy), never simply successful or unsuccessful, never the unwitting agents of impersonal forces at work in society.[7] Finally, in literature it meant that people "who did good things always reaped good results, and cruel people always came to cruel ends."[8]

To maintain such a position Confucianists had to have faith in the fundamental goodness of both man and the universe. Linked together by a myriad of morally impregnated threads, favorable conditions in the universe encouraged favorable behavior in man, while pure thoughts and good deeds among men promoted a more beneficent universe. In human affairs, it therefore followed that right makes might, never the reverse. True, rulers sometimes neutralized the significance of this statement by portraying right and might as synonymous, so that the use of might was justified by its very existence. Still, rulers never ob-

---

5. In pithier Vietnamese: hoc an, hoc noi, hoc goi, hoc mo. Quoted in an unpublished paper by Ngo Vinh Long, "Some Aspects of the Vietnamese Scholar-Gentry Class from 1860 to 1900" (Cambridge, Mass.: June 1969), p. 16.

6. This criticism is accepted by An Khe in his article "Khao ve Triet Hoc Khong Giao" [An Examination of Confucian Philosophy], NP 86 (Aug. 1924), pp. 127–38. The author apparently based much of his discussion on a 1918 study by Hu Shih.

7. So Cuong (Le Du) in his article "Lich Su doi Tay Son" [History of the Tay Son Period], NP 97 (July 1925), pp. 11–28, calls for an end to legitimate-illegitimate historiographical fixations; nevertheless, in this and other NP articles he remains wedded to the underlying ethical principle.

8. A tradition criticized by Viet Sinh (Thach Lam), "Mot cai lam to" [A Major Error], Phong Hoa (Hanoi), 17 Feb. 1933, as quoted in Alexander Woodside, Community and Revolution in Modern Vietnam (Boston, 1976), p. 81.

tained approval for the idea that might makes right, a fact that remained significant in Vietnam beyond the collapse of Confucianism as a state religion.

Constant attention to personal attitude also tended to provide Confucianists with a highly refined sense of justice and injustice, at least if one accepts the proposition that judicial punishment and reward ought to be attuned more to motives than to acts. Thus, Thomas Huxley might have been speaking for a long line of Vietnamese literati when he affirmed that "righteousness, that is, action from right motive, not only became synonymous with justice, but the positive constituent of innocence and the very heart of goodness."[9] Again, this Vietnamese attitude toward righteousness and justice survived the collapse of royal resistance to the French, the destruction of many traditional social relationships, and the seizure of power by a Communist Party allegedly operating from principles of historical materialism.

Thomas Huxley had immediately gone on to argue, however, that in the merely animal world neither the pleasures nor the pains of life are distributed according to desert, and that "if anything is real, pain and sorrow and wrong are realities."[10] Confucianists had always been vulnerable on this question of evil and suffering. In Vietnam, with the monarch reduced to a mere shadow of his former self, the idea of the ruler's good actions warding off evil in society and nature rapidly lost most of its significance. It is hardly surprising, therefore, that Buddhism enjoyed a modest revival in twentieth-century Vietnam, first among the peasants and later among a segment of the educated elite.[11] The emergence of the new Cao Dai religious group in southern Vietnam, mentioned previously, reflected a loss of confidence in Confucianism as a value system, as distinct from a set of moral prescriptions. Cao Dai leaders managed to incorporate the salvationist promises of popular Taoism, Buddhism, and European spiritualism along with the utopianism of K'ang Yu-wei. Meanwhile, Catholicism, operating from the novel proposition that man's "original sin" was responsible for evil, with redemption nevertheless possible in an afterlife, retained a hold on perhaps ten percent of the Vietnamese population. Among intellectuals a vague secular humanism gained currency.[12] And, finally, as we can infer from the autobiographi-

9. Thomas H. Huxley, *Evolution and Ethics and Other Essays* (London, 1894), p. 58. Huxley was much discussed in turn-of-the-century China, and these discussions in turn influenced educated Vietnamese well into the 1920s.

10. Ibid., pp. 58, 71.

11. Chapter 8 has further discussion of some of the intellectual questions raised in a Buddhist context.

12. The short stories of Thach Lam (Nguyen Tuong Lan) (1910–42) provide perhaps the most sensitive Vietnamese intellectual evocations of human suffering, without, however, offering much in the way of solutions. For several translations, see Ngo Vinh Long, *Vietnamese Women in Society and Revolution*, vol. 1, *The French Colonial Period* (Cambridge, Mass.: 1974), pp. 57–65, 123–36.

cal account of Chanh Thi, Marxism-Leninism gained adherents among the poor by linking evil and suffering with the existence of an exploitative colonial land-lord system.

Attempts at Confucian Revival

Confucianism had been around too long in Vietnam to give up without a strug-gle. Probably the most ambitious attempt to state a coherent, contemporary Confucian doctrine was that of Tran Trong Kim, the same man commissioned by the French to write primary school morality texts. Particularly in his two-volume study titled *Nho Giao* [Confucianism], Tran Trong Kim argued the existence of two very different types of knowledge, that obtained through "intuitive insight" (*truc giac*), and that accomplished by the more pedestrian powers of "reason" (*ly tri*).[13] Confucian metaphysics was almost entirely the preserve of intuition, he claimed. One's heart or spirit (*tam*) was Heaven's gift, enabling one to under-stand the universe. Indeed, the universe only existed for man because he had that inner light, that spiritual lodestar, not because of any reality existing indepen-dently of man.[14] In short, Heaven, man, and the universe were linked by means of the intuitive *tam*, and it was the duty of men of good will to seek out and attempt to live according to the major principles governing this relationship. The assertion that these were principles of high refinement, to be comprehended only after long years of studying the Confucian classics, served to separate Tran Trong Kim's formulation from certain Buddhist and Taoist schools which allowed for more direct or non-pedantic routes to intuitive truth.

Another distinction from Buddhism or Taoism was the general Confucian in-sistence that study, no matter how lofty or extended, always be followed by so-cially relevant action (*hoc hanh*). However, in Tran Trong Kim's opinion, because the vast majority of people could not be expected to comprehend the lofty "spir-itual transmissions" (*tam truyen*) of the sages, it had become necessary to de-velop a secondary body of "public transmissions" (*cong truyen*), employing reason for communication and focusing on the five relationships, five virtues, and other "practical" formulas.[15] Spiritual transmission involved a quest for the all-encompassing yet elusive *Dao* (Tao), while public transmissions were clearcut designs for moral and political instruction.[16]

Although Tran Trong Kim did devote space to explaining and defending these moral and political designs, he repeatedly emphasized their derivative character

---

13. Tran Trong Kim, *Nho Giao*, 2 vols. bound as one (Saigon, 1962); first published in 1929–30. Actually, the author had stated some of his arguments as early as 1920. See NP 39 (Sept. 1920), 65 (Nov. 1922), and 66 (Dec. 1922).

14. Tran Trong Kim, *Nho Giao*, vol. 1, p. 92.

15. Ibid., pp. xxi, 136–37.

16. Ibid., vol. 2, pp. 343–44.

and warned that Confucianism would not survive, especially in modern times, if proponents simply limited themselves to "outer" or "public" knowledge. In fact, he was willing to countenance designs of Western origin taking the lead in such areas as social control and economic development, since "reason" had apparently found more favorable conditions for historical refinement in the commercial and industrial West. But, he insisted, "reason" must never be allowed to intrude on the intuitively derived "inner spirit" of Vietnam, which had to remain the domain of those few students of Confucius who understood his metaphysical teachings and who could still conduct their lives according to the harmonious Doctrine of the Mean (*trung dung*), rather than losing their equilibrium and stooping to Western preferences for struggle and survival of the fittest.[17]

Tran Trong Kim's study remained a topic of sporadic intellectual comment and conversation for the next fifteen years. Along with his *Viet-Nam Su Luoc* (An Outline History of Vietnam), *Nho Giao* continued to be used in Republic of Vietnam middle schools until the final days of April 1975. No one else among the collaborator elite bothered to revise or update his arguments, despite (or perhaps because of) more than four decades of revolutionary ferment and anti-imperialist struggle.

Phan Khoi (1887–1960) was the first writer to attack Tran Trong Kim's conception head-on.[18] He pointed out that the author's favorite Sung Neo-Confucian texts were hardly synonymous with the teachings of Confucius, a matter that had received extensive attention in China but apparently was little discussed in Vietnam. He accused Tran Trong Kim of taking words recently coined to express Western concepts, particularly 'intuition' and 'reason,' then thrusting them back across the centuries to rework the teachings of the sages for his own purposes. As for the Doctrine of the Mean, even Confucius considered it an almost unattainable ideal when he proposed it, so that in today's far more difficult circumstances it had to be regarded as totally out of place.

Quite aside from questions of historical accuracy or competing doctrinal interpretation, in Phan Khoi's opinion there were at least two reasons why a Confucianist revival would fail to meet contemporary needs: Neo-Confucianism's underlying spiritualism and occultism ran counter to science and any defense of the ideal aristocracy of superior men was incompatible with democracy. Besides, Confucian writers spent far too much time telling people what to do, rather than uncovering, analyzing, and explaining the reasons *why* a particular action was correct. Less attention should be devoted to a priori pontifications, more to experience and experiment. Whatever failed the test of science should be discarded, no matter how loud the wailing about "national essence." Nevertheless, Phan

17. Ibid., vol. 1, pp. xvi–xvii.
18. Phan Khoi, "Doc cuon *Nho Giao* cua Ong Tran Trong Kim" [Reading Mr. Tran Trong Kim's *Confucianism*], PNTV 54 (29 May 1930), pp. 11–13.

Khoi was of the opinion that the moral self-cultivation and self-improvement (*tu than*) facets of Confucianism would handily survive the test, as had been the case when religion and morality were separated elsewhere. For this reason it was unconscionable for Vietnamese to ignore the Confucian heritage, since it was a part of them and would remain so. "Although you live in this Westernized [sic] environment, to not know Confucianism is to not be Vietnamese," he concluded.[19]

Tran Trong Kim replied to Phan Khoi's criticism by arguing that it was the Sung philosophers who had first properly understood Confucian metaphysics and grasped the true transcendental potential of the ancient teaching.[20] He admitted that 'intuition' (*truc giac*) and 'reason' (*ly tri*) were new terms developed by late nineteenth-century writers in response to Western concepts, yet believed this did not rule out their use in expressing certain earlier tendencies in the Confucian tradition. As for logic and the scientific method, Tran Trong Kim claimed he had nothing against them so long as they did not intrude on the domain of the heart or spirit. Given his wide-ranging, Heaven-linked definition of 'spirit' (*tam*), this remained a major qualification indeed. To bolster his argument, Tran Trong Kim professed to see a growing disenchantment with science in the West.[21] And he concluded by inviting Phan Khoi to keep going on the "left road" while he hewed to the "right one." Hopefully they would meet somewhere along the way and build a house of philosophy together, chuckling about how such diverse routes could lead to the same objective.[22]

Rather than denounce this coy restatement of the Doctrine of the Mean, Phan Khoi picked up the metaphor with obvious delight, titling his rebuttal "An invitation to Tran Trong Kim along with Confucius and Mencius to chat at the house of Mr. Logic."[23] Mostly this was a pedantic demonstration of examples where Confucius and Mencius had allegedly failed to follow basic principles of logic

19. Ibid., p. 13. More sweeping critiques of Tran Trong Kim's *Nho Giao* will be discussed in Chapter 8.

20. Tran Trong Kim also asserted this position in *Nho Giao*, vol. 2, pp. 387–90, 401–03, but Phan Khoi did not have access to the second volume when the debate began.

21. This was probably a reference to the writings of Henri Bergson, which Tran Trong Kim had cited approvingly in *Nho Giao*, vol. 1, pp. xxiv–xxv. Bergson was a favorite philosopher of other Vietnamese traditionalists of this period. See, for example, articles in NP 8 (Feb. 1918), 9 (Mar. 1918), 12 (June 1918), 13 (July 1918), 14 (Aug. 1918), and 150 (May 1930).

22. Tran Trong Kim, "May loi ban voi Phan tien-sinh ve Khong-giao" [Discourse with Mr. Phan on Confucianism], PNTV 60 (10 July 1930), pp. 12–16. The following year, in fact, a journal titled *Khoa Hoc Tap Chi* [Science Magazine] was begun with the stated purpose of popularizing the idea that Confucianists and scientists should join together to build Vietnamese "civilized superior men" (*nguoi van minh quan tu*). From this point on, almost every idea imaginable came to be linked in some way with "science." A copy of the first issue of *Khoa Hoc Tap Chi*, dated 1 July 1931, can be found in AOM Indochine NF 1707, together with an official observation that it does not appear to present any "*caractère tendancieux.*"

23. PNTV 63 (31 July 1930), pp. 13–15; and 64 (7 Aug. 1930), pp. 15–18.

(definition of terms, proposition, syllogism, etc.), instead preferring calculated ambiguity that led to endless scholarly disputes in subsequent centuries. Tran Trong Kim responded with his own intricate explanations of the classical passages in question; in the end, however, he chided Phan Khoi for employing narrow, segmented Western logic when what was really called for was intuition, attention to the spirit of the passage, and some reverence for the mysteries of ancient words. Tran Trong Kim titled his response "An invitation to the Honorable Phan Khoi to return to our [Vietnamese] house to study and chat."[24] The problem of under what kind of roof Vietnamese would communicate had not been resolved.

Most readers were aware of an interesting paradox in this exchange. Tran Trong Kim was mounting a rather tardy defense of Confucianism as a timeless religion, yet he himself had been raised in the French rational tradition and had pursued his career within a pedagogical structure dominated by ethnocentric Frenchmen. On the other hand, Phan Khoi had come to the study of Western science and philosophy only secondarily, having been trained from age six in the Confucian classics and having achieved *tu tai* rank in the now defunct civil examinations. Much of what Phan Khoi said was derived from the writings of Ch'en Tu-hsiu and Hu Shih in China a decade earlier. In short, both men were intellectual hybrids in a period of impatient testing and rapid change.[25]

Nor did either man remain particularly consistent in his thinking. Phan Khoi increasingly took an idealist position, and was thus soon attacked by younger advocates of dialectical materialism. Tran Trong Kim talked of keeping moral education as the "roots" and limiting intellectual education to the "branches," yet the branches he listed became heavy indeed, including industry, economics, military science, mathematics, physics, chemistry, and "all the others."[26] He also wrote sympathetically on Taoism and Buddhism, and by 1936 was clearly losing hope that his Neo-Confucian paragons could make their way in a modern world of chaos and struggle. The basic fault, he now said, stemmed from human cleverness, which led people to kill and destroy in the process of seeking the truth.[27] Gone was the affirmation of mutually reinforcing goodness in heaven, man, and nature.

Other advocates of Neo-Confucian revival tended from the beginning to set

24. PNTV 71 (25 Sept. 1930), pp. 8–11; 72 (2 Oct. 1930), pp. 9–11; and 74 (16 Oct. 1930), pp. 9–13.

25. The paradox was noted in print by Le Tai Truong, "Propose de lettrés," NP (French Supplement) 155 (Oct. 1930), pp. 28–29. He was particularly disturbed to see Tran Trong Kim, "an eminent representative of our new elite," returning to doctrines that the literati had forsaken.

26. Tran Trong Kim, *Nho Giao*, vol. 2, p. 396.

27. Tran Trong Kim, *Quan Niem ve cuoc Nhan Sinh* [Concepts of Human Life] (Hanoi, 1936), p. 6. Tran Trong Kim's discussion of Taoism is in NP 67 (Jan. 1923), 68 (Feb. 1923), 74 (Aug. 1923), and 75 (Sept. 1923); his main study of Buddhism is *Phat Luc* [Buddhist Strength], second printing (Hanoi, 1942[?]).

more modest goals. Either because they themselves no longer had faith in mystical transmissions or because they knew such ideas would be mocked by the majority of young intellectuals, their focus was on the simple social convenience of retaining Confucian ethical and political principles. To counter the argument that "Eastern" principles were inferior or dated, they began a methodical search for European writers who might be used in defense. Probably the most tireless polemicist along these lines was Pham Quynh, who provided readers with scores of explanations, interpretations, and translations on ethical subjects. Thus he found the work of Ernst van Bruyssel, a Belgian conservative, helpful in upholding the sanctity of marriage, denouncing birth control, and decrying the weakening of family ties.[28] The Vietnamese family was further defended against the depredations of individualism by reference to the arguments of the novelist Henry Bordeaux.[29] And to reinforce Confucian teachings on friendship, Pham Quynh reached back to the eighteenth-century writings of Mme Marquise de Lambert.[30]

Pham Quynh's more ambitious philosophical and literary treatises had contemporary social implications too, generally (but not always) in conservative or reactionary directions. One of his paragons appears to have been Charles Maurras, the same Maurras who challenged a whole generation of French bourgeois intellectuals to denounce liberty, equality, democracy, progress, republicanism, and any other belief growing out of the Enlightenment or the 1789 Revolution. In the opinion of Maurras, Descartes and Rousseau had initiated a disastrous era of unbridled individualism leading to the dismantling of authority and hierarchy as epitomized by Cardinal Richelieu.[31] Following Maurras's lead, Pham Quynh attacked Rousseau as highly "destructive" (pha hoai). Emile Zola's naturalism was labeled vulgar, extremist, and decadent; Vietnamese writers were counseled not to follow his path. Victor Hugo was taken to task for ignoring the essential classical heritage, for arguing that there was beauty in chaos, and for saying that rebels and eccentrics ought to be admired. "Such extreme libertarianism cannot help but be dangerous," Pham Quynh intoned, "because any country that takes it seriously loses all sense of discipline."[32]

As for Descartes, he at least was given the courtesy of a Vietnamese translation

28. Pham Quynh, "Gia Toc Luan" [An Essay on the Family], NP 29 (Nov. 1919), pp. 375–81. Based on Bruyssel's book, Le Vie Sociale.

29. Pham Quynh, "Nghia Gia Toc" [The Meaning of Family], NP 2 (Aug. 1917), pp. 89–92.

30. Pham Quynh, trans., "Tinh Be-ban" [The Sentiment of Friendship], NP 41 (Nov. 1920), pp. 369–78.

31. Pham Quynh, Charles Maurras, Penseur Politique (Hanoi, 1943). Robert O. Paxton, Vichy France: Old Guard and New Order (New York: Knopf, 1972), pp. 23–24, 149–50. Almost as if their destinies were linked, in 1945 Pham Quynh was executed by the Viet Minh only seven months after Maurras had been sentenced to life imprisonment by the Gaullists.

32. Pham Quynh, "Van Chuong Phap" [French Literature], NP 53 (Nov. 1921), p. 397.

of one of his most important works, *Discours de la méthode*. Pham Quynh relied on Henri Bergson for a revisionist interpretation of Descartes, however, then added his own facile conclusion that the entire message could be summed up in Chuang-tzu's concept of 'human virtue' (*dao duc*).[33] At other times Pham Quynh sang the praises of such romanticists as Lamartine, Musset, and Vigny. But he congratulated Paul Bourget for demonstrating in his novels that a society that exists and perpetuates itself, even though imperfectly and without much happiness, is still better than indiscipline and chaos.[34]

When defending the continuing relevance of Confucian philosophy per se, Pham Quynh chose to rely not so much on recent Vietnamese or Chinese interpretations as on those of a French orientalist named Edouard Chavannes. Both men alleged hierarchy and obedience to be at the core of the original teachings of Confucius. The father was undisputed master of the family, just as the emperor was master of the nation. Equality was a meaningless concept; rather, one's first responsibilities were to maintain social order and to respect those who personified that order. Most dangerous of all was the notion that the majority could or should select its rightful leaders. In fact, unless the East reasserted the principle of rule by princely, superior men (*quan tu*), just as the West needed to return to the seventeenth-century idea of *noblesse oblige*, there would be endless chatter, moral decay, and rabble in the streets.[35]

Ritual (*le*) also being considered an essential aspect of Confucianism, Pham Quynh and associates of like mind attempted to breathe new life into traditional ceremonies large and small. For the first time imperial honors to Heaven and earth were photographed and explained in exquisite printed detail. Yet, ironically, the camera probably helped to strip away whatever high mystery remained.[36] Again, by way of Western reinforcement, elaborate and simultaneous attention was given to the award of a knighthood from Pope Pius IX to a prominent Vietnamese mandarin of Catholic faith. Pictures featured all the quasi-military regalia, from Napoleonic-age hat and uniform to bejewelled sword and medal.[37] Other articles in *Nam Phong* delineated ranks and privileges of village

33. Pham Quynh, "To Triet Hoc Nuoc Phap: Ong Descartes cung sach *Phuong Phap Luan*" [The Legacy of French Philosophy: Descartes and His *Discours de la méthode*], NP 2 (Aug. 1917), pp. 100–104.

34. Pham Quynh, "L'ordre nécessaire," *Essais Franco-annamites* (Hue, 1937), p. 481. It is worth noting that Pham Quynh gave little attention to such highly regarded contemporaries as Maurras and Bourget as Charles Péguy, Paul Valéry, and Paul Claudel.

35. Pham Quynh, trans., "Khong Phu Tu Luan" [An Essay on Confucius], NP 13 (July 1918), pp. 4–15; idem, "Khong Giao Luan" [An Essay on Confucianism], NP 50 (Aug. 1921), pp. 116–22; idem, "Confucius et le Confucianisme," *Essais Franco-annamites*, pp. 117–25. Pham Quynh also drew extensively from Fustel de Coulanges, especially the latter's study *La Cité Antique*.

36. NP 45 (Mar. 1921), 46 (Apr. 1921), and 48 (June 1921).

37. NP 45 (Mar. 1921). The mandarin was Nguyen Huu Bai.

officials, upheld traditional marriage and funeral ceremonies, and described local temple observances. There was even a long, detailed series on traditional music, opening with the classical Confucian linkage of imperial music (*nhac*) with proper order in the world.[38]

Nevertheless, by the early 1930s some interesting ritual modifications were being introduced. Thus, "His Majesty the Emperor," Bao Dai, whose only remaining function centered on awards and ceremonies, ordered that the traditional kowtow be dispensed with. As if to demonstrate modernity, Bao Dai instructed his "subjects" that thenceforth it would be sufficient to clasp their hands deferentially in front of the chest.[39] Proposals that the kowtow be dropped in standard Vietnamese wedding ceremonies met with stiff resistance, however.[40] In South Vietnam until 1975 children continued to prostrate themselves before parents and in-laws at the appropriate moments in the ceremony.[41] As for the marriage of Bao Dai himself, in 1934, many Vietnamese who otherwise scorned monarchism in general and the Hue puppet court in particular seem to have waxed euphoric over this last display of regal matrimonial fancy.[42]

To sum up, conservatives like Pham Quynh were convinced that secularized Confucianism, stiffened with some compatible Western ideas, was the most effective means to insure social stability and popular discipline in contemporary Vietnam. In their opinion, certain canons of behavior had been disseminated by precept and example so successfully for so long that it would be a crime to discard them now. The content of these canons ultimately mattered less, however, than reviving or reinforcing the habit of behaving in accordance with fixed and unquestioned rules. Although Vietnamese conservative rhetoric about the decisiveness of morality in human affairs gave the appearance of vintage Confucianism, the source of confidence was more modern, involving the social engineer's idea that indoctrination and habit are more potent than physical force in maintaining social control.

Such an orientation led quite naturally to arguments that education was Vietnam's hope for the future—not just any education, of course, but one that preserved an "inner" spirit of submission to authority while gradually introducing "outer" utilitarian components of science and technology. Variations on this inner/outer or "substance/application" (*the-dung*; in Chinese, *t'i-yung*) formula

38. Hoang Yen, "Cam Hoc Tam Nguyen" [Study of Spiritual Aspirations], NP 47–50 (May–Aug. 1921), 52 (Oct. 1921).

39. PNTV, 22 Sept. 1932.

40. PNTV 119 (18 Feb. 1932), 121 (3 Mar. 1932).

41. By contrast, the marriage kowtow was strongly discouraged in Viet Minh zones from 1945 and throughout the North from 1954. (Discussion with Dr. Ngo Van Hoa in Hanoi on 10 Feb. 1978.)

42. PNTV 234 (15 Mar. 1934), 236 (29 Mar. 1934), and 237 (12 Apr. 1934).

can be found in hundreds of Vietnamese essays of the period. This duality, originally derived from Chang Chih-tung's famous "Exhortation to Learn" of 1898, was considered absolutely essential by conservative Vietnamese until at least the late 1930s. Perhaps the most important corollaries involved contrasting "moral education" (*duc duc*) and "intellectual education" (*tri duc*), as well as the personal attributes of "virtue" (*duc*) and "talent" (*tai*). For example, one author, aiming his words at parents of young pupils, equated "intellectual education" with a metaphorical chicken growing fast and perpetually. "Moral education" was the cage into which that chicken had to be placed. Not to expand the cage was to stunt the chicken, but not to have a cage at all was equally irresponsible. Switching metaphors to make his point even more relevant to the tense conditions of the early 1930s, the author concluded:

Having people with "talent" but not "virtue" is like putting a sharply honed knife in the hands of a hoodlum. Naturally, he will use the knife to his own advantage; yet, as sure as it is advantageous to him, it will also be harmful to a great many people around him.[43]

Assuming one accepted the bifurcation of all knowledge, education, and human character, it was still necessary to relate one component to the other. Thus, one writer reached for the traditional assertion that the "heart" (*tam*) provided man with a rich and central potentiality for goodness, yet switched to a more modern frame of reference when stating that "intelligence" (*tri*) served as "advisor," "compass," or developer of "ideology." For example, he said, feelings of loyalty and patriotism came from the "heart," but unless those feelings were guided by intellectually derived perceptions of strategy and historical timing, then failure was inevitable. On the other hand, possessing intelligence without virtuous emotions reduced man to the status of the animals, to the idea that might makes right, and that success can be achieved by mere plotting.[44] Pham Quynh, not the most consistent of writers, once went a bit further in conceding importance to the "mind" in relation to the "heart." No matter how much inner human virtue Vietnamese might possess or acquire, he said, it could never produce national progress unless equal or greater attention were given to development of "the intellect" (*tri thuc*).[45]

In actual fact, until 1925 or 1926 Pham Quynh and other conservatives were probably as responsible as anyone else for reducing that inner sanctum sup-

---

43. Dong Chau (Nguyen Huu Tien), PNTV 162 (4 Aug. 1932), p. 31. There is little doubt he was aiming the knife indictment at young radicals, in particular, members of the newly formed Indochinese Communist Party.

44. Tran Van Tang, "Qua Khu va Hien Tai" [Past and Present], NP 106 (June 1926), pp. 413–33.

45. Pham Quynh, "Van Minh Luan" [On Civilization], NP 42 (Dec. 1920), p. 445.

posedly reserved for the timeless, inner Vietnamese spirit. If an author placed a tag marked "science" (*khoa hoc*) on almost any topic, it could then be treated according to different rules of investigation and discourse from the more routine articles of spiritual reaffirmation. Thus it was that *Nam Phong*, while maintaining a staunch editorial defense of the five relationships and five virtues, went ahead and printed detailed articles on the physiology of the human brain, the findings of modern psychology, recent discoveries in astronomy, and Einstein's theory of relativity.[46] Soon young intellectuals were going further, treating problems like poverty, inequality, disease, crime, and opium addiction as matters to be studied, attacked, and overcome scientifically, not talked about in the shopworn categories of moral rectitude. Even prostitution, seen by Confucian moralists as an obscene violation of rules regarding female behavior, could now be discussed as a product of more fundamental social and economic forces at work in Vietnam and everywhere else.[47]

In retrospect, all attempts to maintain Vietnam as a spiritual preserve for Confucianism were doomed to failure. At least four reasons are apparent. First, Vietnamese like Tran Trong Kim or Pham Quynh were in the unenviable position of defending doctrines already under heavy attack at the source, China. Was Vietnam to become the center and China the periphery? If so, Tran Trong Kim had erred in choosing to devote a mere fifteen pages (two percent) of his study of Confucianism to Vietnamese writers, when an entire third volume might have been more appropriate.

Yet, Tran Trong Kim's choice did point up the second problem of the revivalists. Confucianism, although previously a state religion and a strong influence on popular Vietnamese thinking, was never synonymous with any Vietnamese "national essence." The revivalists knew this, but they lacked the imagination to advance a more comprehensive, convincing philosophy. They were constantly picking up other diverse components (Buddhism, Taoism, epic Vietnamese poems, folksongs, antiforeign struggle), toying with them awhile, then moving on aimlessly. In this respect, they had rather less chance of success than their conservative Kuomintang counterparts in China, who could at least take Chu Hsi as a reasonable starting point, add a bit of Tseng Kuo-fan for identification with nineteenth-century restoration endeavors, and top this off with the latest exhortations of Chiang Kai-shek.[48]

Thirdly, as a result of developments in colonial Vietnam, the very idea of some

---

46. See the following issues of NP: 36, 38, 76, 89–90, 92, 95–96, 101–103, 105, 107–108.

47. Alexander Woodside, *Community and Revolution in Modern Vietnam*, p. 200, quoting Phan Van Hum, *Ngoi Tu Kham Lon* [Sitting in Saigon Central Prison] (Saigon, 1957), pp. 135–37. Originally published in 1929.

48. For the comparable 1930s Chinese effort, see Mary Wright, "From Revolution to Restoration: The Transformation of Ideology," in Joseph R. Levenson, ed., *Modern China: An Interpretative Anthology* (New York: Macmillan, 1971), pp. 99–113.

timeless set of Vietnamese characteristics was being challenged. Nothing was sacred; everything seemed in flux. Bergson and Maurras provided conservatives with up-to-date weaponry, but they were neither Chu Hsi nor indigenous Vietnamese philosophers. In this sense, traditionalism was merely a symbiotic relative of radicalism, as modern in its own way as Marxism-Leninism. It certainly was not the product of serene minds seeking the touchstone of civilization. Nothing illustrates this more clearly than the tendency of some of the most corrupt Vietnamese officials in the colonial administration to chant Confucian formulas loudest and longest. Seemingly unlimited French military and police power provided an effective cover for bureaucratic immorality. Hearing rumors of corruption, a French superior normally preferred to chalk it up to "traditional custom" rather than clean house or even institute a serious investigation. Meanwhile, victims seldom dared to challenge perpetrators openly, knowing that they might end up in much worse condition than before. In short, those who mouthed principles of "benevolence" or "righteousness" preyed on those who might still truly believe—a situation rife with tension and potential confrontation.

Finally, in the deepest sense, the philosophical bifurcation of "heart" and "mind" did not truly satisfy anyone. Traditionally, most Vietnamese had faith in the oneness of life and the wholeness of the universe. They assumed that human perceptions, dreams, values, and beliefs were integrally related to each other, to the social world, and to the heavens beyond. There was a grand design of timeless order, next to which constant changes of nature and man paled in comparison. Now, however, traditionalists told people to live simultaneously in two different worlds with two different mental frameworks. Radical Vietnamese, of course, had no more desire to exist schizophrenically than anyone else. True, the idea that morality could be separated from religion gained support, as did the belief that science would make religion (but not ethics) unnecessary.[49] There was also talk of a special "revolutionary ethics" (*dao duc cach mang*), although what that meant remained subject to diverse interpretations.[50] It would not be oversimplifying too much to suggest, however, that many young Vietnamese intellectuals of the 1920s and 1930s were searching for a religion to replace Confucianism.

The Self and Society

Most Vietnamese intellectuals of the 1920s and 1930s were of the opinion that the previous two generations of educated elite had failed their forefathers by allowing the French to defeat and to colonize Vietnam. More to the point, many

49. See, for example, Ve Thach (Dao Duy Anh), comp., *Ton Giao* [Religion] (Hue, 1929).

50. This term may have originated with Liang Ch'i-ch'ao's "ethical revolution" (*tao-te koming*); if so, it is an interesting example of how important a slight difference in syntax can be. Because Vietnamese normally reverses the modifier-noun word order of Chinese, the meaning of the phrase is substantially altered if the original Chinese syntactic order is retained.

individuals had the feeling that in some way, large or small, they themselves had to begin to right this wrong. This was a burden no determinist philosophy could remove; nor did any objective analysis of French power and Vietnamese weakness eliminate the shame. Only eliminating the foreigner, as in the tenth, thirteenth, fifteenth and eighteenth centuries, could do that.

Why had Vietnam lost to the French? What should (or could) be done about it? Hundreds of answers came forth in publications of the period. Again and again, however, writers returned to the complex relationship between individual motivation and group accomplishment. The easiest thing to assert was that Vietnamese, from monarch to lowliest subject, had been woefully deficient in lofty purpose and too preoccupied by matters of selfish gain or mere physical survival to stand together and fight. This was the familiar dichotomy between "righteousness" (nghia) and "self-interest" (loi). As a corollary, it was often argued that legitimate "public" (cong) identifications and priorities had been swamped amidst the vulgar, selfish scramble for "private" (tu) status, wealth, and power. In the end, it was said, a lot of individuals seeking short-term gratification had provoked long-term disaster for the country.

The favorite remedy among the scholar-gentry was to exhort people to return to the virtues of loyalty, filial piety, self-sacrifice, frugality, and endurance. Enough individuals doing this at once would strengthen the group. This was the assumption on which the late nineteenth-century anticolonial Can Vuong (Loyalty to the King) movement had been grounded, and it helped to account both for the movement's considerable popularity and its ultimate demise.[51] As we have seen, some writers were quite prepared to continue arguing the merits of Confucian moral rearmament throughout the 1920s and into the early 1930s, yet fewer and fewer Vietnamese intellectuals seem to have been persuaded that their country's salvation lay in that direction. When An Khe in 1923 called on his countrymen to uphold righteousness and scorn self-aggrandizement, to change themselves inwardly before worrying about changing others, his words were already plaintive, defensive, almost defeatist in tone.[52] Three years later, when Nguyen Van Vinh, a prominent collaborator intellectual, sought to propose the formation of a society to promote patience, honesty, industry, thrift, loyalty, and charity among the Vietnamese people at large, he was enraged to discover that the most popular quoc-ngu newspaper of the day had no place for his essay or his elaborate draft constitution.[53]

---

51. For further discussion of Can Vuong activities, see Marr, Vietnamese Anticolonialism, pp. 44–76.

52. An Khe, "Quoc Tuy va Van Minh" [The National Essence and Civilization], NP 78 (Dec. 1923), p. 458.

53. In the end he paid to have a pamphlet printed himself. Tan Nam Tu (Nguyen Van Vinh), Thuc Tinh Dong Bao [Awakening sentiment of Countrymen] (Saigon, 1926).

The newspaper's refusal was a result of growing ideological separation, not petty personal intrigue, as Nguyen Van Vinh preferred to believe. Tran Huy Lieu, young editor of *Dong Phap Thoi Bao* [Indochina-France Times], was even at that moment preparing a broad indictment of traditional morality. He was especially troubled by the particularistic implications of the concept of 'fidelity' or 'loyalty' (*trung*):

Reading the history of our land extending back thousands of years, we see only groups of subjects demonstrating faithfulness to their king and never citizens being loyal to their country. That was a wrong ethic. It buried alive countless Vietnamese [potentially?] loyal to their country, fostered slavish obedience to the ruler, and prevented our people from developing an ethic of nationalism. How could such a country expect to compete and survive (*sinh ton*)?[54]

Tran Huy Lieu pointed out that despite apparent defects, not only within "loyalty" but "filial piety" (*hieu*) and other traditional ideas, some contemporaries still talked of retaining the superior Vietnamese moral spirit while borrowing Western material components. "Who knows?" he concluded: "Perhaps it is our morality that is completely outmoded and hence the cause of our tragic loss of sovereignty in recent times."[55]

Having said that, Tran Huy Lieu was rather inclined to downgrade the importance of self-cultivation in achieving national political objectives. Indeed, he suggested that the Confucian *Ta Hsüeh* sequence which had dominated orthodox Vietnamese thinking for centuries might well be turned on its head:

One must have a country before one can have a hearth and home, a hearth and home before one can focus on the self. If one's country is in ruins, can one honestly claim that one's home is at peace, that one's inner self is content?. . .Who among us does not have a wife and children, a father and mother, an extended family? . . .That home and family are to the nation, however, as twigs and leaves are to roots and trunk. If roots and trunk are rotten, what hope is there that twigs and leaves will be fresh and vital?[56]

Such ideas helped to put Tran Huy Lieu in jail in 1929, where he converted to Marxism-Leninism and embarked on a second career as Party journalist, DRVN government minister, and prolific writer and editor on historical subjects.

---

54. Tran Huy Lieu, *Mot Bau Tam Su* [A Gourdful of Confidences] (Saigon, 1927), p. 13. On the other hand, the author affirmed (p. 7) that ordinary Vietnamese had retained a certain skepticism about total loyalty, for example, in the wry popular comment that soldiers who failed to die on the battlefield had difficulty proving their "fidelity." These conditional aspects of feudal loyalty would come to be stressed by Vietnamese historians after 1945. See, for example, Le Sy Thang, "Ho Chu Tich va su nghiep truyen ba chu nghia Mac-Le-nin vao Viet-Nam" [President Ho and the Task of Spreading Marxism-Leninism to Vietnam] NCLS 144 (May–June 1972), p. 15.

55. Le Sy Thang, "Ho Chu Tich," p. 15.

56. Ibid., pp. 20–21.

Whether one abandoned the *Ta Hsüeh* sequence or not, the final result might well be the same. Tran Huu Do, older than Tran Huy Lieu and still inclined to take self-cultivation seriously, revived the ancient proposition of Hsün-tzu that man was superior to other animals primarily because he knew how to form social organizations, not because of any special moral acumen. Then, relying on turn-of-the-century writings of Liang Ch'i-ch'ao, he linked this to Social Darwinian visions of ruthless struggle in which only the fittest survived. The single factor determining which species or human group won out and which was consigned to oblivion was how well they understood the principle of "sticking together."[57] The larger the group, the better its chances for victory. Later, Tran Huu Do emphasized that in the modern world of science and technology it was not so much physical strength as strength through intelligence that provided the key; either way, he claimed, the goal of all this collective effort was power, without which there could be no freedom (citing Kant and Nietzsche for authority).[58] Tran Huu Do left no doubt that he was proposing fervent struggle by the majority of Vietnamese against the French colonial overlords rather than internal or international class struggle. Nevertheless, he too joined the Indochinese Communist Party and, as we shall see later, published several important essays on the historical dialectic and imperialism.

Growing interest in social mechanics was not the monopoly of political radicals. As early as 1918 Than Trong Hue, a ranking collaborator mandarin, criticized his countrymen for allegedly having lost the ability to organize, and solemnly instructed them to emulate the Japanese.[59] Japan continued to be studied and praised for its discipline and dynamism, at least until the occupation of Manchuria, when Vietnamese intellectuals split over the moral question of the ends to which these capabilities were being put.[60] Vietnamese writers proposed a number of smaller scale organizational models for testing, from consumer cooperatives to German-style kindergartens and private nursery schools for children of the urban poor and unemployed.[61]

---

57. Tran Huu Do, *Hoi Trong Tu Do* [Rolling the Drum of Freedom], vol. 3 (Saigon, 1926), p. 102.

58. Tran Huu Do, *Thanh Nien Tu Doc* [Youth Improvement Readings], vol. 1 (Saigon, 1928), pp. 4–7.

59. Than Trong Hue, "Con duong tien bo cua nuoc ta" [Our Country's Progressive Path], NP 8 (Feb. 1918), pp. 61–64, and NP 9 (Mar. 1918), pp. 125–31.

60. PNTV 84 (28 May 1931), 88 (25 June 1931), 106 (29 Oct. 1931), 113 (17 Dec. 1931), and 201 (25 May 1933); Nguyen Gy, *Long Nguyen Vong cua Quoc Dan Viet Nam* (Hanoi, 1933), pp. 11–24.

61. PNTV 30 (28 Nov. 1929), 44 (20 Mar. 1930), 45 (27 Mar. 1930), 46 (3 Apr. 1930), 61 (17 July 1930), 70 (18 Sept. 1930), 121 (3 Mar. 1932), 170 (29 Sept. 1932), and 187 (16 Feb. 1933). For further discussion, see Alexander Woodside, "Development of Social Organizations in Vietnamese Cities in the Late Colonial Period," *Pacific Affairs*, vol. XLIV, no. 1 (Spring 1971), pp. 39–64.

Such attention to new social organizations inevitably raised questions about old familial and quasi-familial relationships. Here conservatives were caught in a serious dilemma, wanting to retain the "spirit" of traditional personal ties, yet often having to concede that successful modern groups demanded impersonal bylaws, membership criteria, functional specialization, and technocratic knowledge. Indeed, the very idea that one's new organizational position could somehow supersede one's previous status as scholar, peasant, artisan, or merchant (*si-nong-cong-thuong*)—not to mention father, son, husband, or wife—was potentially quite disruptive. Iconoclasts picked up this theme with glee, denouncing the familial system for having retarded Vietnamese historical development and launching slashing attacks on such continuing practices as arranged marriages, indentured servanthood, extended-family hierarchies, and village leadership according to status rather than ability. As long as Vietnam remained a family-centered culture, one writer argued, nation and society both would be like a pile of sand—plenty of tiny, hard units, but almost no larger cohesiveness.[62]

What, then, was to provide that cohesiveness? For some, the answer was an almost mystical national awareness. Years before, Phan Boi Chau had taken up the old images of "unity of hearts" (*dong tam*) and "great unity" (*dai dong*) and given them lyric, patriotic significance. He and other scholar-gentry leaders had worked tirelessly to raise political identifications from king to country, from personal loyalty to love of nation. Vietnam's precolonial status as a major power in mainland Southeast Asia had been lauded and credit shifted to the people rather than the ruling dynasties. The geographical shape, size, and specific boundaries of Vietnam assumed new importance. New concepts like "Fatherland" (*To Quoc*), "countrymen" (*dong bao*), and "citizen" (*quoc dan*) had entered the Vietnamese vocabulary permanently. Individuals might not have had a "State" (*Nha Nuoc*) to identify with, but they did have an idealized total community.[63]

Twenty years after Phan Boi Chau, Tran Huu Do was still driving away at the same themes. Like his predecessor, Tran Huu Do was most infuriated by the relative ease with which the Vietnamese monarchy and most of the mandarinate had been deceived, outmaneuvered, overwhelmed, and then enlisted as servants by the French "alien race" (*di chung*). Both were immensely proud of Vietnam's precolonial capacities, especially when confronting the Chinese, yet both believed that the success of French pacification policies had served to expose a number of serious Vietnamese character weaknesses. In proposing remedies,

---

62. Dao Duy Anh, *Viet Nam Van Hoa Su Cuong* [Outline History of Vietnamese Culture] (Hanoi, 1938), pp. 121–22, 326–28. The author was of the opinion, however, that changes in the colonial economic, social, and educational systems were already producing major changes in the Vietnamese family, quite aside from the question of who wanted this to happen and who did not.

63. Marr, *Vietnamese Anticolonialism*, pp. 138–39, 166–67, 210–11, 227–28; Tran Van Giau, SPT-2, pp. 83–86, 159–60.

Tran Huu Do was perhaps more concrete than Phan Boi Chau, often returning to ideas for heightening differentiation between "we" (*ta*) and "outside peoples" (*nguoi ngoai*), that is, between Vietnamese as a group and alien races and nations. Nothing could sharpen this feeling more quickly, he suggested, than foreign travel and study of foreign examples, which would lead Vietnamese to appreciate exactly how their own language, customs, laws, and spirit differed from others'. Tran Huu Do professed not to be worried that some Vietnamese might become too enamored of foreign practices. They could praise another nation to the skies, he said, just so long as they served none but their own.[64]

During the 1920s, however, Vietnamese intellectuals increasingly looked upon nationalism as either outmoded or as only one component in the overall prescription for salvation. They began to suspect that social solidarity stemmed from a number of factors both more complicated than lyric patriotism and more subject to rational analysis and reinforcement. When the French succeeded in smashing the Viet Nam Quoc Dan Dang (Vietnam Nationalist Party) in 1929–30, "unity of hearts" rhetoric went into permanent decline. It was replaced by the concept of *doan ket*—literally, "groups fastened together"—a very different image of human motivation and activity.

Kant versus Bentham

Limiting ourselves for the moment to ethical (as distinct from political) problems of relating the individual and society, Vietnamese intellectuals of this period wishing to part company with Confucianism were attracted by two Western schools of thought: Kantian idealism and utilitarianism. Actually, Kant was probably singled out in the first instance because of certain affinities with Neo-Confucianism, which could now be restated in a more prestigious "Western" philosophical context. Thus, both Kant and the Neo-Confucianists accepted virtue a priori and presented life as a quest for the ultimate good. Kant's call to individuals to act in such a way that what they willed might also be thought of as universal laws was simply a more "rational" expression of the sage in search of the Way (*Dao*)—or so some Vietnamese might feel. As one writer argued by way of concrete example, Kant's principle meant that individual acts as drastic as suicide or as routine as laziness could be firmly classed as immoral, since it was obvious that if everyone acted in these ways the results would be disastrous. Instead, each person had to develop good intent, focus his willpower, and try to live every moment according to the categorical imperative. Duty (*nghia vu*) existed outside and above questions of nature, experience, human emotion, or practical

64. Tran Huu Do, *Hoi Trong Tu Do*, vol. 3, pp. 3–5, 10–14; ibid., vol. 2 (1926), p. 4; idem, *Tieng Chuong Truy Hon* [The Bell Which Calls Up Souls] (Saigon, 1925), p. 16. There is no evidence that the author himself ever traveled out of Vietnam.

achievement.[65] Or, as Pham Quynh had put it fifteen years earlier, Kant made pure morality determine the content of philosophy, rather than the reverse.[66]

However, there was a new and potentially subversive component of Kantian idealism that did not escape Vietnamese readers. Unlike the "humaneness" (*nhan*) of Neo-Confucian philosophy, Kant's pure reason claimed to stand above history, traditional precedent, and custom. At any moment, each individual could *will* a moral ideal that was both rational and unselfish. Those who realized this could experience real exultation and a sense of freedom from routine constraints or desires. Self-determined devotion to principle might thus become a new faith.[67] Going a step further, if enough Vietnamese chose immortality and perfection of mankind as a whole over the transitory happiness of the individual in society, this might be the basis of an ideology of liberation. Nguyen An Ninh clearly had this in mind when he argued passionately the need for each individual to make a conscious choice between filial piety and the just cause.[68]

A French Catholic priest, undoubtedly conversant with the intricate European debates for and against Kant in the previous century, took it upon himself to warn the Vietnamese of hidden dangers. In particular, he said, Kantian idealism left open the possibility of two different groups equally certain of their moral righteousness proceeding to fight each other to the bloody end, and only afterward might it be possible to judge who was right and who wrong. Giving the point contemporary relevance, he labeled one group as people who believed in "determinist morality." Their philosophy deserved condemnation because it lightened personal responsibility for actions, undermined the power of laws, and eroded fear of punishment. Rhetorically the priest asked, "Other than God, to whom is the individual responsible, before what court is he to go to pay for his sins?"[69] Clearly it was the Church for him. Most Vietnamese would never share his implicit answer, or even grant "God" a role, but the question of the individual in relation to various "courts" (History, Fate, Science, the State, the Party, the People) remained a vital one.

Utilitarianism came to Vietnam by many routes and took many shapes. As early as the 1860s Nguyen Truong To (1828–71), a Vietnamese Catholic possessing both Confucian and Western training, argued in memorials to King Tu Duc

65. Do Duc Vuong, *May Thuyet ve Luan Ly* [Some Theories on Morality], pamphlet reprint from the *Bulletin de la Société d'enseignement mutuel du Tonkin*, vol. XVI (Jul.–Dec. 1936), p. 13.

66. Pham Quynh, "Khao ve cac Luan Ly Hoc Thuyet cua Thai Tay" [An Examination of Western Moral Doctrines], NP 49 (July 1921), p. 12.

67. Do Duc Vuong, *May Thuyet ve Luan Ly*, p. 12.

68. Nguyen An Ninh, *Hai Ba Trung* [The Trung Sisters] (Saigon, 1928), pp. 37–38.

69. Rev. Père Hue, "Luan Ly doi voi Khoa Hoc the nao?" [How Does Morality Relate to Science?], NP 49 (July 1921), pp. 14–20.

that the forces of nature had to be studied before all else, since man's supreme position among beings was based on his mastery of steam, water, wind, and rain. Economic production was prerequisite to any social organization, Nguyen Truong To affirmed, after which came laws, political system, and culture (in that order). God created the elements to be used for the betterment of humanity, he said, and those who appreciated this paid first attention to "concentrating strength and amassing profit" (doc suc phu loi), leaving literature, laws, and customs for later. Nguyen Truong To then proposed scores of reforms, from geological surveys and savings banks to expanded foreign trade and modern armament factories.[70] Not surprisingly, very few of his ideas found support at court, and those that did were never implemented systematically.

After the collapse of armed resistance to the French, some Vietnamese literati re-read Nguyen Truong To's memorials and avidly sought out the more recent Chinese reformist publications. By 1905-08 they were clearly cognizant of Adam Smith's thesis that the wealth of nations was founded on "enlightened self-interest." A few even tried to establish small commercial or industrial companies, quite a shock to their contemporaries. As one recent commentator has phrased it:

Up until the beginning of the twentieth century a literatus spoke only about humaneness, righteousness, ritual, knowledge, and sincerity. Where would one ever find him talking about needles and thread, buttons and soap?[71]

Nevertheless, these literati-turned-businessmen were still in many ways bound to their earlier training. What really interested them was the anticipated social response to their teaching by example, not questions of how they themselves might make or sell better needles and thread. Their minds remained fixed on the abstract national advantages of, for example, capital formation, new techniques, reduced reliance on imports, and outmaneuvering the local Chinese. They never faced up to the role of personal gain (loi)—their own or anyone else's—in this grand endeavor. As a result, they not only made poor individual capitalists but failed to advance the discussion of public-private welfare linkages very far.

In the years immediately following World War I a tiny native bourgeoisie tried hard to assert itself. The War had stimulated Vietnamese entrepreneurial activity, and, in the face of renewed French and Chinese competition, the call now went out for people to abandon old anti-mercantile attitudes and join the fray. Vietnamese periodicals were filled with straightforward odes to capitalism. Some articles told readers how to become wealthy. Others provided background information on the growth of industry, transport, and trade in nineteenth-century

70. Tran Van Giau, SPT-1, pp. 381-405.

71. Tran Van Giau, SPT-2, p. 57. For a very brief description of these scholar-gentry business ventures, see Marr, Vietnamese Anticolonialism, pp. 179-81.

Europe, on the functions of money and banking in modern societies, or on the strange commercial schools turning out future entrepreneurs in France. Closer to home, some writers demanded to know why so few Vietnamese had the "stomach for getting rich." By way of contrast, they praised individuals like Bach Thai Buoi who had managed to acquire wealth outside the standard landlord and officeholding scenarios. Proposals were made for a Vietnamese-controlled bank, as well as a merchant association aimed against the Chinese (but not the French).[72] There was even an attempt in Saigon in 1919 to boycott Chinese firms, but it did not succeed.[73]

The highpoint of Vietnamese entrepreneurial proselytizing probably occurred in Saigon in 1924–25 as part of a campaign to eliminate certain French and Chinese monopolies and to loosen civil and economic restrictions in general. This, too, foundered. Vietnamese bourgeois leaders soon lost the initiative to younger activist intellectuals who had less of a stake in the future of native capitalism. With the advent of the Great Depression, another cry was heard for support of Vietnamese companies, many of which were now in danger of bankruptcy. In *Phu Nu Tan Van*, for example, there was special praise for the valiant struggle of the fledgling Bank of Vietnam. A well-known businessman, Diep Van Ky, contributed a detailed essay on money, banking, and currency exchange systems. The precipitous fall in the world price of rice shocked a number of individuals into writing plaintive articles proposing immediate government assistance.[74] Throughout this period and beyond, books and pamphlets were published bearing such evocative titles as "Paragons of How to Get Rich," "Buying Cheap and Selling Dear," "Forty-one Occupations Requiring Little Capital," and "Wealth is Better than Nobility."[75]

Not surprisingly, many Vietnamese traditionalists found such talk repugnant. Often they expressed themselves in simple, passionate comments about how moral standards had degenerated to the point where those who gathered the

---

72. The *Tribune Indigène*, organ of the small Constitutionalist Party of Cochinchina, was perhaps most vociferous in presenting these ideas. However, it is remarkable that the more bureaucratic-oriented Hanoi monthly *Nam Phong* published ten distinctly entrepreneurial articles in the brief period from May 1919 to June 1920. After that, either *Nam Phong*'s editors lost interest or the French overseers advised curtailment.

73. Ralph B. Smith, "Bui Quang Chieu and the Constitutionalist Party in French Cochinchina, 1917–30," *Modern Asian Studies*, vol. 3, no. 2 (1969), pp. 135–36.

74. PNTV 41 (27 Feb. 1930), 231 (11 Jan. 1934), 245–47 (7–21 June 1934), 248 (28 June 1934), and 249 (5 July 1934). The owner-publishers of the PNTV, Nguyen Duc Nhuan and spouse, were prominent Saigon importers and wholesale-retail merchants.

75. Tien Long Thuong Doan, *Guong Lam Giau* (Hanoi, 1929); Dang Huu Nghia, *Mua May Ban Dat* (Hanoi, 1933); Ban Cong Nghe Bien Tap, *Sach Day Lam 41 Nghe It Von* (Hanoi, 1941); Ngo The Pho and Tran Trung Vien, *Giau Hon Sang* (Hanoi, 1936).

An advertisement for Vietnamese textiles. The title reads "Economic Warfare . . . Chinese silk vanquished by 'Fragrant River' silk." Saigon, 1931. Courtesy of the Bibliothèque Nationale.

most money could achieve the greatest power.[76] Nguyen Ba Hoc, whom we have met before, extolled the intimate pleasures of family life as opposed to total preoccupation with the savage competition to get rich.[77] His short stories (a pioneer effort in this genre) regularly explored the tension between traditional values and the enticements of modern education, material convenience, and sensual pleasure.[78] Duong Ba Trac published a book-length essay despairing over the decline of Confucian morality under pressure of bourgeois fixations on money, prestige, and power.[79]

It is important to note, however, that Nguyen Ba Hoc the family man also published an essay on economics—because, he said, "animal desires" (*thi duc*)

76. See, for example, Nguyen Van Minh and Nguyen Van Khai, *Hoc Sinh Tu Tri* [Student Self-Edification] (Hanoi, 1930). Interestingly enough, the authors believed that only the idealistic youth of Vietnam could reconstitute a legitimate elite (*thuong luu*).

77. Nguyen Ba Hoc, "Co gan lam giau" [Endeavoring to Become Rich], NP 23 (May 1919), pp. 404–09.

78. In particular, see Nguyen Ba Hoc's stories in NP 10 (Apr. 1918), 26 (Aug. 1919), 35 (May 1920), and 43 (Jan. 1921).

79. Duong Ba Trac, *Tieng Goi Dan* [A Call from the Rostrum] (Hanoi, 1925).

should not be neglected.[80] His short stories did not really condemn getting rich per se, only the common inability to maintain spiritual rectitude in the process.[81] Duong Ba Trac criticized contemporary requirements for money to obtain formal education for one's children; yet when the time came to propose changes, he lamely suggested increased attention to extra-curricular learning.[82] The monthly Nam Phong, for which both men wrote prolifically, mirrored these growing contradictions in other ways. A debate occurred, for example, over whether people should continue to bring gifts to mandarins or not. In response to criticism, Than Trong Hue and several other officials proposed the formation of a society to protect the "interests" (quyen loi) of mandarins—an idea that would have profoundly shocked all literati only a few decades earlier.[83] Pham Quynh, Nam Phong's editor, accepted the need for students to think of themselves and family before they could think of their country, and he translated an obscure American writer to argue that it might be necessary for Vietnam to pursue Western materialist concepts before returning to Eastern spiritual priorities.[84] Printed side-by-side with articles, poems, and classical passages extolling the five cardinal virtues, such talk must have raised fundamental questions in the minds of readers.

As understood in Vietnam in the 1920s, utilitarianism not only meant that individuals had a "natural" desire to enjoy the pleasures and escape the pains of life, but that this innate tendency, if dealt with rationally and purposefully, could be the foundation of a social system bringing happiness and security to the greatest numbers. A society was most viable (and conceivably most moral) when it made the fullest possible use of individual ingenuity and intelligence to control nature, transform matter, and develop new ways to benefit the many instead of just the few. To begin to accomplish this in Vietnam, the individual had to be freed from traditional particularistic bonds, be encouraged to form entirely new social relationships, and be given the protection of a firm, impersonal legal system.

Even for those who accepted these principles there remained problems, however. Most obviously, a number of writers otherwise supportive of exuberant anti-traditionalism were still troubled by what they regarded as excessive "individualism" (ca nhan chu nghia) among the new generation. For example, Tran Huu Do, who upheld the need to destroy many old attitudes and practices, also felt

80. Nguyen Ba Hoc, "May dieu yeu-luoc ve kinh-te-hoc" [Outline of Economics], NP 45 (Mar. 1921), pp. 200–20; NP 46 (Apr. 1921), pp. 290–95.

81. Indeed, several of Nguyen Ba Hoc's other stories dwell on individuals who accomplish this feat. NP 13 (July 1918) and NP 34 (May 1919).

82. Duong Ba Trac, Tieng Goi Dan, pp. 134–35.

83. NP 26 (Aug. 1919), 27 (Sept. 1919), 28 (Oct. 1919), and 43 (Feb. 1921). Apparently the debate was stimulated by a series of articles in the Courrier d'Haiphong.

84. NP 29 (Nov. 1919) and NP 36 (June 1920). The American was G. L. Dickinson.

the need to caricature those young intellectuals who quoted Greek hedonists or Russian anarchists to excuse egoistic behavior, or those who employed Jeremy Bentham and Adam Smith as sanction for concentrating on personal or family aggrandizement. Still others, he said, took solace in romanticism, composed tear-drenched verses, and wrung their hands at the slightest obstacle. There were also the total cynics, the sarcastic attackers of any coherent position, and those he termed the meek at heart and the resigned fatalists.[85]

Although not entirely comfortable with the idea, Tran Huu Do was willing to agree that each individual acted out of selfish needs and desires. Nevertheless, he added quickly, individuals had to understand that they could not gratify their own needs for long without the protection that a group offered, both against the depredations of other group members (this was the function of laws) and, even more importantly, against the constant threat of attack and subjugation by outsiders. It was not the self and society that were antagonistic, he said, but rather the self and slavish dependence on others, either local dictators or foreign colonialists.[86] He argued that self and society actually complemented each other, made each other possible. Without courageous, dynamic, self-assertive individuals (his favorite examples were Moses, Luther, Columbus, George Washington, and Sun Yat-sen), society would not flourish and the state could not remain independent. Equally, without structure and, above all, a stern legal system applying to everyone, the individual could not hope to find his rightful place in the sun. In a sense the self was the soft, responsive core of Tran Huu Do's ideal construct, while group solidarity was the tough protective shell. Though the self and the group were mutually supportive, group solidarity was paramount in times of great challenge. The liberty of the individual, which John Stuart Mill had considered an end in itself, became for Tran Huu Do a means at best.

The ethical implications of a system revering self-assertion were also troubling to many. At the state level it seemed to mean the law of the jungle. Pham Quynh, for example, who often cited international conflicts as a prime reason why Vietnamese should be content to live under French "protection," was apparently very upset when a member of the French parliament proposed to solve metropolitan financial problems stemming from World War I by simply selling Indochina "like a piece of merchandise" to Great Britain or the United States.[87] On the other hand, for Tran Huu Do such episodes merely reaffirmed that in the real world

85. Tran Huu Do, *Tieng Chuong Truy Hon*, pp. 3–11.

86. Tran Huu Do, *Hoi Trong Tu Do*, vol. 1, pp. 4–7. Here the author's discussion clearly relied heavily on the earlier writings of Liang Ch'i-ch'ao. See Hao Chang, *Liang Ch'i-ch'ao and Intellectual Transition in China, 1890–1907* (Cambridge, Mass.: Harvard Univ. Press, 1971), pp. 95–112.

87. "Dong Phap bao gio van la Dong Phap" [French Indochina Will Always Be French Indochina], NP 37 (July 1920), p. 83.

might makes right. It did no good whatsoever for people who had lost their liberty to sit around discussing the immorality of the chief jailer or his rotten native turnkeys. What was needed was a thorough assessment of the objective situation, careful organization, and a well-executed break-out to regain power from the aliens. In short, it was as "natural" for the French, British, Dutch, and Americans to want to dominate others, to be the masters of large numbers of dependent peoples, as it should be for the dependent peoples to want to throw them out.[88] As we shall see later, very few Vietnamese, including Tran Huu Do himself, could remain satisfied with such statements of moral equivalence between exploiter and exploited.

At the personal level there is not a great deal of evidence that individual freedom, new organizational affiliations, and new judicial procedures produced a "new morality"; on the contrary, stories abounded of young men and women who committed suicide, dissipated themselves with opium, caught venereal diseases, or suffocated in the lucre extracted from their family's tenants and workers. Private organizations tended to become vehicles for simple self-protection or predatory action against others. Thus, in Hue in 1927, there was founded a royal relatives' self-protection society, complete with published constitution and by-laws.[89] Various non-regal lineages proceeded to follow suit.[90] The same pattern of narrow interest identification was apparent in most of the new professional, religious, regional, and school alumni associations. As for the colonial legal system, there is little doubt that it was used more to enlarge the privileges of the few than to defend the rights of the many.

Vietnamese Marxist Ethics

In actual fact, Vietnamese peasants and workers were not sitting around waiting for landlords and businessmen to experience a moral awakening. Increasingly they realized that organized self-protection was a game poor people in colonial Vietnam could play too, albeit never with the same favorable odds as the rich. During the 1920s, organizational forms and much of the underlying ideology remained traditional. Peasants still looked to mutual-aid groups, sworn brotherhoods, and religious sects, while workers tried to cluster together in quasi-familial protective associations. By the end of the 1930s, however, conditions had changed

88. Tran Huu Do, *To Co Mat Quyen Tu Do* [The Causes of Our Loss of Freedom] (Saigon, 1926), pp. 66–67; idem, *Hoi Trong Tu Do*, vol. 2, pp. 5–6. The author also pointed out that the Vietnamese had earlier dominated the Cham, Khmer, and various highland peoples in the same fashion.

89. Dong Ton Tuong Te Pho, *Chuong Trinh* [Program] (Hue, 1930).

90. Cao Thi To Tu, *Cao Gia Toc Bo* [Genealogy of the Cao Family], 2 vols. (Saigon, 1938); *Minh Huong Gia Thanh Hoi Quan* [Ming-Origin Ancestral Honor Association] (Saigon, 1931). ("Ming-origin" refers to families of several different lineages who fled China in the seventeenth century and settled in the Mekong delta area.)

dramatically: most workers and not a few peasants now had some experience with unions, strikes, support groups, demonstrations, and public meetings. Rather than simply wrapping themselves in crypto-royalist symbolism and rhetoric, leaders now knew how to formulate grievances, publicize demands, negotiate settlements—and pick up the pieces when the enemy struck back, as he always did. Many of these skills were learned from the intelligentsia, either through direct association or by emulation. The high attrition rate among radical activists due to jailing, illness, and loss of commitment ensured that the intelligentsia would not monopolize leadership positions entirely.

As growing numbers of Vietnamese came to call themselves Marxists or Marxist-Leninists, they began to approach moral questions from a different perspective. True, many gravitated to Marxism out of a sense of moral outrage at French colonial injustice and exploitation. Ho Chi Minh, for example, was until 1925 almost entirely preoccupied with the inhumanity of colonialism and the need for all oppressed peoples to join together to liquidate this scourge of the earth.[91] Clearly he believed that the Vietnamese had learned something in their several thousand years of social experience, in particular, the sophistry of arguing that one could remove evil from aggression or even render aggression laudable. Addressing himself to conditions in other French colonies as well as Vietnam, Ho Chi Minh stated angrily, "If one has a white skin, one is automatically a civilizer. And when one is a civilizer, one can commit the acts of a savage while remaining the most civilized."[92] "Colonization is theft," another author had affirmed; Ho Chi Minh felt compelled to add "rape, and assassination."[93] Nguyen An Ninh, no less influential than Ho Chi Minh during this period, took up the same attack eight years later and directed it specifically against Social Darwinism.[94] Younger Vietnamese were no less infuriated. One communist activist recalled how upset she had been as a teenager to witness Frenchmen and their lackeys encouraging Vietnamese to scramble and struggle against each other for small amounts of money at an annual festival commemorating victory in World War I.[95] Another

91. Nguyen Ai Quoc, *Truyen va Ky* (Hanoi, 1974). Included are six French-language articles of the period 1922-25, with accompanying Vietnamese translations by Pham Huy Thong. See also Bernard B. Fall, ed., *Ho Chi Minh on Revolution* (New York, 1967), pp. 21-126. While Ho Chi Minh wrote most of these articles for a French Left audience, trying to heighten their anger at what their government was doing to others, there is no reason to believe he did not stand by every word.

92. Fall, ed., *Ho Chi Minh on Revolution*, p. 87.

93. Ibid., p. 110.

94. Nguyen An Ninh, *Ton Giao* (Saigon, 1932), pp. 1-7, 21-27.

95. Ton Thi Que, *Chi Mot Cong Duong* [Only One Road] (Nghe An, 1972), p. 8. A similar revolting experience occurred to Nguyen Thi Minh Khai when she returned from Europe aboard a British vessel and observed colonial couples tossing coins to urchins in the shark-infested waters below. Nguyet Tu, *Chi Minh Khai* (Hanoi, 1976), pp. 73-75.

cadre remembered his satisfaction when for the first time in 1930 plantation workers under his leadership refused to break ranks as the French manager tossed handfuls of coins on the ground in front of them at a *Tet* observance.[96]

While the perennial conflict between oppressor and oppressed remained extremely important to Vietnamese Marxist-Leninists, they had no monopoly over that issue. From a moral viewpoint, at least, it was probably the peculiar Marxist combination of materialist self-interest and idealistic claims regarding the perfection of human character that kept many Vietnamese involved, even at considerable risk to themselves. Thus, on the one hand, individuals were expected—indeed, encouraged—to ascertain and uphold their needs and desires to the fullest extent possible. Human society being organized into economic classes, individuals would normally find the most advantage in joining with those who shared the same relationship to the mode of production—and against those who did not. Consequent struggles for control of the means of production served to propel the advance of human history.

There is no doubt that Vietnamese Marxist-Leninists took this interpretation of self-interest seriously. For example, the ICP's 1932 program called on particular components of the population "to sacrifice because of class affiliation, to struggle because of self-interest."[97] A 1930 internal directive spoke of the need to "exploit every opportunity to draw the masses into struggle in as short a time as possible."[98] The unprecedented use of "exploit" (*loi dung*) in a favorable sense highlighted the shift in political outlook. A Party periodical of the same period printed the following statement on its masthead: "The Communist Party is a growing, developing struggle organization, not a finished group of flawless, ethical beings."[99] Clearly, the individuals who drafted such arguments wanted to create not a bastion for select moral men but an instrument of power. Rather than grouping together as fellow classmates, fellow provincials, or fellow bureaucrats in order to praise each other's conduct and attack that of outsiders, as had been the model before, they would voice the aspirations of specific classes, strata, and minority elements, then try to piece together a viable united front to overthrow the French colonialists and Vietnamese propertied elite.

On the other hand, it cannot be denied that those Vietnamese Marxist-Leninists who chose immortality and perfection of mankind as a whole over salvation of the individual in the immediate world were rated as exemplary revolution-

---

96. Tran Tu Binh, *Phu Rieng Do* (Hanoi, 1971), pp. 96–97. This episode was prelude to a bitter strike and numerous arrests.

97. *Chuong Trinh Hanh Dong cua Dang Cong San Dong Duong* [Action Program of the ICP] (n.p., 1932), p. 34.

98. Instructions for the month of November 1930 from the Northern Region Committee to Party branches. AOM (Aix), GG Series F-7F4, vol. 5.

99. *Co Do* [Red Flag], 3 (3 July 1930), reproduced in AOM (Aix), GG Series F-7F4, vol. 4.

aries.[100] Immortality lay in what one did and what one left behind for subsequent generations.[101] In this sense, exemplary individuals made the moral decision to deny themselves present gains in favor of rewards for posterity, be it their own children and grandchildren or perhaps a more abstract community. While it was never claimed that all Party members met these criteria all the time, the pressure on cadres to lead spotless personal lives and be totally dedicated to the cause was considerable. By the same token, those who opposed the Revolution, for whatever reason, were not only considered morally inferior but were expected to visibly manifest that inferiority. Thus, in March 1945, a French colonel commanding an artillery unit fleeing the Japanese, having approached to purchase food and request safe passage to the Sino-Vietnamese frontier, was described by a Viet Minh cadre as follows:

> His face was flushed from having to carry his potbelly up the stairs. His beard looked like a broom, and his blue eyes appeared to be turning white. His long face was dripping with sweat. Although he tried to maintain a dignified bearing, it only made him look more ridiculous. His normal manner of breathing out fire and brimstone must have been lost somewhere along the trail, for now he simply had the forlorn appearance of a commander beaten in battle.[102]

When the Frenchman saluted rigidly and clicked his heels to signal his departure, the Vietnamese cadre purposefully kept his hands in his pockets. The small Viet Minh unit later ambushed the colonel's column and allegedly reaped 500 rifles, six mortars, and more than 100 horses. Whatever the facts of this entire confrontation, the cadre's description was more an exercise in theater than an attempt at objective reporting.

How, then, did Communist Party ethics differ from Confucian ethics? First of all, whereas the Confucian elite had tended to view the peasants as the passive recipients of a moral indoctrination which could improve their attitudes but not their status, Communist cadres sought to create valued new statuses for the impoverished, and encouraged them "to resist their social degradation, both as a situation and as a category of thought, themselves."[103]

---

100. For a particularly interesting account of ten martyrdoms prior to the August 1945 Revolution, see *Guong Chien Dau cua Nhung Nguoi Cong San* [Struggle Paragons among Communist Individuals], 3rd edition (Hanoi, 1965).

101. Nguyen An Ninh, *Ton Giao*, p. 34. Pham Hung (b. 1912), sentenced to death in 1931 on political charges, used this same argument to convince his cellmates, three common criminals, that they should stop their petty harassment of the Corsican guards, help other prisoners, and learn how to read, on the possibility that their death sentences would be commuted. One was guillotined, but the others survived. Pham Hung, "Trong Xa Lim An Chem" [In the Death Cell], *Tren Duong Cach Mang* [On the Road to Revolution] (Hanoi, 1960), pp. 34–41. Pham Hung is today fourth-ranking leader of the Vietnam Communist Party.

102. Le Thiet Hung, "Lay Sung" [Getting Guns], *Rung Yen The*, p. 46.

103. I have borrowed this argument from Woodside, "Development of Social Organizations," p. 54, but have used it in a rather different context.

Secondly, the centuries-old stigma attached to selfish motivation (*loi*) was significantly reduced. Confucianists had normally argued that nothing good came from legitimizing material or sensual urges. Vietnamese Marxists-Leninists set as one of their most important tasks the "awakening" of great numbers of people to their own material self-interests.[104] Of course, had they not already been convinced that the vast majority of Vietnamese were poor and oppressed, and that causing this majority to become much more conscious of their status was a prerequisite to revolutionary victory, the contrast might well have been less striking.[105] As it was, Party characterizations of the "authentic" interests of various classes and strata changed often, leading one to conclude that applying dialectical materialism in practice was fully as complicated as defining the Way in traditional ideology.

Thirdly, one cannot overemphasize the elements of energy, dynamism, struggle, and progress that pervaded radical formulations of the period, designed specifically to counter alleged traditional preferences for quietude, fatalism, harmony, and comforting repetition.[106] This aggressive reinterpretation of the world applied not only to relations between the individual and society, but also between society and Nature. Briefly stated, it was no longer cosmological ethical interaction that served as the immutable principle, nor even Hsün-tzu's more "modern" organizational concentration, but rather the perceived capacity of man to use his body and mind to confront and overcome most natural and social obstacles. Although some prominent Western scientists, philosophers and artists were coming to question this article of faith, they do not appear to have influenced the thinking of Vietnamese Communists of this period.

Finally, the centrality of the family in Vietnamese society was criticized and a more complex model of social interaction advanced. Henceforth, Marxist-Leninists argued, the individual should also be linked to interest groups, classes, "peoplehood" (*dan toc*), national citizenship, and the exploited majority of humanity in general. Along with this model came a serious effort to organize around ideology, political strategy, and leadership ability rather than personalities, regional ties, or ascriptive relationships. That this endeavor has been far from a total success does not diminish the significance of the relative changes in attitude that occurred. For example, the operative concept of *doan ket*, literally meaning "groups fastened together," should not be confused with either the particularistic,

---

104. Tran Van Giau, SPT-2, pp. 372–73, points up this distinction in relation to a 1936 Taoist text, but his comment applies equally to earlier Confucian writings.

105. In his *Duong Kach Menh* (1926), Ho Chi Minh asserts flatly that "the more a person is oppressed, the more lasting is his revolutionary spirit, and the more determined his revolutionary intent." (Dang Cong San Viet Nam, *Cac To Chuc Tien Than cua Dang* [The Party's Organizational Forebearers] (Hanoi, 1977), p. 24.) One is led to inquire, then, why small peasant proprietors rather than tenant farmers or agricultural laborers seem to have served as the backbone of the Viet Minh.

106. This radical assault on harmony is treated further in chapter 7.

hierarchical family model or the utopian "great unity" (*dai dong*). It seems to imply a social and political structure maximizing common interests yet allowing for objective differences. Nevertheless, quasi-familial viewpoints remain imbedded in the Vietnamese language, and Communist political symbolism reflects that condition. Although the extended family is of far less significance now than before, the nuclear family remains a key social element. As for "great unity," this historically resonant term is often employed when referring to the ultimate dialectical stage, "communism," while at other times writers assert it as a contemporary ideal, or even reality.[107] Thus, past, present, and future sometimes tend to merge in distinctly un-Marxian fashion.

More than any other prominent Vietnamese Communist, Ho Chi Minh was conscious of this continuing ambiguity in social identifications and ideals. He seems to have decided that in the top-priority struggle against the foreigner these internal Vietnamese ambiguities need not always be attacked frontally; indeed, they might occasionally be turned to tactical advantage. We have already seen how Ho Chi Minh, upon returning to Vietnam in 1941, projected a personal image which combined the austere self-improvement ethic of the Confucian literatus with certain new traits such as a passion for punctuality, for physical fitness, and for the simple direct speech of the ordinary Vietnamese villager (which he definitely was not). Ho Chi Minh's status as quasi-familial "Uncle" to his countrymen (who were thus his "nieces and nephews") is also well known.[108] Less well known are the family-like atmosphere that he worked hard to develop among close comrades and his insistence that Party cadres on the move fit themselves properly into the families of local supporters, even if they were only going to be present for a day or two.[109] Family metaphors cropped up constantly in Ho Chi Minh's conversations; in the mid-1930s he criticized Vietnamese comrades in the Soviet Union, saying that a handful of activists who failed to be fraternal towards each other could hardly expect to unite the entire Vietnamese people;[110]

---

107. A variation is the ideal of "One for all, all for one," sometimes used in relation to future social goals, sometimes as a current Party standard. See, for example, Tran Van Giau, SPT-2, p. 375.

108. Until the August 1945 Revolution, the more reverential yet distant term "great-grandfather" (*cu*) was often heard in popular references to Nguyen Ai Quoc (Ho Chi Minh), presumably reflecting his near-legendary wanderings abroad and association with anticolonial literati like Phan Boi Chau and Phan Chu Trinh. After his death, Ho Chi Minh again became officially known as "great-grandfather," but remained "uncle" in informal discussions.

109. Possibly the best available account of personal relations with Ho Chi Minh is contained in Vo Nguyen Giap, *Nhung Nam Thang Khong The Nao Quen* [Unforgettable Months and Years], 2 vols. (Hanoi, 1970 and 1975), translated and published by the Foreign Languages Publishing House as *Unforgettable Days* (Hanoi, 1975). Another valuable set of memoirs is Hoai Thanh et al., *Bac Ho, Hoi Ky* [Memoirs about Uncle Ho] (Hanoi, 1960), translated as *Days with Ho Chi Minh* (Hanoi: FLPH, 1962).

110. Hoai Thanh et al., *Days with Ho Chi Minh*, p. 141.

in October 1946 he appealed for northern, central and southern Vietnamese to regard themselves as three brothers of one family. "Since no one can divide the members of one family," he claimed, "no one can divide our Vietnam."[111]

At the time of the August 1945 Revolution, "Fatherland Altars" (*Ban Tho To Quoc*) were set up in many quarters of Hanoi. While the form was obviously borrowed from traditional ancestral ceremonies, the content aimed at rousing further patriotic enthusiasm, at impressing individuals with the "sacred nature" of new citizenship duties, and at welcoming recruits into the armed forces.[112] In the same way, Ho Chi Minh repeatedly exhorted everyone to be "loyal" (*trung*) to the Fatherland and "pious" (*hieu*) toward the People—a conscious relating of Confucian moral prescriptions and new political identifications.[113] At the most important public appearance of his life, ceremonies of September 2, 1945 establishing the Democratic Republic of Vietnam, Ho Chi Minh presented himself to the people as a new synthesis of ideologies. After some deliberation he had chosen to wear neither the black tunic of the traditional literatus nor the white linen suit of the intelligentsia, but an old worker's cap, a military-style khaki tunic with high collar, and white rubber sandals. Vo Nguyen Giap's further description is worth quoting at length:

The Old Man moved at a brisk pace. This surprised quite a few people then because they did not see in the President the slow and elegant gait of a "nobleman." He spoke with a faint accent of someone from the countryside of Nghe An province. Uncle appeared in this manner in front of one million people that day. His voice was calm, warm, precise and clear. It was not the eloquent voice people were used to hearing on solemn ceremonies. But people immediately sensed in it profound sentiments and a determined spirit. It was full of life, and each word, each sentence pierced everyone's heart. Halfway through reading the Declaration of Independence, Uncle stopped and suddenly asked, "Can you hear what I'm saying?" One million people answered in unison, their voices resounding like thunder: "Y. . .es!!" From that moment, Uncle and the sea of people became one.[114]

When organizing other expressions of public solidarity the Viet Minh sometimes borrowed a leaf from the French book. At a flag-raising ceremony in Hue in late 1945, for example, a Vietnamese journalist recorded the following:

A bugle sounded. All citizens within earshot became silent and turned toward the flagpole. Frolicking children stopped in their tracks. Elders sipping their morning tea stood up. Women on the adjacent river ceased rowing. A rickshaw man pulling a foreigner halted abruptly and stood at attention, leaving his customer to stare at the scene

111. Vo Nguyen Giap, *Unforgettable Days*, p. 348.
112. Ibid., p. 85; idem, *Unforgettable Months and Years*, pp. 55–56.
113. Idem, *Unforgettable Days*, pp. 240–41.
114. Idem, *Unforgettable Months and Years*, p. 27.

in bewilderment. During those two powerful minutes the national flag slowly climbed the pole and fluttered in the breeze, symbolizing the soul and glory of our country.[115]

Even at the height of the patriotic euphoria of late 1945 there were portents of discord, however. Thus, a wealthy practitioner of eastern medicine, after first exhorting people to unite under Ho Chi Minh's leadership, devoted most of his treatise to the need to form private corporations, to learn trades, and to buy domestic pharmaceuticals.[116] A book-length essay, presuming to explain the rights of citizens in the new Democratic Republic, asserted that property was not socially determined but a "natural right," offering the case of Robinson Crusoe as substantiation. The author also argued that employers must have authority to hire and fire employees, and that levying indirect taxes on essentials was a better form of revenue collection than the progressive income tax.[117] While such individuals might continue to march under the DRVN banner, they would soon realize that their vision of the future was not the official one.

Conclusion

Among current students of Vietnam there has been a tendency to assume that Vietnamese attitudes toward ethics and politics have changed very little in the twentieth century, or that they have come full circle after a brief, traumatic interlude during the French colonial era. Such assumptions reflect either wishful thinking on the part of the observer or a failure to understand the devilish plasticity of words and other symbols in sharply altered historical circumstances. Thus, the mere fact that Ho Chi Minh employed such terms as "loyalty," "humaneness" and "virtue" did not make him a Confucian any more than Winston Churchill's or Franklin Roosevelt's use of such terms as "reason," "freedom," and "democracy" made them simple creatures of the Enlightenment. Each became a national leader in part because he knew how to take old symbols and use them creatively according to the political needs of the moment.

Ho Chi Minh had a much more difficult task in one sense. Unlike Churchill and Roosevelt, who were establishment figures, Ho Chi Minh was an outlaw working from the periphery. It was thus essential for him to discredit the moral and political ideals disseminated by the ruling elite—in this case, the French imperialists and their native collaborators. Since the linchpin of the opposing value system was the idea that colonial rule was beneficial to both French and Vietnamese, Ho Chi Minh concentrated his attack there. Although the origins of his anti-imperialism were clearly personal and emotional, by the early 1920s he

115. Hoai Tan, *Trung Bo Khang Chien* [The Armed Resistance in Central Vietnam] (Hanoi, 1946), pp. 14–15.

116. Le Huy Phach, *Tan Dan Phuong Luoc* (Hanoi, 1945). Written largely in verse.

117. Nguyen Bang, *Quyen Cong Dan Trong Chinh The Cong Hoa Dan Chu* [Rights of the Citizen in a Democratic Republican System] (Hanoi, 1945), pp. 9–27.

had fashioned an intellectual paradigm whereby colonial barbarism provided the objective conditions for political action on the part of Marxist voluntarists such as himself. As he wrote at one point, "Colonial atrocities have prepared the soil; it is for socialists to sow the seeds of revolution."[118]

By the late 1930s the seeds had been well and truly sown. In early 1941, when Ho Chi Minh was able finally to return to Vietnam, he spent less time condemning the enemy and more time communicating a set of alternative values. The most important ethical component was "revolutionary heroism" (chu nghia anh hung cach mang). As defined in a host of subsequent speeches and essays, the driving emotion for a Vietnamese revolutionary hero was primordial patriotism; the intellectual framework was scientific socialism. Patriotism was said to be most potent among the peasantry, while scientific socialism was best grasped by the proletariat. The Communist Party, vanguard of the proletariat as well as leader of the peasant masses, was the only organization that could successfully "combine" (ket hop) those critical emotional and intellectual forces. Revolutionary heroism would enable the Party simultaneously to confront powerful enemies and to serve the masses.[119] More than once Ho Chi Minh quoted two lines of Lu Hsün's poetry to explain the Party's dual position:

> Eyes opened wide in defiance, gazing contemptuously
> > at a thousand giants.
> Head bowed, serving as a horse for small children.[120]

It is reasonable to ask whether, after more than three decades devoted mainly to slaying giants, the Communist Party of Vietnam has today lost some of its capacity to respond to popular urgings. Or perhaps the problem is in equating the masses with small children rather than mature adults. Then, too, there can be no denying that the ethics of a party engaged in mobilizing people to seize power are often different from a party in power and likely to remain there for some time. All of these questions carry us well beyond 1945, and are thus merely suggestive. Nevertheless, perhaps they can open avenues of inquiry beyond that of simply comparing Confucianism and Marxism, a subject which has received an inordinate amount of scholarly attention with only mixed results.

---

118. Nguyen Ai Quoc (Ho Chi Minh), writing in La Revue Communiste (Apr. 1921).

119. Van Tao, Chu Nghia Anh Hung Cach Mang Viet Nam [Vietnamese Revolutionary Heroism] (Hanoi, 1972); Nguyen Khanh Toan, "Ho Chu Tich, Nguoi Cha, Nguoi Thay Vi Dai cua Dan Toc, Vi Lanh Tu Thien Tai Doi Doi Kinh Yeu cua Cach Mang Viet-nam" [President Ho: Father, Great Teacher of His People, Forever Beloved, Supremely Capable Leader of the Vietnamese Revolution], NCLS 168 (May–June 1976), pp. 1–7. See also NCLS 93 (Dec. 1966), pp. 1–3; NCLS 99 (June 1967), pp. 1–9; TCVH 2-1977, pp. 17–28.

120. Ho Chi Minh, Tuyen Tap [Selected Works] (Hanoi, 1960), p. 371; Vo Nguyen Giap, Unforgettable Months and Years, pp. 56–57.

4. Language and Literacy

In September 1931, an aging collaborator politician, Ho Duy Kien, during an otherwise routine Cochinchina Colonial Council discussion on primary education, made the mistake of referring to the Vietnamese language as a "patois" similar to those found in Gascogne, Brittany, Normandy, or Provence. For the next few months, from one end of Vietnam to another, the *quoc-ngu* press denounced Ho Duy Kien as rootless (*mat goc*), unpatriotic, and unrepresentative. Writers pointed out that Vietnamese had no less than 17 million speakers, a very long period of development, an abundant oral tradition, and a small but treasured corpus of *nom* (demotic script) literature. Besides, they argued, whatever the past limitations of the native language, the future of the Vietnamese people (*dan toc*) would be partly determined by ongoing efforts to strengthen the connections between the spoken language, the writing system, and the extant corpus of literature.[1]

As no journalists seemed to rush to his defense, Ho Duy Kien requested and received space to explain his "patois" statement.[2] What really counted, he said, was the language of officialdom. Traditionally in Vietnam this had been classical Chinese, with spoken Vietnamese considered vulgar and inadequate, and *nom* merely a type of scholarly recreation. Today, he said, the most useful language was French, not only for officials but also for intellectuals, professionals, and entrepreneurs. Indeed, most of the writers attacking him had gained prestigious positions solely because of their earlier opportunities to master French at school. Yet, they wished now to deny that chance to current primary school children. As for the alleged nation-building powers of language, Ho Duy Kien claimed that the reverse case was historically more accurate. In particular, it was many centuries after the French monarchs had consolidated political and economic power that writers were finally able to bring the French language to full flower. Perhaps five hundred or a thousand years hence the Vietnamese language might also be so fortunate. Meanwhile, however, the position of the Vietnamese people was

---

1. See, in particular, articles in PNTV 101 (24 Sept. 1931), 104 (15 Oct. 1931), and 107 (5 Nov. 1931).

2. *Cong Luan* (Saigon), 21 Oct. and 17 Nov. 1931; PNTV 110 (26 Nov. 1931).

more akin to the Gauls using Latin under the Roman Empire. Today's problems of governing, educating, feeding, and clothing the people had best be handled in French, he concluded.

Twenty years earlier, Ho Duy Kien's "patois" statement might well have passed unnoticed. Most educated Vietnamese assumed that Chinese or French, or both, were essential modes of "higher" communication. A group of Vietnamese literati had indeed begun to explore the patriotic potential of *quoc ngu* writing, but they were effectively silenced in 1908. During World War I the French themselves decided to promote *quoc ngu* as a means to train minor native functionaries and to filter out incendiary ideas emanating from Paris. Then, during the late 1920s, *quoc ngu* writing developed a momentum of its own and a direction quite different from what the French would have preferred. By 1931, despite renewed repression and censorship, a clear majority of the Vietnamese intelligentsia were committed to the rapid development of *quoc ngu* as the modernizing solution, the way to avoid permanent reliance on any foreign language. Fifteen years later spoken Vietnamese, *quoc ngu* script, and the printing press were linked together so tightly that any other solution was deemed anachronistic, perhaps counterrevolutionary. And by the 1960s, only three decades after Ho Duy Kien's bland prediction that the local "patois" would need five hundred years to mature, the Vietnamese language was probably capable of expressing as wide a range of concepts with as much precision and subtlety—depending on the purpose—as many other national languages with far longer heritages of intellectual experimentation, refinement, and dissemination.

What accounts for this tremendous expansion in language competence over such a short period of time? Two factors were critical: the desire of an increasing number of intellectuals to make *quoc ngu* more useful than Chinese or French for defining and disseminating modern Vietnamese culture, and the decision of the newly founded Democratic Republic of Vietnam in 1945 to make the struggle against ignorance and illiteracy one of three top revolutionary priorities (the others being to resist the return of the French and to overcome famine). If *quoc ngu* had remained the concern of only an elite coterie, it probably would not have been able to permanently replace French. On the other hand, the DRVN's mass literacy campaign would have proved to be of far less historical significance without the preceding phase of language experimentation and enrichment.

Intellectuals everywhere have an obvious and particular attachment to words. However, for Vietnamese intellectuals of the 1920s and 1930s words were a consuming passion. It is hard to convey this passion today, especially when writing in another language; however, no study can afford to ignore this subject. Essentially, it was the encounter with French concepts and writing styles, together with a contiguous exploration of current Vietnamese speech, oral traditions, *nom* poetry, and Chinese sources, that provoked excitement, sparked intense debate, and provided the foundation for rapid growth in both language content and form.

Lest one overstate the significance of this quest, it should be pointed out that many Vietnamese intellectuals gravitated to the language question as a substitute for political action. Colonial officials, including the head of the dreaded Sûreté, Louis Marty, often encouraged this tendency. Nevertheless, both Vietnamese and French actors were often aware that words could not be abstracted from social and political context, and that language, oral and written, was ultimately an expression of shared beliefs, fraternal bonds, communal historical ties, and joint expectations. In any event, the line between language development and political action soon became blurred, so that it no longer separated collaborators from anticolonialists, "detached" literary figures from committed revolutionaries. This helps to explain, for example, why Pham Quynh, the primary apostle of *quoc ngu* development in the early period, might subsequently become a ranking collaborator mandarin, whereas some of the young Francophone anticolonial leaders of the 1920s might later devote a fair amount of time to mastering *quoc ngu* and to disseminating ideas in that medium.

Three assumptions concerning language were generally shared by Vietnamese intellectuals of the period 1920–45. First, on the basis of both Confucian precept and Aristotelean logic, they were quite convinced that words must be used correctly in order to communicate properly and hence foster appropriate conduct. Faith in science and the scientific method reinforced this idea. Secondly, the belief was growing that spoken Vietnamese was an important and perhaps even an essential component of national identity. Even intellectuals more at home in French than their mother tongue came to appreciate the significance of the fact that at least eighty-five percent of their countrymen spoke the same language with only minor dialectal variations. And, finally, most Vietnamese intellectuals were aware of the role of mass literacy in the strengthening of nation-states in Europe and Japan in the late nineteenth century. It was a source of considerable chagrin, for example, that by 1933 Vietnam had produced "only" 155 newspapers and periodicals, compared to an alleged 3,812 dailies in Germany in 1926, or 100 dailies for the city of Paris.[3] As the colonial government was proving unwilling to further encourage literacy and publication in Vietnam, intellectuals experimented with private and sometimes illegal alternatives.

By the time Ho Duy Kien stood up to disparage Vietnamese and promote French, the die had already been cast. For Vietnam to become truly "civilized" (*van minh*)—which almost everyone now took to mean a strong, free, and independent nation-state—the majority of intellectuals were certain they had to pro-

---

3. PNTV 232 (18 Jan. 1933), p. 6, lists both *quoc-ngu* and French-language serials published in the colony, including some titles no longer printed as of 1933. This list can be compared with the 97 serials to the year 1930 studied in Huynh Van Tong, *Lich Su Bao Chi Viet Nam* (Saigon, 1973).

mote an even tighter linkage between precise usage, the spoken language, and mass literacy. How that decision was reached and what problems remained to be faced and overcome are important parts of Vietnam's modern intellectual history.

The Language Heritage

Spoken Vietnamese has a long and rich history. A form of proto-Vietnamese probably existed by the fourth century B.C.; whether its primary linguistic affiliation was to a north-south Austronesian grouping including Malay and various dialects of south China, to an east-west Austroasiatic group of Mon-Khmer languages, or to the Sino-Tibetan family, of which Thai is a member, is still being actively debated.[4] Vietnamese was also influenced by the Chinese language during a millennium of colonial rule, although not enough to alter its basic structure.

Once the Vietnamese regained their independence in the tenth century A.D., they continued assiduously to borrow words from Chinese, but insisted on pronouncing them according to their own speech habits. In terms of overall vocabulary, as distinct from phonology, morphology, and syntax, Vietnamese thus came to be more closely related to Chinese than to any other language. Since borrowing occurred over a long period of time and assimilation of loan words proceeded quite gradually, there does not seem to have been any crisis of language development. However, some loan words did remain far less assimilated than others, probably because their function in spoken Vietnamese continued to be subordinate to their function in written Chinese.

As with any spoken language, Vietnamese came to be most versatile in those areas of greatest significance to the gratest numbers of speakers. Students of Vietnam's language and folklore cannot help but be impressed, for example, by the subtlety of expression on matters of life and death, natural (and supernatural) phenomena, agricultural techniques, social customs and family relationships. Often a wide range of words or semantic forms are available to express more or less the same thought, with individuals choosing one or another according to complicated criteria of status, ritual, and style.[5] Changes in twentieth-century lifestyle and attitude have reduced or eliminated some of these subtleties while introducing new ones. Thus, faced with the need to relate wind and rain patterns to crop fertility, a whole series of traditional words, phrases, and formulas have progressively given way to the terminology of the meteorologist (via evening

4. Lieng Khac Van, "A Comparison of Malay and Vietnamese" (M.A. thesis, Macquarie University [Australia], 1977); Vuong Loc, "Glimpses of the Evolution of the Vietnamese Language," *Linguistic Essays* (Vietnamese Studies No. 40) (Hanoi, 1975[?]), pp. 9–15.

5. Two relevant examples, concerning death and procreation, are discussed briefly in Nguyen Tuan, "Ve Tieng Ta" [Concerning Our Language], TCVH 3-1966, pp. 21–22.

radio reports) and the agronomist. Realizing that something is being lost as well as gained, Vietnamese writers, including natural scientists, can still be found rhapsodizing on the powerful images of nature to be found in traditional folk poetry.[6]

Nevertheless, if Vietnam had continued up to the twentieth century with no writing system, the Vietnamese language would have been much the poorer. The key period appears to have been the tenth to fifteenth centuries A.D., when a cluster of aristocratic families led Vietnamese peasants to eject their Chinese overlords, defend the country against repeated counterattacks, and construct an economic, political, and military apparatus unrivaled in Southeast Asia. Although the Chinese rulers had introduced Chinese characters much earlier, it seems that only the tiniest minority of Vietnamese had bothered to master them.[7] Independent Vietnamese rulers systematically fostered knowledge of written Chinese for administrative, religious, and cultural purposes, and they also introduced by stages the Chinese examination system and Confucian mandarinate. By the end of the fifteenth century, unless a young Vietnamese male was born to royalty, his best chance of getting ahead in life (assuming family support) was to devote many years to learning how to read and write Chinese and to attempting to climb the rigorous examination ladder. If he memorized the forms well enough he could achieve mandarin status. If he made even one stylistic error he was likely to be failed, but might still make a reasonable living as a local teacher, scribe, medical practitioner, or fortune-teller.

Whether administering a distant province or instructing children in his home village, the Vietnamese literatus was part of an elite fraternity defining itself largely in terms of the Chinese language. Members demonstrated familiarity with the works of past writers, indulged in elaborate plays on earlier motifs, and criticized the poetry of contemporaries with such wit and panache that friendships were seldom disrupted. In this way, Vietnam developed a literary tradition and a model of the writer as artist. Because the Chinese characters were pronounced according to Vietnamese preferences, and because certain stylistic modifications occurred over time, later scholars came to refer to a hybrid "Sino-

6. Che Lan Vien, "Lam cho tieng noi trong sang, giau, va phat trien" [Making the Spoken Language Clear, Rich, and Expansive], TCVH 3-1966, p. 29; Nguyen Tuan, "Ve Tieng Ta," p. 23; Nguyen Duy Thanh, "Y cua toi ve tieng Viet-Nam" [My Ideas on the Vietnamese Language], PNTV 119 (18 Feb. 1932), pp. 5–10.

7. Interestingly enough, one prominent Marxist writer has suggested that in such a colonial context illiteracy was historically advantageous, since it pushed the Vietnamese to enrich their own oral traditions rather than use Chinese and risk assimilation. Nguyen Khanh Toan et al., *Tieng Viet va Day Dai Hoc Bang Tieng Viet* [Vietnamese and University Teaching in Vietnamese] (Hanoi, 1967), p. 11. The author may be reacting to his own early training and superiority in French rather than Vietnamese.

Vietnamese" (*Han-Viet*) language. However, there would seem to be no more linguistic justification for this term than for a fifteenth-century "Latin-English" versus the Latin written contemporaneously in Rome.[8]

Naturally, the possession of Chinese language competence set the Vietnamese literati apart from the masses. Indeed, a Vietnamese literatus might aspire to a lifestyle having more in common with a literatus in Peking or Hangchow than with an illiterate countryman living just across the paddy field. However, because only a minority of the literati ever achieved mandarin status, while the majority remained part of village life and leadership arrangements rather than gravitating permanently to towns or minor feudal houses, there was a substantial amount of communication between the educated elite and their less fortunate countrymen.

Aside from their roles as local purveyors of wisdom, ritual, and paperwork, the literati delighted in demonstrating artistic prowess on appropriate occasions. For example, while Vietnamese peasants were engaged in such tasks as spinning thread, repairing nets, or making handicrafts, literati might drift in and participate not in the labor but in story recitations, folk-singing, and composition of verses. Some literati improvisations entered the oral tradition, just as some peasant narratives and improvisations came to be used in literature. Thus, in the north-central provinces of Nghe An and Ha Tinh, an entire genre of folk-singing in verse grew up among village women who joined together in the evenings to spin thread and the men (some coming from other villages) who gathered to admire, to court, and to test wits. Certain literati were known throughout the region as aficionados, travelling miles through wind and rain to participate in these exchanges. By the same token, some women developed word skills to the point where they could outmatch any male participants—much to the delight of their peers.[9]

Partly as a means to capture Vietnamese folklore in writing, the literati gradually improvised a separate ideographic system to accord with the sounds and syntax of the spoken language.[10] Known subsequently as *nom*, this unique Vietnamese script unfortunately remained even more unwieldy than the Chinese from which it was spawned. Unlike Japanese *kana* or Korean *hangul*, there was

8. The term "Sino-Vietnamese" continues to be used by most Western specialists, even though this would seem to give too much emphasis to phonology and not enough to syntax, vocabulary, and intellectual content.

9. Ninh Viet Giao, *Hat Phuong Vai* (Hanoi, 1961).

10. In the first instance, Chinese characters probably were used as phonetic signs by officials recording the names of Vietnamese people, places, and things; Buddhist monks may also have written down certain Sanskrit passages in a form capable of being chanted in Vietnamese. John De Francis, *Colonialism and Language Policy in Viet-Nam* (The Hague: Mouton, 1977), pp. 20–28; Dao Duy Anh, *Chu Nom* [*Nom* Characters] (Hanoi, 1975).

no process of character simplification that resulted in a basic set of phonemes or syllables. Some of the problem lay in the tonal and nonagglutinative nature of Vietnamese as contrasted with Japanese or Korean.[11] More important, however, was the attitude of most Vietnamese literati, who continued to regard Chinese as the ultimate in civilized communication and thus considered *nom* a form of recreation. Between the late fourteenth and late eighteenth centuries several Vietnamese monarchs ordered that *nom* be used for administrative and educational purposes, but doubtless to the relief of most literati, these monarchs did not remain in power long enough to ensure implementation. Meanwhile, the minority of literati who took *nom* writing seriously had to be careful not to offend the fraternity or be accused of subversion through circulating "vulgar" texts. Private *nom* literature was also restricted by the fact that Vietnam was a relatively small country lacking the economic base to support a range of prestigious non-official schools or temples, much less large family libraries or professional copying teams.

Despite such disadvantages, *nom* somehow managed to serve as a written vehicle for the spoken language, thus providing yet another link between the peasantry and the elite. Scholars transcribed the songs, narratives, and witticisms of villagers and also wrote down and disseminated their own ideas in *nom*. Since in nearly every village there was someone able to read *nom* aloud or convey the substance in oral synopsis, the literati acquired a greater potential for influencing the attitudes and activities of the masses. In fact, from the fourteenth century this mediating potential took on enough significance to set the central court to worrying about how to control *nom* use. Eventually several monarchs issued edicts specifically banning the printing, sale, distribution, or ownership of *nom* texts.[12] The body of *nom* literature continued to grow, nonetheless.

A few examples will serve to demonstrate the outwardly minor yet ultimately consequential role of *nom* literature. During the Tran dynasty (A.D. 1225–1400) royal edicts were first read aloud in Chinese and then interpreted in spoken Vietnamese, possibly with the aid of *nom* notes.[13] In the early fifteenth century the renowned strategist, statesman, and scholar Nguyen Trai demonstrated an ear for folk expressions in his *nom* work titled *Quoc Am Thi Tap* [National Language Poetry Compilation].[14] *Gia Huan Ca* [Family Training Ode], traditionally at-

---

11. De Francis, *Colonialism and Language*, pp. 28–30.

12. Leopold Cadière and Paul Pelliot, "Premier étude sur les sources annamites de l'histoire d'Annam," BEFEO 1904, 4, p. 631. Nguyen Tung, "Quelques remarques sur les rapports entre littérature sino-vietnamienne et littérature en Nom," *Asie du Sud-Est et Monde Insulindien* 5(3):1973, p. 8.

13. Dang Thai Mai, "Tieng Viet va Day Dai Hoc Bang Tieng Viet" [Vietnamese and University Teaching in Vietnamese], in Nguyen Khanh Toan et al., *Tieng Viet*, pp. 59–61.

14. Nguyen Trai, *Quoc Am Thi Tap* (Hanoi, 1956).

tributed to Nguyen Trai, aimed to disseminate stern Neo-Confucian moral principles to as broad an audience as possible, with particular attention to feminine behavior (see Chapter 5).[15] Later in the fifteenth century King Le Thanh Tong went well beyond Nguyen Trai's experiments, personally organizing and leading a twenty-eight member poetry circle in the creation of a wide variety of verses in *nom*.[16] Yet both men were far better known to posterity for their creative efforts in the Chinese language, Nguyen Trai for his vigorous prose delineations of Vietnamese identity and Le Thanh Tong for his Hong Duc Law Code.

One of the most revealing works from the point of view of language development was *Chinh Phu Ngam* [Lament of a Soldier's Wife], originally composed in Chinese by Dang Tran Con in the early eighteenth century and subsequently translated into *nom* at least six different times. Doan Thi Diem's *nom* version entered the popular tradition and today remains a Vietnamese classic, while the Chinese original continued to be appreciated by the literati.[17] By comparing the various renditions in both scripts, Vietnamese linguists have come to learn a great deal about the range of communication opportunities available at particular points in time, and Vietnamese poets have been able to ponder the distinctions between erudition, wordy obfuscation, and creative brilliance.[18]

Vietnam's most famous literary production in any script is *Truyen Kieu* [The Tale of Kieu].[19] Written in *nom* in the early nineteenth century by Nguyen Du, the story-line of *Kieu* is drawn from an obscure novel of sixteenth-century China. The plot is fanciful, the philosophy escapist, both aspects hardly distinguishing *Kieu* from many other Vietnamese works before or after. Some of the popularity of this 3,254-line poem can be explained by its ambiguous morality, which outraged stiff-backed Confucianists and thus increased the need for oral transmission. However, from the day that Nguyen Du first circulated manuscript copies of *Kieu*, what seems to have most entranced people are the beautiful poetic rhythms, vivid imagery, and penetrating character sketches. No Vietnamese person is untouched by the word magic of *Kieu*. The juxtaposition of certain sounds, the bittersweet evocations of nature, and the personality stereotypes of loyal

15. Nguyen Trai, *Gia Huan Ca* (Saigon, 1953).

16. Maurice Durand and Nguyen Tran Huan, *Introduction à la Littérature Vietnamienne* (Paris: G. P. Maisonneuve et Larose, 1969), pp. 71–74.

17. Dang Tran Con, *Chinh Phu Ngam Khuc* [Lament of a Warrior's Wife] (Saigon, 1950). Hoang Xuan Han, *Chinh Phu Ngam Bi Khao* [Compassionate Study of *Chinh Phu Ngam*] (Paris, 1953). Another *nom* rendition by Phan Huy Ich also has its admirers.

18. Xuan Dieu, "Su Trong Sang cua Tieng Viet trong Tho" [The Brilliance of Vietnamese as Seen in Poetry], TCVH 3-1966, pp. 14–16.

19. Nguyen Du, *Truyen Thuy Kieu*, 8th printing (Saigon, 1968). A good English version is *The Tale of Kieu*, trans. Huynh Sanh Thong (New York, 1973). Often the title *Kim Van Kieu* is employed, indicating three characters rather than one.

PUBLIÉ PAR
Mme HUYNH-KIM-DANH

SAIGON

One of the climactic scenes of
Truyen Kieu, when Kim Trong
and Thuy Kieu dare to break
convention and meet each other
alone. Courtesy of the
Bibliothèque Nationale.

daughter, weak-kneed scholar, playboy, brothel keeper, bandit leader, and jealous wife have all become a part of the Vietnamese language and outlook on life.

In a sense, Nguyen Du was Vietnam's Chaucer, and *Kieu* capped a series of popular works that both reflected and greatly enhanced the development of the vernacular. Nguyen Du loved to participate in local poetry exchanges, and his ear for popular phraseology was unsurpassed among the educated elite. But *Kieu* was also the work of an individual creative artist, transcending speech patterns and *nom* literature of the day. That combination of verbal familiarity and poetic genius ensured that bards of every succeeding generation would memorize and recite *Kieu*. By the same token, however, local poets were not constrained from improvising on Nguyen Du's verses, from further amplifying the characters of protagonists, or from fashioning new scenes entirely.[20] Still other poets continued to write original *nom* poetry, the most famous being Ho Xuan Huong and Nguyen Dinh Chieu. Finally, in the first decades of the twentieth century, *nom* creative efforts merged with new poetic experiments in the romanized script.

20. Ninh Viet Giao, *Hat Phuong Vai*, pp. 15–17, 30–31, 56–58; Nguyen Tuan, "Ve Tieng Ta," pp. 22–25; *Ky Niem 200 Nam Sinh Nguyen Du* [The 200th Anniversary of Nguyen Du's Birth] (Hanoi, 1967), pp. 430–36.

The romanized syllabary had been formulated by seventeenth-century Catholic missionaries to aid in their own study of spoken Vietnamese. Obviously, for them a variant of some European alphabet was more useful than *nom*. Beyond simple language study the missionaries may also have employed their script to prepare sermons and to train Vietnamese auxiliaries.[21] However, despite this promising beginning, for the next two hundred years Catholic tracts and catechisms were published not in Vietnamese romanized script but in Chinese, *nom*, or Latin.

Not until 1861 did the situation change significantly, when the invading colonial forces set up a printing press to publish materials in Vietnamese romanized script as well as in French. Their Vietnamese collaborators took to labeling the former as *quoc ngu* ('national language'), *quoc van* ('national literature'), or *quoc am* ('national tongue')—all terms previously used to identify materials in the *nom* script. Two Vietnamese Catholics, Truong Vinh Ky (1837–98) and Huynh Tinh Cua (1834–1907), labored to raise the romanized script beyond its existing status as a rather crude vehicle for foreign religious and political propaganda, but their translations and codifications were not widely disseminated and their language proposals met with skepticism and distrust. Meanwhile, yet another Catholic, Nguyen Truong To (1828–71), was fruitlessly petitioning the royal court in Hue to accept the idea of an official non-romanized syllabary drawn from Chinese characters but tied to Vietnamese sounds and syntax.[22]

French colonial officials and missionaries of the late nineteenth century took language policy quite seriously, although there were areas of disagreement. Most were convinced that to achieve permanent colonial success required the harsh curtailment of Chinese influences, including the writing system. Missionaries often saw the Confucian literati as the main obstacle to the general Catholic conversion of Vietnam.[23] Hence, in their view, to eliminate the Chinese language was simultaneously to isolate Vietnam from its heritage and to neutralize the traditional elite. On the other hand, as we have seen in chapter 2, Chinese pro-

21. De Francis, *Colonialism and Language*, pp. 48–66. The gifted seventeenth-century Jesuit, Alexandre de Rhodes, is generally credited for consolidating the romanized script, particularly via his *Dictionarium annamiticum, lusitanum et latinum* (1651), to which a grammatical sketch of Vietnamese was appended; Alexandre de Rhodes also prepared a romanized catechism. It would be interesting to compare his use of Vietnamese with that of religious proselytizers elsewhere. See, for example, Charles A. Ferguson, "St. Stefan of Perm and Applied Linguistics," in Joshua A. Fishman, comp., *Language Problems of Developing Nations* (New York, 1968), pp. 253–65.

22. Truong Buu Lam, *Patterns of Vietnamese Response to Foreign Interventions, 1858–1900* (New Haven: Yale Southeast Asian Studies Monograph 11 [1967]), pp. 99–103, contains a translation of Nguyen Truong To's memorial. For discussions of the context see SPT-1, pp. 391–92, and De Francis, *Colonialism and Language*, pp. 101–105.

23. See, for example, the 4 May 1887 letter of Monseigneur Puginier to the Minister of Colonies. AOM NF 541 (3).

vided a sacral veneer to the old moral order. As time went on, both administrators and missionaries had second thoughts about any policy that increased the chances of disequilibrium. Vietnamese conservatives were troubled too. The famous poet Tan Da (1888–1939) unwittingly summarized the entire dilemma when he instructed school children that "We Vietnamese must study French and follow the path of the Sage Confucius."[24] By the late 1920s the French were reintroducing Chinese characters to the primary school curriculum in the forlorn hope that order might be restored.

This is not the place to discuss all the theories, claims, arguments, and contradictions of French colonial language policy.[25] Nevertheless, certain turn-of-the-century attitudes do need to be mentioned. First of all, most French officials still believed that Chinese was incompatible with "progress" and had to go. Secondly, the new native elite had to speak and write French. Thirdly, *nom* was thought to be irrelevant to all but a handful of academicians. Fourthly, the Vietnamese romanized script—increasingly referred to as *quoc ngu*—was believed to be satisfactory for the transmission of very basic concepts to the colonized masses, but by no means was it a candidate to replace either Chinese or French as a vehicle of "higher" communication. Finally, the same generalization was often applied to spoken Vietnamese, which most Frenchmen considered rudimentary, even infantile in comparison to "truly civilized" Western tongues. While none of these French judgments was particularly valid, and while several were gross perversions, they all influenced the course of language development in Vietnam.

Language Alternatives

Meanwhile, some Vietnamese were trying to ascertain for themselves a suitable approach to language development. Whether they gave emphasis to advancement in status, to learning about the new "winds and tides" in the world, or to communicating more effectively with their countrymen, the choice of language(s) was extremely important. At the turn of the century it appeared to many that French was required for personal (and family) success, that Chinese was still necessary for access to a huge reservoir of knowledge—most recently the reformist writings of K'ang Yu-wei and Liang Ch'i-ch'ao—and that *quoc ngu* had considerable potential for mass education and proselytzing. However, for those Vietnamese with ambitions of pursuing all three objectives, this meant mastering three writing systems and two literary traditions (plus *nom* if they were really serious). During the next two decades only a handful of Vietnamese accomplished this feat. By the mid-1920s some intellectuals were moving to cut the Gordian knot.

---

24. (Tan Da) Nguyen Khac Hieu, *Len Sau*, Hanoi, sixth printing, 1925, lesson 21.

25. The most recent discussion can be found in De Francis, *Colonialism and Language*, pp. 69–219.

No fewer than eight language options were theoretically available to Vietnamese of the early twentieth century:

LANGUAGE ALTERNATIVES

	Spoken Language		Writing System
	Mass	Elite	
1.	Vietnamese	Vietnamese/Chinese	Chinese/Nom
2.	Vietnamese	Vietnamese/Chinese	Chinese
3.	Vietnamese	Vietnamese	Nom
4.	Vietnamese	Vietnamese	Simplified Nom
5.	French	French	French
6.	Vietnamese	French	French
7.	Vietnamese	French/Vietnamese	French/Quoc Ngu
8.	Vietnamese	Vietnamese	Quoc Ngu

The first alternative represented the situation prior to French occupation. By 1905, however, even the staunchest monarchists were coming to the conclusion that the *status quo ante* could never be regained, either in politics or language. Reformist literati went further, demanding immediate abolition of the Confucian examination system and replacement of Chinese by some combination of French and *quoc ngu.* The second alternative, which implied systematic fostering of links with contemporary Chinese literary developments, was rendered very difficult by French policy and by the increasing tendency in China to stress the *paihua* vernacular as opposed to the classical literary language. If China had been in a position to reintervene in Vietnam—an idea discussed by people as eminent as Liang Ch'i-ch'ao and Sun Yat-sen—some of the Vietnamese elite might well have hastened to learn characters again.[26] But not until late 1945 did Chinese troops march into the capital of Vietnam again, only to depart a scant nine months later.

In the decades prior to World War I, Vietnamese literati probably took *nom* more seriously than at any time since the short-lived Tay Son dynasty more than a century earlier. *Nom* was indubitably Vietnamese, something that could not be said of Chinese, French, or—at that point—*quoc ngu.* A wide range of poems, ballads, dramas, and prose exhortations were composed in *nom* to expedite dissemination of new ideas about patriotism and modernization. Works in Chinese were also translated into *nom* and then *quoc ngu,* often causing subsequent oral

26. David Marr, *Vietnamese Anticolonialism, 1885–1925* (Berkeley and Los Angeles: Univ. of Calif. Press, 1971), pp. 109–10, 126, 169, 217–18.

versions to achieve more significance than any of the written versions.[27] From the perspective of language style and imagery it was the *nom* poetry of Nguyen Khuyen (1835–1909) and Tran Te Xuong (1870–1907) that captured the imaginations of the most people. Nevertheless, no one seems to have mounted a campaign to make *nom* the national script, nor did scholars devote much time to standardizing *nom* character usage.

As for any dramatic simplification of *nom* (alternative 4 above), although this idea was discussed for decades, no concrete proposals appear to have been disseminated until the late 1920s. At that juncture one author proposed a specific syllabary resembling Japanese *kana*;[28] another devised an alphabet based on the traditional radicals of Chinese orthography, which he then clustered in the manner of characters to make words.[29] Perhaps the most imaginative approach was to employ radicals for individual phonemes and then add another radical for the tone, thus synthesizing different characters for every Vietnamese spoken word. The author of this system had no great ambitions for his new *nom* script, however, merely suggesting that it be employed for decorative or ceremonial purposes, for example at weddings, school graduations, and funerals.[30] That was a sad epitaph for what had been a living, creative mode of expression only a few decades prior.

Complete Vietnamese assimilation to the French language (alternative 5) had been advocated by a number of colonial theorists and officials in the 1860s and 1870s. Although proven by the 1880s to be wildly impractical, even in Cochinchina, it was never quite abandoned as a long-term objective. Indeed, many Frenchmen saw *quoc ngu* as a strictly transitional script, a historical stepping-stone to more general familiarity with the French language, if only in some pidgin variety. However, as Vietnamese intellectuals gained access to unauthorized publications or returned from studies in the *métropole* with incendiary ideas, French confidence in the "civilizing force" of the French language declined precipitously. By the mid-1920s colonial pedagogues had implemented a hybrid French language curriculum for Vietnam, designed to prove that agricultural subsistence and handicraft production equaled modernity, that traditional Vietnamese values had to be preserved, and that the big, wide world beyond was a messy, dangerous place best left to the protecting power.[31]

As it turned out, from 1918 onward almost all Vietnamese focused their atten-

---

27. Ibid., pp. 152–54, 168, 172–79, 226–27, 242–43.

28. Vi Huyen Dac, *Viet Tu: Mot Loi Viet Tieng An Nam* [A System for Writing Annamese] (Haiphong[?], 1929).

29. Nguyen Khac Toan, *Quoc Ngu Loi Chu Nho* [A Chinese-Style System for National Writing] (Hanoi[?], 1931).

30. Nguyen Kinh Chu, *Chu Nom Moi* [A New *Nom* Script] (Nam Dinh, 1932).

31. Gail P. Kelly, "Colonial Schools in Vietnam: Policy and Practice," *Proceedings of the 2nd Annual Meeting of the French Colonial Historical Society* (March 1977), pp. 96–121.

tion on language alternatives 6–8. In that year the Chinese-language civil examinations were abandoned in Annam, the last outpost, and a new colonial Code of Public Instruction took effect, emphasizing 'Franco-Vietnamese' primary schooling. The Entente victory in World War I increased Vietnamese feelings that, like it or not, the French were going to be around for some time to come, and that perhaps the thing to do was to profit from that fact individually and collectively. For many elite Vietnamese this meant, among other things, renewed dedication to learning and using French. For the next decade Vietnamese proficient in French held the political and intellectual limelight. These were not merely the collaborator officials, absentee landlords, and compradors, but also an increasingly vocal group of French-educated lawyers, teachers, and journalists marching to a rather different tune. The problem of language development was never far from the top of the list of items deserving attention.

A favorite venue for discussing and testing language concepts was the education society (*hoc hoi*), discussed in chapter 1. Although most such societies emphasized French language proficiency, they also debated the role of *quoc ngu* instruction and published a considerable number of primers, compilations, and translations in that medium. In March 1925, at the Cochinchina Society for the Promotion of Study, Phan Van Truong delivered a speech that signaled a major shift in the attitude of some Francophones toward spoken Vietnamese and *quoc ngu*. Essentially, he proposed that every relevant publication in French (and other languages) be translated into *quoc ngu*, leading to the time (not too far away, he inferred) when the entire educational program up to doctorate level would be conducted in Vietnamese. "This will make our programs as good as the European programs," Phan Van Truong argued, "and perhaps even better if we really work at it." He particularly excoriated those Francophones, including some political radicals like himself, who portrayed the Vietnamese language as inherently sick and obscurantist, deserving of elimination in favor of the dynamic, progressive French medium. "We may perceive ourselves to be ill, but if we listen to people who urge us to take that arbitrary medicine we'll probably die needlessly," he concluded.[32]

The idea of employing *quoc ngu* for all popular education was not new. Two decades earlier some Vietnamese literati had said much the same thing as Phan Van Truong. They were deeply impressed by what they heard and saw of Japanese educational programs. Many came to equate national power with an alert, informed, literate citizenry. Once they had decided that Chinese characters were no longer appropriate to Vietnam, and that *nom* was not worth overhauling, then the move to some form of romanized script was logical, perhaps inevitable.

Nonetheless, for a Confucian literatus to endorse *quoc ngu*, a system created

---

32. Phan Van Truong, *Viec Giao Duc Hoc Van Trong Dan Toc Annam* (Saigon, 1925), pp. 19, 21.

by alien missionaries and promoted by the colonial authorities as part of a more general policy of cultural pacification, took considerable intellectual imagination and emotional self-control. In effect he was proposing his own demise, since he could probably never master *quoc ngu* in the way he had mastered Chinese and *nom*. The main effort would have to be borne by the next generation, trained primarily in French and *quoc ngu* and treating Chinese and *nom* as historical repositories, more or less the way the modern British elite might treat Latin and Old English.

In 1908, having discovered that the writings of these Vietnamese literati were potentially inflammatory, and that some of these men were involved in clandestine anticolonial activities, the French abruptly put an end to such experiments in education, language, and culture. Literati partisans were thrown in jail or otherwise muzzled. Although some of their publications, documents, and manuscripts continued to circulate covertly, and although the French had no way of blocking oral transmission, it remained a fact that from 1908 to at least 1920 it was impossible to participate in any similar experiments that were not carefully controlled by the colonial authorities.

As we shall see below, a number of educated Vietnamese became excited from World War I onward about the possibility of advancing their country's destiny primarily by means of language development. They wrote in rapturous tones about the "mother tongue" (*tieng me de*) and often attacked the Francophones for "losing their roots" (*mat goc*). Many were sincere. Others were political conservatives who considered the French language and literature to be subversive. Still others saw *quoc ngu* as the keystone of a neo-traditional strategy that could save Vietnam from revolution. None of them could have predicted, however, how some radical Francophones would join in the late 1920s with students emerging from the Franco-Vietnamese schools to seize the initiative in *quoc ngu* development and turn it toward different, often revolutionary objectives. By the 1930s the idea that *quoc ngu* development and dissemination constituted essential components of the struggle for independence and freedom was part of every radical platform. Yet even the most optimistic member of the intelligentsia could not have guessed that only two decades later, citizens of a Democratic Republic of Vietnam would be able to conduct all important affairs—political, military, economic, scientific, and academic—in spoken Vietnamese linked to the *quoc ngu* writing system. Vietnam's previously distinct oral and primary written modes of communication were thus finally united, problems of mass education and indoctrination were greatly simplified, and elite and popular experiences were brought closer together.

Pham Quynh and "Nam Phong Tap Chi" [Southern Ethos Journal]

Upholding the Vietnamese mother tongue was not inherently patriotic, any more than promoting the French language was inherently collaborationist. Until the mid-1920s, in fact, the movement to perfect *quoc-ngu* was spearheaded by one of the colonial regime's most faithful servants, Pham Quynh (1892–1945). Born to a literati family of Hai Duong province (northern Vietnam), this remarkable man went through at least three careers before being executed by the Viet Minh in the August 1945 Revolution. Graduating from the French School for Interpreters in 1908, Pham Quynh worked for a while at the Ecole Française d'Extrême-Orient on Chinese-language texts. During World War I he assisted the Sûreté in preparing a series of anti-German tracts in Chinese for release in Shanghai. This quickly led to a prolific career as journalist, editor, and translator, from which Pham Quynh eventually moved on in 1932 to various mandarin positions at the royal court in Hue.

After having arrested or chased into exile the main leaders of the literati movement of 1907–08, the French realized that many remaining members of the Confucian elite would not be content to simply exist on colonial sinecures or sit around writing classical poetry. They also had to take pains to guide the slowly growing numbers of French-educated Vietnamese. What was needed, in short, was a carefully supervised yet stimulating alternative to the outlawed movement. An air of urgency was added in 1912 as the Sûreté became aware of a batch of new Chinese publications filtering into Indochina that either supported the German case in Europe (and thus, French analysts reasoned, German imperial designs in Asia) or pointed to the advantages of anticolonial agitation and revolt in the event that European hostilities prevented troop reinforcements from being sent to Asia.

One colonial response was to initiate the weekly *Dong Duong Tap Chi* [Indochina Journal], which appeared on 15 May 1913 and continued until 1918.[33] As editor the French selected Nguyen Van Vinh (1882–1936), an early and precocious graduate of the School for Interpreters, marginal participant in the reformist movement of 1907–08, and increasingly vocal advocate of French language, literature, and culture.[34] *Dong Duong Tap Chi* devoted considerable attention to attacking Vietnamese literati who failed to appreciate the benefits of French rule. Phan Boi Chau (1867–1940) was singled out for condemnation, including the charge—quite accurate—that he preferred to learn about the West via Chinese writers and translations rather than bothering to study the French language. "It is hard enough to select primary French concepts and ideals that are digestible to Annamites," wrote an irritated Nguyen Van Vinh, "but if one picks these things up via Chinese books and Chinese characters, with pieces carved off the top and the bottom and strange ingredients added here and there,

33. The publisher was François Henri Schneider, intimate of an earlier governor-general and owner of profitable printing establishments in Hanoi and Saigon. Huynh Van Tong, *Lich Su Bao Chi Viet Nam*, pp. 57–58, 65–66.

34. Other key participants included Phan Ke Binh (1875–1921), Tran Trong Kim (1887–1953), Nguyen Van To (1889–1947), Pham Duy Ton (1883–1924), and Nguyen Khac Hieu (Tan Da) (1888–1939). Pham Quynh was involved in a secondary capacity.

then it is not just a matter of indigestion or choking, but of being poisoned."[35] Nguyen Van Vinh proposed that the Vietnamese Francophone elite replace the traditional literati entirely, since in his opinion the latter were obstacles to progress whether they demonstrated full loyalty to the colonial regime or not.

By late 1915, however, it was obvious to some French officials that *Dong Duong Tap Chi* was failing to provide suitable intellectual inspiration. The resident superior of Tonkin, for example, suggested that a less strident, more discreet, and better organized propaganda vehicle was needed. In Annam conservative mandarins voiced irritation at Nguyen Van Vinh's attacks on all things Confucian, which in their opinion were both unfair and tended to further undermine public order. Governor-General Albert Sarraut was surprised and concerned to receive confidential reports that the library shelves of vaunted Vietnamese scholar families were still stacked with proscribed Chinese texts rather than *Dong Duong Tap Chi*. Worse, candidates of top-level (and still Chinese-language) examinations in Hue had the effrontery to persist in answering questions on "Western learning" by citing K'ang Yu-wei (now regarded as a German mouthpiece by the French) instead of colonially approved source materials.[36]

With the war in Europe grinding on interminably, with the regular French garrison in Indochina reduced to 2,500 men, and with the *colon* community increasingly fearful of any sign of native unrest, Sarraut and his knowledgeable assistant for political and intelligence affairs, Louis Marty, devised a more subtle and sophisticated program to manipulate the Vietnamese elite. Rather than the earlier raucous calls for Westernization or sarcastic attacks on the Confucian literati, Sarraut now favored "East-West reconciliation" and the formulation of unique Indochinese solutions to all problems. For the next few years the key slogan was "Franco-Vietnamese collaboration and harmony" (*Phap-Viet de hue*), which many elite Vietnamese took to mean new interaction producing equal benefit to both parties. Yet for Sarraut and Marty the underlying assumption remained unchanged: French-inspired ideas would help to convert millions of Vietnamese to willing colonial subjects. In this sense they were still products of the French Enlightenment. Not satisfied to rule sullen foreigners by means of threat and coercion, these liberal idealists wished to turn those foreigners into friendly, smiling, understanding (if always junior) partners in an epic historical undertaking. As one report summarized the strategy, there would now be a "conquête morale des habitants après la conquête matérielle du pays."[37]

35. Nguyen Van Vinh, "Goc Luan" [On Origins], *Dong Duong Tap Chi* 2 (22 May 1913).

36. Nguyen Van Trung, *Chu Dich Nam Phong* [The Main Objective of *Nam Phong*] (Saigon, 1974), pp. 247–61. I would like to thank Professor Trung for sharing his ideas and findings with me over the years.

37. "Communication à faire à la presse de 1913 à 1916." Now in the documents collection of the National Library of Vietnam (Hanoi).

Sarraut and Marty selected Pham Quynh as key collaborator in this endeavor, bypassing a number of more senior individuals. First priority was given to organizing a new journal, written primarily in *quoc ngu* but also containing a Chinese section and an occasional reprint of French material. After half a year of screening associates and mapping editorial policy, *Nam Phong Tap Chi* was introduced to the reading public on 1 July 1917.[38] This monthly publication, which lasted until 1934, generally featured sections devoted to expository prose, poetry, short stories, literary criticism, and historical documents. Two years later another important component of the Sarraut—Marty—Pham Quynh program was initiated, the Association pour la formation intellectuelle et morale des annamites (AFIMA). Although similar in many respects to the educational societies discussed in chapter 1, the AFIMA was meant to serve more particularly as a convenient meeting ground for Confucian- and Western-educated members of the Vietnamese elite. It was also used occasionally as a sounding board for colonial policy questions, although its political docility made this something of an exercise in narcissism. In the intellectual and cultural life of northern and central Vietnam, nevertheless, *Nam Phong* and the AFIMA succeeded remarkably until about 1924, after which they were outpaced by a number of more independent-minded intelligentsia groups.

Even in its heyday *Nam Phong's* political platform was too sycophantic to interest anyone except perhaps minor officials and clerks who wanted to know the latest colonial party line.[39] Hense, one must look elsewhere for the journal's undoubted attraction. Quite simply, Louis Marty and Pham Quynh had hit upon language nationalism. The promotion and dissemination of *quoc ngu* literature was presented as an alternative to dangerous political activities. More than that, *quoc ngu* literature was to be the key opening up a vast panorama of knowledge, as well as the vehicle to carry Vietnam from "semi-civilized" (*ban khai*) to "civilized" status. For a brief period the movement to develop *quoc ngu* was effectively portrayed as a dramatic national innovation, a patriotic crusade paving Vietnam's way into the modern world.

---

38. The masthead listed as "founders" Louis Marty, Pham Quynh, and Nguyen Ba Trac (?–1945). The latter individual focused on the Chinese section until his departure five years later for a mandarin position in Hue. Marty probably selected Nguyen Ba Trac mainly because he was a returned student from Japan who had publicly disavowed anticolonialism. As "sustainers" of *Nam Phong*, Governor-General Sarraut and King Khai Dinh were also listed. Archival sources reveal that the Director of Political Affairs, Pierre Pasquier, provided a monthly subsidy of 500 piasters to *Nam Phong*. AOM (Aix) R 19.140.

39. Interviews conducted half a century later with contemporaries of Pham Quynh indicate that most of them ignored *Nam Phong's* political editorials; their favorite was often the poetry section. Nguyen Van Trung, *Pham Quynh: Van Hoc va Chinh Tri* [Pham Quynh: Literature and Politics] (Saigon, 1973), pp. 27–72; Nguyen Van Trung, *Truong Hop Pham Quynh* [The Case of Pham Quynh] (Saigon, 1975), pp. 65–96.

Vietnam's long scholastic tradition had already led many individuals to imbue paper, pen, and ink with quasi-magical significance, to confuse literary production with social action. Now, thanks to modern publishing techniques, it was possible for an otherwise frustrated district official or schoolteacher to see his own creation in print and to know that thousands of contemporaries would see it too.[40] From the colonial point of view, if enough elite members could be convinced that they were fulfilling their patriotic duty by fostering *quoc ngu* literature, then perhaps anticolonial outbreaks could be restricted perpetually to a few embittered dropouts and an occasional peasant jacquerie. The mass of ordinary farmers and laborers were expected to receive at best a few years of training in *quoc ngu*, just enough for them to read and absorb approved concepts and techniques without further need of Confucian- or French-educated mediators. If all went well, the entire process would help to create a new environment unique to colonial Indochina, with elite and mass alike carefully screened from threatening influences emanating from metropolitan anticolonialists, communist revolutionaries, Chinese nationalists, or anyone else.

Pham Quynh's cleverest contribution to this campaign of dissimilation was to associate himself with 'The Tale of Kieu.' Aware that *Kieu* was already widely admired for its rhythms, imagery, and characterizations, Pham Quynh now sought to turn the poem into a cult object, with himself as oracle. Thus, after lauding *Kieu* as the national soul (*quoc hon*), the national essence (*quoc tuy*) of Vietnam, he proceeded to argue that if the literature of Vietnam, particularly 'The Tale of Kieu,' survived, then the language of Vietnam would survive, and so would the country.[41] Several years later a Confucian scholar named Ngo Duc Ke (1878-1929), only recently released from twelve years in prison on Con Son island, angrily reversed those priorities, maintaining that only if the people (*dan toc*) of Vietnam first survived would the language survive, and hence the literature.[42] The battle line was thus clearly drawn between those who argued that an essentially elitist cultural renaissance could save Vietnam and those who believed that only popular mobilization and struggle would accomplish the task.

---

40. Evidence of continuing faith in the intrinsic power of the written word can be found in hundreds of Vietnamese essays and poems of the 1920s. One author capsulized this attitude when he referred emotionally to publishing as the critical watershed between mere thought and action (*su lam*). Tan Nam Tu (Nguyen Van Vinh), *Dan Dao va Dan Quyen* (Saigon, 1926), preface.

41. Pham Quynh, "Truyen Kieu," NP 30 (Dec. 1919), pp. 480-500. There is some evidence that Pham Quynh got his idea for the glorification of *Kieu* from a French article about the Persian masterpiece *Shah-Nama*, by Firdausi. Further extensive discussion of *Kieu* can be found in NP 71, 72, 75, 79, 81, 83, 85, 87, 99, 104, 106, 111, 112, 119, 125, 126, and 134.

42. Ngo Duc Ke, "Nen Quoc Van" [Basis of National Literature], *Huu Thanh* 12 (Dec. 1923); idem, "Luan ve Chinh Hoc cung Ta Thuyet Quoc Van" [Essays on Upright Learning and Heresy in National Literature], *Huu Thanh* 21 (Sept. 1924). Both are reprinted in Dang Thai Mai, ed., *Van Tho Cach Mang Viet-Nam Dau The Ky XX* [Vietnam's Revolutionary Prose and Poetry in the Early Twentieth Century] (Hanoi, 1964), pp. 237-51.

In linking *Kieu*, the Vietnamese language, and the national identity, Pham Quynh was nothing if not audacious. He went beyond mere generalized praise of 'The Tale of Kieu' to a total defense of Thuy Kieu, the prostituted heroine of the story. Thuy Kieu was alleged to combine the best of both Confucian and Buddhist traditions, since she continued to know the difference between right and wrong (Confucianism) even as dark destiny swept her along unchecked (Buddhism). The fact that she had eagerly loved three different men in a period of fifteen years, totally contrary to traditional concepts of chastity, was dismissed disingenuously by Pham Quynh as a "sacrifice to Fate"; he often similarly portrayed his own political collaboration as passive rather than active. Thuy Kieu was said to possess a form of spiritual chastity transcending physical degradation; she had sold herself only because she needed to get enough money to free her father and elder brother from jail. In the same way, Pham Quynh called upon others of his generation to commit themselves to the French in order to bring modern civilization to Vietnam. Providing one's intentions were good, it did not matter what people said.

By the late 1920s, however, a new generation of intelligentsia were rejecting Pham Quynh's reasoning in favor of a new vision of millions of plain people, the previously passive Thuy Kieus of Vietnam, pulling together, organizing, struggling, and defeating the seemingly impregnable colonial system. Although many of these young men and women loved the poetry of Kieu passionately, they argued that Pham Quynh's glorification of the poem and idealization of the heroine was part of a larger strategy aimed at keeping Vietnamese weak and submissive. Whether Thuy Kieu's only choice was prostitution or not, it was essential to show that Pham Quynh was poisonously deceptive in arguing that twentieth-century Vietnamese had no choice except collaboration with the French. In the end, Viet Minh cadres probably chose to execute Pham Quynh as much for his gifted rationalization of collaboration as for his subsequent holding of various court positions.[43]

Ironically, Pham Quynh almost surely considered himself to be a Vietnamese patriot. Often the object of bitter attack, he consistently scorned his critics as jealous, out of touch with reality, or simply dupes of alien revolutionary ideologies. He believed it to be the will of history that France should seize Vietnam and bring it gradually to a modern, civilized state of grace. Yet Pham Quynh never considered himself to be French by any definition. Unlike many other ranking collaborators, he never took up French citizenship, and he severely criticized those who proposed that French be adopted over Vietnamese as the language of the country. It would be like admiring the beauty of another person's

43. For further discussion of the controversies surrounding "The Tale of Kieu," see Jean Chesneaux and Georges Boudarel, "Le *Kim Van Kieu* et l'esprit public vietnamien aux XIXe et XXe siècles," *Mélanges sur Nguyen Du* (Paris: Ecole Française de l'Extrême-Orient, 1966), pp. 153–92.

house, he said, and then feeling that one could abandon one's own house and simply move into the other. Those Vietnamese who seriously tried to "become French" found that they ended up being neither. They were *déraciné*.[44]

Pham Quynh could wax lyrical on the value of linguistic renaissance, as witnessed by the following passage:

> To be Vietnamese we must love and treasure the language of our own country. We must raise the Vietnamese language above both French and Chinese. . . . I am a person who, loving Vietnamese truly, volunteered long ago to devote my entire life to building that language into a literature, so that my country might have a body of writing standing alone, so that my people might not have to suffer the perpetual fate of studying and writing a borrowed tongue.[45]

Although most of the Confucian literati knew this rhetoric to be politically deceptive, they were now tired and insecure, and thus open to the suggestion that modern conditions demanded totally different criteria. As for the young intelligentsia, separated from the Chinese classics, unable to read *nom* literature, bathed in a veneer of French language, seeking psychological release from surrounding injustices, many of them seized on Pham Quynh's vision of salvation through language enrichment. Few could have denied his assertion that

> if you want to know the true spirit of a people, there is nothing so good as listening to popular folksongs and poetry. Mothers singing children to sleep, wives mourning husbands—that is the natural language of a people, from the bottom of their hearts.[46]

Despite this hyperbole, Pham Quynh's attention to popular oral traditions was extremely selective. In particular, although he must have been aware of the thousands of poems, couplets, folktales, and folk expressions that defied stern upper-class instructions about ritual, order, and obedience, Pham Quynh generally chose to ignore them. Instead, he preferred to portray Vietnamese peasants as simple, passive, unassuming, respectful of authority, and resigned to their fate. Little was said of the constant, desperate struggle of these people against the elements; no mention was made of peasant resistance to rapacious tax collectors and corvée organizers; and the crucial role of peasant volunteers and draftees in repelling earlier foreign invaders was noted only in passing.[47] The best that can be said is that *Nam Phong* transliterated a significant number of *nom* poems

---

44. Pham Quynh, "Chu Phap co dung lam Quoc Van An-nam duoc Khong?" [Should French Be Used to Create Annamite National Literature?], NP 22 (Apr. 1919), pp. 279–86. Pham Quynh did endorse large-scale importation of French scientific vocabulary to *quoc-ngu*, however (see discussion below).

45. Pham Quynh, "Su Dung Chu Nho trong Van Quoc Ngu" [The Use of Chinese Words in National Writing], NP 20 (Feb. 1919), pp. 96–97; TCVT-2, pp. 138–39.

46. Pham Quynh, "Chu Phap," p. 280; TCVT-2, pp. 184–85.

47. Pham Quynh, *Le Paysan Tonkinois à travers le Parler Populaire* (Hanoi, 1943).

which, while not usually of folk origin or particularly threatening to the status quo, were deeply appreciated by readers of diverse political persuasions.[48]

Although he might laud Vietnamese folk expressions in principle, and although samples of folk sayings were occasionally collected and reproduced in *Nam Phong*,[49] Pham Quynh's paramount concern was that *quoc ngu* literature rise above its plebeian origins and develop a sense of majesty, ceremony, and refinement. Nor did he hide the socio-political purpose of this exercise. Perhaps daily news accounts, scenic descriptions, or harmless stories of amusement and love could rely largely on "common" (*tam thuong*) language forms, but serious expository prose demanded a different approach entirely. Because he believed firmly in the efficacy of traditional Confucian norms in sustaining social order and upper-class privilege, Pham Quynh argued that Chinese rather than *nom* should be the source of almost all *quoc ngu* vocabulary relating to politics, law, philosophy, or religion.[50] Being a monarchist, he pointed out how starkly different it was to write a sentence about the activities of royalty in simple *nom* style versus the "obviously superior" Sino-Vietnamese style. The alternatives can be translated roughly as follows:

[*Nom*] The Vietnamese King traveled to the northern part of the country and has now returned to the capital.

[*Han-Viet*] His Majesty the Emperor and cortege, having journeyed Northward, are once again in Imperial Chambers.[51]

As it was, some literati participants in *Nam Phong* complained that *quoc ngu* could never possibly achieve the majesty of Chinese. One writer argued that Chinese must be retained for the same socio-religious reasons that European Catholics retained Latin. In Vietnam this meant that the use of Chinese should continue, at least for divination, geomancy, and fortune-telling.[52] Ten years later

---

48. See in particular the *quoc-ngu* renditions of poems by Nguyen Khuyen (1835–1909) and Tran Te Xuong (better known as Tu Xuong) (1870–1907), NP 4–8, 11, 30, 31, and thereafter.

49. See, for example, the codification of more than one thousand proverbs by a mandarin of Thai Binh province, NP 42 (Dec. 1920); see also NP 46, 88, and 144.

50. For abundant examples of this approach to vocabulary development, see the glossary (*tu-vung*) sections of NP 1-18 (July 1917–Dec. 1918), as well as the translations of French political and judicial terminology in NP 41 (Nov. 1920). Vietnamese Communist journals and leaflets distributed ten years later contain different borrowed words of Chinese or Japanese origin, some of them equally jolting to the ear (see AOM [Aix] F-7F4). It would be interesting to study which of these loan words never achieved currency, which later fell into disuse, and which were effectively assimilated to current Vietnamese.

51. In *quoc ngu:* [*Nom*] "Ong Vua Viet-Nam di choi Bac-Ky, nay da ve Kinh roi" versus [*Han-Viet*] "Hoang-Thuong ngu-gia Bac-Ky, nay da hoi loan." Pham Quynh, "Su Dung," NP 20 (Feb. 1919), pp. 91–92. Other attempts at royalist style can be found in NP 6, 9, 11, and 15.

52. Pham Huy Ho, "Viet-Nam ta biet chu Han tu doi nao?" NP 29 (Nov. 1919), pp. 416–19. Additional defenses of Chinese are in NP 21, 24, and 40.

the colonial authorities seem to have reached partial agreement, issuing primary school texts for teaching Chinese on the grounds that knowledge of that language would preserve Vietnamese morality.[53] By that time *quoc ngu* literature had developed its own momentum quite distinct from what either Pham Quynh or the forlorn upholders of Chinese could have wished.[54]

If pushed too far or too fast, Pham Quynh's strategy of employing Chinese loan words for *quoc ngu* risked reader incomprehension. Indeed, when Louis Marty dispatched intelligence agents to various northern provinces to ascertain if early *Nam Phong* articles were being understood, he received criticisms that the language was too high-class, that many words were not in current use, and that most of the foreign geographical terms and personal names were a total mystery.[55] Some years later, young Vietnamese mocked Pham Quynh by commenting that he spoke in as stilted a fashion as he wrote.[56] In fact, however, backed up by colonial pedagogues, Pham Quynh's passion for Chinese loan words threatened to open up yet another chasm between spoken Vietnamese and the primary written medium. Half a century after *Nam Phong's* glossaries were published, many of these borrowed terms could be found in Saigon texts, still with a heavy scholastic crust, still unassimilated to the spoken language.

The problem of how to coin new words produced *Nam Phong's* only real polemical exchange. A plain-spoken Cochinchina soap manufacturer, Nguyen Hao Vinh, attacked the journal for using far too many "Chink words" (*chu Chet*), thus, in his opinion, perpetuating the stupid and dangerous tendency to ape the very people who had repeatedly attempted to assimilate the Vietnamese. Instead, *Nam Phong* should be leading the way in researching, coining, and disseminating neologisms from within the Vietnamese language itself. Only when totally defeated in a specific case, Nguyen Hao Vinh argued, should foreign sources be tapped—and then not by focusing automatically on Chinese, or even

53. Other purposes for studying Chinese were said to be "enrichment of national literature" and access to old family and village records and commercial documents. Le Thuoc and Nguyen Viet Chi, comps., *Han Van Giao Khoa Thu: Lop So Dang* [Chinese Literature Textbook: Third Grade], third printing (Hanoi[?], 1933), preface dated May 1928.

54. It should not be concluded that Chinese writing disappeared overnight. Even among the radical intelligentsia Chinese occupied a minor yet interesting niche until perhaps 1945. Mention has already been made (chap. 1) of commemorative banners in Chinese at the 1926 funeral of Phan Chu Trinh. ICP pamphlets and leaflets of 1930–31 sometimes had Chinese as well as *quoc-ngu* texts; three examples can be found in AOM (Aix) F-7F4.

55. Reports of agents Ngo Vi Lien and Kieu Tuong, 28 August 1917; documents now in the former Archives Centrales de l'Indochine, Résidence Supérieur au Tonkin, Hanoi. TCVH 7-1964, p. 61.

56. Ho Huu Tuong, *41 Nam Lam Bao* (Saigon, 1972), pp. 7–8. The author, who read *Nam Phong* as a teenager, adds wryly that where he lived the journal was only saved from being used as toilet paper because the women of the house thought there was something faintly sacrilegious about throwing anything containing Chinese characters into the outdoor privy.

French, but by identifying whatever language seemed to express the concept most accurately. To hammer his point home, Nguyen Hao Vinh mocked King Khai Dinh for continuing to read speeches in Chinese, and court mandarins for continuing to memorize passages about Mount T'ai Shan, far beyond Vietnam's borders, while remaining hopelessly ignorant of the Mekong delta. Significantly, Pham Quynh chose to delete portions of this paragraph as lacking in appropriate respect for one's superiors.[57]

A ranking court mandarin, Than Trong Hue, was given first rejoinder to Nguyen Hao Vinh. He explained rather lamely that since the Emperor (*Hoang Thuong*) needed to have prepared in advance an exact French translation of each Chinese speech, there was no possibility of his highness extemporizing in Vietnamese. Than Trong Hue also told Nguyen Hao Vinh that he should demonstrate proper deference before even beginning to discuss such matters. Another Hue correspondent to *Nam Phong* went further, suggesting that Nguyen Hao Vinh should be sternly punished by the Cochinchina authorities. The most coherent criticism, however, came from a fellow southerner, Tran Van Don, who pointed out how many Chinese words had been effectively assimilated to spoken Vietnamese over the centuries, to the degree that people no longer thought of them as foreign. There was no logical reason why this should not continue, he said, in the same way that the Japanese still often turned to Chinese (here he was somewhat out of date), or the French to Latin. Nevertheless, his argument was not solely utilitarian. Although a Western-trained physician, Tran Van Don firmly upheld the practice of King Khai Dinh employing Chinese on formal occasions, for the same reasons that the French often inscribed Chinese characters on medals and certificates of merit presented to Vietnamese. Surely Nguyen Hao Vinh was not proposing to smash all morality, the three social relationships, the five virtues, and traditional customs and procedures? he questioned rhetorically. And finally, touching on the matter that had probably prompted Nguyen Hao Vinh to write in the first place, he asked why the people of northern and central Vietnam, who were more assiduous students of the Chinese language, had not been bled white by Chinese merchants as had the people in Cochinchina, who understood little or no Chinese?[58]

At least one writer came to Nguyen Hao Vinh's defense. Chu Lang Ban, publishing his comment originally in a southern paper, agreed that *Nam Phong* used too many Chinese neologisms. Probably the problem of popular assimilation of foreign terms could only be resolved by the effects of time. It was really difficult, he said, to have to wear a French hat, Chinese slippers, and Vietnamese tunic, but eventually everything would sort itself out. Pham Quynh, preferring a chem-

---

57. NP 16 (Oct. 1918), pp. 198–209.

58. NP 17 (Nov. 1918), pp. 256–67. Tran Van Don ignored the role of French economic policy in producing this Chinese commercial differential.

istry metaphor, suggested that Chinese and French language "elements" would combine to produce a new Vietnamese substance entirely different from the two original constituents. The fact that his "formula" failed to include spoken Vietnamese or *nom* was perhaps the most telling indictment of Pham Quynh's language strategy.[59]

In contrast to its approach to word formation, *Nam Phong* exerted a generally creative influence on the development of *quoc ngu* fiction employing Western literary forms. Translations of French dramas and short stories by Molière, Corneille, Voltaire, Rousseau, and Maupassant provided some models, albeit not of the most contemporary variety. Nguyen Ba Hoc (1857-1921) tried his hand repeatedly at original short stories, each being an intriguing if unresolved combination of Confucian parable and personal observation of changes in Vietnamese society.[60] Rather more successful at avoiding classical parallel sentence structure and developing straightforward narration and description was Pham Duy Ton (1883-1924).[61] *Nam Phong* also serialized one of the first Western-style novels in *quoc ngu*, *Qua Dua Do* [The Watermelon] by Nguyen Trong Thuat (1883-1940). Although the story was an escapist adventure, its moral a simple reaffirmation of unswerving loyalty to one's king, the plot was well organized and the language contemporary and easy to understand.[62]

Meanwhile, in 1921, Pham Quynh wrote and published the first serious Vietnamese analysis of the Western novel.[63] Attention was given to structure, style, subject matter, and characterization. His contrast of Western and Chinese novels was also of particular relevance at that point, because the latter were being translated into *quoc ngu* and thus enjoying new influence.[64] On the other hand, Pham Quynh's essay pointedly ignored many aspects of European fiction and literary criticism that he deemed unsuited to the Vietnamese colonial environment. He concentrated almost exclusively on French authors and left out essential English and Russian contributions. And even among the French he chose to disregard

59. NP 18 (Dec. 1918), pp. 320-26; see also NP 19 (Jan. 1919) and NP 20 (Feb. 1919).

60. Nguyen Ba Hoc's stories can be found in NP 10, 13, 23, 26, 35, 45, 46, and 49.

61. NP 18, 20. Nguyen Ba Hoc was a literatus, whereas Pham Duy Ton had graduated from the French School of Interpreters.

62. Nguyen Trong Thuat, "Qua Dua Do" [The Watermelon], NP 103 (Mar. 1926) and thereafter.

63. Pham Quynh, "Ban ve Tieu Thuyet" [A Discussion of the Novel], NP 43 (Jan. 1921), pp. 1-16. Eight years later Pham Quynh expanded this essay and published it separately as *Khao ve Tieu Thuyet* [An Investigation of the Novel] (Hanoi, 1929).

64. The impact at various times of Chinese novels in Vietnam deserves further investigation. For example, the young Ho Chi Minh is said to have much preferred the *Tale of Three Kingdoms* and *Monkey* to the Four Books and Five Classics. Hoai Thanh et al., *Bac Ho, Hoi Ky* (Hanoi, 1960), pp. 19-20. Nguyen An Ninh's father, Nguyen An Khuong, was well known for his *quoc-ngu* translations of Chinese novels.

contemporary writers such as Marcel Proust, André Gide, Henri Barbusse, Colette, François Mauriac, and Jules Romains.

Most significant was Pham Quynh's attempt to convince young Vietnamese writers to pursue certain fictional themes and avoid others. Thus, after dividing all Western novels into three neat categories—*romans passionnels, romans de moeurs,* and *romans d'aventures*—he warned Vietnamese not to fall prey to the first, described the second as being limited merely to individual quests for wealth or fame, and strongly recommended the last category as appropriate to local tastes and levels of literary competence. Even adventure fiction was to be restricted, however. Thus, he said, characters in *romans d'aventures* ought to be ruled by surrounding environmental conditions rather than adopt heroic postures. For confirmation he cited the French critic Ferdinand Brunetière, who claimed that the art of the novel was to demonstrate that man, in spite of his claims, was always at the mercy of the situation confronting him and reacted accordingly. To cap this line of argument, Pham Quynh returned to 'The Tale of Kieu,' recalling the manner in which Thuy Kieu's individual will had always been captive to "fate" (*van menh*).

Pham Quynh might have given the appearance of philosophical determinism, and might even have believed it himself. Nevertheless, he had a social engineer's view of language development. Under French tutelage, and within carefully formulated colonial guidelines, Pham Quynh and his colleagues at *Nam Phong* expected to scan a wide range of foreign and local materials, select appropriate items, translate where necessary, and provide suitable interpretations. To the degree that *Nam Phong* was able to monopolize readership, both the forms and content of *quoc ngu* writing could be carefully regulated. Indeed, viewed very optimistically, *quoc ngu* writing might serve as a methodically constructed sieve through which were sifted all human concepts, old or new, Chinese, French, or Vietnamese. Some would be permitted to pass relatively untouched; others would be given pejorative labels or filtered out entirely. Still others would be consciously altered to "fit conditions" in a permanently colonized Vietnam. It was a scheme befitting modern scientism, but it did not succeed.

The Quoc Ngu Explosion

As it eventuated, *Nam Phong* was unable to monopolize serious reader attention even at the height of its influence from 1917 to 1924. Ironically, French-language publications were most responsible for preventing Pham Quynh's *quoc ngu* sieve from doing its job. Especially in Saigon, Vietnamese intellectuals with a superior grasp of French language and literature offered their own interpretations, selected their own favorite authors, and denounced the whole idea of a "unique" Indochina colonial environment. From late 1923 Nguyen An Ninh and Phan Van Truong were able to publish *La Cloche Fêlée,* a provocative weekly newspaper that not only opposed government economic policies and called urgently for political reforms, but also devoted considerable attention to the writings of Leo Tolstoy, Friedrich Nietzsche, Jean Jaurès, Romain Rolland, André Gide, and Anatole France.[65]

Pham Quynh, perhaps sensing that he had lost the initiative in providing Western ideas for Vietnamese consumption, chose to attack Nguyen An Ninh personally. The latter was both *déraciné* and dangerous, he indicated, a perfect example of why Vietnam should take the *Nam Phong* approach and move slowly and discriminately. The pretext for this assault was Nguyen An Ninh's statement before a magistrate that from age eighteen he had undergone a spiritual crisis, constantly doubting his own ideas and actions, and even considering entering a Buddhist monastery. Taking the robes would have been much more suitable, Pham Quynh opined, than proceeding to write incendiary articles and stir up the populace; even Buddha had felt it necessary to meditate for a long time beneath the Bodhi tree before proselytizing.[66] Contemporary Vietnamese were simply not prepared to handle such turbulent concepts as 'liberty' (*tu do*) and 'equality' (*binh dang*), Pham Quynh emphasized on another occasion.[67]

As mentioned before, Phan Van Truong, Nguyen An Ninh's close associate, led the drive to convince Vietnamese Francophones that they must concentrate on developing *quoc ngu*. Language was the expression of a people's soul, he said, in apparent agreement with Pham Quynh. However, for Phan Van Truong this meant that Vietnamese was capable of rapid, spontaneous and infinite growth, not merely cautious experimentation on the part of the elite. As for the problem of word coinage, although he admitted that translation was corruption in the purest literary sense, it was equally true that all living languages were the product of extensive borrowing. French had a polyglot history and was still subject to change. Vietnamese had borrowed extensively from Chinese, yet that had not made the people Chinese, any more than linguistic affinities had turned the English people into French people or vice versa. In the twentieth century, Phan Van Truong suggested, Chinese could still serve as a fertile source of Vietnamese neologisms because of the monosyllabic correspondence and the many phonemic similarities. On the other hand, Vietnamese intellectuals should also constantly be improving their knowledge of French, as it provided direct entry to the modern sciences, mathematics, and jurisprudence. The concrete objective, he emphasized, was to translate to *quoc ngu* and to publish writings on every conceivable subject, so that "all of our people are able to study." To reach a tiny minority of

65. *La Cloche Fêlée* began weekly publication in Saigon on 10 Dec. 1923. It shifted to biweekly status on 26 Nov. 1925, changed its name to *Annam* on 6 May 1926, and was shut down by the authorities on 2 Feb. 1928.

66. Pham Quynh, "Malaise Moral," NP 106 (June 1926), pp. 53–55. Nguyen An Ninh never felt the need to respond to Pham Quynh.

67. Pham Quynh, "Chu Phap," NP 22.

Francophones was of "very little benefit," Phan Van Truong argued, whereas to popularize via *quoc ngu* was to make the Vietnamese national soul progressively "more alert, more intelligent and more courageous."[68]

In sounding the call among Francophones for serious attention to *quoc ngu*, Phan Van Truong could not help but be painfully aware of how difficult it was for someone educated primarily in French to write in a way acceptable to ordinary Vietnamese. His own occasional use of Western syntax in *quoc ngu* raised eyebrows among even the elite.[69] And his book, titled *Phap Luat Luoc Luan* [Summary Discussion on Law], presumably derived from old Paris study notes, contained many language formulations not likely to be understood by the small number of Vietnamese high school graduates, much less the more significant group possessing three or four years of primary instruction.[70] Nguyen An Ninh was rather more successful. His 1928 drama on the Trung sisters, for example, combined vernacular style with a complex political message.[71] And his 1932 essay on religion managed to cover an ambitious intellectual landscape in reasonably colloquial fashion.[72]

However, it was to fall to a group of even younger Saigon journalists, men in their late teens or early twenties, to start converting Phan Van Truong's popularization proposal to reality. From 1925 to 1929 they unleashed a flood of *quoc ngu* articles, essays, and short stories. Increasingly disenchanted with colonial policies, they saw private *quoc ngu* literary activity and publishing as one way to maintain a degree of intellectual and political momentum. They definitely took to heart the challenge of creating a single, multifunctional, modern standard Vietnamese language.[73] The content was as politically provocative as the censors would permit. For example, they published a large number of *quoc ngu* biographies and short stories of an overtly heroic character, the purpose being to argue that people who merely accepted fate were doomed to destruction, whereas those who struggled were admired and remembered forever, even when they failed (see chapter 6).

68. Phan Van Truong, *Viec Giao Duc*. Significantly, Duong Ba Trac, a prominent Confucian literatus, endorsed most of these ideas the same year. Duong Ba Trac, *Tieng Goi Dan* (Hanoi, 1925), pp. 42, 44, 98, 102, 116–21, 133.

69. Phan Trong Minh, who write the preface to Phan Van Truong's *Viec Giao Duc*, specifically felt called upon to defend Phan Van Truong's syntactical innovations as "new literature."

70. Phan Van Truong, *Phap Luat Luoc Luan* (Saigon, 1926). Despite this language problem the publishers took the risk of printing 5,000 copies.

71. Nguyen An Ninh, *Hai Ba Trung* (Saigon, 1928).

72. Nguyen An Ninh, *Ton Giao* (Saigon, 1932).

73. Probably the most important early vehicle for these young journalists was *Dong Phap Thoi Bao*, published from 2 May 1923 to 31 Dec. 1927. However, the paper with the largest circulation (5,000–15,000 copies) was *Trung Lap Bao* (16 Jan. 1924 to 30 May 1933), controlled and financially subsidized by French commercial interests. Subsequent significant Saigon *quoc-ngu* serials included *Than Chung* (1929–30), *Duoc Nha Nam* (1928–37), and *Phu Nu Tan Van* (1929–34).

Meanwhile, in Hanoi, the alternatives to *Nam Phong* were multiplying too, albeit with less initial excitement and vigor. Nguyen Van Vinh, again backed by François Schneider, edited *Trung Bac Tan Van* (Central and Northern News), and this publication eventually achieved the dubious distinction of being the longest surviving *quoc ngu* daily of the colonial period.[74] It was in his translations of French literature, however, particularly works by Fontaine, Molière, Dumas, and Hugo, that Nguyen Van Vinh outpaced the *Nam Phong* group entirely. Tan Da (Nguyen Khac Hieu) picked up where Tran Te Xuong and Nguyen Khuyen had left off, writing and publishing *quoc ngu* poems that were redolent of *nom* and folk genres, but with less attention to traditional structure and with a new emphasis on artistic introspection.[75] Tan Da simultaneously wrote essays for, or edited, a long series of newspapers and journals.[76] In fact, for most creative writers of the 1920s, it was not the sale of poetry or short stories that kept them alive, but the numerous small fees for producing a steady flow of newspaper articles according to deadlines. A number of writers performed for *Thuc Nghiep Dan Bao* [Producing People's Paper], a Hanoi daily established in 1920 by fifty landowners, merchants, and industrialists to meet the needs of the nascent Vietnamese bourgeoisie. Only in the 1930s were authors able to support themselves, at least in part, through sale of their fiction or poetry.

A still different influence was exerted by Hoang Tich Chu (1897–1932), who brought back from France the model of the journalist as aggressive but politically non-committed professional, totally dedicated to digging out the facts and writing them up in tightly organized sentences devoid of rhetoric or ambiguity. Hoang Tich Chu and those other individuals who heeded his cry demanded that the old parallel sentence be scrapped entirely and that French syntax be integrated with *quoc ngu* wherever possible. He was particularly fond of grammatical inversion to emphasize a point. On the other hand, he denounced those writers who laced their *quoc ngu* sentences with French words or expressions, insisting that they either take the time and energy to translate them or not use them at all. Many Vietnamese conservatives were offended by Hoang Tich Chu's approach, citing China's Hu Shih and Ch'en Tu-hsiu as more appropriate models.[77] Although some of Hoang Tich Chu's language innovations proved indi-

---

74. *Trung Bac Tan Van*, begun originally as a weekly affiliate of *Dong Duong Tap Chi*, became a daily in 1919 and was published until Sept. 1945.

75. Nguyen Khac Hieu, *Tan Da Van Van* [A Tan Da Compendium] (Hanoi, 1952); originally published in three volumes in 1939–40.

76. His journalist involvements included *Dong Duong Tap Chi, Huu Thanh, Dong Phap Thoi Bao,* and especially *An Nam Tap Chi,* which Tan Da edited and published as finances permitted from 1926 to 1933. His success in selling morality texts was noted in chapter 2.

77. *La Patrie Annamite* no. 5 (29 July 1933).

gestible in the long run, the movement to communicate with the least possible ambiguity continued throughout the 1930s and 1940s, permanently altering both written and spoken syntax.[78]

Hanoi also became the favored location for a growing number of Vietnamese novelists and short-story writers. In the late 1920s, as per Pham Quynh's recommendation, they did indeed favor adventure themes divorced from matters of contemporary social and political significance. The emphasis was on murder mysteries, spy intrigues, ghost stories, and dreamlike travel to romantic corners of the world. Love stories filled with tears and pathos also gained currency, the first being a 1925 novel clearly modeled on *Camille*.[79] By the early 1930s, however, the focus was shifting. Although romantic love, psychological introspection, scenic description, and languid travel narratives (inside Vietnam) remained important for at least another decade, writers increasingly felt the need to witness and to judge social questions of the day. The intelligentsia avidly purchased creative fiction, either in long serialized form in newspapers and journals or in final bound form. *Quoc ngu* became far more supple, to the point where each writer could develop his own style and be easily recognized by the reading public.[80]

The same emphasis on freedom and clarity of expression was evident in *quoc ngu* poetry after 1930. Breaking from the strictures of T'ang style that had dominated poetry in Vietnam for centuries, young writers like The Lu, Luu Trong Lu, Tu Mo, Che Lan Vien, Xuan Dieu, and Huy Can experimented with a wide variety of new forms and topics. Traditionalists accused them of being too lazy to learn the old rules, or of merely aping Hugo or Lamartine. They replied that the old poetry rules were actually quite easy to learn, but were simply too restrictive and did not meet current needs:

We live in a time of motors, electric lights, radios, films, and gramophones, quite different from the days of coconut-oil and *mu-u*-oil lamps; yet, [traditionalists] want us to cry, laugh, and love, express regret, anger, or hatred in the same narrow domains, the

---

78. Hoang Tich Chu died prematurely, perhaps because his model of the individual journalist also included opium-smoking, hard drinking, and very little sleep. From 1930 to 1932 in Hanoi he published *Dong Tay* and wrote for *Ngo Bao*.

79. Hoang Ngoc Phach, *To Tam* [Beautiful Heart], tenth edition (Saigon, 1963). Earlier writings by the author can be found in NP 41, 43, 52, 54, and 88. The influence of *To Tam* was still being critically debated in 1933–34. See PNTV 187, 229, 231, and 256.

80. This was true even of members of the same literary group, for example, Nhat Linh (Nguyen Tuong Tam) as compared with Khai Hung (Tran Khanh Du), not to mention authors as stylistically diverse as Ho Bieu Chanh, Nguyen Cong Hoan, Ngo Tat To, or Vu Trong Phung. For English synopses of scores of novels of the 1930s and early 1940s, see Hoang Ngoc Thanh, "The Social and Political Development of Vietnam as seen through the Modern Novel" (Ph.D. diss., Univ. of Hawaii, 1968), pp. 140–268. Moc Khue, *Ba Muoi Nam Van Hoc* [Thirty Years of Literature] (Hanoi, 1942), is an early, thoughtful appraisal of *quoc ngu* literature.

same outmoded frameworks. If we follow that path, we'll do nothing but repeat hackneyed phrases ad nauseam.[81]

In real life, however, most contemporary Vietnamese were using neither coconut oil nor electric lights, but imported kerosene when they could afford it. The writers of "New Poetry" (*Tho Moi*) were in an analogous situation, discarding Chinese and *nom* meters only when it became obvious that Verlaine or Baudelaire could not be adequately translated in that manner.[82] Original creations often bore too heavy an imported stamp, either in their use of run-on lines and caesura or in their self-conscious attempts to be socially relevant. Only in the 1940s did some of the "New Poets" successfully incorporate popular Vietnamese imagery and thematic concerns, and by this time the general public was also somewhat more prepared to accept their freewheeling meters.

By far the most difficult medium to introduce was Western-style drama. That it was a potentially volatile form was evinced by the controversy which developed over the message conveyed by a 1920 Vietnamese rendition of Molière's "Le Malade Imaginaire." One outraged viewer wrote a long letter to *Nam Phong*, linking the stage historically with subversion and corruption and specifically denouncing Molière's irreverent attitude toward death, his failure to maintain class distinctions, and his implication that women should not always obey their menfolk. To allow Vietnamese people to be mesmerized by stage actors, especially in such dangerous times, served only to "pour oil on fire," he concluded.[83]

As it happened, only very small circles in Hanoi and Saigon took Western-style drama seriously in the 1920s and 1930s. Translations remained stilted, and even original creations tended to be brittle drawing-room pieces. Meanwhile, other writers and performers were approaching the problem from the opposite direction, altering the style, costume, presentation, and themes of traditional drama to appeal to contemporary audiences. Vietnam possessed a strong and structurally diverse dramatic tradition, including the popular theater (*cheo*), more formal morality plays (*tuong*), and the highly stylized Chinese opera (*hat boi*). The most important new genre was "reform theater" (*tuong cai luong*), which began in southern Vietnam around World War I, became extremely popular there, and then swept northward in the late 1920s and 1930s.[84] "Reform theater," corre-

81. PNTV 211 (10 Aug. 1933), pp. 304. See also PNTV 210, 213, 215.

82. Nguyen Thi Kiem, "Bai dien thuyet . . . ve 'Loi tho Moi' " [A Speech on the "New Poetry Style"], PNTV 211 (10 Aug. 1933), pp. 8–9; and PNTV 213 (24 Aug. 1933), pp. 9–11.

83. NP 35 (May 1920) includes a general history of drama in France (pp. 377–95), the long letter to the editor by "Nam Minh" (pp. 396–408A), and a detailed rebuttal by Pham Quynh (pp. 408B–408G). See also *Trung Bac Tan Van*, 20 Apr. 1920.

84. Eventually, this new genre came to be called simply *cai luong*. Hundreds of published *cai luong* scripts can be found in the Bibliothèque Nationale (Paris) collection.

sponding roughly to Western light opera or musical drama, gave writers a financial base, allowed actors and actresses considerable interpretive leeway as they traveled from one location to another, and undoubtedly played a major role in disseminating new ideas and language beyond the intelligentsia. Although Vietnamese devotees of Western theater were unhappy with this compromise, particularly the continuing tendency to posture and overact instead of seeking "realist" solutions, they were generally powerless. Only in the mid-1930s did a few writers attempt innovations of their own—for example, one-act plays in verse.[85] After the August 1945 Revolution, stage drama (*kich noi; san khau*) finally achieved acceptance; yet, even today it cannot be said to have outpaced the *cheo* or *cai luong* among the general public.[86]

Vietnamese Semiotics

In the midst of this outburst of journalism, fiction, poetry, and "reform theater" scripts, some Vietnamese took time to analyze the *quoc ngu* writing form itself and to propose changes. This seemed logical when it was considered that the basic syllabary was the product of European ears listening to Vietnamese speech almost three centuries earlier, and then transcribing according to Portuguese language conventions. Rationalizing the *quoc ngu* alphabet by adding or subtracting certain vowels or diacritics was one suggestion often heard in the 1920s. Another idea was to drop the diacritics entirely in favor of extra letters at the end of words.[87] This practice was in fact adopted for Vietnamese telegrams, since it proved impossible to transmit diacritics by either Morse code or teleprinter. Several systems of Vietnamese stenography were also introduced.[88]

Nevertheless, what remains remarkable is how very little the *quoc ngu* writing system was altered up to and beyond 1945. The hyphen between syllables began to fade away. Overlap between the *a* and *o* vowels was eliminated.[89] Southern use of the *hoi* accent rather than the *nga*, reflecting regional speech preferences, gradually receded in publications but continued to bedevil pupils who under-

85. Thus, around 1935 Huy Thong (b. 1916), a member of the New Poetry movement, created two short tragedies in verse, "Anh Nga" and "Kinh Kha." Later, as Pham Huy Thong, he became an archaeologist and vice-chairman of the Vietnam Social Sciences Committee.

86. Moc Khue, *Ba Muoi Nam Van Hoc* [Thirty Years of Literature], pp. 69–81, has a provocative discussion of failures and successes in drama.

87. Le Mai, *Quac Am Tan Che* [A New System of National Language] (Saigon, 1927[?]).

88. NP 50 (Aug. 1921). Vu Tran, *Quoc Ngu Viet Tat* [Abbreviated National Writing] (Hanoi, 1921). The preface to the latter manual asserts that "civilization" demands a Vietnamese capacity to take quick notes at lectures, meetings, and political assemblies.

89. For example, Ho Chi Minh's earlier pseudonym, Nguyen Ai *Quoc*, had often been written as Nguyen Ai *Quac*.

standably wanted to write as they spoke.[90] On the other hand, as literacy became more widespread, other *quoc ngu* imperfections probably exerted a feedback effect, altering Vietnamese speech patterns to accord with the written medium.

Certainly there is abundant evidence that *quoc ngu* publications helped to expand the range of spoken Vietnamese. Although there had always been specialized styles of speech and vocabulary according to social function, now the language became both more complicated and less compartmentalized. To the peculiar speech patterns of the literatus, Buddhist monk, artisan, peasant, or petty merchant, for example, were now added the rhetoric of the political activist and the terminology of doctors, lawyers, engineers, and entrepreneurs. Words such as 'struggle' (*dau tranh*), 'germ' (*vi trung*), 'suspended sentence' (*tu treo*), 'pedagogy' (*su pham*), 'electric battery' (*pin*), and 'company' (*cong ty*), either coined locally or in Japan and China, were promoted by the small groups of Vietnamese who needed them most. The remarkable thing, however, is the number of these words that became part of the general oral vocabulary. At a different level, the increased availability of dictionaries and glossaries gave individuals access to the vocabularies of other groups. Thus, by 1945 it was possible to estimate that the Vietnamese language already possessed 40,000 scientific and technical terms. By 1969, with the aid of systematic government language and education programs, this figure had jumped to 250,000.[91] Obviously, no one used more than a tiny fraction of this total in everyday conversation, but the fact that they could seek out a particular term and understand its meaning served to alter the course of Vietnamese language development.

There was in Vietnam no institution similar to the Académie Française; instead, words were simply coined by the thousands each year and then left to survive or perish in the language marketplace. Although this produced considerable confusion, and caused Pham Quynh to propose an official institution of some sort to deal with the problem, the majority of Vietnamese intellectuals of the late 1920s and 1930s clearly believed creative spontaneity to be an integral part of language growth.[92] Debate continued, of course, since most intellectuals also wanted to agree on certain principles of word formation.[93] Even after the Demo-

---

90. An early discussion of the question of *hoi* versus *nga* can be found in PNTV 251 (26 July 1934).

91. N[guyen] K[hanh] T[oan], "The Vietnamese Language," *Viet Nam Courier* 49 (June 1976), p. 21. Nguyen Khanh Toan et al., *Vietnamese and Teaching in Vietnamese in D.R.V.N. Universities*, 2nd edition (Hanoi: FLPH, 1969), p. 54.

92. Phan Khoi, "Ve cai y kien lap hoi 'Chan Hung Quoc Hoc' cua ong Pham Quynh" [On Pham Quynh's Idea of Establishing a Society for the "Promotion of National Learning"], PNTV 70 (18 Sept. 1930), pp. 9–11.

93. See, for example, articles in *Tri Tan* (Hanoi) no. 9 (1 Aug. 1941), and no. 11 (22 Aug. 1941).

cratic Republic of Vietnam settled on a formula, debate continued over rules of implementation and possible exceptions.

Possibly the clearest formulation prior to 1945 was advanced by Phan Khoi:

All words that can be spoken in our language (*tieng ta*), should be. When our language lacks the capacity, or tends toward lack of clarity, incompleteness, or verbosity, then Chinese [loan words] should be employed. When Chinese is unsatisfactory, then we should be willing to use French [loan words] as well as [those of] other foreign languages.[94]

This meant, for example, that the indigenous words for *father* and *mother* were quite suitable, so that there was no need to use the loftier Chinese derivatives. On the other hand, Vietnamese words for *religion, virtue, study, conscience, politics, philosophy,* and *science* had been successfully incorporated from Chinese at one time or another. Even if an early Vietnamese equivalent were to be uncovered, there was no point in discarding an already acceptable term. Chinese, however, clearly lacked appropriate words for many new concepts. For example, Phan Khoi pointed out that the French word *cas* contained aspects of circumstances, space, and time that no indigenous or Chinese word could match; hence, it was probably best to convert it to *ca* and assimilate it to Vietnamese. Ironically, in this case, other language forces were at work, and Phan Khoi's proposal was ignored in favor of a word coined earlier in Japan, which subsequently gained standard usage in Vietnam.[95]

In the most basic sense, Phan Khoi was arguing for word coinage along utilitarian philosophical lines. If precise communication was critical to Vietnam's future, then those who coined words for different reasons, be they emotional gratification or social control, ought to be effectively countered. The principle of precision meant, for example, that contemporaries who called the bicycle *xe may* ('machine vehicle') were wrong; rather, it should be *xe dap* ('treading vehicle'). This modification was soon in common use. At a more subtle level, Phan Khoi cited cases where incorrect terminology could be politically damaging. Thus, some Vietnamese had taken to referring to the colonial administration as the *tan*

94. Phan Khoi, "Su dung chu Tau trong tieng Viet-Nam" [Using Chinese Words in the Vietnamese Language], PNTV 121 (3 Mar. 1932), pp. 5–7. Much subsequent debate hinged on what was unclear, incomplete, or verbose in Vietnamese coinages as opposed to Chinese or French ones. For example, Ngo Quang Chau, in his work *Luan Ve Tieng Nam* (Hanoi, 1940[?]), criticized his peers for not working much harder to find "ordinary" Vietnamese expressions. This was the starting point of DRVN neologism policy after 1945. Nguyen Khanh Toan et al., *Tieng Viet va Day Dai Hoc bang Tieng Viet* (Hanoi, 1967), pp. 76–136; idem, *Linguistic Essays*, pp. 124–47.

95. That word is *truong hop*, which Phan Khoi had rejected because it lacked the time dimension of *cas*. A Western word that did take up and retain an important place in the Vietnamese vocabulary was *logic* (*lo gich*).

trao or *tan trieu* ('new dynasty'), as if the French were simply replacements for the house of Nguyen. Among other things, this led Vietnamese peasants to continue to regard taxes as obligatory dues owed by subjects to their feudal lords, instead of coming to believe in the responsibilities of free citizens in a democracy. At this juncture in Phan Khoi's argument, it should be noted, the text was censored.[96] On the other hand (Phan Khoi continued on another occasion), there were times when the people knew enough to ignore officially inspired terminology. Hence, even while the Hue court persisted in entitling the country *Dai Nam* ('Great South'), most individuals preferred *Viet Nam* ('Southern Viet')—both because they knew there was nothing "Great" about the country's current colonial status, and because "Great" required some comparative context that was hardly self-evident.[97]

Of course, Phan Khoi realized that there was more at stake in language usage than simple accuracy. A central problem in Vietnamese was status terminology. Long characterized by extremely intricate but essential rules of hierarchy, by the 1920s and 1930s the Vietnamese language was beginning to change along with social attitudes. Most obvious was the downgrading of strict conventions concerning the monarch and his family and ancestors. Phan Chu Trinh had set the new tone in 1922 when he wrote from France a caustic open letter to King Khai Dinh that pointedly ignored most of the traditional slavish terminology.[98] Writers and orators in Cochinchina were soon poking fun at the Nguyen family, but in central and northern Vietnam the threat of being charged with linguistic *lèse-majesté* kept people more cautious until the mid-1930s.

A more serious question pertained to native officials who demanded extreme language deference, and the majority of Vietnamese who continued to accomodate them. Here it is worth observing that the colonial system often perpetuated the forms while objectively undermining the substance. For example, in line with traditional rules of *kieng ten* or *huy ten* 'name taboo,' a newly arrived district mandarin might distribute to subordinates a list of words that could not be uttered because they were included in his name(s) or those of members of his family, alive and deceased. Any person coming from another district had to be extremely circumspect in speech; he had to ascertain the local taboo words and avoid using them lest he get into trouble. Yet it was equally well known that subordinates often used the name-taboo custom to mock superiors out of earshot,

---

96. Phan Khoi, "Theo thuyet chanh danh soat lai may cai danh tu nguoi minh thuong dung" [Rechecking Nouns in Common Use According to the Concept of Correct Names], PNTV 69 (11 Sept. 1930), pp. 11–13.

97. Phan Khoi, "Dinh chinh lai cach xung ten cua nguoi Viet-Nam" [Rectifying Name Usage among Vietnamese], PNTV 58 (26 June 1930), pp. 11–12; PNTV 59 (3 July 1930), pp. 9–10. The first point had already been made by Phan Boi Chau in 1905. Marr, *Vietnamese Anticolonialism*, p. 118.

98. Phan Chu Trinh, *Thu That Dieu* [Seven-Point Letter] (Hue, 1958).

simply by substituting derogatory words for the real ones. Hence, a ranking mandarin collaborator in Hue became His Excellency Nguyen Huu *Boi* 'playboy,' while the governor of Ha-Dong province was known as Hoang Trong *Cu-Li* 'coolie.'[99]

In different areas of Vietnam particular words were always mispronounced, simply because some powerful official, perhaps fifty or a hundred years earlier, had possessed that word as his personal name. By contrast, the French exalted the names of their officials, giving them to streets, bridges, and schools. Obviously, two very different recognition patterns were involved, the former emphasizing discreet silence, the latter public exposure and verbal repetition. By the 1930s educated Vietnamese were converted to the Western approach, and were demanding that public places be named for Vietnamese luminaries rather than French admirals and governors-general.[100]

As distinct from mandarins of the "protected" royal administration, Vietnamese occupying clerk positions in the French colonial hierarchy were generally unable to demand the adherence of their subordinates to name-taboo protocol; worse still, their French superiors insisted on calling them by the familiar *tu*, and, of course, paid them only a fraction of what their French counterparts received. All of this probably increased their need to have fellow Vietnamese address them by fancy job titles, for example, "Mr. Postal Supervisor" or "Exalted Translator Mandarin." Even the socially reformist journal *Phu Nu Tan Van* [Women's News] indulged in an elaborate discussion of how to properly translate the French title *Assesseur*. If such linguistic palliatives were still inadequate, a Vietnamese functionary could join one of many new religious and social organizations and eventually be referred to as "Grand Chamberlain" or "Honorable Mr Chairman."[101]

The pretensions of office were only the tip of the iceberg. That status was a fundamental aspect of the Vietnamese language is reflected by the fact that there was no pronoun *you*, and by the strong preference for avoiding the use of *I*. A wide range of quasi-familial terms were employed instead, almost all of them implying a vertical relationship based on age, social class, job function, sex, or moral judgment. As Vietnamese intellectuals came to question traditional social patterns, they naturally explored the role of language as both inhibitor and instigator of social change. Thus, the prominent young writer Tran Huy Lieu, wishing to give the lower classes more social significance, criticized the practice

99. Their real names were Nguyen Huu *Bai* and Hoang Trong *Phu*. Phan Khoi, "Tuc Kieng Ten" [The Custom of Name Taboo], PNTV 90 (9 July 1931), pp. 5–8.

100. As Phan Khoi pointed out, this meant that even the direct descendants of Vietnamese luminaries would have to break tradition and utter the forbidden names. However, he specifically exempted the names of the Nguyen kings when proposing the elimination of all name taboos.

101. PNTV 103 (8 Oct. 1931). See also Alexander Woodside, "The Development of Social Organizations in Vietnamese Cities in the Late Colonial Period," *Pacific Affairs* XLIV, no 1 (Spring 1971), pp. 46–48.

of calling peasants by the non-descript term *ke* 'person,' of referring to artisans as *chu* 'father's younger brother,' and of merchants being downgraded to *con* 'children.' Meanwhile, he said sarcastically, even the wives of the outmoded literati class were still being addressed as *ba* 'grandmother' or *co* 'paternal aunt.'[102] Phan Khoi hypothesized that once upon a time all Vietnamese had simply called each other *may tao* 'you and me,'[103] but that the development of social classes and perfection of ritual had eliminated that practice in favor of the current multitude of status pronouns. Although troubled by the broader implications of this hypothesis, i.e., that language becomes more restrictive the more "civilized" the society, Phan Khoi limited himself to proposing several modest reforms. These included: upgrading the first-person singular *toi*, which at one time had probably been limited to the "ruler-subject" (*vua-toi*) relationship; limiting the derogatory third-person singular *no* to animals; and employing the term *ho*, traditionally meaning 'family' or 'clan,' for the third-person plural 'they.'[104] Within a decade or two these suggestions were commonly in use.

Intellectuals of more radical bent than Phan Khoi wanted to go further. They were faced, for example, with the dilemma of how a modern political leader should refer to his followers and vice versa. The term *dan* 'people' had already broadened beyond the original concept of 'children of the ruler' to imply a common ethnic identity. The next step was to give *dan* the meaning 'citizens of a modern state.' Perhaps unwittingly, the French made this transformation easier by employing *dan* and the newly coined term *cong dan* 'citizen' to try to convince Vietnamese to pay their taxes more quickly and to obey all colonial laws (see chapter 2). A large instruction manual prepared by a prominent French official was titled *Dan Que Nen Biet* [What Rural People Should Know]. In the body of the text, however, the translator had real difficulty in selecting pronouns. Perhaps in frustration, he often used the politically neutral *nguoi* 'person' to address the reader. Occasionally he slipped and used *nguoi nha que* 'country bumpkin.' On the other hand, when the author's purpose was to encourage the local elite to set up primary schools drawing on village funds, the honorifics *lao thanh* 'old and wise' or *tien sinh* 'sir' were offered as inducement.[105]

---

102. Tran Huy Lieu, *Mot Bau Tam Su* (Saigon, 1927), p. 11.

103. At the time Phan Khoi was writing, *may tao* was used only in situations of closest friendship or as a slur. Hence political prisoners often demanded that guards not employ the *may tao* relationship. Luu Dong, *Buoc Dau Theo Dang* [First Step in Following the Party] (Hanoi, 1961), p. 56.

104. Phan Khoi, "Phep lam Van: Cach dat Dai Danh Tu" [Rules of Writing: The Use of Pronouns], PNTV 73 (9 Oct. 1930), pp. 13–14. It is worth noting that the author gave equal heed to recent changes in *pai-hua* pronoun usage in China and to French language practices.

105. Pierre Grossin, *Dan Que Nen Biet* [Rural People Should Know], third printing (Hanoi, 1928). The term *tien sinh* (Chinese *hsien-sheng*) had been encouraged by Sun Yat-sen in China and enjoyed a brief period of use among educated Vietnamese.

When addressing a public gathering, the prudent solution was to refer to everyone as *ong ba* 'grandfather and grandmother,' plus whatever additional pronouns, higher or lower, were deemed appropriate for a particular audience. The more democratic orators gradually shifted to *anh chi em* 'older and younger brothers and sisters'; others preferred the term *cac ban* 'friends' when addressing strangers, but this sounded far too impersonal when the aim was to win people over or to rouse them to action. During the August 1945 Revolution the term *dong chi* 'comrade' was expanded beyond formal party membership to the public at large, assuming some of the political mystique of *citoyen* in 1789 France or *tovarich* in 1917 Russia. However, it was not long before "comrade" also took on a ritualized character, or was absorbed into the mainstream by the simple device of appending another pronoun, for example, *anh dong chi* 'elder brother comrade.' Ho Chi Minh, who probably understood the meaning of the word *comrade* better than any other Vietnamese, preferred to style the Vietnamese citizenry as *chau* 'nieces and nephews' and to be called *bac* 'elder paternal uncle.'

Despite the continuance of many traditional pronouns, the more extreme quasi-familial usages were being whittled down or confined to historical discussions. Thus, a primary school pupil would still refer to himself as *con* 'child' when addressing his teacher, but a university student could use *toi* 'I' when talking with his professor. The leader of a voluntary organization—a youth group, for example—would probably ask that he be called *anh* 'elder brother' rather than something more lofty.[106] Even the rigidly structured Catholic Church saw changes, priests now being styled *cha* 'father' rather than *co* 'paternal great-grandfather.' *Bam* was abandoned as an additional honorific when talking to the rich and powerful.[107] Changes went further in the Democratic Republic of Vietnam after 1945, with the "grandfather-grandmother" usage being restricted largely to real family relationships; persons of status demanded less language deference, and, more importantly, subordinates were far less willing to accord it to them.

As some Vietnamese women began to object in print to their traditional position of inferiority (see chapter 5), it was inevitable that this, too, would be linked to the language question. Thus one prominent female writer, Mme Nguyen Duc Nhuan, criticized her peers for referring to themselves in print as *em* 'younger sister' or sometimes even *con* 'child' or *to* 'servant.' "Don't depreciate yourselves that way," she counseled. Instead, women should use *toi* 'I' just like the men and

---

106. Vu Dinh Hoe, *Nhung Phuong Phap Giao Duc o cac nuoc va van de Cai Cach Giao Duc* [Education Methods in Various Countries and the Question of Educational Reform] (Hanoi, 1945), p. 124.

107. For a more detailed discussion of pronoun references, at least as employed in the Republic of Vietnam before its demise in 1975, see Laurence C. Thompson, *A Vietnamese Grammar* (Seattle: Univ. of Washington Press, 1965), pp. 248–52, 294–306; see also Buu Lich, *Van De Than Toc* [The Question of Lineages] (Saigon, 1966).

thus help to raise their collective status.[108] Although Mme Nguyen Duc Nhuan was obviously limiting her proposal to educated women—and would have been quite offended if her female servants had styled themselves *toi*—the idea did spread, and the use of *toi* became one of the emblems of a liberated woman of any class. Nevertheless, when conversing with their husbands, Vietnamese wives continued to style themselves 'younger sister' and husbands were still called 'older brother.' The best that women could gain on this front was a reduction in derogatory pronouns used by husbands toward wives.[109]

Although Vietnamese intellectuals of the 1930s often criticized the traditional extended family system and argued that new socio-economic conditions must produce new patterns of family interaction, no one seems to have proposed that the traditional hierarchical kinship terminology be altered fundamentally. For example, Vietnamese parents were repeatedly chastised for clinging to outmoded customs and attitudes regarding their children, especially in the areas of education, occupational preference, marriage, and post-marital decision-making, yet I have found no suggestion in publications of the period that the constant verbalization of domination/submission be modified, or even that, after reaching adulthood, sons and daughters might stop styling themselves 'children' when talking to their parents. Nor, apparently, was there any attempt to simplify the roster of twenty or more pronoun references for particular categories of uncle, aunt, niece, nephew, and cousin.

Only as concerns name taboo within the family was there some change. As Phan Khoi pointed out, the replacement of Chinese characters by the *quoc ngu* syllabary made it difficult, if not impossible, for a child reciting a lesson in school to eschew any mention of the names of his parents and grandparents. Previously, the pupil might have been permitted to mispronounce a Chinese character representing his father's name, for example, altering *ca* to *co*, or *an* to *yen*. Now that written and oral mediums were united, however, teachers expected every pupil to recite and spell uniformly.[110] Phan Khoi might have added that the same pressure was also exerted on adult journalists, essayists, poets, or anyone else who wrote for public consumption. A few writers tried to avoid using certain words in print, but even they abandoned the practice by the 1930s.[111] Other innovations besides *quoc ngu* compounded the problem, for example, the need to fill out job

---

108. Mme Nguyen Duc Nhuan, " 'Toi' hay la 'em' " [Using "I" or "Younger Sister"], PNTV 71 (25 Sept. 1930), p. 22. Actually, the author favored *ta* over *toi*, but admitted that the former might be too haughty.

109. A male writer urged husbands to drop the *may tao* relationship when talking to wives because of its implied arrogance. If husbands did this, he suggested, then perhaps wives would stop such derisive references to them behind their backs as *no* or *thang do*. Dang Van Bay, *Nam Nu Binh Quyen* [Equal Rights for Both Sexes] (Saigon, 1928), p. 21.

110. Phan Khoi, "Tuc Kieng Ten," pp. 7–8.

111. For example, in the long letter to *Nam Phong* by Dr. Tran Van Don, cited in n. 59, the author insisted on writing *nho* as *nhu*, presumably out of respect for one of his parents or ances-

applications or medical forms, to respond to official queries about family background, to carry accurate identification papers. Nevertheless, at home the personal names of one's parents and grandparents generally continued to be taboo, and the idea of naming a newborn infant after any close relative remained repulsive.

Vietnamese pronouns had long been employed to symbolize moral judgments or to demonstrate particular emotions, as well as to convey more obvious age, class, status, sex, and kinship distinctions. Thus, if a speaker wanted to castigate someone, he might use *may* for 'you' or *no, han,* or *thang* for 'he.' Much of the Vietnamese swearing vocabulary was (and is) rooted in denigration of a person's kith and kin. At a more subtle level, writers could indicate their own attitude toward a particular character by their choice of pronoun. Historians, who had long divided historical personages into "legitimate" (*chinh*) and "spurious" (*nguy*), naturally selected pronouns that heightened the moral color of their narrative. This approach could prove amusing on occasion, as when an authorized colonial school text instructed pupils that from 1914 to 1918 in Europe a lot of countries had "fought like bandits with each other" (*danh giac voi nhau*).[112]

Once again, Phan Khoi was ready with a reform proposal. Historical figures should be referred to simply by their names, he said, thus avoiding the pronoun problem entirely. Phan Khoi singled out the contemporary historian Tran Trong Kim for criticism, citing his use of "grandfather" (*ong*) to herald the "good" actors and his coy dropping of pronouns or use of *thang* to indict the "bad" ones.[113] Phan Khoi's attitude was adopted by many realist novelists and short-story writers of the late 1930s, as they tried to allow readers to form their own moral opinions about particular characters rather than stacking the deck from the beginning with loaded pronouns. This position did not fare well in the 1940s and beyond, however. In the dominant school of social realism, for example, while criteria for labeling individuals as good or bad changed considerably, the requirement to provide clear-cut labels was reimposed with a vengeance.

Mass Literacy Efforts

While the intelligentsia experimented with new language forms, the Vietnamese public at large developed a thirst for reading and writing unmatched anywhere else in Southeast Asia. Perhaps the earliest concrete indication of this enthusiasm

---

tors. However, that alteration was apparently not retained in his essays on general medicine in PNTV a decade later.

112. DIRIP, *Van Quoc Ngu* [Learning the National Script] (Saigon, 1942), p. 115. It is possible that the Vietnamese author was slipping a wry message of non-association past his French masters.

113. Phan Khoi, "Dinh Chinh lai," p. 10. Apparently, Tran Trong Kim dropped most of the "grandfather" honorifics in the second printing of his influential *Viet-Nam Su Luoc* [Outline History of Vietnam]. Phan Khoi meanwhile broke his own rule by insisting that Phan Chu Trinh be referred to as *tien sinh* rather than *thay.* PNTV 121 (3 Mar. 1932), p. 5.

Cover of one of the most widely published *quoc ngu* literacy primers, compiled by Nguyen Ngoc. Note the display of Chinese characters for added solemnity, a practice that receded quickly in the 1930s. Courtesy of the Bibliothèque Nationale.

was the proliferation of introductory *quoc ngu* manuals. Generally, each manual was about twenty-four pages long and sold for between .06 and .12 piasters. It featured the alphabet in big letters, a variety of the more difficult Vietnamese dipthongs and tripthongs, some writing exercises, and a few concluding reading lessons.[114] Between 1920 and 1940 at least eighty-eight different manuals in 364 editions were published, with a minimum total of 3.7 million copies.[115] About fifteen titles boasted twenty or more editions and cumulative printings of 100,000 to 200,000 copies. As might be expected, most of these large-circulation texts had been approved for use in the colonial public schools.[116] However, two Catholic *quoc ngu* primers published in Qui Nhon achieved a combined circulation of at least 392,000 copies between 1920 and 1936. And several manuals claiming more

114. There were intriguing exceptions to this pedagogical pattern. One self-instruction primer, Tran Ha Thanh, *Hoc Tieng Me De* [Studying the Mother Tongue], 20,000 copies (Cholon, 1930[?]), for example, organized Vietnamese words in large grids, the first letter or syllable varying alphabetically down the left margin and the last across the top. The second half of the booklet was filled with ads for Sino-Vietnamese medicines. Frenchmen also put forth *quoc ngu* study systems, particularly in the early stages. In 1912, for example, F. H. Schneider devised a technique for learning *quoc ngu* without a teacher, meant especially for officials already competent in Chinese and *nom*. AOM (Aix) R 19.127.

115. These figures are based on my admittedly incomplete examination of holdings in the Bibliothèque Nationale (Paris) in 1971–72. See chapter 1 for a general discussion of publications.

116. This was definitely true of the two largest circulation manuals of the 1920s: Nguyen Ngoc, *Van Quoc Ngu* [Learning the National Script] (Hanoi, n.d.); and Do Than, *Méthode Prati-*

A father points his son toward the village school, first stop on the road to modernity. Tran My Nguyen, comp., *Hoc Quoc Ngu Chi Nam* (Hanoi, 1927). Courtesy of the Bibliothèque Nationale.

than 100,000 copies were clearly designed as much for home use as for school instruction.[117]

It is remarkable how so many of these introductory *quoc ngu* manuals managed to convey a sense of anticipation and excitement amidst the simple letter clusters and rote exercises. On the cover of one primer, for example, was the picture of a proud father leading his son to school.[118] Another primer had a delightful drawing of three children studying together.[119] Some of the passages for recitation pointed out how literacy was the key to opening a vast treasure-house of knowledge; others emphasized the patriotic significance of finally linking spoken and primary written language systems. While some of the hyperbole was designed merely to improve commercial sales, there can be no doubt that publishers were responding to a more fundamental upsurge in public demand

---

que pour l'Etude du Quoc Ngu (Hanoi, n.d.). During the 1930s, however, the colonial government published its own larger version, which combined introductory *quoc ngu* instruction with a more extensive series of reading and recitation exercises. DIRIP, *Van Quoc Ngu*, 13th printing (50,000 copies) (Hanoi, 1940).

117. See, for example, *ABC Van Quoc Ngu* [Learning the ABCs of the National Script], 15th printing (10,000 copies) (Saigon, Xua Nay, 1939).

118. *Au Hoc Quoc Ngu Chi Nam* [Guide to Childhood Study of the National Script], 2nd printing (20,000 copies) (Hanoi, 1927).

119. *Quoc Ngu Vo Long [National Script Primer]*, 9th printing (10,000 copies) (Hanoi, 1929).

for *quoc ngu* instruction, a demand confirmed in scores of newspaper and journal articles of the period.

Until about 1930 there was a tendency among the Vietnamese intelligentsia to assume that public and private school instruction combined with some manuals for home study were sufficient to overcome the problems of mass illiteracy. Indeed, a significant expansion was underway in the numbers of Vietnamese capable of reading (see chapter 1). However, from the early 1930s, most intellectuals were dissatisfied with the pace of progress and convinced that more imaginative solutions were needed. This period also saw a growing intelligentsia desire to "go to the people," not just selling them newspapers or making speeches, but living among the masses, understanding conditions, and perhaps forming organizations. Private *quoc ngu* instruction was both an often-heard request of workers and peasants and something the intelligentsia was uniquely qualified to undertake. Conservative Vietnamese often saw such instruction as an opportunity to induce the lower classes to use their leisure time constructively rather than wasting it by drinking, gambling, or "disturbing social order and paralyzing the nation's moral system."[120] Radical Vietnamese saw literacy instruction as a bridge to broader political education, as well as a legal cover for recruiting followers who would help them challenge the existing order.[121]

As might be expected, teachers and journalists were the first to push hard for further mass literacy initiatives. Some of them had already published *quoc ngu* primers.[122] During 1935 they campaigned vigorously for the government to alleviate the plight of students forced to drop out of school because of continuing adverse economic conditions. In September 1936 a Provisional Committee for Free Education was established in Hanoi to try to improve and expand the private schools.[123] In 1937 a society against illiteracy was proposed, by means of which everyone competent in *quoc ngu* would be mobilized to teach wherever needed. Illiteracy had to be considered as serious a threat as cholera, the author of the proposal argued, since it, too, could retard people or even lead to the extermination of an entire nationality.[124]

120. Trong Duc, "Van De To Chuc Nhung Thi Gio Ranh Viec cua Binh Dan o Xu Ta" [The Question of Organizing the Spare Time of the Common People in Our Country], *Vai Van De Dong Duong* [Some Indochina Questions] (Hanoi, Feb. 1945), p. 123.

121. For example, *Su That* 1 (5 Sept. 1936), suggested that a workers' union could increase its membership in a single factory from twenty to three hundred simply by starting night classes and setting up a reading room.

122. Nguyen Cong Hoan, *Van Chu Viet Nam* [Learning Vietnamese Words], 1st printing (5,000 copies) (Hai Duong, 1929); Le Mai, *Van Quoc Ngu*, 28th edition (50,000 copies) (Saigon, 1929); Nguyen Khac Hieu, *Len Sau*, 6th printing (5,000 copies) (Hanoi, 1925).

123. The secretary of this committee was a young teacher named Vo Nguyen Giap. *Le Travail* (Hanoi) 2 (23 Sept. 1936).

124. X. N., *Luttons contre l'Analphabètisme qui paralyse notre peuple* (Hanoi: An Thinh, 1937). Although the author cited the Soviet Union and China as places where "armies of mili-

During this period various groups of Vietnamese intellectuals tried to get government permission to form a private organization of this type, but met with no success. Finally, with the aid of some timely lobbying among French Popular Front leaders in Paris, a group of fifteen prominent Hanoi intellectuals was given permission to establish the Association for the Dissemination of Quoc Ngu Study (Hoi Truyen Ba Hoc Quoc Ngu).[125] Chairman of the association was Nguyen Van To (1889–1947), a conservative scholar employed at the École Française d'Extrême-Orient, but also acceptable to radical Vietnamese because of his moral integrity and patriotism.[126] Radicals held the key positions of secretary and treasurer. Vo Nguyen Giap was assistant treasurer, and the headquarters of the association was at the private school where he taught. Presumably, the French expected that several government functionaries, among whom the most prominent was Tran Trong Kim, Tonkin primary school inspector, would exert a restraining influence.

Radical members of the association's leadership committee held the initiative for fourteen months, during which time they adhered scrupulously to the bylaws and concentrated on selecting young, upright, patriotic teachers for the night classes. They also publicized the organization's instructional methods and objectives far beyond the few cities in which they were allowed to begin courses.[127] Significantly, conservative members of the association were not alienated and generally chose to stand for re-election in April 1939.[128] Even avowed anti-communist journals regularly gave the association favorable publicity.[129] After the outbreak of war in Europe in September 1939, most of the radicals ended up in jail or in the mountains. However, several covert members of the Indochinese Communist Party, as well as a number of sympathizers, continued to play key roles in the association.[130]

---

tants" had organized literacy classes among the people, he was careful to suggest that for Indochina it was advisable to have colonial officials involved in every echelon of the proposed society.

125. Draft bylaws were submitted for government approval on 19 May 1938. A public discussion was held in early June, and Résident-Supérieur Chatel gave formal permission on 29 July 1938. Bylaws of Hoi Truyen Ba Hoc Quoc Ngu (Hanoi, 1938); Tin Tuc (Hanoi) 9 (4 June 1938). At about the same time a "Société des amis de l'école populaire" was formed in Saigon to expand both quoc ngu and French instruction. Les Critiques (Saigon) 11 (20 July 1938). However, I have been unable to discover whether it enjoyed any success.

126. Nguyen Van To was destined to be executed by the French nine years later.

127. The Central Committee of the ICP carefully instructed its members in August 1938 to obey the association's bylaws to the letter so that the French would have no excuse for shutting it down. Vu Huy Phuc, "Vai net ve Phong Trao Thanh Toan Nan Mu Chu o Viet Nam" [Some Comments on the Movement to Wipe Out Illiteracy in Vietnam], NCLS 30 (Sept. 1961), p. 34.

128. Notre Voix (Hanoi) 16 (30 Apr. 1939).

129. Chinh Tri Tuan Bao (Hanoi), 23 Mar. 1939.

130. These included Dang Thai Mai, Ton That Binh, and Tran Van Giap. Further information on 1938–39 association activities is available in Tin Tuc 24 (6 Aug. 1938), 27 (20 Aug. 1938), 31 (3 Sept. 1938), 35 (17 Sept. 1938), and 41 (8 Oct. 1938); Notre Voix 12 (2 Apr. 1939) and 20 (28 May 1939).

The Association for the Dissemination of Quoc Ngu Study organized its first classes in September 1938. Four hundred people, aged six to "over thirty," signed up. One hundred had to be dropped for lack of suitable teaching space.[131] By December a leftist youth journal was complaining about colonial obstructionism and scare tactics, especially in the countryside. "If they don't want to meet their [literacy] responsibilities," the editors grumbled, "then at least let others get on with the work."[132] By January 1939 Hanoi enrollments had climbed to 1,300, and classes were also underway in Haiphong and Viet Tri. A special appeal was issued for women to get more involved in the movement, no matter what the opposition from either family members or local authorities.[133] By May 1939, similar classes were being taught in central Vietnam, especially in and around the royal capital of Hue.[134] However, during the years 1938–39 almost all attempts to set up classes in rural areas were stymied.

Perhaps because known Communists in the association were eliminated after September 1939, the French relaxed their policy and allowed private *quoc ngu* classes to be established in some provincial towns of northern and central Vietnam. The fall of France to the Germans and the establishment of an uneasy Japanese–Vichy partnership in Indochina led to further improvements for the association. *Quoc ngu* instruction was now seen by the French as part of a larger strategy to involve the Vietnamese in a type of cultural nationalism compatible with French political interests, but divorced from the Japanese concept of a Greater East Asia Co-Prosperity Sphere.[135] As the wartime colonial budget could not begin to meet Vietnamese popular educational aspirations, a select number of voluntary organizations were allowed to expand their activities substantially.[136]

131. *Tin Tuc* 35 (17 Sept. 1938). The authorities had insisted that all regulations applying to private schools be adhered to by the association, which excluded classes on worksites or in village communal halls.

132. *The Gioi* (Hanoi) 5 (1 Dec. 1938).

133. *The Gioi* 7 (1 Jan. 1939).

134. *Notre Voix* 20 (28 May 1939). Court functionaries and private school teachers cooperated in establishing literacy classes in central Vietnam. CMCD-9, p. 171. One key location appears to have been the Thuan Hoa private school in Hue, run by Ton Quang Phiet, a former political prisoner and continuing clandestine member of the ICP. Thuan Hoa Hoc Hieu, *Hoc Sinh Nghi He* (Hue, 1937), pp. 12–13, has a list of school teachers.

135. Japanese authorities in Indochina from September 1940 allowed the French to continue routine colonial administration, but also set up Japanese-language classes and subsidized publication of Japanese textbooks as part of a more general effort to woo the local populace. The French responded by promoting native functionaries to higher ranks, expanding primary education, and giving some private organizations more freedom to function. Office of Strategic Services, *Programs of Japan in Indo-China* (intercepts of shortwave broadcasts) (Honolulu, 1945).

136. Besides the Association for the Dissemination of Quoc Ngu Studies, these included the Boy Scouts, the Catholic Youth Organization, Thanh Nien Tien Phong (Vanguard Youth), and various other groups authorized by the French commissioner of youth and sports.

In July 1944 a general meeting of the Association for the Dissemination of Quoc Ngu Studies was held in Hanoi, attended by seven hundred representatives from different parts of the country. After this meeting and the attendant publicity, there was an upsurge in local requests for teachers. During the next twelve months the association recorded 1,971 volunteer teachers engaged in instructing 59,827 students. Some 175,000 *quoc ngu* primers were printed and distributed free to students during this period, quite an accomplishment considering the shortage of paper and the rampant inflation. During this period, too, the association was finally able to set up four branches in southern Vietnam.[137] Nevertheless, Nguyen Van To, chairman of the association, was acutely aware that the needs of village people were still essentially unfulfilled, since most rural classes were still taking place in provincial centers.[138]

Besides recruiting volunteer teachers, starting classes, and supplying free books and writing materials to students, the association performed a major service to future cadres by devising certain pedagogical techniques better suited to mass literacy efforts. Association teachers were expected to be both strict and approachable. Classes were meant to be serious and carefully structured: students walked single-file in and out of the room, monitors were appointed, and there were group recitations and periodic examinations. Corporal punishment was allowed for boy students, but girls were to be rebuked verbally and adults were only to be chastised gently. According to the association's pedagogical manual, because many students came from poor families, they had a tendency to be "sloppy and mischievous." Nevertheless, a teacher who spent most of his time maintaining discipline was obviously doing something wrong. Nor were teachers to insist on being called by traditional honorific titles. They were also to permit curious outsiders to observe classroom proceedings. Each association branch was told to prepare contingency plans for dealing with neighborhood ruffians who might try to disrupt proceedings, steal supplies, or threaten students on their way to and from classes. Teachers were asked to meet with each other once a week to learn from each other's experiences. Area directors were selected to visit classes regularly, keep records, distribute supplies, and counsel teachers. They were to resolve problems not by acting as superior to inferior, but by stimulating collective discussion.[139]

137. This compared with thirty branches in the north and fifteen in central Vietnam. There were also branches for Vietnamese residing in Phnom Penh and Vientiane. Vu Huy Phuc, "Vai net," p. 35. Wartime activities of the association can be followed in the fortnightly Hanoi journals *Thanh Nghi* and *Tri Tan*.

138. *Thanh Nghi*, 5 Feb. 1945. The association's projects to establish mobile libraries, exhibitions, and teacher-training courses were also still in the planning stages.

139. Hoi Truyen Ba Hoc Quoc Ngu, *May dieu can thiet cac Thay Day Giup Hoi Nen Biet* [Important Things Teachers Helping the Association Need to Know] (Hanoi, 1940).

The association also helped to break new ground in the methodology of language instruction. For example, rather than induce students to recite the spelling of each word in a ritual lilt, as had been the practice, students were encouraged to sound out words by syllables. This was particularly effective with Vietnamese, as there were very few disparities between sound and script. Even more important, the association experimented with the use of traditional poetry meters to fashion jingles that helped students to remember what they had learned. Thus, when studying how to write the alphabet, the following ditty recalled the distinction between o and a, i and t:

> o and a are different letters,
> Because a has a fishhook on its side.
> i and t both have hooks,
> But small i has a dot and long t a cross.[140]

Despite this concession to popular poetry, the Association for the Dissemination of Quoc Ngu Studies retained a firmly elitist orientation. For example, teachers were not asked to research the local environment or to prepare lessons of value to the particular audience. At most, students might be given several exercises dealing with how to use the train and postal services.[141] The bulk of the reading lessons, however, continued to uphold the virtues of diligence, neatness, and social harmony.[142] Like primary teachers almost everywhere else in the world, they held to the curious assumption that to train the hand to write correctly was simultaneously to discipline the mind and to promote civilized conduct.[143]

Meanwhile, Communist Party members jailed or forced to flee to the mountains in 1939–40 were not entirely idle on the literacy front. Actually, a number of cadres imprisoned a decade earlier had often whiled away the time by either teaching or studying *quoc ngu*.[144] And participants in the "soviet" movement of Nghe An and Ha Tinh provinces in 1930–31 had made a point of organizing *quoc ngu* classes.[145] Now, however, they tended to approach cultural advancement in general, and literacy instruction in particular, far more diligently and

---

140. Vu Huy Phuc, "Vai net," p. 34 (written in verse).

141. Tran Van Giap, Hoang Xuan Han, and Vu Hy Truc, *Van Quoc Ngu* (Hanoi, 1939).

142. Hoang Dao Thuy, comp., *Truyen Anh Em Bac Ben* [A Story of Brothers and Sisters at Bac Ben], 2nd printing (Hanoi, 1944).

143. Surprisingly enough, two decades later National Liberation Front literacy teachers were being told exactly the same thing. *ABC Writing Instruction* (Rach Gia, 1966) (translated by U.S. intelligence).

144. See, for example, Pham Hung, "Trong Xa Lim An Chem," *Tren Duong Cach Mang* (Hanoi, 1960), pp. 34–41.

145. Trung Chinh, "Tinh Chat Doc Dao cua Xo Viet Nghe Tinh" [Unique Characteristics of the Nghe Tinh Soviets], NCLS 30 (Nov. 1961), p. 13.

methodically. Considerable ingenuity was demonstrated in the fashioning of study materials. Before long several colonial prisons had clandestine *quoc ngu* newspapers circulating among the interns.[146]

One of the first things Ho Chi Minh did upon his return to Vietnam in 1941 was to organize a literacy class at his Pac Bo headquarters near the Chinese border. "You must study in order to know . . . and you must know in order to carry out a revolution," he instructed his students. During this period Ho Chi Minh also typed out a number of essays and poems for cadres to use in teaching. He insisted that all Party members become literate, and that all literate cadres form classes wherever they might go.[147] One of the first graduates of Ho Chi Minh's literacy class was employed to read copy submitted by writers for *Cuu Quoc* [National Salvation], the main Viet Minh newspaper. If this man was unable to explain the content of a prospective article to Ho Chi Minh, it was sent back for revision.[148]

It was in the Viet Minh liberated zones that learners often became active participants in the educational process rather than passive recipients of information. This was particularly important in mountain areas, where the vast majority of residents spoke something other than Vietnamese as their first language. They wanted to know how to romanize words in their own particular language, and ethnic Vietnamese working among them were happy to oblige, not least of all because it facilitated study of the language by outsiders. It was not long before each of the major languages spoken by the mountain peoples of northern Vietnam had a romanized script and some basic instruction materials. All Viet Minh literacy work, Vietnamese or other, was carried out in conditions that would have made most members of the Association for the Dissemination of Quoc Ngu Studies blanch. Flat rocks, tiles, or banana leaves made acceptable writing surfaces. There was no shortage of chalk in the limestone mountains, and a number of tropical plants made good ink. As Viet Minh units could seldom stay in one place for very long, it was sometimes necessary to hide books and writing materials at key locations for a variety of people to use. Ferry crossings, rest stops, and wood-cutting areas were favorite points. Even when marching it was possible to study,

---

146. Perhaps the best-organized classes and printing operations were those inside Son La prison, 125 miles west of Hanoi. Dang Kim Giang, "Truong Quan Chinh Trong Nha Tu Son La" [A Military-Political School inside Son La Prison], in *Nguoi Truoc Nga, Nguoi Sau Tien* [The Front Rank Falls, the Rear Advances] (Hanoi, 1960), pp. 53–58; Xuan Thuy, "Suoi Reo Nam Ay" [The Bubbling Spring in That Year], in *Len Duong Thang Loi* (Hanoi, 1960), pp. 63–68.

147. Phan Ngoc Lien, "Tim hieu ve Cong Tac Van Dong, Giao Duc Quan Chung cua Ho Chu Tich trong thoi gian Nguoi o Pac Bo" [Investigating President Ho's Mass Mobilization and Education Efforts While He Was at Pac Bo], NCLS 149 (Mar.–Apr. 1973), pp. 14–15.

148. *Nhan Dan* (Hanoi) 2537 (1 Mar. 1961).

for example, by hanging a few words on each person's back and then shuffling the line occasionally.[149]

These two literacy endeavors, one legal and essentially urban, the other clandestine and carried out mainly among mountain peoples, came together during the August 1945 Revolution. One of Ho Chi Minh's first acts as provisional president of the Democratic Republic of Vietnam was to declare a nationwide campaign to wipe out illiteracy.[150] It seemed a wildly utopian objective, especially if conceived in ordinary pedagogical terms. The responsible government agency was allocated an amount of money that could at best have employed 1,000 teachers—when the minimum needed was 100,000. A partial solution was to rely entirely on voluntary teachers, and to use the money for publishing textbooks (2.5 million copies in fourteen months) and for organizing teacher training courses. However, Ho Chi Minh sounded the broader call, ideally tuned to the spirit of those days:

> People who cannot yet read and write must put all their effort into it. If the wife can't read, then the husband should instruct her. If the younger brother can't read, then the elder brother must help. If parents can't read, then it is up to the children to teach them. Employers must instruct employees, and the rich must open classes in their homes to teach unlettered neighbors. Landlords, plantation and mine supervisors, and factory managers must open classes for their tenants and workers. Women, especially, need to study, since they have been held back so long. Now is the time for you sisters to work to catch up to the men, to demonstrate that you are a part of the nation, with the right to elect and to be elected. In this entire endeavor I hope that the youth of both sexes will show particular energy and enthusiasm.[151]

Between September 1945 and December 1946 the Department of Mass Education reported 95,665 voluntary instructors as having taught 2,520,678 people how to read and write. While it is impossible to verify such figures, there can be no doubting the intensity and scope of the literacy movement during this period. One characteristic of newly independent Vietnam was the barefooted peasant walking to evening classes, tiny oil lamp in one hand, battered *quoc ngu* primer in the other. Classes were held in village communal houses (*dinh*), pagodas, private residences, shops, and offices. It was not unusual to see three generations of one family sitting side by side, laboriously scratching out the lesson on slate boards or scraps of paper. For those who could not or would not attend evening sessions, there were special classes at the marketplace, in the rice fields, and

---

149. FLPH, *Struggle Against Illiteracy in Viet Nam* (Hanoi, 1959), pp. 15–16, 24.

150. Three decrees issued 8 September 1945 established a Department of Mass Education (Nha Binh Dan Hoc Vu), instructed each village to have at least one class underway within six months, and made *quoc ngu* studies compulsory in all regions of the country. Vu Huy Phuc, "Vai net," p. 36.

151. Nha Binh Dan Hoc Vu, *Van Quoc Ngu* (Hanoi, 1945), p. 1.

A popular woodcut promoting
mass literacy in the Democratic
Republic of Vietnam. Courtesy
of l'Ecole Française d'Extrême-
Orient, Paris.

aboard fishing boats. Study words were scrawled on the sides of buildings and
train cars, and even on the mud-encrusted flanks of water buffalo. A team of
fishermen hauling in nets or a group of girls transplanting rice might have ten
different syllables painted on their conical straw hats. Flat wicker baskets with
words painted on them were strung from trees along the road or at ferry crossings, and people were not supposed to proceed until they had recited to the
satisfaction of a young, enthusiastic village member.

Some local revolutionary committees went further, for example, refusing to
allocate communal land to families with illiterate members, or preventing people
from signing documents that they could not read aloud. Some villages set up
"gates for the blind," through which all the illiterate had to pass while children
mobilized for the occasion jeered at them. Widely circulated poems challenged
the old to catch up with the young, wives to surpass husbands, betrothed to insist
that prospective mates learn how to read and write. To cite one example:

It's not worth much, the hibiscus flower,
With its bright red color but no scent.

Study words hung for the benefit of passing farmers. The sign says, "My neighborhood is determined to wipe out illiteracy before September 2nd" (Vietnam's Independence Day). FLPH, *Struggle Against Illiteracy in Viet Nam* (Hanoi, 1959).

> Likewise, dear girl, your beauty is worth nothing,
> If your mind is still a blank![152]

While such social and psychological pressures appear to have been quite effective in the short run, they could easily become onerous if institutionalized. There was a danger of this from the moment in October 1945 when the Department of Mass Education decided that the entire population of Vietnam was going to learn to read and write by 8 September 1946. When it became obvious that this was not going to happen, and particularly after the outbreak of war in the north in December 1946, the Department revised its approach without abandoning its ultimate objective. The slogan "Studying is Patriotic" now was phrased in more concrete terms: "We must be literate to emerge victorious in the Resistance."[153] There was also less compulsion and more explanation of the practical benefits of

152. FLPH, *Struggle Against Illiteracy*, p. 26.

153. In Vietnamese the two slogans are "Di hoc la yeu nuoc" and "Co biet chu khang chien moi thang loi." Vu Huy Phuc, "Vai net," p. 38.

literacy. More attention was devoted to what happened after a student completed his or her first class of three or four months. A whole system of complementary classes was organized, with elementary courses in hygiene, science, history, geography, civics, and mathematics. After the signing of the Geneva Peace Accords it was possible to mount yet another campaign in Vietnam north of the seventeenth parallel. By the end of 1958 it was claimed that 93.4 percent of the lowland population aged twelve to fifty could read and write.[154] Not surprisingly, following the 1975 liberation of South Vietnam, one of the first decisions of the new regime was to institute a mass literacy and complementary education campaign.

The Interplay of Sound and Script

Viet Minh leaders were aware that even if their most optimistic literacy projections were confirmed, a substantial proportion of mass education would still have to be accomplished by means of spoken Vietnamese. More than that, Viet Minh cultural cadres would have to understand and appreciate popular oral traditions sufficiently to relate them selectively to revolutionary objectives. Without this effort—not easy for radical intellectuals who previously had tended to disparage Vietnamese folk traditions—it would be impossible to mobilize the rural masses.

During the years 1943–45 there was an outpouring of poems, songs, stories, and aphorisms on a variety of patriotic and social revolutionary themes.[155] Some were initiated by well-known literary figures; others blossomed anonymously and spread quickly by word of mouth or by means of crude flyers and local news sheets. Perhaps the most interesting creations were those that employed traditional stylistic criteria to convey entirely new ideas. For example, the same 6-8 poetic meter used by *nom* writers and unlettered peasants for centuries was now put in the service of modern epidemiology, explaining orally and effectively the relationship between germs, poor hygiene, and unboiled water, and between failure to be inoculated and the existence of cholera.[156] Another poem targeted the common housefly:

154. Vu Huy Phuc, "Vai net," pp. 37–42; FLPH, *Struggle Against Illiteracy*, pp. 21–57.

155. The overall relationship between Vietnamese popular culture and revolutionary mass mobilization in the 1940s is a topic whose complexities I am not prepared to handle in this study. One place to begin is with Vietnamese proverbs (*tuc ngu*) and folk songs (*ca dao*). The earliest *quoc ngu* compilation is probably Nhuyen Van Ngoc, *Tuc Ngu Phong Dao* [Proverbs and Folksongs] (Hanoi, 1927). Truong Chinh, *Nhung Bong Hoa Dai: Phe Binh* [Wild Flowers: Literary Criticism] (Hanoi, 1941), is perhaps the first serious intellectual assessment of Vietnamese folk songs.

156. "Vi trung benh ta rat mau" [Germs Cause Cholera Very Quickly], a poem of which 34 lines were recalled for my benefit by Mrs. Uyen Loewald, who learned it while living in a Viet Minh liberated zone in the late 1940s. A more complete study of this topic would require, among other things, a checking of hygiene primers of the 1920s and 1930s for any evidence of similar or identical poems.

What are you carrying in your baggage, Mr. Fly?
I'll bet it's loaded with dangerous illnesses.
See, here's some cholera, there's some TB,
And there are some inflamed eyes and sore throats.
Typhoid, dysentery, scabies. . . .
There's not a soul who hasn't been bothered by you.
Although you may change your form,
Even become immortal,
The meek and the fierce,
The young and the old,
The high and the low,
Must know you as the envoy of Hell.
The more civilized we become,
The more fear we have of you.[157]

Vietnamese culture was rich in musical forms to link with poetry meters and thus further improve the chances of popular transmission. These included folk songs (ca dao), folk opera (cheo), and reform theatre (cai luong). A new form that gained popular acceptance in this period was the marching song, often on patriotic historical themes.[158] One song, "A Call to Youth" (Tieng Goi Thanh Nien), by Luu Huu Phuoc, swept the country in 1945 and served as a rallying cry for an entire generation of Vietnamese. One indication of its importance was the decision of Ngo Dinh Diem, head of the pro-American Republic of Vietnam from 1955 to 1963, to alter the title and some of the words of the song and to declare it the national anthem.[159] Meanwhile, Viet Minh and subsequent National Liberation Front adherents continued to march to the original words.

For a crucial sixteen months, from August 1945 to December 1946, the Democratic Republic of Vietnam had control of Hanoi's reasonably modern printing presses and radio broadcasting facilities. When forced to flee the city, Viet Minh units carried much of this equipment with them, and continued to both publish and broadcast in the mountains until their victorious return to Hanoi in 1954. Their ability to use language for purposes of mass mobilization and mass education was certainly one key to their success.

If one compares the Vietnamese language of the mid-1940s with that of a quarter-century earlier, it is apparent that people were now able to communicate more effectively on a wider range of topics. This was important, not only to the cognitive process of forming ideas, but also to the political process of changing

157. "Chu Ruoi" [Uncle Fly], a poem recalled by Mrs. Uyen Loewald.
158. Three of the most effective writers of marching songs in the early 1940s were Luu Huu Phuoc, Van Cao, and Do Nhuan. Tu Ngoc, "Nhan xet chung ve nen Am Nhac Viet Nam tu 1930 den nay va anh huong qua lai giua no va Van Hoc" [General Remarks on Vietnamese Music from 1930 to the Present, as well as its Interaction With Literature], TCVH 5-1970, pp. 28–37.
159. Thus in Saigon-held areas the song became known as "Citizens!" (Nay Cong Dan Oi!).

society. After the August 1945 Revolution, conditions were ripe to link cognitive and political components of language development in Vietnam. Language aided Vietnamese peasants to become more aware of the world beyond the village. It helped them to rationalize their environment and to begin to organize and to control their destinies. However, language also remained a weapon of political orthodoxy, whether of the old Confucian or—increasingly after 1945—the new Marxist-Leninist variety. This contradiction between greater popular awareness and elite desires to regulate the content and forms of expression is still unresolved. It is not a problem unique to Vietnam, but one encountered by almost every society that takes to heart the idea of linear progress by means of mass education.

5. The Question of Women

One evening a schoolteacher of philandering tendencies left home without telling his wife when he'd be back. Following traditional norms, she faithfully held back dinner untill 11:00 P.M., then sent an older child to try to locate papa and ask him to come home. When papa was nowhere to be found, mama heeded the hunger pangs of her children and put dinner on the table. Then, at 2:00 A.M., with everything cleaned up and the children asleep, papa returned. Although his wife proceeded to bring everything out to serve him, he was angry that she and the children had already eaten. "I don't care what time it is," the husband growled, "You must wait for me. By what right do you eat ahead and expect me to take leftovers?" When his wife meekly countered that perhaps he should let her know when he was going or coming, the husband exploded, accusing her of forgetting "the three submissions" and "four virtues," of expecting him to obey her, and of being polluted by Western ideas picked up at school.

At this point the schoolteacher's wife was expected to make the appropriate gestures of surrender, especially since the children and several boarding pupils had been awakened by the noise and were listening intently. However, she chose to dispute that comment about Western "pollution." "Your remark impugns my dignity, and you have no right to talk like that," she said. For the husband, this was it. He shifted the pronominal reference for his wife to the derogatory *may*, threatened dire physical retribution, and ordered her out of the house as if she were the merest servant. Still the wife spoke back, and he beat her severely, stopped only by the neighbors who rushed in. Yet it did not end there, since the husband, feeling exposed and above all wishing to uphold his status as a schoolteacher of traditional demeanor, carried the argument to everyone he met in the village, using a host of classical expressions to bolster his case. By contrast, his wife was expected to stay at home most of the time, so that few villagers ever heard her side of the dispute. Almost by reflex the village, including the sharp-tongued women in the marketplace, supported the husband. The wife was marked down as a mulish, Westernized oddity probably deserving of divorce.[1]

This story, recounted in 1928 by a male schoolteacher named Dang Van Bay,

---

1. Dang Van Bay, *Nam Nu Binh Quyen* (Saigon, 1928), pp. 24–29.

highlighted the author's more abstract discussion of the issue of sexual equality. Dang Van Bay, like most other Vietnameses intellectuals of the period, was acutely aware that Vietnamese society was being altered substantially, and that as a result interpersonal relations neither could nor should remain the same. How to understand those changes, what attitude to take, and where to go in the future were problems receiving considerable attention.

Dang Van Bay was also representative in selecting the Vietnamese family system as one of the most important verbal battlegrounds. This should not surprise us, considering how traditional Vietnamese formulations provided the family with near-religious status and endowed the father with quasi-priestly functions. In any serious effort to alter the self and society—which even Confucian traditionalists were now granting was necessary—relations between parents and children, husbands and wives, and older and younger siblings would have to be reanalyzed completely. The various roles of women was one obvious place to begin.

Historically speaking, Vietnamese women had never been reduced to cremating themselves along with their husbands as in India or in Champa. They had never worn a veil as in Islamic countries, nor bound their feet as in China. There is some evidence that in prehistoric times they enjoyed equality, even power. Women were certainly active members of the work force. Nevertheless, Chinese colonial administrators (111 B.C.–A.D.939) and, especially, subsequent Vietnamese monarchs went to considerable lengths to convince women that they were by nature inferior, that their roles were rigidly circumscribed, that they should always follow and never lead. While never completely successful, particularly among peasant women, such sustained indoctrination did have a major impact. Women internalized submissive norms almost to the point of believing them to be natural law, and only some disputatious folk songs and risqué poetry gave evidence of alternative values.

With the early years of the twentieth century, however, came the first basic questioning of all aspects of Vietnamese society, including female dependency. By the 1920s, "women and society" had become something of a focal point around which other issues often revolved. Hundreds of books, pamphlets, and articles were published on all sides. Women became conscious of themselves as a social group with particular interests, grievances, and demands. It was often pointed out that if all Vietnamese were oppressed to some degree, then Vietnamese women were the most oppressed of all. Counterattacks on such thinking helped expose the degree to which the French colonial regime and many Vietnamese collaborators were wedded to the pre-modern, conveniently exploitative aspects of Neo-Confucianism.

Almost inevitably, debates over women's rights (*nu quyen*) led rapidly to the question of distinctions among women (as well as men). Whereas in the 1920s there were two primary sides to the issue, moderate feminist and traditionalist, in the 1930s a third position won adherents by focusing on the severe privations encountered by women who worked in factories and mines, on plantations, as tenant farmers, or as servants, concubines, and prostitutes. Such women might still join with their more fortunate upper- and middle-class sisters on some issues. However, when it came to plotting how to get rid of the French and seize control of the means of production, they had more in common with their lower-class husbands and brothers. It was expected that women participating equally in these dangerous struggles would reap equal benefits—an assumption that did not always prove correct. Nevertheless, by 1945 Vietnamese women had come a long way toward understanding themselves in the modern world and acting on that understanding. Equality of the sexes (*nam nu binh dang*) and contributions of women to the new society served as powerful, perhaps essential, weapons in the post-1945 Resistance War.

Traditional Attitudes

Most of the dogma on what a proper Vietnamese woman should be and do was taken from orthodox Confucian texts. Foremost was the principle of chastity (*trinh*), not only the defense of virginity before marriage, but also absolute faithfulness toward one's husband, alive or dead, and a purity of spirit that was meant to transcend worldly desires.[2] Next came the eminently practical "three submissions" (*tam tong*), whereby a woman's life was divided into childhood, marriage, and widowhood, and she was ordered to obey three masters in se-quence—father, husband, and eldest son. Having comprehended the "three sub-missions," there followed a long list of feminine do's and don't's, often gathered together under the rubric of the "four virtues" (*tu duc*): labor (*cong*), physical appearance (*dung*), appropriate speech (*ngon*), and proper behaviour (*hanh*). In work, one mastered cooking, sewing, and embroidery, but normally not reading or writing. In physical appearance, one learned to be attractive to one's husband but not enticing to others. In speech, one was self-demeaning and rigidly polite rather than assertive or imaginative. And in behaviour, one was always honest and loyal to one's superiors.

Beyond such platitudinous designs there existed hundreds of more precise oral prescriptions that fathers and mothers repeated to their daughters, not to men-tion an abundance of precedents drawn from classical and popular sources and recited to children by relatives, teachers, and village elders. Thus, the maxim "Men and women should remain physically distant," while intended primarily as a warning to girls about the lustful designs of men, also served as justification for keeping women protected and socially retarded. To reinforce this taboo, each

---

2. It is worth mentioning that this primary stress given to chastity reflected the Sung dynasty teachings of Chu Hsi, not those of Confucius, Mencius, and other earlier philosophers.

village had concrete historical examples of the unguarded flower that had been violated by the wayward bee, of the purest, fragile drop of rain that had been sullied with ugliest dirt.

Once married (by means of parental negotiations, of course), a woman was to remember, "If your husband is angry, refrain from talking back. Boiling rice doesn't burn when you lower the flame."[3] Women's work, which could range from the cultural amusements of the upper class to the weeding, transplanting, fuel gathering, water fetching, cooking, sewing, and domestic animal raising of most peasant women, never carried with it the prestige or remuneration of men's work. Then, too, a woman was expected to be pregnant as often as possible. Physical complications often combined to weaken her health permanently. On the other hand, if a couple was unable to produce children after a few years, pressure quickly increased to seek out and add a concubine to the family. Romantic novels to the contrary, concubines were usually treated very poorly, akin to indentured servants, so that there existed a class of women inferior even to other women.[4]

Actually, it was necessary for the wife or concubine to have a male child, for, as the saying went, "One boy and you can inscribe a descendant; ten girls and you can write nil." Another more colloquial expression was "A hundred daughters are not worth a single testicle." Women were demeaned at every turn with such phrases as "Heaven above and Earth below, men honoured and women reviled." At festival times, it was women who put in extra hours to prepare special foods but men who made the offering to the ancestors and received the blessings of prosperity in return. Mothers accomplished most of the essential socialization of children, but fathers and paternal ancestors received the credit for sons who subsequently scored well in civil examinations and daughters who managed to satisfy their in-laws. In such an environment it was the unusual woman indeed who acquired any formal education and came to be respected for her intelligence and initiative.

Nevertheless, once married, many a Vietnamese woman found that the hardest cross to bear was not her husband's anger, the occasional presence of a concubine, or the lack of intellectual challenge, but rather the harsh, intolerant ways of the mother-in-law. It was considered routine for mothers-in-law to haze a new arrival mercilessly, and many found pleasure in continuing the practice indef-

3. For a more complete discussion of such proverbs and of premodern values in general, see Cong-Huyen-Ton-Nu-Thi Nha Trang, "Traditional Roles of Women as Reflected in Oral and Written Vietnamese Literature" (Ph.D. dissertation, University of California, Berkeley, 1973). See also Mai Thi Tu and Le Thi Nham Tuyet, *Women in Viet Nam* (Hanoi, 1978), pp. 11–92.

4. This distinction was well summarized in the traditional saying, "A wife is married, but a concubine is bought." For further discussion of such customary distinctions, see Pham Trong Thieu, "Noi ve Nu Quyen o Viet-Nam" [A Discussion of Women's Rights in Vietnam], NP 93 (March 1925), pp. 227–37.

initely. Some of the angriest folk songs dealt with this relationship. Thus, one song concluded that mother-in-law and daughter-in-law, in their roles as mistress and servant, "can never have anything good to say about each other."[5] Another, in repudiation of filial norms, declared:

> Out of affection for my husband I must wail at
> mother-in-law's death,
> I and the old woman were definitely not relatives.[6]

Vietnamese Confucian mandarins and scholars realized that their one-sided, stern and simple maxims directed at women put a strain on credibility. Their answer was to reinforce the system from more subtle angles. One of the more interesting examples of coherent feminine instruction was *Gia Huan Ca* [Family Training Ode], traditionally ascribed to Nguyen Trai, the renowned fifteenth-century strategist, statesman, writer, and moralist. Written in *nom* (demotic characters) rather than Chinese characters, it was clearly meant to be circulated widely among the people, by rote recitation if not reading. Various segments of this 796-line poem did indeed enter the popular oral tradition. As in medieval Europe, one of the author's techniques was to place women on a pedestal, to glorify their oppression. Female chastity, for example, was put almost on a par with such masculine qualities as loyalty (*trung*) and righteousness (*nghia*). If she conducted herself properly, a daughter might even have a chance of being remembered:

> Behold virtuous women of true chastity,
> Whose iron will shields them from lustful fires.
> A pious, gentle daughter gives her parents peace of mind,
> Brings praise to her family and a thousand years' continuity.[7]

If a woman was unlucky enough to be married off to a man with a passion for wine, women, or gambling, the important thing was to conceal the husband's weaknesses and thereby preserve the man's family honor.[8] And, while *Gia Huan Ca* gave mothers considerable responsibility for educating children, it was also

5. Nguyen Van Ngoc, comp., *Tuc Ngu Phong Dao*, vol. 1 (Saigon, 1967), p. 226. (First published in 1928.)

6. Ibid., p. 338.

7. Nguyen Trai, *Gia Huan Ca* (Saigon, 1953), p. 12. Recent research indicates that this poem may have been written in the seventeenth century and subsequently attributed to Nguyen Trai. Other well-known traditional propaganda poems for women included Le Quy Don's *Me Khuyen con ve nha chong* [Mother's Advice on Her Daughter's Going to the Husband's Home]; Ly Van Phuc's *Phu cham tien lam* [Father Outlines the View Ahead], and Tuy Ly Vuong's *Nu pham dien nghia* [An Elaboration of Feminine Ideals].

8. Nguyen Trai, *Gia Huan Ca*, p. 15.

they who would be held culpable if offspring turned out spoiled or ungrateful.[9]

At various times in succeeding centuries Vietnamese male literati embellished *Gia Huan Ca* and added perspectives of their own. Dang Tran Con, in his eighteenth-century *Chinh Phu Ngam* [Lament of a Soldier's Wife], criticized the endless warfare of the period, yet also idealized the women who stayed home faithfully to pine for their husbands and attend to the chores.[10] As we have seen in the preceding chapter, Nguyen Du, with his immortal *Truyen Kieu* ('The Tale of Kieu') of the early nineteenth century, created a scholarly storm for over a century with, among other things, his revisionist interpretation of chastity. Nonetheless, the basic tenets of female passivity, of a daughter's piety toward her parents, and of fidelity to one's mate were upheld and perhaps even enhanced by the tremendous popularity of this work.[11]

In the 1850s there appeared Nguyen Dinh Chieu's *Luc Van Tien*, dealing with the misfortunes of a young scholar (Luc Van Tien) and the girl who loved him from a distance, Kieu Nguyet Nga. Written at a time when Vietnam was facing imminent invasion from the West, *Luc Van Tien* was uncompromising in its adherence to traditional norms, including female subservience. Thus, having only looked at Luc Van Tien and exchanged poems once, Kieu Nguyet Nga yet felt the obligation to attempt suicide when her chastity and fidelity to him were jeopardized. Saved by Kuan-yin, the Buddhist Goddess of Mercy, the heroine was eventually reunited with her idealized lover.[12] Indeed, the response to life of these two well-bred individuals was so nearly ideal that one may assume that the author was engaged in an elaborate allegory, pointing out the evils of contemporary society and the corresponding need, in his opinion, for strict reassertion of traditional ethics. He himself lived by what he preached, refusing any compromise with either the corrupt Vietnamese mandarinate or the arrogant French colonizers.

Well into the twentieth century the ideals of chastity and political rectitude were firmly linked to each other. The story was often told, for example, of the mandarin who, having cooperated with the invading French in the early 1860s, wanted to reverse his position entirely. Instead of being welcomed, he was roundly condemned with the phrase, "Once a girl is spoiled, she can hardly call

9. Ibid., p. 20. For a more thorough discussion of *Gia Huan Ca*, see Nha Trang, "Traditional Roles of Women," pp. 15–46.

10. Dang Tran Con, *Chinh Phu Ngam* (Saigon, 1950). Although the original work was written in Chinese, it was quickly translated into *nom* by Doan Thi Diem, a female contemporary of Dang Tran Con and herself a striking exception to the general education rule.

11. Nguyen Du, *Truyen Thuy Kieu*, 8th printing (Saigon, 1968). Nguyen Du, *The Tale of Kieu* (New York: Random House, 1973). For a further detailing of the ethical questions, see Nha Trang, "Traditional Roles of Women," pp. 83–155.

12. Nguyen Dinh Chieu, *Luc Van Tien*, 4th printing (Saigon, 1946). See also Nha Trang, pp. 48–81.

herself a virgin!" The mandarin returned to his home village, wrote a public apology, and committed suicide. Ironically, a few years later the official who had condemned the 'spoiled' mandarin committed suicide under similar conditions.[13] Tran Huy Lieu, whom we have met already as a young intellectual organizing Phan Chu Trinh's "state funeral" and challenging the traditional precedence given to personal and family matters, still chose to lead off one of his most important nationalist essays in 1927 with the comment, "A young woman who doesn't keep her virginity should be ashamed of being a female, just as a young man who doesn't sort out his innermost thoughts is wasting himself as a male." The author went further, in fact, and equated his own decision to voice his deepest feelings in print with a woman's once-in-a-lifetime decision to surrender her virginity.[14] For modern Vietnamese women successfully to disassociate these images in the public mind was indeed a challenge.

Nevertheless, it would be wrong to assume from the above brief discussion that Confucian moralists had succeeded entirely in propagandizing pre-modern Vietnamese women into submission. Among the plain people in particular there remained a frankness of expression and diversity of life experience that defied regimentation. Each Confucian platitude, for example, could be turned on its head at the right opportunity. Thus, the saying about a hundred girls not being worth a single testicle was countered by "A hundred boys are not worth a girl's earlobe." Another poem humorously rated a woman at the price of a finely-crafted sleeping mat, whereas a whole bundle of men was only good for putting in a cage and letting the ants pick at them. As for concubinage, rather than be forced into that onerous position, poor girls were advised to assuage their hunger by chewing on a fistful of fig leaves.[15] In marathon folk-singing encounters, women were able to publicize their own skills, criticize men's conduct, deftly propose marriage, and even hint of continuing attraction to someone other than their own husbands.[16]

Many folk-songs were intimately related to labor activities, and it was pride in their work that probably did more than anything else to keep women from suc-

---

13. Even in 1974 in Saigon this story was reprinted favorably. Nguyen Duy Oanh, *Chan Dung Phan Thanh Gian* [Portrait of Phan Thanh Gian] (Saigon: Ministry of Education, 1974), p. 148. My thanks to Tran My Van for bringing this to my attention.

14. Tran Huy Lieu, *Mot Bau Tam Su* (Saigon, 1927), preface page. It is, perhaps, more than a human-interest sidelight that about fifty years later Tran Huy Lieu's son Tran Thanh Cong told a foreign correspondent how he had been conceived in 1944 when his father's comrades cut an opening in a prison camp fence and arranged a meeting for Tran Huy Lieu with his wife. Tiziano Terzani, *Giai Phong! The Fall and Liberation of Saigon* (New York: St. Martin's Press, 1976), p. 199.

15. Le Thi Nham Tuyet, *Phu Nu Viet Nam qua cac Thoi Dai* [Vietnamese Women Across the Ages] (Hanoi, 1973), p. 150.

16. Ninh Viet Giao, ed. and comp., *Hat Phuong Vai* (Hanoi, 1961), pp. 13–15, 36–47.

cumbing completely to the dominant ethic implying female guilt or inferiority.
Besides the routine tasks mentioned previously, women usually took the lead in
raising silkworms, spinning, weaving, food processing and preservation, selected
handicraft production, and the marketing of surplus goods. It seems clear that
small groups of women traveled some distance to engage in commerce, despite
Confucian instructions about men handling all extra-family affairs. When men
were away at war or studying (often fruitlessly) for the civil examinations,
women took the economic initiative entirely. Wives also maintained regular contact with maternal relatives, contrary to Confucian norms, and it was not unusual
for them to spend months in the village of their own parents.

Generally, the poorer the family the more likely husband and wife were to rely
heavily on each other, to share tasks, and thus to take superior-inferior strictures
with a grain of salt. On the other hand, wealthier families had perhaps three
generations and various collateral elements and servants under one roof, with all
the role differentiation and vertical organization implied by that situation.
Whether or not the poor peasant woman in a nuclear family was therefore "better off" than the second or third wife in a wealthy extended family is an open
question. We should not forget that the peasant family's existence was often
highly precarious, subject to the destructive whims of flood, drought, pestilence,
and war. It was in these times, especially, that young daughters were sold as
concubines, slaves, or prostitutes. And even in quieter periods there was little to
prevent a powerful mandarin from taking a fancy to a tenant's wife or daughter
and simply appropriating her. The mandarin's son who raped a peasant girl from
an impoverished family might get off scot-free or be asked to pay a token sum.
In such ways the traditional socio-economic structure reinforced demeaning attitudes toward women, and attitudes provided justification for structure.

What the majority of Vietnamese women lacked was not involvement in production, for as one folk-song put it:

> My body toils at a hundred different tasks,
> In the morning I'm out in the ricefields,
> In the evening I'm working the daughter-in-law patch.[17]

Rather, they lacked control of the means of production, they were excluded from
key decision-making, their work was considered less valuable, and their occupational alternatives to laboring in the fields and at home were more circumscribed
than was the case for men. If they wished to exercise power, it had to be via their
menfolk. This was reflected, for example, in the many folk-sayings about wives
slaving so that their husbands might become mandarins. If her husband were

---

17. Le Thi Nham Tuyet, *Phu Nu Viet Nam*, p. 83. The key words are *ruong lua* (ricefields)
and *ruong dau* (daughter-in-law fields), the latter being a metaphorical reference to a host of
very real chores in and around the house.

successful, a wife reaped some reflected glory; and it was not unusual for her to manage her husband's business affairs and even some of his official duties. Perhaps the entire relationship was summed up in the adage, "A man's property is his wife's work."[18] The same principle applied to mothers and sons. Vietnamese tradition abounded with mothers who made endless sacrifices for their sons, especially the eldest, and with men who were motivated more by the desire to repay maternal kindnesses than to obey stern paternal injunctions.

At an earlier stage in Vietnamese history male and female roles had been far less differentiated: matrilineal and patrilineal ties were of roughly equal importance; female gods of fire and fertility ranked as high as male gods; fathers took on many of the responsibilities of caring for infants; women married the brother of a deceased husband (as men might marry the sister of a deceased wife); and positions of leadership were open to individuals of both sexes. Despite later Confucianist denunciations of such practices as "barbaric," and repeated royal proscriptions, residual forms persisted in many localities. Besides, every Vietnamese individual remained familiar with at least two or three female culture giants.[19] Most famous of all were the Trung sisters, who had led a short-lived rebellion against the Chinese overlords in the first century A.D. A popular cult developed around the spirits of these two women, and individual villages also kept alive the names and exploits of their twenty or more female lieutenants.[20]

Two centuries after the Trung sisters, another young woman, Trieu Thi Trinh, took up the same challenge. Although she, too, failed to dislodge the Chinese, the stories that grew up about her tell us much about both the dreams of Vietnamese women and of the fears of the men who fought, followed, or heard of such women in subsequent centuries. According to a late eighteenth-century account, for example, Trieu Thi Trinh was nine feet tall, had three-foot-long breasts and a voice like a temple bell, and was able to eat several pecks of rice and walk five hundred leagues in a single day. Yet she was also said to possess a beauty that could shake the soul of any man. Following repeated altercations with her (evil) sister-in-law, Trieu Thi Trinh killed her and took to the forest, where she soon gathered together a hardy band of braves to harass the Chinese. When her brother counseled that women were not supposed to act in such a way, Trieu Thi Trinh replied:

I only want to ride the wind and walk the waves, slay the big whale of the Eastern sea,

---

18. Ngo Vinh Long and Nguyen Hoi Chan, *Vietnamese Women in Society and Revolution,* vol. 1: *The French Colonial Period* (Cambridge, Mass.: Vietnam Resource Center, 1974), pp. 12–13.

19. Le Thi Nham Tuyet, *Phu Nu Viet Nam,* pp. 29–72.

20. Ibid., pp. 109–11; Ly Te Xuyen, *Viet Dien U Linh* [Vietnamese Palace Spirits] (Hanoi, 1972), pp. 48–49.

clean up our frontiers, and save the people from drowning. Why should I imitate others, bow my head, stoop over and be a slave? Why resign myself to menial housework?[21]

Her brother, deciding that she must be another gifted commander like the Trung sisters, joined up.

Soon Trieu Thi Trinh was riding into battle on a war elephant, breasts strapped over her shoulders, golden tunic glistening in the sun. At first the Chinese underrated her because she was a woman, but after a few confrontations they were terrorized at the very thought of coming under her gaze. Her army was not equipped for seige tactics, however, and rapidly lost discipline while waiting for the Chinese to emerge from their walled fortress. Then, too, Trieu Thi Trinh was said to fear anything impure, smelly, or dirty, so that when the Chinese commander finally ordered his troops to surge out of the fort, they went naked, yelling and kicking up dust like wild animals. This allegedly caused Trieu Thi Trinh to ride off in disgust, which produced panic among her forces and led to her being surrounded and committing suicide. She continued to pursue the Chinese commander in his dreams, however, and a pestilence was blamed on her. His solution was to order woodcarvers to make hundreds of penis images and hang them over doors. Three centuries later, Trieu Thi Trinh appeared in the dreams of yet another (male) Vietnamese opponent of Chinese rule, offering not disease but spiritual support. During the independent Ly (A.D. 1010–1225) and Tran (1225–1400) dynasties she was honored by the central court with various posthumous titles.[22] As Le dynasty (1428–1788) scholars moved to bring Vietnamese practices into conformity with Neo-Confucian doctrine, they must have agonized often about what to do with Trieu Thi Trinh. It is not insignificant that she survived all their manipulations.

To summarize, Vietnamese mandarins and scholars—all male—had nurtured and refined a clear system of oppression for Vietnamese women. While this varied according to class, all women were to some degree affected. Coming into the twentieth century, Vietnamese women had ample reason to protest. That they were able to do so effectively, however, was in part due to the fact that they had never been fully cowed, and that men had never treated them entirely as chattel.

Opening Gambits

A new generation of Vietnamese literati emerged in the first decade of the twentieth century, determined to work for national independence and to modernize

---

21. Ly Te Xuyen, *Viet Dien U Linh*, p. 120.

22. Ibid., pp. 119–25. Visual representations of the Trung sisters and Trieu Thi Trinh can be found in Maurice Durand, *Imagerie Populaire Vietnamienne* (Paris, 1960), pp. 225–29, 231, 235, and 412.

Vietnamese society.[23] At first dimly, later more coherently, some of them came to understand that any serious cultural revolt required an attack on the subordination of women, just as any serious national struggle had a far better chance of succeeding if women were actively involved. Besides, anger at French colonial exploitation of Vietnamese often opened male eyes to other forms of exploitation, including that of women by men, just as women often saw most quickly and perceptively the base character of the colonial relationship. While it took women another two decades to gain their own public voice and begin to organize effectively, there seems little doubt that by 1905-10 old attitudes were already undergoing change among at least a minority of the population.

During this period women were recognized as part of the national polity, at least in theory. Concrete proposals were made for expanding their educational opportunities. At the short-lived but highly influential Dong Kinh Nghia Thuc (Eastern Capital Non-Tuition School) women were encouraged to attend public lectures on history, culture, and politics—at the time a radical innovation. Larger, less scholastic gatherings were organized outside, including dramatic presentations recounting legends surrounding the heroic Trung sisters.[24] Two women, educated daughters of literate families, were allowed the unprecedented honor of participating at the school as teachers of Chinese and quoc-ngu (romanized script).[25] Nonetheless, men occupied all leadership positions at the school, and it was the men who were thrown in jail by the French at the time of the inevitable crackdown.

Phan Boi Chau (1867-1940), who seems to have been more concerned than most of his male contemporaries with the status of Vietnamese women, wrote a fascinating drama, or *tuong*, concerning the Trung sisters.[26] The characters were essentially colonial and anticolonial archetypes in first century A.D. costume. Almost certainly, Phan's main purpose was to focus on the role of Vietnamese women in the forthcoming anticolonial struggle. He posed a situation where women's actions stemmed more from the same patriotic principles that motivated their fathers, husbands, and brothers than from deference to Confucian concepts of female servitude and obligation. Specifically, whereas most writers continued into the twentieth century to emphasize Trung Trac's faithful desire to revenge her husband who had been executed by the Chinese governor-general,

23. David G. Marr, *Vietnamese Anticolonialism, 1885-1925* (Berkeley and Los Angeles: Univ. of Calif. Press, 1971); see, in particular, chapters 4-8.

24. Tran Huy Lieu, ed., *Lich Su Thu Do Ha-Noi* [History of the Capital City of Hanoi] (Hanoi, 1960), pp. 151-52.

25. Tran Huy Lieu et al., CMCD-3 (Hanoi, 1958), p. 31.

26. Phan Boi Chau, *Tuong Trung Nu Vuong; Truyen Pham Hong Thai* [Drama of the Trung Monarch; Story of Pham Hong Thai] (Hanoi, 1967), pp. 15-106. Written about 1911 in Siam, the play was apparently smuggled into Vietnam in various hand-written copies after 1913; subsequent oral transmission produced differing versions.

Phan depicted this as merely the catalyst energizing her preexistent love of country and her desire to expel the foreign invader. And whereas Trung Trac's younger sister, Trung Nhi, had long been portrayed as joining the struggle out of sisterly obligation, Phan placed this motivation second to that of patriotism.[27]

On the other hand, Phan Boi Chau still employed stereotyped female characteristics to make the Trung sisters more "realistic" to his audience. Trung Trac cried pitifully when her husband's body was brought home. In later adversity she temporarily lost her nerve, and her younger sister had to bolster her courage with the appeal, "Come now, we can't give way to ordinary female emotions. We've got to get out and take care of military matters."[28] Fifteen years after Phan wrote these lines, Tran Huu Do, a man of similar political inclination, was still using the female metaphor to represent some of the worst human attitudes to be combatted, for example, passivity, physical and spiritual weakness, sensualism, and narrow-mindedness.[29] In Tran's large pantheon of Western heroes worthy of emulation, only one, Joan of Arc, was a woman, while among Vietnamese historical giants only the Trung sisters ranked with the men. The best that can be said for Tran Huu Do on this matter is that he did not attack the tentative efforts of Vietnamese women to assert themselves, and, by the late 1930s, had successfully eliminated psychological stereotypes from his writings.

The French, after having closed the Dong Kinh Nghia Thuc in early 1908 and then jailed or otherwise neutralized most Vietnamese scholars of anticolonial tendency, moved gradually to promote more politically palatable alternatives. Most important from an intellectual perspective, at least for the seven or eight years following its creation in Hanoi in July 1917, was the monthly *Nam Phong* [Southern Ethos], discussed previously. The editor, Pham Quynh (1892–1945), felt himself eminently qualified to comment on just about every facet of human existence, including the roles of women in various societies East and West, old and new. In a 1917 essay titled "The Education of Women and Girls," Pham Quynh sketched out a very cautious reform concept that for the next decade or so gained adherents among upper-and middle-class Vietnamese of both sexes before being severely attacked and largely discredited.[30]

Apparently, the stimulus for Pham Quynh's article was his concern that newfangled ideas of "male-female equal rights" (*nam-nu binh quyen*) were begin-

27. Phan Boi Chau was not the first to so depict the Trung sisters. Leaders of the Tay Son movement in the late eighteenth century did likewise, and they may well have gotten it from pre-Confucian Vietnamese folklore. Alexander B. Woodside, *Vietnam and the Chinese Model* (Cambridge, Mass.: Harvard Univ. Press, 1971), p. 46.

28. Phan Boi Chau, *Tuong Trung Nu Vuong*, p. 83.

29. Among Tran Huu Do's thirteen available publications I counted no fewer than ten pejorative references to women.

30. Pham Quynh, "Su Giao-Duc Dan Ba Con Gai" [Education of Women and Girls], NP 4 (Oct. 1917), pp. 207–17; reprinted in Pham Quynh, TCVT 1 (Saigon, 1962), pp. 17–35.

ning to seep into Vietnam at the very same time that the old ethical standards were in an obvious state of decline. If women were really to aspire to "self-rule and self-protection," he said, they would need a careful educational regimen or they would fall quickly into the pits of decay and despoilation. On the other hand, he attacked those Vietnamese of "medieval mentality" who felt that the only solution was to keep women illiterate and unaware. Such limited vision, he argued, would lead only to further demoralization; besides, it was unrealistic in the long run. Thus Pham Quynh—backed by members of the French colonial administration—set out a policy of extreme gradualism in dealing with modern opportunities for Vietnamese women.

The key to Pham Quynh's concept was the differentiation of female curriculum according to class. He devoted more than half his essay to a careful delineation of upper-class (including *haut bourgeois*) female instruction on the one hand, and middle class instruction on the other. No mention was made of instruction for lower-class women, either because Pham Quynh considered them irrelevant or because he knew that their families would seldom be able to spare them from the fields and household chores. For the upper class he proposed opening a special private academy for women, with one section of standard classes for young people and a second section of lectures and discussions for more advanced girls and adult women. The bulk of instruction would be in Vietnamese and would emphasize *quoc-ngu* literature, beginning with *Truyen Kieu, Chinh Phu Ngam, Luc Van Tien,* and other works "appropriate to women's nature." Some of the more intelligent students could study a little Chinese, and maybe even some French literature. Nevertheless, he intoned somberly, girls would only have a limited period in their lives for study, and then it would be time for marriage— a new life entirely.

For middle-class girls, Pham Quynh thought it necessary to seek more "practical" results. For him this meant special attention to the first of the traditional female virtues, *cong,* or 'labor,' as distinct from appearance, speech, and behaviour. 'Labor' meant classes in sewing, weaving, and embroidery, plus arithmetic, to meet presumed middle-class preoccupations with buying and selling and maintaining accurate account ledgers. By contrast, upper-class girls were permitted to study the natural sciences, hygiene, geography, and history—if only to participate later as adults in polite social conversation. And, while the upper class might study Chinese or French literature, middle-class girls would have only a smattering of French language such as to allow them to engage in direct commercial relations with the French.

In subsequent years Pham Quynh wrote or translated other articles of relevance to the women's issue. His famous defense of the prostituted Thuy Kieu leaned rather heavily on Western romanticism, lyricism, and the culture of despair, a departure indeed from his policy-oriented discussion of proper ethics and social practicality in women's education.[31] Having idealized the personal sensitivity and unbelievably diverse emotional life of Thuy Kieu, Pham Quynh apparently saw nothing unusual in turning around and denouncing contemporary talk of "freedom and equality," in particular, the desire of certain women to do something other than enable a family to function effectively.[32] To the degree that he was willing to give women any modern intellectual or political role at all, it was as hostesses of salons—after they had helped their husbands to start a career, had families underway, and had sponsored fashionable charities.[33]

Among *Nam Phong* contributors as a whole, differences of outlook concerning women were even more obvious. For example, when Hoang Ngoc Phach, a education student soon to make a name as a pathfinding Vietnamese novelist, condemned 'The Tale of Kieu' and more recent romantic fiction for undermining the effectiveness of long-standing Confucian ethical prescriptions for women, leaving them more vulnerable than before, he was immediately taken to task by several upper-class female readers. Essentially, they told him that women did not need male moral guardians to decide what they should or should not experience. They considered Hoang Ngoc Phach's remarks extremely patronizing, and the sexual double standard—as it applied to literature, at least—quite out of keeping with the age.[34]

Meanwhile, Nguyen Ba Hoc, the well-known literatus, continued unabashedly to defend arranged marriages and to chide Pham Quynh publicly for proposing modern schooling for a minority of Vietnamese women when, he said, the entire country remained so underdeveloped and even educated men were unable to find suitable employment. Besides, "The higher that women are able to study, the more income they will squander, the more their sensual desires will be inflamed, the more destitute they will end up." Women will lose all sense of decency if they act like men, Nguyen Ba Hoc concluded.[35] At about the same time, by way of contrast, a ranking collaborator mandarin, Than Trong Hue, was arguing that

31. Pham Quynh, "Truyen Kieu" ['Tale of Kieu'], NP 30 (Dec. 1919), pp. 480–500 (also available in TCVT 3, pp. 79–131).

32. Pham Quynh, "Dao Duc Luan" [An Essay on Ethics], NP 21 (Mar. 1919), pp. 186–91; also, TCVT 2, pp. 233–44.

33. Idem, "Dia Vi Nguoi Dan Ba trong Xa Hoi Nuoc Ta" [Position of Women in Our Society], NP 82 (Apr. 1924), pp. 269–84. Pham Quynh had been deeply impressed—one might say overwhelmed—by the hostess of a salon to which he had been invited in Paris in 1922. See NP 90 (Dec. 1924), pp. 477–78.

34. Hoang Ngoc Phach, "Van Chuong voi Nu Gioi" [Literature in Relation to Women], NP 41 (Nov. 1920), pp. 379–83; replies by Miss Nguyen Dong Khang and Mrs. Dam Phuong appear in NP 42 (Dec. 1920) and NP 43 (Jan. 1921) respectively.

35. Nguyen Ba Hoc, "Ban ve Nghia Tu Do Ket Hon" [Discussion of the Meaning of Free Marriage], NP 27 (Sept. 1919), pp. 231–35. Nguyen Ba Hoc, "Thu Tra Loi Ong Chu But *Nam Phong*" [Letter Responding to the Editor of *Nam Phong*], NP 40 (Oct. 1920), pp. 322–24.

classical Confucian instructions about women remaining at home had never been carefully observed in Vietnam, and should certainly not be revived now. It had long been quite normal for Vietnamese women to work in the fields, to fashion handicrafts, and to market surplus commodities, he pointed out. "Whatever jobs men can handle, women can too," Than Trong Hue asserted, and this had to be remembered when formulating government policy or organizing groups of citizens.[36]

Later, *Nam Phong* did work out a hybrid conservative stance, essentially combining quaint odes to some unique "Eastern" feminine spirit with distinctly European attacks on women's emancipation. Thus, on the one hand, there appeared a thirteen-part idealized and romanticized translation and commentary on various Chinese women of yore.[37] The editors even reached back two millenia to resurrect and translate a set of Han dynasty feminine instructions.[38] On the other hand, obscure Western writers like Henri Marion, Gina Lombroso, and Félix Pécaut were imported and translated to demonstrate that many people in the "civilized world" also continued to uphold a family-centered existence for women and to oppose free marriage, sexual equality, and coeducational schools.[39] Perhaps these two cultural strands were brought together most cleverly in a five-part serialized translation of "The Diary of a Henpecked Husband," which was in reality a slashing caricature of urban modernized women in contemporary China.[40]

At the behest of the Governor-General, in 1918 Pham Quynh traveled south to Cochinchina and attempted to stimulate interest among some of the older scholar families in closer collaboration with the French. He gave special attention to the family of Nguyen Dinh Chieu, author of *Luc Van Tien*, and still, thirty years after his death, a symbol of stubborn southern refusal to "assimilate" to direct colonial rule. Several descendants firmly declined, but Suong Nguyet Anh (1864–1921), fifth daughter of Nguyen Dinh Chieu and independently known for her

---

36. Than Trong Hue, "Con Duong Tien Bo Cua Nuoc Ta," [Our Country's Progressive Path], NP 8 (Feb. 1918), p. 64.

37. Tung Van (Nguyen Don Phuc), "Dan Ba Dong Phuong" [Eastern Women], NP 101 (Dec. 1925), intermittently thereafter to NP 123 (Nov. 1927). A 1931 reprinting of this series, in five small volumes, includes an introduction denouncing the contemporary idea that women must be "equal" and out in society. See also the poetic creations on women in NP 57 (Mar. 1922) and NP 83 (May 1924).

38. Dong Chau, trans., "Loi Ran Dan Ba Con Gai" [Advice to Women and Girls], NP 130 (June 1928), pp. 568–76. Of a similar nature are the translations of Chu Hsi's poetry on "family education" in NP 7 (Jan. 1918).

39. See translations and interpretations in NP 49 (July 1921), 99 (Sept. 1925), and 149 (Apr. 1930).

40. Lac Kho, "Nhat Ky So Vo" [Diary of a Henpecked Husband], NP 124 to 128 (Dec. 1927–Apr. 1928). I have been unable to identify the original Chinese author.

poetry in both Chinese and *nom*, agreed to participate. The result was Vietnam's first periodical aimed specifically at women, entitled *Nu Gioi Chung* [Women's Bell], published in Saigon each Friday in *quoc ngu*, and financially controlled by Henri Blaquière, director of *Le Courrier Saigonnais*.[41]

In the first issue of *Nu Gioi Chung*, dated 2 February 1918, Suong Nguyet Anh thanked the governor-general for his attention, stated her willingness to co-operate in his program of educational reform, especially of expanded *quoc-ngu* training, and promised to avoid "political" questions. Emphasis in her periodical would be given, she said, to upholding moral standards, to instruction in daily work tasks, to promotion of commerce and handicraft production, and to the general "expansion of contacts among people."[42] Suong Nguyet Anh probably hoped that *Nu Gioi Chung* would become a national women's journal. Her poems often evoked images of solidarity among Vietnamese of north, center, and south.[43] In 1918, however, the number of women proficient in *quoc-ngu* was still quite small, and the editor's extreme caution on political matters presumably reduced the readership even further. To make matters worse, a number of subscribers failed to pay their bills. At the end of 1918, after less than a year of publication, the weekly was terminated.

Suong Nguyet Anh remained in most ways an upholder of traditional values. Indeed, the fact that when her husband died early she had vowed never to re-marry, upholding the widow-image for all to see, was clearly another facet of her appeal.[44] The constant emphasis in her articles on the roles of daughter, wife, and mother within the Vietnamese family carried a special message of authority. More than one admiring writer compared her with the idealized figure of Kieu Nguyet Nga in her father's classic *Luc Van Tien*.[45] Nevertheless, the fact that a woman had taken editorship of a major periodical, however briefly, provided concrete impetus for other upper-class matrons to venture beyond the family. Fifteen years later Phan Van Hum, Trotskyist intellectual, was still trying to explain to himself and his readers how one traditionally inclined woman could inspire so much non-traditional behaviour. His answer, hardly adequate, yet not without cultural significance, was that Suong Nguyet Anh, although very hard on herself, tended to be quite lenient toward others. Specifically, while not appearing

41. Huynh Van Tong, *Lich Su Bao Chi Viet-Nam tu Khoi Thuy den 1930* (Saigon, 1973), pp. 100–102.

42. *Nu Gioi Chung*, no. 1 (2 Feb. 1918). Each issue had eighteen pages (eight devoted to advertising) and cost .40 piaster, a prohibitive amount for all but a few potential readers.

43. See, for example, the poem sent as first anniversary greeting to *Nam Phong*, reprinted in NP 14 (Aug. 1918), pp. 111,–12.

44. Nam Xuan Tho, *Suong Nguyet Anh* (Saigon, 1957), pp. 13, 22–23, 27–28.

45. Ibid., p. 28. To compound Suong Nguyet Anh's personal tragedy, her daughter died in childbirth, and she took responsibility for raising the surviving granddaughter.

to consider the personal effects of sexual repression, she remained sensitive to the problem elsewhere and never demanded that all widows avoid remarriage.[46] To the degree that this was true, male traditionalists sensed a threat, and began publishing rebuttals even before *Nu Gioi Chung* had closed its doors.

Textbooks and Manuals for Women

During the 1920s there was a gradual increase in the number of girls attending primary schools. By 1930, French administrators recorded 40,752 girls undergoing public or private instruction.[47] At least an equal number were probably being taught basic *quoc-ngu* at home, or at the informal study associations beginning to crop up in many localities. The colonial authorities supported basic instruction for women, but within a very limited framework. As one ranking French administrator phrased it, a good young Vietnamese rural woman should be "nimble, clean, kitchen-wise, and proficient in sewing, and should even know how to read and write *quoc-ngu.*" She should also definitely "take pleasure in bearing lots of children" and, in between, perhaps, take up weaving.[48] Actually, as indicated before, most pupils came from a minority of upper- or middle-class families. In a country of perhaps twenty million, there was obviously much to be done before anyone could take pride in the educational statistics.

Nevertheless, a market of modest proportions had developed for the first time in *quoc-ngu* textbooks to be sold to female students. This demand was accentuated by the cries of Vietnamese traditionalists that feminine norms were being neglected in the already available textbooks, and that women were being corrupted by the romantic poems, novels, and short stories sold outside school walls. The typical plot of these romantic potboilers involved a worthy young man and a beautiful girl falling in love, but then being forced to part due to social restrictions. There followed pages and pages of heartbreak, after which the hero or heroine often died of despair or sought consolation in religion or aimless drifting. While there might sometimes be a certain amount of social commentary exposing corruption, dissipation, or selfishness, characters were almost always manipulated by forces beyond their control, and the outcome was meant to be pathetic.

As might be expected, the predominant topic of texts designed to counter such influences was *luan ly*, or ethics. Apparently, the first textbook of this kind was published in Hanoi in 1918, entitled *Reading Lessons in Feminine Moral Con-*

46. Phan Van Hum, "Suong Nguyet Anh va Dao Tam Tung" [Suong Nguyet Anh and the Three-Submission Ethic], PNTV 243 (24 May 1934), pp. 13–14.
47. Out of a total of 435,782 primary pupils. See "Tableau Statistique de l'Enseignement en Indochine," AOM, NF 1323.
48. Pierre Grossin, *Dan Que Nen Biet*, pp. 61–62.
49. Phan Dinh Giap, *Nu Hoc Luan Ly Tap Doc* [Reading Lessons in Feminine Moral Conduct] (Hanoi, 1918).

As can be seen from this literacy primer cover, some Vietnamese authors still wanted to keep girls sewing while their brothers studied. Courtesy of the Bibliothèque Nationale.

duct.[49] One thousand copies were printed, at .25 piasters each. During the next decade or so, about twenty-five other such texts specifically for young women appeared on sale, sometimes in multiple editions. Quantities ranged from the ordinary 1,000 copies per edition to 5,000 or even 10,000 copies. Traditionalist authors, who in this type of publication definitely predominated, tended to structure book lessons according to the standard "three submissions" and "four virtues." For example, a woman teacher in Lang-son divided her published recitation lessons into five imperatives: at home, follow your father's instructions; upon marriage, follow your husband; guard your pregnancy; and look after the family, including second wife and servants; and when your husband dies, follow your son. For a woman, being a wife was "as natural as eating food." Had not the great Napoleon said that in life there were only two things eternally precious: courage in men, and chastity in women? Only if women revered the old could they comprehend the new. To clinch the argument, she invoked Trung Trac as the supreme example of Vietnamese feminity.[50]

50. Dinh Chi Nghiem, *Dao Nam Huan Nu* [Male Ethics and Female Training] (Hanoi, 1927). Like many others, the author relied on poetry to reach her pupils and facilitate memorization.

Ironically, some authors who profited from the fashion for romantic literature also saw a bit of money to be gained from pompous moralizing for young women. Tran Phong Sac, a classics teacher best known for his Chinese-style dramas on romantic themes, published a book titled *Nu Trung Ba Hanh* [One Hundred Lessons on Proper Feminine Behavior], complete with 100 Chinese characters for everything from chastity to affection.[51] Tan Da (Nguyen Khac Hieu), already famous for his beautiful, bitter, highly individualistic poetry, put together several morality books for children, including one specifically for girls, which were later picked up by the colonial authorities, reprinted many times, and presumably helped to keep the author alive in his declining years.[52]

Several other textbook authors took a more practical line with female readers, but the underlying philosophy was the same. For example, Do Duc Khoi, in a text also enjoying the profitable imprimatur of the French educational authorities, started with the simple maxim that a woman's place is in the home, and hence while at school she should study only those subjects that might make her a better housewife.[53] Lessons dealt with such matters as personal hygiene, contagious illness (one sparse lesson), and the benefits of letting light and air into the house, keeping a proper bed, kitchen cleanliness, abstaining from liquor, providing milk for children, and eating a balanced diet of eggs, meat, and vegetables. Since the majority of Vietnamese families could seldom afford milk, meat, or eggs, the author clearly was aiming his message at upper- and middle-class women.

While potential readers must have been somewhat receptive to family-centered prescriptions (or there would not have been so many publications for sale), this does not mean they were isolated from the broader political and social currents of the day. As we shall see, women responded in an organized way from the mid-1920s. This also helps to account for the fact that several textbook authors, although sharing many of the traditional assumptions outlined previously, parted sharply with the majority of writers when it came to matters of Vietnamese identity and history and attitudes toward the French colonial overlords. Trinh Dinh Ru (1893-1962) managed in Haiphong in 1926 to publish a female primary school text with numerous patriotic implications, and with subtle alterations in traditional outlook based on a perceived need to mobilize women for future struggle. The first lesson had a father being chided by traditionalist neighbors for sending his two daughters to school. The father defended his decision by saying, "You still don't understand. These days, daughters should be taken just as

---

51. Tran Phong Sac, *Nu Trung Ba Hanh* (Saigon, 1922). The other side of the coin was for someone to publish a manual on male etiquette for dealing with females of various ages and social levels. See Ha Phi Phi, *Doi Dai Phu Nu* [Behavior toward Women] (Hanoi, 1928).

52. Tan Da's text for women is *Dai Guong Truyen* [Tales of Great Paragons] (Hanoi, 1925).

53. Do Duc Khoi, *Nu Hoc Thuong Hanh* (Hanoi, 1926).

seriously as sons. . . . A country that really wants to overcome ignorance must not only have boys studying, but also girls." Lesson three, titled "If you love your country you must study," managed to point out deftly that "boys and girls born in Vietnam are all children of the same house. Hence, we must all love our country in the same way as we love our mother." The author added a small paragraph at the foot of the text chastising those Vietnamese who had been deceived into calling France the "Motherland." After all, he said, "We are born in Vietnam, and that makes Vietnam our Motherland. Those who keep on referring to France as the Motherland are really wrong! Only French people can properly call France the Motherland."[54]

Numerous lessons in Trinh Dinh Ru's textbook were devoted to those Vietnamese, especially women, who had struggled against the Chinese. The Trung sisters were praised for sustaining the spirit of independence, even though they had been defeated. Young readers were encouraged to visit the Trung sisters' temple and commemorate them every February 5th. Trieu Thi Trinh was also lauded, and quoted to the effect that if all the men were scared, then women must rise up. There was even a lesson about the female writer Ho Xuan Huong, who, though not a resistance figure, had written some very earthy, sometimes scatological poetry in the nineteenth century, and had severely criticized prevailing attitudes toward women.[55] Finally, as if to bring matters almost up to date without incurring immediate censorship, Trinh Dinh Ru devoted one of his last lessons to the uplifting story of a Japanese girl who had donated all her savings to the fight against the Russians in 1904.

Several years later Trinh Dinh Ru addressed himself to the new group of young female teachers then taking up positions at the primary school level. While admitting that all teachers were severely restricted by the government curriculum, he gave the young women pointers on how, particularly in moral instruction and history, they might yet exercise some creative initiative and thus convert their jobs from minor sinecures to positions of true social significance. Rather than simply follow official material in a perfunctory manner, as was apparently quite common, Trinh Dinh Ru encouraged women teachers to employ examples from personal experience, to convert bland generalities on paper to questions of immediate relevance, and to take an activist role in correcting the bad characteristics of their pupils. Then, too, women teachers should engage in

---

54. Trinh Dinh Ru, *Nu Sinh Doc Ban* [Reader for Female Students] (Haiphong, 1926). Another writer refers to Trinh Dinh Ru's wife in the same laudatory category as Suong Nguyet Anh and Dam Phuong, so it may well be that she had an important role in this and other publications. Dang Van Bay, *Nam Nu Binh Quyen*, p. 7.

55. As a Confucian scholar, Trinh Dinh Ru felt constrained to add that, although Ho Xuan Huong's style was indeed brilliant, it was too bad that so many of her poems lacked propriety.

discussions and prepare and publish more of their own books for feminine instruction rather than depend on men.[56]

In 1927, Phan Boi Chau was heard from again on the subject of women, this time publishing a brief primary school text.[57] Since writing his play about the Trung sisters, however, Phan had been captured by the French, put on trial in Hanoi, and sentenced to life imprisonment, subsequently commuted to loose house arrest in Hue. Partly for these reasons, but also perhaps because he had not worked out in his own mind the degree of change necessary in Confucian values, Phan Boi Chau wrote with extreme discretion when addressing his young feminine audience. The basic message was that they should try to be "mothers to the nation." Like most other textbooks of the period, lessons were structured according to the "three submissions" and "four virtues." Yet, under *ngon*, or 'appropriate speech,' the example of Madame Roland and her impassioned advocacy of Republican democracy was cited approvingly, along with that of Cheng Yu-hsiu, a young Chinese woman who had taken part in the 1911 Revolution, studied law in Paris, and participated in various international conferences.[58] Obedience to one's parents and parents-in-law was firmly upheld, yet husbands and wives were encouraged to share tasks with each other, both within the house and out in the village or society at large. Special attention was given to motherly responsibilities, including teaching children to serve their country.

Finally, Phan Boi Chau provided a series of lessons on achieving unity (*hop quan*), with striking images of communal labor in cutting trees, hauling in fishing nets, and rowing together against a storm. If girls were teased with the question, "Do you have a husband yet?" they should reply, "Yes, his surname is Viet and his given name Nam." This husband was more than three thousand years of age, had resisted the Han dynasty and beaten the Ming, yet did not look old, Phan added vividly. Now, the husband/country would gain unified help from women in taking on other enemies—or such was the definite implication of the last lesson. Huynh Thuc Khang (1876–1947), well-known scholar, publisher, and political figure in his own right, added a laudatory postscript to Phan Boi Chau's lessons, suggesting that they could serve the same pedagogical purpose for contemporary women as the Three-Character Classic (*San-tzu Ching;* in Vietnamese, *Tam-Tu Kinh*) had served previously for men.

56. (Ngau Tri) Trinh Dinh Ru, "The nao la co Cong voi Xa Hoi? Loi Noi Thang cung cac Nu Giao Su" [How Can One Serve Society? A Frank Discussion with Female Teachers], PNTV 51 (8 May 1930), pp. 5–7.

57. Phan Boi Chau, Nu Quoc-Dan Tu Tri, 2nd printing (Hue, 1927), pp. 3–16.

58. Phan Boi Chau was under the misapprehension that Cheng Yu-hsiu had subsequently died in an airplane accident. In 1933, however, she passed through Vietnam, creating a stir with her remark that perhaps Japanese aggression was a blessing in disguise, as it would lead the Chinese people to unite and fare better in the life-and-death struggle that must follow. PNTV 190 (9 Mar. 1933).

After the violent confrontations of 1930–31, French administrators and Viet-namese collaborators tried to refute the arguments of writers like Trinh Dinh Ru and Phan Boi Chau on their own philosophical terrain. For example, in a text for third- and fourth-year female instruction, Vu Nhu Lam argued that every nation took the family as its base. Any girl who did not love her home (nha) could obviously never love her country (nuoc). He asked more pointedly, "Unless you obey the words of your father and mother, how can you know how to obey the laws of the State?"[59] As we shall see, even as these lines were being written, some young Vietnamese women were coming to deny the logic of the framework within which both sides were functioning.

Among other new genre was female hagiography. In the late 1920s at least thirteen such books appeared, exhorting Vietnamese women to follow specific historical or near-contemporary examples. Seven titles were promptly banned in Annam, but presumably continued to be sold and circulated elsewhere. At first the emphasis was on Chinese and Korean heroines who had taken some role in overthrowing the Ch'ing dynasty or in resisting Japanese colonial rule.[60] Perhaps the most popular example was Cheng Yu-hsiu, mentioned above, who had "not only fulfilled her obligations to her family but had also studied to great heights."[61] Madame Roland also received book-length attention as the "first true heroine of Europe," and someone even dared to translate a Chinese biography of "Three Brave Heroines of Russia."[62] Very soon, however, the focus shifted almost entirely to Vietnamese women, the Trung sisters and Trieu Thi Trinh naturally getting most prominence, but Doan Thi Diem, Bui Thi Xuan, and Ho Xuan Huong not far behind.[63] Reviving Bui Thi Xuan on the printed page was a direct and conscious slap to the puppet court in Hue, since she had led Tay Son armies against the Nguyen more than a century before and had finally been executed

59. Vu Nhu Lam, Nu Sinh Doc Ban [Reader for Female Students] (Nam Dinh, 1932), p. 21.

60. Hoang Thi Tuyet Hoa, Giam Ho Nu Hiep [Mme Mandarin the Heroine] (Saigon, 1928); Ngoc Son and Doan Hiet, trans., Guong Ai Quoc [Patriotic Paragons] (Saigon, 1928); Hue Dich, Trieu Tien Nu Cach Menh Mac Tu Oanh [Muk Cha-yŏng: Female Korean Revolutionary] (Hanoi, 1927).

61. Nguyen Hoc Hai, Trinh Duc Tu: Trung Hoa Nu Kiet [Cheng Yu-hsiu: Chinese Heroine], 3 vols., 2nd printing (n.p., 1929). Forty years later the Communist Party activist Ton Thi Que re-called being so excited after reading this biography that she was unable to sleep. Ton Thi Que, Chi Mot Con Duong (Nghe An, 1972), p. 14.

62. Phan Thi Bach Van, Guong Nu Kiet [Heroic Feminine Paragon] (Saigon, 1928); Ngoc Son and Doan Hiet, trans., Than Thu Do [Spirits of the Capital], 2 vols. (Saigon, 1928–29). Perhaps partly in response, French colonial textbooks were soon glorifying Joan of Arc.

63. Nguyen An Ninh, Hai Ba Trung (Saigon, 1928); So Cuong, Nu Luu Van Hoc Su [History of Literature by Women] (Hanoi, 1929). Three thousand copies of this book on the literary contribu-tions of Vietnamese women were printed, priced at .35 piaster each. See also Nguyen Kim Dinh, Gai Anh Hung Nuoc Nam [Vietnamese Heroines] (Saigon, 1928).

by elephant trampling—the opposing troops thinking enough of her courage to insist on eating her liver and heart.[64]

In 1930 there appeared a novel about a fictional Vietnamese woman named Nguyen Tuyet Hoa which perhaps summarized the outlook of many upper- and middle-class writers of the day.[65] The cover depicted the heroine herself, wearing modified Western dress and holding a book in one hand and a sword in the other. From poor beginnings she had gone to school to learn weaving. Then, somehow, she opened a factory and started an association to enable young women, spinsters, and widows to find work, learn a craft, exercise, and study a bit (including the four virtues). Profits and losses of the association were shared equally. At one point the heroine traveled to Japan to study advanced techniques and to buy looms. Later she sent several other women to learn how to manufacture the machines domestically. Of course, in reality, French mercantile interests had prevented any of this happening for Vietnamese men, much less women, so the entire story was rather fanciful. As for the sword, toward the end of the story there was vague mention of practicing the Japanese martial arts in order to "punish the wicked," including those who "robbed, deceived, and cheated the people, causing pain to society."[66] Indeed, the book/sword image appeared to harken back to debates between literati reformists and activists more than two decades prior. If so, the author's sympathies were clearly reformist in character.

At another level, yet sharing the same self-conscious assertion of Vietnamese identity, were Vietnam's first modern cookbooks, which appeared in the 1920s. While still aimed at upper- and middle-class readers, there was no attempt to promote curiosity foods or esoteric menus. Recipes were kept simple and explanations concise. It was as if this particular generation had just discovered that Vietnamese cuisine was unique and felt the need to write it down firmly rather than rely largely on oral transmission as in centuries past. Thus, the introduction to one cookbook pointed out that each country had its special customs, clothes and foods, which should not be denigrated in any way.[67] Cooking was not to be frowned upon, but only cooks who did their work badly. At the top of the list of requirements were clean hands and a hygienic kitchen, a new emphasis entirely.

Simple manuals on modern hygiene and family medicine became another unique area of publishing interest. Women probably read and used these books as often as men. Texts on Eastern medicine, both Chinese and Vietnamese, ex-

---

64. Another source of the period has Bui Thi Xuan being burned alive. See the brief discussion in Le Thi Nham Tuyet, *Phu Nu Viet Nam*, pp. 117–18.

65. Truong Hoan, *Nguyen Tuyet Hoa*, 5 vols. (Saigon, 1930).

66. Ibid., p. 154.

67. R. P. N., *Sach Day Nau An Theo Phep Annam* [Teaching One to Cook Annamite Fashion] (Saigon, 1929).

panded greatly during 1925–30 in terms of diversity and numbers of copies published.[68] Beginning about 1925, texts on Western medicine entered the field. Initially these tended to be written by French physicians resident in Indochina and translated by Vietnamese subordinates.[69] One such volume, apparently quite popular, even tried to tackle the more fundamental problem of preventive medicine, explaining how illnesses began and putting first emphasis on endemic and epidemic diseases.[70] Soon, qualified Vietnamese doctors were writing manuals on their own, usually more concise and more attuned to what a middle-class family was likely to have on hand.[71] Finally, there were books written by lay persons, which attempted to combine traditional moralizing with a smattering of basic hygiene and preventive medicine, for example, extolling the values of sleep, exercise, and eating in moderation while condemning liquor, promiscuity, gambling, and opium.[72]

Books and pamphlets on the previously tabooed subjects of sexual hygiene, pregnancy, childbirth, and venereal disease also appeared for the first time, occasioning angry outbursts from traditionalists. One of the earliest publications attempted to neutralize criticism from Sinophiles by simply translating a recent text from China.[73] Several diagrams of sexual anatomy were included. Another early and detailed manual on pregnancy and infant diseases, written by a Vietnamese physician, chose to defend public discussion of such topics from an implicitly political position, stating that "our race will day by day grow stronger when we finally pay attention to child care and the prevention of child-deforming illness."[74] Both Eastern and Western medical books gave social diseases cau-

68. Most striking was the fat compendium put out annually in *quoc-ngu* by the famous Chinese Tiger-Balm medicine king. By 1931 this combined almanac, manual, and company advertisement was 370 pages long, and 100,000 copies were being printed. Luong Y Vi-Te Sanh, *Nhi Thien Duong* [Second Paradise] (Saigon, 1931).

69. See, for example, A. Sarramon, *Sach Duong Sanh Cho Gia Quyen* [Manual for Nurturing the Family], trans. Nguyen Binh (Saigon, 1925). This ambitious, well-illustrated manual on illness, first aid, health, and hygiene sold at the high price of 1.20 piasters, yet was printed to the tune of 5,000 copies.

70. Quan Bac-Si Devy, *Cho Khoi Om Dau* [Avoiding Illness], trans. Do Vong, 4th printing (Hanoi, 1928).

71. Hoang Mang Luong, comp., *Thuoc Gia Dung Va Phep Cuu Cap* [Family Medicines and Forms of Remedy] (Hue, 1927).

72. N. H. N., comp., *Ve Sanh Nguoi, Di Doan Minh* [Human Hygiene, Personal Beliefs] (Sadec, 1929).

73. Nguyen Van Khai, trans., *Nam Nu Hon Nhan Ve Sinh* [Marriage Hygiene for Men and Women], 2nd printing (Hai Phong, 1924). The translator also added a short poetic preface justifying the topic.

74. Nguyen Van Luyen, *San Duc Chi-Nam* [Guide to Childbirth] (Hanoi, 1925). This volume was still being reprinted in Saigon in 1957 despite major medical advances in the intervening three decades.

tious attention.[75] In 1929, however, discretion was thrown to the wind in a booklet containing lurid descriptions of common venereal diseases.[76] The compiler, a prominent writer and publisher of romantic, sometimes pornographic fiction, seemed far more interested in sensation and in scaring parents and young people than in discussing treatment or cures.

Early Women's Organizations

With men still dominating writing for the growing female readership, the next obvious step was for women to form their own organizations, support each other, articulate their own positions in their own materials, and perhaps even reach a national audience of both sexes. Women certainly were not getting far in already existing organizations. For example, the prestigious Association for the Support of French Studies apparently failed to admit one female among 145 members accepted between 1908 and 1929.[77] Perhaps bourgeois male attitudes were best revealed by Nguyen Van Vinh in his elaborate bylaws for a proposed new study society. Article nine included the principle of "no discrimination as between men and women," but then immediately turned around to state that all women wishing to be admitted "will first have to seek permission from their husbands."[78] The prejudice against women leaving their homes at all remained very strong, especially if it entailed being in the company of men. Those who dared to break this convention risked being labeled immoral, or even being beaten by their husbands.

Surprisingly, one of the first women's organizations emerged in the very center of traditionalism, the royal capital of Hue. In early 1926 Mme Nguyen Khoa Tung (better known by her pen name of Dam Phuong) and several score other women in and around Hue founded the Nu Cong Hoc Hoi, or "Women's Labor–Study Association."[79] On June 28, 1926 they arranged a solemn opening cere-

75. Truong Minh-Y, *Ve Sanh Can Yeu* [Essential Hygiene] (Saigon, 1928); Tran Phong Sac, *Ve Sanh Thuc Tri* [Practical Hygiene] (Saigon, 1928).

76. Nguyen Manh Bong, comp., *Hoa Lieu Benh Phiem Dam* [General Discussion of Venereal Diseases] (Hai Phong, 1929). A later (1931) edition contained pictures of venereal diseases in various stages.

77. *Phap Hoc Bao Tro Hoi* (Hanoi, 1930), pp. 12–16.

78. Tan Nam Tu (Nguyen Van Vinh), *Dan Dao Va Dan Quyen* (Saigon, 1926), p. 81.

79. Mme Dam Phuong (Nguyen Khoa Tung) was related to the royal family and had been able to study Chinese as a youth. Dao Hung, "Ba Dam Phuong Va Nha Nu Cong Hoc Hoi o Hue" [Mme Dam Phuong and the Women's Labor-Study Association in Hue], PNTV 69 (11 Sep. 1930), pp. 14–17. Apparently about forty-five when the association was founded, Dam Phuong usually appended the title *nu-su* (in Chinese, *nü-shih*) to her pen name. This term, which had come back into vogue in China a generation earlier, was meant to indicate either a single or married woman possessing literary skills. In Vietnam it enjoyed a certain currency in the 1920s, but then faded from sight.

mony for the public, at which Phan Boi Chau gave the principal address—in itself something of a challenge to the French Resident Superior and his collaborator mandarins, given Phan's formal status as a condemned criminal.

Phan Boi Chau lauded the establishment of the association and cited numerous antecedents in Japan, China, England, and the United States. Although he had been asked to speak on the subject of morality, he proceeded to argue for a subtle merging of traditional and modern values, a selective appreciation of Eastern and Western concepts of female behavior. For example, he said, it was definitely wrong for Vietnamese women to continue meeting only in kitchens and to waste their time playing cards. If young men or women had talents for other, broader endeavors, it was wrong to yoke them indefinitely to the family. In fact, in the most pressing interests of national survival, Vietnam *and* Vietnamese women had no choice but to change.

Nevertheless, Phan Boi Chau argued, the wrong changes could impede national progress. Thus it was not authentically Vietnamese for young men and women to imitate the dancing customs of England and the United States by hugging each other around the floor; nor was it proper to waste money on perfume, lipstick, and rouge, especially when other Vietnamese were going hungry. Then, too, struggling for individual liberties was right and necessary, but it should not take precedence over authentic service to the country. If one was in the position of being a parent or a child, a husband or a wife, it was truly important that one take one's responsibilities seriously. Attack those who abuse their position or exhibit a slavish mentality, he said, but do not claim that there are no legitimate roles as parent, child, husband, wife.

Several times Phan Boi Chau pointed out that survival of the Women's Labor-Study Association was not going to be easy. It was totally unprecedented, for one thing, and it was positioned right in that heart of darkness, the royal capital. There would inevitably be discordant voices from within the organization; yet, with enthusiasm and fortitude, much could be accomplished. After all, women's productivity would be essential to the future economic growth of the country, and they did have a political role—although Phan suspected that the recent precedent of the Soviet Union, where women were party leaders and government functionaries, was perhaps "too advanced" for Vietnam. Finally, in an elaborate but vivid metaphor designed partly to evade the police agents and censors, Phan Boi Chau pointed dramatically to some cut lotus flowers in a vase in front of the rostrum. It was fine, he said, for those "Eastern" lotuses to receive some fresh "Western" water. But the existence or lack of such "Western" water was not what would induce the inevitable wilting and death of those flowers; rather, it was the fact that they had been taken from the broad reaches of their natural, free environment and forcefully imprisoned in an artificial vase. *That* was the source of their agony, not the type of water they received. Clearly, Phan was indicating the "artificial" and oppressive colonial regime as the prime enemy, and asking his audience to take that issue most seriously, while placing matters of cultural change—including women's rights—in a secondary position.[80]

In the first four years or so of its existence the Women's Labor–Study Association never took a firm stand on this issue. We may speculate that Mme Dam Phuong, energetic and respected chairperson of the association, shared Phan Boi Chau's sentiments, yet felt that an upper- and middle-class public organization under close colonial scrutiny was hardly the place to air them. The association did cooperate discreetly with a more radical Hue study group led by Dao Duy Anh.[81] It also gave preferential attention to domestic Vietnamese products, and members more than once argued in favor of a women's "Buy-Vietnamese" campaign.[82] Finally, Dam Phuong's own son, best known by his pen name of Hai Trieu (1908–54), was a leader in the clandestine leftist Tan Viet Party, and in January 1930 participated in its reorganization along Marxist-Leninist lines.[83]

Nevertheless, in her role as leader of the association, Dam Phuong consistently limited herself to urging better educational opportunities for women, to defending the primacy of family responsibilities in the life of women, and to traveling north and south to stimulate formation of other women's groups. None of this seemed threatening to the colonial authorities or to collaborator publicists, at least at first.[84] Nor did they find anything particularly upsetting in her definition of the basic objective of the association, which was "to build for women a sense of self-development by means of new occupational skills and within the parameters of both Eastern and Western virtue and independence."[85] It was the "socially acceptable" occupational skills she was referring to, such as sewing, weaving, and the raising of silkworms. These skills should be stressed in any educational curriculum, along with ethics, applied economics, and literature. Like contemporary women in China, she argued, Vietnamese women should reject the traditional "three submissions," reject such old sayings as "Only an unskilled girl is possessed of true virtue," and be ready to read deeply and travel broadly. But the supreme

---

80. Phan Boi Chau, *Nu Quoc Dan Tu Tri*, pp. 18–27.

81. For example, advertisments for Dao Duy Anh's "Quan Hai Tung Thu" publishing endeavor were included in the association journal, *Phu Nu Tung San*.

82. See, for example, the 3 June 1927 letter from Bich Van, association member in Nam Dinh. Hoi Nu.Cong Hue, *Nu Cong Thuong Thuc* [General Knowledge about Women's Work], vol. 2 (Hue, 1929), pp. 30–31.

83. Hai Trieu (real name, Nguyen Khoa Van), along with other Tan Viet members, joined the Indochinese Communist Party later the same year. As we shall see, he played an important role as Party journalist and literary critic until his death in 1954.

84. For example, the editors of *Nam Phong* welcomed the association's foundation enthusiastically, and pointed out that Mme Dam Phuong was well known to readers already. NP 106 (June 1926), p. 514. Dam Phuong's earlier contributions can be found in NP 13 (July 1918), 43 (Jan. 1921), and 49 (July 1921).

85. Speech given 13 September 1926. Phan Boi Chau, *Nu Quoc Dan Tu Tri*, p. 29.

obligation of a woman was still to be a good mother, or, more precisely, a "citizen mother" (*me quoc dan*). While it would be up to the next generation, the children, to determine whether Vietnamese society advanced or declined, whether the family system flourished or withered, the mothers were the ones who would "serve as both pathfinders and protectors in . . . a period of transition."[86]

Since the colonial regime was not providing satisfactory education by anyone's definition, the association organized some classes of its own in Hue, raised silkworms, and disseminated practical information on household skills, especially cooking.[87] Dam Phuong's speaking trips and the dissemination of association literature helped stimulate formation of other small groups around the country, in such places as Da Nang, Hoi An, Saigon, Can Tho and Go Cong.[88] The Go Cong organization, deep in the Mekong delta, apparently took a different tack from that in Hue, concentrating almost entirely on publication of books of special interest to women. A 1929 advertisement of their Nu Luu Tho Quan (Women's Press) boasted sixteen titles already in print and nine in preparation. Press representatives were listed in seven other locations throughout Vietnam, and there were even two student outlets in Paris.[89]

By 1929 the French colonial authorities were increasingly worried that such social, educational, and intellectual organizations had definite political implications—and with good reason. Even the cookbooks were now devoting prominent advertising space to the overtly anticolonial publications of Phan Boi Chau, Tran Huy Lieu, and Dao Duy Anh.[90] The women's question itself was rapidly becoming a focus for national discussion, a matter on which intellectuals of diverse backgrounds could communicate and, conceivably, reach agreement as to pro-

86. Dam Phuong, *Phu Nu Du Gia Dinh* [Woman's Role in the Family], vol. 2 (Saigon, 1929), p. 10. Thirteen years later, based largely on her experience with eleven sons and daughters, Mme Dam Phuong wrote a manual for pre-school training, titled *Giao Duc Nhi Dong* [Educating Young Children] (Hanoi[?], 1942).

87. The association's report for April 1929, for example, lists classes in *quoc-ngu* and weaving, and reports a sale of silkworms with the modest profit of 2.00 piasters. Three recipes are also printed. Nhu Man, ed., *Phu Nu Tung San*, vol. 1 (Hue, May 1929), pp. 36–39.

88. The Da Nang organization is mentioned in the weekly newspaper *Thanh Nien Tan Tien*, no. 11 (31 Jan. 1929). Hoi An (or Faifo) boasted an organization of fourteen members and circulated a pamphlet titled *Nu Cong Hoc Hoi Faifo* [Faifo Women's Labor-Study Association] (1926). The Saigon group centered around planning and publication of *Phu Nu Tan Van*, discussed below. Mme Huynh Ngoc Nhuan led the formation of a private girl's school in Can Tho, stressing cooking, embroidery, literature, and music (mentioned in Mme Nguyen Hao Ca, *Phu Nu Viet-Nam* [Vietnamese Women] [Saigon, 1930(?)], p. 14).

89. Dam Phuong, *Hong Phan Tuong Tri* [Mutual Knowledge for the Fair Sex] (Go Cong, 1929). The previous year, Nu Luu Tho Quan had printed and circulated 10,000 copies of a four-page advertisement requesting long-term subscriptions. Phan Thi Bach-Van, *Chinh Nghe Xuat Ban* [A Legitimate Publishing Effort] (Go Cong, Dec. 1928).

90. R. P. N., *Sach Day Nau An Theo Phep Annam*.

grams for change. While presumably the Sûreté had followed the development of women's activities from the very beginning, the only firm evidence prior to 1929 of high-level administrative concern was consistent promotion of some of the more traditionalist textbooks, mentioned previously, and, in Annam at least, the overt banning of a score or more books directed at women.[91] Indirect colonial influence was exerted by wealthy Vietnamese functionaries who donated money to groups like the Women's Labor-Study Association.[92]

On the other side of the fence, an increasing number of women were beginning to criticize the moderate public positions of leaders like Dam Phuong and to propose more fundamental institutional changes. In a February 1928 letter to association members, Dam Phuong felt the need to defend herself against unnamed individuals who argued that women's rights rather than work skills and education should be the rallying cry. Dam Phuong was prepared to grant that women's sharing of political power was a legitimate long-term objective, but talking about it was not very meaningful until the "body" had been given new skills and the "soul" had been renovated by serious education. "Women's rights" handed out on scraps of paper would not mean anything; without training and mental preparation, Dam Phuong asserted, Vietnamese women would not know what to do with them.[93]

Such reasoning did not satisfy the critics. Tran Thi Nhu Man, editor of the association's short-lived journal, *Phu Nu Tung San* [Women's Review], aired differences publicly in a long essay analyzing and condemning the Vietnamese family and social systems, both traditional and contemporary. She and others were coming to the opinion that one-sided chastity, arranged marriages, and female occupational and educational restrictions would have to be tossed out the window along with the more obvious "three submissions" and "four virtues."[94]

In late 1929 and 1930, a time of overt nationalist and communist challenges to the status quo, the colonial authorities were not prepared to allow a public dialogue of this kind to continue. Besides, they may have suspected the Hue

---

91. A brief biography of a Korean woman who fought Japanese colonial rule was the first specifically women-oriented book banned in Annam, in an edict dated 8 Oct. 1927. Five books of the Nu Luu Tho Quan (Go Cong) were banned in 1929. Trung Ky Bao Ho, *Nghi-Dinh Cam Cac Thu Sach Va Cac Thu Bao Chi Khong Duoc Truyen Ba, Phat Mai Va Tang Tru Trong Hat Trung-Ky* [Edict Banning Specific Books and Periodicals from Circulation, Sale, or Possession in Central Vietnam] (Hue, 1929[?]).

92. Tran Ba Vinh, conservative delegate to the colonial Grand Council, offered a "friend's" 2,000 piasters to buy land and construct a headquarters for the association. Mme Tran Van Chuong, wife of a prominent collaborator lawyer (and mother of the future Mme Ngo Dinh Nhu), collected 230 piasters from well-connected friends in Bac Lieu. A Vietnamese technician in Dong Hoi, sent money and encouraged the association to *uphold* the "three submissions." *Nu Cong Thuong Thuc*, vol. 1, pp. 38-40; *Phu Nu Tung San*, no. 1, May 1929, pp. 36-37.

93. *Nu Cong Thuong Thuc*, vol. 1, pp. 25-28.

94. *Phu Nu Tung San*, no. 1 (May 1929), pp. 1-35.

Women's Labor–Study Association of being a recruiting ground for revolutionary groups. Thus, Tran Thi Nhu Man's publications were banned, and the association temporarily ceased to operate. When the association was permitted to reopen in late 1930, Dam Phuong had been replaced as chairperson, the conservative colonial delegate Tran Ba Vinh was supervising allocation of a government subsidy, and the French Resident Superior was publicly warning members against consorting with any "declared enemies of family, society, and peace." The association journal in 1931 featured ninety-one recipes in place of the normal lead essay of social commentary. So that no one could mistake the new policy, an association member appended to the recipes a defense of the "four virtues" and a denunciation of those women who talked loosely of following Western ideas, demanding freedom and equality and the like. "With our *men* still lacking in talent," she concluded, "who would dare say anything about *women*?"[95]

Whatever energy remained with the Hue association was directed to organizing a women's handicraft fair for late 1931. Significantly, the leaders of this project saw themselves as women of status and wealth with an obligation to help the less fortunate. They announced philosophically, "When our homeland creates individuals, it divides them according to work roles, some spiritual, others material." Everyone shared "equal responsibility," however. More concretely, the leaders hoped the fair would give "working women" a chance to demonstrate their skills, "women of capital" an opportunity to put their money into viable businesses, and "students" a chance to observe the range of occupations open to them in the future. To show its support, the government offered the newly constructed Annam Representative Assembly building as a site for the fair. On 22 December 1931 Governor-General Pasquier and a large retinue of assistants, members of the royal family, and journalists attended a special preview and purchased a variety of handicrafts. Sampling the home-made sweets, French officials were heard to say that they tasted "as good as Western candies."[96]

Apparently, many women did not consider handicrafts or French praise of their sweets to be matters of highest priority. From a paid-up membership list of eighty-seven in 1929 the Hue Women's Labor–Study Association dropped to fifty-four members two years later. Class attendance fell by two-thirds.[97] From a vanguard women's group, capable of exciting interest all around Vietnam, the association by 1932 was just another circle of cautious bourgeois matrons with too much time on their hands. In 1934 the association was reported to be operating a

95. *Nu Cong Thuong Thuc*, vol. 3, 1931; Dao Hung, "Ba Dam Phuong," pp. 14–17.

96. "Mot Cuoc Dau Xao, My Nghe Phu Nu Tai Hue: Lam The Nao Cho Phu Nu Duoc Giai Phong?" [Women's Craft Exposition in Hue: How Can Women Obtain Liberation?], PNTV 98 (3 Sept. 1931), pp. 1–2; also PNTV 102 (1 Oct. 1931), p. 9, and PNTV 115 (7 Jan. 1932), pp. 13–14.

97. *Nu Cong Thuong Thuc*, vol. 2, pp. 30–32, and vol. 3, p. 39. Dao Hung, "Ba Dam Phuong," p. 15.

small store, but otherwise "close to death." The bell of Hue's Thien Mu pagoda was "sad and sleepy," providing no impulse to action.[98] Clearly the vibrant, committed women of Hue and vicinity had gone on to other alliances and conceptual frameworks.

Other women's groups of the late 1920s seem to have suffered a similar fate. The Go Cong Women's Press, which was operating in the supposedly more lenient legal environment of Cochinchina, fared even worse than the Hue association. First its books were banned from circulation, then the press was closed down, and finally the editor, Phan Thi Bach Van, was taken to court for the crime of "disrupting peace and security in the region by means of literature and ideas." Mme Bach Van was fined 2.50 francs and the publishing house ordered to disband permanently.[99] Groups in Da Nang and Hoi An apparently simply vanished, unnoticed and unmourned. Only the *Phu Nu Tan Van* group managed to push ahead, with results that deserve exploration in more detail.

Phu Nu Tan Van

The establishment in Saigon in May 1929 of a highly successful weekly periodical, *Phu Nu Tan Van* [Women's News], signaled a new phase in discussion of social issues in general and the roles that Vietnamese women might play in particular. Read avidly by both sexes, *Phu Nu Tan Van* served above all as a testing ground for new ideas, from baby beauty contests to dialectical materialism, from graphic arts (e.g., advertising design, cartoons) to first-hand reporting of the destitute lives of female miners, agricultural laborers, beggars, and prostitutes. Because the target audience was not the tiny, well-educated elite element (which in any event was still more at home in French) but rather the tens of thousands of functionally literate young women and men emerging from between three and six years of schooling, *Phu Nu Tan Van* articles were generally kept brief, the vocabulary unceremonious, the message straightforward.[100] Circulation figures suggest that it did its job quite well. *Phu Nu Tan Van* averaged 8,500 copies a week for over two years, dropped to 5,000 as the effects of the Depression reached Indochina, and then survived at about 2,500 copies until finally being shut down by government order in December 1934.[101]

98. Interview with Miss Tuyet Tam, PNTV 236 (29 Mar. 1934), as well as first-hand observations of Nguyen Thi Kiem, PNTV 244 (31 May 1934).

99. PNTV 39 (13 Feb. 1930) and 40 (20 Feb. 1930). At the same court session Phan Dinh Long, publisher of the Dan Tri Thu Xa series in Can Tho, was sentenced to six months in jail on similar charges. PNTV 218 (28 Sept. 1933) has a photograph of Phan Thi Bach Van on its cover.

100. A somewhat less stimulating daily periodical, *Phu Nu Thoi Dam* [Women's Discourse], was begun in Hanoi in December 1930 and survived until June 1934. A third periodical, *Phu Nu Tan Tien* [Women's Modern Advance], began publishing in Hue in mid-1932 but apparently collapsed soon after.

101. Individual copies were thirty-four pages long and sold for .15 piaster until March 1934, when the price was dropped to .10 piaster. There was a lapse in publication from December 1930

Other than format, the key to *Phu Nu Tan Van*'s popularity was timing. By 1929 the Vietnamese intelligentsia already understood the importance of women being energized and organized. However, because there was as yet no new consensus on the proper roles of Vietnamese women in given circumstances, *Phu Nu Tan Van* was able to assume an eclectic posture, print a wide range of opinions, and then benefit from the subsequent debates, which were not limited to major writers but often included many unsolicited manuscripts and letters from readers as well. As the period 1929–34 was otherwise one of systematic colonial repression, we may assume that the government censor and the publisher of *Phu Nu Tan Van* shared a tacit agreement whereby "non-violent" advocacy of social and cultural reform was acceptable in place of political discussion and activity.[102] Indeed, both censor and publisher may have seen gradual changes in the status of women as one safety valve against violent revolution. As it turned out, however, the women's question served to highlight a whole range of other social issues, from the patriarchal family system to current religious practices, from educational literature to the function of sports and hygiene in developing a strong, dynamic citizenry. From these issues it was only a small step to advocacy of total social upheaval—a step that *Phu Nu Tan Van* ended up taking, tactfully but unmistakably, in the last two years of its existence.

From start to finish the primary organizer and supervisor of *Phu Nu Tan Van* was the publisher, Mme Nguyen Duc Nhuan. She was backed financially by her husband, a major Saigon importer, wholesaler, and retailer. His company bought advertising space regularly, as did a number of other firms, the most prominent being Job cigarettes, Nestlé condensed milk, the Bank of Vietnam, and Citroën automobiles. Printing was sub-contracted to the firm of Mme Diep Van Ky, herself a successful entrepreneur. Without all these financial arrangements, fairly reliable even in the worst days of the Depression, Mme Nguyen Duc Nhuan would not have been able to attract such a top-ranking editorial staff or commission so many articles from outside journalists and cultural luminaries.[103]

It is possible to delineate four phases in the five-and-one-half-year existence of *Phu Nu Tan Van*. For the first twelve months or so the emphasis was on debate among established Vietnamese personalities, naturally almost all male. The tone

---

to May 1931. During June 1932 a four-page daily version of *Phu Nu Tan Van* was published too, apparently to try to refute widespread criticism of the publisher's financial dealings in conjunction with the big Saigon Women's Fair the previous month.

102. The head of the Saigon censorship bureau, M. Edouard Marquis, was certainly well known to the local journalist community, witness his attendance and speech at a dinner inaugurating *Phu Nu Tan Tien* in March 1932 (PNTV 123 [17 Mar. 1932], p. 19). Meanwhile, however, copies of PNTV were often confiscated when circulated beyond Cochinchina. In late 1929 students at the Collège du Protectorate in Hanoi were punished for possessing copies of PNTV. *Hoc Sinh*, no. 4 (15 Dec. 1929).

103. Thieu Son, "Mot Doi Nguoi" [A Person's Life], *Pho Thong*, no. 13, (Saigon, 15 June 1959). The author contributed often to PNTV.

was set by the publisher writing to a number of "celebrities" (danh nhan) to solicit their comments on the women's question and future editorial policy. Of the twelve individuals whose replies were published, only one, Dam Phuong, was female.[104] Opinions ranged from that of Bui Quang Chieu, who bluntly pointed out that upper-class Vietnamese men had quite enough troubles dealing with colonial masters and lower-class challenges—let alone female malcontents—to that of Diep Van Ky, who denounced the idea of a period of "tutelage" for women ("That is the argument of rulers being uttered by the ruled!") and intimated that both female *and* national liberation would come only by forceful action.

Lead editorial content was usually the prerogative of Mme Nguyen Duc Nhuan, while Dao Trinh Nhat (1900–51) seems to have been given responsibility for other week-to-week decisions. Phan Khoi was star essayist, but six or seven other men and women provided regular columns and feature stories.[105] Reader response was extremely gratifying, and there was a flood of requests for back issues. A three-week map- and picture-drawing contest for children drew 1,115 entries.[106] Contests of this sort, mainly for adults, became a regular feature, and prizes included such eminently bourgeois items as a big wall clock or a 280-piaster hardwood liquor cabinet. A poll was taken to determine the ten most favored "people's representatives" if and when the French allowed some degree of self-rule—an example of how *Phu Nu Tan Van* was able to skate on thin political ice occasionally.[107]

Even as dreams of political liberalization were being entertained, however, ruthless government suppression of Vietnamese nationalist and communist organizations was causing *Phu Nu Tan Van* to draw back from serious advocacy of progressive causes. For the remainder of 1930 there was increased emphasis on learning the matronly arts (embroidery, sewing, weaving, cooking), on raising

104. This series appeared from PNTV 1 (2 May 1929) to PNTV 14 (1 Aug. 1929), with additional comment by the editors in PNTV 12, 15, and 18. In order of appearance the contributors were: Tran Trong Kim, Phan Van Truong, Nguyen Van Ba, Nguyen Van Vinh, Dam Phuong, Pham Quynh, Bui Quang Chieu, Huynh Thuc Khang, Phan Boi Chau, Nguyen Phan Long, Cao Van Chanh, and Diep Van Ky. Other individuals, including women, were asked, but they declined or did not respond.

105. For the first few years these participants included Trinh Dinh Ru (ethics and education), Trinh Dinh Thao (law), Dr. Tran Van Don (hygiene and medicine), Ho Bieu Chanh (serialized novels), Miss Bang Tam (general science), and Cao Thi Ngoc Mon (family administration).

106. Five hundred twenty-three entries had to be disqualified because they were not from children. PNTV 4 (23 May 1929).

107. The list of twenty candidates, all men, was announced in PNTV 50 (1 May 1930) and results published in PNTV 64 (7 Aug. 1930). There were 1,594 responses, 1,234 being declared acceptable by contest rules. Highest vote-getters were Phan Van Truong, Huynh Thuc Khang, Nguyen Phan Long, and Diep Van Ky. Significantly, seven out of eight of those candidates who were listed as mandarins or colonial representatives failed to make the top ten.

money for suitable charities, and on contemplating abstract problems of language enrichment and Confucian epistemology. Perhaps the nadir was reached with the *Phu Nu Tan Van* issue of 18 September 1930, which instructed everyone to be happy despite increasingly disturbing events, replayed the now tired tune about the need to form organizations, and announced that Vietnamese employees—not inmates—at the notorious Con Son (Poulo Condore) prison island, having just been granted permission to set up for themselves a small library, would appreciate donations of books and periodicals. Even in these dark times, however, it should be noted that circulation figures remained reasonably high, partly because the editors were allowed to print details of government capture, trial, and punishment of Vietnamese revolutionaries. Such printed accounts were sought particularly in northern and central Vietnam, where censorship remained more stringent than in the south. *Phu Nu Tan Van* photographs of the twenty condemned Vietnamese Nationalist Party activists helped contribute to their immortality, just as the journal's narration of the suicide of the fiancée of Nguyen Thai Hoc, one of the condemned activists, helped to disseminate this poignant story from one end of the country to the other.[108]

The third phase of *Phu Nu Tan Van* activity began in May 1931 after a five-month publishing hiatus. It was marked by increasing awareness and concern about the Great Depression, which at that moment was reaching Indochina with a vengeance. Journalistic attention was thenceforth given to the falling price of rice, to company bankruptcies, to growing unemployment, and to the drop in school enrollments. However, until early 1933 *Phu Nu Tan Van* was generally unable to offer new insights on these very serious developments. The staff, though clearly aware of radical proposals for action, opposed them. A spate of lead editorials cautioned against precipitous social change; there was an even more dogged preoccupation with private fund-raising; Mme Van Dai and Mme Phan Van Gia reasserted conservative prescriptions for female behavior; and Thieu Son's sparkling but conceptually hollow essays took on special prominence.[109]

Ironically, what was to be the biggest organizational success of moderate and conservative women affiliated with *Phu Nu Tan Van* served to undermine their public credibility and helped lead to their editorial eclipse. Instancing the work of Yvonne Sarcey in France and the Hue handicraft exposition the previous year,

108. Thieu Son, "Mot Doi Nguoi," mentions the impact of this PNTV coverage beyond southern Vietnam. *Sach Choi Xuan Nam Tan Vy* [Amusements for Spring 1931] (Hanoi, 1931) demonstrates both visually and intellectually the influence of PNTV in the north. Reports of 1930 confrontations are found in PNTV 40–42, 44, 47, 52–53, 55, 58–59, 61, 63, 69, 72, and 75. Unlike its clearly sympathetic attitude toward the nationalists, PNTV was generally hostile in its reporting of 1930 communist activities.

109. Mme Van Dai joined the Viet Minh about twelve years later and was accepted into the Communist Party in 1948, an interesting conversion discussed below.

Phu Nu Tan Van masterminded a Women's Fair *(hoi cho phu nu)* in Saigon in May 1932. There were scores of stalls selling female handicrafts and food delicacies, speeches by the French governor of Cochinchina and four Vietnamese women, and a wide variety of games and contests. The fair drew large, enthusiastic crowds and reported a comfortable profit of 7,600 piasters. However, immediately thereafter the fair's management was attacked by a number of Saigon newspapers. In particular, they accused the husband of *Phu Nu Tan Van*'s publisher, M. Nguyen Duc Nhuan, of using the occasion to reap selfish business advantage. Although the journal fought back, even to the extent of publishing a daily supplement for one month, it was clearly a jolting and demoralizing episode for those who had dominated *Phu Nu Tan Van* since its inception. During the last half of 1932 a number of younger, more radical women were thus able to assert themselves in print.

Finally, in early 1933, a dramatic shift in *Phu Nu Tan Van* editorial policy became apparent. The emphasis was now on penetrating journalistic encounters with individuals of all classes, forthright sociological discussions of prostitution, religious escapism and faith-healing, attacks on fascism, and critiques of bourgeois feminism. Most surprisingly, a long series of popularized accounts of world philosophy ended by asserting that dialectical materialism was the culmination of humankind's effort to both comprehend and remake reality. The leader of this editorial coup seems to have been Nguyen Thi Kiem (equally well known by her poetry penname of Manh Manh), supported by Nguyen Thi Chinh (Mme Ta Thu Thau) and Phan Thi Bach Van.[110] Probably out of fear of colonial retribution, most of *Phu Nu Tan Van*'s earlier matronly contributors vanished. So, too, did Phan Khoi, the journal's prime cultural arbiter up until then. His place was soon filled by Phan Van Hum (1902-45), a Trotskyist philosophy teacher just returned from France. In November 1933 the editors formalized the break by printing direct attacks on Phan Khoi by Phan Van Hum and Hai Trieu, son of Dam Phuong.[111]

Why Mme Nguyen Duc Nhuan permitted the young radicals to seize the initiative is not entirely clear. Perhaps, in addition to having been put on the defensive by the outcry surrounding the Women's Fair, she was simply willing to go along with the intellectual mood of the day and see what the French censors would do. In reality, it was the group of Marxists coalescing around the newspaper *La Lutte* that soon provided most of the radical initiative, rather than the editors of *Phu Nu Tan Van*.[112] Nevertheless, those who did read *Phu Nu Tan*

---

110. Other writers included Phan Thi Nga, Nguyen Thi Nguyet, and Bich Van.

111. PNTV 224 (9 Nov. 1933) and 225 (23 Nov. 1933). Phan Van Hum was a great admirer of Nguyen Thi Kiem's "new poetry" *(tho moi)*, perhaps especially because he himself was skilled only in traditional styles. Ho Huu Tuong, *41 Nam Lam Bao* (Saigon, 1972), pp. 72-73.

112. Daniel Hémery, *Révolutionnaires Vietnamiens et Pouvoir Colonial en Indochine*, pp. 57-63.

Van were obviously motivated. In June 1933, for example, the editors reported that eighty-five readers' manuscripts had been received in the previous month alone.[113] Circulation was less than one-third of 1929–30 averages, yet this had already been the case before the radical coup. Mme Nguyen Duc Nhuan may have been impressed, too, by the new editorial team's systematic attempts to build contacts outside Cochinchina. During 1933–34 there was a notable increase in information, organizational notes and manuscripts emanating from women in Hanoi, Hue, and Phnom Penh. Although the objective of converting *Phu Nu Tan Van* into a truly national women's journal was never realized, the sharing of ideas and the personal ties that resulted proved of considerable value to other groups in the Popular Front period that followed.[114]

How did *Phu Nu Tan Van* elucidate the women's question? As might be expected, this subject was treated quite differently in 1933–34 from what had been the case in 1929–32. Broadly speaking, the editors of the first few years saw themselves as purveyors of an infinite variety of new information for and about women. This ranged from the very immediate and serious (for example, protecting the foetus or treating infant diseases) to the distant and arcane (for example, circus women with beards, or royal perversions toward women throughout history). If there was a dominant theme, it was the improvement of female educational opportunities, formal and informal. As the Depression worsened in 1932, attention centered on the need for women to acquire practical, marketable skills in order both to supplement declining male incomes and to provide women with the alleged key to personal independence. Nevertheless, when pressed, *Phu Nu Tan Van* editors continued to argue that home and family were the prime obligations of a Vietnamese woman. Outside occupations or cultural and social activities were to be undertaken only after one had proven oneself as wife and mother. The editors also opposed "free marriage," i.e., young men and women falling in love and getting married without waiting for parental "orders" (*lenh*); and they hinted that "equal rights" (*binh quyen*) was a non-issue, since Vietnamese men hardly benefitted from whatever suffrage or other legal arrangements existed in the colony.[115]

In 1933–34, however, faith in formal education vanished, and occupational

113. PNTV 204 (15 June 1933).

114. In August 1933, after receiving some indication that the colonial authorities would stop obstructing routine mailings of PNTV outside Cochinchina, PNTV attempted a circulation blitz focused on Hanoi. Overall publishing figures climbed to 5,000 but then dropped back below 3,000 by the end of the year. A PNTV delegation sent northward in September 1934 caused considerable comment and resulted in a number of provocative articles.

115. "Nam Nu Binh Quyen va Hon Nhon Tu Do: *Phu Nu Tan Van* Khong He co su Chu Truong Ay" [Equal Rights for Men and Women and Free Marriage: *Phu Nu Tan Van* Has Never Taken Such a Position], PNTV 129 (28 Apr. 1932), pp. 1–2; P. Nguyen Huu Luong, "Cai Be Trai Cua Cuoc Phu Nu Van Dong" [The Other Side of Women's Activism], PNTV 138 (9 June 1932), pp. 18–19.

independence came to be seen as the prerogative of only a tiny minority of women. Indeed, as the mass of poor Vietnamese women became the primary ideological concern of *Phu Nu Tan Van*, readers were warned about the tendency of females with any schooling or financial means to separate themselves from their sisters, to become not a worthy vanguard but individualistic, self-seeking parasites on the backs of others. This tendency was given the pejorative label of "feminism" (*phu nu chu nghia*), a specifically bourgeois phenomenon to be resisted steadfastly. In its place, the editors called on readers to commit themselves to a fundamental restructuring of the economic system such that the vast majority (i.e., peasant and proletarian women as well as men) could reap the rewards. Only socialism could bring about real female equality, they hinted clearly.[116]

Even in its last year of publication, however, *Phu Nu Tan Van* was hardly a vehicle for lower-class women to express themselves directly, much less an organ of socialist struggle. It remained essentially one means for the Vietnamese intelligentsia to better understand themselves and perhaps alter behavior. From beginning to end it was at once catalyst, conceptual testing ground, and disseminator of new ideas—indeed, perhaps the best example of this type of journalism ever to emerge in Vietnam. Rather than the dry theoretical essays on women's liberation via education, occupation, or economic restructuring, it was probably the attacks on sexual segregation, polygamy, wife-beating, religious escapism, and superstition that had the most effect. There were also sensitive treatments of birth control, female psychological disorders, and suicides among young Vietnamese women. Attempts were made to delineate coherent female positions on literature, aesthetics, ethics, and entrepreneurship. As might be expected, there was a strong element of Western faddishness too, reflected, for example, in the ads for stylish Parisian frocks and Radium face cream, the special fascination for American aviatrixes, and the repeated calls for Vietnamese women to learn to play tennis. Even at this time, however, limits were drawn. Western customs declared unsuitable for Vietnam included ballroom dancing, painted fingernails, beauty contests, and the expressing of male admiration of females by means of whistles, catcalls, or pinching. By way of promoting occasional syntheses, *Phu Nu Tan Van* played a key role in popularizing the *ao dai* dress, a stylish modification of the traditional upper-class gown still worn today on social occasions.

Between 1929 and 1934, if *Phu Nu Tan Van* is any indication, at least some Vietnamese women gained considerable confidence, a better sense of proportion, and new visions of future action. One small measure of this was the journal's

116. Key editorials attacking "feminism" and emphasizing economic and class factors in the oppression of women can be found in PNTV 220, 236, and 237. Markings on PNTV 237 (12 Apr. 1934) indicate that it was viewed by someone in the office of the French Chef de Cabinet at some point prior to being placed in the Dépôt Legal.

cover. For the first sixteen months the cover had always featured a drawing of three obviously well-off Vietnamese women (representing south, center, and north) gazing pensively at a copy of *Phu Nu Tan Van*. Underneath was a stanza of poetry: "Powder and lipstick serve to embellish the Motherland, making clear the countenance of Vietnamese women."[117] Subsequently, both drawing and poem were discarded in favor of a straightforward table of contents, presumably to emphasize subject matter over style. Finally, in August 1933, cover photographs of individual Vietnamese women were introduced, soon followed by groups of women at work or participating in sports activities. "Powder and lipstick" had given way to images conveying intelligence, determination, and productivity.

Public oratory was one test of female nerve that *Phu Nu Tan Van* encouraged from its inception. Characterizations of timid, note-bound matrons addressing politely bored friends were supplanted by young women standing alone in front of mixed crowds and speaking impromptu. Reaction to these new, energetic, publicly involved females was not all positive, to say the least. *Phu Nu Tan Van* itself was accused of encouraging women to abandon their families, and a caricature of the liberated Vietnamese woman emphasized her alleged desire to be equal with men in gambling, extramarital sex, and conspicuous consumption.[118] Eventually, the editors of *Phu Nu Tan Van* decided that the best defense was a good offense. They responded in detail to articles in other publications that condemned or mocked female activism, and when rumor campaigns occurred they brought the matter out into the open for all to judge. Thus, when Nguyen Thi Kiem was the object of covert criticism for "loose behavior" during her highly successful 1934 speaking tour of central and northern Vietnam, even though she had taken the precaution of asking her father to accompany her, Mme Nguyen Duc Nhuan wrote and published a sturdy rebuttal.[119]

In its 20 December 1934 issue, *Phu Nu Tan Van* announced a three months' closure, supposedly to reorganize in anticipation of new, more liberal censorship regulations. Apparently, the colonial authorities used the pretext of a three-year-old charge of slandering Bui Quang Chieu to keep the journal from continuing.[120] Nevertheless, one cannot help but sense that *Phu Nu Tan Van* had

117. *Phan Son To Diem Son-Ha, Lam Cho Ro Mat Dan Ba Nuoc Nam.* "Countenance" (*Mat*) also has the undermeaning of "true value."

118. P. Nguyen Huu Luong, "Cai Be Trai," pp. 18–19. The author half-humorously threatened a movement to demand male equal rights if too many women entered the work force.

119. PNTV 264 (25 Oct. 1934). During her trip Nguyen Thi Kiem gave several speeches on male attitudes concerning "progressive" women, which probably helps to account for the rumors. See PNTV 243, 247, 253, and 259.

120. Huynh Van Tong, *Lich Su Bao Chi*, p. 176. In April 1935 two additional issues of *Phu Nu Tan Van* did appear, with Mme Nguyen Duc Nhuan still listed as publisher, but minus all radical contributors. Not long after, according to Phuong Lan, *Nha Cach Mang Nguyen An Ninh*

reached something of an internal impasse. Had it continued to move to the left, it would have lost any remaining bourgeois backers, including Mme Nguyen Duc Nhuan herself; had it kept its intellectually eclectic, politically noncommittal attitude, the young radical editorial team would have lost interest—as would have many of the intelligentsia readers, for that matter. In short, *Phu Nu Tan Van* had the curious honor of helping to pave the way for an outpouring of more focused, politically inspired essays, articles, and short stories by and for women in the subsequent Popular Front period, but not being able to participate itself.

The Moderate Legacy

Having referred to a moderate stance on the women's question, it is necessary to define more clearly what this meant, and then to judge what influence moderate arguments may have had on Vietnamese women (and men) subsequently. Historically, the moderate position had its nascence in the 1907 Dong Kinh Nghia Thuc, assumed organized form in the 1926 Women's Labor-Study Association, and probably attained a zenith of respectability several years later during the early years of *Phu Nu Tan Van*. After that, the moderate position was challenged with increasing severity. As we have seen with *Phu Nu Tan Van*, and as we shall see with later Marxist formulations, it was not difficult to attack bourgeois women for ignoring problems of class exploitation, or for proposing educational and occupational reforms that in a colonial context, and during a serious worldwide depression, could hardly be expected to benefit more than a tiny minority. Nevertheless, moderates did manage to raise other questions, particularly of a social and cultural character, that could not be answered entirely by reference to dialectical materialism. They touched on problems that had been with Vietnamese women before the French arrived, and would be with them to some extent after all the foreigners had been forced out.

The most important single contribution of moderate writers was reducing Confucian ideas on the status of women from timeless dogma to a somewhat quaint collection of historically-determined homilies. This was nowhere more evident than in the 1928 essay by Dang Van Bay entitled *Nam Nu Binh Quyen* [Male-Female Equal Rights], mentioned at the opening of this chapter.[121] Women were not by nature inferior to men, the author asserted; their current "weaknesses" were a product of cultural conditioning. Thus, if Vietnam had had two thousand years of matrilineal rather than patrilineal history, the saying "One boy and you can inscribe a descendant; ten girls and you can write nil" would have been reversed. Dang Van Bay even hinted that fairness would require passing on the names of both father and mother, but backed away from that proposal as "creating too many complications" in speech and in recording of documents. It

---

[Nguyen An Ninh the Revolutionary] (Saigon, 1970), pp. 124–25, the entire Nguyen Duc Nhuan family moved to France.

121. One thousand copies of this sixty-page essay were printed.

was sufficient, he said, for everyone to realize that patrilineage was a mere inci-
dental, especially in Vietnam, with its superabundance of Nguyen surnames.

Chastity remained a more volatile question, but Dang Van Bay was undaunted. If, he argued, one considered chastity in its full moral definition, with
its strong emphasis on fidelity, on keeping one's word, on cultivating a clean
mind, then surely that principle should apply equally to men as well as women.
Even in the narrow physical sense of female virginity, a very brief period was
being considered, from puberty to marriage vows; and hence it was wrong to
condemn a woman for life because of once giving way to human emotions.
Many women rich in spirit, true to the larger concept of chastity, had been badly
treated by men, and deserved sympathy, not rejection. Besides, it had long been a
part of the social conditioning of Vietnamese men to tease and pressure young
women into vulnerable situations. If virginity were to be upheld—as the author
felt it should be—then men would have to observe the same limitations on their
passions as women, and not treat women as something to be assaulted, penetrated.[122]

The premise on which Dang Van Bay based his entire essay was that all
human beings should be treated justly and equitably (*cong-binh*), which meant
treating none as slaves or material objects.[123] In an optimistic syllogism reminiscent of the early Confucian classics, the author argued that "Although Heaven
tells us that Boys are Boys and Girls are Girls, Heaven also teaches us that Humans are Humans and Animals are Animals. Never has anyone been able to
affirm that Humans are Animals."[124] Historically, this basic principle had been
sadly violated, and Vietnamese women had been placed in a distinctly inferior
category. When it came to advocating contemporary changes, however, Dang
Van Bay equivocated. Thus, even though he argued in principle for free choice
by two potential marriage partners, in practice he cautioned young people to
heed the matchmaking initiatives of their elders. As for parents, he merely urged
them to conduct marriage negotiations on a higher plane, to seek virtuous, compatible mates for their children rather than jockey for the best social and economic position. In this way, too, he added lamely, relations between daughters-in-
law and mothers-in-law were bound to improve, since the former would be serving the latter out of love and respect rather than dried-up, mindless servitude as
in the past.[125]

122. By way of contrast, a prominent moderate female contemporary of Dang Van Bay
strongly advised young women to "revere chastity above all gold and jade," not to trust young
men, since they were sexually aggressive by nature, and to remember always the tragic consequences of unwed pregnancy. Mme Nguyen Hao Ca, *Phu Nu Viet Nam* (Saigon, 1930[?]), pp.
16–22.

123. Dang Van Bay, *Nam Nu Binh Quyen*, p. 4.

124. Ibid., p. 7.

125. Ibid., pp. 42–43, 48–56.

As for husbands and wives, Dang Van Bay beat a hasty retreat to the ancient Chinese formula of individual moral regeneration. That is to say, husbands were encouraged to reform themselves inwardly so that their wives would accept their leadership willingly, and so that the family and thus the nation would find new life, prosperity, and happiness. No longer should husbands refuse to take the words of their wives seriously. No longer should they use demeaning personal pronouns toward them, or they would find their wives secretly using scornful pronouns for them when speaking with others. Husbands should behave toward wives according to the principle of "conciliation" (hoa), while wives should observe the principle of "obliging consent" (thuan). Becoming even more explicit, the author stated, "Going out and facing the earth's wind and waves is the husband's responsibility; managing domestic affairs is the wife's. Thus tasks are divided and the job accomplished."[126]

Many Vietnamese women, moderates included, were not prepared to wait for this alleged male moral awakening. They took to heart Phan Boi Chau's advice to pull themselves into women's collectives, teach each other, share labor, and take both happiness and sorrow together. They pondered the implications of Phan Boi Chau's final comment on the women's question:

In getting things going, the real core will be the spontaneous strength of you women yourselves. If you want to know whether the journey is long or short, there is no better way to find out than to get up and set out. A day on the road is worth more than a year of reading geography books. If you want to know whether you are skillful or clumsy at a particular occupation, best jump in and try it out. A year of practice is worth ten years in technical schools. . . . Talking about swimming yet fearing to jump in the river, or wishing to climb but being afraid of mountains will never get you anywhere! . . . Sisters, don't put your hopes in today's educational system, for it is completely rotten; don't depend on the family, for its future is uncertain; and don't look to the officials, for they are in the dark and want to keep you there, too. The real way, the only way, to strengthen your intellect is through practical execution (thuc hanh), relying on your intuitive knowledge, and on your perception of the new winds and tides about in the world.[127]

After thirty years of painful concrete experience, Phan Boi Chau had come to advocate not only spontaneous action but the importance of understanding those new "winds and tides." In the essay cited above, he did not limit himself to exhortations to action, but also tried to provide a serious anthropological and historical framework as well as a learned and slashing attack on Vietnamese traditionalists. Nevertheless, Phan Boi Chau remained in many ways a prisoner of Confucianism.

126. Ibid., p. 58.

127. Phan Boi Chau, Van De Phu Nu [The Question of Women] (Saigon, 1929), pp. 30–31. Three thousand copies of this book were printed and sold for .30 piaster each. The book was promptly banned in Annam.

The first modern institutional critique of female oppression was that of Tran Thi Nhu Man, mentioned previously as editor of the short-lived women's journal in Hue. Citing the Iroquois Indian research of Lewis Henry Morgan, she made a brief case for sex equality in primitive times, moved on to evidence of matrilineage in early China, speculated on why women had become the personal property of men, mentioned how capitalism had forced women into the factories (but also increased their consciousness), and concluded her historical review with favorable references to Marxist prescriptions for "socializing the family." The bulk of her essay, however, was a searing and specific critique of the traditional exploitation of Vietnamese women, followed by some proposals for equal opportunity and freedom to select one's own mate and to take on responsibilities beyond the family. "In contemporary Vietnamese social conditions," she stated, "a woman must not live only for the family, but also for herself and for society."[128] And of those three reference points, the author concluded, society was now the most crucial.

For many moderate Vietnamese women, the logic of both Phan Boi Chau's and Tran Thi Nhu Man's arguments led directly to Marxism. However, few dared to travel that road themselves, particularly after the violent events of 1930–31. Instead, they continued to seek alternatives. Thus, articles on women obtaining higher education and coveted professional status did not disappear overnight. The fact that only one woman was to be found in a 1936 list of the twenty top professionals trained in France must have been discouraging, nevertheless.[129] Other women saw commercial entrepreneurship as the key, and somehow managed to nurse businesses through the Depression and the economic disruptions of World War II. Yet, there were probably fewer successful Vietnamese businesswomen in 1945 than there had been in 1930. Perhaps a three-act play of 1944, titled "New Women," summarized the mood best. In this drama the Vietnamese heroine, after guiding a newspaper through diverse obstacles and facing up to new political and social pressures, is finally forced to shut down by the authorities. The similarity to *Phu Nu Tan Van*'s experience was obvious, as was the fact that no female-operated journal had risen to take its place in the intervening decade.[130]

Another possibility was to link oneself more closely to French feminists. In 1935 there appeared in Hanoi a fortnightly journal titled *Fémininds*, published by and for the wives of French *colons* and functionaries, but including articles on "indigenous" women as well. The symbol of bourgeois Vietnamese feminism was now Bao Dai's young wife, the "Empress" Nam Huong. One Vietnamese male author, after stating that women must voice their grievances loudly lest men

128. *Phu Nu Tung San*, no. 1, p. 32.

129. She was Hoang Thi Nga, with a 1935 doctorate of science in Paris. "Etat des Indochinois diplômes, 1936–45," AOM NF 1193.

130. Vu Dinh Long, *Dan Ba Moi* [New Women] (Hanoi, 1944).

think they are content to be oppressed, proceeded to dedicate his book to Nam Huong, "the most advanced woman of our country."[131] A woman less able to voice grievances loudly could hardly have been imagined. Nevertheless, like her husband, Nam Huong did lend her name often to sports activities, and this was the place where Vietnamese and French women came together most successfully.[132] Just prior to the outbreak of World War II yet another cautious effort to promote "women's rights" began, this time in the form of a set of novels.[133] It apparently vanished amidst the government's new repressive measures of September 1939. During the War the Vichy administration devoted considerable attention to Joan of Arc, but this probably only served to reinforce Vietnamese interest in the Trung sisters and Trieu Thi Trinh.[134]

Faced with dangerous Marxism on the left and scant success with alternative "social" activities, many moderate women retreated to the family. That they were not comfortable with traditional patterns, however, is evident from publications of the period. For example, in child pedagogy, rather than force girls down the old prescribed path, one prominent bourgeois matron encouraged mothers to allow daughters to develop whatever aptitudes were demonstrated in early years. "Frying fish and cooking rice can be learned later, with only a few months' rigorous application," she added brusquely.[135] The fact that she mentioned only drawing, music, and literature as acceptable alternative aptitudes, however, kept her proposal from raising any eyebrows. Another author offered mothers a twelve-year regimen for improving the intelligence quotients of their children, pointedly contrasting this approach (which was based on recent child psychology research in France and America) with traditional pedagogical precepts.[136]

Perhaps most revealing, however, was a little manual entitled *Gia Dinh Dam Am va Hanh Phuc* [Sweet and Happy Family], written, the author admitted, because there was so much current evidence of family strife even to the point of "terrible tragedy and bloodshed."[137] What emerged was sixty-three slightly pa-

131. Nguyen Van Thuong, *Cam Hue Nu Si* [Miss Cam Hue] (Hanoi, 1935), frontispiece.

132. The journal *Fémininds*, mentioned above, emphasized sports as well as design and short stories. See also Nguyen An, *The Thao Phai Dep* [Exercises for the Pretty Gender] (Hanoi, 1940). Phan Thi Nga, previously active with *Phu Nu Tan Van*, assisted in preparing this and other female physical education manuals.

133. The series was to be titled "Women's Library," with fortnightly printings from June 1939. At least two titles are available: Mai Huong, *Song Long* (Hanoi[?], 1939), and Linh Chi, *Nga Ba Duong* [Three-Cornered Intersection] (Hanoi[?], 1939).

134. Repeated ceremonies for Joan of Arc are reported in the weekly illustrated magazine *Indochine* (Hanoi), especially during 1942.

135. Mme Nguyen Hao Ca, *Phu Nu Viet Nam*, p. 15.

136. Dam Quang Thien, *Mot Phuong Phap Do Tinh Than Do cua Con Tre* [A Technique for Measuring Children's Intelligence] (Hanoi, 1932).

137. K. B. Nhon, *Gia Dinh Dam Am va Hanh Phuc* (Saigon, 1936). For a similar (though less imaginative) defense of family harmony in the same year, see Mme Le Trung Ngoc, *Nu Luu*

thetic arguments for reasserting family hierarchy and traditional role acceptance. The wounds of the Depression were obvious, however. Thus, wives were urged to be understanding when husbands were unemployed, and not to grieve when jewelry was pawned to pay the bills. There was no point in reviling the rich, much less attacking them physically, since they were not aware of their evil ways and, besides, had worked hard to accumulate their property. Nor was suicide an acceptable recourse, in the author's opinion; it made one lower than chickens and ducks, who at least had the graciousness to give meat in repayment for being fed and protected. Then, too, who was to say that death brought happiness? It might well bring agony, especially since the netherworld was said to have rich and poor people, too. Returning to the present, the author advised wives to keep silent when husbands lost their tempers. If it came to a beating, wives should hope for a switch to the rump rather than a less discriminating assault that would only result in "senseless expenditure for medical care."

During the early 1940s a quasi-traditional mood seized a fair portion of the Vietnamese intelligentsia. Non-Marxist attitudes toward women accordingly moved even further to the right. A number of books glorifying the "Heaven-determined function" (thien chuc) of woman within the family were published or simply reprinted from a decade earlier.[138] In primary and secondary school curricula, teachers were advised to exercise increased discrimination between boys and girls, the former getting more instruction in crafts, physical education, science, and the humanities, the latter more training in home economics, child-care, and family hygiene.[139] Vietnamese history and folklore were employed yet again to try to convince women that they should be proud of their roles as mothers, wives, and—occasionally—defenders of the patrimony.[140] What was new, however, was the general admission by bourgeois writers that their own class was corrupted, lacking in purpose, existing from day-to-day on the trivia of life. Now, instead of constantly deriding "country bumpkins" (nha que), bourgeois writers romanticized the Vietnamese peasant. The manners and attitudes of bourgeois women were excoriated as never before, and matrons were sternly advised to emulate peasant women in their alleged spirit of self-sacrifice and quiet home-making satisfactions. One author even invoked the specter of Social Darwinism, quoting Theodore Roosevelt on the dangers of national extinction if women

Phan Su [Obligations of Womanhood] (Hanoi[?], 1936). The author was the wife of a ranking mandarin.

138. Trinh Le Hoang, *Nghe Thuat Lam Me* [The Art of Being a Mother] (Hanoi, 1941); Dung Kim, *Phu Nu voi Gia Dinh* [Woman in Relation to the Family], 2nd printing (Hanoi, 1941[?]), 3rd printing, 1943; Nguyen Khac Hieu, *Dai Guong* [Great Paragons] (Hanoi, 1942), 4,000 copies.

139. Vu Dinh Hoe, *Nhung Phuong Phap Giao Duc o cac Nuoc va Van De Cai Cach Giao Duc* (Hanoi, 1945), pp. 114–20.

140. Le Van Hoe, *Luoc Luan ve Phu Nu Viet-Nam* [General Essay on Vietnamese Women] (Hanoi, 1944).

failed to give enough attention to bearing and rearing children and to long-term population expansion.[141]

The influence here of contemporary fascist ideology hardly needs remarking upon. What is more significant is the way in which acceptance of the bankruptcy of bourgeois ideology and renewed interest in traditional formulas led some Vietnamese women in precisely the opposite political direction. Thus, Mme Phan Anh, although similarly inclined to stress historical traditions, moral indoctrination, and housewife training, saved her highest-priority recommendations for economics. Vietnamese women, she said, must respond forthrightly to wartime inflation, commodity shortages, and basic production requirements. She chided traditionalists for tending to idealize the family roles of women, then proceeded to declare their attitudes functionally irrelevant. Dire necessity was forcing more women into the work force, and women were wanting to speedily acquire new proficiencies, no matter what traditionalists said or did.[142] Writing in early 1945, the precise time when more than one million Vietnamese were dying in a war-induced famine, including tens of thousands in the streets of Hanoi, Mme Phan Anh apparently was prepared to support whatever group seemed most capable of mass mobilization of women and men alike. Along with her husband (who was minister of youth affairs in the Japanese-sanctioned Tran Trong Kim government), Mme Phan Anh soon joined the Viet Minh.

Besides economic production and political mobilization, the ongoing involvement of some bourgeois women in local charities provided a potential meeting ground with the Viet Minh. Although moderates and radicals had parted company ten years earlier in their respective attitudes toward philanthropic work, contact with orphans, destitute coolies, or starving peasants might still be a profoundly moving experience for anyone. As conditions worsened, even those conservatives who focused primarily on female childbearing, child-rearing, and homemaking tasks began to urge bourgeois women to visit the hovels of the poor. Thus, the author who had quoted Theodore Roosevelt about the perils of declining population quantity and quality also appealed to the matrons of Hanoi: instead of continuing to focus on acquiring the property of unfortunates or expecting to order people around with the wave of a hand, they ought to take themselves to the "dark and smelly" homes of poverty-stricken, diseased mothers, of poorly fed, unclad children, and try to do some good.[143] And Mme Van

141. Thai Phi, *Mot Nen Giao Duc Viet-Nam Moi* [A New Vietnamese Education System], 4th printing (Hanoi, 1943), pp. 128–36. This essay was apparently written in March 1941.

142. Ba Phan Anh, "Kha Nang cua Phu Nu" [Capabilities of Women], *Vai Van De Dong Duong* [Some Indochina Questions] (Hanoi, Feb. 1945), pp. 99–103. One of a set of articles from *Dac San Thanh Nghi* (Hanoi) of the same month. See also her article on the need for women to read and write *quoc ngu*, in *Thanh Nghi* (Hanoi), no. 26 (1 Dec. 1942).

143. Thai Phi, *Mot Nen Giao Duc*, p. 134.

Dai, who had vanished from the pages of *Phu Nu Tan Van* after the radical coup, choosing instead to write for more cautious publications and to involve herself in ongoing charity activities, took a dramatic step in 1944 or early 1945 when she secretly accepted from the Viet Minh the responsibility for organizing an orphanage in Hanoi. With the outbreak of full-scale fighting in December 1946 she led three hundred children to a mountainous liberated zone, joined the People's Army, and eventually gained admission to the Communist Party.[144]

Marxism and the Women's Question

Vietnamese women, like Vietnamese men, came to Marxism from a variety of backgrounds and for a variety of reasons. If there was a predominant factor, however, it was outrage and frustration at the way in which the strong treated the weak in colonial society. Depending on personal experience, anger might focus first on the local policeman, tax collector, moneylender, landlord, plantation overseer, factory manager, military superior, school principal, family patriarch, husband, or mother-in-law. Needless to say, victimization did not always result in political radicalization. Many men and women turned inward upon themselves, temporarily or permanently, and this helps to explain the undoubted attractions of spiritualism, romantic individualism, hedonism, and opium smoking in the 1920s and 1930s. Nevertheless, it was the alternative—that is, increased sensitivity to the torments of others as well as a desire to find protection in numbers—that proved the more significant response by the 1940s.

This tendency to generalize grievances cannot be overemphasized. Without it, the Vietnamese would never have been able to mount a sophisticated mass attack on French rule. Thus, even though Ho Chi Minh began his life of struggle by simply condemning foreign brutality, by 1925 he was clearly cognizant of other important forms of human aggression and injustice as well—including ill-treatment of women by men.[145] By the same token, Vietnamese women who may have begun by feeling hindered or harrassed by parents, relatives, husbands, or in-laws often came to empathize with and show solidarity toward jailed anti-colonial activists, striking coal miners, or starving peasants.

Marxism obviously endorsed such expansion of political consciousness among the exploited, regardless of class, sex, or nationality. More than that, however,

144. LT-2, pp. 184–88. As Mme Van Dai continued to publish prolifically on the family, motherhood, and other "women's matters," a comparison with her earlier writings would be quite instructive.

145. It should be remarked, however, that Ho Chi Minh still tended to link all forms of aggression in colonial society to the presence of foreign overlords. See, for example, Bernard Fall, ed., *Ho Chi Minh on Revolution*, pp. 29–30, 109–15. French brutalization of Vietnamese women was a theme stressed equally by the Vietnamese Independence Party (Viet Nam Doc Lap Dang) in Paris in the late 1920s. AOM NF 645(?).

Marxism offered an ideological framework linking all types of exploitation to the existing mode of production, and suggested ways by which the oppressed might vanquish their oppressors and establish a system of true equality. To the degree that they were members of an inferior caste—or "slaves of slaves," as one commentator put it—Vietnamese women certainly were not averse to seeing the world in dichotomous terms.[146] More to the point, they had little difficulty imagining an epic confrontation between a minority of imperialists and "feudalists" on the one hand, and the vast majority of exploited people (of both sexes) on the other. It is thus far from accidental that particular female aspirations and general political objectives came to be expressed in identical terms, for example, liberation (*giai phong*), equal rights (*binh quyen*), equality (*binh dang*), and self-rule (*tu chu*).

Where the Marxist concept of liberation parted company with other concepts was already the subject of public debate in Vietnam in the early 1930s. Thus, Phan Khoi, who thought of himself as a moderate progressive, found himself harshly taken to task by Nguyen Thi Chinh for arguing that alterations in the Vietnamese "philosophy of life" (*nhan sanh quan*) held the key to women's liberation. Rather, it was "objective" historical progress and the economic mode of production, she said, that determined everyone's "subjective" philosophy of life:

> We are now in the historical stage of monopoly capitalism and statist economies, with decisions being made by a minority of financial and political leaders. The majority of people do not decide things; they only follow. Rice is to be .60 piasters per *gia* [approx. 40 litres]. Right. Train tickets are to rise three cents. Right. A box of matches is one cent. Right.[147]

The way to change this situation, Nguyen Thi Chinh concluded, was for the majority—the mass of men and women—to join in political struggle against the minority. This would bring women out of the kitchen; philosophies of life would be altered; and the entire socio-economic system would be transformed. Moreover, this process (including women's liberation) would not take half a century as Phan Khoi had predicted, since objective, systemic progress was operating on a much faster timetable than any highly relativistic proposals for attitudinal change.[148]

Whatever the "objective" and "subjective" conditions, Vietnamese trying to make a revolution knew that they could not afford to remain complacent about

146. The "slaves of slaves" status is discussed in Arlene Eisen Bergman, *Women of Vietnam* (San Francisco: People's Press, 1974), pp. 38–57.

147. Nguyen Thi Chinh, PNTV 162 (4 Aug. 1932), p. 10. Phan Khoi's original essay is in PNTV 158 (7 July 1932), and 160 (21 July 1932).

148. Phan Khoi appended a brief rebuttal to Nguyen Thi Chinh's article, accepting historical progress as the "root." However, he continued to ignore the economic mode of production, and repeated his opinion that discussion of philosophies of life was very important.

the status and role of women. Accordingly, the Indochinese Communist Party immediately upon its formation in 1930 issued several proclamations putting the struggle for equality of the sexes among the ten principal tasks of the revolution.[149] Two years later the Party's "Action Program" repeated this commitment, condemned the imperialists for preserving and reinforcing feudal restraints on women, and mentioned that "the most advanced sisters in Indochina have already engaged themselves in the heroic struggle." More concretely, the "Action Program" asserted that "the most miserably oppressed group of all" in Indochina was the women working in factories and on plantations. Demands included elimination of all laws and customs sanctioning sexual inequality (specifically citing arranged marriages, bride harrassment, polygamy, concubinage, and fathers having automatic custody of children in divorces or separations), four months' paid maternity leave, and establishment of free childcare centers at worksites.[150]

By the time of the Popular Front (1936–39) the Indochinese Communist Party had further refined its platform on women. For "ordinary sisters" (*chi em binh dan*), a category meant to include the mass of female workers and peasants, the Party now demanded equal pay for equal work, eight weeks' paid maternity leave, implementation of recently enacted laws forbidding the employment of women in mines or on night shifts, and extension of legal protection (maximum hours, minimum wages, civil treatment) to domestic servants and wet nurses. For bourgeois women, the Party stressed equal inheritance rights and access to positions in government bureaus and private offices, rather than having to stay at home or compete frantically for the limited number of existing jobs as teachers and shop accountants. On behalf of all women, regardless of class, the Party called for elimination of polygamy, broader educational and occupational training opportunities, individual freedom to marry or divorce, and the granting of universal adult suffrage.[151]

During the Popular Front period, too, several authors picked up where Tran Thi Nhu Man had left off in 1929 and provided detailed expositions of the women's question from a Marxist perspective. Nguyen Thi Kim Anh, after a rather routine portrayal of the status of women in primitive communist, slave, feudal, and capitalist periods, warmed to the subject of twentieth-century middle-class feminist and female proletarian activities in Europe and America. Predictably, she condemned feminists for focusing so much attention on female

149. Ho Chi Minh, *Selected Writings, 1920–1969* (Hanoi, 1977), pp. 39–41; *An Outline History of the Vietnamese Worker's Party* (Hanoi, 1970), pp. 163–72.

150. *Chuong Trinh Hanh Dong cua Dang Cong San Dong Duong* [Action Program of the Indochinese Communist Party] (n.p., 1932). An English translation of a French version is available in Robert Turner, *Vietnamese Communism* (Stanford: Hoover Institution Press, 1975), pp. 318–33.

151. Cuu Kim Son and Van Hue, *Chi Em Phai Lam Gi?* [Sisters, What Is to Be Done?] (Hanoi, 1938), pp. 18–22.

suffrage, which within a bourgeois democratic framework would simply give more power to a minority. By contrast, she said, women like Clara Tetkin, Kroupskaya (Lenin's wife), Rosa Luxembourg, and Alexandra Kollontai had seen the advantages of joining with proletarian men to overthrow the old order and establish socialism. The Third International had on the one hand succeeded in overcoming narrow male jealousy and hatred of women competing for scarce jobs, and on the other hand managed to convince women that they need not segregate themselves in particular occupations or remain aloof from unions and political organizations composed largely of men.

Needless to say, Nguyen Thi Kim Anh lauded recent female advances in the Soviet Union. Nevertheless, any thoughtful reader of the statistics cited could see that the struggle was far from over. For example, even though the Stakhanovite movement had demonstrated that women were not necessarily weaker in work capacity than men, and even though women now made up the majority in many Soviet factories, men for some reason still constituted more than sixty percent of the university student population and eighty-four percent of Communist Party membership. Then, too, procedures for marriage and divorce, extremely simple in the early 1920s, had been tightened up by the 1930s. Perhaps most revealing, however, was the fact that the Soviet government was now offering financial inducements to women to bear more children.[152]

As for Vietnam, Nguyen Thi Kim Anh argued that French colonialism, by relying heavily on both feudal and capitalist ideologies, caused women to be "the most exploited group of all, both in the family and in society."[153] If women were to become a major force in the Vietnamese national liberation struggle, preparatory to marching side by side with women elsewhere in the international socialist struggle, then it was imperative for revolutionaries to pay attention to special female grievances arising from this double bind of feudal and capitalist conditions.[154] In a series of newspaper articles of the same period, Nguyen Thi Kim Anh directed her most scathing remarks against certain female intellectuals, who, she said, mixed reactionary, fascist, feudal, and capitalist concepts to assist men in preventing their wives, sisters, and daughters from joining the women's liberation effort.[155] Nonetheless, she must have known that many Indochinese Communist Party members remained little moved by the plight of women, that they often

152. Nguyen Thi Kim Anh, *Van De Phu Nu* [The Question of Women] (Cholon, 1938). As nothing further is known about the author, one should not rule out the possibility that Nguyen Thi Kim Anh was a pseudonym for a man writing on the subject of women.

153. Ibid., p. 48.

154. Ibid., pp. 51–52.

155. Nguyen Thi Kim Anh, *Dan Chung* (Saigon), nos. 16 (14 Sept. 1938), 17 (17 Sept. 1938), and 19 (24 Sept. 1938). The attack was triggered by an article by Tuyet Dung, in *Doc*, no. 19. This exchange is discussed in Nguyet Tu, *Chi Minh Khai* (Hanoi, 1976), pp. 89–94, with the faint suggestion that Nguyen Thi Kim Anh was in fact Nguyen Thi Minh Khai.

tended to limit female activists to support roles, and that, in a few cases, they kept more than one wife.

Perhaps the most impressive Vietnamese Marxist study of the women's question prior to the August 1945 Revolution was that prepared by Cuu Kim Son and Van Hue and published in two volumes in Hanoi in 1938.[156] The first volume, *Doi Chi Em* [Sister's Life], opened with a description of the conditions of Vietnamese women according to the following categories: proletarian, servant, peasant, petty merchant, intelligentsia, and feudal-capitalist. The bulk of this volume was devoted to a discussion of socio-cultural institutions which continued to inhibit all Vietnamese women to some degree or another, particular attention being given to engagement ritual, marriage, divorce, polygamy, intra-family hierarchy, prostitution, and restricted educational opportunities. Significantly, the authors remained convinced of the value of the institution of marriage; however, they proposed that it be transformed from a mechanism of patriarchal continuity, property control, and labor exploitation to a means for promoting monogamous love and happiness. They credited journals like *Phu Nu Tan Van* and novels like *Doan Tuyet*, by Nhat Linh, for greatly increasing public understanding of the personal tragedy inherent in so many arranged marriages. At least among intelligentsia families, it was said, parents now tended to consult daughters on selection of a marriage partner. But they were still shocked at the idea of daughters taking the initiative, that is to say, meeting young men on their own, falling in love, and only then seeking formal approval.

Surprisingly, Cuu Kim Son and Van Hue invoked the psychological theories of Sigmund Freud and Wilhelm Reich (1897–1957) when explaining to parents the particular needs and sensitivities of adolescents. They even talked of a "sexual crisis" in Vietnam stemming from the sustained repression of normal human instincts.[157] Nguyen Thi Kim Anh had also described in positive terms the freedom of young men and women in the Soviet Union to meet each other at cinemas, dance pavilions, sporting events, and cultural centers.[158] Such ideas were

---

156. Cuu Kim Son and Van Hue, *Doi Chi Em* (Hanoi, 1938). The brief introduction to *Doi Chi Em* consists mostly of an article translated from Truong Chinh's *Rassemblement* (16 Mar. 1937). Cuu Kim Son was one pen name of Tran Duc Sac. Better known by the pseudonym of Van Tan, he was assistant editor of NCLS until 1976. Van Hue was in reality Pham Van Hao, who took the name Hue from his wife. Until 1975 he was head of the Revolutionary Museum in Hanoi.

157. Cuu Kim Son and Van Hue, *Doi Chi Em*, pp. 15–17, 21–24. Specifically, the authors felt the stifling of sexual instincts to be one cause of masturbation (at that time in the West still thought to be destructive to the nervous system), prostitution, venereal disease, rape, and the taking of religious vows of chastity. Non-Marxist Vietnamese intellectuals were also fascinated by Freud and contemporary Western sexual imagery. See, for example, the large drawing of an Asian girl in modern bathing suit sitting on the beach and enjoying the feel of a big wave splashing up between her thighs, in *Thanh Nien* (Hanoi), no. 11 (7 Apr. 1934).

158. Nguyen Thi Kim Anh, *Van De Phu Nu*, pp. 30–31.

still shocking to most Vietnamese, including the intelligentsia, and conservatives delighted in seizing upon them to prove that communists advocated "free love" or "jungle behavior" rather than rules of proper human conduct as passed down through the ages. As it turned out, Freud ended up being more often denounced than endorsed by Vietnamese Marxist writers.[159] Yet one cannot help but wonder if Viet Minh success a few years later in recruiting and motivating adolescents was due in some measure to Popular Front discussions of this sort.

It would be wrong to convey the impression that Cuu Kim Son and Van Hue were total iconoclasts. For example, they suggested that it was not the concept of a separately defined, female morality that was outmoded, but only its traditional Confucian component. Although the "three submissions" would have to be eradicated entirely, the "four virtues" might be given new meanings: "labor" (cong) should be extended far beyond the home to include factory and professional work, social and political involvements; "physical appearance" (dung) need not always stress pleasant expressions and languid motions—when the occasion warranted, they said, women ought to look angry, show eagerness, or move aggressively; "appropriate speech" (ngon) no longer meant being sweet and comforting all the time—women also had to learn how to talk boldly and eloquently when trying to convince people to join the liberation struggle, or firmly and bluntly when telling husbands they were wrong; and "proper behavior" (hanh) did not have to signify slavish obedience, but could mean resolute commitment to the struggle for freedom and independence, in fact, a readiness to resist all attempts at exploitation. To summarize, Cuu Kim Son and Van Hue quoted Lenin urging every housewife to become capable of managing state affairs.[160] Unfortunately, the authors never spelled out how these new "four virtues" for women differed substantially from male attributes; this led to the inference that some portion of the old content was still valid, or even that women were expected somehow to fulfill both old and new ideals simultaneously. At the very least, the authors must have sensed that employing old formulas for new purposes ran the risk of mental confusion, or of old content slipping back in later through the rear door.

Cuu Kim Son and Van Hue probably believed that only commitment to action and the accumulation of experience could solve such problems. In their second volume, Chi Em Phai Lam Gi? [Sisters, What Is to Be Done?],[161] they argued that true women's liberation could only come as an adjunct to liberation of the "proletarian class and working masses" in Indochina and throughout the world. Women in Western capitalist countries mught appear to be liberated, but in real-

159. For one of the earliest Marxist attacks on Freud, see X. X., "Triet Hoc voi Cuoc Doi" [Philosophy and Life], PNTV 209, 210, 211 (22 July to 10 Aug. 1933).

160. Cuu Kim Son and Van Hue, Doi Chi Em, pp. 12–13.

161. Idem, Chi Em Phai Lam Gi? (Hanoi, 1938).

ity they were still bound by economic chains. Among other things, the authors pointed to the tendency of women in capitalist societies to marry men of their own class, to seek out wealthy "sugar daddies," or to slide into prostitution when no other employment opportunities were available. Nevertheless, Cuu Kim Son and Van Hue did praise Vietnamese women of bourgeois and petit bourgeois backgrounds who had taken the first initiatives in the late 1920 and early 1930s. In a colonial situation, and particularly with the Popular Front government in office in Paris, there was still merit in women organizing to demand short-term, limited freedoms in a capitalist context.

Where bourgeois Vietnamese women had gone wrong, Cuu Kim Son and Van Hue claimed, was in paying far too much attention to altering customs and far too little to promoting economic and political changes. Even with customs, they remarked sarcastically, there had been a lot of talk and little action, so that it had been left to lower-class wives or mistresses of Frenchmen to first ride bicycles, to refuse to blacken their teeth, and to wear Western clothing. Such reluctance to take chances was understandable, the authors commented, since bourgeois women often benefited from the existing system.

Despite such deficiencies, Cuu Kim Son and Van Hue proposed that sympathetic bourgeois and petit bourgeois women join together with lower-class women, agree to emphasize common grievances, and progressively organize an "Indochina Women's United Front" (*Mat Tran Thong Nhat cua Phu Nu Dong Duong*). Upper-class participants could contribute useful "theoretical" knowledge, and they also had proven abilities in writing, publishing, and public speaking. On the other hand, some lower-class women already possessed valuable experience in organizing local grievance committees, tax protests, and mass demonstrations.[162] Thus the authors suggested that in a city such as Hanoi separate groups be formed by petty merchant women, female teachers and nurses, and students. Individuals of different backgrounds might also organize around particular issues, for example, female literacy, occupational training, social services, sports, and anti-fascism or anti-superstition campaigns. Each group would subsequently appoint delegates to a Hanoi women's league (*lien doan*), which in turn would link up with other cities and provinces to form regional and national organizations. This was the "horizontal" technique of organizing, Cuu Kim Son and Van Hue emphasized, as distinct from the "vertical" technique, which would have involved women students of each district forming branches (*chi hoi*), then appointing delegates to provincial associations, and so on up to a national women's student union. The latter approach was said to be too time-consuming—but a more important and unspoken reason, in all likelihood, was that vertical links for all such united-front networks, male and female, were the prerogative of the Indochinese Communist Party. The authors also did not men-

162. Nguyen Thi Kim Anh, *Van De Phu Nu*, pp. 52–55, makes much the same point.

tion proletarian women in this detailed schema, apparently because they were supposed to join labor unions composed of both sexes.

Did class-based organizations meet the specific needs of women or not? On this question, Vietnamese Marxist writers were not entirely consistent. The basic hypothesis was that women, at least outside the feudal or bourgeois classes, were far more oppressed by their class enemies than by men. Only when private property was abolished could women truly be free. The class struggle was thus a movement for women's liberation, and vice versa.[163] In any event, it was claimed, economic changes in colonial Indochina were already making it impossible for men to keep women subservient.

> In order to survive, women are now forced to leave families to work in factories and mines. Daily they rub shoulders with men and toil as men do, and thus come to understand their true value. Knowing that they must work to eat, women no longer simply *follow* their fathers and mothers, *follow* their husbands and sons, as though they were in a state of perpetual bondage.[164]

Nevertheless, the same authors admitted that a few proletarian men still sought concubines when first wives appeared unable to provide male heirs. Although theory specified that all such feudal attitudes were to vanish as the economy was further transformed, readers were urged to take a non-determinist stance and to regard the liberation of women as a high-priority matter.[165] Nguyen Thi Kim Anh got closer to the core of the matter when she emphasized that even in the Soviet Union, vanguard of the international proletarian movement, women maintained organizations to protect their particular rights and interests (*quyen loi*). Surely such organizations were all the more important in Vietnam, where both feudal and capitalist attitudes toward women were still rampant. As long as women avoided the mistake of opposing males per se and sought only to combat the reactionary viewpoints held by many people of both sexes, they would find themselves able to march side by side with men in the overall campaign for freedom, equality, and improvement of living standards.[166] Nevertheless, one cannot help but suspect that a number of Vietnamese Marxists failed to get the point entirely. Cuu Kim Son and Van Hue, for example, chose to refute not the argument that a woman's primary role was in the home,

---

163. Cuu Kim Son and Van Hue, *Chi Em Phai Lam Gi?*, pp. 12–13, 16.

164. Ibid., p. 4; emphasis in original.

165. Ibid., pp. 5, 32–34. Polygamy continued to pose a problem in the 1940s and 1950s for the Communist Party, especially in mountain regions. See Duong Thi An's sharp comments in *Nguon Vui Duy Nhat* [The Sole Source of Joy] (Hanoi, 1974), p. 109.

166. Nguyen Thi Kim Anh, *Van De Phu Nu*, pp. 34, 52–54. "Freedom, equality, and improvement of living standards" was the ICP's broadest united-front formula during this period. Almost as an afterthought the author mentioned that Vietnamese women had already demonstrated a capacity for heroic struggle during more than four thousand years of national history.

but only the conservative assertion that modern women were incapable of fulfilling that role properly. They also did not see the illogic of first asserting that women's weaknesses were socially determined, then turning around to speak of certain natural feminine strengths such as virtue, patience, and loyalty. And when they referred to the women's movement as a component (*bo phan*) of the much larger popular movement, the effect was to downgrade the particular concerns of women.[167]

For some Marxists the shock of seeing (or reading about) young Vietnamese women asserting themselves was clearly more cultural than political. Nhan Chi (apparently a Thanh Hoa provincial cadre) sarcastically equated earlier women's journals with nostrums for venereal disease, and warned readers not to be fooled by urban feminists who "use their thighs and breasts to carry out 'charity' work or 'sports' activities."[168] After blandly asserting that sexism was negligible among the proletariat, he still worried that too many wives protesting the actions of their husbands could disintegrate the proletarian movement. Halfway through Nhan Chi's essay it became clear that he was primarily interested in explaining the development of industrial capitalism in Europe, not the women's question in Vietnam. Male chauvinism was obviously not limited to moderates and traditionalists.

Whatever the ambiguities, women did join the Indochinese Communist Party. The highest-ranking female Party member of the 1930s was Nguyen Thi Minh Khai (1910–41). As a student in the provincial town of Vinh, Nghe An province, she was deeply influenced by a number of young radical schoolteachers, two of whom later became secretaries-general of the ICP.[169] Her father, a railway clerk, allowed Nguyen Thi Minh Khai to use an upstairs room in the railroad station to hide forbidden literature and to convene study sessions among her peers. Classmates joked that the old patriot Phan Boi Chau had "snatched away" her soul with his stirring poetry written from exile. As Nguyen Thi Minh Khai became more involved in political organizing, her mother's occupation as petty trader provided her with a convenient cover for trips to distant towns and provinces. However, she was compelled to hide from her parents any nighttime activities, and she came under increasing pressure to marry into a mandarin family and settle down. In early 1930 she "emancipated" (*thoat ly*) herself from her family and left to take up a new life as a professional revolutionary.[170]

---

167. Cuu Kim Son and Van Hue, *Chi Em Phai Lam Gi?*, pp. 34, 38, 41.

168. Nhan Chi, *Chi Em Lao Kho Voi Xa Hoi* [Working Women and Society] (Thanh Hoa, 1938), pp. 4, 11, 24.

169. These were Tran Phu (1900–31), who died in prison, and Ha Huy Tap (?–1941), who was executed by a firing squad.

170. Nguyet Tu, *Chi Minh Khai*, pp. 9–41. Most other young Vietnamese women trying to engage in convert political activity faced exactly the same obstacle, since it was unthinkable that

Selected to train and to work in the Hong Kong bureau of the Comintern, Nguyen Thi Minh Khai was detained by the British in April 1931. By speaking Cantonese convincingly, she managed to avoid being turned over to the French authorities, and wound up spending three years in various Chinese Kuomintang prisons. Upon her release in Shanghai in 1934 she reestablished contact with the ICP, was smuggled aboard a Soviet ship to Vladivostok, and soon was studying in Moscow. In August 1935 Nguyen Thi Minh Khai was able to address the Seventh Congress of the Comintern. It was an unprecedented opportunity, she told the audience proudly. She used it both to stress the greater oppression of women workers and peasants in colonial and semi-colonial societies and to chide the congress for not having more female delegates from advanced Western parties. Apparently a public success, she was sought out by other delegates and photographed talking with Lenin's wife, Krupskaya. At about this time she also married Le Hong Phong, head of the Party's Overseas Leadership Bureau.[171]

After her return to Vietnam via Berlin, Paris, Singapore, and Hong Kong, Nguyen Thi Minh Khai became part of the leadership group that worked hard to implement the Comintern's new anti-fascist popular front strategy. In her role as undercover member of the Southern Region Committee, located not far from Saigon, she specialized in expanding rural contacts, recruiting women, compiling instructional materials, and organizing training sessions. Early in 1939 Nguyen Thi Minh Khai was selected Secretary of the Saigon–Cholon Party branch, where she apparently had to cope with considerable disunity as a result of local Trotskyist successes and the rapidly changing international situation. Early in 1940 she bore a daughter, whom Le Hong Phong was never able to see, for he had been jailed soon after the outbreak of war in Europe, and was destined to die from torture in 1942. Nguyen Thi Minh Khai herself was captured in late July 1940, tried on charges of attempting to overthrow the colonial regime, and executed on 28 August 1941.[172]

Perhaps more representative of early female Party members was Nguyen Thi Nghia. Although she had been born to a well-to-do family in Ha Dong province and had received a primary school degree, she chose to "proletarianize" herself by working in factories and preaching revolution. Responsible for maintaining contact between the ICP Central Committee and the Nghe-Tinh region during the critical year 1930, she was captured in December and bit off the front of her tongue in attempted suicide. Tortured mercilessly, she feigned muteness to avoid betraying Party secrets. Only when she knew she was dying did Nguyen Thi

---

a respectable unmarried or widowed woman would travel alone at night or meet secretly with a group of men. See Ton Thi Que, *Chi Mot Con Duong*, pp. 15–16.

171. Nguyet Tu, *Chi Minh Khai*, pp. 41–75. Nguyen Thi Minh Khai's pseudonym at that time was Phan Lan.

172. Ibid., pp. 76–136.

Nghia reveal to her startled cellmates that she could talk, simply telling them to remain loyal to Party and country. An emotional funeral was conducted by the female prisoners, and once each week for a year they "communed" (*cau dong*) with the spirit of Nguyen Thi Nghia by means of carefully organized seances.[173]

The Nghe-Tinh uprising also marked the first real influx of lower-class women to the Party, not least of all because they were allotted shares of land along with the men and were allowed to participate in political meetings and literacy classes. A leaflet distributed at this time, addressed specifically to women, argued that sexual equality would be part and parcel of the ultimate revolutionary victory, which, however, could only be won at the price of great struggle, sacrifice, suffering, and loss of life.[174] Undoubtedly sensing some social and political significance, French officials commented more than once on female involvement in the Nghe-Tinh uprising.[175] In one particular confrontation colonial soldiers tried to break up a demonstration by tearing off the clothes of one female activist in front of her peers. To show they could not be cowed in this way, other women proceeded to strip off their clothing in solidarity, then marched to jail with the first activist, chanting Communist Party slogans en route.[176] Only Vietnamese peasant women had nerve enough to do such a thing; urban feminists would probably have scattered in total confusion.

Sometimes sexist attitudes of the enemy could be used to advantage. Because the colonial police still tended to assume that politics was a man's business, the Party regularly assigned women to secret liaison and leaflet-distribution tasks. An innocent-looking girl on a bicycle or an old betel-chewing lady carrying fish sauce to market was less likely to be stopped and searched. Female stereotypes could also be combined with class stereotypes, for example, a clandestine Communist covering herself with gold jewelry and playing the role of a provincial social climber.[177] However, none of this solved the problem of male Party mem-

---

173. Ton The Que, *Chi Mot Con Duong*, p. 95. The author, who was in prison with Nguyen Thi Nghia, indicates that the seances were a device to impress the guards. One can assume, however, that at least some of the prisoners also believed in spirit communion.

174. Translated leaflet titled "Aux Compatriotes féminins," in AOM NF 2634. Original probably seized Jan. 1931.

175. Le Thi Nham Tuyet, *Phu Nu Viet Nam*, pp. 199–200. Pierre Brocheux, "L'implantation du mouvement communiste en Indochine française: le cas du Nghe-Tinh (1930–1931)," *Revue d'Histoire Moderne et Contemporaine* XXIV (Jan.–Mar. 1977), p. 64.

176. Le Thi Nham Tuyet, *Phu Nu Viet Nam*, pp. 200–201. Having women in the forefront was not entirely accidental. A Communist Party "Plan to Mobilize Peasant Demonstrators," circulated in northern Vietnam in September 1930, suggested that women speakers were particularly effective in convincing colonial soldiers of a group's non-antagonistic intent. AOM (Aix) F-7F4, Sep.–Oct. 1930 folio, item 18.

177. Nguyen Thi Dinh, *No Other Road to Take* (Ithaca: SEAP, 1976), pp. 27–29. This is a translation of *Khong Con Duong Nao Khac* (Hanoi, 1969), memoirs of the deputy commander of the People's Liberation Armed Forces.

bers themselves continuing to cast women participants in stereotyped support roles—for example, cooking meals for cadres, mending clothes, or making a bit of money by growing and selling vegetables—and it was the unusual man indeed who overcame traditional ideas about the uncleanliness of women and nursed them when they were sick or washed their undergarments.[178]

The one sure way for a female Party member to obtain more recognition was to succeed in organizing other women. By 1937–38 a number of young women were concentrating on this task and producing results. Central Committee resolutions of 1937 and 1938 stressed the female constituency and instructed all Party echelons to establish specialized women's committees. When planning and implementing strikes at locations where women formed the bulk of the work force (for example, the Nam Dinh textile factory or the Hai Phong spinning mill), the Party could hardly have done otherwise. At the large and historic 1938 May Day rally in Hanoi several thousand women, arrayed in paramilitary fashion alongside other groups, yelled predetermined slogans and listened to their own representative, Miss Bao Tam, demand the "progressive eradication of barriers differentiating men and women."[179] *The Gioi* [World],[180] the Party's bimonthly for young people, featured a women's column not too different from that of *Phu Nu Tan Van* four years earlier. Young women were urged to be daring (*bao dan*) rather than dependent (*y lai*), to "grab hold of their own lives, futures, and happiness"—in short, "to have the courage to liberate themselves." There was an admiring article on the wife of the Comintern's popular-front strategist, G. Dimitrov, as well as favorable references to the Trung sisters and Joan of Arc. Other articles made it clear that Vietnamese women were already active in denouncing the current fascist offensive in Spain, in raising money to aid Chinese victims of Japanese aggression, and in multiplying the number of informal literacy and occupational training classes in Vietnam.[181]

With the harsh colonial crackdown of late 1939 and 1940, many female activists found themselves in jail just like the men. Those able to evade capture soon focused on organizing local branches of the Viet Minh Women's Association for National Salvation. However, a new avenue of advancement was opening up in small Viet Minh "armed proselytizing" units, the forerunners of the Vietnam People's Army. Of a group of twenty-one formed in Thanh Hoa in July 1941, for example, five were women, and the famous armed proselytizing unit inaugurated by Vo Nguyen Giap on 22 December 1944 included three women among

178. Ton Thi Que, *Chi Mot Con Duong*, p. 45; Nguyet Tu, *Chi Minh Khai*, p. 104.

179. Cuu Kim Son and Van Hue, *Chi Em Phai Lam Gi?*, pp. 34–36; Le Thi Nham Tuyet, *Phu Nu Viet Nam*, pp. 203–05. The latter source also indicates that forty percent of the members of Party-initiated worker-peasant "mutual aid associations" in the period 1936–39 were women.

180. *The Gioi* (Hanoi) began publishing in September 1938 and closed down in August 1939.

181. *The Gioi*, issues of 15 Sept., 1 Dec., and 15 Dec. 1938, and 1 Jan. 1939.

its thirty-four members. According to General Giap, the ability of these women to both handle firearms and explain current political developments made a deep impression on villagers.[182] Probably the best known female military cadre of the early period was Ha Thi Que (b. 1922), who in 1943 shifted from her position as local women's organizer to conduct classes on military and political subjects for men and women in the Central Committee's "secure zone" (an toan khu). By Ha Thi Que's own account, it was not an easy task. Twice she was accused by women of "husband-stealing," simply because she was young, the classes had to be conducted at night, and she was in a position to tell men to do things. She remembered thinking to herself:

Stealing a person for the revolution is nothing to be ashamed of. I have no other desire. Surely the wives will eventually understand.[183]

Women's Union organizing and women's military activity came together in 1945. Both civilian and military groups were important in seizing government grain supplies during the famine that swept northern Vietnam early in the year, and both participated in subsequent attacks on local colonial offices and disarming of colonial militia units. Nguyen Thi Hung, for example, specialized in the meticulous planning of assaults on granaries in Hung Yen province. This included encouraging public participation, mobilization, attack, division of rice, transport, selecting alternate escape routes, and ambushing pursuing enemy units. When almost nine months pregnant, Nguyen Thi Hung led a mass demonstration to take power in Kim Dong district.[184] Meanwhile, Truong Thi My, former worker in a Haiphong silk filature, was given exactly eighteen hours to organize a mass march on Hanoi from nearby Ha Dong province. She not only did that, but then marched back to Ha Dong to seize local power.[185] During those same critical days, Nguyen Thi Dinh was Viet Minh banner-carrier at the head of several thousand peasants who marched many hours to seize the Ben Tre provincial administration. Nguyen Thi Thap was on the uprising committee in My Tho province, and Nguyen Khoa Dieu Hong was a principal speaker at the mass meeting in the Hanoi opera house on 17 August 1945, when political initiative in the capital swung permanently to the Viet Minh.[186] A week later Duong Thi An

---

182. Vo Nguyen Giap, Tu Nhan Dan Ma Ra [Coming from the People] (Hanoi, 1964), p. 168.
183. Ha Thi Que, "Rung Yen The," Rung Yen The (Hanoi, 1962), p. 89. Ha Thi Que had already been through two brief courses in military subjects, the more advanced focusing on Mao Tse-tung's doctrines concerning strategy and tactics. She mentions, too, that she was the second "liberated woman" to work in the secure zone, the first being Mme Bay, wife of Hoang Quoc Viet. Le Thi Nham Tuyet, Phu Nu Viet Nam, p. 214, indicates that women soon constituted twenty percent of the membership of armed units in the secure zone.
184. Truong Thi My and Nguyen Thi Hung, Niem Tin Khong Bao Gio Tat [Feelings of Trust Never Extinguished] (Hanoi, 1967), pp. 73–88.
185. Ibid., pp. 41–54.
186. Le Thi Nham Tuyet, Phu Nu Viet Nam, pp. 215–19.

wore a uniform and pranced her horse as part of a Liberation Army unit descending to the delta and heading for Hanoi. "Maybe women along the road didn't see a Trung sister on an elephant," she commented a quarter-century later, "yet they were stunned and excited to see a woman handle a horse well."[187]

On 11 September 1945, only nine days after establishment of the Democratic Republic of Vietnam, the first general conference of the Women's Association for National Salvation was convened,[188] and before the end of that year women were fighting and dying to defend the Republic in southern and central Vietnam.[189] In January 1946 ten women were elected to the first DRVN National Assembly (out of a total of 403). By the end of 1946 more than one million women had joined the women's association or other Viet Minh affiliates, and the association was reorganized, becoming the Vietnam Women's Union (*Hoi Lien Hiep Phu Nu Viet Nam*), which has continued to function to the present day. Also, between September 1945 and December 1946, perhaps 1.25 million women, or almost twenty percent of the adult female population, participated in literacy classes to the point of obtaining some sort of reading certification.[190]

Conclusion

Twenty-six years later, in 1973, a leader of the Vietnam Women's Union told an American visitor to Hanoi, "We have equality, but we are not yet equal."[191] That brief, frank remark tells us a great deal. On the one hand, if we look back fifty years most Vietnamese women at that time had no inkling of what sexual equality meant. If they had heard of the idea, they either opposed it or believed that Vietnamese women were totally unprepared. A sense of distress, self-pity, and powerlessness was the most that could be seen, summed up best by the following popular refrain:

> I am like a well by the road.
> A clever man will use it to wash his face,
> A rude one to wash his feet.[192]

The traditional assumption that an unmarried female was "like a dais not nailed down," that only within the framework of marriage could young women find a secure base from which to live and act, was still unchallenged. Those very few

187. Duong Thi An, *Nguon Vui Duy Nhat*, p. 107.

188. Dang Lao Dong Viet Nam, *Cuoc Van Dong Cach Mang Thang Tam o Ha-Noi* [Activating the August Revolution in Hanoi] (Hanoi, 1970), p. 155.

189. Le Thi Nham Tuyet, *Phu Nu Viet Nam*, pp. 230–231.

190. Ibid., pp. 225–27.

191. From discussion in June 1973 with Dee Donovan, as quoted in Bergman, *Women of Vietnam*, p. 209.

192. Le Thi Nham Tuyet, *Phu Nu Viet Nam*, p. 156.

women who refused to be "nailed down" risked being categorized along with prostitutes and mistresses of Frenchmen.

By the 1930s, married and unmarried women alike had discovered that they could organize themselves effectively, help one another, and gain a public hearing for specific grievances. Increasingly they came to the conclusion that the prevailing ethic of sexual inequality was grounded on women's lack of multiple opportunities, whether economic, educational, or political. If they wanted to be equal—and more and more young women did—they would have to obtain extra-familial responsibilities and prove themselves to their still skeptical male contemporaries, not to mention the older generation of both sexes. No sooner did they attempt this, however, than it became painfully obvious that the achievement of almost anything significant (by either men or women) was blocked by the colonial condition and by internal class distinctions. For some women, to understand this was to retreat to the relative security of the family. For others, it meant they would have to struggle for national liberation and working-class liberation in order to achieve women's liberation. The Indochinese Communist Party provided the obvious (though dangerous) vehicle.

Vietnamese Marxist-Leninists were also able to argue that women's energies and skills had always been employed to create surplus value, but that in slave, feudal, or capitalist economic conditions they were systematically denied power, status, and personal satisfaction commensurate with their labors. In a socialist system, however, things would be different. While it is not possible to assess the validity of that claim in any detail here, a few points do deserve mention. Certainly women became more involved in extra-family production in the various zones controlled by the Communist Party from 1944 onward. The money or work points earned belonged to them, not to their parents or husbands. Women also achieved equal rights under the law, and were given special protection in matters of marriage, working conditions, and maternity leave.[193] Women gained considerable power in the lower echelons of the Party and government as well as in all echelons of trade unions, rural cooperatives, and militia organizations. Finally, women obtained greater educational opportunities and eventually came to constitute the majority in certain professions, for example, medicine, teaching, and laboratory sciences.

Today, young women still consult their parents on key matters pertaining to schooling, occupation, or matrimony, and wives still defer to their husbands in many ways. Mothers remain closer to children than do fathers. And it is the female cadres who make tea and serve guests arriving from a distance. Nevertheless, if a woman chooses to disagree with her parents, husband, or male co-work-

---

193. One of the key legislative acts, titled Law on Marriage and the Family, was passed by the DRVN National Assembly in December 1959. See *Nhan Dan*, 29 Dec. 1959.

ers, she is no longer at an automatic disadvantage. She can seek support from her teachers, from local Women's Union representatives, or from Party officials. Largely for this reason few parents dare to pressure a daughter entirely against her will. A husband who abuses his wife risks stern rebukes from outside. A wife, if she wishes, can institute divorce proceedings at no special penalty to herself. A female worker who feels she has been bypassed for advancement because of her sex is able to raise the matter forthrightly and without fear of retaliation.

Where does all this leave the women of Vietnam? Clearly, tremendous changes in attitude and objective status have occurred in the past fifty years. However, as Premier Pham Van Dong has admitted bluntly, "Much is left to be done so that our women can fully play the role due to them in all fields and at all levels."[194] In particular, only a handful of women have made it to the Party Central Committee, and there are none in the fourteen-member Political Bureau or the nine-member Secretariat.[195] Four decades after Nguyen Thi Minh Khai was given the responsibility of secretary of the Saigon–Cholon Party branch (only to die before a firing squad for her efforts), no other woman has achieved a comparable rank. In short, although women have taken the socialist maxim to heart and have worked according to their abilities, they have yet to receive commensurate benefits.

The Vietnam Women's Union cannot be faulted. It continues its efforts to alter female consciousness, to mobilize public support, and to intervene in situations of obvious injustice. Something is still amiss, however. Often it seems that Vietnamese women are being called upon to assume a double burden. They are still expected to be good daughters, wives, and mothers on the one hand, and they must also hold down full-time outside jobs. This means, for example, that when a woman finishes eight hours of shopwork, she may have to stop by the market, pick up the children at the nursery, cook the dinner, and clean up afterwards. Considerate husbands may assist in one or more of these family tasks, but there are no economic, institutional, or moral factors to make them bear the burden equally. Women are strongly encouraged to take outside political, military, social, educational, and cultural responsibilities more seriously, but men generally have more time (and residual energy) to devote to such things.

Today in Vietnam it seems that almost all men (and many women) still assume that females are endowed with certain "natural" capabilities in the areas of home, family, and education. This appears to be true among the top leadership as well as among ordinary workers and peasants. Thus Le Duan, secretary-general of the Party, has instructed educational cadres as follows:

194. Pham Van Dong, interview in *Le Monde* (Paris), 16 April 1977.
195. Fourth Party Congress results, in *Quan Doi Nhan Dan*, 23 Dec. 1976.

Women are very good and highly suited to teaching. Good teaching needs good feelings and deep love for children. . . . There should be many women in this field, because education for children is, above all, education by emotion.[196]

In line with this thinking, the government is working hard to expand the number of childcare centers; yet there does not seem to be any plan for men to share responsibility for running them. Indeed, as women move into some new occupational fields, there may be a tendency for men to avoid those specialities as "women's work." In short, even though functions continue to change, attitudes do not keep pace.

During thirty years of life-and-death struggle against the French and then the Americans, traditional female attributes such as chastity, obedience, and self-denial were often transposed to the political realm and used to bolster new ideals, for example, love of country, unswerving loyalty to the Party, and postponement of personal happiness until group objectives could be fulfilled. Bao Dinh Giang, writing about developments in his home village in Southern Vietnam from 1940 onward, fondly recalled his sister memorizing every line of Nguyen Dinh Chieu's *Luc Van Tien* and reciting key passages for all to hear. Above all, he remembered the moral of the story: "Young men put loyalty and filial piety first; young women cultivate the virtue of chastity."[197] Thanks to the teachings of Ho Chi Minh, however, his sister had learned to "merge" the concept of chastity with defense of the nation. While there is no doubt that this happened not only to Bao Dinh Giang's sister but to hundreds of thousands of other young Vietnamese women as well, the story cannot be said to end there. In particular, now that "independence and freedom" have been achieved and "building socialism" has become the paramount goal, some writers continue to posit a "uniquely Vietnamese" female character that retains more than a hint of traditional morality. It will be interesting to see if tomorrow's Vietnamese women owe more to Nguyen Dinh Chieu or to young radicals of the 1930s like Nguyen Thi Minh Khai and Nguyen Thi Kim Anh.

196. Le Duan, *Thau Suot Duong Loi cua Dang, Dua Su Nghiep Giao Duc Tien Len Manh Me, Vung Chac* [Itemizing the Party's Line, Causing Educational Undertakings to Advance Strongly and Surely] (Hanoi, 1972), pp. 24–25.

197. Bao Dinh Giang, "Khi Hat Giong da Gieo Xuong" [When the Seeds Were Sown], in *Len Duong Thang Loi* [On the Road to Victory] (Hanoi, 1960), p. 137.

6. Perceptions of the Past

Young Vietnamese intellectuals developed a passion for heroes in the 1920s. They read Chinese historical novels in translation, and were thrilled by the courage and righteousness of the military leaders.[1] They also marveled at the audacity of Christopher Columbus, the idealism of Abraham Lincoln, and the patriotic zeal of Sun Yat-sen. Finally, they rediscovered Vietnamese heroes, most obviously the leaders of ancient struggles against the Chinese and the Mongols, but increasingly those who had fought the French as well. Once the colonial authorities understood this trend they banned the more volatile biographies.

Meanwhile, a young journalist and schoolteacher named Dao Duy Anh was drawing a rather different lesson from the past. Convinced that the key historical ingredient was knowledge, not willpower, Dao Duy Anh and a small circle of friends began to compile, publish, and distribute a series of *quoc ngu* books which presented the ideas of Lamarck, Darwin, Comte, Marx, and H. G. Wells, as well as providing more general descriptions of modern psychology, economics, sociology, anthropology, political science, and law.[2] At the end of most texts was a glossary, in the same manner as *Nam Phong* a decade prior, but often containing concise new *quoc ngu* definitions of such terms and concepts as "consciousness," "class," "objective," "subjective," "ideology," "economic aggression," and "proletariat." Even when simply translating or summarizing the arguments of others, Dao Duy Anh and friends conveyed intellectual excitement. Having first cast their net widely, they then pulled it closer to hand with trenchant studies of

---

1. Moc Khue, *Ba Muoi Nam Van Hoc* (Hanoi, 1942). Bui Cong Trung, "Tu Long Yeu Nuoc Chan Chinh toi da di den Chu Nghia Cong San," *Nguoi Truoc Nga Nguoi Sau Tien* (Hanoi, 1960), pp. 8–10.

2. Remarkably, the series was published in the royal capital of Hue, bastion of cultural conservatism. It was printed with the assistance of Huynh Thuc Khang, editor of *Tieng Dan* [Voice of the People], and released under the Quan Hai Tung Thu (Broad Visions Edition) label. A list of nineteen titles is on the inside cover of Ve Thach (Dao Duy Anh), *Ton Giao* [Religion] (Hue, 1929). Dao Duy Anh later indicated that he had been responsible for twelve titles, his comrades seven. Le Thanh, *Cuoc Phong Van Cac Nha Van* [Interviews with Writers] (Hanoi, 1943[?]), p. 161.

religion, nationalities (*dan toc*) and imperialism, at which point the colonial authorities terminated the series and arrested Dao Duy Anh.[3]

These two threads—the one idealistic and inspirational, the other analytical—continued to wind through Vietnamese writings about history in the 1930s and 1940s. On the one hand, the past was seen to possess great potential for motivating people and for legitimizing particular courses of action, and on the other hand, it might serve as objective guide, or at least suggest what was likely or unlikely to happen. In either case the touchstones were the present and the future.

The Nineteenth-Century Legacy

Taking history seriously was not new in Vietnam. For many centuries the royal court had maintained detailed records, and the king had often consulted ancient texts for both policy guidance and policy justification. Local scholars wrote poetry suffused with historical nuance, prepared glosses and interpretations of the Chinese classics for students, and collected data on everything from old tropical medical remedies to popular folk songs and ghost stories. Some families and clans kept careful genealogical and biographical records (*gia pha*), and even the poorest uneducated farmer was probably able to recount his lineage to the third or fourth generation, knew the basic ritual history of his village back to the tutelary diety, and could identify several Vietnamese culture heroes who had fought the Chinese, Mongols, Cham, or Khmer.

As we have seen (chapter 2), nineteenth-century Vietnamese scholars approached most intellectual questions via Sung Neo-Confucianism, and history was no exception. Hoping to extend the tenure of their specifically Vietnamese dynasty beyond what might otherwise be expected, Nguyen rulers sifted the historical chronicles of Ssu-ma Kuang (1019–86) for choice precedents. Because history had no existence apart from morality, a precedent lacking the proper pedigree was unlikely to be suggested by court officials. Chinese precedents, having the best pedigrees, tended to monopolize the attention of the king and his advisers, although Vietnamese experience did manage to intrude occasionally. Buddhist and Taoist precedents were suspect, despite the strong impact of these religions in Vietnam in earlier centuries and despite their continuing relevance to the people at large.[4] Examples from "barbarian" countries were rigorously ex-

---

3. He was charged with helping to organize the Tan Viet Cach Mang Dang [New Vietnam Revolutionary Party], detained for a year, then given a three-year suspended sentence.

4. John K. Whitmore, "The Vietnamese Confucian Scholar's View of His Country's Early History," in J. Hall and J. Whitmore, eds., *Explorations in Early Southeast Asian History: The Origins of Southeast Asian Statecraft* (Ann Arbor: Univ. of Michigan Papers on South and Southeast Asia, 1976), pp. 193–203.

cluded until the policy situation was practically hopeless, even though for centuries Vietnam had maintained a degree of contact with Southeast Asia and the West. At a time, therefore, when Vietnam was facing a grave and unprecedented challenge, the Vietnamese elite sneered at alternative explanations and remained profoundly confident that it possessed the only true and legitimate doctrine.

Approaching history as a subcategory of Confucian doctrine also influenced Vietnamese judgments on their ability to alter events—in short, their degree of free will. Nineteenth-century palace historians were so conditioned to thinking of the Chinese as superior that it was necessary to explain past Vietnamese victories over Chinese forces in terms of the latter's temporary weakness rather than the former's strength. They were also familiar with the grand deterministic design of Shao Yung, wherein time was divided into thirty 10,800- and 129,000-year cycles linked to the *Book of Changes*, and Vietnamese events were sometimes interpreted on that basis. King Tu Duc (r. 1847–83), for example, found this formula helpful in explaining the fall of the Le dynasty (1428–1788), since it eliminated the need to grant the detested peasant-oriented Tay Son movement any accomplishments.[5]

Nevertheless, it was not in the interest of the monarch to allow mindless determinism to usurp his own role of influencing Heaven's actions through royal sanctity. As Tu Duc said, relying on such formulas would be like "putting on a blindfold and arguing about which items were white and which were black. Even if correct it would be pure luck!"[6] In fact, to the degree that highly literate kings like Minh Mang (r. 1820–41) and Tu Duc took a direct supervisory and editorial role in the writing of palace history, they were able to select their own precedents from a large, antiquated, idealized, and mostly Chinese literary treasure house, both to judge the past and to justify their personal decisions. Not surprisingly, they also made sure that the histories emphasized the legitimate accession of their own dynasty, the total illegitimacy of any competitor or any popular uprising, and the need for unity and stability in facing foreign dangers.

Local Vietnamese literati were capable of picking their own precedents and of making their own judgments. As it became obvious that the Nguyen dynasty was being outmaneuvered and humbled by the French, literati used impeccable classical citations to urge different courses of action upon the court. This failing, some harkened back to the earlier Le dynasty, even to the point of supporting pretenders to the throne. The Confucian idea that each man—not only the king—must assume responsibility for changing himself, his family, and the world beyond was reasserted forcefully. The French nonetheless moved onward to phys-

---

5. SPT-1, pp. 178–80, 191, 211–12.
6. From the *Kham Dinh Viet Su Thong Giam Cuong Muc* [A Mirror of Vietnamese History Prepared by Imperial Order], cited in SPT-1, pp. 180–81.

ically occupy and then "pacify" Vietnam. As the new century dawned, young scholars finally went outside the previous Neo-Confucian canon and sought precedents from a much broader range of sources.

Contact With Western Historiography, 1900–25

Deeply shaken by defeat, yet still steeped in the five relationships, five virtues, and five elements, some Vietnamese literati sought alternative frameworks for human existence and action. Agonizing self-doubt became the impetus to critical inquiry and, eventually, new hopefulness. Attacks on classical studies, on the traditional political system, and on alleged Vietnamese psychological weaknesses were all first mounted effectively in the brief period 1902–08, then forced by French and puppet royal court reaction to assume more diffuse, less challenging postures. In the 1920s critics again gained the initiative, in far more favorable social and political circumstances, and the old ways of thinking were never able to recover.

Among his many credits, Phan Boi Chau (1867–1940) may be considered Vietnam's first modern historian. First and foremost an anticolonial proselytizer and organizer, Phan sought in almost all of his writings to rouse patriotic sentiment, denounce French exploitation, and propose solutions to Vietnam's modern quandary. Within that overall framework he attempted at various points to explore Vietnamese history, not simply as a rhetorical device, but to test new hypotheses, to clarify ideas in his own mind, and to urge readers to go further on their own.[7] He abandoned the old historiographical framework of dynasties, individual rulers, and good or evil advisors. One alternative was topical, using such categories as establishment or reestablishment of the fatherland, ethnic and population information, geography and natural resources, times of great change, prominent military and literary personalities, physical expansion and frontier maintenance, tributary relations, and contacts with the West. Another alternative had even more radical implications, since it incorporated linear-progressive and Darwinian-struggle conceptions of history. Vietnam's time line was divided into six periods: animal, animal–primitive, primitive, primitive–developing, developing, and civilized. In the first decade of the twentieth century Vietnam was said to be in the developing period, with "civilization" possible only after Vietnamese sovereignty had been regained.

7. Works by Phan Boi Chau of particular historiographical significance are *Viet-Nam Vong Quoc Su* [History of the Loss of Vietnam], written in 1905, and *Viet-Nam Quoc Su Khao* [A Study of Vietnam's National History], written in 1909. SPT-2, pp. 159–72, has a perceptive analysis of Phan Boi Chau's historical outlook. See also David Marr, *Vietnamese Anticolonialism, 1885–1925* (Berkeley: Univ. of Calif. Press, 1971), pp. 114–19, 148–49. Later publications by Phan Boi Chau are also of some historiographical interest; see, for example, *Van De Phu Nu* (Saigon, 1929), pp. 1–13.

The contrast with previous cyclical or golden-age conceptions of history was dramatic. Along with many others of his generation, Phan Boi Chau was deeply impressed by recent Chinese and Japanese interpretations of the works of Charles Darwin and Herbert Spencer. Indeed, as it turned out, Social Darwinism continued to filter to other Vietnamese groups as well, becoming the single most disruptive counterperception of history and society until the late 1920s (see chapter 7). At first, "survival of the fittest" assumed the shape of the grim reaper, and engendered the fear that Vietnamese had perhaps awakened too late and were threatened with extinction. Yet, to refuse to struggle was sure suicide and, besides, a denigration of one's heroic ancestors. Later the feeling grew that knowledge of how to struggle, how to progress in even the most difficult circumstances was not a secret monopolized by any one nation, people, or ruling class, but an open book available to all who bothered to seek it out. Most importantly, progress was made by masses of people struggling to survive and flourish, not by a handful of rulers and sages seeking to bring Heaven and earth into harmony by proper ethical conduct. Once this idea took root and began to be widely disseminated, the focus shifted to the question of which modern philosophy explained the most about the contemporary world and was most appropriate to Vietnamese needs.

Phan Boi Chau's generation made the study of Western history, philosophy, and political theory emotionally acceptable, indeed a patriotic necessity. It had become possible to assimilate previously "barbarian" ideas while continuing to remain Vietnamese and, in the case of many, continuing to hate specific Western practices in Indochina. For example, based on comparative historical analysis as well as personal observation, Phan Boi Chau drew the conclusion that the previous Vietnamese concept of the state, emphasizing a particular relationship between ruler and subject, had to be discarded in favor of a state defined in terms of citizenry, territory, and sovereignty. Of these three components, citizenry was most important—people who were alert, increasingly well educated, and motivated by generalized patriotism rather than personal fidelity to a leader.

It would be a mistake to think of Phan Boi Chau and other literati as having broken the Confucian connection between politics and morality. While Phan discarded dynastic history and downgraded Chinese precedents in favor of Vietnamese ones, many of his causal explanations were quite within tradition. Although he sought to define a national history of Vietnam, with special attention to mass unity (or lack thereof) in times of foreign confrontation, his vision of what the masses might be thinking and wanting to do was very limited. Phan was particularly anxious to assert that "man makes the times," and it was individual heroes that fascinated him; as a result, there was almost no discussion of larger social and economic forces. Nor was success a condition for hero status. The two crucial elements were that a hero's motives be pure (thus presumably excluding the Caesarian–Napoleonic thread in Western hero literature) and that he be somehow linked to the masses by "like-mindedness" (*dong tam*), an emotionally evocative but essentially idealistic concept. Only much later did Phan come to emphasize the possibilities inherent in the concerted actions of a large number of "small" heroes. By that time a new generation of intelligentsia were pursuing that idea on their own, and from a potentially more radical perspective.

New Intellectual Perceptions of the Past

Many young Vietnamese intellectuals would have preferred to wipe the slate clean, to forget the past. They wanted Vietnam to draw its strength from the future, and to "let the dead bury their dead," as Karl Marx once phrased it.[8] If that future was to see Vietnam achieving a "higher" revolution, then new, ahistorical answers to its problems were required.[9]

In truth, such attempts to dismiss the past were indirect testimony to its ongoing potency. Whether attacking history or simply trying to ignore it, these young men and women remained aware of how the past bore down on the present. The desire to start anew—which generally implied Western solutions—stemmed from the belief that Vietnam's reservoir of written and oral tradition was extremely burdensome.

Nevertheless, it eventually became apparent to most intellectuals that they could not deny their past entirely and remain Vietnamese. New identities could not be manufactured out of whole cloth, and to attempt to do so was not only disorienting for the individual but risked alienating him permanently from the masses, a self-defeating exercise if he had aspirations to transform society. Then, too, by choosing not to investigate the past, intellectuals often had difficulty determining to what extent they themselves remained prisoners of tradition. In fact, some of those who mocked the past most vigorously showed indirect evidence of sustaining strong traditional outlooks.[10]

If one appreciated that the past was very much alive, formidable in ways not always comprehended, and if one was determined to alter temporal realities, then it became necessary to delineate, analyze, and argue rejection or acceptance of particular historical legacies. In the words of Thach Lan, people had to understand "why we are like we are today," not as a prelude to acceptance, but in

---

8. Karl Marx, *The Eighteenth Brumaire of Louis Bonaparte* (Moscow: Foreign Languages Publishing House, 1948), p. 19.

9. Nguyen Duc Quynh, "Mot Loi The" [A Vow], *Tieng Tre* [Young Voice] (Hanoi), vol. 2, no. 7 (9 Jan. 1936).

10. This was perhaps most obvious in the writings of Hoang Dao, theoretician of the 1930s Tu Luc Van Doan (Self-Reliance Literature Group). In his *Muoi Dieu Tam Niem* [Ten Points to Ponder] (Hanoi, 1938[?]), for example, Hoang Dao called for a "total acceptance of what is new," but then reverted to "inner rectification" and the old *Ta Hsüeh* formula to explain what he meant. Most of his "revolutionary" program turned out to be yet another exercise in moral exhortation, perhaps less convincing than that of Tran Huu Do a decade earlier.

order to recognize weaknesses and to build a new ideological foundation.[11] This could be disconcerting for even well-educated Vietnamese. Thach Lan, for example, wanted to continue to believe in reincarnation, yet realized that because such a concept often led the "poor to bow their heads before the rich, the weak before the strong," it had to be condemned.[12]

Ultimately, the intelligentsia wanted to subdue the past, not eliminate it. It was sensed that one measure of man's advance was in the way he controlled his myths, distinguished areas of behavior, and brought more and more of his activity under the rule of reason. In reevaluating history, intellectuals wanted to develop a usable past which could connect them with and help to propel them into a worthy future.[13] To do that required a comparative framework. Western history served this purpose admirably, especially when backed up by residual knowledge of Chinese history and some attention to modern Japan. Vietnamese traditionalists found this approach to history profoundly unsettling, as it undermined faith in allegedly timeless values and institutions. Eventually, however, they too could be observed casting about for contemporary foreign ammunition to support their own interpretations of Vietnamese history.

An Overview of Publications, 1912–44

Books and pamphlets dealing primarily with history, biography, or traditional Vietnamese literature were a small but significant part of the publishing explosion described previously (chapter 1). A cursory survey of more than 9,000 quoc-ngu publications surviving from the three decades prior to the August 1945 Revolution reveals at least 294 titles in these categories (see Table 1).[14] The total number of historical books and pamphlets printed exceeded 530,000 copies.[15] When one remembers that in the mid-1920s probably no more than five percent

11. Thach Lan (Cao Van Chanh), "Luan Ly va Kinh Te," PNTV 36 (9 Jan. 1930), p. 6.

12. Thach Lan, "Cac Gia Tri Cu o Dong Duong Bi Do" [The Old Values in Indochina Are Overturned], PNTV 54 (29 May 1930), p. 18. His reincarnation example was provoked by French colonial attempts to stimulate a Vietnamese Buddhist revival (see chapter 7).

13. One of the first to sketch such an approach in Vietnam was Nguyen An Ninh. See his public address of 15 Oct. 1923, reprinted in La Cloche Fêlée 5 and 6.

14. A complete analysis would probably double or triple the number of titles on historical subjects. In particular, Mme Christiane Rageau of the Bibliothèque Nationale (Paris) has identified 271 quoc-ngu anthologies of traditional Vietnamese literature, whereas I located only 60. Glancing rather hurriedly at the 1,200 or so Buddhist, Taoist, Catholic, and Cao Dai texts, I came to realize that some of these works deserved more careful attention. Chinese traditional histories and literature were excluded as well. In retrospect, a count should at least have been kept of quoc-ngu translations of Chinese historical fiction, for example, the Tale of Three Kingdoms, since various Vietnamese radicals indicated later how avidly they read such materials in preference to arid colonial school texts.

15. This figure is based on the handwritten notations on many of the titles in the Bibliothèque Nationale collection, the result of their having been submitted by publishers as part of the French

Table 1. Partial Survey of Histories, Historical Dramatizations, Biographies and Traditional Vietnamese Literature, 1912–44

Biographies

Vietnamese personalities	80	
Modern Chinese personalities	16	
Western personalities	18	
Other (Gandhi)	1	
Subtotal	115	(39%)

Vietnam Histories and Historical Dramatizations

Translations of major traditional sources into *quoc-ngu*	6	
General textbooks and popularized summaries	11	
Specific historical period	10	
Specific subject concentration	11	
Provincial histories/geographies (northern provinces: 6; central: 21; southern: 5)	32	
Others (regional, district, village, family, etc.)	11	
Subtotal	81	(27.5%)

Quoc Ngu Renditions of Traditional Literary Works

Luc Van Tien	13	
Truyen Kieu	7	
Thach Sanh	10	
Pham Cong Cuc Hoa	10	
Quan Am Thi Kinh	5	
Cung Oan Ngam Khuc	4	
Hoa Tien	4	
Others (Phan Tran, Chinh Phu Ngam, Nhi Do Mai)	7	
Subtotal	60	(20.5%)

Traditional Literary Compilations, Textbooks, Reference Works	17	(6%)
Non-Vietnamese History (excluding biography)	21	(7%)
Total	294	(100%)

Note: Different editions of the same publication are counted separately.

government's Dépôt Légal system. It is surely conservative. For example, an official 1931 French report lists 415,000 *quoc-ngu* elementary school textbooks on history and geography being printed in 1925–30 alone; most of these would not show up in my estimate. AOM NF 2695.

of the Vietnamese population, or 750,000 people, could be considered literate in any language, such attention to the past is even more striking and deserving of explanation.

The first interesting clue is that 142 titles, or almost half of those located, were published in the brief period 1925–30. Forty-eight (16%) were published in 1912–24 and 104 (35%) in 1931–44. The late 1920s were years of intense soul-searching and growing political consciousness among urban Vietnamese in general and members of the new intelligentsia and nascent working class in particular. For some this included rediscovery of the Vietnamese past, or at least certain parts of it, after having had to recite lessons in colonial primary schools about "our ancestors the Gauls" and having been instructed to refer to France as the "Motherland." Equally important, however, was the effort to reach out to the histories and recent experiences of other countries, places as outwardly unrelated as Turkey and China, Poland and America.

The largest category of historical publication, and also a main cause of the 1925–30 bulge, was that of biographies and biographical dramas or fiction—some 115 of them, or thirty-nine percent of the total. Thirty-five were devoted to foreign individuals and eighty to Vietnamese, the interest in foreign paragons being very strong in the late 1920s but then practically disappearing after 1930.[16] Among foreigners, Sun Yat-sen led the field with six biographies, a reflection of the intense intelligentsia interest in Chinese revolutionary precedents which led some to form a clandestine Vietnamese party modeled on the Kuomintang and doomed to destruction in 1929–30. Christopher Columbus and George Washington enjoyed three biographies each; Lord Nelson, Abraham Lincoln and V. Lenin followed with two. Others given full-length attention were J. J. Rousseau, Madame Roland, Li Yüan-hung, Huang Hsing, Ts'ai Ao (who had helped overthrow Yüan Shih-k'ai), Feng Yü-hsiang (the "Christian general"), Chiang Kai-Shek, Louis Kossuth, and Mahatma Gandhi. There were also four compilations of stories about individual modern Chinese and Korean women, one on individual Soviet women, one on Chinese youth heroes, one on European writer-activists, and, lastly, a colonial textbook on such authorized French heroes as Joan of Arc, Cardinal Richelieu, and Napoleon Bonaparte.[17]

16. By way of comparison, Dr. A. Reid has indicated (personal correspondence) that for Malaya and Indonesia during the same general period there was probably a significantly lower proportion of publications on indigenous historical personalities.

17. If one were to survey Vietnamese periodicals of the same general period with the same intent, the following foreign individuals would surely be added to this list: Pigneau de Behaine (a French bishop who assisted the Nguyen dynasty to power), Baden-Powell, Fridtjof Nansen, Thomas Edison, Woodrow Wilson, Rabindranath Tagore, Anatole France, Adolf Hitler, Leon Trotsky, and Mao Tse-tung. As a further point of reference, spirit mediums of the Cao Dai Church summoned the following foreigners in seances: Mencius, Joan of Arc, Descartes, Shakespeare, Li Po, Pasteur, Victor Hugo, Sun Yat-sen, and Lenin. Victor Oliver, *Cao Dai Spiritism* (Leiden: E. J. Brill, 1976), p. 10.

Twenty-nine different Vietnamese personalities were the objects of full-length publications. The focus was overwhelmingly on leaders of anti-foreign struggles, dynastic founders, and military figures. The Trung sisters, who had led a famous if unsuccessful revolt against Chinese colonialists of the first century A.D., were given pride of place with eleven publications, all admittedly more mythical than factual in content. Tran Hung Dao, thirteenth-century leader of a protracted, victorious struggle against the Mongols, and also someone whose personality and actions were rather more adequately transmitted over time, had seven titles. Six publications were devoted to Le Van Duyet, a distinctly secondary historical figure who had helped Gia Long establish and consolidate the Nguyen dynasty. This is largely explained by his Mekong delta regional identification, a sentiment consciously fostered by some wealthy delta landowners with approval from the French. Going a bit further, however, the fact that Le Van Duyet's tomb had been flattened by Gia Long's son Minh Mang in retaliation for the actions of others occurring after his death, had long been considered a prime example of royal immorality. Recalling this episode poignantly was thus a device for raising ethical issues in general and criticizing Nguyen monarchs in particular. Indeed, one author took the next logical step and included Le Van Khoi, adopted son of Le Van Duyet and one of the leaders of an uprising against Minh Mang (hence the tomb incident), in his roster of "southern" heroes. He hinted that the causes of revolt had been mandarinal oppression and court obscurantism. Contemporary political implications were not left in doubt when the last pages of the book attacked Bao Dai, current Nguyen puppet. Part of this was censored.[18]

Le Loi, victor over the Ming and founder of the Le dynasty (1428–1785), was the object of four biographies or biographical dramas, while Ly Thuong Kiet, eleventh-century Vietnamese commander against the Sung armies, had three publications. Traditional resistance to Chinese domination was rounded out with books or pamphlets on Trieu Thi Trinh, Bo Cai Dai Vuong, Ngo Quyen, Le Hoan, Dinh Tien Hoang, and Quang Trung.[19] It is worth remarking that Vietnamese heroes of this stature were also increasingly being allowed into the carefully screened and approved colonial school texts for children. Why the French permitted any of this is an intriguing question. They must have known that stories of traditional armed resistance to northern colonialists might stimulate opposition to the more immediate western variety.[20] Perhaps they felt that stressing the "Chinese threat" together with a strong dose of traditionalist ethics (which,

18. Vuong Quang, *Viet Nam Danh Tuong* [Famous Vietnamese Military Leaders] (Saigon, 1928).

19. For striking visual evidence of nineteenth- and twentieth-century attraction to heroes of this nature, see Maurice Durand, *Imagerie Populaire Vietnamienne* (Paris: Ecole Française d'Extrême-Orient, 1960), pp. 172, 205, 225–36, 412.

20. The Sûreté kept particularly close watch on the local Tran Hung Dao cults, trying to insure that they remained religious rather than political. AOM (Aix) F-7F59.

ironically, originated in China) was the best available antidote for contemporary "red" doctrines or other radical influences emanating from Canton, Shanghai, or Peking.[21] This may also help to explain why the censors in 1926 allowed three instant biographies of Phan Chu Trinh (1872–1926) to be published, even though he had once been sentenced to death for subversive teachings. His consistently non-violent approach might help to head off a new and potentially revolutionary confrontation.[22]

If such was the French calculation, it was proven wrong on all counts. Vietnamese Boy Scout troops, formed with colonial encouragement in the early 1930s and bearing such glowing names as Hung Vuong (a prehistorical Vietnamese dynasty) or Lam Son (the original guerrilla stronghold of Le Loi), later provided hundreds of healthy, motivated, disciplined cadres for the Viet Minh. A Cub Scout song concluded its account of the crucial thirteenth-century naval victory over the Mongols with the following words: "Oh! Brothers and sisters! Even now, whenever one goes on the Bach Dang river, does anyone forget?"[23] After 1935, censorship restrictions were eased enough to allow publication of a number of biographies dealing sympathetically (though still cautiously) with Vietnamese who had fought the French only decades earlier. Most popular was Hoang Hoa Tham (De Tham), the stubborn Yen The guerrilla leader finally killed in 1913 after more than twenty years of overt and covert resistance.[24] Others given some biographical attention included Hoang Dieu, Ton That Thuyet, King Ham Nghi, Phan Dinh Phung, and Luong Ngoc Quyen, the latter having been killed as recently as 1917.[25] Seven persons who had accepted foreign involvement or intervention received biographical attention at one time or another.[26] Indeed, it is a

21. This would seem to have been the position of Pham Quynh, who had the ear of influential French administrators. At one point he proposed that statues of the elder Trung sister be displayed—even though no one knew what she looked like. He got the idea when in the Pantheon in Paris viewing a statue of St. Geneviève, who was credited with resisting Attila the Hun. NP 73 (July 1923), p. 15.

22. In contrast, Phan Chu Trinh's friendly political opponent, Phan Boi Chau, could not receive book-length biographical treatment until early 1945, courtesy of a Japanese publishing house in Hanoi.

23. *Muon Tro Nen Huong Dao Sinh* (Hanoi, 1934). Hoi Huong Dao Nam Ky, *Ky Niem Dai Hoi Soi Con tai Gia Dinh, 25-12-1942* [Recalling the Cub Scout Assembly at Gia Dinh, 25 Dec. 1942] (Saigon, 1943).

24. Three popularized versions appeared in 1935, each being careful to draw much of its material from already published sources by French authors. A few years later the Viet Minh named an armed resistance zone after Hoang Hoa Tham.

25. Brief descriptions of the activities of these individuals are available in Marr, *Vietnamese Anticolonialism* (page numbers in index).

26. These were: King Gia Long, Vo Tanh, Nguyen Van Tuong, King Dong Khanh, Truong Vinh Ky, Do Huu Phuong, and Nguyen Truong To. The latter's position is somewhat ambiguous, since his 1860s memorials proposed short-term foreign involvement as a way, he hoped, of warding off long-term subjugation.

remarkable indication of Vietnamese preoccupations in the decades preceding 1945 that only three full-length biographies were devoted to individuals in no real way linked to the "foreign question."[27]

Why were biographies so popular? Undoubtedly, one factor was Chinese attention to biography, from which traditional Vietnamese had developed their own genre. In the fourteenth century a Tran dynasty official, Ly Te Xuyen, had compiled the *Viet Dien U Linh* [Vietnamese Palace Spirits], a fascinating hodgepodge of stories about long-dead military commanders, loyal retainers, local earth and water deities, and apparitions from royal dreams.[28] Each spirit discussed by Ly Te Xuyen had already survived at least two centuries due to popular support, court sponsorship, or a combination of both. The Trung sisters were present, as was Bo Cai Dai Vuong, Ly Thuong Kiet and five or six other individuals connected with epic struggles against the foreigner. On the other hand, at least four Chinese colonial officials were remembered favorably (especially Si Nhiep from the first century A.D.); there was praise for a Vietnamese official who allegedly had served Ch'in Shih Huang-ti (r. 222–210 B.C.), and frank admiration for a captured Cham queen who drowned herself rather than marry the Vietnamese king.

What united everyone in the *Viet Dien U Linh* was posthumous power, an ability to protect, to inspire, to urge others to great accomplishments. In this way, for example, a local delta spirit called up effectively by a seventh-century T'ang administrator could much later be invoked by Vietnamese commanders as they prepared to attack enemies in the nearby mountains. A number of spirits were known to have proven their potency in the epic thirteenth-century confrontation with the Mongols. As centuries passed, the Vietnamese court would raise the honorific titles of some spirits, demote others, and add spirits that had been previously overlooked. Didactic stress also changed perceptively. In 1919 a traditional scholar, Ngo Giap Dau, brought forth yet another compilation of *Viet Dien U Linh* stories, which was probably consulted by at least some of the authors of new biographical publications.

The early twentieth century was a time of profound psychological shock and disorientation for many Vietnamese, often summarized in the phrase "loss of country" (*mat nuoc*). By the mid-1920s, however, writers had managed to shift the emphasis to the positive, to the "calling up of souls" (*goi hon*), with full knowledge of the popular religious implications of such rhetoric. "Calling up

27. These three were: King Le Thanh Tong (r. 1460–97), who nevertheless did spend some of his time annihilating the state of Champa; Hai Thuong Lan Ong, an eighteenth-century author of medical treatises; and Nguyen Du, author of "The Tale of Kieu."

28. Ly Te Xuyen, *Viet Dien U Linh* (Hanoi, 1972). Trinh Dinh Ru, the translator from Chinese, and Dinh Gia Khanh, the current editor, consulted eight different texts dating from 1771 onward.

souls" meant above all the search for heroes, old and new, Vietnamese and foreign—not just any heroes, but activists, men and women who had seen a need and proceeded to do something about it. Most revered of all were those individuals who had demonstrated great courage against seemingly insurmountable odds. Columbus was admired because, against the common grain, he had developed the conviction that the earth was round and then had staked his life on that conviction. He had sailed into the unknown, overcome mutiny among his disbelieving crewmen, and returned triumphant (albeit not in full circle).[29]

Young intelligentsia writers steadily pushed the argument further, however, often in prefaces or conclusions to particular biographies. How many readers were prepared to *follow* the heroic example of a Le Loi, a Garibaldi, or a Pilsudski and seize independence for their country? writers would ask bluntly. If readers were dedicated enough, and if they banded together tightly, surely nothing could stop them.[30] "We ourselves are the deities, the spirits *(ong than)* who will determine our own fortune or misfortune," one writer intoned.[31] Another, who soon after became a well-known Indochinese Communist Party essayist, summarized the point by quoting the Marquis de Lafayette: "Should a country desire Liberty, have the People want it and that will be sufficient."[32] Nevertheless, effort still preceded accomplishment; thus, two other writers were led to cite Lord Nelson and Abraham Lincoln as the most pertinent examples for young Vietnamese of the late 1920s. Although their actions had made victory possible, they had died violently before personally being able to savour the fruits.[33] As it became apparent by 1929 that thousands of Vietnamese were serious, that they were prepared to die or be jailed activating such seeming hyperbole, the colonial authorities banned at least thirty biographies published in the previous four years.[34] This led one journal to complain about the government both blocking Vietnamese from their own history and limiting them to French history. The editors added sarcastically that the authorities had better go further and excise "those most glorious chapters, the revolutionary accomplishments of the French people."[35]

29. Tran Minh Khiem, *Vuot Bien Ra Khoi* [Spanning the Ocean] (Saigon, 1928). After reading everything he could find on Columbus, one Vietnamese high school student took to drawing pictures of the earth with wings on the covers of all his books. Luu Dong, *Buoc Dau Theo Dang* (Hanoi, 1961), p. 11.

30. See, for example, Duong Ba Trac, *Tieng Goi Dan* (Hanoi, 1925), pp. 5, 17, 24, 81–82, 100.

31. Tran Tuan Khai, *Hon Tu Lap* [Self-Creating Soul], vol. 1 (Ghandi) (Hanoi, 1926), preface.

32. Hai Trieu, *Muon thi Duoc: Ai-nhi-lan Cach-Mang Luoc Su* [Seek and Ye Shall Have: A Brief History of the Irish Revolution] (Gia Dinh, 1928).

33. Lam Van Ly and Tran Huy Lieu, *Anh Hung Yeu Nuoc: Ong Nap Nhi Ton* [A Patriotic Hero: Lord Nelson] (Saigon, 1928).

34. Trung-Ky Bao-Ho, *Nghi-Dinh Cam cac thu Sach va cac thu Bao, Chi Khong duoc truyen ba, phat mai va tang tru trong hat Trung-ky* (Hue, 1929).

35. PNTV 49 (24 Apr. 1930), p. 8.

In retrospect, many Vietnamese writers have judged such preoccupation with individual will, or even a collective attack based solely on psychological readiness, to be at best a naïve if perhaps necessary phase, at worst potentially self-destructive. It was naïve because it ignored differences of space and time. For example, if young Vietnamese had bothered to investigate Josef Pilsudski further (one prominent Vietnamese Marxist historian has opined), they would have found that he represented Polish landlord and bourgeois interests against Polish peasants and workers, and that he took help from Western countries as part of the overall imperialist effort to isolate the Soviet Union. Glorification of willpower was potentially self-destructive because it put a premium on grand gestures—for example, assassinations or attempted coups, necessarily the work of an elite, clandestine apparatus—thus inevitably downgrading ideology, proselytizing, training, public demonstrations, and strikes. Finally, it left little room for analyzing historical trends, domestic or international, or for weighing advantages and disadvantages of various actions at any given time.[36] In short, fascination with the power of the will led all too often to adventurism.[37]

Even in the late 1920s, however, all was not epic biography and psychological uplift. As can be seen from Table 1, diverse local histories and geographies were coming out, often sponsored by local French administrators or wealthy Vietnamese grouped together in educational societies. Traditional Vietnamese literary works enjoyed great popularity up to 1930, often being published in runs of 3,000–5,000 copies. After 1930 they were outshone by the new creative poetry, novels, short stories, and critical essays of young contemporary authors. Yet all the traditional works listed in the table remained familiar to Vietnamese, if not from printed versions then because of the many dramatic variations (*cheo, tuong, cai luong*) that had grown up. After 1945, and especially after 1954, full-length editions were reprinted in both Hanoi and Saigon.

Luc Van Tien, composed by the blind scholar-poet Nguyen Dinh Chieu just prior to French occupation of the Mekong delta, had the curious distinction of being both avidly promoted by the colonial authorities and retaining considerable popularity among Vietnamese patriots. The former saw it as the epitome of Confucian morality, which in many ways it was; the latter focused on the particular message of fidelity and sacrifice for a just cause. Besides, it was beautiful poetry, and the man who created it had tried to live by what he preached.[38]

---

36. SPT-2, pp. 545–600, has perhaps the most detailed analysis of this overall question as it relates to the 1920s.

37. Oddly enough, at one point a major journal controlled by the French authorities printed an article lauding power of the will as exemplified by four contemporary personalities: Lenin, Mussolini, d'Annunzio, and Kemal Attaturk (NP 72 [June 1923], pp. 471–80). By the early 1930s the French and most Vietnamese were no longer making that kind of mistake.

38. Tran Nghia, "Nhin lai viec su dung noi dung *Luc Van Tien* duoi thoi Phap Thuoc" [Recalling the Use of *Luc Van Tien*'s Content during French Rule], TCVH 1-1965, pp. 57–65.

Ornate cover of one of the many editions of *Luc Van Tien*, by Nguyen Dinh Chieu. Hero and heroine are exchanging commitments in the form of a poem and a flower. Courtesy of the Bibliothèque Nationale.

Debates on Vietnamese History

Throughout the 1930s, novelists, poets, political essayists, and social critics all enjoyed more attention and sparked more controversy than writers of history. Nevertheless, history was hardly ignored, and by the early 1940s there was a clear resurgence of interest in specifically Vietnamese historical events and interpretations of the past.

The one historical topic that concerned almost everyone from the first years of the twentieth century was whether the French had entered and remained in Vietnam as friends or as foes. Even a cursory review of publications in the period 1912–44 reveals a fundamental cleavage on that issue. In the history texts employed in Catholic schools, for example, King Tu Duc was pictured as undeserving of the throne in traditional ethical terms, the French were described as heroic liberators, and those Vietnamese who chose to resist were labeled aggressive pirates (*giac*), spurious elements (*dang nguy*), or perpetrators of disorder (*loan*).

The Vietnamese people at large were said to be deeply appreciative of the hospitals, schools, and railroads bestowed on them by the beneficent foreigner.[39] By contrast, toward the end of a half-poetic, half-narrative account of traditional Vietnamese resistance to foreign intervention, another author managed to slip in the following passage:

The French forces suddenly, without provocation, came and destroyed our fortresses, stole our country, made us lose many soldiers and commanders, and caused our people to cry out in confusion. Surely that is reason enough for us to consider them major enemies.[40]

Numerous other examples of this starkly conflicting vision of French colonial penetration and rule could be cited. It is worth remarking, however, that diverse students of recent Vietnamese history apparently never sat down to argue the merits of each other's positions on the colonial question and then put their ideas together under one cover. Part of the problem was censorship, of course; nevertheless, such a hypothetical book might have been passed in 1925–28, and it almost surely could have been published in 1935–38. We must tentatively conclude that one side or the other, or perhaps both, did not consider the effort worthwhile. So sharp were the emotional and intellectual differences that communication was not possible.

In 1935 there was a brief minor exchange concerning King Ham Nghi's 1885 flight from Hue and direct participation in the Can Vuong resistance. After one author had lauded this action in a loose biography of Ham Nghi,[41] another author went to the trouble of publishing a pamphlet arguing that the biography was unscholarly, that it "soiled Vietnam's history," and that, in any event, it was silly and stupid for the Can Vuong to spill blood resisting the French.[42] Ngo Tat To (1894–1954), who wrote about Vietnamese history prolifically, but who would become famous as an anti-feudal novelist, entered the fray and lifted the question beyond the motives or actions of a young monarch and a few mandarins hiding in the hills. Someday, when it was possible to write patriotic history without restriction, he intimated, researchers would demonstrate that the anti-French struggle of the late 1880s was widespread, not just the work of a disgruntled former palace elite.[43] However, he also repeatedly stressed the objective futility

39. E. Quyen, *Su Ky Nuoc Annam* [History of Annam], 6th printing (Qui Nhon, 1930), pp. 90–117.

40. Nghiem Xuan Lam, *Loi Nuoc Non* [Words of the Motherland] (Hanoi, 1926), p. 45. The front cover of this publication has a penned notation and signature indicating that it was looked over by someone in the "First Bureau, First Section" of the French administration.

41. Phan Tran Chuc, *Vua Ham Nghi* [King Ham Nghi] (Hanoi, 1935[?]).

42. Nguyen Trieu Luat, *O Phan Tran Chuc boi nho Quoc Su* [Mr. Phan Tran Chuc Soils Our National History] (Hanoi, 1935).

43. Ngo Tat To and L. T. Sinh, *Vua Ham Nghi* [King Ham Nghi] (Hanoi, 1935).

of Vietnamese with spears fighting foreigners with rapid-fire rifles and mobile artillery—or, as he phrased it, of "eggs going up against stone."[44]

From the early Nguyen dynasty onward there had existed the awkward historiographical question of how to treat the late eighteenth century peasant-oriented Tay Son movement and the short-lived dynasty established by one of its leaders, Quang Trung (Nguyen Hue). Strict attention to national chronology, long a function of court historians and inevitably tied to matters of dynastic mandate, would seem to have required acceptance of Tay Son legitimacy for at least the period 1789-1802. However, such was Nguyen hatred of the Tay Son, such was their lingering fear of the social forces involved, that court historians were ordered to label them outright usurpers. On the other hand, to downplay the massive Tay Son victory over the invading Ch'ing, Nguyen historians cited moral and cosmological indications that the old Le dynasty, which the Ch'ing were professing to uphold, was undeserving of further popular backing and had in fact lost the mandate of Heaven. Where the mandate resided for thirteen years remained deliberately unclear.[45]

Interestingly enough, modernizing literati of the first two decades of the twentieth century seem to have missed the important social and political lessons contained in the Tay Son experience. Perhaps the Nguyen court historians had done their work well; perhaps peasant uprisings were still too unsettling even for the likes of Phan Boi Chau. At any rate, books into the early 1920s continued to canonize Gia Long and his commanders, especially Le Van Duyet and Vo Tanh, while either ignoring or denigrating the Tay Son. Often there was a quaint new twist. Unlike nineteenth-century Nguyen histories, which tended to be militantly anti-Christian, most texts of the first half of the colonial period directed lavish praise toward Pigneau de Behaine, Bishop of Adran, for his assistance to Gia Long (Nguyen Anh) against the Tay Son. The story of Pigneau taking Gia Long's son and heir, little Prince Canh, to France for an audience at the soon-to-vanish court of Versailles was romanticized into an allegory on contemporary French tutorship and eternal Vietnamese loyalty. It was the perfect historical vignette for French purposes, complete with Canh's Confucianist respect for his foreign teacher and Gia Long's later sorrow that neither of them quite lived to share in his victory.[46]

---

44. Ngo Tat To, comp., *Nhung Tran Do Mau Hoi Nguoi Phap Moi Sang Ta* [Bloody Battles When the French First Came], 9 vols. (Hanoi, 1935), conclusion.

45. SPT-1, pp. 181, 202–205. However, Tran Van Giau does cite one occasion when Gia Long, having to explain why he himself had not restored the Le as he too originally promised, stated flatly that he had taken the mandate from the Tay Son and not the Le.

46. Le Van Thom's *Gia Long Phuc Quoc* [Gia Long Restores the Nation] (Saigon, 1914) is quite straightforward in stating that the French administrator and historian P. Cultru suggested to him the idea of proving the "non-ingratitude" of Gia Long in regard to Pigneau. He also includes a picture of the statue in Saigon of Pigneau sheltering an adoring Canh, which was finally re-

Vo Tanh, one of Gia Long's best-known lieutenants, prepares to commit suicide rather than surrender to the Tay Son. Courtesy of the Bibliothèque Nationale.

By the mid-1920s, however, it was impossible to sustain this image. "Franco-Vietnamese collaboration" was under increasing political challenge, the search for alternative visions of the world well underway. In the historical realm, an important early nineteenth-century narrative devoting considerable attention to Tay Son success in attracting popular support and driving out the Ch'ing was translated into *quoc-ngu* and published.[47] To make sure that the popular anti-colonial implications were appreciated, the twentieth-century translator added

moved by the victorious Communists in 1975. Another publication, a traditional opera (*tuong*) written by Dang Thuc Lieng and Nguyen Vien Kieu on the Pigneau–Gia Long relationship, had the contemporary message in its title: *Phap Viet Nhut Gia* [French and Vietnamese as One Family] (Saigon, 1918). But even the arch collaborator Pham Quynh was disconcerted to hear Frenchmen asset that Vietnamese assistance in the Great War represented repayment of a debt incurred when Pigneau assisted Gia Long. "Phap Du Hanh Trinh Nhat Ky" [Diary of a Voyage to France], NP 83 (May 1924), p. 370.

47. Ngo Thoi Chi et al., *Hoang Le Nhat Thong Chi* [History of the Imperial Le Dynasty] (Hanoi, 1926). A second printing came out the next year. The translator, Cat Thanh, also hoped that the reading of history (as well as natural sciences, ethics, and geography) would provide an

both a preface and a postscript reinforcing precisely these points. Perhaps antic-ipating this book, Le Du, a well-known literatus, wrote an article calling for an end to the adjective "spurious" (*nguy*) affixed to everything pertaining to the Tay Son. He lavished praise on Quang Trung as an invincible military commander, masterful diplomat, and domestic reformer comparable to twentieth-century leaders in "civilized" (*van minh*) countries. If Quang Trung had not died pre-maturely, Le Du asserted, Vietnam would have gotten back some northern border territories lost to China in earlier centuries.[48] Tran Huy Lieu (1902–69) lauded Quang Trung's replacement of Chinese writing by Vietnamese *nom* char-acters as well as his alleged desire to return to the "original teachings" of Con-fucius and Mencius.[49] Two other historical texts tending to enhance the Tay Son position were translated and published.[50] An illegal Communist tract of 1930 went a step further, specifically condemning the colonial schools for continuing to support Gia Long.[51]

By 1930, Quang Trung had been publicly rehabilitated to the extent that it was necessary for the authors of a textbook employed in colonial baccalaureate studies to insert in their fifth printing a completely new section, ranking him among the seven "great heroes" of Vietnamese history. Since they also retained Gia Long on this same roster, however, the basic question was still avoided.[52]

---

antidote to the romantic, escapist novels and short stories then beginning to flood the market. A 1963 Hanoi retranslation mentions that Cat Thanh had completed his version as early as 1912; I have yet to find a published copy of that date.

48. So Cuong (Le Du), "Lich Su Doi Tay Son" [History of the Tay Son Period], NP 97 (July 1925), pp. 11–28. Three years later another writer in the same journal compared Quang Trung favorably with George Washington and Napoleon Bonaparte. Thien Dinh, "Lich Su Tay Son" [History of the Tay Son], NP 135 (Nov.–Dec. 1928), pp. 417–26.

49. Tran Huy Lieu, *Mot Bau Tam Su* (Saigon, 1927), p. 12.

50. One was the *Dai Nam Quoc Su Dien Ca* [Ode to the History of Greater Vietnam] (Hanoi, 1926), a historical narrative in poetic form. A better organized and annotated version was pub-lished in Saigon in 1931, in a printing of 5,000 copies. Although a nineteenth-century court-initiated work, it still contained a passage describing the Tay Son mass mobilization and victory over the Ch'ing. The other text was titled *Thanh Khi Tuong Cau* [Chosen Affinities] (Hanoi, 1928). The translator, Ton Quang Phiet (1900–73), commented that on the face of events de-scribed therein it was completely wrong to label the Tay Son a "spurious dynasty." Ton Quang Phiet later became a member of the standing committee of the DRVN National Assembly and secretary-general of the Vietnam-China Friendship Association.

51. *Tieu Hoc Sinh* (Saigon[?]), 11 May 1930. Copy in AOM (Aix) F-7F4, vol. 2, item 14.

52. Phan Ke Binh and Le Van Phuc, *Nam Hai Di Nhan Liet Truyen* [Stories of Outstanding Heroes of the South Seas], 5th printing (Hanoi, 1930). The other five "great heroes" were Trung Trac, Bo Cai Dai Vuong, Dinh Tien Hoang, Ly Thai To, and Le Loi. Whether the Nguyen court opposed use of the revised version of this text in Annam is unknown. As of 1929 a songbook approved for use in Annam schools still castigated the Tay Son as "bandits" and praised Pigneau. Nguyen Trung Phan and Nguyen Trung Nghe, *Sach Day Hat Tieng Nam* [A Vietnamese Song-book] (Hue, 1929).

Tran Trong Kim (1883–1953)—colonial schools inspector, historian, and subsequently prime minister by Japanese fiat for a brief period in 1945—attempted a rationalization of this equal praise of both houses. By his version of orthodox reckoning, the Le dynasty was legitimate until 1788, which necessarily made the Trinh and Nguyen seignorial families usurpers, even though they both stopped short of seizing the throne for themselves. In such times of general disorder, with "kings not acting like kings and subjects not acting like subjects," the Tay Son, as they moved closer to full power, could be considered no worse than the others. However, once the Le king went running to the Chinese for help and once the Ch'ien-lung emperor sent troops into Vietnam, it was up to someone to throw out both the Le pretender and the Ch'ing aggressor. Quang Trung did this and thus was clearly a national hero and legitimate dynastic founder, on a par with Dinh Tien Hoang and Le Loi. After his premature death, however, serious corruption and disorder occurred in Tay Son ranks. Thus it was, according to Tran Trong Kim, that the ordinary people looked anxiously for better leadership, so that they "could work and live in peace." Because he fulfilled this fundamental need, Gia Long was able to fight his way northward (admittedly with French assistance), found his dynasty in 1802, and be remembered as the reunifier of Vietnam.[53]

In 1932, single-minded Gia Long advocates returned to the fray, publishing a musical drama (cai luong) spiced with battles against the Tay Son and featuring a touching scene in which Gia Long gives his son Canh to Pigneau.[54] Several years later this was countered with an historical novel centering on Quang Trung's expulsion of the Ch'ing.[55] At the level of historical scholarship, however, perhaps the key blow was struck in 1944 by Hoa Bang, whose widely read book not only described the actions of Quang Trung and his immediate associates but tried to place everyone within the military and diplomatic context of that period.[56] It was a reasonably competent history rather than simply a biographical panegyric. Nevertheless, the polemic over Quang Trung and Gia Long flared up once again in the 1960s in the form of a fascinating argument in print conducted

53. Tran Trong Kim, Viet-Nam Su Luoc, 6th printing (Saigon, 1958), pp. 367–69, 385–405. First published in Hanoi ca. 1928.

54. Tan Dan Tu and Phan Van Trinh, Gia Long Tau Quoc [Gia Long Flees the Country] (Saigon, 1932). This effort coincided with conservative attempts to promote Bao Dai as a "Vietnamese Meiji Emperor."

55. Nguyen Tu Sieu, Viet-Thanh Chien Su [History of Vietnam-Champa Wars] (Hanoi, 1935–36). Serialized in ten parts, each costing three xu.

56. Hoa Bang (Hoang Thuc Tram), Quang Trung Nguyen Hue: Anh Hung Dan Toc [Quang Trung Nguyen Hue: National Hero] (Hanoi, 1944), two different editions. In a third edition, published in 1950 in the French-controlled zone, the author found it necessary to add a special preface denying that he was preaching war or supporting one dynasty over another. After a brief period as "citizen Vinh Thuy" in the DRVN, Bao Dai, the last Nguyen king, had again become a French puppet.

across the seventeenth parallel between the editorial secretary of the Historical Institute in Hanoi and a Catholic priest and teacher in Hue.[57] Not long after the 30 April 1975 liberation of Saigon, Gia Long Avenue was renamed Ly Tu Trong Avenue, after a young Indochinese Communist Party cadre executed in 1931. The symbolism was almost as obvious as the changing of John F. Kennedy Square to Paris Commune Square.

Meanwhile, having settled in 1940–41 on a strategy of peasant mobilization and people's war, there was more that Vietnamese Marxist-Leninists could gain from the Tay Son experience than simply another anticolonial hero. The Tay Son came to be regarded as proto-revolutionary, in the manner of Chinese Communist Party interpretations of the T'ai-p'ing upheaval of the mid-nineteenth century. The reactionary Nguyen and the imperialist French were said to have thwarted momentous social and economic changes, of which the Tay Son were only a part. Tay Son cultural sensitivities were given special attention, their emphasis on popular traditions and full conversion to an orally linked script being considered vital precedents. Most important, however, were the military lessons. There seems little doubt that Vo Nguyen Giap (b. 1911) (who by the late 1930s had both taught history and examined peasant conditions and attitudes in some detail) saw the Tay Son as a specifically Vietnamese example of what could be accomplished if one combined a mass political base with tactics of surprise, flexibility, and strategic momentum.[58] On the other hand, since the Tay Son had eventually been defeated, Vo Nguyen Giap and other military commanders were not foolish enough to emulate them completely; indeed, they probably learned more from trial and error than from any book, Vietnamese or Western.

History as Process

While the search for heroes occupied center stage, another type of history was entering from the wings. It emphasized not emotions, not the destinies of great men, but impersonal forces and broad shifts in human affairs. What lured intellectuals like Dao Duy Anh (mentioned at the opening of this chapter) was the historical dialectic, the idea that change produced contradictions which resulted in permanent transformations. Here was an effective rebuttal to the argument, well entrenched in both elite and popular Vietnamese traditions, that there really was no present or future—only the past, happening over and over again. Time-

57. See especially Nguyen Phuong, *Bach Khoa* (Saigon), nos. 148 and 149 (March 1963), and Van Tan, NCLS 51 (June 1963), pp. 3–11.

58. Both General Giap and his key lieutenant Van Tien Dung (b. 1917) subsequently referred to the Tay Son experience often in their discussions of military strategy. However, the most comprehensive analysis from a military perspective is Nguyen Luong Bich and Pham Ngoc Phung, *Tim Hieu Thien Tai Quan Su cua Nguyen Hue* [Understanding Nguyen Hue's Military Genius] (Hanoi, 1971). For an interesting analysis of both Tay Son and T'ai-p'ing precedents, see Alexander B. Woodside, *Community and Revolution in Modern Vietnam* (Boston: Houghton Mifflin, 1976), pp. 239–45.

lessness was also being used as an argument against militancy and for the colonial status quo. For example, the prominent French historian Charles Maybon urged his Vietnamese students to accept certain inflexible principles before attempting "scientific history." These included recognition of the fact that "human psychology has not changed, external physical laws have not changed, and the grand principles governing the universe have remained the same from the very beginning to today."[59] Faced with increasing Vietnamese interest in Social Darwinian concepts of struggle and progress, Pham Quynh went to the trouble of translating and printing a contemporary Chinese refutation of evolution based on Chuang-tzu's ancient cyclical concept of history.[60]

However, with the Chinese Revolution, the Great War, and the Russian Revolution fresh in their minds, most young Vietnamese had little use for Chuang-tzu's cycles. Dao Duy Anh's small group in Hue was probably the first to attempt a dialectical approach to history and society.[61] After that effort was halted by the authorities, the initiative passed to Saigon and a group of young radicals recently returned from Paris. Although best known for their acid criticism of contemporary colonial policies, particularly via the journal La Lutte, a number of these young men were attracted to broader philosophical questions as well. In 1933 one of them published the most cogent review of the history of Western philosophy to be seen in Vietnamese to date.[62] The author was particularly concerned with contrasting the "static" formulations of Aristotle with those of Hegel; he then argued that the dialectical materialism of Marx was the capstone of man's epic philosophical quest. One of his colleagues, Phan Van Hum, brought the issue closer to home in November 1933 with a public critique of the idealistic historical outlook of both Tran Trong Kim and Phan Khoi.[63] The stage was thus set for a wide-ranging attack on idealism that continued through the 1930s.

59. Charles B. Maybon, "Phep lam Su va Su Viet-Nam" [Historiography and Vietnamese History], NP 130 (June 1928), pp. 531–48. Translation of a lecture originally given in Hanoi in 1907.

60. Chuong Hong Chieu, "Hoc Thuyet Tay voi Hoc Thuyet Tau: Darwin va Trang Tu" [Western and Chinese Theories: Darwin and Chuang-tzu], NP 87 (Sept. 1924), pp. 216–26. (Concepts of struggle and progress are discussed further in chapters 7 and 8.)

61. See, in particular, three titles published under the pseudonym of Ngo Nhan: Lich Su Nhan Loai [History of Mankind] (1928), Xa Hoi [Society] (1929), and Sinh Ton Canh Tranh [Struggle for Survival] (1929); see also Tinh Tien, Van De Sinh Menh [The Question of Human Life] (1929). In Hue in 1929 Tran Thi Nhu Man also published her essay on the family and society, drawing extensively from the theories of Lewis Morgan and Emile Durkheim. "Gia Dinh va Xa Hoi," Phu Nu Tung San, no. 1 (May 1929), pp. 1–35. Dao Duy Anh and Tran Thi Nhu Man were married, as one can discover in the preface to Dao Duy Anh, Tu Dien Truyen Kieu ["The Tale of Kieu" Dictionary] (Hanoi, 1974).

62. Signed by "X. X.," this discourse appeared as a series of articles in PNTV, beginning with issue no. 198 (4 May 1933) and continuing sporadically through no. 226 (30 Nov. 1933). "X. X." may have been Ho Huu Tuong.

63. Public lecture reprinted in PNTV 224 (9 Nov. 1933). See chapter 3 for a discussion of the 1930 polemic between Tran Trong Kim and Phan Khoi.

Surprisingly, it was left to the Confucian-educated pamphleteer, Tran Huu Do, to publish the first detailed explanation of how the dialectic was meant to work in both the physical and social realms.[64] In stark contrast to his series of booklets published a decade earlier (see chapter 7), which had been based largely on the turn-of-the-century ideas of Liang Ch'i-ch'ao, Tran Huu Do now eagerly accepted Hegel and Marx as mentors. His theoretical exposition focused on laws of perpetual change, dynamic interrelationships, and contradictions. Among the natural sciences he selected examples from atomic physics, thermophysics, paleontology, and biology. Perhaps his most original contribution was to describe the complex, rapidly evolving ecological relationship between plants, deer, tigers, and humans in Rach Gia province of southern Vietnam. In economics, Tran Huu Do cited the relationship of fertilizer to rice output to market price in Cho Lon. In history, the dialectic was used to explain the progressive demise of the extended family system, the supersedence of kings and popes by oil magnates and auto tycoons, the decline and fall of the Ch'ing dynasty in China, and the victory of the 1917 Revolution in Russia. Tran Huu Do's Vietnamese prose was more down-to-earth than that of intellectuals returning from Paris. We can also assume that readers were titillated to see a classically trained literatus turning Marxist dialectician.

Several years later, Tran Huu Do applied his new dialectical tools to a topic of major concern to radical Vietnamese—the history of Western colonial expansion and the twentieth-century crisis of capitalism.[65] Titled simply *De Quoc Chu Nghia* [Imperialism], this book sketched the European quest for overseas markets and raw materials, described diverse forms of economic, political, and cultural aggression, and explained the Great War of 1914–18 as a self-destructive contest between capitalist giants. Tran Huu Do then brought events up to date with a ringing defense of the Soviet Union and a bitter attack on fascism. Looking to the future, he predicted yet another major imperialist war, the eventual overthrow of the entire capitalist system, and the creation of a communist "world of great unity." This millennium (which probably owed as much to K'ang Yu-wei as to Karl Marx) was characterized by elimination of private property, social classes, and exploitation, the removal of distinctions between town and countryside and manual and mental labour, and indeed the extinguishing of the "individual, selfish psychology of humankind." Once these feats were accomplished, the cultural level of humanity would be "a hundred, a thousand, a million times higher than that of the present."[66] Presumably without any sense of irony, the last page of

64. Tran Huu Do, *Bien Chung Phap* [Dialectics] (Saigon, 1936); preface by Phan Van Hum, 2,000 copies printed. The author promised sequels on historical materialism and social philosophy, but I have been unable to ascertain if they appeared.

65. Tran Huu Do, *De Quoc Chu Nghia* [Imperialism] (Saigon, 1938[?]). The first half of this 74-page book may be in large part a translation of some uncited French publication.

66. Ibid., p. 74.

Tran Huu Do's book was devoted to an advertisement for various Eastern medicines to cure venereal diseases, urinary infections, and opium addiction.

It was Dao Duy Anh who finally managed to approach specifically Vietnamese history from a dialectical perspective. In 1938 he published *An Outline History of Vietnamese Culture*, which for the first time treated the Vietnamese past as constantly developing rather than as a timeless repository of things either liked or disliked.[67] While Dao Duy Anh's presentation was far from comprehensive, particularly in the realm of popular culture versus that of the traditional elites, his style was crisp, his use of sources competent, and his categories and interpretations quite different from any previous history of Vietnam. The twenty-page conclusion remains one of the most trenchant statements ever formulated on the cultural postures available to Vietnamese intellectuals prior to the August 1945 Revolution.

From the late 1920s a debate had been going on concerning the relevance of Confucianism to contemporary Vietnam. The overall effect was to reduce Confucianism from the level of either religion or ethical paradigm to a collection of philosophically diverse and historically bound writings and ideas. The next step was to place Confucian thought squarely within a world historical framework, rather than continuing to argue that there was a fundamental difference between East and West. This was accomplished in 1938 by Dao Duy Anh in a thoughtful essay titled *A Critical Discussion of Confucianism*.[68] Ten years earlier Dao Duy Anh had already argued that Confucianism was irrevocably linked with feudalism, and thus those who argued for its retention anywhere in the twentieth century were either idealistic or reactionary, or both. Now he proceeded to analyze the reasons why Confucianism was doomed no matter how hard its proponents tried to salvage it. For example, he outlined the inevitable ideological impact in Vietnam of an expanded monetary economy, of the growth of new urban centers, of peasants "leaving bamboo enclosures and rice paddies" to enter factories, and of women having to "abandon bedroom nooks and kitchen crannies" to eke out a living in the outside world. Even at the royal court in Hue, Dao Duy Anh pointed out, it had been decided in 1919 to postpone indefinitely the monarch's obeisances at the Temple of Confucius. The reasons given at the time indicated that no one believed any more that such acts would influence external reality, especially the material conditions of ordinary people. True, some sectors of society continued to call for a Confucian revival, to construct their own temples, to condemn young people for disrespect, and to preach harmonization of transcen-

---

67. *Viet-Nam Van Hoa Su Cuong* (Hanoi, 1938; republished in Saigon, 1951). In the preceding eight years Dao Duy Anh had also compiled and published the highly respected *Han-Viet Tu Dien* [Sino-Vietnamese Dictionary], 2 vols. (Hanoi, 1932), and *Phap-Viet Tu Dien* [Franco-Vietnamese Dictionary] (Hanoi, 1936).

68. Dao Duy Anh, *Khong Giao Phe Binh Tieu Luan* (Hue[?], 1938).

dental spirit with scientific practice. These efforts were supported by the French colonialists, he said, for the same reasons that Chiang Kai-shek worked in China to revive Confucian rituals and ethical principles. Neither the French nor Chiang would be successful in the long run.[69]

Faith in the historical dialectic could alter one's entire world view. Writing in 1933, one journalist pointed out how only ten years earlier Vietnamese writers had still lumped outside influences together under the poetic but diversionary rubric of "European rains and American winds." Now, however, they approached events in terms of struggle, imperialism, international markets, and economic depression. That was progress, he said, and there would be more of it.[70] Vietnamese women were chastised for drawing the battle lines between Eastern and Western, old and new, good and bad rather than conservative versus progressive.[71] Abstract ideals were far less important than determining what was "suitable" (thich hop) to a given historical period.[72] Thus, when a conservative Vietnamese landlord tried to picture Mirabeau as a revolutionary deserving of contemporary emulation, he was taken to task for daring to apply hopelessly outmoded bourgeois criteria to a time of international proletarian ascendancy.[73] Another writer, observing how many young urban Vietnamese were attracted to romantic individualism, agreed that such a tendency had been highly progressive in nineteenth-century Europe in helping to smash classicism, but suggested that in the twentieth century a firm commitment to realism and mass culture was required.[74]

In the 1930s it was still easier for many Vietnamese intellectuals to identify idealistically with various European schools of thought than it was to test specific concepts against current Vietnamese reality. This led Dao Duy Anh to criticize some of his peers as follows:

They know Plato and Aristotle well, they memorize Thomas Aquinas, they are infatuated by Pascal and Descartes, but they don't think they need to study Sakyamuni, Laotzu or, above, all, Confucius. They don't sense that what they idolize and preach under the label of "humanism" is in fact the ideology of the old [Western] aristocracy and power elite, no more relevant to contemporary Vietnamese than the "humanism" of Confucianism belonging to the old [Eastern] ruling monarchs and officials![75]

69. Ibid., pp. 132–52.

70. PNTV 232 (18 Jan. 1933).

71. Dat Si Tu, Van De Phu Nu Giai Phong [The Question of Women's Liberation] (Saigon, 1932), p. 5.

72. Do Duc Vuong, May Thuyet ve Luan Ly [Some Theories on Morality] (Hanoi, 1936), p. 20.

73. Thach Lan, "Cac Giai Cap" [Social Classes], PNTV 7 (10 Apr. 1930), pp. 13–14. Not surprisingly, the censor blanked out the concluding portion of this article.

74. Thanh Tam, "Van Hoc Lang Man" [Romantic Literature], PNTV 219 (5 Oct. 1933), pp. 12–13.

75. Dao Duy Anh, Khong Giao Phe Binh Tieu Luan, pp. 150–52.

Dao Duy Anh might well have added Rousseau, Hegel, Darwin, and Marx to his European list. He also treated the major Asian philosophers in acultural fashion, as if their impact on Vietnam was no different from that on China, Japan, or Korea. In plain fact, neither Dao Duy Anh nor any of his contemporaries had reached the point in 1938 where they could meticulously compare and contrast Vietnamese experience with that of other societies. Eleven years later Dao Duy Anh was still pleading for more attention to comparative history, in this case, his discovery that dialectical concepts existed in early India and China, not only the West, and his hypothesis that they might have influenced Vietnamese thinking.[76]

Seeking a Synthesis

Despite continuing difficulties, most Vietnamese intellectuals of the late 1930s were prepared to adopt a conscious stance toward history rather than simply to uphold or denounce tradition. They were no longer either cultural purists or rebels, but individuals aware that Vietnam was already quite different from what it had been only twenty years earlier. They accepted Tran Huu Do's argument that "in this world nothing is fixed; there are only processes (qua trinh). . . . If we want to explain any phenomenon, we must first investigate its origins, its growth, and its annihilation."[77] Precisely because the world was changing so rapidly, however, intellectuals found themselves having to act on the basis of very limited empirical investigation. Later, to meet the needs of a society in the midst of war and revolution, the range of enquiry was also narrowed substantially.

As ideological sophisticates, Vietnamese intellectuals knew quite well that the past could be interpreted in different ways. One person's hero could be another's villain. A landlord or an official was not likely to see things in the same way as a peasant or worker. This was evident, for example, when the colonial authorities in July 1939 organized an observance of the 150th anniversary of the French Revolution. As might be expected, the authorities and their Vietnamese associates focused on the storming of the Bastille and later Napoleonic glories. It all had a patriotic and idealistic ring. By contrast, the Indochinese Communist Party chose to stress class conflict in the French Revolution and the contributions of Robespierre.[78] Such differences over remote history could also take on practical political significance. In 1940, the Corsican head warden of Hanoi prison used his proud Napoleonic heritage constantly to mock and degrade the Vietnamese inmates, and although incarcerated students undoubtedly remained a bit awed by Napoleon and ashamed that Vietnam possessed no comparable giant, one jailed

76. *Tim Hieu* 4 (Sept. 1949) and 5 (Oct. 1949). *Tim Hieu* was distributed by the Marxist Study Association of Interzone IV (north-central Vietnam).

77. Tran Huu Do, *Bien Chung Phap*, p. 10.

78. *Demain* (Hanoi) 35 (14 July 1939). *Notre Voix* (Hanoi) 26 (14 July 1939). *Dan Chung* (Saigon) 72 (5 July 1939).

student finally got up the nerve to tell the head warden sarcastically that, since Napoleon had ended his days a prisoner on St. Helena, presumably not *all* inmates were animals as asserted. One year later, when the Corsican head warden was gleefully predicting that Hitler would crush Stalin, Vietnamese Communist prisoners kept their own hopes alive with thoughts of Napoleon's earlier defeat on the same terrain.[79]

As the world became engulfed in war, radical Vietnamese tried to learn from the very recent past as well. The Indochinese Communist Party paused for a moment to assess the fifteen-year history of Marxism-Leninism in Vietnam.[80] Vo Nguyen Giap pored over maps and descriptions of the Chinese struggle against Japan. In a 1939 publication he paid special attention to Chu Teh's strategy of protracted resistance.[81] Within a year he was in the mountains trying to devise a similar strategy for Vietnam. Soon he was joined by Ho Chi Minh, who amidst all his other duties somehow found time to compile two guerrilla warfare manuals based on personal observations in Yenan, as well as to translate an ancient military text by Sun-tzu and a short history of the Communist Party of the Soviet Union.[82]

It became common practice in the Viet Minh to criticize all significant political or military events, a form of instant historical analysis which often resulted in nothing more than the passing of an oral or handwritten report to the next higher echelon. In some cases, however, more ambitious investigations were ordered with an eye to uncovering errors, reassessing doctrine, and improving training curricula for future cadres. Such were the objectives of a careful study of the 1940 Bac Son uprising near the Sino-Vietnamese frontier, the results of which were considered important enough to be printed and distributed four times in four years.[83] Participants in unsuccessful operations were expected not merely to assign blame to one person or another, but to analyze what had happened from an objective perspective. Thus, Tran Huy Lieu, one of the leaders of a March 1945 uprising at Nghia Lo prison one hundred miles northwest of Hanoi, tried to explain to himself, to his Party comrades, and to the public at large why events had gone out of control and a large number of inmates were killed without achieving the desired results.[84] His account was both vivid history and a valuable case study for future cadres.

79. Luu Dong, *Buoc Dau Theo Dang* (Hanoi, 1961), pp. 11, 53, 66, 90, and 92.

80. *Dan Chung* 41 (3 Jan. 1939) and 42 (7 Jan. 1939).

81. Van Dinh (Vo Nguyen Giap), *Muon Hieu Ro Tinh Hinh Quan Su o Tau* [Understanding Clearly the Military Situation in China] (Hanoi, 1939).

82. Phan Ngoc Lien, "Tim Hieu ve Cong Tac Van Dong, Giao Duc Quan Chung cua Ho Chu Tich trong thoi gian Nguoi o Pac-Bo," [Investigating President Ho's Mass Mobilization and Education Efforts while at Pac-Bo] NCLS 149 (Mar.–Apr. 1973), pp. 13–21, 30.

83. Tong Bo Viet Minh, *Bac Son Khoi Nghia* [The Bac Son Uprising], 4th printing (Hanoi, 1946). Half of this 39-page booklet is a description, half a discussion of lessons to be learned.

84. Tran Huy Lieu, *Nghia Lo Khoi Nghia* [The Nghia Lo Uprising] (Hanoi, 1946).

Most Vietnamese intellectuals did not become directly involved with the Viet Minh until the summer of 1945 and thus had no opportunity to participate in such early operational critiques. Rather, the period 1940–44 saw them stepping back from political affairs, trying to size up what had already happened and hoping to find where Vietnam specifically might fit into the scheme of things. Partly this was simple self-protection, since both the Vichy French and the Japanese could be extremely ruthless with anyone who threatened public order; and partly there was the feeling that Vietnam's immediate fate was being decided on distant battlefields, not inside the country, and thus this was perhaps the time to take a longer, more reflective look at events.

There is evidence, however, that even before the war the Vietnamese intelligentsia was losing whatever political élan it may have possessed, splitting up ideologically and simultaneously shifting its attention increasingly to literary, cultural, and historical questions. Political differences aside, Vietnamese intellectuals had reached something of a saturation point with Western ideas. Having tended to separate themselves from their own past for a decade or more, they now wanted to reverse the process, at least to the point of being able to understand in detail how Vietnamese society differed from other societies.

In such conditions it naturally became quite fashionable to both read and write about Vietnamese history. A poll of readers conducted in southern Vietnam in 1942, for example, listed five historical titles among the ten most respected books. First and third were Tran Trong Kim's *Confucianism* and *An Outline History of Vietnam*, evidence that the conservative message had gained a new lease on life.[85] Dao Duy Anh's *Outline History of Vietnamese Culture* was also in the top ten, however, and it was to be the radical intellectuals who contributed the larger proportion of new historical studies in this period. Thus, Ngo Tat To took time away from his efforts in creative fiction to publish annotated *quoc ngu* translations of surviving literature of the Ly (A.D. 1010–1225) and Tran (1225–1400) dynasties.[86] He also published a discussion and compilation of *nom* literature from the fifteenth to the nineteenth century.[87] One reason for doing all this, he said, was to make available materials that fewer and fewer people could read in their original forms.

The most striking evidence of popular interest in the past was the success of a weekly journal published in Hanoi from 1941 to 1945, titled *Tri Tan* [To Know the New].[88] In one sense the title was quite misleading, since wartime censorship ruled out any wide-ranging discussion of current events; nor could *Tri Tan* be

85. *Thanh Nghi* 22 (1 Oct. 1942). "The Tale of Kieu" was second.
86. *Van Hoc Doi Ly* [Literature of the Ly Period] and *Van Hoc Doi Tran* [Literature of the Tran Period] (Hanoi, 1941).
87. *Thi Van Binh Chu* [The Literature of Binh Chu], 2 vols. (Hanoi[?], 1941).
88. The first issue of *Tri Tan* appeared 3 June 1941, sold for 12 piasters, and contained twenty-four pages. Apparently 1,500–2,000 copies of each issue were printed.

considered innovative or intellectually exciting in the manner of *Phu Nu Tan Van* [Women's News] a decade earlier. What must have attracted readers were the many detailed yet purposefully non-specialized articles on Vietnamese history, culture, language, and literature. The roster of individual contributors was very diverse, ranging from the conservative pedagogue Duong Quang Ham to the young university radical Nguyen Dinh Thi. At least two participants, Tran Van Giap and Nguyen Van To, were employed at the Ecole Française d'Extrême-Orient and had published extensively in French. They saw *Tri Tan* as a means to disseminate in *quoc ngu* some of the scholarly historical findings of the previous decade.[89] Nevertheless, the preference in *Tri Tan* was to dramatize and to romanticize the past rather than to analyze it. This was suggested by a regular front-cover drawing of a stack of books, some spectacles, and an open Chinese text upon which rested a fragile lily flower. It was also evident in the tabloid-like attention to human-interest vignettes and apocryphal stories. Perhaps this is what led Dao Duy Anh to criticize some of his colleagues for not going back to original sources, for failing to subject documents to critical analysis, for giving too much credence to oral history, and for allowing personal prejudice to get in the way of "scientific" interpretation.[90]

Significantly, the main scholarly publications of this period dealt with the Chinese classics and Chinese history. *Quoc ngu* translations appeared of the *Ta Hsüeh, Analects, Mencius, Book of Changes, Book of Poetry*, and *Doctrine of the Mean*. A serious study of Taoism was published.[91] The well-known Trotskyist intellectual Phan Van Hum researched and published a thoughtful discussion of Buddhism.[92] Dao Duy Anh contributed *An Outline History of China*.[93] Dang Thai Mai began exploring the important historiographical debates that had taken place in China from 1928 onward.[94] He also translated short stories by Lu Hsün and successfully transmitted to Vietnam some of the literary theories of the May Fourth generation.

Possibly the most impressive philosophical work of the era was Phan Van Hum's 500-page exposition on Wang Yang-ming.[95] Having access to a four-vol-

89. Other *Tri Tan* participants included Hoa Bang, Nguyen Huy Tuong, Dao Duy Anh, Hoang Thieu Son, Le Thuoc, and Phan Van Hum.

90. Le Thanh, *Cuoc Phong Van Cac Nha Van* (Hanoi, 1942), p. 177.

91. Ngo Tat To and Nguyen Duc Tinh, *Lao Tu* (Hanoi, 1942). The publishers, Mai Linh, promised future studies of Confucius, Mencius, Chuang-tzu, Hsün-tzu, Han Confucianism, Sung Neo-Confucianism, and Wang Yang-ming, but I have been unable to ascertain if any of these actually appeared. For further discussion of this book, see SPT-2, pp. 377–85.

92. *Triet Ly Phat Giao* [Buddhist Philosophy] (Saigon, n.d.).

93. *Trung Hoa Su Cuong* (Hue, 1943). The author relied heavily on Chinese and French sources, with little interpretation of his own.

94. *Thanh Nghi* 25 (16 Nov. 1942).

95. *Vuong Duong Minh* (Hanoi, 1944). Other works in this Tan Viet series dealt with Aristotle, Descartes, Kant, Nietzsche, Bergson, Einstein, Buddhism, and metaphysics.

ume compendium of Wang Yang-ming's writings published in Shanghai in 1935, as well as to recent Chinese scholarly interpretations, Phan Van Hum gave about equal attention to biography and to intellectual exposition. He was particularly anxious to simultaneously place Wang Yang-ming within the context of his times and to demonstrate to Vietnamese intellectuals the contemporary relevance of Wang's philosophy of uniting theory and practice (see chapter 8).[96] Ironically, just as Phan Van Hum was devoting himself to the ideas of Wang Yang-ming, his old protagonists in the Indochinese Communist Party were preparing to engineer a revolution and seizure of power.

For all the philosophical spadework and obvious public interest, Vietnamese intellectuals were still having real difficulty interpreting their own history. One exception was the thoughtful study *Xa Hoi Viet Nam* [Vietnamese Society] by Luong Duc Thiep.[97] Although similar in content to Dao Duy Anh's *Outline History of Vietnamese Culture*, Luong's work was even more inclined to test everything in terms of the historical dialectic. His analysis of the nine centuries prior to 1802 was especially provocative. Without using the term, Luong Duc Thiep suggested that the Asiatic mode of production had been responsible for inhibiting progress in Vietnamese agricultural technology, commerce, and industry. In spite of that retardation, however, Vietnam had undergone two major transformations during that period: the establishment and successful defense of a Vietnamese monarchist state (eleventh through thirteenth centuries); and the subsequent emergence of a Vietnamese people (*dan toc*), reaching culmination in the late eighteenth-century Tay Son movement and defeat of the Ch'ing invaders. After that, Vietnamese society rapidly fell behind developments in the West, leaving the way open for French conquest and exploitation. Luong Duc Thiep concluded his book by predicting that international and local contradictions had become so sharp that the dialectic would manifest itself very soon, producing yet another turning point in history. Since the Vietnamese bourgeoisie had shown itself quite incapable of leadership, the future was in the hands of the workers (*tho thuyen*).

National, Scientific, and Mass History

While Luong Duc Thiep's 1944 prediction may have been comforting to ICP members, they were already trying hard to ensure that the wheel of history actually turned—and against the French and Japanese. They had also decided that "working class" leadership meant very little without a mass following. That led them directly to the peasantry.

In seeking ways to communicate with Vietnamese peasants, ICP members dis-

---

96. In an appendix Phan Van Hum extracted a previously unpublished essay by Phan Boi Chau also stressing Wang's unity of theory and practice.

97. *Xa Hoi Viet-Nam* (Hanoi, 1944; republished in Saigon, 1971).

covered yet another use for history. It provided a convenient bridge across which intellectuals could go to appreciate mass attitudes, and across which the masses might go to grasp new ideas of struggle and progress. Previously the Vietnamese intelligentsia had treated most peasant customs with ill-disguised contempt. Now it was possible to place all customs in historical perspective. Cadres of urban intellectual background could now be seen practising certain basic peasant rituals, such as smoking a water pipe, chewing betel, or drinking homemade brews of one kind or another. However, they continued to draw the line at "superstitious" customs.

As for the peasants, although it was still futile to quote Hegel, Marx, or Lenin to them, this did not mean that they were incapable of grasping new concepts. Provided that the symbols were familiar and the implications concrete, Vietnamese peasants demonstrated a remarkable capacity to alter selected attitudes and behavior patterns. History provided one means by which Communist cadres could assure peasants that some existing beliefs were quite acceptable, that not everything was being challenged. More than that, the ICP now endorsed the idea that certain peasant attitudes were at the heart of Vietnamese capacities to survive and flourish.

Realizing how little they knew about peasant culture, Communist cadres of intelligentsia background labored to master the subject with the same passion shown during "proletarianization" a decade earlier. Much of this was accomplished inductively, while working, fighting, or relaxing side by side with peasant recruits or sympathizers. However, intellectuals in the Viet Minh's National Salvation Cultural Association (Hoi Van Hoa Cuu Quoc) were also able to approach the problem deductively, relying on an increasing body of published and unpublished collections of folksongs, popular poems, peasant aphorisms, and local ritual. Not surprisingly, new meanings were often discovered. For example, Nguyen Dinh Thi used folk materials to demonstrate that Vietnamese peasants had an essentially optimistic, struggle-oriented, patriotic character regardless of time or place. Some of the pitfalls of this approach were evident in the snatches of poetry that he cited to prove personality ideals. Thus, poems praying for rain were said to demonstrate profound peasant understanding of nature. The tendency of oral literature to modify sad or distasteful historical facts was a form of peasant optimism, of refusing to accept fate blindly. When Nguyen Dinh Thi summarized his argument, nevertheless, he talked of the need to "look life straight in the eye, to perceive exactly the problems that need solving, and then to vault into life."[98] Whether one could continue to pray for rain and "look life straight in the eye" was not discussed.

98. HT-5, pp. 517–30. Nguyen Dinh Thi in 1963 was general secretary of the Vietnam Association of Writers.

Nowhere was the shift more apparent than in the interpretations now given by Viet Minh intellectuals to 'The Tale of Kieu.' Brandished by conservative collaborators in the 1920s, wept over by romantics in the 1930s, Vietnam's primary epic traditional poem was now provided with anti-imperialist credentials. For example, Hoai Thanh (b. 1909), severely attacked by Marxists in the 1930s as an advocate of a cultural world beyond "mundane" economics, was now warmly endorsed when he represented the rebel leader Tu Hai, Kieu's lover, as a model of timeless Vietnamese heroism. Hoai Thanh further claimed that the author, Nguyen Du, had managed to "overcome the obstacles between past and present" despite the great material and intellectual changes occurring in the 130 years since the creation of *Kieu*. Hoai Thanh concluded with a profoundly idealistic message of comfort to his generation:

And so it seems we are not so lost after all. Behind us we have the immense history of our people. Between us and that immense history there is still a road we can travel, still spiritual cords attaching us. Because we can still love Nguyen Du we are not yet in the position of abandoned children in a strange country. We can share our happiness and sadness, our hopes and dreams, with someone in the past.[99]

Even Dao Duy Anh, one of the earliest defenders of the historical dialectic, appeared bewitched by the magic of *Kieu*, arguing that Nguyen Du was the first Vietnamese author to succeed in crossing class barriers, as a result sowing in people's hearts enduring faith in the creativity of their language and "shaking the souls" of each subsequent generation.[100]

One of the practical means by which radical intellectuals and peasants (or workers) came to share something in common was by organizing historical commemorations. Actually, as early as 1929, Vietnamese Marxist-Leninists were commemorating specific Western, Chinese, and Vietnamese historical events. By 1931 the French Sûreté felt compelled to warn local officials to be particularly vigilant on twenty-seven days of the calendar year.[101] Besides eleven rather obvious Western revolutionary anniversaries, three Chinese events were noted: the 1911 Revolution; Sun Yat-sen's death in 1925; and the 1927 Canton Uprising.[102] Death dates were predominant among the Vietnamese events, those commemorated including the Trung sisters, the 1885 defenders of King Ham Nghi, three patriotic literati (Phan Chu Trinh, Ngo Duc Ke, Luong Van Can), two intelligentsia activists (Pham Hong Thai, Nguyen Thai Hoc), and a group of Commu-

99. HT-5, pp. 506–16. Originally published in *Thanh Nghi* 36 (May 1943). As of 1963, Hoai Thanh was general secretary of the Vietnam Union of Literary Artists.

100. *Khao Luan ve Kim Van Kieu* [An Examination of the *Tale of Kieu*] (Hue, 1943).

101. AOM (Aix), Résident Supérieur Tonkin F-50.

102. See also the 1929 handwritten pamphlet on the Canton Uprising in AOM (Aix) F-7F4, vol. 1, item 8.

nist revolutionaries executed in Phu Tho in November 1930.[103] Two events, the 1802 enthronement of Gia Long and the 1883 Harmand Treaty making protectorates of Annam and Tonkin, were to be remembered in negative fashion each year.

By 1944 the ICP was able to add a number of events of its own to the historical calendar. These included formation of the Party and establishment of the Nghe Tinh soviets in 1930, the Bac Son and Nam Ky uprisings of 1940, and the organization of the first national-salvation platoon in September 1941. Among the many ICP cadres killed by the French in the previous fifteen years, a few were singled out and in effect given status as revolutionary martyrs.[104] In 1954 the opportunity came to name streets, bridges, and schools in northern Vietnam after both ICP-initiated events and Party heroes. Twenty-one years later the chance finally came in the South as well.

Among all ICP leaders of this period, Ho Chi Minh was probably the most confident practitioner of the new history. Selectively combining antitraditionalism with nationalistic appreciation of Vietnam's past, he set the tone for almost all subsequent Viet Minh historiography. Much of his message was conveyed orally. Vo Nguyen Giap recalls, for example, how on nights in the mountains in 1941, when it was too cold to sleep, a fire would be built, and Ho Chi Minh would narrate to cadres the history of the world, "as if telling folk tales." Each time he took pains to link international events to those in Vietnam, and to conclude by predicting that conditions would be very favorable for revolution within four or five years.[105] Soon after, Ho Chi Minh found time to compose a 236-line poem titled "The History of Our Country from 2879 B.C. to 1942." Typed out on his own portable typewriter and disseminated via Viet Minh training classes, the poem stressed resistance to foreign aggression and, above all, the peasant-based Tay Son defeat of the Ch'ing.[106] Some persons who were present at recitations of this poem recall it ending with a firm forecast that Vietnam would achieve independence in 1945.[107] One cadre even remembers double-

103. See also the 1929 handwritten pamphlet on Pham Hong Thai in AOM (Aix) F-7F4, vol. 1, item 9.

104. Although there was no set list so far as I know, the following Party members probably were already being commemorated posthumously in the mid-1940s: Le Hong Son, Ngo Gia Tu, Chau Van Liem, Ly Tu Trong, Ha Huy Tap, Nguyen Thi Minh Khai, Nguyen Nghiem, Tran Phu, and Hoang Van Thu. See *Guong Chien Dau cua Nhung Nguoi Cong San* [Struggle Paragons among Communist Individuals], 3rd edition (Hanoi, 1965).

105. Vo Nguyen Giap, "Father of the Vietnam Revolutionary Army," in Hoai Thanh et al., *Days with Ho Chi Minh* (Hanoi, 1962), pp. 198–99.

106. Phan Ngoc Lien, *Tim Hieu ve cong tac*, pp. 14–16.

107. Vu Anh, "From Kunming to Pac Po," in Hoai Thanh et al., *Days with Ho Chi Minh*, p. 176.

checking with Ho Chi Minh to see if he really wanted to print such a prognostication, especially after having just criticized some local activists for setting a date for an armed uprising.[108] Unfortunately, no printed version of this poem appears to have survived. Perhaps it is most significant that, whatever the exact content of the poem, ICP members looked on it as a talisman, motivating them to accomplish the anticipated event and legitimizing the prophet when and if the event occurred.

Much of the Viet Minh cultural effort involved a conscious pouring of new wine into old bottles, a metaphor in fact used by more than one subsequent analyst in the DRVN. This involved selective redemption of the past, the salvaging of some bottles and the bypassing of others. Thus, while Vietnamese resistance to foreign intervention was declared the glorious, continuous thread linking all epochs and all classes, there was little discussion of the millennium of successful Chinese control, the bitter internal wars, the near annihilation of the Cham, or the ability of foreigners to repeatedly find Vietnamese collaborators. When such distasteful matters had to be raised, they were treated as feudal episodes, historically bound. Vietnamese heroes as historical entities were praised as never before, but the actions of their posthumous spirits were either relegated to the museum category of feudal superstition or treated as symbolic reflections of continuing popular respect. This was a reversal of the fourteenth-century *Viet Dien U Linh*, which judged individuals primarily on their posthumous powers and thus included a number of spirits which appeared to have had insignificant temporal lives.

Nevertheless, the human mind is not a collection of wine and bottles. Or, to demonstrate the ultimate inadequacy of the metaphor, one may say that no conceptual wine is ever entirely new, since the act of linguistic transfer involves accommodation. And no cultural bottle remains entirely inert, but rather works its chemistry on the wine to some degree or another. Finally, both wine and bottles exist in a constantly changing environment, the river of time that Heraclitus spoke of so long ago. Hence, even if the chemistry remains reasonably stable, the external conditions existing when the bottle is opened and the wine drunk surely constitute a critical factor in determining the value of the experience.

Although many Viet Minh intellectuals presumably remained fascinated by problems of change and continuity, their publications took on an increasingly idealistic and formalistic tone. They were responding in part to an ICP policy statement of 1943 which called for a new culture possessing exclusively na-

---

108. Unpublished memorandum of Le Quang Ba, as discussed in Phan Ngoc Lien, *Tim Hieu ve cong tac*, pp. 17, 21–22.

tionalistic, scientific, and mass traits (see chapter 8). Vietnamese history was often distilled into two categories: building and defending the nation.[109] Whichever category a particular event might fit into, the implicit message was that of a timeless Vietnamese spirit and tradition (*truyen thong*) operating outside the historical dialectic. When the dialectic was invoked, it usually had a heavy teleological bias—in other words, later history was made the goal of earlier history; for example, the passing of the Vietnamese feudal literati and the failure of bourgeois Vietnamese to assert national leadership were often regarded as confirming the leadership credentials of the proletarian ICP. Each time a new ideological "line" (*duong loi*) was promulgated, selected historical events were wheeled out to help prove its validity. Paradoxically, twenty years of intelligentsia separation from the living, breathing, overwhelming past of Vietnam now enabled members to adopt a distinctly utilitarian posture, to exploit history without feeling exploited by it.

Radical Vietnamese who continued to believe in the future-opening potential of historical study (as distinct from its ideological or didactic capacities) were faced with a difficult choice: they could defer their serious work until such time as the anti-imperialist struggle was victorious, in the interim becoming cultural cadres and churning out whatever was called for; or they could research, write, and publish outside the Viet Minh, in which case their efforts might be ignored or, worse yet, be cited by the French or collaborator groups as evidence that the Viet Minh had failed to mobilize the best minds available. Most appear to have put themselves at the service of the Viet Minh, at least until 1949-50. Those others who remained aloof do not seem to have published much that was original. While a number of historical publications eventually appeared in Hanoi and Saigon, particularly during 1950-51, most seem to have been the fruit of work accomplished before 1945, and many were simply reprints.

Viet Minh victory in the August 1945 Revolution posed the ultimate teleological problem. For those who took an active role, this was in all likelihood the most inspiring, exhilarating moment of their lives. As a result, histories written by these people have tended to convert Vietnam's entire past into a mere backdrop for the Revolution. For committed Communists, the efforts of diverse radical intellectuals and anticolonial activists of the 1920s and 1930s had the historical purpose of bringing the ICP to power. Some have even suggested that all this activity was aimed at helping one man, Ho Chi Minh, achieve his historical destiny.[110] Once his destiny had been fulfilled and he had departed this earth, Ho Chi Minh was placed in a crystal sarcophagus to be viewed by Vietnamese in

109. An earlier non–Viet Minh version had three categories: building, defending, and expanding the nation. See Khuong Viet, *Tri Tan* 7 (18 July 1941).

110. Occasionally the argument has gone one step further, with Ho Chi Minh's life being synonymous with the Vietnamese revolution, or even with modern Vietnamese history (see, for

perpetuity. For those less inclined to physical symbols, one writer argued that "Time may erase everything, but Uncle Ho's love of man is free from time and space."[111] Party Secretary Le Duán simply affirmed that Ho Chi Minh "will live forever."[112]

Ho Chi Minh may indeed enter the Vietnamese pantheon at the level of the Trung sisters, Tran Hung Dao, Le Loi, and Quang Trung. Surviving leaders of the ICP and Viet Minh struggle of the 1930s and 1940s are anxious, however, that much more be remembered by subsequent generations than the achievements of one man. They want to convey as much of the agony and the ecstasy as possible. They are particularly worried that citizens of an independent Vietnam, not having experienced the degradations of colonial and semi-feudal rule, will become self-centered and complacent. Thus in 1971, Duong Thi An, a ranking female cadre, publicly criticized her own son, a civil engineer, for failing to recognize how much his parents, relatives, and older Vietnamese people in general had sacrificed so that he could be happy. For her son, she lamented, book accounts of oppression and revolution were "like mere legends or fairy tales."[113]

Nevertheless, Duong Thi An did go to the trouble of narrating an account of her experiences to 1945. Hers was only one out of eighty-two memoirs concerning the fifteen years prior to the August Revolution published with Party encouragement by 1976.[114] How much the past can be sustained, and in what form, is impossible to judge at this point. More importantly, one must ask whether the new generation will *want* to sustain the past as seen by its elders, or rather try to advance some important new interpretations. To the degree that conditions have changed and different conceptual problems arisen, this will prove to be one test of its ability to relate to both the universal and the particular in human experience.

---

example, NCLS 145 [July–Aug. 1972], p. 61); nevertheless, glorification of Ho Chi Minh was never so great as that of Stalin in the Soviet Union, Mao Tse-tung in China, or Kim Il-sung in Korea.

111. Song Tung, in *Vietnam Courier* 47 (Apr. 1976), p. 29.

112. *This Nation and Socialism Are One* (Chicago: Vanguard Books, 1976), p. 219. Edited with an introduction by Tran Van Dinh.

113. Duong Thi An, *Nguon Vui Duy Nhat* (Hanoi, 1974), pp. 5–8. The author, a member of the Nung minority and wife of General Chu Van Tan, was active in the Women's Union in various highland regions. Her son had complained of her not being at home in Hanoi more often.

114. TCVH 2-1977, pp. 17–28. The Vietnam People's Army has had a parallel memoir-producing effort. Province cultural bureaus also encourage local activists to relate their stories, but many of these have yet to be published.

7. Harmony and Struggle

In 1924 a middle-aged practitioner of Eastern medicine named Tran Huu Do (1885–1939) began to castigate his countrymen for failing to pull themselves together to oust the French. Although drawing heavily from turn-of-the-century Chinese publications, particularly those of Liang Ch'i-ch'ao, he aimed his message at the new Vietnamese intelligentsia, and employed a hard-hitting *quoc ngu* essay style. By 1928 Tran Huu Do had thirteen tracts in circulation, of which no fewer than 25,000 copies had been printed.[1] Early that year the French decided to confiscate as many of Tran Huu Do's pamphlets as they could find, and to sentence him to eighteen months in prison for "preaching hatred" and "inciting the Annamite people to revolt."[2] Soon thereafter Tran Huu Do sought and was granted membership in the Indochinese Communist Party. His son Tran Bach Dang was active in the Viet Minh and came to occupy important positions in the National Front for the Liberation of South Vietnam.

At first glance Tran Huu Do would not seem to arouse much intellectual interest. Born and raised in the lower Mekong delta province of Go Cong, he never had the chance to take the traditional civil examinations or to meet the cream of Vietnam's Confucian literati located far to the north. His knowledge of Chinese was good, but his writings of the 1920s contained nothing that had not been said twenty years earlier by the generation of Phan Boi Chau and Phan Chu Trinh. Nevertheless, we know he was read by many young men and women fresh from colonial schools, and his transition from Confucianism to Marxism-Leninism is sufficiently documented to give us some important insights on ideological developments of the period.

Tran Huu Do was very much an intergenerational figure—fifteen years younger than most patriotic literati, but fifteen years older than most members of

1. Each print run was of either 1,000 or 2,000 copies, except for one run of 5,000. At least four pamphlets went into second editions, indicating that they were in fact being purchased and not just gathering dust in shops or in the author's home.

2. *La Jeune Indochine* (Saigon), no. 7 (22 Dec. 1927), no. 10 (12 Jan. 1928), and no. 11 (19 Jan. 1928). Phan Van Hum, *Ngoi Tu Kham Lon* (Saigon, 1957), pp. 101–102, reports seeing Tran Huu Do walking the Saigon Central Prison terrace three afternoons per week in late 1928, a privilege granted to only four political prisoners.

the new intelligentsia. Also, as a southerner without any examination degree pretensions, he was perhaps less tied to orthodox Confucianism than many other
writers of the same age group living in Tonkin or Annam.[3] Acutely aware that
the old learning was fading rapidly, Tran Huu Do nonetheless retained enough
faith to want to transmit part of it in *quoc ngu* to the next generation. He happened to publish at a time when the French had temporarily relaxed censorship
restrictions, and when the trial of Phan Boi Chau as well as the public funeral for
Phan Chu Trinh had sparked curiosity among the intelligentsia concerning political and ideological developments prior to World War I.

Essentially, Tran Huu Do told young Vietnamese that although the many collaborator mandarins, insipid moralists, and proponents of vague harmonizing
philosophies who called themselves Confucianists deserved to be condemned and
isolated, a few others among the older generation, who had placed achievement
of independence and freedom above all else and who had tried to use their Confucian training to those ends, deserved both praise and understanding. As with
the new intelligentsia, patriotic literati like Phan Chu Trinh and Phan Boi Chau
had demanded that any traditional attitudes standing in the way of independence and freedom be discarded, and that any Western ideas and techniques
crucial to survival and growth in the twentieth century be assimilated. It was
thus feasible to be both patriotic and avant-garde, to detest the French for colonizing Vietnam and to love them for their modern wisdom. This was a message
the intelligentsia needed to hear, as it gave them a legitimate link with the past.

Tran Huu Do may simply have been restating old ideas, but his writing style
was immediate and forceful. He avoided flowery images, attacked subjects frontally, used popular metaphors to hammer down key points, and never let a Chinese or Western quotation pass without explaining it in colloquial Vietnamese.
Again and again he warned readers that they existed in a dog-eat-dog environment. Vietnamese would have to prove to themselves, to the French, and to the
rest of the world that they had the capacity to struggle and to win. Tran Huu
Do's tone was reasonably confident, whereas similar Vietnamese writings twenty
years earlier had often had an air of desperation. Clearly he put more hope in
the new intelligentsia than did older surviving literati like Phan Boi Chau.

One of Tran Huu Do's favorite metaphors was that of small boats in stormy
waters. For example, when struggling for independence from the French it
would be wise to train rigorously and accumulate experience methodically, in the
same way as boatmen first learned how to cross rivers and navigate canals, then
attempted travel along the coast, and only afterward ventured out into the open
sea. One's attitude during such training and accumulation of experience was cru-

---

3. It would be particularly revealing to compare Tran Huu Do with northern contemporaries,
for example, Duong Ba Trac (1884–1944), Hoang Tang Bi (1883–1939), Nguyen Khac Hieu
(1888–1939), and Doan Nhu Khue (1883–1957).

cial. Thus, if a boatman became fearful of the choppy waves in the river, he would not readily attempt the coastline or ocean. Ultimately he had to be mentally prepared to face and to surmount waves terrible beyond imagination. It would do no good in the midst of a storm to stand and curse the wind, the waves, the breadth of the ocean, the small size of one's boat, or the ineptitude of one's fellow sailors. Nor would it help to repeatedly flee back to port when the storm clouds appeared on the horizon, as one would then never reach the distant goal.[4]

Sometime around 1930 Tran Huu Do exchanged his Social Darwinism for the historical dialectic.[5] The circumstances surrounding this apparent conversion remain obscure. Perhaps he debated the relevant issues with Communist Party cadres in jail. Perhaps he was influenced by Vietnamese Marxists recently returned from Paris, several of whom were accomplished dialecticians. Whatever the case, Tran Huu Do soon was admitted to membership in the ICP and participated actively in the Popular Front movement prior to his death in 1939.[6] Yet, he remained more an idealist than a materialist, more concerned with the struggle for survival and dominance than with the economic mode of production. And he never wavered in placing voluntarism over determinism. Other Vietnamese wrote more cogently as convinced Confucianists, Social Darwinists, or Marxist-Leninists, but Tran Huu Do tells us more about intellectual transition, about serious-minded people trying to grapple with the realities of late colonial Vietnam and coming up with ideas that bore different traces, and that were never meant to be hewn in stone.

Nineteenth-Century Attitudes

Prior to the twentieth century the notions of avoiding discord, of promoting an agreeable whole, and of accepting one's role within that whole were important components of Vietnamese moral and religious philosophy. Cosmological teachings emphasized not resistance but adaptation to the flow of nature. To buck the current meant drowning, or at least capsizing. The earth did not belong to man; man belonged to the earth. Man did not weave the web of life; he was merely a strand in it.

This was not a static or quietist philosophy, although twentieth-century intellectuals often saw it that way. Vietnamese peasants had long ago perceived the sequence of day and night, of wet and dry seasons, of birth and death, as parts of a much larger, albeit still mysterious, design. They appreciated that change was an inherent element of life, and were quite capable of altering behavior to try to

---

4. Tran Huu Do, *Hon Doc Lap* (Saigon, 1926), pp. 15–17; idem, *Tieng Chuong Truy Hon* (Saigon, 1926), p. 8.

5. See chapter 6 for a discussion of Tran Huu Do's later publications on the historical dialectic and capitalist imperialism.

6. LT-2, pp. 168–69.

meet new conditions, whether this be a raging flood, a civil war, or a foreign invasion. Beyond that, there was a messianic thread in popular Vietnamese thinking which sanctioned heroic, altruistic behavior in certain circumstances. A man (or woman) who understood this tradition might be able quickly to mobilize thousands of peasants armed with bamboo spears, staves, and knives.

As for the Confucian elite, they were fascinated with the problem of reconciling observable change with harmonious existence. They found the classic *Book of Changes (Dich Kinh;* in Chinese, *I Ching)* useful for explaining dynamic flux and cyclical movements in the universe—and it even suggested a periodic need for dynastic revolution. Confucian philosophy had retained to the nineteenth century a contradiction between acceptance of evil in nature and optimistic expectations of promoting rectitude and harmony. The latter position had occasionally led Vietnamese literati to challenge the existing state apparatus by means of a "righteous uprising" *(khoi nghia).* To have any hope of winning, such a scholar-rebel would have to convince Vietnamese peasants that his grasp of reality was superior to that of the incumbent ruler, and that the world after rebellion would be far better than anything previously experienced. Many "righteous uprisings" occurred; very few were successful.[7]

Vietnamese rulers possessed in practice an ingenious, reasonably flexible ideology to both "explain" nature deductively and promote social order. Their buttresses were two additional classical Chinese texts, *Ta Hsüeh* (Vietnamese *Dai Hoc)* [The Great Learning] and *Chung Yung* (Vietnamese *Trung Dung)* [The Doctrine of the Mean], which emphasized that man's special task was to relate the world of day-to-day subjective phenomena to a larger, essentially predetermined reality. For the elite, this meant both studying the words of the sages and quietly meditating on the "inner principle of things"; for the masses, it meant internalizing a host of prescriptive maxims and social formalities (see chapter 2). Hovering above everyone and accessible only to the rarest and most superior of men was the Way *(Dao; Tao),* an immutable norm, an objective principle transcending all diversions, all vicissitudes of life. The Doctrine of the Mean, with its summary of the intimate relationship between self-cultivation, ethics, and metaphysics, also provided convenient points of contact with Taoist naturalism and Buddhist psychology. Sung Neo-Confucianism made that linkage more explicit.

A nineteenth-century Vietnamese could be forgiven, therefore, for failing generally to discriminate the Confucian "mean" from the Taoist principle of "nonaction" *(vo vi; wu wei),* or the Buddhist idea of compassion from Mo-tzu's idea of

---

7. An excellent example of a nineteenth-century literatus who refused to accept the status quo was Cao Ba Quat (1809–54), killed attempting to mount an uprising against the Nguyen dynasty. Because he left behind such a wealth of poetry it is possible assess his attitudes and motivations rather carefully. See Vu Khieu, ed., *Tho Chu Han Cao Ba Quat* [The Chinese Poems of Cao Ba Quat] (Hanoi, 1976).

universal love. He simply believed that imbalance was normally to be avoided, as it meant man against man, man against nature, in either case a separation between the self and the "other." Besides, *yin-yang* (Vietnamese *am-duong*) doctrine suggested that an excess of anything might well lead to its opposite. Although there might be certain times when it was necessary to employ one's moral powers recklessly, to use physical force to the utmost, to die a righteous death rather than suffer dishonor (after all, even the Doctrine of the Mean spoke of the superior man being firm in his energy, "standing erect in the middle without inclining to either side"[8]) behind every turbulent initiative stood the conviction that harmony was being served, that the "natural" balance would soon be restored for the good of all concerned. To risk a modern metaphor, it was as though the universe were fitted out with a benign gyroscope upon which all things animate and inanimate could depend for final guidance. The idea that nature and human society were perpetually unharmonious or that the most zealous, ruthless, and competitive would inherit the earth was quite repulsive.

The World Askew

Harmony received a severe blow in the period of French conquest. The world seemed out of joint, the gyroscope off its pivot. Crude barbarians and fawning Vietnamese were taking control, with no sign that a proper mean, an ethical balance was ever to be regained. At most one could satisfy one's own conscience, and perhaps posterity, by fighting and dying in protest. More likely one searched desperately for an inner harmony which could be cultivated apart from the seemingly evil and disorienting outer world. New interest was shown in Buddhism and Taoism. Individual mystics appeared in many localities, offering syncretic roads to salvation. However, centuries of Confucian dominance had made their mark. With no church institution or spiritual hierarchy separate from the state, quietism and mysticism remained largely private alternatives, or at best, regional phenomena, never spawning a national movement.

By the first decade of the twentieth century it was apparent that some literati were prepared to downgrade the idea of cosmic-social sympathy in favor of the Western-derived concepts of bitter struggle and linear progress. This proved to be yet another blow to harmony, although at the time the colonial authorities limited the impact by punishing the literati proponents, by curtailing circulation of Chinese publications, and by offering their own version of Western science and philosophy. Besides, even the most brilliant literati participants in the Dong Kinh Nghia Thuc educational effort were unaware of the full political and social implications of these new ideas. When they eventually understood, not a few recoiled in shock and sought less disruptive solutions.

The colonial authorities were not averse to Vietnamese assimilating ideas of

8. James Legge, trans., *The Four Books* (New York: Paragon Books Reprint, 1966), p. 359.

struggle and progress, providing it was understood that the French were far ahead and thus deserved to rule. As early as 1886 the French Resident-General, Paul Bert, instructed a prominent Vietnamese collaborator in the historical dialectic as seen by a confirmed imperialist:

If, 400 years before Christ, when our ancestors were subsisting on fruits, and when Confucius was writing the *Book of History*, a Chinese fleet had invaded our shores, bringing to these rude tribes an already refined civilization, advanced arts and sciences, a strongly organized social hierarchy, and an admirable moral code, Chinese influence would have implanted itself legitimately and would have been dominant for a period that no one can imagine. Now today a reverse phenomenon has come about.... Now the eternal law of history has intervened. In our turn, we arrive with our fleets, our equipment both pacific and warlike, and we legitimately acquire our commanding influence.... This will not last, I am sure, but it is a necessary stage: Annam cannot escape this fatality.[9]

Paul Bert went on to claim that among Western imperialists the French were the most flexible and benevolent and had the most affection for the vanquished. He insisted that a true Vietnamese patriot would seek to utilize this fortunate accident, rather than "running into the brush [and] exciting poor peasants to get themselves killed and ruined."[10]

Paul Bert's argument had a frankness bred of complete confidence. Several decades later, however, the French were not nearly so sure that history was going their way. Some went as far as encouraging the Vietnamese to abandon thoughts of struggle, to return to ideals of harmony and order that had served them well in pre-colonial times and let France bear the burden of defending Indochina from contemporary predators.[11] Others reaffirmed the necessity for Vietnamese to struggle, but not physically. Pure Science was the key to success, one colonial administrator emphasized.[12] Since the Renaissance, he argued, the West had be-

9. The full translation of this letter from Paul Bert to Truong Vinh Ky is reprinted in John De Francis, *Colonialism and Language Policy in Viet-Nam* (The Hague: Mouton, 1977), pp. 119–21. The French original is contained in Joseph Chailley, *Paul Bert au Tonkin* (Paris: Charpentier, 1887), pp. 325–29.

10. John DeFrancis, *Colonialism and Language*, p. 121.

11. See, for example, Pierre Pasquier, *L'Annam d'autrefois* (Paris: Challamel, 1907). During his later tenure as governor-general of Indochina (1928–34), the author worked hard to revive interest in traditional concepts of social harmony and order. While not particularly successful among Vietnamese intellectuals, Pasquier did convince some foreign observers that France had found a solution to colonial strife and turmoil. Thus, one well-known world traveler began his account by claiming that "between the India of unrest and stormy China is an oasis of peace and beauty—French Indo-China" (Maynard Owen Williams, "By Motor Trail Across French Indo-China," *National Geographic* [Oct. 1935], p. 487).

12. E. Vayrac, "Bai hoc cua Rabelais: Nguoi An-Nam lam the nao doi moi duoc van minh cua minh" [The Lesson of Rabelais: How Annamites Can Change Their Civilization], NP 140 (July 1929), pp. 1–25. Trans. Pham Quynh.

come "Lord of the World" because it focused on developing intellect and human virtue far above other peoples. Although most of the contemporary world was suffering from the actions of insane people, dreamers, social inferiors, and professional agitators run amok, the French could help the Vietnamese to rise above all that by means of the study and application of Science. Indeed, nationalities that did not learn Science were doomed. "Being the fittest or being exterminated: the Universe has only these two roads. That is natural law," the administrator warned.[13] Nevertheless, he added, it was very important not to try to jump into areas one did not comprehend or try to force reality in one's own direction. To be victorious over nature, he said, it was essential to follow nature's laws, which included the principle that everything advanced one step at a time, never in leaps and bounds.

Vietnamese collaborators endorsed such arguments at every opportunity. For them, French modernity not only explained the original imperialist attacks and Vietnamese loss of sovereignty, but also justified continued French protection and tutelage. Vietnam was obviously weak, underdeveloped, and vulnerable. If the French departed, Vietnam would simply be attacked and devoured again. Up until 1918 the German Kaiser was seen to be the main threat. After 1918 matters became rather more complicated, with Japanese imperialists, Chinese warlords and revolutionaries, Russian Bolsheviks, and Wilsonian self-determinists being cited as menaces. Vietnamese were still told to be thankful that it was the "humanistic" French who had colonized them and not one of the more rapacious breeds. Even if one chose to dispute French humanism, was it not better to have the whole Vietnamese family under one master rather than be divided up forcibly and parcelled out as servants to many different masters?[14]

Most Vietnamese collaborators wanted to believe that France offered not only protection but progress. *Nam Phong*'s original editorial prospectus in 1917, for example, stressed that France had undertaken to teach Vietnam the "difficult craft of being a nation in this world of survival of the fittest (*canh tranh sinh ton*.)"[15] Morality primers of the 1920s repeated that theme often. Thus, the famous poet Tan Da instructed eight-year-old children that, even though it was inevitable in this world of harsh competition that stronger races would put weaker ones "into their pouch," Vietnamese ought to be grateful to France for letting them advance on the long road to civilization.[16] Nguyen Trieu Luat suggested that if the Vietnamese studied long and hard they could someday reach the level of French men and women and be "let loose." Until that day, however,

---

13. Ibid., p. 9.

14. Phan Dinh Long, *Cay Kim Chi Nam* (Saigon, 1928), pp. 14–17.

15. NP 1 (July 1917), pp. 1–7.

16. Tan Da (Nguyen Khac Hieu), *Len Tam*, 5th printing (Hanoi, 1926). By 1935 at least 20,000 copies of this primer had been published.

all talk of independence was "insane."[17] Occasionally authors adopted a curious racist posture, arguing that whereas the black, brown, and red races were known to be "stupid and lazy," the white and yellow races were very clever.[18] Presumably, white and yellow races working together were unbeatable. As late as 1942, Vietnamese readers were being encouraged to demonstrate gratitude for being able to "take cover under the Tricolor's shadow" while learning how to survive amidst the great powers.[19] By that time, however, such words must have rung hollow to even the most devoted collaborator. Not only had the Depression undercut his economic status and the French government refused him significant political gains, but now the French Third Republic itself had been extinguished by the Germans, the Indochina authorities subordinated to the Japanese. The French obviously were having difficulty proving their own ability to survive, much less to protect and nurture others.

Struggle as a National Norm

Social Darwinism reached far beyond apologies for French colonial rule. It was used to explain almost any phenomenon, from Vietnamese ability to adapt clothing to tropical conditions,[20] to the need to abandon name taboos in the Vietnamese language.[21] Businessmen justified their competitive practices, authors defended literary fashions, students crammed for examinations, all in the name of survival of the fittest. Inevitably there was doctrinal confusion. Thus, Vietnamese women were urged simultaneously to produce more children, to back up their husbands, to criticize men, to abandon slavish attitudes, to take part in sports, and to be more aggressive—in each case with Social Darwinian justifications.[22] There were also clear differences on where to draw the doctrinal line. On matters of education, for example, Tran Trong Kim, although agreeing that Vietnam had to assimilate Western knowledge in order to survive, still argued that the elite must not stoop to crass struggle or it would never be able to sustain the respect of the lower classes.[23] By contrast, Vu Dinh Hoe defined the problem in broader terms:

The object of education is not to satisfy man's fondness for knowledge. Rather, education should forge individuals into components possessing sufficient means to act, to struggle externally and internally, and thus to live. Knowing how to live vigorously, in both the

17. Nguyen Trieu Luat, *40 Bai Quoc Su* [Forty National History Lessons] (Hanoi, 1926), pp. 102–103.

18. Nguyen Van Hung, *Dong Au Tu Tri* (Hanoi, 1930 [?]), lesson 19.

19. Viet Bao, *Phap Viet Phuc Hung Ca* (Hanoi[?], 1942), p. 13.

20. Tri Duc Hoc Xa, *Loi Hoa* [Flowery Words] (Nam Dinh, 1934), pp. 161–62.

21. Phan Khoi, "Tuc Kieng Ten," PNTV 90 (9 July 1931), p. 8.

22. PNTV 26 (24 Oct. 1929), 60 (10 July 1930), 92 (23 July 1931), 93 (30 July 1931), and 194 (6 Apr. 1933). Bui Vo Lo, *Van De Phu Nu Giai Phong* [The Question of Women's Liberation] (Saigon, 1932), pp. 16–18.

23. Tran Trong Kim, *Nho Giao*, vol. 1, pp. xiv–xv.

material and spiritual sense, such individuals would be of benefit to themselves and to the group.[24]

This was precisely the sort of argument that caused Vietnamese traditionalists great anguish. Europeans did indeed teach their children that "life is a battlefield," Tran Van Tang admitted. Yet it had brought them only religious strife, class antagonism, the mad scramble for colonies and, most recently, the obscene carnage of the Great War. People, money, machines—even art and aesthetics— were put at the service of struggle. Although Europeans engaged in frantic quests for new philosophies from Catholicism to Protestantism, from spiritualism to humanism, from monarchism to democracy to communist utopianism, no one was able to prove real progress. In truth, because people were increasingly transfixed by external knowledge (tri) and personal advantage (loi), thus tending to ignore the inner spirit (tam), the empathy which distinguishes mankind from animals, there was simply more exultation of evil, more dissatisfaction with one's station in life, more social disorder (loan).[25]

While many Vietnamese intellectuals sympathized with Tran Van Tang's anguish, they saw very little in reality to suggest that the meek would inherit the earth. Few would have denied Dao Duy Anh's assertion that because of new objective conditions the "non-action" of the Lao-tzu and the Doctrine of the Mean of Confucius, the "pacifism" (phi chien) of Mo-Tzu, and the "compassion" (tu bi) of Sakyamuni were all wild and woolly dreams that had to give way to attitudes of resolute, enthusiastic struggle.[26] Another author summed up the feelings of his generation even more cogently:

Life is not the endurance of suffering but resistance to it, not enjoyment of quietude but active involvement, not acceptance of the present but the constant search for a better future.... Life is a fierce war. To try to escape is the same as a soldier deserting the battlefield.[27]

What made such a grim vision bearable, of course, was the assumption that the future would be better than the present—in short, the idea of linear progress. Even Vietnamese traditionalists could be found stumbling into endorsements of

24. Vu Dinh Hoe, Nhung Phuong Phap Giao Duc o cac Nuoc va Van De Cai Cach Giao Duc (Hanoi, 1945), pp. 107-108.

25. Tran Van Tang, "Qua Khu va Hien Tai," NP 106 (June 1926), pp. 413-33.

26. Dao Duy Anh, Viet-Nam Van Hoa Su Cuong (Saigon, 1951), p. 327; see also Ngo Tat To and Nguyen Duc Tinh, Lao Tu (Hanoi, 1942), pp. 114-23, particularly their criticism of Taoist "non-action" as opposing not only struggle but also the laws which regulate struggle; they argue that such ideas would lead Vietnamese back to a primitive existence no better than that of the Eskimos, the aborigines, or the "savages" of the central highlands of Vietnam.

27. Do Duc Vuong, May Thuyet ve Luan Ly (Hanoi, 1936), p. 7.

the "law of natural progress" (*le tien hoa tu nhien*),[28] although it was more consistent for them to reassert Chuang-tzu's concept of the "circular void" (*vong oc*), with its provision for flux and cycles, and to deny that Darwin had proven anything other than that there was biological adaptation among obscure flora and fauna.[29]

It is important to realize that Social Darwinism as perceived in Vietnam was quite different from either the teachings of Herbert Spencer or subsequent popularizations in Europe and America. In large part this was because of the screening influence of Chinese writers, particularly Liang Ch-i-ch'ao and Yen Fu.[30] For the generation of Phan Boi Chau and Phan Chu Trinh, even when it denounced tradition or endorsed Western ideas, Chinese formulations still seemed vaguely superior and certainly more comprehensible. Younger Vietnamese had much less cultural deference for things Chinese, but they appreciated that both countries shared the same basic aspirations for independence and freedom in a world dominated by imperialism. Social Darwinism as reinterpreted by Liang Ch'i-ch'ao and Yen Fu appeared on the one hand to explain the tremendous explosion of Western collective energy and on the other to offer a scheme whereby both China and Vietnam might be transformed to survive the onslaught and eventually become powerful and prosperous in their own right.

Herbert Spencer's grand biological metaphor for human society, with its stress on assertiveness, organic group interrelationships, and the actualization of potentialities within competitive conditions, seemed to explain a great deal for Chinese and Vietnamese alike. By contrast, they either ignored or downgraded Spencer's emphasis on the efficacy of liberalism, particularly with regard to individual liberties and laissez-faire economics; they dismissed Spencer's suggestion that nationalism was outmoded, that the "militant" stage of evolution characterized by wars and brute coercion was giving way progressively to an "industrial stage" characterized by healthy economic competition.[31] Vietnamese readers of the

28. See, for example, Nguyen Gy, *Long Nguyen Vong cua Quoc Dan Viet Nam* (Hanoi, 1933 [?]), pp. 1–2. Pham Quynh at one point agreed that the doctrine of natural selection seemed to imply that the French language would inevitably replace Vietnamese. He resolved this dilemma by telling his compatriots to put "sentiment" ahead of "personal advantage" and uphold Vietnamese rather than French. NP 22 (Apr. 1919), pp. 285–86.

29. Chang Hung-chao, "Hoc Thuyet Tay voi Hoc Thuyet Tau: Darwin va Trang Tu," NP 87 (Sept. 1924), pp. 216–26. This is a translation by Pham Quynh of a contemporary Chinese article.

30. For an earlier discussion of this question, see David G. Marr, *Vietnamese Anticolonialism, 1885–1925* (Berkeley: Univ. of Calif. Press, 1971), particularly pp. 100–101, 114–19, 173–75, and 227–28.

31. For the Chinese case, see Hao Chang, *Liang Ch'i-ch'ao and Intellectual Transition in China, 1890–1907* (Cambridge, 1971); and Benjamin Schwartz, *In Search of Wealth and Power: Yen Fu and the West* (Cambridge: Harvard, 1969).

1920s, of course, could look to the terrible bloodletting of World War I for confirmation of Spencer's error.

How could Vietnam under the colonial yoke produce dynamic, assertive citizens? In the first instance, Vietnamese would have to jettison a number of beliefs and customs long regarded as true or sacred, but now seen as contributing to their degradation and their inability to regain independence. Thus, Tran Huu Do chose to attack gerontocracy, the willingness of sons to submit to fathers, Buddhist-Taoist quietude, faith-healing, and fortune-telling.[32] He devoted twelve pages to exposing the "perils of premature marriage," arguing that it hindered education, perpetuated bad health and hygienic practices, and reduced work output. Besides, he claimed, there was a positive statistical correlation between late marriage and advanced civilization.[33] Tran Huu Do was especially concerned to legitimize the martial arts, which for him meant condemning the orthodox Confucian inclination to regard any threat to the body as unfilial, as an unwarranted jeopardizing of family property. Ingrained timidity thus led elders to continue to utter such phrases as, "Let the other's spittle dry on your face," or "take a step backward to make it easier on yourself." If young Vietnamese followed that advice, Tran Huu Do warned, then they deserved enslavement. Rather, they should accept the necessity of spilling blood for national independence, and get on with the struggle.[34]

Members of the new intelligentsia could be even more stinging than Tran Huu Do. Tran Huy Lieu, for example, recalled painfully the words of an unnamed Frenchman: "Only when Annamese dogs are finished eating [French] shit will the Annamese people be done with wanting to be slaves."[35] Specifically, those of his generation who were lured by talk of Franco-Vietnamese cooperation had to come to their senses and understand that what was being proposed was "cooperation" between an emaciated, sweating Vietnamese rickshaw driver and his fat, cigar-puffing colonial passenger, or between a painted native prostitute and her long-nosed, curly-haired foreign paramour. Nor was it enough, Tran Huy Lieu emphasized, for Vietnamese to indulge themselves in bitter ethical condemnations of the French and then plead inability to act:

It is the way of the great powers for the strong to oppress the weak, the clever to oppress the ignorant. It is the way of the oppressed nations to make themselves indepen-

---

32. Tran Huu Do, *Thanh Nien Tu Doc*, vol. 2 (Saigon, 1928), pp. 64, 67; idem, *To Co Mat Quyen Tu Do* (Saigon, 1926), pp. 23-24, 48-49; idem, *Hoi Trong Tu Do*, vol. 3 (Saigon, 1926), p. 16.

33. Tran Huu Do, *Thanh Nien Tu Doc*, vol. 2, pp. 90-101. Apparently this argument was condensed and adapted from an essay by Liang Ch'i-ch'ao.

34. Tran Huu Do, *To Co Mat Quyen Tu Do*, pp. 20-23.

35. Tran Huy Lieu, *Mot Bau Tam Su* (Saigon, 1927), pp. 34-35.

dent and powerful. We know now the causes of our nation's loss, so what do we plan to do about it?[36]

In suggesting that weak, ignorant, and oppressed nations could somehow turn the tables on the strong, clever imperialists, Tran Huy Lieu was obviously going beyond Herbert Spencer. Probably this stemmed from his enthusiastic reading about heroes of victorious national liberation struggles, for example, Washington in America, Garibaldi in Italy, and Pilsudski in Poland (see chapter 6). It may also have reflected popular millenarian beliefs inside Vietnam. Whatever the origins, from the late 1920s onward it was an article of faith among the Vietnamese intelligentsia that effort is determined by its challenge, that the greater the opposition the harder people will struggle to overcome it. The image of river water pushing harder against dikes the higher they are raised was often invoked. At some point in time a break was inevitable.[37] Vietnamese traditionalists used the same metaphor, but for a different purpose, suggesting that it was wisest to divert some of the water upstream rather than try to keep building the dikes higher and higher.[38] All seemed to agree, nevertheless, that adversity tempers men and helps make them great.[39]

Looking to their own past, Vietnamese saw some grounds for optimism. Had not the Viet people managed to avoid assimilation during a millennium of Chinese rule? Had not Vietnam mounted its own march to the south, in the process eliminating the kingdom of Champa and wresting the lower Mekong delta away from the Cambodians?[40] Some authors went further, picturing Cambodia and Laos as traditional Vietnamese vassals and even arguing that Siam and Burma

---

36. Ibid., p. 19. Tran Huy Lieu and a small group of friends also translated or interpreted in print some of Liang Ch'i-ch'ao's writings, explained the democratic republicanism of Sun Yat-sen, Huang Hsing, and Ts'ai Ao, and formulated their own tentative response to current Vietnamese conditions. Their publications often appeared in Saigon under the Cuong Hoc Thu Xa (Power Study Library) label.

37. It is interesting to compare this Vietnamese metaphor with that of Mao Tse-tung on the strength of a river increasing as mountains push in and constrict its flow. See Frederic Wakeman, Jr., *History and Will: Philosophical Perspectives of Mao Tse-tung's Thought* (Berkeley: Univ. of Calif. Press, 1973), pp. 202–203.

38. NP 35 (May 1920), pp. 408F–408G. Trinh Dinh Ru employed the metaphor in yet a third way, arguing that Vietnamese men and women should work together to raise up the dikes against contemporary perils, but to do this only when the current was not too strong. PNTV 12 (18 July 1929), pp. 5–6.

39. *Tri Tan* 1 (3 June 1941). PNTV 257 (6 Sept. 1934) has a particularly striking article on Fridtjof Nansen's epic three-year struggle with polar ice.

40. Ngo Van Trien, *Lich Su Nam Tien cua Dan Toc ta* [History of the Southward Advance of Our People] (Hanoi, 1929); Lieu Thanh Ban, *Ly Thai Ton: Binh Chiem Thanh* [Ly Thai Ton: Pacifying Champa] (Saigon, 1930); PNTV 36 (9 Jan. 1930), p. 6; NP 8 (Feb. 1918), pp. 61–62.

had once been tributaries.[41] Partly as a result of these numerous struggles with their neighbors—and long before arrival of modern nationalist ideology, it was pointed out—the Vietnamese developed a central state apparatus and a strong sense of patriotism. In short, by almost all the accepted criteria—ethnicity, language, history, culture, religion, customs, political system, and legal tradition— Vietnam could be considered to have become a nation well prior to French colonization.[42] If the Viet people had not evolved successfully in this way, one writer concluded, they would still be "eating ashes and groping for rice husks" in the jungle, merely another small tribe like the Meo, Muong, Man, or Moi.[43]

Nevertheless, such past accomplishments had not counted for much when facing the French. The disaster was even more striking if one contrasted Vietnam and Siam. One writer remarked ruefully that the former had slid from freedom to servitude, whereas the latter had risen from tributary status to being an independent state recognized throughout the world.[44] Clearly Vietnam still had to unlock and apply some important secrets of modern national power if it were ever to reverse its fortunes. Above all, most writers affirmed, the Vietnamese people would need to unite, assert their vital energies, rid themselves of feelings of passivity or fear, and employ the "laws" of natural selection and survival of the fittest to national advantage. "Nature red in tooth and claw" would have to be faced and overcome.

Intragroup Conflict

As mentioned above, Herbert Spencer was not particularly interested in competition between nations. Broadly speaking, he held that successful competition between individuals of the human species and between their various economic subgroupings was the key to human evolution. Although Chinese and Vietnamese interpreters of Social Darwinism might downgrade discussion of competition inside their respective countries, they could not ignore it entirely. The younger the Vietnamese writer, the more likely he was to tackle this problem head-on. Tran Huu Do, reflecting older preferences, focused almost exclusively on struggle directed at those outside the group (i.e., the colonialists) rather than struggle between group members. He never gave his opinion on whether that significant component of the population who actively served the *di chung*, the French aliens, was objectively a part of the enemy camp and thus to be struggled against, or perhaps was capable of reform and redemption. Instead, he recalled

---

41. Tran Huy Lieu, *Mot Bau Tam Su*, p. 19; Duong Ba Trac, *Tieng Goi Dan* (Hanoi, 1925), pp. 5, 24.

42. Pham Quynh, "Doc Sach co Cam," NP 149 (Apr. 1930), p. 307.

43. Duong Ba Trac, *Tieng Goi Dan*, p. 7. The author's term for "evolution" (*thien dien*) was the same as that used by Yen Fu. Most writers preferred *bien hoa*.

44. Phan Dinh Long, *Cay Kim Chi Nam*, p. 17.

the Vietnamese (and South Chinese) folktale of the stork and the giant clam, each of whom was trying to eat the other. The stork got his sharp beak inside, but was pinned before he could paralyze the clam. Neither animal would give an inch, and as a result a fisherman came along and seized them both for dinner. In the same manner, Vietnamese "storks" and "clams" had made it all too easy for the French "fisherman."[45]

On the other hand, Tran Huy Lieu, sixteen years Tran Huu Do's junior, was much less reticent about condemning Vietnamese collaborators. Perhaps because he and many of his young intelligentsia colleagues initially had put so much faith in the ability of the nascent Vietnamese bourgeoisie to challenge the French, Tran Huy Lieu concentrated his fire on Bui Quang Chieu and the Constitutionalist Party. He accused the Constitutionalists of false nationalism, of employing patriotic rhetoric as a smokescreen, and of occasionally supporting popular issues that would not enrage the French colonial authorities but avoiding risky, important issues like the plague.[46] Meanwhile, far to the north in Hanoi, other young writers were starting to heap scorn on those Vietnamese who glorified resistance to the Chinese or confrontations with the Cham, Khmer, and Siamese but refused to apply these lessons to the French. In the wake of this criticism more than a thousand clerks, primary school teachers, colonial army personnel, and village functionaries were recruited to the clandestine Vietnam Nationalist Party (Viet Nam Quoc Dan Dang). With little idea of what they wanted to do other than to lash out at the colonialists, and perhaps to support Sun Yat-sen's "Three Principles of the People," Nationalist leaders lost their sense of direction in the face of ruthless Sûreté counteraction.[47] Although survivors were unable to rebuild the party structure, a sharp line had been drawn once again between the sunshine patriots and those prepared to risk everything in the struggle for independence.

Only among the Vietnamese bourgeoisie was there an occasional attempt to apply Social Darwinism to questions of individual status. Thus, in a delightful full-page advertisement inside the front cover of a political tract, a Vietnamese prosthodontist explained how he had seen the need for a medicine to alleviate tooth pains and gum inflammation. By employing the philosophy that "in my work, if you want to live you must struggle, and keep struggling until you have achieved your objective victoriously," our friend had managed to become sole agent for the appropriate medicine.[48] The organ of the Constitutionalist Party,

45. Tran Huu Do, Hoi Trong Tu Do, vol. 3, p. 4.

46. Tran Huy Lieu, Mot Bau Tam Su, pp. 35–39.

47. Significant publications by this group include Nhuong Tong, Dan Toc Chu Nghia [Nationalism] (Hanoi, 1927); Dat Cong and Mong Tien, Guong Thieu Nien [Young Paragons] (Hanoi, 1927); and a translation from Sun Yat-sen's writings, entitled Dan Sinh Chu Nghia [People's Livelihood] (Hanoi, 1928).

48. Van Dau, Chanh Tri Nguyen An Ninh [Nguyen An Ninh's Politics] (Saigon, 1937). See also the advertisement by a large trading company in Cuu Kim Son and Van Hue, Chi Em Phai Lam

after denying the existence of social classes in Vietnam, proceeded to claim that "the landlord is most often at bottom only a tenant who has succeeded, as the mandarin is only the son of a peasant who has passed the literary examinations."[49] Yet another Saigon man of means broadened the argument, saying that "one must have poor people and rich people if there is to be struggle to achieve happiness." The poor should realize, he added, that the rich had endured considerable privation and overcome many obstacles to reach their current position.[50]

The majority of Vietnamese intellectuals were deeply troubled by such logic. It was one thing to acknowledge that international politics functioned according to the principle that "the strong wins; the weak loses" (manh duoc yeu thua), quite another to apply the same principle to domestic relations. The image of everyone clawing at each other to gain precedence in society was still offensive; yet, how could a "scientific law" be true at one level of human activity and not at another? That Charles Darwin had neither used the term "survival of the fittest" nor applied his theory of natural selection to human social organization was not widely known in Vietnam.[51] Some of the most well-read intellectuals thus put themselves in conflicting positions. Tran Trong Kim, after citing scientific research on the blue fly, reluctantly accepted the idea that all living beings were involved perpetually in struggle and natural selection. Nonetheless, he criticized "science" for increasing people's sensual expectations, for helping the strong get stronger, and hence for heightening conflict within society.[52] Many authors explained the success or failure of particular organizations inside Vietnam in more-or-less Machiavellian fashion, yet bemoaned the decline of Confucian morality instruction. Le Du, for example, upheld the violent overthrow of the Le dynasty by the Tay Son with the assertion that "society is nobody's special property; he who is strong and vigorous is its master."[53] On many other occasions, however, Le Du voiced fears of moral decay and preached contemporary social harmony.

Great Harmony

There was an alternative tradition in Vietnam, to which disadvantaged people in particular often looked for guidance. This tradition drew selectively from Buddhism, Taoism, animism, faith-healing, and Neo-Confucian morality (especially the principle of righteousness). Often the catalyst was an individual monk, her-

Gi? (Hanoi, 1938), p. 70, offering specialized assistance to small merchants so that they would not be ruined in this period of "survival of the fittest and the strong defeating the weak."

49. La Tribune Indochinoise (Saigon), 10 Aug. 1931.

50. K. B. Nhon, Gia Dinh Dam Am va Hanh Phuc (Saigon, 1936), pp. 13, 18.

51. Apparently the first Vietnamese study of Charles Darwin and his theories did not appear until 1944, when Nguyen Dinh Thi published the book Dac-uyn [Darwin] under the auspices of the Hoi Van Hoa Cuu Quoc. Unfortunately, I have been unable to locate a copy.

52. Tran Trong Kim, Quan Niem ve cuoc Nhan Sinh (Hanoi, 1936), pp. 8-9, 12,16.

53. So Cuong (Le Du), "Lich Su Doi Tay Son," NP 97 (July 1925), p. 27.

mit, spirit medium, or medical practitioner. Although philosophical content varied widely from one place to another, most believers looked to a magic future of "great harmony" (*dai dong*) in which all wrongs would be righted and everyone would live in peace, brotherhood, abundance, and beauty. The orthodox Confucian establishment in Vietnam found this tradition objectionable and potentially treasonous. Official response varied, however, from execution of adepts to uneasy endorsement of local spirits. Vietnamese villagers in general tended to accept the ideological supremacy of Confucianism when the state was well run (that is to say, when major economic and military programs were being accomplished without too heavy a drain on local resources), but they were prone to recant in times of prolonged misfortune.

To the degree that French colonization was seen as a disaster by ordinary Vietnamese, it also dealt a blow to Confucianism and stimulated the resurgence of syncretic ideologies. More than that, the late nineteenth and early twentieth century witnessed the emergence (or reemergence) of scores of millenarian groups throughout Vietnam, offering exactly what the Nguyen dynasty was no longer capable of offering—solidarity, justice, and salvation. Generally, each group boasted a charismatic leader with mystical powers and possible imperial aspirations. There were elaborate oaths, rituals, and regalia, as well as colorful legitimizing myths linking the golden past to the glorious future. Some groups attempted to challenge local colonial authority and were dispersed or subdued. Others focused more on prayer, ceremony, and modest welfare benefits for members. Even the smallest and most innocuous group was kept under Sûreté observance, however.[54]

Confucian literati had been known to affiliate or cooperate with syncretic groups in the past. The collapse of armed resistance to the French made this all the more likely.[55] However, it was left to some retired colonial functionaries and wealthy landowners to establish the largest, most successful syncretic religious group of the twentieth century—the Cao Dai. Building on a highly eclectic tradition unique to the Mekong delta, and adding components from Western Catholicism and seance ritual, the Cao Dai religion was notable for its opulent ceremonies, intricate hierarchies, strong patron-client ties, intimate séances, and firm promises to restore morality on earth and harmony in the universe. From 1925 it captured the imagination of hundreds of thousands of southern Vietnamese farmers, tenants, and agricultural laborers. French administrators were not sure how to react. Some favored the Cao Dai as an alternative to more radical Vietnamese organizations, while others were concerned that the hierarchy

---

54. SPT-1, pp. 443–554; Georges Coulet, *Les Sociétés secrètes en Terre d'Annam* (Saigon: C. Ardin, 1926).

55. Phan Boi Chau, for example, sought out Buddhist and Taoist priests in southern Vietnam in 1904. Marr, *Vietnamese Anticolonialism*, pp. 103–105.

was not under sufficient colonial supervision. As it turned out, both opinions were correct. In Cochinchina (but not elsewhere) the Cao Dai became a viable conservative alternative to Marxism-Leninism. On the other hand, some Cao Dai leaders became increasingly disenchanted with French colonial policies and increasingly attracted to the Japanese.[56]

Although most Vietnamese intellectuals scorned Cao Dai pageantry and superstition, they were fascinated by its success at mobilizing the masses. Some Saigon intellectuals began dabbling in Cao Dai religious politics. A more characteristic response was to investigate the ideological roots of Vietnamese popular religion in general, with an eye to identifying and upgrading components considered suitable to modern conditions. Buddhism attracted by far the most attention, perhaps because it had an abundant and sophisticated philosophical corpus, unlike popular Taoism or the local spirit cults. Then, too, Vietnamese were aware of the Buddhist revival movement already underway in China, led by a monk named T'ai Hsü. A few Vietnamese monks traveled to China and returned with the intention of "revitalizing" (chan hung) or "actualizing" (hien dai hoa) Buddhism, making it more responsive to the contemporary needs of society. In 1925 and 1926 secular intellectuals were surprised to see groups of monks attending political meetings.[57]

It was not until 1934 that Buddhist associations were established in all three regions of Vietnam. The delay reflected a recurring dilemma for all those Vietnamese who wished to mobilize large numbers of people for particular purposes. If they went ahead without government approval, they might well recruit an enthusiastic following, but would then always be vulnerable to official harrassment or punishment. As we shall see below, one group led by Nguyen An Ninh did grow up rapidly in Cochinchina in the late 1920s without government sanction, and was thence branded a "secret society" and effectively repressed. The alternative, of course, was to apply for legal recognition by the colonial authorities, who would then carry out a meticulous investigation and generally withhold approval until satisfied that the project was harmless.[58] After the smash-

56. Jayne Werner, "The Cao Dai: The Politics of a Vietnamese Syncretic Religious Movement" (Ph.D. thesis, Cornell University, 1976), pp. 1–211.

57. Tien Lu Dong Tu, ed., Chan Hung Phat Giao [Revitalizing Buddhism] (Hanoi, 1927). See also Trinh Van Chan, "Buddhism and Politics in South Vietnam" (M.A. thesis, Howard University, March 1971), pp. 34–36.

58. The Tonkin Buddhist Association, for example, had its application rejected in 1933 but approved in 1934, apparently after the Sûreté became convinced that no "non-religious" activities were involved. Records indicate that it soon enrolled 20,000 members willing to pay dues of 1 piaster per year, 700 who paid 30 piasters, and 200 who paid 50 piasters. Association publications offer regular evidence of backing for both the French Protectorate and King Bao Dai. The French were especially pleased when the association publicly pledged loyalty at the outbreak of war in Europe in September 1939. AOM (Aix) G-G Indochine, series F-7F59.

Cover of a popular Buddhist text, the *Quan Am Dien Ca* [Verse Story of Kwannon], in this case edited by Huynh Tinh Cua. Courtesy of the Bibliothèque Nationale.

ing of Nguyen An Ninh's group, and especially after the nationwide violent upheavals of 1930–31, most intellectuals of Buddhist sympathy opted for legal recognition. Once recognized, lay members concentrated on printing and distributing *quoc ngu* scriptures and sermons as well as subsidizing new schools for monks and nuns. The clergy devoted its time to meditation, study, translation of Chinese-language texts, codification of monastic rules, and simplification of rites. Although professing a new, positive attitude to worldly needs, Buddhist associations appear to have lagged behind even the Catholic Church in terms of concrete social achievements.[59]

The closest that colonial Vietnam came to possessing a Buddhist mass movement was in 1939, with the appearance of the Hoa Hao. This mystical sect had its roots in the centuries-old sacred attraction of the Seven Mountains (That Son) which jut up from the Mekong plain between southern Vietnam and Cambodia. Its immediate origins, however, lay with the psychological transformation of Huynh Phu So (1919–47), the frail, haunted son of the chief of Hoa Hao village

59. SPT-2, pp. 229–39. Alexander B. Woodside, *Community and Revolution in Modern Vietnam* (Boston: Houghton Mifflin, 1976), pp. 192–200.

(Chau Doc province). Word of his visions, prophesies, and healing powers spread like wildfire through western Cochinchina. When in August 1940 he predicted the imminent humbling of the French by the Japanese, the Sûreté put Huynh Phu So in a psychiatric ward. His disciples simply considered this another worldly test of their heaven-inspired leader and stepped up proselytizing activities. In 1942 the Japanese liberated Huynh Phu So from the French as he was about to be banished to Laos. Thenceforth, from a Kenpeitai building in Saigon, Huynh Phu So disseminated prophesies of damnation for non-believers and independence for Vietnam. The French had to be content with striking at the "Mad Monk's" disciples in the countryside.[60] Unlike the Cao Dai, the Hoa Hao eschewed elaborate temples and complex hierarchies in favor of individual spiritual enlightenment and direct communion with the Almighty. Like the Cao Dai, however, the Hoa Hao tapped traditions specific to the Mekong delta and never tried hard to gain mass followings in central or northern Vietnam.

While Buddhist organizations remained of only limited national significance, Buddhist philosophy did command considerable attention among Vietnamese intellectuals. This was particularly true when debating the issue of social harmony versus social struggle.[61] If, as Buddhists argued, man perpetually creates his own wretched condition, is constantly the victim of his own cleverness, then he cannot expect to avoid misery by violent struggle, by cutthroat economic competition, or by any other appeal to selfish rewards. The only solution short of death or returning to the womb is to limit one's desires, support the oppressed, eliminate inequalities, and use the admitted benefits of modern science to build a better life for everyone. Although one Buddhist writer admitted that there was some risk of social chaos in preaching such a doctrine, given existing sharp disparities in wealth and privilege, he appealed to rich people to think from the perspective of the lower classes, and to recognize that any individual's day in the sun was limited. Misfortune would have to strike, if not in one's own life, then probably during the lives of one's children or grandchildren. Instead of constantly finding excuses to keep the lower classes deprived, rich people should accept the idea of a classless society producing abundance and happiness for all. A "fair and equal society" was man's ultimate means to escape suffering and turmoil.[62]

Although many elite Vietnamese found such a humanist vision satisfying, the individual who made the most serious attempt to test its practicality was Nguyen An Ninh (1900–43). Born to a prestigious literati family, trained in the best

60. A. M. Savani, *Notes sur le Phat Giao Hoa Hao* (Saigon[?], 1951), pp. 1–21. In September 1945 the Hoa Hao refused to accept ICP leadership of the anticolonial struggle and were soon making tacit arrangements with the French. The Viet Minh accused Huynh Phu So of treason and apparently executed him in 1947.

61. It was also true when debating scientific objectivity, a subject discussed in chapter 8.

62. Bui The My, *The Gioi Bat Binh* [A World of Inequality] (Saigon, 1928).

French schools, confidant in Paris of both Phan Chu Trinh and Ho Chi Minh, Nguyen An Ninh was for many the perfect model of the young patriotic intellectual. In the years 1923–26 he used his considerable gifts as a writer, editor, and public speaker to challenge the Cochinchina authorities and shame the Vietnamese bourgeoisie. Thrown into jail for his efforts, Nguyen An Ninh wrestled with the problem of how to reach a mass constituency. Already vaguely familiar with popular religious beliefs, he now earnestly began studying religion in general and Buddhism in particular. After release from jail and a brief visit to France, Nguyen An Ninh took up residence in a small village not far from Saigon, arranged his house in Buddhist fashion, shaved his head, wore the simple black pajamas characteristic of southern peasants, and began to bicycle around the countryside selling his own brand of medicinal ointment. A network of disciples quickly materialized, most of them expecting wondrous social and political solutions from their leader. Instead, Nguyen An Ninh was jailed again and hundreds of peasants rounded up for interrogation and possible trial.[63]

It is difficult to know to what degree Nguyen An Ninh was merely using popular religion as a political vehicle and to what degree he himself took Buddhist teachings seriously. Certainly he was not a true believer. Nevertheless, he was sincerely impressed by Buddhism's attention to human oppression, by its idealism, and by its psychological subtlety. Probably he saw himself engaged in a human experiment, trying to unite certain universal and particular beliefs so as to make them meaningful to Vietnamese intellectuals and peasants alike. By 1932 Nguyen An Ninh had moved away from Buddhism in favor of Marxism. Yet, Buddhism still seemed of sufficient importance to him five years later to occasion a book-length critique.[64]

What bothered Nguyen An Ninh almost from the beginning was alleged Buddhist quietude, a mental detachment that often led believers to accept evil without struggling against it. The proposition that individuals could effectively separate themselves from love, anger, pleasure, and beauty was already suspect. More importantly, it seemed wrong from a social viewpoint to counsel Vietnamese that it was better to endure evil than to employ violence or to risk bringing violence upon oneself.[65] In a system composed of "victors and vanquished, oppressors and oppressed, masters and slaves," passivity might mean suicide. The French seemed to want to shield the Vietnamese from the lessons of Prometheus stealing heaven's fire, of David slaying Goliath.[66] In short, it appeared essential to

63. Nguyen Dai Dao, *Ong Nguyen An Ninh Duoc Tha* [Mr. Nguyen An Ninh Has Been Released] (Saigon, 1927). Le Van Thu, *Hoi Kin Nguyen An Ninh* [Nguyen An Ninh's Secret Society] 2nd edition (Saigon, 1961), pp. 1–72. *Dien Tin* (Saigon) 944 (1 Sept. 1974).

64. *Phe Binh Phat Giao* [A Critique of Buddhism] (Saigon, 1937). SPT-2, pp. 241–42, 293–301.

65. *Hai Ba Trung* (Saigon, 1928), p. 40.

66. *La Cloche Fêlée* (Saigon), 19 May 1924. SPT-2, pp. 475–76.

"use strength to try to overcome suffering, to encourage friends to combine forces and struggle with life, thus building hope for subsequent generations."[67] Nguyen An Ninh broadened his criticism beyond Buddhism, accusing all major world religions of having run out of ethical steam, of dissipating their righteous anger in favor of insipid determinism and bland homilies, usually in support of the status quo. Like many of his contemporaries, Nguyen An Ninh was searching for a new public religion to reinvigorate the sense of human virtue, of moral legitimacy, of single-minded advancement of good and defeat of evil. And like many others, Nguyen An Ninh found some key answers in jail.

Prison

No experience more defined the nature of Vietnamese revolutionary leadership than prolonged detention in colonial prisons. Jails were to the Vietnamese what the Long March was to the Chinese. They were seen both as microcosms of colonial society and universities of revolutionary theory and practice. It was as if the French had purposefully designed laboratories to test their Vietnamese enemies' will to struggle. As one Communist activist told his parents just after getting out of jail in 1939, "It is the karma (kiep) of people who have lost their country either to be crushed underfoot like worms and crickets or to make a revolution that smashes the cangue and chains which imprison them."[68]

From another perspective, colonial jails in Indochina might be described as fulfilling a religious function. They forced a significant segment of the Vietnamese intelligentsia to withdraw from the world, endure privation, sort out their thoughts and attempt to master the self and external reality. In this sense, prisons were not unlike Zen monasteries, except that the acolytes were not there by choice and those in charge were seen not as teachers but as the enemy. A similar comparison might well be made with basic training camps devised by elite military units to disorient and then reprogram and remotivate young recruits. In neither case, however, would brutalization extend nearly as far as it did in colonial jails.

The first large contingent of political prisoners entered the system in 1929–31. Probably totaling about 10,000, these detainees were a far from homogeneous lot in terms of social origin, ideological inclination, or organizational affiliation. By almost all accounts, however, members of the fledgling Indochinese Communist Party took the initiative from 1930 in trying to devise techniques for not only withstanding life in prison but using the occasion to political advantage. Of course, if all of these people had been kept in prison indefinitely, their political impact on colonial society would have been minimal; however, some were let out

67. *Ton Giao* (Saigon, 1932), pp. 53–54.
68. Truong Sinh, in *Len Duong Thang Loi*, pp. 45–61.

after only a year or two of detention, and the vast majority had been released by the end of 1936. A second wave of political jailings occurred after the outbreak of war in Europe. This time, however, detainees had a better idea of what to expect, and there were plenty of hardened veterans to provide guidance to the neophytes. During World War II hundreds of political prisoners were either released or managed to escape. Those remaining behind bars were all liberated as part of the August 1945 Revolution.

A Vietnamese entering the colonial prison system for the first time found himself stunned, disoriented, degraded, and forced to look at humankind in a different light. If he entered jail with lingering visions of cosmic harmony, he soon became convinced that tension and conflict were the natural order of things. If the detainee was an intellectual, he discovered that certain of his most treasured attributes were worthless, whereas characteristics previously despised or ignored proved extremely valuable. Social class and formal education counted for little; ingenuity and resourcefulness counted for a great deal. Unlike lower-class prisoners, jail for an intellectual was probably the first time he learned whether or not he was capable of standing up under severe physical strain. Not surprisingly, some individuals accepted as leaders in the world at large were found wanting in prison, just as other individuals who had previously attracted no attention, and were perhaps unaware of their own potential, emerged as pillars of strength and masters of operational maneuver behind bars.

The story of colonial prisons was conveyed far beyond jail walls, both by word of mouth and in print. Probably the first detailed published account of jail experiences was that of Phan Van Hum, titled *Ngoi Tu Kham Lon* [Sitting in Saigon Central Prison].[69] Although incarcerated for only eleven weeks in late 1928, Phan Van Hum left no doubt in the reader's mind that his outlook had been altered permanently. He conveyed the shock of being stripped and searched, of being yelled at constantly and rapped on the head for the slightest error in prison procedure. Life was quickly reduced to the lowest common denominators: eating, sleeping, defecating, avoiding punishment, and attempting to deal with scabies, fever, and other ailments. Prisoners competed vigorously for an extra morsel of tough pork, for preference in the twice-weekly baths, for the least uncomfortable sleeping positions. They were known to kill each other over a few cigarettes. Trustees sold their souls to the authorities for the smallest privileges. Vietnamese guards, treated with obvious contempt by the French, Corsican, and Senegalese guards, vented their spleen on the inmates and extorted "protection"

---

69. *Ngoi Tu Kham Lon* (Saigon, 1929; 2nd edition, 1957). Originally serialized in January 1929 issues of *Than Chung* (Saigon). The author, a comrade of Nguyen An Ninh, had been arrested after an altercation with native colonial police in which, as he put it, he had rejected Christ's admonition to turn the other cheek.

money from prisoners' families. And above it all sat the chief warden, seemingly oblivious to the constant struggle below but in fact dependent on that struggle for his continued control.

Despite this grim picture, Phan Van Hum saw some cause for hope. Common criminals often shared their food, meager property, and hard-earned knowledge with new inmates. Although leaders were quick to resort to violence to maintain the pecking order, the system did have its own ethics. Special hatred was reserved for spies and informers. When exposed, they would be beaten severely, even if it meant that the perpetrators had to spend a month in solitary confinement as a result. Yet an informer who begged forgiveness was beaten much less severely, and certain human worms were not worth risking solitary confinement for. One of the latter, for example, was forced to prostrate himself in front of the fetid toilet and mock his paternal ancestors to the fourth generation.[70] Although Phan Van Hum was bothered by some of the other practices of prison gangs (which he felt owed more to romantic Chinese novels and dramas than to anything contemporary and vital), his main desire was to convince gang members and comrades outside that if they wanted to risk their lives it was better done in the service of high national ideals than to revenge a petty slight or to obtain another cigarette.

From a personal point of view, Phan Van Hum believed that his character had been subjected to a grueling test in jail and had been found vulnerable but not entirely unworthy. He admitted that in the early stages of incarceration he had been made to feel very ashamed of himself. He remained fearful of the repercussions for his family. However, he had eventually worked out responses that seemed appropriate, and he obviously hoped his readers and his family would agree. The essential problem, Phan Van Hum suggested, was to struggle to keep one's mind pure, upright, and alert while one's body was being defiled and broken. For external substantiation he cited Confucian teachings on how to become a sage, the Greek myth of Prometheus, Christ carrying his own cross to Calvary, *The Brothers Karamazov* by Dostoyevsky, the experience of a Vietnamese mystic jailed a decade earlier, and the contemporary example of Mahatma Gandhi.[71] His favorite metaphor was that of a circus acrobat walking a tightrope, tipping one way and then the other, but always seeking dynamic equilibrium.[72] Many

70. Ibid., pp. 96–100.

71. Ibid., pp. 43, 47, 144, 154. Two years later, Bui Cong Trung, a student jailed after returning from Moscow, had mental visions of Christ's torment prior to crucifixion, of himself observing several Vietnamese anticolonialists going to the guillotine in 1916, and of German communists who had befriended him in Europe being jailed and tortured. To sustain morale, he tried to recall everything his father and mother had taught him, carved a revolutionary star on the wall, whistled the "Internationale," created poetry, and caught bedbugs. Bui Cong Trung, "Phai Song" [We Must Live], in Bui Cong Trung and Truong Sinh et al., *Nguoi Truoc Nga Nguoi Sau Tien* (Hanoi, 1960), pp. 27–32.

72. Phan Van Hum, *Ngoi Tu Kham Lon*, p. 145.

Vietnamese were afraid to climb onto the tightrope of life, he said. Those who tried often lacked the proper attitude. Faced with unexpected challenges, they lost their balance and fell. Enough Vietnamese would have to master the art, however, or Vietnam would remain forever enslaved.

Phan Van Hum's 1929 book was followed by scores of other jail exposés. Content varied according to individual temperament, prison location, and current censorship guidelines.[73] Most shocking was *Nguc Kontum* [Kontum Prison], written by Le Van Hien, a Communist Party member arrested in Nghe An and transported to the central highlands in late 1930.[74] Along with 296 other detainees, mostly participants in the Nghe Tinh soviets, Le Van Hien was marched sixty kilometers to the mountains north of Kontum to construct a section of Colonial Route Fourteen. Six months later less than half that number of people stumbled back to Kontum, the rest having died of dysentery or malaria, been beaten to death by the montagnard guards, or been shot when unable to stand and walk. In December 1931, when the French tried to send some of the survivors plus new arrivals back to the construction site, prisoners mounted a demonstration and hunger strike. The French shot and killed fifteen prisoners, and were then able to truck two hundred others to the site. However, the strike and killings at least brought matters to the personal attention of the governor-general, resulting in a marked improvement in working and living conditions.

More importantly, Kontum taught survivors, and other Vietnamese who would listen, the suicidal implications of meek compliance. As the author pointed out more than once, most detainees were only too happy to get out of the jam-packed cells in Vinh, and they were mentally prepared to work hard as part of their proletarianization experience. Their first rude awakening came when the French lieutenant commanding the montagnard guards pulled out his pistol and shot a prisoner who collapsed while marching. After that the prisoners were terrorized and dehumanized in a hundred additional ways. Although individually they devised tricks to avoid beatings or to gain a few extra minutes' rest, collectively they were quite incapable of resistance. Only when back in Kontum Prison did the survivors have time and energy to assess the horrible episode, organize themselves and plot counteraction. When the confrontation came, individual spokesmen stepped forth in full consciousness of impending death, managed to utter a few words, and were shot down one after the other.[75]

---

73. Most of these accounts were put forth in periodicals, but I have located six published in book form. Jail exposés should be distinguished from prison poetry and from autobiographies written in prison, both of which have longer traditions in Vietnam.

74. *Nguc Kontum* (Tourane [Da Nang], 1938). *Le Travail* (Hanoi) in 1938 also serialized a French translation of *Nguc Kontum*.

75. One of those individuals was Truong Quang Trong, a former medical student in Hanoi. He was said to have kept his spirits up by wearing inside his shirt an embroidered vest given to him by his fiancée. Another leader killed was Dang Thai Thuyen, whose father, Dang Thai Than, a

Nevertheless, the ultimate test for a political prisoner was not to stand bare-handed in front of enemy rifles, but to face up to interrogation and possible torture. This test was generally a private one, and it demanded not merely physical courage but emotional control and mental agility. The prisoner's objective was to avoid divulging secrets, just as the interrogator's was to ferret them out. The fate of one's closest comrades, perhaps the very survival of the revolutionary structure, rested in the mind and body of one person undergoing incredible trauma. Some early prisoners tried to outfox the enemy by fabricating stories, but this only whetted the interrogator's appetite and led to many additional sessions.[76] Later, prisoners realized that the first problem was to ascertain what the enemy already knew and what he was looking for before admitting to anything.[77] Even the most masterful cover story was of little use without detailed, sustained corroboration from other detainees.[78] Eventually, one might admit to personal responsibility without involving any other activists—either that or one acted dumb, enduring torture if necessary, until the Sûreté gave up or death ended the contest. Some prisoners, fearing that the next torture session would cause them to break, committed suicide.[79]

The clash of wills between prisoners and jailers became the object of much discussion among Vietnamese revolutionaries. Not a few memoirs and short stories, some rather more credible than others, focused on this topic.[80] Often the issue was broadened beyond concrete problems of preserving clandestine networks or protecting one's fellow prisoners to attempting to shame the enemy, or at least to render him vulnerable in the eyes of other Vietnamese. Thus, a revolutionary who not only endured torture but somehow enraged or unnerved his torturer was likely to be immortalized. A fourteen-year-old female prisoner was urged not to cry or the enemy would not fear her.[81] Some authors claimed that successful tests of will with the enemy while in jail represented proof of communism's "objective progress" over other ideologies.[82] Others suggested a more rudi-

---

disciple of Phan Boi Chau, had also died violently after being trapped by a colonial patrol in 1909. See ibid., pp. 42–44; AOM A-50 (34), carton 24.

76. Phan Van Hum, *Ngoi Tu Kham Lon*, pp. 47, 56–57, 111, 133.

77. Luu Dong, *Buoc Dau Theo Dang* (Hanoi, 1961), pp. 34, 36–37, 50–51.

78. Van Tien Dung, in Le Thiet Hung et al., *Rung Yen The* (Hanoi, 1962), pp. 127–34, describes how his elaborate cover story was blown by a comrade who eventually broke under torture.

79. Ton Thi Que, *Chi Mot Con Duong* (Nghe An, 1972), p. 94. Ngo Vinh Long and Nguyen Hoi Chan, *Vietnamese Women in Society and Revolution* (Cambridge, Mass.: Vietnam Resource Center, 1974), pp. 183, 191–92, 204.

80. Vietnamese "jail literature" deserves detailed attention in its own right, and it might well lend itself to comparison with similar writings in other countries.

81. Ngo Vinh Long and Nguyen Hoi Chan, *Vietnamese Women*, pp. 153–56, 174, 179, 192.

82. See, for example, TCVH 2-1977, pp. 17–28.

mentary lesson: "As the enemy has made waste of us, we will make waste of them."[83] Whatever the validity of particular published accounts, there can be no doubt that any revolutionary who conducted previous activities to perfection but then faltered inside prison could never be given significant responsibility again, just as any average member who withstood all trials in prison was worthy of great respect and trust after release.

In reality, prison life was likely to become all too routine after the first few months. Prisoners needed to have a purpose or they would stagnate physically and mentally. It was here that communist intellectuals demonstrated particular initiative. Because the problem of regaining or sustaining one's health was common to everyone, individuals competent in French made a point of trying to befriend the prison doctor. Sometimes it was possible to become an orderly and thus help to dispense whatever medicines were available. Of equal importance, inmates grouped together to enforce basic rules of sanitation. In the best-organized cell blocks seriously ill inmates were given round-the-clock attention and provided with extra food taken from the daily rations of cellmates.

Prisoners also discovered that a well-organized and motivated cell block could often fend off some of the worst excesses of individual guards and perhaps obtain minor concessions from the chief warden. As one participant phrased it:

Struggle, repression; new struggle, repression again—but struggle for the right to live went on. As a result of each struggle, we scored small concessions for the improvement of our daily life.[84]

Another activist recalled how the women's ward of Vinh prison was organized according to the principle: "Unity is life, division is death."[85] Over time a number of chief wardens apparently decided that trying to uncover and destroy these internal networks was more trouble than tacitly accepting their authority and discussing issues with their representatives. Inmate leaders considered this a signal victory; wardens regarded it simply as a device to promote order and reduce violence. Wardens may have had second thoughts, however, when inmate organizations began to establish regular liaison with comrades outside and to effect prison escapes.[86]

Those who entered prison without any manual skills were soon learning and

83. Ngo Vinh Long and Nguyen Hoi Chan, *Vietnamese Women*, p. 164.

84. Hoang Quoc Viet, in *A Heroic People: Memoirs from the Revolution*, 2nd edition (Hanoi, 1965), p. 167. The author, subsequently a key ICP Central Committee member, was recalling life on Con Son island, 1931–36.

85. Ton Thi Que, *Chi Mot Con Duong*, p. 88. For an example of a prison struggle effort that failed, see Luu Dong, *Buoc Dau Theo Dang*, pp. 54–77.

86. For an example of the meticulous planning involved in escape operations, see Van Tien Dung, in Le Thiet Hung et al., *Rung Yen The*, pp. 134–42. Among other things, the reader comes

improvising. Knives sharp enough to shave off hair were honed from tin strips.[87] Needles and thread were fashioned, clothing sewn, and sandals made. Where the jailers would permit, prisoners grew vegetables, raised poultry, prepared vermicelli (on a handmade machine), and contrived simple medicines. Perhaps the ultimate example of prisoner ingenuity was to use the profusion of larvae in the prison store of dried fish on Con Son island as quality feed for poultry.[88]

Con Son island in the early 1930s was a key testing ground for Communist Party operations. Perhaps because the minimum term for Con Son convicts was five years, people tended to spend less time wondering when they would be released and more time trying to do something meaningful. It is also remarkable how many messages and study documents were smuggled onto the island, usually with the assistance of sympathetic guards or clandestine French Communist Party members working aboard supply ships.[89] Cigarette wrappers or scraps of tissue paper were used to write out tiny circulating copies of study materials, after which the original was sequestered against the likelihood that copies would eventually be discovered and confiscated. When this did once happen and the French demanded to know where the original was hidden, prisoners teased them by claiming that students returned from Moscow had written them from memory.[90] As early as 1932, French administrators were complaining that Vietnamese who knew little of Communist theory and practice when they entered prison were already completely trained and capable of carrying on individual propaganda missions.[91]

Revolutionaries arrested at the outbreak of World War II were even more intent on making use of their time in jail. Clandestine journals were composed by hand and distributed inside several prisons. Lessons were prepared on how to mobilize different sectors of the population, how to avoid capture, give public speeches, write leaflets, and draw posters. Some inmates were able to entice military guards studying for promotion to show them basic weapons texts or to demonstrate the manual of arms. On labor details outside the walls a few prisoners were able to remain unsupervised long enough to practice crawling, rolling, fall-

---

to appreciate why the author became chief of general staff of the Vietnam People's Army. Two other detailed accounts of jailbreaks are contained in Nguyen Tao, *Chung Toi Vuot Nguc* [We Escape from Prison] (Hanoi, 1977), pp. 29–49, 270–87.

87. Phan Van Hum, *Ngoi Tu Kham Lon*, pp. 34–35.

88. Hoang Quoc Viet, *A Heroic People*, pp. 169–70.

89. Pham Hung, behind bars from 1931 to 1945, recalls cultivating a French guard who eventually provided him with regular radio news reports. "Trong Xa Lim An Chem," [In the Death Cell] in Pham Hung et al., *Tren Duong Cach Mang* (Hanoi, 1960), pp. 34–41. The author is currently fourth ranking member of the ICP Political Bureau.

90. Hoang Quoc Viet, *A Heroic People*, p. 172. Study materials on Con Son included *Anti-Dühring, State and Revolution*, and *Fundamental Principles of Marxism-Leninism*.

91. "AAPCI: Les faits de mois de janvier 1932," AOM SLOTFOM, III, 48.

ing to the ground, marching, simple squad formations, and evasive maneuvers. Training preference was given to individuals selected for escape attempts or reliable cadres whose sentences happened to be nearing an end. Each comrade would try to convey to such persons the essence of his own experience to date, share special morsels of food, take on extra chores—in short, put himself emotionally into the other individual's body.[92]

Friendships forged behind bars were often the closest of any in the revolutionary movement. Thus, it is not entirely coincidental that a number of subsequent ICP Political Bureau members were together on Con Son island in the early 1930s, or that another group of ICP leaders first worked with each other inside Son La prison in the early 1940s.[93] A third group of significance has been the veterans of Ba To prison (Quang Ngai).[94]

Ho Chi Minh did not belong to any of these prison fraternities. Perhaps that was a minor advantage, at least when combined with the fact that he had indeed suffered imprisonment elsewhere, at the hands of the British (1931–33) and the Chinese Kuomintang (1942–43). On both occasions he was reported dead, yet reemerged. When Ho Chi Minh appeared for the first time before large crowds in August and September 1945, his legend—especially accounts of his indomitable will and indestructability—had preceded him.[95]

Vietnamese Communist Concepts of Struggle

The Marxism-Leninism studied by Vietnamese in jail or overseas insisted that the laws of nature and the laws of human society not be confused. It was unscientific and indeed reactionary to suggest that human history could be explained in biological or zoological terms. Man was distinguished from other animals by his ability to produce his means of subsistence. A particular mode of production indicated a particular mode of life. Social relationships, or forms of human cooperation, were in themselves a type of productive force. As the production forces

---

92. Dang Kim Giang, in Bui Cong Trung et al., *Nguoi Truoc Nga Nguoi Sau Tien* (Hanoi, 1960), pp. 53–58; Xuan Thuy, in Chanh Thi et al., *Len Duong Thang Loi* (Hanoi, 1960), pp. 63–68.

93. The Son La group deserves particular study. As early as April 1945 members clearly saw themselves as a fraternity. See Nguyen Van Rang, in Le Thiet Hung et al., *Rung Yen The*, pp. 64, 84. A big reunion of Son La prisoners was held in 1977 and a collection of Son La poetry published. See Ty Thong Tin Van Hoa, *Suoi Reo* [Bubbling Spring]. Surviving Son La veterans include Le Duc Tho, Van Tien Dung, and Xuan Thuy.

94. Ba To veterans include Tran Van Tra, Pham Kiet, and Nguyen Don. See Pham Kiet, in Le Thiet Hung et al., *Rung Yen The*, pp. 5–18; and Pham Kiet, *Tu Nui Rung Ba To* [From the Ba To Highland Forests], 4th printing (Hanoi, 1977).

95. Ho Chi Minh's poems composed during his 1942–1943 incarceration were later compiled, translated (from Chinese), and published as *Nhat Ky Trong Tu* [Prison Diary] (Hanoi, 1960). For a recent translation to English by Huynh Sanh Thong, see David Marr, ed., *Reflections from Captivity* (Athens, Ohio: Ohio Univ. Press, 1978), pp. 59–98.

of a nation developed, so too did the division of labor, which in turn led to clashes of interest. In the modern era, the primary clash of interest was between capitalists and proletarians. In colonies such as Indochina, therefore, the primary struggle was between the imperialists and their lackeys on the one hand, and the working class on the other. This struggle would be won by the colonized, as part of a global proletarian victory over capitalism.

Armed with French Communist Party and Comintern publications arguing the above, Vietnamese intellectuals began about 1930 to denounce Social Darwinism as reactionary capitalist propaganda designed to legitimize ruthless exploitation of the lower classes. This must have puzzled many Vietnamese, since writers like Phan Boi Chau, Tran Huu Do, and Tran Huy Lieu had hardly projected the aloof determinism or bourgeois individualism of Spencer, and had argued not for capitalist reformism but for anticolonial revolution. Marxism-Leninism could be seen as correcting Social Darwinian deficiencies, however. As understood in Vietnam, Social Darwinism meant that one human being was expected to dominate another, one group to amass the force necessary to coerce other groups, one nation to acquire sufficient overt power to cow or destroy enemy nations. By contrast, Communists argued that those who monopolized the guns yet lacked tight control of the means of production might hold on to political power for a while but eventually were doomed to defeat. If the vast majority of Vietnamese who actually grasped the tools of production could somehow confront the tiny minority of French and Vietnamese who exploited them for surplus profit, victory was certain.

Looking further ahead, most radical Vietnamese were attracted to the idea that human nature was perfectable, given victory of the proletariat and the benefits of modern science and industry: two human beings amidst material plenty need not fall into a superior-inferior relationship. In this sense, therefore, the current heightening of class consciousness was aimed at the extinction of all classes, the sharpening of struggles aimed at an ending of struggle.[96] During the socialist stage, one author cautioned, there would still be important contradictions between man and nature, but man would be better able to deal with such problems once he did not have to expend energy on class struggle.[97] As for the ultimate stage, that of communism, Vietnamese authors drew upon a variety of essentially millenarian terms, including "great harmony" (*dai dong*), "equality" (*binh dang*), and "total altruism" (*hoan toan bac ai*). One author warned, however, that communism did not mean that all wishes would be fulfilled, or that all

96. Hong Phong, *Chanh Tri Kinh Te Hoc Chi Nam* [A Guide to Political Economics] (Saigon, 1937), p. 34; Son Tra, *Giai Cap La Gi?* [What Is a Class?] (Tourane [Da Nang], 1938), pp. 4–5.

97. Pham Van Dieu, *Bien Chung Duy Vat Luan* [An Essay on Dialectical Materialism] (Saigon, 1937), p. 31.

individuals would have the same intelligence, abilities, or training. The important thing would be for everyone to have equal opportunity.[98]

There can be no doubt that many Vietnamese Communists sustained their spirits in jail or in underground hideouts by telling themselves that imperialism was the last stage of capitalism, that the French imperialists were outwardly strong but inwardly suffering from grave contradictions, and that they, the vanguard of the proletariat, were part of a vast international movement destined to bury capitalism and create a communist paradise on earth. Almost surely the ethical advantages of this position counted for more than the historical determinism. Very few Vietnamese had ever been comfortable with Social Darwinism's indifference, even the sanction that it provided for brutish behavior. Assuming that nature was characterized by naked conflict, pain, sorrow, and wrong, it did not necessarily follow that human beings had to follow nature's rules.[99] On the contrary, the majority of human beings might band together to destroy a social system that encouraged barbarism and to replace it with one that promoted civilized behavior.

This was certainly the conclusion drawn by Ho Chi Minh, almost a decade before other Vietnamese had had any reliable exposure to Marxism-Leninism. By his own admission, Ho Chi Minh was attracted to the Communist Third International in 1920 not by ideas such as the historical dialectic, surplus value, or modes of production, but by Lenin's attack on imperialist oppression and support for revolutionary movements of national liberation.[100] Both then and thereafter, the first question Ho Chi Minh would address to foreign comrades was, "If you do not condemn colonialism, if you do not side with the colonial people, what kind of revolution are you waging?"[101] To his own people five years later Ho Chi Minh began to suggest that the revolutionary firmness of a social class is deter-

98. Do Thi Bich Lien, *Binh Dang* [Equality] (Phu Ly, 1938). This author, like many other radical Vietnamese of the period, was particularly attracted to *Anti-Dühring*, by Friedrich Engels. See also Bui Cong Trung, "Phai Song." p. 32; Hoang Quoc Viet, *A Heroic People*, p. 172; and Son Tra, *Giai Cap La Gi?*, p. 6. Phan Van Hum, *Bien Chung Phap Pho Thong* [Popular Dialectics] (Saigon, 1936), pp. 12–13, describes how a taxi-driver friend in Brussels spent three years working his way through *Anti-Dühring*, then used it to plan a successful confrontation with the police. *Anti-Dühring* had the advantage of being concise and sharply worded, yet of ranging equally across philosophy, political economy, and socialism. Engels' attack on Dühring's "Force Theory" also served as an antidote to Spencer, Nietzsche, Liang Ch'i-ch'ao, Tran Huu Do (prior to 1930), and anyone else who appeared to place political and psychological causation ahead of social and economic causation.

99. In the West this position had been argued effectively by Thomas Huxley. However, Huxley appears to have excluded indigenous non-European peoples from under his ethical umbrella. See *Evolution and Ethics and Other Essays* (London: Macmillan, 1894), pp. 16–20.

100. Ho Chi Minh, *Selected Works*, vol. 4 (Hanoi, 1962), p. 499.

101. Bernard Fall, ed., *Ho Chi Minh on Revolution* (New York: Praeger, 1967), p. 24.

mined more by the degree of oppression it suffers than by the actual mode of production involved. More precisely, because Vietnamese workers and peasants were *both* suffering extreme oppression at the hands of the French colonialists and Vietnamese landlords, they would tend to unite their struggles rather than divide them.[102]

In addition to the moral incentives, Marxism-Leninism opened up important new avenues of organized struggle. Whereas previously Vietnamese anticolonial intellectuals had focused on publishing, forming study groups, and perhaps plotting armed uprisings, now they also took the lead in organizing labor unions, strikes, peasant demonstrations, and even grievance committees within the colonial army. Strikes may not have been particularly successful in forcing concessions from mine and factory managers, but they did prove excellent opportunities to identify, recruit, train, and test Party members. In the context of the times, strikes also gave strikers the sense of participating in a much larger movement. When in 1929 a pamphlet distributed at the Saigon oil refinery boldly proclaimed, "For the common happiness, strike and achieve a great victory," it was trying to link the efforts of a few hundred Vietnamese workers to a momentous national and international struggle.[103] When word of the huge peasant demonstrations and violent French repression in Nghe An and Ha Tinh provinces reached factory and mine laborers in the north, they tried frantically to mount support actions, arguing that to sit quietly while such events were underway would cause the imperialists to "lose respect" (*khinh nhon*) for the power of the worker-peasant alliance. Without such action, they said, the imperialists would return to exploiting workers much more severely than at present.[104]

Even in the midst of the epic confrontations of 1930–31, however, some Vietnamese Communists were concerned to keep moving on secondary fronts. Thus the Party worked ceaselessly to discredit French government initiatives, for example, the Indochina exhibit at the 1931 Colonial Exposition in Vincennes, or the visit to Indochina of Minister of Colonies Paul Reynaud the same year.[105] At local levels, Party members were instructed on how to enter a village for the first time and how to convene a meeting, distribute leaflets, organize a demonstration, and avoid a bloody confrontation with native soldiers (see chapter 9).

---

102. Ho Chi Minh, *Duong Kach Menh* [Road to Revolution], originally printed in Canton in early 1927 for use in training classes. Only excerpts have been made available to the public subsequently, for example, in *Hoc Tap* (Hanoi), no. 2, 1961, pp. 50–58. See also discussion in Huynh Kim Khanh, "Vietnamese Communism: The Pre-Power Phase (1925–1945)" (Ph.D. diss., Univ. of Calif., Berkeley, 1972), pp. 58–69.

103. Annex to 19 Nov. 1929 note from the governor-general to the minister of colonies. AOM (Aix) G.G. Series F-7F2.

104. AOM (Aix) G.G. Series F-7F4, vol. 4.

105. *Quoc ngu* leaflets attacking the Exposition and Reynaud's visit are in AOM SLOTFOM, carton 12.

Vietnamese Communists, in short, aimed to develop a wide spectrum of struggle options, then to select and modulate them according to concrete conditions. This contrasted sharply with the remaining non-communist militants, who continued to talk (if not necessarily act) in terms of "stick-and-stone" confrontations, or of "hard defeating soft."[106] In the early 1930s, nevertheless, most Vietnamese Communists did maintain a dichotomous view of class struggle that tended to inhibit flexibility. The overriding contradiction, and thus the principle struggle, was between propertied and non-propertied peoples. From this it appeared to follow that "Only poor, miserable people can know how to love other poor, miserable people."[107]

Later in the 1930s Vietnamese Communists conveyed a more graduated concept of class. Besides the standard subcategories for capitalists and proletarians and routine discussions of "intermediate" classes, a distinction was now often made between Vietnamese peasants of some means and the vast majority of poor and landless peasants. Writers also pointed out how individuals might belong to two different classes at the same time. Thus, a railroad mechanic who continued to own a hectare or two of rice land was simultaneously a proletarian and a landlord, assuming he rented his land to others. On the other hand, the tens of thousands of peasants who tilled their own fields in season but then tried to find employment as coolies, artisans, or miners at other times of the year were given the label of semi-proletarian.[108]

Such theoretical problems of class delineation did not assume major operational importance until the land reform period of 1953–56, when class and social strata definitions worked out by the central leadership were disseminated to Party cadres in every northern Vietnamese village as a guide to land confiscation and redistribution activities. Simultaneously, however, peasants were encouraged to make their own judgments by means of "denunciation of suffering" sessions and People's Courts directed against landlords. Poor and landless peasants often ended up denouncing middle and rich peasants as well as landlords, contrary to government intentions. Matters became so tense that apparently some Party leaders argued for a shift away from overt class confrontation and toward education, negotiation, and routine law enforcement procedures.[109] Because the overall ob-

---

106. The "stick-and-stone" image was used by Nhuong Tong, as cited in Huynh Kim Khanh, "Vietnamese Communism," p. 124. "Hard defeats soft" comes from Hoang Dao, *Muoi Dieu Tam Niem* (Saigon, n.d.), p. 41.

107. This was the headline on *Lao Nong* 4 (30 Jan. 1930), contained in AOM (Aix) G.G. Series F-7F4, vol. 1.

108. Hong Phong, *Chanh Tri Kinh Te Hoc Chi Nam*, pp. 6–7; Son Tra, *Giai Cap La Gi?*, pp. 14–16; Truong Chinh and Vo Nguyen Giap, *The Peasant Question* (Ithaca, N.Y.: SEAP, 1974), pp. 16–18.

109. Such a proposed shift was roundly criticized by Ho Viet Thang in a speech given 28 Feb. 1955 and published in *Nhan Dan* (Hanoi), 6 Apr. 1955.

jective was not merely to transfer property but to bring about a political, social, and psychological revolution in the countryside, class struggle was allowed to continue unimpeded for three years. At the end of that time several ranking leaders took responsibility for "excesses," and an attempt was made to correct the more obvious injustices. Nevertheless, the Party was satisfied that it had broken the power of the landlords, and that poor and landless peasants, perhaps sixty percent of the population, had become energetic defenders of the new order.[110]

In the intervening period, from 1940 to 1952, Vietnamese Communists purposefully downgraded class struggle in favor of national struggle. The theoretical justification involved reemphasizing Lenin's linkage of the proletarian struggle in advanced countries with liberation struggles among oppressed nationalities. However, during these years Vietnamese Communists received much less support than before from their proletarian allies in France and the Soviet Union. More to the point was Ho Chi Minh's conviction that if they failed to lead a victorious national liberation struggle they might never have the opportunity to engineer a victorious class struggle. To counter the colonial strategy of "divide and rule," Ho Chi Minh urged Vietnamese of all classes to be considerate of each other's interests and to compromise with each other. Although his strategy involved the fashioning of ever broader united fronts (see chapter 9), it had an important "divide-and-rule" component too, based on Lenin's advice to undermine powerful enemies by exploiting the smallest rift. Identifying principal and secondary contradictions thus became an integral part of national as well as class analysis in Vietnam.

It would be wrong to characterize Ho Chi Minh or any other major Vietnamese Communist leader as a nationalist. As early as 1922, Ho Chi Minh considered nationalism to be a dangerous siren capable of luring colonized peoples away from communism.[111] This judgment was presumably corroborated by the violent split between the Kuomintang and Chinese Communist Party in 1927. From 1930 the Indochinese Communist Party denounced not only collaborator nationalists like Pham Quynh and Bui Quang Chieu but also those survivors of the Vietnam Nationalist Party who refused to see the light and convert. Among unaffiliated intellectuals, Marxism-Leninism became increasingly attractive, although Nietzsche continued to enjoy support.[112] At a less philosophical level, Vietnamese Communists were uncomfortably aware of how many intellectuals

110. Christine White, "Class and Revolution: Land Reform in the Democratic Republic of Vietnam (1953–1956)" (paper presented at the Asian Studies Association of Australia Conference, Sydney, May 1978).

111. Ho Chi Minh, *Oeuvres Choisies*, vol. 1, pp. 12–13. Article originally published in *l'Humanité* (Paris).

112. Phan Van Hum, *Ngoi Tu Kham Lon*, pp. 48, 54, 152. Luu Dong, *Buoc Dau Theo Dang*, pp. 9, 11–13, 18–19.

remained fascinated by the success of militaristic nationalism in Turkey, Thailand, and Japan, not to mention fascism in Italy and Germany. They denounced Nietzsche as a racist, took a firm antifascist position, and emphasized ongoing national liberation struggles in such countries as China, India, the Philippines, Mexico, Argentina, Cuba, and Ethiopia.[113]

During the Popular Front period, the ICP encouraged people to love and uphold the Vietnamese "patrimony" (*To Quoc*), but not at the expense of other ideals. Specifically, Vietnamese needed to know that it was wrong to want to dominate other countries or peoples, and they should never forget that the ultimate objective was a worldwide "common patrimony."[114] This basic position was carried into World War II. At a practical level, Vietnamese Communists from 1940 were forced to develop more amicable relations with various highland minorities if they were to have any hope of building and defending liberated zones.[115] As late as September 1945, nevertheless, one could still find an otherwise Marxist-Leninist interpretation of the "nationalities question" arguing that the future of "small and weak nationalities will be determined by their capacity to struggle."[116] The Social Darwinian undertones were unmistakable.

Toward a Mass Concept of Struggle

As World War II neared an end, the readiness of Vietnamese to struggle became obvious. Most widespread was the desire to struggle against individual frailty, to try to improve one's health, one's physical strength, one's martial prowess—and thus one's ability to deal with external reality. Beyond that was the conviction that strong individuals make strong countries. Previously, colonial administrators had complained that Vietnamese culture was heavily biased against both physical education and the martial arts.[117] During World War II, however, tens of thousands of young Vietnamese participated energetically in a variety of French- and Japanese-sponsored sporting, scouting, and paramilitary groups. The Viet Minh generally chose not to attack such activities frontally, instead recruiting

113. Bui Cong Trung, in Bui Cong Trung et al., *Len Duong Thang Loi* (Hanoi, 1960), pp. 31–33; Vo Ba Phan, *Van Dong Giai Phong Dan Toc* [Activating National Liberation] (Saigon, 1937).

114. *The Gioi* (Hanoi), no. 4 (15 Nov. 1938).

115. It is instructive, for example, to contrast Le Van Hien's 1938 racist attitude toward his Montagnard guards in Kontum with subsequent Viet Minh stress on cooperation among "fraternal nationalities."

116. Quoc Thuy, *Van De Dan Toc* [The Nationalities Question] (Hanoi, 1946). Text completed Sept. 1945.

117. Indochine Française, *Le Comité Central d'Instruction Physique et de Préparation Militaire de l'Indochine* (Paris, 1931), pp. 5–6. The authors, while indicating a readiness to encourage Vietnamese physical education and paramilitary acivities, also pointed out that it was hardly in the French interest to train indigenous personnel capable of "constituting cadres for revolutionary formations."

individual members and in some cases winning over entire groups after the Japanese *coup de force* of March 1945. While one should not overstate the changes, there can be no doubt that the model Vietnamese youth of 1945 was muscular, firm of step, bronzed by the sun, and able to defend himself.[118]

There was also a tremendous thirst to possess and to learn how to use firearms. The French had long maintained very tight restrictions on civilian ownership of guns, ammunition, and explosives.[119] In the hills of northern Vietnam, however, the minority peoples retained an assortment of hunting rifles and muskets. During World War II the Viet Minh also managed to acquire a very limited stock of Kuomintang, French, Japanese, and American firearms. Wherever a Viet Minh squad went, though it usually possessed only two or three guns, citizens were encouraged to hold them, practice the manual of arms, and perhaps learn how to disassemble, clean, and reassemble the various models. The handful of available pistols were given nicknames by Viet Minh leaders, and soon developed long revolutionary pedigrees independent of their temporary custodians. With an average of only four or five rounds per weapon, the main effect clearly was symbolic. Nonetheless, villagers responded with alacrity, sometimes drilling far into the night. As they marched to and fro they yelled out:

> One, Two, One, Two,
> With one heart we march forward.
> Don't let enemy forces escape;
> We're resolved to sacrifice.
> One, Two, One, Two.[120]

The readiness and capacity of tens of thousands of Vietnamese to fight was first put to the test in and around Saigon in September 1945, following Allied (British) refusal to recognize the Viet Minh's Southern Region Provisional Administrative Committee and arming the resident French community instead. The militant spirit of the day was captured by Hoc Tu, a Vietnamese journalist, who provided blow-by-blow battle accounts and asserted that "all the people of southern Vietnam see that it is *necessary to die, and want to die.*"[121] With no apparent sense of contradiction, he also judged that the approximately two percent of the Vietnamese populace prepared to ally with the French and thus sell out their country would have to be exterminated. To help meet the foreign threat, "southward-advance" (*nam tien*) units were mustered and dispatched from various

118. Many elders also picked up this mood—perhaps an indication that the change was not as dramatic as it seemed at the time.

119. Pierre Grossin, *Dan Que Nen Biet* (Hanoi, 1928), pp. 58–60, 163–64.

120. Ha Thi Que, in Ha Thi Que et al., *Rung Yen The*, p. 89. Early Viet Minh weapons training and use is recalled by Le Thiet Hung in ibid., pp. 30–50. See also Tran Do, "Cong Tac Doi," in Chanh Thi et al., *Len Duong Thang Loi*, pp. 83–99.

121. Hoc Tu, *Nhung Ngay Dau cua Mat Tran Nam Bo* [First Days on the South Vietnam Battlefront] (Hanoi, 1945), p. 7. Emphasis in original.

northern cities and towns. Years later, Vo Nguyen Giap recalled how moved he was to see battalions of young men marching south, singing new revolutionary songs as they went. Practically none of them had ever been in battle, and most were venturing beyond their home region for the first time, he added.[122] He might also have added that very few ever lived to see their homes again.

The urge to be strong, to march in unison, to use firearms, to die for one's country if necessary—these were all important components of the Vietnamese struggle ideology of 1945. They were hardly unique to Vietnam, however, and they could also dissipate almost as rapidly as they had formed. What *was* truly remarkable in Vietnam was the manner in which the Viet Minh—an organization with no governing background and very little military experience—was able to both perpetuate the feverish mood of struggle and to give it direction. In a situation where breast-beating sentiments could easily have led to win-or-lose adventurism, mutual recrimination, and loss of strategic momentum, the Viet Minh found a formula that combined the advantages of both popular spontaneity and focused action.

Besides drawing on their own theoretical and practical experiences, it would seem that the Viet Minh leaders were particularly indebted to Chinese Communist Party and Chinese Red Army precedents. In a Red Army manual translated and distributed by the Vietnam Liberation Army in September 1945, for example, great stress was placed on the need to grasp the meaning of *protracted* struggle, neither expecting quick results nor growing apathetic over time. Since the vast majority of citizens still lacked firearms, it was essential for everyone to recognize that there were many other ways to struggle effectively, not only with bamboo spears or tools, but also by cutting telegraph wires, destroying bridges and roads, poisoning the enemy, and spreading rumors.[123] Ho Chi Minh had a flair for making even the most pedestrian tasks sound exciting and important. From the earliest days of the August 1945 Revolution he convinced people that the struggles against the "famine bandit" (*giac doi*) and the "ignorance bandit" (*giac dot*) were just as essential to ultimate victory as the struggle against the "invader bandit" (*giac xam*). In many other ways the initial zeal to confront and destroy the enemy was translated into a wide range of functions for young and old, male and female, rich and poor, educated and uneducated. By the time fighting spread across the entire country in December 1946, millions of Vietnamese understood the concept of people's war.

Besides the singular efforts of Ho Chi Minh, it fell to several thousand ICP members to communicate such a multifaceted idea of struggle and to start converting it to reality. As might be expected, former political prisoners were given most of the key leadership positions. Party cadres who had survived incarceration

---

122. Vo Nguyen Giap, *Unforgettable Months and Years*, trans. Mai Elliott (Ithaca, N.Y.: SEAP, 1975), p. 71.

123. Viet Nam Giai Phong Quan, *Chien Thuat Co Ban* [Fundamental Tactics] (Hanoi, 1945).

with their reputations intact or enhanced had that unique combination of inner fire to turn the world upside down and readiness to obey the collective will. To avoid physical and psychological annihilation they had been forced to master the self, almost to the point of inhumanity. They were quite prepared to sublimate everything to struggle, to revolutionary tension. Jail graduates had also learned the value of patience, ingenuity, and flexibility when facing seemingly intractable obstacles. Not least of all, they understood the fallacy of dealing with human problems as one would with problems in nature. As regards the colonial enemy, for example, one former prisoner explained that it was one thing to struggle against waves in the sea and quite another to struggle against oppressors who were endowed with intelligence and who knew their jobs very well.[124]

The Viet Minh did not convey a single concept but rather a variety of different ones according to the needs of the moment and, one must imagine, differing interpretations among the leaders. Most highly regarded was altruistic struggle, in which an individual consciously engaged in activities that made other persons of his group more likely to survive at the price of making himself more likely to die.[125] However, the Viet Minh gave equal or greater attention to cooperative struggle, to pooling capacities in order to overcome obstacles that no individual or small group could hope to overcome. The slogan "All for one, one for all" was often used in this context.

Yet a third approach was that of "emulation" (*thi dua*), borrowing from Soviet experience. Here an individual (or small group) was encouraged to compete, to try hard to equal or excel others, but in such a way that the collective good was overtly enhanced. Material or spiritual benefits to the competitor were meant to be seen primarily as recognition for furthering collective objectives and only secondarily as rewards for outperforming one's peers. In this context, "Emulation is patriotic" soon became a key Viet Minh slogan, and Ho Chi Minh devoted his 1949 Tet poem to the topic:

> If each individual practices emulation,
> If each branch does the same,
> If each day sees emulation campaigns,
> We will surely win;
> The enemy will surely be defeated.[126]

While this was far from the idea of survival of the fittest, it was also far from traditional concepts of self-denial or harmonious interaction. The pursuit of self-

---

124. Luu Dong, *Buoc Dau Theo Dang*, pp. 39–40.

125. This type of behavior, quite inexplicable in terms of survival of the fittest, is now being taken seriously among some Western biologists, geneticists, and sociologists who study the evolution of social animals.

126. Quoted in Ha Minh Duc, "Bac Nam sum hop" [North and South Reunited], TCVH 1-1976, p. 37.

interest was no longer to be considered the root of all evil but rather a human trait (at least until the communist millennium) that needed to be channeled in certain directions in order to benefit both the individual and society.

It should not be thought that harmony was banished from the Vietnamese vocabulary. Particularly as the Viet Minh became more an organ of state power and less of a united front, renewed emphasis on harmonious relations could be observed. Eventually, arguments would be made for harmony between higher and lower echelons of organizations, between trade unions and directors of state enterprises, and between husband and wife. General Van Tien Dung employed the idea of musical harmony to prepare combat units for the Spring 1975 Offensive:

> If you musicians are all in agreement, then your conductors, the Central Military Committee and the General Command, are prepared to raise the baton at the proper time, when the opportune moment arrives.[127]

General Secretary of the Communist Party Le Duan went so far as to assert that Vietnamese culture was a "harmonious blend of the original cultures of the many fraternal nationalities," quite ignoring the long history of struggle in which the ethnic Vietnamese had emerged on top.[128]

Such rhetoric reflected the transition from revolution to order. It did not necessarily signal a return to traditional concepts of harmony, however. For one thing, harmony had come to imply solidarity against some other force, not a natural mean, a principle of non-action or an indiscriminate humanism. Also, harmony had to be worked for; it did not occur spontaneously. Finally, harmony was subordinate to the dialectic, thus signifying only temporary resolution of (non-antagonistic) contradictions. Only in this light can it be understood, for example, why the Vietnamese Communist delegates to the Paris Peace negotiations insisted on the use of the terms "reconciliation" (hoa giai) and "concord" (hoa hop) in the final January 1973 agreement to define the intended relationship between Vietnamese organizations that had been fighting each other for decades. As it turned out, continuing antagonism between the United States and the DRVN prevented any serious test of this policy. The Communists then followed another dictum, that of refusing to wait passively for contradictions to work themselves out, and delivered the coup de grâce in early 1975.

Only a few months before that coup de grâce, Tran Van Giau, a well-known Communist intellectual had summarized for me the anti-imperialist experience by saying, "Water wears down rock." He probably knew that he was paraphrasing an ancient Taoist text, which brilliantly contrasts the 'weakness' of water with

---

127. Van Tien Dung, *Our Great Spring Victory* (New York: Monthly Review Press, 1977), p. 28. Trans. by John Spragens, Jr.

128. Le Duan, *This Nation and Socialism Are One* (Chicago, 1976), p. 189.

its observable capacity to attack that which is hard and strong.[129] This general principle had indeed helped to inspire both Chinese and Vietnamese practitioners of people's war. Yet the man I talked to was by no means a Taoist, but a complex, sometimes paradoxical product of many historical influences; he was acutely aware that over time the character of both the imperialist "rock" and the anti-imperialist "water" had changed. At any rate, in March and April 1975 it was thousands of tanks that broke the will to fight of the Saigon army, not peasants armed with bamboo spears.

Having devoted so much thought and energy to anti-imperialist struggle, Vietnamese Communists were not particularly well prepared in 1975 to deal with other dialectical problems. Less than a year after reunification, for example, Le Duan told a French journalist that it was proving "more difficult to combat nature than the American aggressor."[130] To this he might well have added the problem of how to position Vietnam in the Sino-Soviet struggle, and of how to reconstruct the Vietnamese economy without either promoting class struggle or going too far into debt to foreign interests. As Vietnamese Communists had learned thirty-five years earlier when building the Viet Minh, to be willing to struggle was only the beginning: ultimate success depended on knowing when, where, and how to struggle.

129. D. C. Lau, trans., *Lao Tzu Tao Te Ching* [Master Lao's Canon of Taoist Virtue] (Harmondsworth, Middx.: Penguin, 1970), chap. LXXVIII.

130. François Nivolan, *Le Figaro* (Paris), 12 Mar. 1976.

8. Knowledge Power

In early September 1939, excited students at the Thang Long High School in Hanoi converged on the classroom of their young history teacher, Vo Nguyen Giap, to hear what he had to say about the news of war in Europe. They were disappointed when he stuck firmly to the syllabus and lectured on mid-nineteenth-century transformations in French capitalism. Undaunted, however, the students quickly surrounded him after class and asked a chorus of questions about the meaning of the war, about whether they should be happy or sad, optimistic or pessimistic. Mindful of Sûreté informers, and perhaps stunned by Stalin's agreement with Hitler, Vo Nguyen Giap paused several moments; he seemed about to launch into a long discussion, but then changed his mind and simply advised his students to consider the war as being forced upon them, as certainly no occasion for joy nor an event on which to pin their hopes for national independence.

Four months later these same students were astonished to hear that their teacher, unlike most other known ICP members, had managed to evade the Sûreté and flee the city. A flood of rumors followed: Vo Nguyen Giap had been picked up by a Russian airplane; he was in charge of building a terrible new weapon; he was establishing a fully-equipped Red Army unit on the Sino-Vietnamese border. These rumors were soon overshadowed by news of the French capitulation in Europe, the Japanese attack on Lang Son and the Vichy-Tokyo agreement to share the spoils in Indochina. By late 1940 a number of Vo Nguyen Giap's students had decided to link up with the underground remnants of the ICP, but they did not see their teacher again until August 1945, when he arrived with Ho Chi Minh and units of the Vietnam Liberation Army.[1]

It was not entirely by accident that Vo Nguyen Giap left his position as history teacher and became a military commander. Much of what he had done since he was a teenager seemed a prelude to that decision. Born to a literati family in Quang Binh province in 1911, Vo Nguyen Giap was subsequently able to attend the prestigious Quoc Hoc school in Hue. Along with other bright young men and

---

1. Luu Dong, *Buoc Dau Theo Dang* (Hanoi, 1961), pp. 12–24. The author joined the anti-imperialist youth organization immediately after seeing a trainload of wounded colonial soldiers—mostly Vietnamese—arrive in Hanoi station from the late September 1940 battle at Lang Son. He was soon captured and incarcerated.

women in Hue, he assisted the famous literatus Huynh Thuc Khang to edit and publish the newspaper *Tieng Dan* [Voice of the People], joined the clandestine New Vietnam Revolutionary Party (Tan Viet Cach Mang Dang), and was duly arrested in late 1930 or early 1931. Upon release, Vo Nguyen Giap departed for Hanoi and a multifaceted life as a law student, high school teacher, journalist, editor, and a member of the Indochinese Communist Party.

During the Popular Front period (1936–39), still not thirty years old, Vo Nguyen Giap was identified prominently with many different intelligentsia causes, including the campaign for greater freedom of the press, the effort to get the French Left to pay more attention to colonial questions, and the establishment of the Association for Diffusion of *Quoc Ngu* Study.[2] By early 1937 he also had developed a particular interest in the living conditions of Vietnamese peasants, and presented a report on this topic to Justin Godart, French government delegate touring Indochina.[3] Later the same year he collaborated with Truong Chinh in writing the first detailed study in Vietnamese of rural socio-economic relations, titled *The Peasant Question*.[4] Simultaneously, Vo Nguyen Giap was following events in China as closely as available sources would permit, focusing above all on the strategy and tactics of the Red Army.[5]

Only a month or two before the outbreak of war in Europe, Vo Nguyen Giap published *The Main and Proper Road: The Question of National Liberation in Indochina*.[6] This was an ingenious attempt to strike a path somewhere between the pro-Japanese elements led by Prince Cuong De and the militant antiwar sentiments expressed by the Trotskyists. By concentrating on the immediate threat to Indochina posed by the Japanese "dwarf animals," and by suggesting that the French "colonial reactionaries" might well choose to align with the Japanese rather than arm the local populace for resistance, he in effect narrowed the problem to how, when, and where the ICP itself would launch an armed struggle. He called for an immediate strengthening of Party operations, to enable it simultaneously to withstand colonial assault and to continue to explain to the Vietnamese public what was happening locally and overseas. "A political strategy is only as good as the people who carry it out," he stressed.[7] Within months of

2. *Le Travail* (Hanoi) 20 (29 Jan. 1937); *Rassemblement* (Hanoi) 3 (1 May 1937).

3. *Le Travail* 21 (5 Feb. 1937).

4. Qua Ninh and Van Dinh (Truong Chinh and Vo Nguyen Giap), *Van De Dan Cay*, 2 vols. (Hanoi, 1937 and 1938); republished as one volume (Hanoi, 1959); trans. Christine Pelzer White, *The Peasant Question* (Ithaca, N.Y.: SEAP, 1974).

5. Van Dinh, *Muon Hieu Ro Tinh Hinh Quan Su o Tau* (Hanoi, 1939). Vo Nguyen Giap may also have compiled *Tau Nhat: Ai Duoc Ai Thua?* [China and Japan: Who Will Win and Who Will Lose?] (Hanoi, 1937).

6. Van Dinh, *Con Duong Chinh: Van De Dan Toc Giai Phong o Dong Duong* (Hanoi, 1939).

7. Ibid., p. 22.

writing those lines the Party apparatus was being torn apart by the Sûreté. Vo Nguyen Giap's own wife was arrested and tortured, and eventually died in prison. The Comintern's defense of Stalin's pact with Hitler added to the confusion among both Party members and sympathizers. Nevertheless, the faint path sketched by Vo Nguyen Giap in mid-1939 (presumably with Party approval) was destined to become the road pursued by the Viet Minh from 1941 and the highway marched by the Democratic Republic of Viet Nam from 1945.

Vo Nguyen Giap associated whatever he learned with the necessity for action. Like most others among the Vietnamese intelligentsia he wanted consciously to grapple with life rather than merely to live it. This posed a host of particular problems, some of which have been discussed in earlier chapters. Taken together, however, they amounted to yet another problem. By 1939 the intelligentsia had access to a wide range of knowledge and were conscious of differing ways of ordering it. Yet, few individuals had found time to sort out the available writings, teachings, observations and stray experiences. By design or default, the majority was content with ambivalance. It was often the necessity for action that revealed a preference for one idea over another. As we shall see, those Vietnamese most conscious of this dialectic between theory and practice were the ones most likely to benefit from both the information available and the experiences thrust upon them.

What every member of the intelligentsia wanted was a set of beliefs that both explained reality and provided the means to alter it. However, each time the emphasis shifted from the absorbing of new facts and theories to their imaginative application to local conditions, a formidable obstacle emerged: all conventional forms of action were monopolized or guarded jealously by the French and their native subordinates. At such junctures, individuals or groups were forced to make difficult decisions. If they pushed onward, it had to be either within or outside colonial law. Either way, to make the experience meaningful, considerable energy had to be expended in unconventional directions. Thus, Ho Chi Minh, son of a mandarin and graduate of Quoc Hoc school in Hue, decided in 1911 to sign on as a cook's helper aboard a French ship in order to learn the ways of the outside world. So too, intellectuals confined to a few square meters of jail space in the 1930s tried to give their minds leeway and to increase their practical skills by organizing clandestine classes on everything from world history and philosophy to how to draft propaganda leaflets and evade police dragnets.

As might be expected, many well-meaning Vietnamese intellectuals who intensely disliked the status quo still could not bring themselves to tread such exceptional paths or take such personal risks. They tended to flit in and out of action according to external circumstances. The *degree* of commitment to change thus came to distinguish the few from the many—without, however, necessarily separating them.

Jumping Out of One's Shadow

In 1923 the French governor of Cochinchina, Maurice Cognacq, made the mistake of telling Nguyen An Ninh, "We don't need intellectuals in this country. If you wish to be one, go to Moscow!"[8] Instead of taking Cognacq's advice, Nguyen An Ninh launched a devastating attack on all power-wielders who believed that they could withhold knowledge from those who craved it. In the West, he said, it went back as far as the Biblical myth picturing intelligence as the snake that had driven humankind from Paradise. In the East it was imbedded in orthodox Confucianism, which always placed nebulous "virtue" (*duc*) above "intelligence" (*tri*) or "talent" (*tai*).

From the turn of the century, literati like Phan Chu Trinh and Phan Boi Chau had been determined to comprehend the strange "winds and tides" alive in the larger world of which Vietnam was now clearly a part. Nguyen An Ninh's father in fact had assisted scores of young Vietnamese to travel illegally to Japan for study. Men of that generation condemned the traditional examination system for producing too many gifted memorizers, yet hardly anyone competent to undertake methodical investigations of nature or society. Graduates were expected to be subtle arbiters of conduct and managers of royal policy. The concept of "intelligence" was taken to mean skillful handling of men, not the accumulation, ordering, and testing of information about the objective world.

Only in the late 1920s did a number of Vietnamese writers go further, however, and insist that "intelligence" be placed *ahead* of "virtue." Utilizing Yen Fu's triad of "physical," "intellectual," and "moral" education, they argued that no idea or institution could be accepted a priori. Everything, including "virtue," had to run the gauntlet of scientific analysis. Intellectual enquiry thus became the keystone to the arch.[9] Not surprisingly, Vietnamese traditionalists were revolted. They did not like the idea of three categories in the first place, since it implied that there were other important goals in life besides "virtue." Forced by current convention to accept the categories, they confined themselves to arguing that moral education be placed at the top.[10] Some went further, taking an overtly antagonistic view of intelligence. One author cautioned that the brighter and the more curious a child, the more prone he was to mischief or rebellion.[11] A 1937 pedagogical manual rejected the intellectual approach entirely, simply instruct-

8. *La Cloche Fêlée* (Saigon), 7 Jan. 1924.

9. Phan Khoi, "Doc cuon *Nho Giao* cua Ong Tran Trong Kim," PNTV 54 (29 May 1930); and PNTV 64 (31 July 1930). For Yen Fu's earlier formulation, see Benjamin Schwartz, *In Search of Wealth and Power: Yen Fu and the West* (Cambridge, 1964), pp. 85–90.

10. Tran Van Tang, "Qua Khu va Hien Tai," NP 106 (June 1926), pp. 417–25; Tran Trong Kim, *Nho Giao*, vol. 2 (Saigon, 1962), pp. 393–96.

11. Tuy Lan, *Gia Dinh voi Hoc Duong co nen Hop Tac Khong?* [Should the Family and

ing teachers to employ a very firm voice and to tell pupils, "We must do this . . . We do not want to do that . . . We should not lie . . . We all have to devote ourselves to revering our mothers and fathers."[12]

Such attitudes were ridiculed by members of the intelligentsia. They wanted to investigate everything, from Descartes to sexual hygiene, from philosophical Taoism to the significance of Vietnamese lullabies. It was as if they were trying to seize hold of several millennia of knowledge in a few years. The mood was at once self-deprecating, in terms of assumed Vietnamese ignorance, and grandly optimistic, in the belief that progressive accumulation of knowledge led inevitably to individual and group power. Vietnamese had long been like the frog at the bottom of the well, looking upward and remaining sublimely confident that the entire world was a blue circle encompassed by yellow bricks. Now, however, it was necessary for Mr. Frog to jump out of that well, feast his eyes on new horizons, and draw entirely new conclusions.[13] Another image was that of a child wandering aimlessly in a dark jungle who suddenly hacked his way out and discovered a clear path. It was almost like "jumping out of one's shadow to find some elements of truth," the author added, citing Albert Einstein as the most brilliant practitioner of this art.[14]

One real danger, of course, was that the practitioner might jump so far out of the Vietnamese cultural context that he made himself irrelevant. As early as 1920, Nguyen Ba Hoc, a conservative literatus, was cautioning the new generation with a metaphor of his own. Vietnam was like a grand old house left behind by parents for their children. After allowing the house to become infested with termites and start falling apart, the children had cast their eyes longingly at someone else's beautiful house, and decided to destroy their own to build one like it. Little did they know that they lacked the appropriate skills and materials, so that once they put everything up it failed to fit. Thus, when the winds and rains came they were forced to rush around frantically, like birds who had lost their nests.[15]

Ten years later Pham Quynh was decidedly less poetic, warning intellectuals that to borrow an ideology completely from outside was treason to the nation.

School Cooperate?] (Hue [?], 1930), pp. 8–9. The author added that the problem was greatly compounded by evil outside agitators talking to pupils and having them spread leaflets in school. Those pupils who did not turn over leaflets to their teachers were to be expelled.

12. Dao Dang Hy, *Su Pham Thuc Hanh Khai Yeu*, 2nd printing (Vinh, 1937), p. 49.

13. See, for example, Tran Huy Lieu, *Mot Bau Tam Su* (Saigon, 1927), p. 6. The frog in the well (*toa tinh quan thien*) was an ancient Chinese and Vietnamese metaphor to indicate narrow perspectives.

14. Truong Truc Dinh and Nguyen Dong Ha, "Mot Cai Hoc Thuyet Moi: Thuyet 'Doi Dich' cua ong Einstein" [A New Concept: Mr. Einstein's Theory of Relativity], NP 76 (Oct. 1923), pp. 316–26.

15. Nguyen Ba Hoc, "Thu tra loi ong Chu But *Nam Phong*" [A Reply to the Editor of *Nam Phong*], NP 40 (Oct. 1920), pp. 322–24.

Ironically, he himself continued to offer up as his patriotic alternative a Chinese-derived amalgam of Confucianism, Taoism, and Buddhism.[16] By that time, too, the colonial authorities had curtailed study in France and upgraded the "Eastern philosophy" curriculum component in Vietnamese schools—for fear, they said, that young people would continue to "let their intellects wander, thus forgetting home and country."[17]

While most Vietnamese intellectuals had no trouble seeing through the arguments of Pham Quynh or the French colonial authorities, Nguyen Ba Hoc's "old and new houses" required a serious response. Some writers simply asserted that Vietnam could never regain its independence unless it tossed out the old and accepted the new. Yet, independent or not, very few Vietnamese wanted to become yellow-skinned Frenchmen. Other writers saw the house metaphor as being too static, too dichotomous. Switching to a biological metaphor, they expressed confidence that natural selection would gradually ensure that some new plants flourished, while others would find the soil unsuitable and perish. It was quite wrong for anyone to try to play God and screen the plants in advance, however.[18] If in a particular realm of knowledge or behavior it eventually became obvious that old and new were in hopeless opposition, canceling each other out, then it was appropriate to choose one or the other.[19]

What was really required was an understanding of the process of intellectual development within a specific society (Vietnam) rather than prolonged discussion about ideal types labeled "old" and "new," "Eastern" and "Western." As Huynh Thuc Khang, yet another literatus, saw fit to lecture the French governor-general in 1930:

> Man's ideas evolve with the social milieu, and in times of crisis sweep the masses up in the impetuous torrent, drawing them along with the irresistable current. The only opportune policy is to open wide the gates to the tempestuous waters, which, if savagely blocked, will overflow and cause irreparable devastation.[20]

Minus the hyperbole, which was undoubtedly related to the upheaval and repression then occuring in nearby Nghe An and Ha Tinh provinces, Huynh Thuc Khang seemed to be saying that French and Vietnamese historical actors might succeed in avoiding war or violent revolution, but only if they allowed maximum

---

16. Thuong Chi (Pham Quynh), "Doc Sach co Cam," NP 149 (Apr. 1930), p. 310.

17. Résidence Supérieure au Tonkin, Circulaire aux familles au sujet de l'envoi des étudiants indochinois en France (Hanoi, 1930).

18. Hoang Dao, Muoi Dieu Tam Niem (Saigon, n.d.), pp. 16–17 (originally published about 1938).

19. Phan Khoi, "Tuc Kieng Ten," PNTV 90 (9 July, 1931), p. 5.

20. Letter dated 15 Sept. 1930 to Governor-General Pasquier. AOM (Paris) Indochine 54, dossier 632.

intellectual and political freedom, and even then the evolving social milieu would be final arbiter.

For a lot of young inquiring Vietnamese intellectuals, their first serious crisis occurred within the family. Some parents and relatives openly disparaged the ideas that young people brought home. A much more common response, however, was to permit sons and daughters, nieces and nephews to pursue their own thoughts so long as they made no move that disrupted basic family customs and expectations. As one writer commented ruefully, this tactic produced a lot of young Vietnamese who talked convincingly, for example, about individualism as a means to develop talent and stimulate progress, yet meekly proceed to obey every instruction at home. They were like stallions who pawed the ground furiously yet went absolutely nowhere, he added.[21]

What to do when faced with this family problem was a matter of intense discussion. Phan Boi Chau, certainly no individualist, bluntly counseled young people to avoid dependence on one's parents, to defer marriage, and to concentrate first on making one's own living. Once a person had done that, he or she could seek out like-minded individuals and form organizations of real social and political significance.[22] For thousands of individuals arrested in 1929–31, the dilemma was more immediate and agonizing. Phan Van Hum, for example, described two cases in which the Sûreté imprisoned elderly parents in order to obtain confessions from sons. Hundreds more people were thus jailed in the service of filial piety. By way of contrast he cited the well-known story of Nguyen Trai, who, having begged to follow his mandarin father into servitude in China in the early fifteenth century, was sternly instructed to stay and help save his country, and in this manner also revenge his father.[23]

The solution for some young Vietnamese was to "emancipate" (*thoat ly*) themselves entirely from family and locality. In the first instance this was not entirely voluntary. For example, students expelled from colonial schools as a result of demonstrations during the late 1920s were often too afraid or too proud to face their parents. Students in France sometimes found that it was impossible or undesirable to continue receiving support from home. Still others decided quite consciously to put as much distance between themselves and their families as

21. Hoang Dao, *Muoi Dieu Tam Nien*, p. 15. This tension was the motive force behind a number of novels and short stories published by the Tu Luc Van Doan, of which Hoang Dao was a member. See also articles by Pham Ngoc Thach in *Le Cahier Bleu* (Hanoi) 1 (Nov. 1933) and 2 (Dec. 1933).

22. Phan Boi Chau, *Van De Phu Nu* (Saigon, 1929), pp. 25–28.

23. Phan Van Hum, *Ngoi Tu Kham Lon* (Saigon, 1957), pp. 105–106. Nguyen Trai became principal advisor to Le Loi, eventual victor over the Ming colonialists and founder of the Le dynasty (1428–1788).

possible, not necessarily out of feelings of antagonism, but as an essential part of finding a new direction in life. In the event of arrest or other misfortune, this separation might also serve as a protective shield for both the individual and his family. Whatever the case, once "emancipated," intellectuals might try to imitate what they understood to be the Western model of a lone, inner-directed, and iconoclastic rebel, or they might seek out an alternative reference group as Phan Boi Chau had advised. Popular novelists like Nhat Linh and Khai Hung explored the former option with considerable flair, suggesting how fragile and vulnerable as well as how assertive or creative such individuals were likely to be.[24] In real life, nevertheless, Nhat Linh and Khai Hung formed the Self-Strengthening Literary Group (Tu Luc Van Doan) and worked hard to keep it functioning. In one of Nhat Linh's most successful novels, Doi Ban [Two Friends], he also suggested that any intellectual truly committed to the ideals of Vietnamese freedom and independence might well have to join an unspecified nationalist organization in South China.[25]

Radical intellectuals who opted for "proletarianization" (vo san hoa) in the late 1920s were not only following Comintern encouragement but also trying to prove that their bourgeois or feudal upbringing could be thrust aside, that they were able to make a living with their hands, and that they might find acceptance in a new reference group of miners, factory workers, or coolies. By the early 1930s the Indochinese Communist Party appears to have formulated guidelines on "emancipation." Members were encouraged (but not ordered) to "sacrifice the family," which naturally led some anticommunists to label them antifamily. On the other hand, it was quite common to recruit new members from among one's siblings or cousins, the assumption being that they were much less likely to be Sûreté agents. Amongst close comrades there was no shame in expressing continuing love for family members, especially one's mother.[26]

In the late 1930s the colonial authorities paroled many political prisoners back to home villages with the expectation that the extended family together with the local notables would help keep them in line. Even where this tactic failed, the

---

24. Nhat Linh and Khai Hung, Doi Mua Gio [Stormy Life] (Hanoi, 1935); Nhat Linh, Doan Tuyet [Breaking Away] (Hanoi, 1935); Khai Hung, Thoat Ly [Emancipation] (Hanoi, 1936).

25. Doi Ban (Hanoi, 1937[?]). Nhat Linh [Nguyen Tuong Tam] had to follow his own suggestion during World War II after his tentative contacts with the Japanese incurred the wrath of the French Sûreté. He returned with the Chinese Kuomintang and assorted Vietnamese nationalists in September 1945.

26. Professor Van Tao, in a February 1978 discussion with the author, cited examples of political prisoners who depended on memories of long-suffering, unselfish mothers for moral sustenance. The image of patriotic mothers encouraging children to grow up to defeat the enemy was also common. See, for example, the lullaby written by a Son La prisoner, in Ty Thong Tin Van Hoa Son La, Suoi Reo (Son La, 1977), pp. 16–17.

wounds to both family and parolee were considerable.[27] Throughout the Viet
Minh period (1941–54), "emancipation" was almost a revolutionary rite of passage, with Party members either requesting or being asked to leave the people,
places, and objects they had known from birth.[28] Unlike the intellectuals of the
1920s and 1930s, however, these generally were individuals who had already
been enrolled and tested at the local level, who had a rather firm idea of what
was expected of them and were simply going to a position where they would be
more effective and less of a risk to the local apparatus.

What the most gifted young intellectuals of the 1920s and 1930s wanted was
to be able to stand aside without losing touch, to be objective but not detached.
They saw the risks of cultural alienation, but also the dangers of being hamstrung
by traditional commitments.[29] Finding a solution was not easy. What eventually
saved many intellectuals was a combination of old literati *noblesse oblige* and the
new Western (not solely Leninist) model of an elite, aggressive vanguard party.
For the vast majority of Vietnamese intellectuals the purpose of "jumping out of
one's shadow" was not to obtain some abstract truth but rather to see the world in
such a way as to alter it. Often the objectives were said to be the gaining of a new
"compass" to life as well as a comprehensive "formula" for national salvation.[30]
Admittedly, it was sometimes hard to ascertain where messianic zeal left off and
scientific understanding took over. Tran Huy Lieu, for example, while admitting
that popular superstitions were debilitating to national strength, still firmly asserted the socio-political advantages of "having religion."[31] Years later, in 1960,
Ho Chi Minh again employed the compass metaphor to explain the utility of
Leninism, then added that Leninism was also "a radiant sun illuminating our
path to final victory, to socialism and communism."[32]

Until the late 1920s there existed among most Vietnamese intellectuals a naïve
confidence that words on paper had a special, almost autonomous power to alter
reality. Ideas were to be communicated in print to the multitudes, to penetrate
their souls and stimulate a sweeping transformation of society. Thus, when in

27. Truong Sinh, in Chanh Thi et al., *Len Duong Thang Loi* (Hanoi, 1960), pp. 45–61, provides a poignant description of the family arguments and tears that accompanied his decision to
break parole and escape in September 1939 rather than face probable reincarceration.

28. See, for example, Truong Thi My, in Truong Thi My and Nguyen Thi Hung, *Niem Tin
Khong Bao Gio Tat* [Feelings of Trust Never Extinguished] (Hanoi, 1967), pp. 5–21.

29. Daniel Hémery, *Révolutionnaires Vietnamiens et Pouvoir Colonial en Indochine* (Paris,
1975), pp. 67–68, particularly mentions Nguyen An Ninh and Phan Van Hum as appreciating this
dilemma.

30. Phan Dinh Long, *Cay Kim Chi Nam* (Saigon, 1928); Cao Chanh, *Phuong Cham Cuu
Quoc* (Saigon, 1926); Tran Trong Kim, *Nho Giao*, vol. 1, p. xv.

31. Tran Huy Lieu, *Mot Bau Tam Su*, pp. 18–19.

32. *Selected Works* (Hanoi, 1977), p. 252.

1926 Cao Chanh called for a "national citizen's education effort," he meant the publication of hundreds of *quoc ngu* pamphlets, repeated exhortations to self-respect, and each individual telling himself twice a day, "The Vietnamese people will be able to be their own masters." Cao Chanh also challenged his compatriots to answer such questions as, What is a citizen? What is a human being? What is an official, a government, a society? Being quite certain that most people could not give firm replies, he argued that a lot of book-learning had to be accomplished before anyone embarked on resolute political action.[33]

If the French had continued the policy of mild liberalization begun in 1925, particularly on matters of primary interest to the Vietnamese intelligentsia, Cao Chanh's scholastic approach to change might have retained more support. Already in 1926, however, conflict was apparent. By 1928, outspoken intellectuals had reason to feel threatened, and from 1929 until at least 1933 the colonial administration hounded all opponents into oblivion, or at least silence. This French response forced individuals to explore much more urgently the linkage between theory and practice. For example, after reviewing in print the historic achievements of Western civilization, one intellectual decided that the central message for Vietnamese was the need for an "ideal" (*ly tuong*), which had to be implemented in society by means of "power," which produced a "revolution."[34] Another writer summed up the difficult yet necessary task as follows:

Having been born men, we must live within the realm of ideas. If we want our ideas to be independent, we must know how to observe and to test. Once we have done this and passionately believe (*tin me*) a particular idea, we must be decisive and have the courage to carry it out in practice.[35]

At what point, however, did one's knowledge, ideals, or beliefs reach the level where one was capable of acting effectively? That was a question over which Vietnamese intellectuals continued to differ sharply. Some members of the fledgling Vietnam Nationalist Party decided in 1929 that the time had come to demonstrate willpower by means of violent action.[36] Aware that such feelings were widespread, Dao Duy Anh saw fit to caution his generation as follows:

---

33. Cao Chanh, *Phuong Cham Cuu Quoc*, preface. Cao Chanh further suggested that Vietnam needed to reach the educational level of late eighteenth-century France before it could be "free" in the manner of the 1789 Revolution. Such ideas owed a lot to Phan Chu Trinh: indeed, the author dedicated his pamphlet to Phan, who was at that time dying of tuberculosis in a Saigon hospital.

34. Tinh Tien, *Van Minh Au My* [European and American Civilization] (Hue, 1928), conclusion.

35. Tran Dinh Nam, *Tri Khon* [Intelligence] (Hue, 1928), conclusion. Seventeen years later the author accepted the post of minister of interior in the short-lived Japanese-sponsored Tran Trong Kim cabinet.

36. As early as July 1927 a group identifying itself as either the Annam or Vietnam Nationalist Party was distributing leaflets among native colonial soldiers in the French concession in Shang-

The youth of our country cannot be said to lack enthusiastic life purpose (*chi khi*) and durable spirit. However, the majority are far more ready to act than they are to *know*, such that when they do start acting they are sure to be defeated.[37]

Such measured statements did not prevent Dao Duy Anh from being arrested and given a three-year suspended sentence (see chapter 6). Although that brush with colonial law appears to have pushed Dao Duy Anh further toward scholastic pursuits, some of his comrades drew a different conclusion and opted for lives as professional revolutionaries.

The Information Explosion

Whatever Governor Cognacq's wishes or Nguyen An Ninh's frustrations, the French did permit the Vietnamese to publish extensively from 1924. Not only the more controversial publications deserved attention in this respect: a number of books and articles appearing during the periods of tightest censorship (1929–33, 1940–44), though of no direct political import, added significantly to the reservoir of information and expertise available to literate Vietnamese. For example, besides the profusion of basic hygiene and sex-education texts discussed in chapter 5, there also appeared more advanced *quoc ngu* studies on the prevention, detection, and treatment of specific diseases, including tuberculosis, cholera, syphilis, and trachoma. In 1930 an impressive eighteen-volume medical encyclopedia was published, which devoted separate volumes to such specialties as surgery, dermatology, ophthalmology, gynecology, and epidemiology.[38] Following a centuries-old precedent, texts on indigenous Vietnamese and Chinese medical remedies were also compiled.[39] It was not until the 1950s, however, that serious efforts were made to correlate new Western and traditional Vietnamese and Chinese medical practice.

Mathematics texts, published as early as 1911, became increasingly numerous and sophisticated after 1926. General science texts followed the same pattern, although no *quoc ngu* expositions of physics, chemistry, biology, or other specific scientific disciplines seem to have appeared. The emphasis tended to be on practical applications of science, for example, the nature and uses of electricity, ker-

---

hai, asserting that "the day has arrived when we must struggle to the death to liberate our country from slavery." AOM (Paris).

37. Dao Duy Anh, *Dan Toc* [Peoplehood] (Hue, 1929), p. ii.

38. Tran Duc Tam, ed., *Than Ho Menh Ra Doi* [The Means of Self-Protection Comes to Life] (Haiphong, 1930). An encyclopedic medical dictionary (Pham Khac Quang and Le Khac Thien, comps., *Danh Tu Y Hoc* [Vocabulary of Medicine] [Hanoi, 1944]) began to appear years later, but the Bibliothèque Nationale seems to have only the first volume (for the letters A and B).

39. A representative text is Nguyen An Nhan, *Sach Thuoc Kinh Nghiem* [Empirical Medicine] (Hanoi, 1929). More remarkable is Nguyen Van Huynh, ed., *Y Te Nam Cham* [Magnetic Medicine] (Hanoi, 1933), which contains 1,140 medical treatments used by the Muong minority of north-central Vietnam.

osene, and explosives, or the characteristics of various exotic plants.[40] Most representative were the diverse agricultural extension guides aimed at increasing rice output, improving the quality of livestock, or introducing farmers to the commercial potential and proper cultivation of such crops as corn, coffee, tea, tobacco, and coconuts.[41] One of the most interesting was titled *Some Secrets about Azolla*, introducing farmers to a particular type of organic fertilizer that twenty-five years later finally received the official attention it deserved and began to be grown and applied throughout the DRVN.[42]

Yet another means to disseminate specialized information was the calendar-almanac. The one prepared for the year 1930 by the Trung Bac Tan Van publishing house, for example, had sections listing local market days and festivals, explaining forestry regulations as well as telegraph and mail order procedures, and touting the government's agricultural, medical, and veterinary services. It also included sections on how to organize one's time efficiently, how to pour concrete, how to play a number of card games, and how to tell one's own fortune.[43] The chief editor, Nguyen Van Vinh (1882–1936), one of the best known Western-educated figures of the previous generation, was roundly criticized by younger intellectuals for giving legitimacy to fortune telling. Critics also pointed out the significance of government censors passing such "superstitious junk" while simultaneously banning what was loosely termed "communist" literature.[44]

To enable village notables, landlords, and rich peasants to understand and enforce regulations as well as take advantage of specialized services, colonial administrators prepared a variety of handbooks in French and had them translated into *quoc ngu*.[45] Particular attention was devoted to land measurement, property and inheritance laws, and the petitioning of officials beyond the village or canton level. Most ambitious was *Rural People Should Know*, a 167-page manual covering not only those topics in detail, but also instructing people on what to do in the event of fire, flood, or epidemic, describing each form of colonial taxation, and explaining the host of identification certificates that each individual was supposed to acquire from the time he was born to the time he was buried.[46] Readers were repeatedly told not to be dirty, to obey every law or face the consequences, and to be grateful that one's taxes were being used to public benefit. In fact, however,

40. Le Van Kinh, *Khoa Hoc Tung Dam* [Science Notes] (Saigon, 1934).

41. A cursory survey turned up 29 texts on applied agriculture published between 1925 and 1944.

42. Nguyen Cong Tieu, *Nhung Dieu Bi Mat ve Beo Dau* (Hanoi, 1934). 10,000 copies.

43. *Nien Lich Thong Thu: Nam Canh Ngo 1930* [Calandar-Almanac: Year of the Horse 1930] (Hanoi, 1929). 50,000 copies.

44. PNTV 66 (21 Aug. 1930), 73 (9 Oct. 1930), 76 (30 Oct. 1930), 79 (27 Nov. 1930), and 109 (19 Nov. 1931).

45. A cursory survey turned up eighteen such manuals published between 1924 and 1936.

46. Pierre Grossin, *Dan Que Nen Biet*, trans. Nguyen Van Nghi (Hanoi, 1928).

almost all the colonial services mentioned were quite beyond the means of the poor and landless peasants who constituted about three-fifths of the total population. Two exceptions were enlistment in the colonial army and signing up as a contract laborer in Cochinchina or New Caledonia.

Urban Vietnamese, too, had a range of practical guides from which to choose. Most seem to have been aimed at small traders and shopkeepers (see chapter 3), but there were also *quoc ngu* guides for journalists, clerks, accountants, stenographers, typists, draftsmen, building contractors, auto mechanics, chauffeurs, and photographers.[47] Significantly, there were very few manuals for artisans or small manufacturers. One exception was a text ambitiously titled *Science and Industry*.[48] Concerned both by unemployment triggered by the Great Depression and by Vietnam's reliance on consumer goods from France, the author, a chemical engineer, limited himself to providing instructions on how to manufacture soap, toothpaste, shampoo, face powder, hair dye, granulated sugar and lubricating oils. During World War II the French in Indochina were forced to improvise techniques for producing some of the items previously imported, but very little of this experimentation seems to have made its way into Vietnamese publications.[49]

It was from periodicals that the average literate individual probably learned the most about Western scientific and technological discoveries. Early issues of *Nam Phong*, for example, explained to readers the development of the submarine, airplane, telephone, camera, and concrete. At a somewhat more theoretical level, *Nam Phong* editors and translators offered brief histories of modern astronomy, physics, and biochemistry. Pasteur's progress in germ theory was outlined. Tuberculosis, a serious problem in Vietnam, was given special attention. Einstein's theory of relativity was characterized. The functioning of the human brain was described and a long, rather diffuse essay on psychology serialized.[50]

About a decade later, the weekly *Phu Nu Tan Van* was pursuing some of the same topics, but from a more popular perspective and with the advantage of smoother *quoc ngu* prose. Dr. Tran Van Don, for example, provided scores of articles on pregnancy, child care, and general hygiene. Various techniques for avoiding or terminating pregnancies were outlined, occasioning sharp criticism from some readers. Readers were informed of the nutritional value of unpolished

---

47. Counting the commercial guides, I saw thirty-two such urban-oriented handbooks published between 1921 and 1944.

48. Lam Van Vang, *Khoa Hoc va Cong Nghe* (Saigon, 1931). A second edition was printed in 1932; and a revised edition, titled *Tieu Cong Nghe* [Small Industry], appeared in 1936.

49. One exception was Nguyen Quoc Luong, *Xe Chay Bang Hoi Than* [Vehicles Running on Coal Gas] (Hanoi, 1942[?]), which offered detailed illustrated instructions on how to convert motor vehicle engines to run on coal or charcoal.

50. Almost all of these articles appeared in *Nam Phong* between July 1917 and December 1921, after which less and less attention was given to science and technology.

rice, as well as that of the lowly bindweed (*rau muong*). Beyond such individual advice, however, *Phu Nu Tan Van* pointedly criticized the colonial authorities for inadequate attention to preventative medicine. Such diseases as malaria, tuberculosis, cholera, syphilis, rabies, and leprosy could be controlled, the editors pointed out, if the government were willing to mount serious campaigns. When these criticisms apparently fell on deaf ears, some writers took more militant positions, suggesting that only overthrow of the imperialist system could clear the way for effective public health programs. The same transition could be observed on the subject of modern technology. *Phu Nu Tan Van* began its life in 1929 singing the praises of airplanes and motion pictures and brimming with ideas about young Vietnamese learning how to manufacture everything that was imported. It went out of existence in late 1934, preoccupied with the plight of those millions of Vietnamese who had access to nothing more than a hoe or a hammer.

Whatever their political persuasion, Vietnamese intellectuals of the 1920s and 1930s were fascinated with news from overseas. Stories ranged from the bizarre (the existence of bearded women in Europe)[51] to the gravest problems of war and peace. Events in France received the most coverage, as might be expected.[52] However, developments in China and Japan were never ignored. The United States also was a place to watch, whether for its youthful exuberance, its outrageous fads, or the power of Wall Street. With each advance of fascism, Italy and Germany became of more interest and concern. Those Vietnamese who wanted to read fascist, anti-communist, or anti-Semitic publications found that they were readily available among French *colons* in Indochina.[53] India received attention mainly because of two men: Rabindranath Tagore and Mahatma Gandhi. Very little concern was shown for Southeast Asia beyond Indochina.[54]

The Soviet Union received Vietnamese attention almost from the moment Tsar Nicolas II abdicated. *Nam Phong* praised Kerensky and attacked the "extremist revolutionaries" led by Lenin. Several months after the Bolsheviks seized power, however, *Nam Phong* included a surprisingly straightforward description of Lenin's calls for peace, land, and bread, together with his assertion that the

---

51. PNTV 84 (28 May 1930).

52. For example, between October 1934 and June 1937 the important left-wing newspaper *La Lutte* (Saigon) devoted about half its total foreign coverage to France. Daniel Hémery, "Journalisme révolutionnaire et système de la presse au Vietnam dans les années 1930," *Les Cahiers du Cursa* (Amiens), no. 8 (1978), p. 84.

53. Several local French periodicals were apparently established specifically to advocate these views. See *La Lanterne* (Cholon), published from 1933 to 1935, and *Salut Public* (Hanoi), published in 1939.

54. There were occasional articles on royal activities in Thailand, and the 1925-1926 upheavals in the Dutch East Indies received very sympathetic treatment in one booklet. Chau Van Sanh, ed. and trans., *Luoc Su Cach Mang o Nam Duong Quan Dao* [Summary History of Revolution in the South Seas Archipelago] (Saigon, 1929).

entire war was being fought by workers and peasants on behalf of capitalists who sat at home, ate well, wore good clothes, and improved their margins of profit. Subsequent issues rectified this slip, condemning the Bolsheviks for signing a separate peace with Germany, supporting the Allied intervention in Russia, and mocking Soviet sailors who visited Asian ports and apparently had the temerity to advise rickshaw pullers not to serve as beasts of burden.[55]

During the 1920s, young Vietnamese in France obtained a broad range of information on the Soviet Union. As is well known, Ho Chi Minh took the further step in 1923 of actually traveling to Moscow under Comintern auspices. The following year, after having moved on to Canton, Ho Chi Minh had published in Paris a very favorable description of the Comintern's "Toilers of the East University."[56] It was not long before scores of Vietnamese intellectuals were on their way to Moscow to observe, study, train, and exchange ideas. By 1930, sufficient numbers of students had returned to Vietnam (from France and China as well as the Soviet Union) to be able to stimulate reasonably informed discussion about Soviet and Comintern policy and performance. In 1931, the Sûreté also discovered that French Communist tracts were being expertly camouflaged inside innocuous publications, for example, the essays of the seventeenth-century moralist Fénelon, or sets of logarithm tables.[57] During the mid-1930s the weekly Saigon newspaper *La Lutte* served as (among other things) a forum for lively debate over Stalin's political conduct (see chapter 9).

Even when behind bars, radical Vietnamese often went to great lengths to obtain and circulate information about international affairs. Thus, Le Van Luong managed to follow the 1933 Berlin trial of Georgi Dimitrov by means of Paris newspapers smuggled into death row of Saigon Central Prison.[58] Three political detainees in Hanoi's Hoa Lo prison pooled their last pennies to arrange purchase of several newspapers describing Hitler's 22 June 1941 attack on the Soviet Union.[59] By 1943, ICP cadres in several prisons had reliable enough access to foreign news reports that they were able to feature regular overseas columns in clandestine newspapers. In Son La prison one creative individual summarized the international news in long poems for memorization and recitation. At the end of 1943 he pictured the German armies retreating on the Russian front, British and American aircraft bombing Berlin, guerrillas attacking in Yugoslavia, the

55. NP 2 (Aug. 1917), 7 (Jan. 1918), and 9 (Mar. 1918).

56. Article translated and reprinted in *Cach Mang Thang Muoi va Cach Mang Viet-Nam* [The October Revolution and the Vietnamese Revolution] (Hanoi, 1967), pp. 13–15. See also Ho Chi Minh, *Selected Works*, vol. 1 (Hanoi, 1960), pp. 80–84.

57. AOM (Aix) Résident Supérieur au Tonkin F-50. Message from P. Arnoux to the resident-superior et al., 19 Mar. 1931.

58. Le Van Luong, "San Sang len May Chem" [Ready to Mount the Guillotine], in Pham Hung et al., *Tren Duong Cach Mang* (Hanoi, 1960), pp. 41–51.

59. Luu Dong, *Buoc Dau Theo Dang*, pp. 91–93.

Japanese losing the Gilbert Islands, and the Congress Party demanding that Great Britain grant independence to India.[60] Pham Kiet, about to be shifted from one place of detention to another in late 1943, laboriously copied details of Allied-Axis battle information on cigarette papers, rolled them tightly, covered them with wax, and inserted the tiny cylinder in his anus. As it turned out, his new comrades had almost nothing else to read throughout 1944.[61]

Science and Objectivity

If there was one facet of the Western historical experience that most excited the Vietnamese intelligentsia, it was the development of science (*khoa hoc*). Besides the obvious relevance to problems of military and economic power, scientific methodology seemed to be at the heart of man's capacity in recent centuries to break conceptual barriers, to smash myths that had held him back for so long. Going one step further, many Vietnamese intellectuals considered science as the new and universal solution to man's age-old dilemma of seeing the world in subjective fashion. After all, if the scientific and technological revolutions proved anything, it was that such things as matter, energy, atoms, molecules, cells, and bacteria existed independently of man's perception of them, and that devising techniques to harness these "unseen" objective phenomena was essential to human progress.

The intelligentsia were painfully aware that Vietnam had not accomplished much in the experimental sciences. This was attributed variously to primitive economic conditions, Confucian orthodoxy, and (more recently) French colonial obstructionism. An occasional writer could be found defending Vietnamese traditional medicine, especially the discovery, testing, and utilization of a wide variety of tropical plants.[62] However, others stressed how almost all traditional medical practitioners had continued to accept patently unscientific concepts derived from ancient texts, had refused to subject their own findings to outside testing, and had thus failed to establish a common, cumulative body of expertise.[63]

While the term "science" soon came to mean many things to many people, everyone agreed that it signified systematic inquiry, careful measurement, and logical presentation. The traditional tendency to express oneself with calculated ambiguity was roundly condemned. In every field of knowledge it was now necessary to define terms, state propositions, attempt syllogisms, and make deduc-

---

60. Ty Thong Tin Van Hoa Son La, *Suoi Reo*, pp. 9-13.

61. "Nhung Nguoi Tu An Tri 'Cang' Ba To" [Prisoners Detained at Ba To], in Le Thiet Hung et al., *Rung Yen The* (Hanoi, 1962), pp. 5-18.

62. PNTV 76 (30 Oct. 1930), 80 (4 Dec. 1930). An acknowledged medical luminary was Le Huu Trac (1720-91), better known as Hai Thuong Lan Ong, whose 28-volume treatise demonstrates a definite ability to observe, record, and assess clinical data. *Thuong Kinh Ky Su* [Essays on Returning to the Capital] (Hanoi, 1959). Originally completed in 1782.

63. Luong Duc Thiep, *Xa Hoi Viet Nam* (Hanoi, 1944), pp. 254-58.

tions—all of which would then be subjected to external evaluation.[64] This system was not bound by limitations of history or culture, a point that impressed even traditionalist Vietnamese occasionally.[65] Armed with this belief, writers proceeded to launch appeals to investigate empirically every facet of Vietnamese reality. The "truth" (su that) might prove uncomfortable; it might violate longstanding customs and codes of behavior—yet it had to be faced if Vietnam was to survive and prosper.

Sometimes a traditionalist writer could be found denying that science had produced any leap in man's understanding of reality. Thus, Newton's gravitational laws were said to be no substantial improvement over the ancient Chinese principle that all nature interacts sympathetically. Because Darwin had failed to show the origins of life, because mathematicians were incapable of defining infinity, because physicists could not demonstrate ultraviolet light, they were not really so much better than the classical philosophers. As for that current giant, Albert Einstein, he had merely confirmed Chuang-tzu's assertion that there were no absolutes.[66] For two other writers in the same journal, however, Einstein's theory of relativity suggested something more provocative. Henceforth, they said, everyone would need to be more precise in making assertions. For example, if a friend stated that the road from Hanoi to Saigon was long, one needed to ask, "In relation to what?" Compared to a stroll from Peach Street to Dong Xuan Market in Hanoi, it was indeed long; but compared to a trip from Europe to America, it was not. They went on to explain that this principle applied to time as well as space, so that when defining one's exact position it was actually necessary to speak of four dimensions.[67]

During the colonial period only a handful of Vietnamese acquired the expertise in physics and mathematics to fully appreciate four-dimensional thinking. However, a great many intellectuals were impressed by the ability of scientists to develop unambiguous terms and symbols to communicate their findings to other scientists, thus permitting independent testing and the successful transit of cultural and linguistic barriers. Phan Van Truong suggested that hundreds of teachers, journalists, lawyers and other professionals take up the scientific challenge when translating from foreign languages to Vietnamese.[68]

64. Phan Khoi, "Moi Tran Trong Kim," PNTV 63 (31 July 1930), p. 15.

65. See, for example, Tran Trong Kim, Pham Duy Khiem, and Bui Ky, Viet Nam Van Pham [Vietnamese Grammar] (Hanoi, 1940), p. vi, in which Tran Trong Kim pointedly rejects the argument that Western grammatical methods are inappropriate for analyzing the Vietnamese language. "East or West, reason is the same," he asserts.

66. Tran Van Tang, "Qua Khu va Hien Tai," NP 106 (June 1926), pp. 413–33. Chuong Hong Chieu, "Hoc Thuyet Tay voi Hoc Thuyet Tau: Darwin va Trang Tu," NP 87 (Sept. 1924), pp. 216–26.

67. Truong Truc Dinh and Nguyen Dong Ha, NP 76 (Oct. 1923), pp. 316–26.

68. Viec Giao Duc Hoc Van Trong Dan Toc Annam (Saigon, 1925), pp. 11–12.

What struck Vietnamese most forcefully, however, was the purpose and method with which an Einstein or a Marie Curie worked. They seemed to combine an inner passion to achieve with an outer refusal to be swayed by subjective considerations. Trying to benefit from their example, Phan Van Hum devised his own file-card system to record every bit of significant data that came to his attention. Being of philosophical bent, he focused on different nuances of meaning as encountered in French, Chinese, and Vietnamese publications. In 1934 he recommended the filing system to his readers, explaining how to organize one's external findings on the one hand and add personal assessments on the other, thus achieving insights over time that were greater than the mere sum of the accumulated parts. Phan Van Hum also encouraged every literate Vietnamese to write down thoughts regularly, either in the form of a diary, as book reviews, or as reflective essays. This practice, he said, would force clarification of personal attitudes and provide invaluable training in communication.[69] In subsequent decades thousands of Vietnamese did precisely what Phan Van Hum had recommended, collecting notes, keeping diaries, and reformulating ideas, either for their own edification or possible publication. Leading intellectuals continued to provide pointers on how to order one's desk and papers so as to be "master of one's work." Although one could not expect to be a Darwin or Mendeleyev and achieve perfect classification systems, any sensible filing procedure would reap rewards.[70]

On other occasions, writers emphasized the capacity of science to carry man beyond the realm of common sense and random speculation. While any person might sense the principle of unceasing motion after looking at the rivers, clouds, and stars, Phan Van Hum pointed out that it took someone of scientific aptitude and skill to demonstrate that the earth itself was moving in at least three directions simultaneously, or that mountains were the product of countless years of upheaval and erosion.[71] Nor did astronomers or geologists jump into such problems precipitously. Scientists took pains to define issues carefully, to state limitations, before proceeding to investigate and analyze.[72]

The opposite of science was "superstition" (me tin), which Vietnamese intellectuals felt a strong personal and social obligation to expose at every opportunity. Novelists and short-story writers were particularly devastating in their attacks on

---

69. PNTV 241 (10 May 1934) and 242 (17 May 1934).

70. La Vinh Quyen, "Nep lam viec khoa hoc tren 'ban giay' " [Scientific Work Habits at One's Desk], Van Hoa Nghe Thuat 11 (1978), pp. 9–10. Karl Marx's study is also described as an outwardly modest and somewhat jumbled place, but actually having all materials "arranged according to the inner logical discipline of [his] research."

71. Bien Chung Phap Pho Thong (Saigon, 1936), pp. 8–11.

72. Phan Van Hum, in PNTV (12 Apr. 1934).

This cover of a geography text on Ben Tre province conveys some of the intellectual excitement and confidence of the era. Courtesy of the Bibliothèque Nationale.

fortune-telling, geomancy, and quackery.[73] Essayists like Tran Huy Lieu made biting references to ignorant peasants who put their faith in magical banners and amulets when trying to assault French colonial troops.[74] Vietnamese women were considered more prone to superstition than men, thus requiring special educational attention.[75] Often one test of a liberated woman was her ability to overcome fears of ghosts and walk alone at night.[76]

Intelligentsia condemnations of superstition tended to degenerate all too easily

73. See, for example, Vu Trong Phung, *Giong To* [The Tempest] (Saigon 1966), pp. 234–43, 281 ff. The Lu, *Vang va Mau* [Gold and Blood] (Saigon, 1962; originally published in 1934), is a suspense novel built entirely around the idea of science and logic overcoming evil spirits.

74. Tran Huy Lieu, *Mot Bau Tam Su* (Hanoi, 1927), p. 17.

75. See articles in the following issues of PNTV: 48, 54, 72, 201, 225, and 243. Ironically, a subsequent ICP booklet aimed especially at women printed an advertisement for "scientific fortune-telling" only three pages after having linked continuing female superstitions to Depression setbacks in female education. Cuu Kim Son and Van Hue, *Doi Chi Em* (Hanoi, 1938), p. 42.

76. This was a practical necessity for members of clandestine organizations. Ha Thi Que, in Le Thiet Hung et al., *Rung Yen The*, pp. 85–86, recalls how she finally mustered the courage to walk past a particular haunted banyan tree in her nighttime missions for the ICP.

into ridicule directed at the prototypical "country bumpkin" (người nhà quê), the individual who lived most of his life within a few miles of his home village and who appeared unaffected by modern trends. Hoang Dao seemed to appreciate this problem when he cautioned his peers that it was not enough to mock superstitious people. Somehow, he said, one had to declare war on the ghosts and devils who still ruled the minds of the vast majority of Vietnamese, interfering with everything from pregnancy and birth to death and interment.[77] He had no practical suggestions, however, for how to attack ghosts without offending believers.

Like many other intellectuals of his generation, Hoang Dao was certain that objective laws existed to explain everything in the universe. Although many things remained unclear, someday all the secrets of nature and society would be understood. In the meantime science could be used to comprehend, conquer, and change specific components of nature and society. Through this dual process of investigation and action, man-made laws and institutions would be improved so as to eventually conform with the results of natural law.[78] In this way, too, all religious superstitions would disappear.[79] Yet, there was more than a hint of religious fervor in these intelligentsia arguments. The old spirits who had helped to explain the world previously were in effect to be replaced by the single god of Science, who would not only explain but liberate. Moreover, this was not a mere provincial or national god, but one apparently accepted by advanced people throughout the world.

While there was comfort in contemplating a future organized according to scientific laws, Vietnamese intellectuals were not unmindful of a paradox. Science also accepted that "truth" was inherently bound to conditions of time and space, and was always concrete, never abstract.[80] Scientific truth, being a very transitory phenomenon, could hardly provide believers with a sense of certainty. Apart from grand designs of timeless order, all ideas were ephemeral creatures of changeable circumstance. As might be expected, this idea appealed to Vietnamese Buddhist writers, who saw in it a modern substantiation of Buddha's ancient teachings on the impermanence of things. Their confidence thus bolstered, Buddhists went on to reassert the basic unreality of things. Totally depen-

77. Hoang Dao, Muoi Dieu Tam Niem, pp. 49–52. A simple procedure for critically assessing ghosts and other "illusions" had been proposed by Nguyen Trong Thuat in NP 103 (Mar. 1926), but it seems to have been ignored.

78. See also Nguyen Tu Thuc, Noi Chuyen Dao Nuoc Minh [A Discussion of Our Country's Religions] (Saigon[?], 1929); and Luong Duc Thiep, Duy Vat Su Quan [Historical Materialism] (Hanoi, 1945), pp. 29–30. NP 42 (Dec. 1920), pp. 446–56, has a relevant translation from Charles Moureu, La puissance de la science.

79. Nguyen An Ninh entered a mild dissent on this point, suggesting that some small superstitious component would probably remain. Ton Giao (Saigon, 1932), p. 58.

80. Pham Van Dieu, Bien Chung Duy Vat Luan, 2nd printing (Saigon, 1937), p. 41.

dent on his senses, which were notoriously unreliable, man could never transcend his subjective self. The only solution was to extinguish one's desires, thus escaping not only impermanence and unreality but human suffering as well.[81] Writers of Taoist persuasion quickly joined in, arguing that the reality of dreams was no less valid than waking reality, that man's inner spirit (*tam*) and Nature (*van vat*) were one and the same.[82]

In the opinion of other Vietnamese writers, such Buddhist and Taoist arguments represented deliberate obfuscations. It was one thing to accept the impermanence of truth, quite another to assert the unreality of things. Science insisted that there was an objective world which existed independently of man's consciousness. While no one could presume to assert the absolute identity of thought and reality, clearly the systematic quest for truth could produce major rewards. What was needed was for more people to immerse themselves in the concrete problems of the day, not retreat to a "paradise of the mind."[83]

Dialectical Materialism

Although a few Vietnamese were able to study Marxist-Leninist doctrine in Paris, Moscow, or Canton in the 1920s, the real impact inside Vietnam came in the 1930s. One of the earliest known texts to be translated into *quôc ngu* was Bukharin's *ABCs of Communism*, prepared for clandestine distribution in September 1929.[84] Because possession of any document arguing even the philosophical merits of dialectical materialism was sufficient grounds for arrest until 1933, most serious study occurred behind bars or within small study groups convened secretly by returned students. From 1933, however, books and articles began to be published legally in Cochinchina which explained the world in dialectical materialist fashion while coyly omitting the more offensive terminology and making no reference to particular sources. Thus, Cao Hai De said nothing of Marx or Lenin when he argued that socialism was the child of capitalism, that the proletariet was trying to liberate itself by destroying the capitalists, and that nationalities (*dân tôc*) were struggling to free themselves from worldwide capitalist oppression.[85]

81. Three Buddhist journals discussed these questions intensively in the mid-1930s: *Tu Bi Am* (Saigon), *Vien Am* (Hue), and *Duoc Tue* (Hanoi). SPT-2, pp. 271–95.

82. Nguyen Duy Can, *Toan Chan Triet Luan* [Essay on Authentic Philosophy] (Hanoi[?], 1936); SPT-2, pp. 366–71.

83. Phan Van Hum, "Ta voi ngoai ta" [The Self and Other], PNTV 262 (11 Oct. 1934). Thien Chieu, *Tai sao toi da cam on Dao Phat* [Why Did I Thank Buddhism] (My Tho, 1936).

84. Titled *Cong San Chu Nghia So Hoc* [Elementary Communism], a copy can be found in AOM (Aix), G.G. Indochine F-7F2.

85. *Tu Tuong Xa Hoi* [Social Thought] (Ben Tre, 1933). See also Phan Van Hum's discourse in PNTV 224 (9 Nov. 1933), as well as the related articles by "X. X." beginning in PNTV 198 (4 May 1933).

With the advent of the Popular Front government in France in 1936, Vietnamese radicals threw caution to the wind, publishing a large number of translations, synopses, and reformulations of basic Marxist-Leninist texts. Perhaps the first full-fledged Marxist study to appear in *quoc ngu* legally was *Dialectical Materialism*, by Pham Van Dieu.[86] Following a routine discussion of the mode of production and the division of labor, the author became more eloquent as he discussed the differing world views of rich and poor people. The impoverished were automatic materialists, he said, being forced to spend most of their time worrying about food, clothing, and housing. They had no trouble understanding that the body ultimately controls the will. In Russia they had moved to overthrow the capitalists not because they saw Marxism as a new religion but because they were hungry, cold, and anguished. Pham Van Dieu then went on to assert that poor people who worked directly with nature were likely to have a better grasp of reality than rich people who studied nature indirectly if at all. For centuries the rich had disseminated mystical beliefs to try to deceive the poor, while the latter unfortunately had focused too much on mere short-term gratification of the senses. Now, however, armed with the "scientific law" of dialectical materialism, the poor were on the offensive worldwide. In Vietnam, similarly armed, readers could immediately perceive why certain individuals were socialists and others idealists.[87]

During 1937 and 1938 a score more books and pamphlets of this type appeared, bearing such titles as *Summary Examination of Class Struggle*,[88] *What Is Communism?*,[89] *A Synopsis of "Das Kapital,"*[90] and *Popularized Marxism*.[91] Most authors drew liberally from available French sources, but the acts of translation and synopsis, not to mention the addition of local examples, often gave these publications a distinctly Vietnamese flavor. For example, Son Tra, in *What is a Class?*, began by pointing out that only ten years earlier intellectuals had talked simply about the nation, about Vietnamese countrymen from king to commoner aligning against the foreigner. They refused to accept the existence of social classes. Now, however, the focus had shifted dramatically: not only Vietnamese communists but Vietnamese fascists, monarchists, and Catholics openly admitted

86. *Bien Chung Duy Vat Luan* (1st ed., 1936; reprinted 1937). The author appears to draw from Russian as well as French sources. Another 1936 publication was Tran Huu Do's *Bien Chung Phap* (discussed in chapter 6), which, however, did not deal with materialism.

87. In the spirit of 1936 Saigon, Pham Van Dieu listed both ICP and Trotskyist leaders as "socialist." He aimed his "idealist" epithet at Cao Dai leaders.

88. Pham Van Dieu, *Luoc Khao ve Giai Cap Dau Tranh* (Saigon, 1937).

89. Huynh Van Tai, *Cong San la Cai Gi?* (Saigon, 1937).

90. Hoang Du, *Tom Tat Sach Tu Ban Luan cua Marx* (Hanoi, 1937[?]).

91. Hai Trieu, *Chu Nghia Mac-Xit Pho Thong* (Hue, 1938).

that there was a class system. Where they differed, Son Tra emphasized, was in communist readiness to fight the exploiting classes as part of the historical effort to eventually eliminate class struggle, whereas the ruling elements talked incessantly about the necessity of "class harmony" if one wanted to build a rich and powerful country.[92]

A favorite method of bringing dialectical materialism home to ordinary Vietnamese readers was to start by inquiring, "Why are some people rich and others poor?" The idea that such discrepancies were preordained by Heaven, or that certain families deserved their wealth because of past actions, was refuted with simple arguments drawn from Marx. To add credibility, ICP publications invariably pictured the Soviet Union as a place where the labor theory of value, class conflict, proletarian consciousness, and socialist heroism had all been demonstrated in fact. The poor Russian masses, after perceiving the true nature of feudal and capitalist exploitation, had overthrown the autocracy, seized control of the means of production, established a workers' democracy, and laid the foundations for socialism, thus becoming the gallant vanguard and model for all mankind.[93] Vietnamese Trotskyist publications naturally took issue with ICP descriptions of recent events in the Soviet Union, but they were in substantial agreement on the significance of the October 1917 Revolution (see chapter 9).

This persistent linking of what was happening in faraway Europe with the destiny of Vietnam and the Vietnamese people would not have been convincing without the prior impact of the Great Depression. Economic conditions in the colony had worsened dramatically from mid-1931, forcing hundreds of thousands of people off the land, out of work, or into bankruptcy. Some months before, the ICP had alerted members to what was happening elsewhere and had predicted the disruptive effect on Indochina.[94] Before long, Vietnamese newspapers and periodicals were filled with accounts of the collapse of the rice and rubber markets, business layoffs, mortgage foreclosures and groups of people wandering the countryside in search of the means of survival. There appeared a new genre of fiction which portrayed the plight of the poor in painful detail.[95]

---

92. [Nguyen] Son Tra, *Giai Cap la Gi?* (Tourane [Da Nang], 1938), pp. 3–5. A follow-up booklet in the same series was *Chinh Phu la Gi?* [What Is a Government?], by Trieu Van.

93. Tran Huu Do, *De Quoc Chu Nghia* (Saigon, 1937[?]), pp. 41–58; Hong Phong, *Chanh Tri Kinh Te Hoc Chi Nam* (Saigon, 1937); Tan Cuong, *The Gioi Cu va The Gioi Moi* [The Old World and the New World] (Hue [?], 1937); D. K. and T. K., *Cach Day 21 Nam* [Twenty-One Years Ago] (Hanoi, 1938).

94. *Cong San*, no. 1 (n.p., 1 Feb. 1931). Available in SLOTFOM, series 5, carton 13, document 64.

95. One of the earliest in this genre was Son Vuong, *Chen Com Lat* [An Unsalted Bowl of Rice] (Saigon, 1931). The cover has a stark drawing of a father preparing to hang himself as his two

Musical dramas about street beggars, unemployed heads of family, and pathetic suicide pacts were performed by well-known singers in Saigon.[96]

It was stunned merchants and landowners who wrote most of the early essays attempting to fathom the Depression and suggest suitable responses. Generally they stressed the global dimensions of the disaster, called for French government help, proposed that Vietnamese entrepreneurs band together more tightly, and urged the wealthy to reduce conspicuous consumption and underwrite private charity programs for the poor.[97] Occasionally, their lurking fear of what the lower classes might do was expressed openly. One writer, for example, ruminated that "laws and guns" might not be of any use when people were starving.[98]

Writers less wedded to the existing system spent an increasing amount of time simply wandering among the victims of the Depression, gaining concrete impressions and gathering information for publication. Some of the best articles focused on a single individual or family, the objective being to sustain emotional interest as well as to provide convincing detail. Letters to the editor from underprivileged readers often had the same effect.[99] For the first time, photographs of tattered street beggars, of desperate women and children hovering around the marketplace hoping for scraps, appeared in popular Vietnamese journals.[100] Another innovation, perhaps the most penetrating of all, was the critical cartoon. In late 1933, for example, one cartoonist pictured a surly mandarin telling an obviously undernourished and helpless mother and child, "With big stomachs like that, how dare you whine about being hungry!"[101] The Tet 1933 issue of *Phu Nu Tan Van* featured a cartoon contrasting the unemployment, floods, business failures, and suicides of 1932 with what the editors hoped would symbolize the new year,

---

emaciated children lie sleeping on a mat nearby. See also the tentative short stories in PNTV 150 (23 June 1932), 199 (12 May 1933), 204 (15 June 1933), and 215 (7 Sept. 1933).

96. Huynh Ha wrote and directed three such *cai luong* in 1933: "Vong Co That Nghiep" [Unemployment Song], "Vien Dan Vo Tinh" [The Indifferent Bullet], and "Bat Com That Nghiep" [Unemployment Bowl of Rice]. Performers included Phung Ha and Nam Chau. There was undoubtedly an element of commercialism in some of these Depression-oriented works. As late as 1937, the sheet music for the "Unemployment Tango" was being sold for .20 piaster. *Tango That Nghiep* (Saigon, 1937).

97. Cao Hai De, *Dieu Tra va Giai Quyet Van De Kinh Te Khung Hoang* [Investigating and Solving the Economic Depression Problem] (Saigon, 1932). Tieu Minh, *Quang Minh* [Brightness] (Go Cong, 1932). Bich Son and Yen Son, *Bot An Xai Giup Dong Bao Bi Nan vi Kinh Te Khung Hoang* [Eat Less and Help Countrymen Suffering from the Economic Depression] (Phan Thiet[?], 1932).

98. Dong Hai Thon Phu, *Vuot Qua Duong Kinh Te Khung Hoang* [Leaping across the Economic Depression Road] (Hanoi, 1933).

99. See PNTV 159 (14 July 1932), 183 (29 Dec. 1932), 235 (22 Mar. 1934), 256 (30 Aug. 1934), and 268 (29 Nov. 1934).

100. PNTV 128 (21 Apr. 1932).

101. *Thanh Nien* (Hanoi), no. 12 (21 Nov. 1933).

including new factories and shops, day-care centers, and crowds of graduating primary and high school students.[102] Ten months later, however, the editors printed two large, foreboding cartoons of unemployed workers and intellectuals.[103] Finally, in early 1934, they angrily denounced colonial tokenism, endorsed dialectial materialism, and called for poverty-striken Vietnamese women and men to join together to eliminate economic oppression.[104]

By the mid-1930s Vietnamese writers of differing political inclinations were in agreement that the Depression had caused fundamental changes, demanding serious analysis. One moderate author probably voiced the general sentiment when he began his essay on monetary policy by saying:

> In recent years Vietnam has been roused from its sleep behind thick bamboo hedges. Economic waves have hit us repeatedly, forcing everyone from merchants to peasants to wail and to moan. What has caused all this? What is the solution?[105]

A prominent Hanoi businessman claimed that the Depression was worse than the biblical Great Flood, as absolutely no one had escaped its effects. His solution was to reassert human virtue, to encourage Paris and London to lead a peaceful international economic recovery, and to propose the formation of hundreds of mutual-aid societies among Vietnamese farmers, merchants, and laborers. Members of these societies would need a new spirit of "universal patriotism," he stressed, enabling them to comprehend that the French economy had to be defended above all if the Indochinese economy was to recover. Given effective cooperation, he predicted recuperation in five years and a "bustling, sumptious, prosperous and happy" Indochina in ten years.[106] Seldom was a prediction proven so wrong.

On the other side of the political fence, ICP writers placed the Depression within the predictable Marxist-Leninist historical context, to include the vigorous Western capitalist search for raw materials and new markets, the emergence of competing colonial spheres, the imperialist bloodletting of 1914–18, the upsurge of a socialist alternative, and the anticipated collapse of world capitalism.[107] Of more practical consequence, however, were the essays that discussed how Indochina in particular fitted into the world capitalist system, and then proceeded to employ the tools of dialectical materialism to explain social and economic developments inside the colony. Thus, the recent waves of dispossessed farmers and

102. PNTV Special Tet Issue, 19 Jan. 1933.
103. PNTV 221 (19 Oct. 1933).
104. PNTV Special Tet Issue, Feb. 1934; PNTV 236 (29 Mar. 1934).
105. Tran Nhuoc Thuy, *Van De Tien Bac* [The Question of Money] (Hanoi, 1934), preface.
106. Nguyen Ban, *Cuu Nan Kinh Te Khung Hoang* [Rescue from the Economic Depression] (Hanoi, 1935). An informative twenty-page "Honor Roll of Meritorious Builders of the Indochina Economy" is appended to the author's essay.
107. Tran Huu Do, *De Quoc Chu Nghia*, pp. 1–40.

ruined artisans were linked to much broader capitalist historical trends.[108] The heightened exploitation of Vietnamese female laborers, servants, and petty traders was tied to market forces unleashed by the Depression.[109] Other writers concentrated on increasingly sharp contradictions between landlords and tenants or agricultural laborers.[110] There were also investigations of specific French colonial policies—for example, Truong Chinh's and To Dan's careful, concise attack on the head tax.[111] In the interests of building a common front against fascism, however, some obvious implications of Marxist-Leninist doctrine for Indochina were ignored or stated only in the most general of terms.

Some of the best writing on the material conditions of different classes of Vietnamese was done by novelists, none of whom chose to accept the discipline of any political party in the 1930s. Khai Hung, for example, wrote knowingly about the privileged milieu of northern mandarin and landlord families. Nhat Linh captured the more intense, urgent life of the petit bourgeoisie. His younger brother, Thach Lam, explored the further reaches of urban poverty, including the lives of unemployed clerks, destitute widows, and struggling prostitutes. Still others focused on rickshaw pullers, coal miners, gamblers, petty thieves, and smugglers. Nguyen Cong Hoan and Ngo Tat To ventured successfully beyond the towns to write about the increasingly tense world of the village notable, moneylender, poor peasant, and agricultural laborer.[112] As works of art, these publications ran the gamut from romantic to realist to naturalist; taken together, they provided a devastating indictment of colonial society, even though their political message tended to be vague or non-committal. By 1940, although many literate Vietnamese were probably still unable to explain dialectical materialism—much less apply the theory to Vietnamese conditions—there was hardly anyone who had not come to empathize with the plight of the poor and downtrodden as seen through *quoc ngu* fiction.[113]

Who (or What) Makes History?

Taking the historical materialism of Karl Marx at face value, Vietnamese might have been forced to conclude that major advances in the capitalist mode of pro-

---

108. See, for example, Nhan Chi, *Chi Em Lao Kho voi Xa Hoi* (Thanh Hoa, 1938), pp. 11–22.

109. Cuu Kim Son and Van Hue, *Doi Chi Em* (Hanoi, 1938), pp. 3–9, 32–40.

110. Truong Chinh and Vo Nguyen Giap, *The Peasant Question*, pp. 17–19, 28–43, 66–77.

111. Qua Ninh (Truong Chinh) and To Dan, *Mot Du An Cai Cach Thue Than* [A Proposal to Reform the Head Tax] (Hanoi, 1938). The authors proposed substitution of a steeply progressive income tax. Numerous shorter articles on the above topics appeared regularly in ICP-controlled periodicals, such as *Tin Tuc* (Hanoi), *Dan Chung* (Saigon), and *Dan* (Hue).

112. Hoang Ngoc Thanh, "The Social and Political Development of Vietnam as seen through the Modern Novel" (Ph.D. diss., Univ. of Hawaii, 1968), pp. 182–259.

113. To what degree each of these writers of fiction mirrored reality or even had that intent is a separate question which deserves more investigation.

duction would need to occur in their country before a working class of sufficient size and self-consciousness could be generated to smash the imperialists—either that, or Vietnam would be required to wait for the French proletariat to seize power in the metropole and (presumably) dismantle the colonial system. By the early 1930s, however, it was obvious that neither the Vietnamese bourgeoisie nor the Vietnamese proletariat was going to grow very large under French colonial rule, and that the French proletariat was no closer to victory than it had been a decade or two earlier. For the mode of production to work its magic, Vietnamese might have to remain colonial subjects for another hundred years or more.

Karl Marx was far from being a mechanical determinist, however. Although certain that in history lies the meaning of human existence, Marx also believed that once man came to an understanding of his past he could locate the present stage of his journey and know by what means he had to travel to reach its end. History thus commanded action; but the actor, knowing, could determine history. It was for this reason that Engels quoted Hegel approvingly in the assertion that "Necessity is blind only in so far as it is not understood."[114] Lenin, of course, went even further in endorsing voluntarism and in rejecting any evolutionary interpretation of Marx.

When the time came in the early 1920s for Ho Chi Minh to grapple with these problems, the stunning success of Lenin and the Bolsheviks in Russia appeared to have already dealt a sharp blow to those socialists who stressed the importance of the capitalist mode of production and the overall size and sophistication of the working class. Of greater significance was the formation of a highly disciplined proletarian vanguard party, which could transform the unconscious spontaneity of the masses into fully conscious revolutionary theory and practice. If the Bolsheviks could seize power in semi-feudal Russia, there was no reason why a similar party could not eventually do likewise in Vietnam.

As a dedicated internationalist Ho Chi Minh nonetheless accepted that any such victory in Vietnam would be both difficult to engineer and hard to defend without a parallel victory of the French proletariat over the French bourgeoisie. In 1924 he stated the problem with characteristic pungency:

> Capitalism is a leech with two suckers, one attached to the metropolitan proletariat, the other to the proletariat in the colonies. If we want to kill the animal, we must cut off both suckers simultaneously. If only one is cut off, the other will continue to suck the blood of the proletariat; the animal will continue to live, and the cut-off sucker will grow again.[115]

Ho Chi Minh was prepared to take up his half of the challenge immediately.

114. *Anti-Dühring* (London: Lawrence and Wishart, 1934), p. 128. Translated by Emile Burns.

115. *La correspondence internationale*, no. 46 (1924).

Already in 1921 he had predicted the day when millions of Asians formed a "colossal force" to eliminate one of the necessary conditions of capitalism—imperialism—and thus aid their Western brothers in the total emancipation.[116] Nonetheless, to build such a force required communist vanguards, which in turn required Comintern approval and assistance. In subsequent years Ho Chi Minh often chided his European Comintern associates for not devoting enough attention to the colonies. Eventually, in 1941 he went ahead without apparent reference to higher authority, although certainly convinced that a Viet Minh victory in Vietnam would be of service to the cause of proletarian internationalism.

It is important to remember that, long before coming to Marxism-Leninism, Ho Chi Minh was very familiar in both theory and practice with problems of determinism and free will. Broadly speaking, the classical Confucian texts and history books which he had read as a boy taught that whereas the "Way of Heaven" (Dao Tròi) definitely existed above all mortals, that did not mean that it was entirely *beyond* them. Some human beings had the capacity to understand the Way and thus influence temporal and even cosmological reality. A ruler, in particular, was expected to demonstrate this understanding by means of virtuous conduct; only thus could he be said to deserve the "Mandate of Heaven" (Mênh Tròi) and be blessed with loyal officials and industrious subjects. When there was order in the world, the ruler's power to make history was very seldom questioned; when there was upheaval and fratricide, however, each disciple of the Way was supposed to analyze causes, make judgments, and take appropriate actions. The majority might well find doctrinal reasons for continuing to support the ruler, perhaps from a more conditional position; a minority might try to take events into their own hands. Whatever the case, history taught rulers and ruled alike that from very ancient times there had been cycles of virtue and decadence which coincided with periods of peace and disorder. A ruling dynasty might extend its lease on power through virtuous acts, but it could not expect to hold power indefinitely.

Though a classically educated Vietnamese might be unfortunate enough to live during a period of decadence and disorder, at least there was an abundant corpus of historical precedent to help him make personal choices. Some of these models clearly suggested that "destiny" (dinh mênh) existed apart from individual effort: if so, then one could either wait for events to sort themselves out, or one could act forthrightly according to one's inner perception of the Way, letting destiny make itself felt in its own time. Other models stressed the atunement of one's actions with external reality—in short, of doing "all things according to the times" (tuy thoi). While this principle had an obvious deterministic thrust, if an individual perceived the world to be turned upside down, it might also legitimize

116. *Revue Communiste* (May 1921), as reprinted in Daniel Hémery, "Du Patriotisme au Marxisme," *Le Mouvement Social* 90 (Jan.–Mar. 1975), pp. 49–51.

surprising changes in behavior. Perhaps the best known philosophical effort to reconcile destiny and individual responsibility was that of Chu Hsi, who bluntly advised no one to be so rash as to stand under a precipitous wall and assert that everything depended on the Mandate of Heaven. "Whenever a man has done his very best, there he has his destiny alone," Chu Hsi added.[117]

Going further along the voluntarist path, at least one nineteenth-century Vietnamese literatus had implied that a "destiny" which cannot be perceived in advance is almost the same as not having one at all. Not only should one focus solely on human virtue, but perhaps one could also recognize that the outcome was primarily of human derivation.[118] As mentioned previously (chapter 2), Nguyen Dinh Chieu had pointedly condemned Catholicism for being other-worldly and determinist, not to mention traitorous. The fact that he used the term "Way of Heaven" for Catholicism (as opposed to the legitimate "Way of Man" [Dao Nguoi] of Confucianism) suggested a major reinterpretation of the relationship between the universe and man—which, unfortunately, Nguyen Dinh Chieu never explained further.

Ho Chi Minh was also intimately aware of a number of less orthodox teachings and stories which downgraded determinism almost entirely in favor of "willpower" (y chi), the capacity of certain individuals to overcome the worst historical odds, sometimes by magical means. Often Taoist in origin, these ideas were deeply embedded in Vietnamese folklore and popular fiction. Many Confucian literati were influenced as well.[119] It should not surprise us, therefore, that as a youth Ho Chi Minh delighted in hearing such exciting folktales, and preferred reading *Monkey* or the *Romance of the Three Kingdoms* to the Neo-Confucian canon. He also knew all the stories of Vietnamese heroes, from the distant Trung sisters to anticolonial literati like Phan Dinh Phung, who had fought and only recently died in the hills not too far from his home.

Ho Chi Minh grew up amidst Confucian literati who not only knew all these precedents well, but who, in the face of relentless French pressures, were being forced to make agonizing decisions that would carry weight far beyond their own homes. His mandarin father, his great-uncle, several of his early teachers, and numerous family friends each had to choose between resistance and collaboration, withdrawal and participation. As a boy he sat with fascination at Phan Boi Chau's feet, listening to him recite poetry. As an adolescent he was enrolled in a program of French studies leading to an official position, but later dropped

117. Chu-tzu Ch'üan-shu [Complete Works of Master Chu] as quoted in Wing Tsit Chan, *A Source Book in Chinese Philosophy* (Princeton: Princeton Univ. Press, 1963), pp. 627–28.

118. Nguyen Duc Dat, *Nam Son Tung Thoai* [Collected Conversations of Nam Son], as discussed in SPT-1, pp. 123–26. Tran Van Giau points out, however, that Nguyen Duc Dat simultaneously professed belief in the divination concepts of Tung Chung-shu.

119. See SPT-1, pp. 117–23, 456–57, 468–69.

that to wander south and eventually to Europe.[120] Consciously or not, Ho Chi Minh's life had taken on the character of a twentieth-century Gautama in search of enlightenment.

While Ho Chi Minh was still an adolescent, Phan Boi Chau and other members of his literati generation were seeking inspiration from recent Chinese reinterpretations of Social Darwinism (see chapter 7). Like Liang Ch'i-ch'ao, Vietnamese literati picked up and quickly elaborated on the themes of human dynamism, struggle, and progress. Also like Liang, however, they preferred to ignore Herbert Spencer's "Olympian detachment," his claim to be describing the impersonal forces of social evolution. From their point of view it seemed obvious that if neither China nor Vietnam had benefitted from this evolutionary process for centuries, then the conscious wills of contemporary men and women would have to be aroused to ward off disaster.[121] One of the key slogans of Vietnamese patriotic literati thus became "Heaven helps those who help themselves."[122] In that spirit a new textbook on Vietnamese heroes, circulated at the short-lived Dong Kinh Nghia Thuc school in 1907, concluded as follows:

Amidst these European winds and American rains, who knows but that there may be men who on behalf of their country will sweep away the fog, lift up the clouds, and create a radiant and expansive horizon for us all![123]

Thrown into confusion in 1908 by sharp French counteraction, however, many Vietnamese literati fell back on deterministic interpretations of reality. Most readily available was the "Will of Heaven," an explanation repeated by some traditionalists for another four decades.[124] Others came to accept French arguments about the inevitable advance of Western civilization and the consequent benefits of colonial tutelage. Even Phan Boi Chau, who found both these positions quite repugnant, and who insisted on retaining the idea that willpower could move mountains, admitted by 1914 that the actions of his small anticolonial group had only one chance in ten thousand of achieving Vietnamese independence. His

120. Hoai Thanh et al., *Bac Ho, Hoi Ky* (Hanoi, 1960), pp. 5–27.

121. For an excellent discussion of Liang Ch'i-ch'ao's attack on "fate" and promotion of voluntarism, see Hao Chang, *Liang Ch'i-ch'ao and Intellectual Transition in China, 1890–1907* (Cambridge, Mass., 1971), pp. 177–89.

122. As late as 1929 Phan Boi Chau was still employing this slogan to summarize his advice to the younger generation. PNTV 10 (4 July 1929), pp. 10–11. Ngoc Son and Doan Hiet, *Guong Ai Quoc* (Saigon, 1928), p. iii, modifies the slogan to "Help yourself first and Heaven will help you thereafter."

123. *Nam Quoc Vi Nhan Truyen* [Stories of Vietnamese Heroes], quoted in Dang Thai Mai, *Van Tho Cach Mang Viet-Nam Dau The Ky XX* (Hanoi, 1964), p. 75.

124. The most coherent exposition of this concept can be found in Tran Trong Kim, *Nho Giao*, vol. 1 (Saigon, 1962), pp. 85–87, 179–80, 190. On the other hand, the same author's memoirs, written in 1949, emphasized the Buddhist concept of Karma. Tran Trong Kim, *Mot Con Gio Bui* (Saigon, 1969).

only defense was that he had to act in a righteous fashion, without reference to victory or defeat.[125] By 1919, his followers all dead, imprisoned, or demoralized, Phan Boi Chau was forced to live from hand to mouth in Hangchow.

Despite this impasse, however, Phan Boi Chau had already made one significant contribution to voluntarist thinking in Vietnam. He had started by 1914 to shift the focus away from the very few "superior men" (*quan tu*) who projected their wills across history, to the proposition that millions of people needed to be convinced of their capacity to make history if Vietnam was ever to be independent. Characteristically, he couched his explanation in historical terms, contrasting the social needs of the past with those of the present and future. In olden days, he claimed, individual capacity was often decisive simply because the magnitude of organization was small, perhaps that of a tribe, clan, or minor principality. At the current level of struggle between nations, however, it was clearly the ability of great masses of people to mobilize that provided the margin between victory and defeat.[126]

Later Vietnamese writers took this message to heart, often under the rubric of enhancing the "people's spirit" (*dan khi*), and by the late 1920s scores of *quoc ngu* publications were urging readers to exercise willpower. At first the problem was viewed primarily as one of acquiring certain new personality traits and casting off old ones. Thus, Vietnamese were urged to emulate Columbus, Magellan, and David Livingstone in their willingness to advance into the dangerous unknown (see chapter 6). Vietnamese also needed to cultivate a sense of militant fervor, a total belief in their cause, and be ready to live on hope, the expectation of great achievements, rather than quick gratification. Sometimes these odes to self-confidence verged on the mystical, as when Tran Huu Do recalled the classical Chinese fable of the hunter who shot an arrow at what he *thought* was a tiger but actually turned out to be a rock. The hunter's commitment was such that, amazingly, the arrow pierced the rock. However, when the man tried to duplicate the performance, *knowing* that it was a rock, it proved quite impossible.[127]

To balance such visions, Tran Huu Do also extolled the merits of calm perseverance, of responding to inevitable setbacks with rational self-criticism rather than panic or frustration. Moses, one of his favorite examples of fortitude, had devoted forty grim years to leading his people out of bondage. More recently, had not Bernard Palissy taken eighteen poverty-stricken years to fashion a radical new method for firing pottery? Had not those teams of men trying to lay a cable across the Atlantic Ocean been thwarted seven times before finally devising a

125. SPT-2, pp. 126–27, 130, 151–53, 162–66. Significantly, Tran Van Giau supports Phan Boi Chau's reasoning, but criticizes as short-sighted and adventuristic similar arguments made only a decade later by the Viet Nam Quoc Dan Dang and other nationalist groups.

126. Dang Thai Mai, *Van Tho Cach Mang*, pp. 211–21.

127. *Tu Co Mat Quyen Tu Do* (Saigon, 1926), pp. 41–46.

technique to do the job successfully?[128] "Defeat is the mother of victory" came to summarize such historical examples for an entire generation of Vietnamese.

As did Phan Boi Chau, Tran Huu Do oriented his entire discussion around national independence, warning that much work, conflict, pain, and imprisonment would precede achievement of that treasured goal.[129] He reaffirmed the need for a multitude of "ordinary heroes" rather than a single grand leader who might not be able to fill all the complex requirements of modern struggle.[130] Real progress might not be evident for thirty years or even a century; and for each hero who lived to tell of his exploits, there would be many of equal temper who died. Like Jesus on the cross, death could not be equated with failure. Tran Huu Do further cautioned his readers that once they had taken the first steps along this dangerous road there would be no turning back.[131] One might enter the struggle of one's own free will, but the nature of the colonial system made it impossible to simply opt out at a later date.

Among personality traits said to be obstructing Vietnamese progress, writers of the late 1920s generally cited selfishness, petty status-seeking, social divisiveness, lack of individual initiative, unwillingness to risk one's life for a lofty principle, and the inability to sustain transcendent or universalistic purpose. There continued to be confusion, however, about why such alleged deficiencies existed, much less what to do about them. On the one hand, current biographies of past Vietnamese heroes clearly suggested that there had been no lack of idealistic, determined, resourceful leaders during earlier periods of crisis; moreover, these leaders had often found sufficient numbers of Vietnamese of similar temperament to accomplish great collective feats. But other essayists, attracted to the idea that psychological characteristics are socially determined, suggested that the offending traits would disappear as the conditions which spawned them were transformed.[132] Still other writers were of the opinion that within any society at any particular point in time a wide range of character traits could be identified. If, for some reason, the peculiar historical conditions did not seem to be throwing forward the appropriate personalities, then it was the solemn responsibility of patriotic intellectuals to highlight the need.[133]

At root, each of these intellectuals was asserting a natural right to choose his own destiny. Further, each believed that the *degree* of personal commitment was as important as the content. As Nguyen An Ninh phrased it,

128. *Hon Doc Lap* (Saigon, 1926), pp. 18–20. These examples were taken from the writings of Liang Ch'i-ch'ao.

129. *Hoi Trong Tu Do*, vol. 2 (Saigon, 1926), p. 4.

130. Tran Huu Do, *To Co Mat Quyen Tu Do*, pp. 59–60.

131. Idem, *Hon Doc Lap*, pp. 22–23.

132. Tran Huy Lieu, *Mot Bau Tam Su* (Saigon, 1927), pp. 2–19.

133. Duong Ba Trac, *Tieng Goi Dan* (Hanoi, 1925), pp. 6–54, suggests this line of reasoning, except that, in accordance with the Doctrine of the Mean, the author counsels his contemporaries not to go too far in any one direction.

for human beings, living is like gambling. In gambling there are only two doors: winning and losing. In life there are also only two doors: life and death; good and evil. If one fails to choose, if one does not resolve one's own course, one still ends up going through one of those doors to honor or dishonor, greatness or cowardice. There is one difference, however. For a gambler, holding the same cards as "the house" means defeat. For a person, having the determination to live and to do right is the path to victory.[134]

Not satisfied with better than even odds, Nguyen An Ninh went on to argue that "If you believe in a lofty cause, a job that must be done, then, although it may take several hundred years, the fact of putting all your strength into it will give you power to overcome even T'ai Shan mountain."[135]

Occasionally, collaborator Vietnamese could also be found endorsing the power of the will. In 1923, for example, an extraordinary article appeared in the government-subsidized journal *Nam Phong* describing how the Great War had thrust forward such leaders as Lenin, Kemal Attaturk, d'Annunzio, and Mussolini, men who had suffered much, who were products of their time, yet who had the forcefulness and insight to capitalize on initial successes and turn dreams into reality. "The river brought them along, but eventually they harnessed the river," the author summarized, consciously attempting to reconcile the philosophical positions of Tolstoy and Carlyle. Although avowedly anticommunist, the author still placed Lenin above the others because of his ability to predict conditions for revolution in Russia and to formulate a policy placing power in the hands of the Bolsheviks.[136]

Radical or conservative, no Vietnamese intellectual wished to disparage anyone who seemed to know how to predict developments and formulate sound political strategies. However, rather than wait for a Vietnamese Lenin or Mussolini to appear, the emphasis was on locating lots of men and women of fervent, rash, abiding sentiment, yet also flexible, ready to admit errors and to act to correct them. In short, the ideal member of the intelligentsia was one who combined passionate commitment with cool, critical, and informed analysis.

The dynamic tension (if not contradiction) between passionate commitment and cool analysis became evident by the mid-1930s. Most radical Vietnamese intellectuals thought of themselves as anti-imperialist, antifeudal and—to the degree their knowledge and experience permitted—scientific. Even those who knew very little about the established scientific disciplines were firm believers in "scientism" (*khoa hoc chu nghia*), although that term did not appear to be used extensively. That is, they placed all reality within a universal order, and deemed all aspects of this order—biological, physical, social or psychological—to be knowable only by the methods of science. While scientific laws of nature and of

134. *Hai Ba Trung* (Saigon, 1928), p. 45.

135. Ibid., p. 62.

136. Hong Nhan, trans., "Thoi The voi Anh Hung" [The Times in Relation to Heroes], NP 72 (June 1923), pp. 471–79 (adapted from an article by Ludovic Naudeau).

human society need not necessarily coincide, scientism did require the acceptance of matter as the only reality and the denial of the separate existence of soul or spirit.

If matter was the only reality, how did it relate to human willpower? This key question was raised occasionally but apparently never discussed critically. As early as 1921 Pham Quynh provided a useful description of the physiology of the human brain and mentioned Western research linking biology, neurology, and psychology. However, he dropped the subject precisely at the point of relating sexual and other biological instincts to broader human behavior, jumping instead to a more comfortable discussion of moral and intellectual controls over the psyche.[137] Nguyen Trieu Luat was somewhat less reticent a few years later, introducing Nam Phong readers to a wide range of Western psychological terminology and conceptions, including the unconscious, the ego, individual personality, and the physiology of perception.[138] Although mentioning instincts and seemingly accepting that human beings sought pleasure and avoided pain, Nguyen Trieu Luat was far more eager to discuss man's "superior inclinations," including his fertile imagination, his quest for truth and beauty, and his urge to pursue the unknown and the dangerous. Perhaps the closest he came to assessing personally the welter of conflicting arguments among Western psychologists and philosophers was to argue that the "body" and "mind" needed each other in the same way as a mandolin needed strings. Then, however, he further suggested the need for "someone to pluck the strings and press the frets." Whether that "someone" was an external God or an internal élan vital was left deliberately unanswered.

Six years later the issue was still bothering Nguyen An Ninh. Although believing fervently in the ascendancy of scientific methodology and expertise, he was disturbed by any proposition that the "body" and the "mind" were totally linked, since that appeared to eliminate man's ability or necessity to choose good reject evil. He wondered, too, whether the status previously accorded in the West to a monotheistic God—transcendent source of all power, and hence jealous custodian of free will—was now unfortunately being granted to Science.[139]

Perhaps the closest that Vietnamese writers came to serious exploration of biological and psychological interrelationships was in the fiction of the late 1930s. This was a direct outgrowth of the depictions of unemployed and dispossessed victims of the Great Depression discussed previously. The main purpose was to demonstrate how a life of grinding poverty or adverse psychological conditioning (or both) could make spiritual concerns almost irrelevant. Thach Lam, for exam-

---

137. NP 36 (June 1920) and 47 (May 1921).

138. See "Tam Ly Hoc," NP 89 (Nov. 1924), 90 (Dec. 1924), 92 (Feb. 1925), 95 (May 1925), 96 (June 1925), 101 (Dec. 1925), 102 (Jan.–Feb. 1926), 103 (Mar. 1926), 105 (May 1926), 107 (July 1926), and 108 (Aug. 1926).

139. Ton Giao (Saigon, 1932), pp. 35–36.

ple, described the torment of a jobless husband whose wife had just felt compelled to sell her sexual favors to obtain food for them both. First throwing the
food on the floor, then picking it up and wolfing it down, the husband recalled
how in the past he had despised those individuals who scrambled constantly for
the next meal and ignored important spiritual questions entirely.[140] Other writers
evoked the petty cleverness of various elements of the *lumpenproletariat* or the
battered stoicism of poor peasants. When several literary critics questioned the
value of doting on the seamier side of life, the scene was set for a battle of pens
between "materialists" and "idealists."

Amidst these polemics it soon became apparent that the "materialists" were
not especially eager to stress the idea that "mind" is determined by "body," or
even that proposition that the mass of poor Vietnamese were motivated primarily by basic material needs. Significantly, the debate quickly took on a strong
literary flavor, with questions of real living conditions and real attitudes among
ordinary peasants and workers being largely ignored. Much of the argument
centered on the relationship between individual creativity and historical progress. Under the banner of "Art for humanity's sake," the foremost representative
of the "materialists," Hai Trieu (1908–54), began by quoting Bukharin to the
effect that art is both a product of society and a means for the "socialization of
sentiment." Both the origins and the end purpose of art thus lay within society,
but there apparently was something titled "sentiment" which was not entirely
material in derivation.[141] Several years later, still drawing from Soviet sources,
Hai Trieu offered a more dynamic image, saying that writers should consider
themselves "engineers of the soul." Unlike mechanical engineers, or military officers who issued commands, or priests who mouthed dogmas, creative writers
aimed to reach and stimulate the inner recesses of the human psyche. Thus they
needed to be indirect, flexible, subtle, and clever in approach. Nevertheless, the
creative product had to be "social realism," and it ought to stem more from the
objective situation than from the author's subjective feelings.[142]

Vietnamese "idealists" upheld the existence of external masterpieces in art,
declared that talented individuals should be free to pursue whatever muse they
wished, denounced any proposition that art is a product of social conditioning,
and, of course, ridiculed the notion that "spirit" is entirely dependent on "matter." They endorsed the idea that contemporary artists had a solemn responsibil-

---

140. *Gio Dau Mua* [First Wind of the Season] (Saigon, 1965), pp. 69–84 (originally published
in 1927).

141. "Nghe Thuat vi Nghe Thuat hay Nghe Thuat vi Nhan Sinh" [Art for Art's Sake or Art for
Humanity's Sake], in Vu Dinh Lien et al., ed., HT-5, pp. 467–74. Originally published in *Doi Moi*
(1935).

142. "Di toi Chu Nghia Ta Thuc Trong Van Chuong" [Advancing to Realist Literature], in Vu
Dinh Lien et al., ed., HT-5, pp. 463–66. Originally published in *Tao Dan* (1939).

ity to help create a fuller, more beautiful life for everyone, but argued that the initiative must come from within, not be ordained from without. Finally, most Vietnamese idealists championed the Promethean vision of civilization as the product of a determined, energetic humanity clashing with a malevolent universe; in their eyes, civilization was the ultimate expression of man's will to overcome death and nothingness, not some crude amassing of technical and organizational achievements.[143]

Although Vietnamese Marxist-Leninists would never cease attacking idealism, it seems clear that the closer they looked at their own culture and the harder they worked at mass mobilization, the more idealistic their own publications became. Eventually they accepted 'The Tale of Kieu' as an eternal masterpiece, endorsed the idea of a timeless Vietnamese spirit, and fashioned their own approved pantheon of immortal Vietnamese heroes (see chapter 6). It is also probably fair to say that most Vietnamese Marxist-Leninists were never determinists except in their certainty that history ultimately belonged to them. While everything was supposed to depend on concrete historical conditions, there was no chance of those conditions proving unfavorable in the long run; nor was society likely to undergo mere evolutionary change. Contradictions might take some time to develop, but they would be resolved abruptly and violently.[144] Besides, Ho Chi Minh had already suggested that the more oppression a social class suffers, the more committed it becomes to revolutionary struggle. Presumably transferring Newton's Third Law of Dynamics to social theory, yet another writer asserted that wherever there is ruling-class pressure one will always find counterpressure from the exploited classes, which results in historical progress.[145]

No Vietnamese Marxist-Leninist was supposed to sit idly by and wait for these contradictions to work themselves out. It was the responsibility of the proletarian vanguard not only to explain contemporary society but to change it.[146] By "thrusting one's hands into action," Phan Van Hum affirmed, one could "help speed up the dialectical process."[147] Human progress was qualitatively different from progress elsewhere in nature precisely because of the role of ideologically-

143. Hoai Thanh, Le Trang Lieu, and Luu Trong Lu, Van Chuong va Hanh Dong [Literature and Action] (Hanoi, 1936). Two other prominent idealist writers of this period were Phan Khoi and Thieu Son.

144. For substantiation, one author cited the 1789 and 1917 Revolutions, the snapping of engine belts after extensive wear, and the brief episode of death after a lifetime of gradual body deterioration. Pham Van Dieu, Bien Chung Duy Vat Luan, 2nd printing (Saigon, 1937).

145. Hoang Tan Dan, "Phai co Van Hoa Binh Dan" [We Must Have a Popular Culture], PNTV 235 (22 Mar. 1934), pp. 13–14.

146. Pham Van Dieu, Bien Chung Duy Vat Luan, pp. 43–44. This was a conscious variation on Marx's famous eleventh thesis on Feuerbach, which the author also quoted.

147. Bien Chung Phap Pho Thong (Saigon, 1936), p. 39.

focused effort and willpower, and above all the "action power of the masses."[148] If enough Vietnamese joined the struggle, it would be possible to "push the wheel of history straight up the progressive road."[149] Clearing away obstacles and shoving hard, "victory over the future" could be secured.[150]

By the early 1940s ICP leaders were arguing that "socialist realism" demanded revolutionary optimism. Thus, any fictional portrayal of the downtrodden Vietnamese peasantry had to suggest growing consciousness, imminent struggle, and eventual liberation. Writers of non-fiction who employed the analytical tools of dialectical materialism but came up with results which did not appear to serve the immediate revolutionary cause (as defined by the ICP) were severely criticized. In 1944, for example, Luong Duc Thiep published *Vietnamese Society*,[151] a serious Marxist study of his country's history, social structure, and popular culture. Although he predicted an imminent turning point in Vietnamese history, he based this on an assessment of broad domestic and international trends, not the activities of any particular political organization. His tone was that of an interested observer, not a direct participant. Publications by Luong Duc Thiep and other members of the Han Thuyen group were soon labeled by the ICP as "mechanistic materialism," "distortions of Marxist theory," and—gravest of all—as providing witting or unwitting assistance to the enemy.[152] The days when members of the Vietnamese intelligentsia might try to stand aside to analyze reality were over.

ICP cultural and intellectual policy was set forth in a five-page Central Committee pronouncement of 1943, titled "Theses on Vietnamese Culture."[153] The implied purpose was to define a context and promulgate a strategy whereby the ICP, working through the Viet Minh, could regain the initiative lost among urban literate Vietnamese since 1939. Although the preamble made the necessary bow to economic determinism, most of the analysis of current conditions was politically oriented. French and Japanese cultural policies were denounced, a roster of "destructive" philosophical tendencies was established, and cadres were ordered

148. Hong Phong, *Chanh Tri Kinh Te Hoc Chi Nam*, p. 5.

149. Bui Cong Trung, "Ban qua ve Nghe Thuat" [A Discussion of Art], in Vu Dinh Lien, et al., ed., HT-5, pp. 475–79. Originally published in *Tao Dan*, no. 6 (1939).

150. Ty Thong Tin Van Hoa Son La, *Suoi Reo*, p. 24.

151. *Xa Hoi Viet-Nam* (Saigon, 1971; originally published in Hanoi, 1944).

152. Truong Chinh, writing in *Tien Phong*, no. 2 (1 Jan. 1945); reprinted in Dang Lao Dong Viet Nam, *Ve Su Lanh Dao cua Dang Tren Mat Tran Tu Tuong va Van Hoa 1930–1945* [The Party's Leadership on the Ideological and Cultural Front, 1930–1945] (Hanoi, 1960), pp. 187–93.

153. "De Cuong ve Van Hoa Viet-Nam," in *Ve Su Lanh Dao*, pp. 182–87. These theses were almost surely drafted by Truong Chinh and cleared by Ho Chi Minh prior to their discussion and ratification by the Central Committee. They show evidence, too, of ICP familiarity with the results of the CCP's May 1942 Yenan Conference on the Problems of Art and Literature.

to orient everything around the revolution for national liberation. All cultural activity was thenceforth to be measured according to the degree that it stimulated simultaneously a sense of patriotism, mass consciousness, and scientific objectivity. Following national liberation, the ICP would lead a full-fledged cultural revolution aimed at creating a socialist culture.

The "Theses on Vietnamese Culture" appear to have remained the definitive Party statement on this topic until Truong Chinh's far more detailed formulation of 1948, titled *Marxism and Vietnamese Culture*.[154] In between, of course, the Japanese had surrendered, the DRVN had been founded, and the Protracted War of Resistance had begun. Nonetheless, Truong Chinh still felt the need to attack the now defunct Han Thuyen Marxist group once again. Aside from his more obvious intent of warning Vietnamese intellectuals that only the ICP could interpret Marxist theory correctly, Truong Chinh was anxious to insure continuing acceptance of revolutionary voluntarism over determinism of any hue. As he described it, the Vietnamese proletarian vanguard had created the appropriate doctrine, struggled to gain the cultural and ideological initiative, and instilled in the masses the consciousness and the will to overthrow the exploiting classes, destroy the old mode of production, and build a new society. As a result,

the ideological struggle has been changed into an armed struggle; attacks with pens have been replaced by attacks with weapons. *Revolutionary culture has thus preceded economic reality* and exerted a powerful influence back on society.[155]

The following year, Hai Trieu, who ironically had been the ICP's banner-carrier against the idealists in the 1930s, endorsed voluntarism to the point where historical materialism seemed to lose almost all significance.[156] Borrowing in part from some recent essays on "autodynamism" by a French Communist named Georges Politzer (1903-1942), Hai Trieu condemned the "economic fatalism" that had infected too many European Marxists since the early twentieth century.[157] Such people failed to perceive how "spirit" could turn around and influence "matter"

154. *Chu Nghia Mac va Van Hoa Viet-Nam*, 2nd edition (Hanoi, 1974). Originally read at the National Cultural Conference, July 1948. An abbreviated French version can be found in *La Nouvelle Critique* 51 (Jan. 1954), pp. 77-100.

155. *Chu Nghia Mac va Van Hoa Viet-Nam*, p. 17 (my emphasis).

156. Hai Trieu, "Luat Anh Huong Tro Lai cua Tinh Than qua Vat Chat va Tac Dong cua Con Nguoi trong Qua Trinh Phat Trien Xa Hoi" [The Law of Reverse Influence of Spirit on Matter and the Impact of Man on the Process of Social Development], *Tim Hieu*, nos. 1 and 2 (Mar.–May 1949), pp. 24–31. This was the publication of the Fourth Interzone's "Marxist Research Branch," an ICP cover name until 1951.

157. Hai Trieu had perhaps read some of Politzer's essays prepared for popular education in France in 1935–36. Among Parisian intellectuals Politzer was best known for his criticism of Bergson and his attacks on bourgeois philosophy. In the Resistance under German occupation, Politzer was captured and executed in 1942. *Encyclopaedia Universalis* (Paris, 1972), vol. 13, pp. 246–47. My thanks to Pierre Brocheux for bringing sources on Politzer to my attention.

or how ideas alone could motivate human beings across space and time. Revolutionary consciousness and willingness to sacrifice could make the difference between defeat and victory. To make his point, Hai Trieu contrasted the poor performance of French colonial mercenaries with the calm readiness of Viet Minh soldiers to strap on explosives and throw themselves against enemy vehicles. The mercenaries were acting "mechanically as animals," while the Viet Minh volunteers were "sacrificing themselves self-consciously as human beings," he asserted.[158] From a more theoretical perspective, Hai Trieu affirmed that collective willpower had been the cause of countless social changes, and that individual leaders were capable of speeding or slowing the wheels of history. From this it also followed that those social classes, ethnic groups or nations that had lost their "autodynamism" might well disappear, leaving behind only some stone tablets or decaying architectural monuments.

Collective willpower had to be focused on particular targets or it would prove ineffective. Although mobilizing the masses was seen to be of prime importance, the ICP did not ignore the advantages of intelligentsia participation (see chapter 9). In 1944, Dang Thai Mai urged members of the intelligentsia to choose between being pen-and-ink prostitutes for the ruling class or keeping some measure of "pure, chaste spirit" by joining with the vanguard elements of society to help fashion a new, advanced culture. Intellectuals could be of great service, providing they did not retain too high an estimate of their creative potential. As Dang Thai Mai gently phrased it,

genius is not some person extracting from his mind completely new ideas to change the world entirely, to remake society; rather, genius is simply a person experienced in the life of society who can perceive amidst mass tendencies an appropriate method to solve crises of the period.[159]

Thousands of intellectuals did indeed join various Viet Minh organizations in 1944 and 1945, serving as instructors, propagandists, administrators, staff officers, and technicians. Although extremely valuable, they continued to pose problems for the ICP. For example, Truong Chinh in 1948 sternly instructed Viet Minh writers to stop distinguishing between art and propaganda, and to accept the principle that true art always serves the "just cause" (*chinh nghia*). The same principle applied to science. Individuals who claimed that there was such a thing as "pure science," to be pursued above national or class interests, were quite possibly serving either the imperialist enemy or a tiny minority of the population who wished to exploit the majority. Although the ultimate liberating powers of

158. Hai Trieu, "Luat Anh Huong," p. 30.
159. "Ban ve Nguyen Tac Sang Tac," in Vu Dinh Lien et al., ed., HT-5, p. 489. Originally published in *Van Hoc Khai Luan* [An Outline of Literature] (Hanoi[?], 1944). As a clandestine Party member teaching and writing in Hanoi, Dang Thai Mai had to choose his words carefully.

science were reaffirmed, Truong Chinh warned that no one should therefore conclude that it was necessary for the DRVN to be in the scientific forefront in order to be able to defeat its enemies.[160]

Truong Chinh also placed limits on objectivity, one of the most treasured ideals of Vietnamese intellectuals in previous decades. For example, writers might describe a Viet Minh military defeat, but only in the context of demonstrating the brave sacrifices of Viet Minh soldiers, of analyzing the causes of defeat, finding some measure of success, and describing how everyone refused to be demoralized and eagerly studied the battle so that they could be victorious in future engagements. Cadres were encouraged to be critical, to point out weaknesses; but those who used these opportunities to promote divisiveness were threatened with imprisonment. Looking at the problem another way, Truong Chinh advised that there were some truths that did not merit discussion or, if worthy, needed to be raised at the right time and place, and in the right manner. By the same token, although all "superstitions" were still to be condemned in principle, those which did not undermine revolutionary policy were to be tolerated in practice.[161] This was meant as a concession to united-front activities, and there can be no doubt that it helped promote political unity. Another convenience was to distinguish "religion" from "superstition." The former was eventually assessed in strictly determinist fashion, as a "social objective phenomenon whose appearance, development, and disappearance have deep social origins and are not dependent upon the subjective will of any group of individuals."[162] The latter, apparently, was more vulnerable to determined action. As late as 1977, however, the list of superstitions to be "strictly prohibited and eliminated" still included fortune-telling, astrology, physiognomy, necromancy, going into trances, drawing lots before idols, making amulets, exorcism, worshipping ghosts, burning incense or sacrificial paper articles for spirits, and treating diseases with witchcraft.[163]

Within that small circle of ICP members who had already survived many trials together and developed a sense of mutual trust and respect, there probably continued to be frank and fruitful intellectual discussions. One can infer this, for example, from a careful reading of the memoirs of military commanders, who were often faced with the practical philosophical problem of how to know and master reality with only very limited resources, and who understood the value of careful planning and correct timing as well as appeals to heroism and self-sacrifice. Thus, for Vo Nguyen Giap, the key to revolutionary genius was not virtue, not willpower, but the capacity for accurate prediction. He stressed how difficult it was to sort things out as they actually happened, in contrast to the ease with

160. Truong Chinh, *Chu Nghia Mac*, pp. 69–74, 92.
161. Ibid., pp. 93–98.
162. *Nhan Dan* (Hanoi), 4 July 1955.
163. *Quan Doi Nhan Dan* (Hanoi), 24 Mar. 1977.

which one might perceive an "inevitable" sequence of events in retrospect. It was essential for a revolutionary leader to "uncover the universal and particular law of things while immersed in a jumble of false phenomena which are difficult to discern, and while surrounded by innumerable intertwined relationships all moving and evolving continuously."[164] Overall revolutionary questions might well depend on this talent, Vo Nguyen Giap suggested, adding that reality and time provided severe tests for each prediction.[165]

Vo Nguyen Giap's obvious candidate for recognition as a revolutionary genius was Ho Chi Minh, who in turn had modeled himself on Lenin. Even with such a man at the helm, however, Vo Nguyen Giap affirmed that events sometimes had a way of getting ahead of the ability of mere mortals to dissect them and act appropriately. In summarizing the events of early 1946, for example, he commented:

> The wheel of history seemed to revolve at full speed. For the revolutionaries, each day, each hour seemed to go by too quickly. Time was in a hurry.[166]

Thirty years later, one of Vo Nguyen Giap's closest associates, Van Tien Dung, had very similar thoughts as he directed the final campaign to liberate South Vietnam. While giving due credit to mass fervor, determination, and endurance, he also explained the need to study conditions, to plan meticulously, and to allow for the intrusion of new, unpredictable factors as events unfolded. He spoke of the "opportune moment" (*thoi co*) as priceless to those who wished to "shake the heavens and rock the earth." Like a great many Vietnamese, he thought nostalgically of how much Ho Chi Minh, who had died in 1969, would have enjoyed setting foot in Saigon. Unlike many, however, Van Tien Dung then immediately turned his mind to checking if the electric power and water systems were functioning properly in the newly liberated city.[167]

164. *Unforgettable Months and Years* (Ithaca, 1975), p. 45.
165. Ibid., p. 45.
166. Ibid., p. 77.
167. *Our Great Spring Victory* (New York, 1977), pp. 56, 59, 137, 173, 186, 247, 261.

9. Learning from Experience

On 15 August 1945, Communist cadres in the outskirts of Hanoi listened to Allied radios report the unconditional surrender of Japan and Allied plans to send Chinese Nationalist and British troops into Indochina to disarm the enemy.[1] Following national strategic guidelines disseminated in March 1945, the Northern Region Committee of the Indochinese Communist Party, meeting a few miles from Hanoi, decided on its own initiative to seize power in the city. The closest Liberation Army units were at least one hundred kilometers from Hanoi, however, and there were probably not more than several score firearms in the hands of local Party members or Viet Minh united-front participants. A hastily formed Military Revolutionary Committee concluded that the best tactic was to organize mass demonstrations which could then be transformed into revolutionary assault forces led by Party cadres and small units of armed Viet Minh. The Committee hoped that all this could be accomplished without provoking serious Japanese counteraction.

Lacking knowledge of local Japanese intentions, however, the Military Revolutionary Committee avoided fixing an exact timetable. Above all, it had to ascertain the degree to which the Japanese would back up the Vietnamese administrators, police, and militia who had been sharing power with them since the 9 March *coup de force* that had removed the French from the equation. A first indication came the next day, when collaborator administrators asked to meet Viet Minh representatives and revealed that the primary Japanese concern was to avoid a direct military confrontation pending surrender to the Chinese. That night a Japanese army officer was killed in a Hanoi theater by Viet Minh activists, and there was no apparent retaliation. On 17 August, Vietnamese administrators organized a public meeting at the big opera house in the center of the city. After the proceedings were under way, Viet Minh red flags with yellow stars sprouted amongst the audience, causing no little excitement. Then, while police

---

1. The following brief account of events in Hanoi in late August 1945 is derived primarily from Ban Nghien Cuu Lich Su Dang Thanh Uy Ha-Noi, *Cuoc Van Dong Cach Mang Thang Tam o Ha Noi* [August Revolution Activity in Hanoi] (Hanoi, 1970), pp. 113–46. See also *Trung Bac Chu Nhat* 259 (26 Aug. 1945) and 260 (2 Sept. 1945).

stood by, armed cadres seized the rostrum, outlined the Viet Minh program for national independence, and converted the assembly into a demonstration that marched through the downtown area, yelling, "Overthrow the puppets!" The crowd got larger as it went, and some militiamen were seen to join in. Neither the Japanese nor the collaborator administration moved to block the proceedings.

Assessing these events on the night of 17 August, the ICP's Northern Region Committee set 19 August as the day for a Viet Minh mass meeting in Hanoi that would then be converted into a general uprising. Japanese installations were to be avoided, and no attempt was to be made to seize weapons from Japanese troops. If the Japanese still chose to counterattack, it was anticipated that uprising participants would have to withdraw to the suburbs, fight guerrilla style, and await the arrival of Liberation Army units from the mountains.

The eighteenth of August was devoted to spreading the word, sewing flags, sharpening knives, and identifying targets. Viet Minh cadres were able to commandeer autos and drive through a number of nearby provinces showing the flag and urging people to both seize local power and to march on Hanoi. Several district and provincial offices were indeed seized that very day, another example of local political initiative that quickly gathered momentum and essentially eliminated the collaborator administration throughout northern Vietnam by 24 August. Meanwhile, in Hanoi, a group of young Viet Minh activists and some citizens from nearby Ha Dong province made a show of force on 18 August that could well have upset plans for the following day, yet ended up confirming the Military Revolutionary Council's assessment of Japanese intentions. With an eye to obtaining firearms, the group marched on the headquarters of the collaborator militia and was blocked by a unit of Japanese soldiers. The lieutenant colonel in command of the Japanese troops requested to parley with a ranking Viet Minh representative. This was arranged, and an informal bargain was struck whereby the Japanese would not counter Viet Minh activities as long as the Viet Minh endeavored to prevent attacks on Japanese personnel.

On the morning of 19 August, Hanoi was already bedecked with Viet Minh flags. Tens of thousands of peasants poured into the city armed with machetes, sickles, bamboo spears, and a sprinkling of firearms. From 11:00 A.M. a loudspeaker system operated in front of the opera house. The crowd continued growing, half in the white shirts and white tunics of the townspeople, half in the black or brown shirts and blouses of the country people. Members of the Military Revolutionary Committee led a flag-raising ceremony and singing of the Viet Minh anthem. They then explained the significance of the unconditional Japanese surrender and called for establishment of a democratic republic to insure civil rights, improve popular livelihood, and mobilize the entire country to safeguard independence. People were subsequently urged to divide into two large groups led by armed Viet Minh to seize specific objectives. The first group marched on the viceroy's residence and took it against only nominal militia resistance. Soon members of the ICP's Northern Region Committee were using the viceroy's telephone to order provincial administrators to surrender to local Viet Minh representatives.[2] Meanwhile, the crowd moved on to liberate the mayor's office, the treasury (but not the Bank of Indochina, guarded by Japanese troops), the post office and the city's central police station.

More trouble was encountered by the second crowd, which marched on the same militia headquarters that had been the object of dispute the previous day. Initially, the Vietnamese commander of the post refused entry. Then he agreed to parley. Finally he assembled his men and stood by while they were addressed by Viet Minh cadres. At that point, however, Japanese infantry, reinforced by tanks, surrounded the installation and sent several officers in to order the Viet Minh to turn over the weapons to them. A responsible cadre reiterated the proposition that the Viet Minh would not threaten the Japanese pending their repatriation, providing they did not interfere in the course of the uprising. This exchange led to a higher-level Viet Minh delegation being dispatched straight to the Japanese general staff headquarters. Apparently, the Japanese commanders were sufficiently satisfied as to the Viet Minh intention and capacity to point the guns in other directions that they ordered their troops to withdraw from around the militia headquarters. However, a further Viet Minh proposal that the Japanese turn over their own weapons was rejected.

On 22 August, Major Archimedes Patti, representing U.S. interests, flew in from Kunming and landed at Hanoi airfield. Jean Sainteny, informally representing the French government, was allowed to come on the same plane but was subsequently treated guardedly by all other parties concerned. Ho Chi Minh arrived from the mountains on 26 August, and the first Liberation Army units marched in five days later. Amidst huge public celebrations the founding of the Democratic Republic of Vietnam was declared on 2 September 1945. Bedraggled Chinese regiments entered Hanoi a week later and began to requisition buildings and to loot private property as well as to disarm Japanese units. At the end of the month, reports began to arrive of violent confrontations in Saigon between French *colons* rearmed by the British and followers of the revolutionary council assembled by the Viet Minh. Soon thousands of Hanoi youths were volunteering to fight in the south. The stage was set for thirty more years of upheaval and strife, in which first the French and then the Americans tried to ignore the August 1945 Revolution and to turn back the clock.

Events in Hanoi were not sufficient in themselves to propel Ho Chi Minh, the ICP, and the Viet Minh to national power. And the DRVN could hardly expect to remain in existence merely because it controlled a number of public buildings, possessed a few thousand more firearms, and had contact with American, Chi-

---

2. The viceroy himself, Phan Ke Toai, had already made clear his willingness to cooperate with the Viet Minh. He has continued to occupy various government positions to this day.

nese, and French representatives. Already before the events of August 1945, a Viet Minh administration was functioning in six mountain provinces of northern Vietnam, a Liberation Army of perhaps one thousand men and women had been trained and seen battle, and hundreds of ICP cadres had spread through the villages of the Red River delta to help organize a bewildering array of united-front groups. A similar process took place on a smaller scale in several provinces of central Vietnam. In the south, for a variety of reasons to be discussed later, ICP cadres encountered much less favorable circumstances, and were only able to pull together an ad hoc anticolonial coalition in the wake of the news of Japan's surrender.

From March to September 1945 there was an upsurge of patriotic fervor and social commitment unparalleled in the history of Vietnam. As those Vietnamese in their fifties and sixties still remember, it was as if both individuals and the nation had been born anew. This spiritual phenomenon was not limited to Viet Minh participants. It was also more a spontaneous reaction to complex events than the result of anyone's planning. Nevertheless, once this outburst of sentiment became manifest, Viet Minh leaders understood its significance better than any others and moved with alacrity to channel it in specific directions.

Theory and Practice

In the twenty years separating the August 1925 Revolution and the trial of Phan Boi Chou, described at the opening of this book, the Vietnamese intelligentsia's perception of the world and its capacity to act on the basis of that perception had altered dramatically. In 1925, no one, including Ho Chi Minh, envisaged a revolutionary strategy of the type employed in 1945. Had someone been so farsighted it would not have meant much, as a number of changes would have to occur—not least of all the establishment and testing of a revolutionary vanguard—before there was a prospect of success.

In one sense, all Vietnamese revolutionary endeavor to 1945 can be defined in terms of the arduous working out of a knowledge and action dialectic. Events conspired to insure that there would be no easy choices. Those who tried to learn from experience might still fall prey to perils not exactly of their own making, from tuberculosis or malaria to torture or nervous breakdown. Those who survived and persevered eventually played critical roles in the modern history of Vietnam.[3]

Unlike some of the topics discussed previously—for example, ethics, language, women's rights, and history—there was no systematic debate in Vietnam about what might be called the philosophy of praxis. The Vietnamese intelligentsia was heir to a tradition that assumed the literate elite to be prominently involved in

---

3. Admittedly, a proper test of this thesis would involve far more detailed investigation of revolutionary activities than is possible here. My purpose is simply to raise some salient questions.

public affairs. Until very recently, in fact, study had been almost synonymous with preparation for the civil examinations; the successful minority became mandarins, the unsuccessful majority performed quasi-official duties in home villages. On the one hand, Vietnamese literati were encouraged to believe that the Chinese classics held the key to all life's challenges; while on the other hand, the *Book of History* warned that "To know is easy, to act is difficult." The practical effect was to put a premium on individuals who knew how to cite classical precedent to bolster particular cases.

As far as I can discover, it was not until 1943 that a Vietnamese writer brought forth Sun Yat-sen's reversal of the *Book of History* passage.[4] Arguing that "to know is difficult, to act is easy," Sun aimed his fire at the traditional tendency to honor generalists and deprecate specialists. Although everyone obviously ate food, it required physiologists, biologists, chemists, physicians, and dieticians to ascertain the effects of particular foods on people and thus plan the optimum diet. Although everyone used money, it was the economists and financiers who knew why and how money circulated in society. Relating Sun's points to Vietnam, the author of the 1943 essay pointed out that many people still placed the traditional medical practitioner ahead of the medical school graduate, the itinerant building contractor ahead of the modern architect. Economic affairs were still characterized by the shifty, quick profiteer, not individuals who knew how to think responsibly and plan ahead. Political affairs demonstrated an extreme paucity of individuals with sound theoretical footing, he added.

Even more notable was the relative lack of interest in Vietnam in Wang Yang-ming, called by one Western scholar "the greatest theoretician of practice in Chinese history."[5] Phan Boi Chau must have been aware of Wang's popularity in Japan and must have heard arguments that Wang's philosophy helped to pave the way for the Meiji Restoration. Yet, as noted below, the only record of Phan's interest was one brief discussion in an unpublished manuscript. It is equally surprising that Phan Chu Trinh, Huynh Thuc Khang, or Tran Huu Do did not have their curiosity piqued by Liang Ch'i-Ch'ao's acknowledged intellectual debt to Wang Yang-ming. Ironically, the first individual to write about Wang in any detail seems to have been the Western-trained conservative Tran Trong Kim.[6] His 1929 effort was entirely descriptive, and probably largely a translation of an unspecified Chinese study. To the degree that Tran Trong Kim revealed any per-

4. Phan Quan, Biet Kho Lam De: Hoc Thuyet cua Ton Van" [To Know Is Difficult, to Act Is Easy: Sun Yat-sen's Doctrine], *Thanh Nghi* (Hanoi) 28 (1 Jan. 1943), pp. 2–4.

5. Frederic Wakeman, Jr., *History and Will: Philosophical Perspectives of Mao Tse-tung's Thought* (Berkeley: Univ. of Calif. Press, 1973), p. 238.

6. Tran Trong Kim, *Nho Giao*, vol. 2, 4th printing (Saigon, 1962), pp. 228–306. NP 109 (Sept. 1926), pp. 245–57, also contains a translated synopsis of Wang Yang-ming's teachings.

sonal judgment at all, it was in favor of Wang's concept of "innate knowledge" (*luong tri*), not his "unity of knowledge and action" (*tri hanh hop nhat*).

It was not until fifteen years later that the talented Vietnamese Trotskyist Phan Van Hum found time to write and publish a mammoth five-hundred-page study of Wang Yang-ming.[7] More than half of the book was biographical, designed to show how Wang's life experience had influenced his philosophy. In a subsequent key discussion of Wang's concept of the "unity of knowledge and action," Phan Van Hum rejected both the *Book of History*'s assertion and that of Sun Yat-sen.[8] Whether one placed knowledge over action or vice versa, he said, the unfortunate effect was separation. Wang Yang-ming had rightly insisted that cognition and experience proceed together, one reinforcing the other.[9] In this, Wang anticipated the empiricism of Francis Bacon, and even the praxis of dialectical materialism. Phan stressed that Wang was not proposing some mystical oneness of knowledge and action but rather a dynamic, creative integration. To add authority to his study, Phan Van Hum appended a section from Phan Boi Chau's unpublished manuscript on the *Book of Changes*, which cited Wang Yang-ming to criticize those who claimed one could think without doing.[10]

While not one to despise book learning, Phan Boi Chau had always treated ideas as tools of concrete political action. For him, the main concern of anyone who took pursuit of the *Dao* seriously was to cope with situations by the performance of deeds. Thinking was essential in the planning stages of anticolonial operations, for example, but later on it might well stand in the way of action and prohibit the necessary response. Such arguments became more pronounced in Phan's writings the more desperate his position became. In 1919 he admitted political failure and ceased advancing new ideas or plans for overthrowing the French.[11] Nonetheless, even after being captured, tried, and forced to remain in Hue, Phan Boi Chau continued vigorously to advise the new intelligentsia on the efficacy of action and experience over quiet study and theorizing.[12]

Ho Chi Minh left Vietnam for Europe in 1911, in part because he felt activist

---

7. Phan Van Hum, *Vuong Duong Minh* [Wang Yang-ming] (Hanoi, 1944). A less impressive effort by Dao Trinh Nhat was serialized in *Trung Bac Chu Nhat* (Hanoi) from issue 83 (19 Oct. 1941) to 158 (23 May 1943).

8. Phan Van Hum, *Vuong Duong Minh*, pp. 341-58.

9. By contrast, Phan Quan, "Biet Kho Lam De," p. 3, had argued that some individuals must specialize in "knowing" and others in "doing." For example, it was not necessary for a scientist to be an engineer or the reverse.

10. Phan Van Hum, *Vuong Duong Minh*, pp. 493–96. Another appendix describes the spread of Wang Yang-ming's doctrine to Japan.

11. David G. Marr, *Vietnamese Anticolonialism, 1885–1925* (Berkeley: Univ. of Calif. Press, 1971), pp. 196–98, 238–40.

12. Phan Boi Chau, *Van De Phu Nu* (Saigon, 1929), pp. 30–31.

literati like Phan Boi Chau had reached an impasse. He didn't know what was needed, but he was pretty sure some of the answers were to be found in the West. As he also told a friend, it seemed desirable to observe the French and other Western peoples on their home ground before formulating any plan to help his countrymen.[13] Ho Chi Minh appears always to have had boundless curiosity about other peoples, languages, and cultures.[14] He was an avid reader, and took abundant notes—traits that proved valuable when he began to write numerous articles in French condemning specific colonial practices in places like Dahomey, Algeria, and Syria as well as Indochina.[15]

In late 1924, as a member of the Comintern mission to China, Ho Chi Minh had his first opportunity to reach beyond articles and speechmaking to recruitment and training of Vietnamese revolutionaries. His 1925 breakthrough—what one observer has called the first successful combination of theory and practice in the Vietnamese revolution—was to convert members of the Association of Like Minds (Tam Tam Xa), a small terrorist group, to the Comintern cause.[16] During the next few years about three hundred additional Vietnamese studied in Canton under Ho Chi Minh's supervision; most returned quickly to Vietnam to begin political organizing in schools, factories, mines, and plantations. Ho Chi Minh called his organization the Vietnam Young Revolutionary Comrades' League (Viet Nam Thanh Nien Cach Menh Dong Chi Hoi), or Youth League for short. This name had obvious appeal to the young intelligentsia, who probably made up ninety percent of the total membership in 1928. Within the Youth League Ho Chi Minh also identified a small, select Communist Youth Group (Thanh Nien Cong San Doan), designed to be the nucleus of a future communist party.[17]

Ho Chi Minh's first publication aimed specifically at a Vietnamese audience was *The Road to Revolution*.[18] Designed principally as a training manual for Youth League recruits, the style was simple and straightforward. On the cover

13. Tran Dan Tien, *Nhung Mau Chuyen ve Doi Hoat Dong cua Ho Chu Tich* [Various Anecdotes on Chairman Ho's Life Activities] (Hanoi, 1969), p. 11.

14. By contrast, Phan Boi Chau never seems to have made a serious effort to go to Europe, and never became very proficient in French. It is perhaps symbolic that from 1919 to 1924 Phan lived most of the time in the beautiful, historically resonant city of Hangchow.

15. Eventually Ho Chi Minh collected what he considered his most telling arguments and published them as *Le Procès de la Colonisation Française* (Paris, 1925).

16. Professor Tran Van Giau, discussion with the author, Ho Chi Minh City, 1 Feb. 1978.

17. Studies relating to the Youth League are fairly numerous. William J. Duiker, *The Rise of Nationalism in Vietnam, 1900-1941* (Ithaca, N.Y.: Cornell Univ. Press, 1976), pp. 191-214, provides a useful introduction.

18. Nguyen Ai Quoc [Ho Chi Minh], *Duong Kach Menh* (Canton, 1927). Excerpts and discussions have appeared in numerous publications, for example, *Hoc Tap* (Hanoi) 2-1961, pp. 50-58, and Tran Van Giau, *Giai Cap Cong Nhan Viet Nam* [The Vietnamese Working Class] (Hanoi, 1961), pp. 380-86. A complete version is available to a select readership in Dang Cong San Viet Nam, *Cac To Chuc Tien Than cua Dang* (Hanoi, 1977), pp. 15-81.

was a drawing of a shackled man, together with the Vietnamese version of Lenin's famous dictum, "Without a revolutionary theory there can be no revolutionary movement."[19] Inside, Ho Chi Minh pointedly criticized spontaneous outbursts such as the 1908 tax demonstrations in central Vietnam and the 1916 march on Saigon Central Prison. He disapproved too of isolated acts of violence, citing De Tham's 1908 attempt to poison a French military garrison, but clearly having Phan Boi Chau's later operations in mind as well. Perhaps the following passage best summarized Ho Chi Minh's outlook:

Because they do not comprehend developments elsewhere in the world, our people do not know how to compare, how to formulate a strategy. When it is not time to act, they do; when it is time to act, they don't. Revolutionaries must understand the international movement and present a coherent policy to the people.[20]

Ho Chi Minh's stress on mental preparation was unmistakable. In the introduction to *The Road to Revolution* he offered the following cause-and-effect sequence to individual Vietnamese: read the book, ponder it carefully, "wake up," link with others of similar inclination, and proceed to "make a revolution." The body of the text included rudimentary Leninist arguments in favor of heightening consciousness, identifying with workers and peasants (the "main force" of the revolution), and building an elite vanguard party. However, there was another thread to Ho's book which owed far more to his Vietnamese upbringing than to Lenin. Ho Chi Minh obviously assumed that the individuals to whom he was addressing himself already possessed a clear awareness of right and wrong together with a profound sense of grievance at the subjugation of their country by the French. Like Phan Boi Chau, Ho insisted that each person reflect on the moral issues at stake, heighten his devotion to principle, and harness his righteous indignation to the revolutionary cause. Thus, *The Road to Revolution's* preface was mainly a list of twenty-three ethical maxims for prospective revolutionaries. The only maxim that might have been out of place in a Confucian primer or boy scout manual was "Know how to keep secrets."[21] Later, Ho Chi Minh distilled revolutionary morality to "industriousness, frugality, incorruptibility, and correctness" (*can, kiem, liem, chinh*).

To ignore this aspect of Ho Chi Minh's ideology would be a mistake. As far as

19. Le Sy Thang, "Ho Chu Tich va Su Nghiep Truyen Ba Chu Nghia Mac-Le-nin vao Viet-Nam," NCLS 145 (Jul.–Aug. 1972), p. 53.

20. Excerpt reprinted in *Ve Su Lanh Dao cua Dang Tren Mat Tran Tu Tuong va Van Hoa, 1930–1945* [Party Leadership on the Ideological and Cultural Fronts, 1930–1945] (Hanoi, 1960), pp. 22–23. Ho Chi Minh may have been thinking particularly of 1912–14, when the Vietnam Restoration Society (Viet Nam Quang Phuc Hoi) smashed itself to pieces in small armed attacks on the colonial administration and was thus incapable of taking advantage of the opportunity provided by the outbreak of war in Europe.

21. "Uncle Ho in Canton," *Vietnam Courier* 48 (May 1976), pp. 26–27.

he was concerned, revolutionary success depended to an important degree on persuading individual militants to behave in upright, exemplary fashion. To know and to alter reality required a kind of virtue, a revolutionary sincerity which had nothing to do with dialectical materialism. Armed with that virtue, one was able to distinguish transitory self-interest from persistent commitment to lofty ideals; with that knowledge, one strengthened the inner will, which in turn enhanced the prospects for achieving a "unity of hearts" (*dong tam*) and a "unity of purpose" (*dong chi*) with others.[22] Ho Chi Minh probably did not expect every Vietnamese to unite as one on this basis, but he certainly intended it for his revolutionary vanguard.

Lenin must have seemed to Ho Chi Minh the perfect historical actor, his will overcoming mechanical materialism, his character inspiring other authentic revolutionaries, his mind grasping broad movements in human affairs and designing appropriate strategies. According to this model, moral and intellectual understanding had to be fulfilled in action or it meant nothing. However, in Ho Chi Minh's early writings we do not see Marx's particular concept of praxis, that is, the will to action in order to *test* belief and obtain additional grounds for further action. Rather, Ho Chi Minh's emphasis was on completing acts once begun. For example, when comparing the American Revolution with the Russian Revolution, he argued that the former was still unfinished, having left the workers and farmers in misery, whereas the latter had accomplished all its objectives, driving out the monarch, the capitalists, and the landlords and even being able to assist people elsewhere to do likewise. "If we are prepared to sacrifice to make a revolution, then we must carry it to the end," he concluded.[23] Action for Ho Chi Minh was more a matter of implementing Leninist theory in Vietnam than a solution to the problem of objective truth, of man proving the "reality and power, the 'this-sidedness' of his thinking in practice."[24]

Meanwhile, the picture inside Vietnam was much less clear. During the 1920s most Vietnamese intellectuals were unsure of themselves in both theory and practice—not to mention the relationship between the two. There was a widespread assumption that if enough people thought seriously about such things as independence, freedom, equality, justice, and civilization, then eventually they would come to be. Thus, action in the 1920s often meant assimilating new ideas and preaching their significance to others—in short, bringing light to darkness.

22. It is worth noting that this concept of "unity of purpose" (*dong chi*), which has an ancient pedigree, was used by Japanese, Chinese, and Vietnamese communists to translate the term "comrade." As we have seen, Ho Chi Minh included the words *dong chi* in the title of his first revolutionary organization.

23. Le Sy Thang, "Ho Chu Tich," p. 53. Of course, Ho Chi Minh accepted that there would be two stages to this revolution.

24. Marx's second thesis on Feuerbach, in *The German Ideology* (New York: International, 1947), p. 197.

For more radical individuals, action also meant challenging the French "civilizing mission," demonstrating to themselves and to anyone else who would listen that Vietnam did not need colonial tutelage, that the French in fact were not preparing the Vietnamese for eventual independence but trying to condition them to indefinite servitude.

Nguyen Trieu Luat was one of the few writers to raise the problem of praxis, as part of his general description of Western psychology. He defined "perception" (tri giac) as equalling sensation plus experience. With the aid of this formula he then explained such concepts as memory, imagination, creativity, judgment, and willpower. His model of volition, however, was strictly a one-way process, involving conception, deliberation, resolution, and practice; there was no provision for practice to influence either the form or the content of the other steps.[25]

Perhaps the only exceptions to this general pattern were those young intellectuals who accepted the advice of the Sixth Comintern Congress to "proletarianize" themselves in mines, factories, or plantations. The main purpose was supposed to be learning from practical experience, altering in the process one's prior way of thinking and behaving. The second objective was to bring revolutionary theory to the working class and to organize and lead the workers in struggle. It seems clear that most intellectuals engaged in "proletarianization" ended up reversing these priorities.[26] Implicitly, the workers had more to learn from the radical intelligentsia than the other way around. Although many "proletarianized" intellectuals did master new skills and come to empathize more with the plight of their unlettered and exploited countrymen, there is no indication that those experiences changed their theoretical premises to any significant degree.

By late 1928 the French authorities apparently had decided that the Vietnamese intelligentsia needed to be taught a stern lesson. Mere intent to eliminate the colonial system became sufficient grounds for violent punishment. In February 1929, the killing of a French labor recruitment officer was used as pretext for attacking the entire Vietnam Nationalist Party.[27] Up to that point, the Nationalists had in fact spent almost all of their time publishing, proselytizing, recruiting, and organizing. Only a small minority had argued in favor of violent action, the rest preferring to prepare for more favorable conditions in the future. However,

25. Nguyen Trieu Luat, "Tam Ly Hoc" [Psychology], particularly the section on perception in NP 102 (Jan.–Feb. 1926) and that on volition in NP 109 (Aug. 1926).

26. Indeed, writing retrospectively, the introduction to a recent set of six memoirs on proletarianization activities of the late 1920s does reverse these priorities. Tran Hoc Hai et al., Vo San Hoa [Proletarianization] (Hanoi, 1972), p. 8.

27. Although the authorities decided within a week or two that the killing of Hervé Bazin had been without political motive, and was merely the result of a rivalry among gangs involved in the lucrative plantation coolie recruitment business, political arrests, trials, and convictions continued. AOM SLOTFOM, series III, carton 39, case 3.

as the Sûreté proceeded to hunt down one component after another, the future darkened, and talk of quick counteraction became more prevalent. On 9 February 1930, those Nationalists still at large attempted an uprising but were quickly defeated.

French *colons*, now thoroughly frightened, demanded and got a policy of total suppression of malcontents. With every passing week the political climate became more tense. None of the many books and articles discussed in previous years had prepared Vietnamese intellectuals for this situation. Not surprisingly, many of the older, the wealthier, or the more timorous moved frantically to cover their tracks. Others reacted in the opposite fashion, becoming so obsessed with the need for action that it clouded their judgment and led them to make some of the same mistakes as the Nationalists. The French managed to retain the strategic initiative at all times, while intelligentsia-inspired actions often tended to be precipitous, poorly planned, or directed at the wrong targets. In the midst of failure it was not unusual to see staunch anticolonists switch abruptly to self-pity, mysticism, random violence, or suicide.

The Lessons of Nghe-Tinh

Immediately following the abortive Nationalist Party uprising of February 1930, Vietnamese laborers at a number of locations around Indochina mounted strikes to both protest French repression and demand better working conditions. These were by no means the first workers' strikes; but their timing, relative size, and persistence gave the French additional reason for concern. Simultaneously, fresh signs of rural unrest were noted in several provinces. The Sûreté assumed that the newly unified Communist Party was masterminding this activity, whereas in fact it had barely begun to disseminate its line and to move leading cadres into position when the strikes began. Although the Communist Party was to be lauded or blamed for many things throughout the remainder of 1930, a great deal of what happened was out of its hands.

From 1925 the Youth League had aimed much of its propaganda and recruiting efforts at the small Vietnamese working class, with only limited success. By early 1929 some members were arguing that the fault was with the League, not the workers. A particularly determined group in northern Vietnam sent a delegation to League headquarters in South China, describing in glowing terms recent strike actions at French-owned mines, railway yards, and textile plants. Gaining confidence, they ridiculed the upper-class, educated backgrounds of the Youth League's founders and demanded that the entire leadership be subjected to a thorough grilling and rectification session conducted by their peers. What they wanted, aside from more power within the organization, was a new policy giving prime attention to obvious, tangible proletarian interests, international and domestic, before spending time and energy cultivating other classes and groups. In short, they demanded a full-fledged Leninist proletarian vanguard party, not a diffuse association of radical leftists, as had been the case. Their position was given important support by some of the student converts to Marxism-Leninism returning from Moscow or Paris, and by the fact that the Comintern, reacting to failures in China, was currently stressing strict proletarian hegemony and preparation for an international revolutionary upsurge.

In defense, the Youth League leadership argued that the Vietnamese proletariat was still extremely small (less than two percent of the population by the most generous definition) and not fully cognizant of its historical role. The level of comprehension of communist theory remained very low, far too low to form a truly Leninist revolutionary party. What the young upstarts were proposing, in effect, was "leftist adventurism," a subjective attempt to leap ahead of Indochina's objective historical conditions. To try to pursue this line might well be disastrous.

Whatever the merits of either case, Youth League members inside Vietnam began flocking to the banner of the proletarian-firsters. When it became impossible to ignore these defections any longer, arrangements were made for Ho Chi Minh, authorized representative of the Comintern, to come from Thailand to chair the famous reconcilation conference of early February 1930, at which a single Communist Party was indeed founded.[28] A written general appeal was issued to "workers, peasants, soldiers, youths, and pupils" in the first instance, and "oppressed and exploited compatriots" secondarily.[29] Overall, the conference was a victory for the proponents of immediate proletarian mobilization, a fact which became more obvious as the Party Central Committee was moved from South China to Haiphong and then Saigon.

History ordained an immediate and extremely harsh test for this infant Communist Party. The atmosphere inside Vietnam was charged with an anticipation and fear not seen since 1908. Although Party members began in March and April 1930 to spread the proletarian line, to participate in strike activities, and to step up the organization of "red workers' unions," very few could be said to have gained control over the pace and direction of local events; nor was the Party prepared to coordinate a national strike movement. At the same time, rural Vietnamese, increasingly sensitive to what was happening beyond village hedges, began to take up some of the worker's slogans, to seek out Party members, to

28. From February to October 1930 it was known as the Vietnam Communist Party. However, the Comintern decided in favor of Indochinese Communist Party in order to make it synonymous with the entire French colony and implicitly downgrade patriotic motivations. For a detailed discussion of 1929–30 organizational shifts, see Huynh Kim Khanh, "Vietnamese Communism: The Pre-Power Phase (1925–1945)" (Ph.D. diss., Univ. of Calif., Berkeley, 1972), pp. 97–123, 134–39.

29. Text in *Hoc Tap* (Hanoi) 5-1971; translation in Bernard B. Fall, ed., *Ho Chi Minh on Revolution* (New York: Praeger, 1967), pp. 129–31.

formulate their own grievances, and to push the local authorities harder for redress.

Matters came to a head on May Day, 1930. This anniversary had obvious significance for Vietnamese radicals of diverse tendencies. More particularly, 1 May 1930 had been selected by the new Communist Party as its first opportunity to demonstrate proletarian power nationwide; but most important was that this particular May Day seems to have caught the imagination of tens of thousands of Vietnamese peasants throughout the nation. Whereas the urban manifestations came and went, the rural ones triggered a long series of major confrontations. In southern Vietnam, for example, the initial peasant marches in Long Xuyen and Cao Lanh sparked six weeks of similar actions in many other Mekong delta locations. The violent colonial countermeasures which followed forced peasants to switch to smaller hit-and-run raids on administrative bureaus. Not until the summer of 1931 were Cochinchinese authorities satisfied that they had forced a return to law and order. May Day in northern Vietnam saw about a thousand peasants march toward the Thai Binh provincial government, carrying a large red flag and holding banners listing specific grievances. They were dispersed by a French officer shooting the flag bearer and troops firing into the crowd; several hundred participants were arrested soon after.[30]

The largest demonstrations of May Day 1930 occurred in Nghe An province of central Vietnam. In one case the French Resident in Vinh was stunned to see an aggregation of several thousand peasants and railway and match factory workers present him with a long list of grievances. Several kilometers away, in front of the Ben Thuy sawmill, a similar demonstration found itself the target of a volley from colonial troops; seven were killed, eighteen wounded, and many others arrested. On the same day, fifty kilometers away, about three thousand villagers swept onto the grounds of the Ky Vien plantation, owned by a particularly detested retired Vietnamese official, and proceeded to sack and burn it. Despite colonial countermeasures, demonstrations continued in Nghe An and adjacent Ha Tinh province throughout May, June, and July. The Nghe An provincial committee of the Communist Party, sensing solid rural revolutionary potential, turned more and more of its attention to the villages, where it distributed leaflets, made speeches, and encouraged the formation of "red peasant associations." By August 1930 the Nghe An provincial committee had wittingly or unwittingly committed the entire Party to a massive violent confrontation with the French.

The "Nghe-Tinh soviet" movement that ensued has been the object of considerable study and debate.[31] The movement involved not only new and larger

30. Ngo Vinh Long, "Peasant Revolutionary Struggles in Vietnam in the 1930s" (Ph.D. diss., Harvard University, 1978), pp. 1–9, 72–93.

31. The classic exposition in a Western language is Tran Huy Lieu, *Les Soviets Du Nghe-Tinh de 1930–1931 au Viet-Nam* (Hanoi, 1960). In Vietnamese, see NCLS 30–34 and 108. Milton

rural demonstrations, but the complete disintegration of colonial control in a number of districts and serious efforts by peasant associations to establish and operate alternative village institutions. Meanwhile, the Communist Party's provincial committee tried to coordinate activities, issuing instructions on village political administration, self-defense, the opening of free *quoc ngu* classes, and the elimination of "superstitious and depraved customs." It also declared the abolition of all colonial taxes, seizure and redistribution of communal lands held by local officials and landlords, reduction of land rents, suspension of debt repayments, and distribution of rice stores held by wealthy villagers to poor and hungry families.[32] Much of this was already being done without Communist Party encouragement. Indeed, some poor peasants went further, confiscating the private fields of landlords and killing or evicting village notables. The main activities, however, were the convening of large village meetings, which usually continued well into the night in a festival atmosphere, and the organization of various schemes to foil the ever-increasing number of colonial troops brought in to quell the uprising.

Events in Nghe-Tinh put all Vietnamese radicals in an agonizing position. Very few believed the peasants had any chance of success, but to do nothing while the French organized countermeasures amounted to crass betrayal. The situation was particularly ironic for the young proletarian-firsters, as workers' strikes and related political agitation had been largely responsible for stimulating overt peasant activity at this particular time.[33] Further, the Nghe An provincial committee was to some degree carrying out general Communist Party Central Committee instructions to form a worker-peasant alliance. As individual Party members and family contacts brought word of the enthusiastic rural response, it seemed natural to devote more effort to establishing peasant associations. When peasants continued to struggle despite sharp colonial retaliation, it was obvious that the Party had to stick with them to help organize the best defense possible in the circumstances.

Osborne, "Continuity and Motivation in the Vietnamese Revolution: New Light from the 1930s," *Pacific Affairs* (Spring 1974), pp. 37–55, provides a helpful introduction to French archival sources on Nghe-Tinh. Pierre Brocheux, "L'implantation du mouvement communiste en Indochine française: le cas du Nghe-Tinh (1930–1931)," *Revue d'Histoire Moderne et Contemporaine*, vol. XXIV (Jan.–Mar. 1977), discusses relevant socioeconomic questions. See also Ngo Vinh Long, "Peasant Revolutionary Struggles," pp. 9–64.

32. Tran Huy Lieu, "Van De Chinh Quyen Xo-Viet" [The Question of Soviet Political Power], NCLS 33 (Dec. 1961), pp. 1–7.

33. There were serious grievances among Nghe An and Ha Tinh peasants, and occasional violent outbursts prior to the early 1930 workers' strikes. Looking back further, these two provinces had particularly strong anticolonial traditions. However, there can be little doubt that the Nghe-Tinh rural upheaval of 1930–1931 was related directly to events at the sawmill, match factory, and railroad works, not least of all because most of the workers visited their home villages rather frequently.

French Communist Party leaflets printed in Vietnamese in 1931 (complete with glue on the back), designed to be smuggled into Indochina. The first caption reads: "Workers-Peasants-Soldiers! Your wives and children, sisters and brothers are hungry and ill-clothed because of the imperialist, feudalist system of the royal court. Join together to wipe out those who suck the blood of your relatives!"

However, the further one was from the actual scene, the more likely one was to label the Nghe-Tinh upheaval as "rash adventurism" or "premature activism"—a prescription for disaster in either case. Students of colonial military and administrative organization were acutely aware of the reserve powers of the French to drown a strictly regional uprising in blood. Comintern observers and Communist Party members in South China reacted most negatively. In Haiphong, the Party's Central Committee sent Nguyen Phong Sac to Nghe-Tinh to try to control developments, but he apparently arrived too late to alter the course of events. In September, the Central Committee (having shifted to Saigon) sent an urgent letter criticizing the Nghe-Tinh decisions, but *also* offering concrete suggestions on how to operate a proper soviet system now that bitter conflict was certain. It was already looking further ahead, arguing that "when the soviets are defeated by the French their meaning will [nevertheless] have made a deep imprint on the people"—thus benefitting the Party and the peasant associations in subsequent struggles.[34]

From early September 1930, Communist Party branches throughout Vietnam

34. Trung Chinh, "Mot vai y kien," [Some Opinions], NCLS 30 (Sept. 1961), p. 3.

Having risen, the masses yell: "Follow the Nghe-Tinh example! Workers-Peasants-Soldiers, eliminate the gang of imperialists, mandarins, capitalists, and big landlords!" Courtesy of Archives Nationales de France.

distributed leaflets containing glowing accounts of the struggle underway in Nghe-Tinh and urging people to provide overt support.[35] In a choice between offering to march at the head of the masses in a hopeless challenge to colonial hegemony or trailing behind them, gesticulating and criticizing, the Party opted for the former.[36] None of the leaflets proposed that soviets be established elsewhere, although some did hold out the prospect of a nationwide revolutionary upheaval. The immediate strategy was to use concrete information coming from Nghe-Tinh to heighten political consciousness, to encourage workers and peasants to joint Party-led organizations, and to try to mount sympathy strikes and demonstrations that would at least siphon off some colonial police and military units from the main arena.

All of these objectives were met in Quang Ngai province, four hundred kilometers south of Nghe-Tinh. There a handful of Communist Party members were able to combine optimistic accounts of what was happening elsewhere with expositions of local grievances to spark numerous peasant demonstrations and sack-

35. AOM (Aix), G.G. series, F-7F4, vols. 4 and 5 contain several score leaflets of this type distributed in September–October 1930.

36. Whether anyone saw the parallel with Marx's dilemma at the time of the formation of the Paris Commune in 1871 is unknown. Certainly the comparison was made later.

The opposite view according to a colonial leaflet of late 1930. The caption has the man in the middle saying, "We destroy all schools because communism can only succeed among the ignorant. Education is our enemy." Courtesy of Archives Nationales de France.

ings of government buildings. The colonial authorities found the peasants of Quang Ngai extremely difficult to subdue; eight months later they finally managed to enforce a sullen peace.[37] Elsewhere the Party's strategy faltered badly. In four other provinces of central Vietnam a total of seventy persons were arrested before planned demonstrations could go ahead. In southern Vietnam it proved impossible to organize any large-scale actions because the authorities were still hounding participants of the demonstrations occurring four months earlier.

The most notable failure, however, was in northern Vietnam, where the new Communist Party was supposed to be strongest. Only in Thai Binh province, site of the May Day demonstration mentioned previously, was it possible to bring together about a thousand persons to march on the Tien Hai district office. After initially refusing orders to shoot into the crowd, Vietnamese colonial soldiers finally opened fire, killing eight and wounding thirty. Quite troubled by their inability to mount a series of demonstrations in diverse localities in the manner of Nghe-Tinh, Party members immediately attempted to rectify the problem by means of criticism and self-criticism sessions.[38] By late October, aware that the peasants of Nghe-Tinh were now being killed by the hundreds, northern Party members were issuing leaflets and documents that contained an air of desperation.[39] No significant demonstrations resulted, however.

Meanwhile, in Nghe-Tinh in September 1930, the French had employed aircraft on several occasions to bomb and strafe demonstrators. The following

37. Ngo Vinh Long, "Peasant Revolutionary Struggles," pp. 65–71.
38. AOM (Aix) G.G. series, F-7F4, vol. 4, items 17 and 18.
39. AOM (Aix) G.G. series, F-7F4, vol. 5, items 2, 10, 12.

month they unleashed a Foreign Legion battalion, whose commander ordered his men to kill nine out of ten of all prisoners taken. Search-and-destroy tactics became routine for all colonial units. A series of new forts were constructed. Village officials were made personally responsible for the actions of every inhabitant, a policy that led many of them either to resign or flee to the nearest colonial garrison. Indecisive mandarins were replaced, an anticommunist political party begun, and population control and food denial programs established. Nghe-Tinh peasants responded by abandoning large demonstrations in favor of hit-and-run operations and small marches composed of people who knew how to disperse quickly and evade the enemy. They also turned inward, demanding more rice and money from wealthy villagers, imprisoning and in some cases torturing their own leaders—including Communist Party members—who happened to be of landlord or rich-peasant background. Eventually, it was famine that forced most peasants to submit. All told, colonial forces probably had killed at least 3,000 inhabitants of Nghe-Tinh, while the peasants had killed less than 130 people. French officials admitted vaguely to holding 3,000 to 4,000 prisoners.[40]

The lessons of Nghe-Tinh were being absorbed even while the conflict was still underway. For example, whereas Communist Party leaflets of April-May 1930 generally exhibited a narrow proletarian preoccupation, those of four months later reflected amazement at the size and momentum of the Nghe-Tinh peasant movement. When it proved impossible to generate similar movements elsewhere (except in Quang Ngai), Party members did not condemn the peasants but rather themselves for being so inept and unprepared. Perhaps most impressive was the staying power of the Nghe-Tinh peasants, their refusal to collapse into confusion or apathy after the first French attacks. Careful students of Nghe-Tinh also noted how the peasants had not stopped at highly visible and cathartic anticolonial, antitax and antilandlord actions, but had gone on to create alternative social institutions, including village administrative committees, self-defense units, *quoc ngu* schools, and welfare networks. It began to appear that the theory of a revolutionary alliance of workers and peasants was indeed practicable in Vietnam. More succinctly, if it took the French twelve months to quell uprisings in three provinces, that clearly suggested the need to plan and prepare for future uprisings that involved peasants of many provinces in all three regions.

Of course, by late 1931 most surviving Party members were forced to discuss such ideas in jail, without any idea of when they would be free to try again. Aside from that, Nghe-Tinh had exposed a number of serious weaknesses. For example, most people had not really expected the French to resort to such calcu-

40. Osborne, "Continuity and Motivation," pp. 46–48. AOM (Paris), SLOTFOM, series III, carton 48. Nguyen Duy Trinh, in Tran Dang Ninh et al., *Con Duong Cach Mang* [The Path to Revolution] (Hanoi, 1979), pp. 67–83. Ton Thi Que, *Chi Mot Con Duong* (Nghe An, 1972), pp. 42–77.

lated, sweeping brutality. This was a lesson the Party would remember a decade later when instructing Viet Minh participants in the art of guerrilla warfare, including methods of obstruction and evasion. Poor peasants also needed to be convinced not to alienate everyone in the village who was better off than they, but instead to focus their discontent on the French, the mandarins, and those landlords and village officials who refused to help the revolutionary cause. By severely harassing even middle peasants in early 1931, Nghe-Tinh activists had exacerbated internal differences and made it easier for the French to restore local control by employing a policy of divide and rule.[41] Further, many Vietnamese city folk were shocked at stories of roving peasant gangs arbitrarily confiscating private property and meting out summary punishments. Colonial apologists naturally used these stories to attempt to discredit Vietnamese radicals in general and the Communist Party in particular.

Significantly, the Communist Party never disassociated itself from any of the events of Nghe-Tinh. On the contrary, it proudly incorporated all the strikes, demonstrations, meetings, confiscations, and punishments into its version of Vietnamese revolutionary history.[42] It admitted major errors, but claimed to have learned how to avoid them in the future. Most importantly, it had been seen to stick close to the newly awakened if "imperfectly conscious" peasantry, sharing both their dreams and their sufferings, rather than standing on the sidelines with an "objectively correct" analysis of society. Ironically, the colonial authorities greatly enhanced the Party's image among poor peasants elsewhere in Vietnam by publicly assigning sole responsibility for the events of Nghe-Tinh to the "alien Bolsheviks." Increasingly, the Party took on the aura of champion of the rural poor, the only political organization prepared to go down the line for them. This undoubtedly strengthened the Party's position in subsequent struggles, even though the Party discouraged poor peasants from confiscating landlord properties and made no secret of its ultimate objective of land socialization.

Perhaps the most subtle lesson of Nghe-Tinh had to do with problems of leadership. Although the Communist Party was profoundly impressed by the power of an aroused peasantry, it was also acutely aware that it had been unable to adequately predict, plan, or coordinate events at the provincial level, much less implement a viable national strategy. It had been placed too often in a position of

41. There is some evidence that animosities remained sufficiently deep inside many Nghe An villages so as to inhibit Communist Party activities in the province until 1945. Ban Nghien Cuu Lich Su Dang, *So Thao Lich Su Tinh Dang Bo Nghe An* [Preliminary History of the Nghe An Provincial Party Branch] (Nghe An, 1967), pp. 43–101. Truong Chinh, *Cach Mang Dan Toc Dan Chu Nhan Dan Viet-Nam* [The Vietnamese People's Democratic National Revolution], vol. 1 (Hanoi, 1975), pp. 260–62.

42. Eventually the Communist Party claimed to have led the entire movement, which seems to me a considerable overstatement. See, for example, *Nhung Su Kien Lich Su Dang* [Historical Facts about the Party], vol. 1: 1920–45 (Hanoi, 1976), pp. 181–274.

responding to the actions of others instead of controlling the pace and direction of events; this had proven particularly debilitating after the French swept in and executed a policy of "white terror." At that point there was a need to wind down the struggle effort, to consolidate, to protect certain core political gains rather than continue "demonstrationism without a way out."[43]

Part of the solution lay in better organization. The Comintern, initiated by Lenin and subsequently controlled by Stalin, was naturally very insistent about the need for a tighter, more disciplined approach to reality. Vietnamese Communists took such advice seriously when patiently rebuilding the Party in 1932–34. Nonetheless, some leaders realized that it was unrealistic to expect the ICP to mount a future challenge to colonial rule primarily by means of organization. The enemy could not be matched echelon for echelon. If this small, poorly armed, perpetually harassed party was ever to succeed, it would have to be in the first instance an ideological conquest, convincing hundreds of thousands of people to anticipate and even rehearse a revolution, but simultaneously persuading them to *hold* that power in readiness pending the opportune moment. What the Party needed, in short, were the advantages of local, spontaneous revolutionary initiatives without the disastrous implications of poorly timed, isolated uprisings. It was not a problem to be resolved perfectly, even in 1945.

"Stalinists" and "Trotskyists"

On 22 May 1930, in front of the Elysée Palace in Paris, about 150 Vietnamese students and workers mounted a vigorous demonstration against death sentences handed down on participants in the abortive Vietnam Nationalist Party uprising three months earlier. Forty-seven protestors were arrested and nineteen leaders deported to Saigon. Most of these young men were already committed to one side or the other in the increasingly bitter confrontation between Stalin and Trotsky, between Comintern and Left Opposition.[44] Together they would reshape radical politics in Cochinchina. In opposition they would expose a number of key problems concerning the nature and direction of the Vietnamese revolution.[45]

As it began among a handful of Vietnamese in France, this debate probably owed more to the desire to participate in what was obviously an international ideological event of the first magnitude then to any careful consideration of what the event meant for Vietnam. As individuals, the debaters were on good terms

43. This is one of a number of harsh Comintern criticisms delivered to an ICP leader in May 1931. Tran Huy Lieu, *Lich Su Tam Muoi Nam Chong Phap* [History of Eighty Years against the French], vol. 2, pt. 1 (Hanoi, 1958), pp. 94–96.

44. Daniel Hémery, "Du patriotisme au marxisme: l'immigration vietnamienne en France de 1926 à 1930," *Le Mouvement Social* 90 (Jan.–Mar. 1975), pp. 3–54.

45. The most detailed and perceptive discussion of radical political developments in Cochinchina in the 1930s is Daniel Hémery, *Révolutionnaires Vietnamiens et Pouvoir Colonial en Indochine* (Paris: Maspéro, 1975).

with each other and remained so for some years. Their willingness to demonstrate side by side in Paris was prelude to a remarkable political alliance in Cochinchina that lasted until 1937. Already in April 1930, however, Ta Thu Thau, the leading Trotskyist, was raising in print the central issue of *what kind* of revolutionary effort ought to be mounted in Indochina now that the "petit bourgeois nationalists" appeared to have been destroyed. For him, the primary threat was an alliance between French capitalism and the native bourgeoisie, the latter using Vietnamese nationalism to deceive workers and peasants into accepting its leadership. If this was true, then Vietnamese adherents of the Comintern position were playing into the hands of the enemy by accepting the necessity of a bourgeois democratic revolution. Instead, Ta Thu Thau argued, they should work for the international proletarian revolution directly, thus avoiding both the fruitless armed adventurism of the petit bourgeois nationalists and the sly reformist nationalism of the bourgeoisie.[46]

Following French destruction of the Nghe-Tinh soviets in 1931, Vietnamese Trotskyists criticized the Indochinese Communist Party for possessing a leadership riddled with petit bourgeois nationalists and thus prone to violent adventurism. In their opinion the ICP had also ignored the economic struggle of the workers and placed too much faith in the peasants. Perhaps because some ICP returned students agreed with this assessment, and also because the Comintern was taking a similar line privately, the ICP made no direct rebuttal. By 1933, in fact, ICP members in Saigon were openly working together with a group of Trotskyists to publish the newspaper *La Lutte* and to advance a joint slate of "workers' candidates" to the Municipal Council. Soon they had managed to outmaneuver the southern Vietnamese bourgeoisie on its own political turf, the restricted native electorates of the Municipal Council and the Cochinchina Colonial Council. In 1936, immediately following the Popular Front electoral victory in France, this unusual *La Lutte* group took another important step, spearheading what amounted to a semi-legal challenge to the existing colonial system. A call went out for the autonomous convening of a representative "Indochinese Congress." Hundreds of local action committees were formed and lists of popular grievances compiled for presentation to the authorities. When the colonial government counterattacked in September 1936, the struggle shifted quickly to organization of workers' strikes and demonstrations, which sometimes achieved modest economic gains but generally failed to extract any significant institutional concessions from the Blum Cabinet.[47] The amount of bloodshed when compared with Nghe-Tinh was extremely small, a reflection both of colo-

46. Hémery, "Du patriotisme au marxisme," pp. 42–44.
47. Hémery, *Révolutionnaires vietnamiens*, pp. 44–63, 281–394.

nial restraint imposed from Paris and increased discipline on the part of Vietnamese strikers and demonstrators.

By mid-1937 the marriage of convenience between the ICP and the Left Opposition in southern Vietnam had come unstuck. The former was committed to the popular-front concept despite the lack of colonial concessions; the latter now felt compelled to denounce the popular-front concept as a betrayal of the working class.[48] Beyond that, however, the connection with the Trotskyists was now a distinct embarassment to just about all ICP members except those who were on the *La Lutte* team. Stalin's 3 March 1937 speech on Trotskyism and the Comintern's huge propaganda blitz justifying the Moscow trials probably forced a showdown. Just to make sure, the French Communist Party sent a deputy, Maurice Honel, to Indochina with instructions to terminate the relationship permanently.[49]

Even without external pressure, however, the split was inevitable. As discussed below, theoretical differences by 1937 had taken on serious practical consequences. From a tactical point of view as well, the ICP no longer needed the Trotskyists in the way they had two or three years earlier. National and local ICP networks had been restored and expanded to well beyond 1930 levels, in part thanks to the highly visible, audacious efforts of the *La Lutte* group.[50] ICP members elsewhere had learned a great deal from watching the *La Lutte* group in action, particularly how to mount legal and semi-legal campaigns. The Party now had its own stable of well-known polemicists, editors, and speechmakers. It was displaying a collective political confidence and maturity quite lacking before. Since for various reasons the Trotskyists had never been able to offer serious competition in northern and central Vietnam, it remained only for the ICP to stand up to them in the south.

Although some of the barbs aimed by ICP and Trotskyist writers at each other were admittedly incongruous in a Vietnamese setting, it would be a mistake to

48. From September 1936, one group of Trotskyists led by Ho Huu Tuong had already begun sniping at the French Popular Front and related issues via the newspaper *Le Militant*. In *La Lutte*, conflict was largely avoided until the March–April 1937 polemic between Nguyen An Ninh and Ta Thu Thau. In late May, the ICP began publishing *L'Avant Garde* as a means to counter *Le Militant*. The next month the three remaining ICP members on the *La Lutte* editorial team withdrew.

49. Tran Huy Lieu et al., CMCD-7, pp. 107–08. With a hint of irony, perhaps, the authors add that Honel was purged in 1939 for opposing the Molotov-Ribbentrop pact. Honel's visit was July–September, not "early 1937" as stated by the authors.

50. Other factors included spontaneous local initiatives to form cells and subsequently seek higher echelon approval, the return of more cadres from training in the Soviet Union, the gradual release or parole of most ICP members from jail, and the excitement generated by the May 1936 Popular Front victory in France.

dismiss the entire dispute as intellectual froth. On the contrary, what began as a seemingly innocuous rhetorical exercise in faraway Paris eventually served to highlight important issues, leading the two groups in very different directions and ending in a bloodletting.

Already in 1932 the ICP's "Action Program" declared that armed insurrection had to be made integral to the bourgeois democratic revolution. The program also promised self-determination for the peoples of Cambodia and Laos and gave new attention to ethnic minorities inside Vietnam.[51] With Comintern advice and assistance, the ICP patiently developed a clandestine apparatus extending from Moscow via France, South China, and Thailand to regional, provincial, and district committees inside Vietnam. Party cadres penetrated existing organizations or established new ones, identified the "most advanced" individuals to form Party cells, and thus endeavored to control (or at least guide) a wide range of political, social, and cultural activities.[52]

Vietnamese Trotskyists believed ethnic politics to be of minor consequence compared with class politics, and in any event a phenomenon that would vanish in the worldwide proletarian revolution. Although not averse to armed insurrection in principle, they took the white terror of 1930–1931 to mean that conditions were far from ripe. Besides, they were concerned that the revolution produce the Red Army, not the reverse. The success or failure of the subsequent socialist transformation of society might well hinge on which came first. As for clandestine operations, while Trotskyists did take some security precautions, they felt much more comfortable operating in the public arena, disseminating publications, addressing meetings, and leading demonstrations. They argued that organization and strategic line ought to be secondary to political agitation among the people. Perhaps more than ICP members they were fascinated by the dialectic between ideas as a product of the economic substructure and ideas that became a "material force" once they penetrated the consciousness of the masses. In either case, an idea, to come alive, could never be kept a secret, the exclusive property of a few leaders.[53]

It may be that consistent Trotskyist advocacy of working-class interests and a direct march to the dictatorship of the proletariat played a key role in reducing

51. *Internationale Communiste* (Paris) 24 (15 Dec. 1932), pp. 1273–87. English translation in Robert F. Turner, *Vietnamese Communism: Its Origins and Development* (Stanford: Hoover Institution Press, 1975), pp. 318–33.

52. Huynh Kim Khanh, "Vietnamese Communism," pp. 213–54; Hémery, *Révolutionnaires vietnamiens*, pp. 48–49.

53. Nguyen Thi Chinh, in PNTV 162 (4 Aug. 1932), pp. 9–11. Pham Van Dieu, *Bien Chung Phap Duy Vat Luan*, 2nd printing (Saigon, 1937), pp. 44–45. Nhi Nhi, *Ai Lam That Bai Cach Mang Tau?* [Who Caused the Defeat of the Chinese Revolution?] (Saigon, 1938), pp. 13–16.

the ICP's proletarian preoccupations. The political limitations of the Vietnamese working class must have been all the more obvious when the ICP was forced to divide that tiny constituency with someone else. Of course, the policies enunciated at the Seventh Comintern Congress in 1935 provided the ICP with further impetus to pursue a united-front strategy, just as it gave some Vietnamese proletarians more reason to follow the Trotskyists. During World War II new Trotskyist nucleii seem to have emerged in the north among Hanoi workers and Hon Gay coal miners. Overall, however, Vietnamese workers remained remarkably quiet after 1939. The 1945 Revolution would not come from the factories, repair shops, mines, or plantations.

Vietnamese Trotskyists were quite prepared to agitate in rural areas, and they upheld the worker-peasant alliance, but they rejected the idea of building revolutionary bases in the "semi-feudal" countryside. In 1936–1937 Trotskyists demonstrated a capacity to stimulate strikes in villages adjacent to Saigon. They tried also to assist tenants and agricultural laborers to extract better contracts from some of the big landlord estates further from the city. However, these initiatives were regarded as extensions of more important efforts in cities and towns, and were not to be allowed to take on a distinct character or to dilute proletarian revolutionary ideology. Although not stated, there was the clear assumption that peasants made fickle allies because of their superstitious outlook, provincialism and readiness to be bought off with a bit of land. The sooner they could be converted into agricultural proletarians as part of the socialist revolution, the better it would be for all concerned.[54]

Many ICP members had a very similar view of the peasantry, but their commitment to engineering a national revolution ahead of a socialist revolution led them in a different operational direction. It seemed obvious that to be able to seize power the ICP would need considerable peasant support. In this sense the 1917 Russian precedent was not particularly applicable, as the French would always be able to crush an uprising in two or three cities of Indochina. Even if temporarily successful, the lack of simultaneous peasant uprisings in the countryside would make it feasible for the colonialist-landlord coalition to mount an effective counterattack.

The crucial question was how to attract and mobilize the peasantry without alienating other potential allies, and without precipitating violent confrontations

---

54. This position is implicit in criticism of Comintern-CCP policy in China, particularly the 1928 retreat from the cities and subsequent attempts to form rural soviets. Nhi Nhi, *Ai Lam That Bai*, p. 8, for example, ridicules the Chinese soviets by comparing them with a hypothetical Vietnamese attempt to establish revolutionary bases in Dong Thap Muoi and Ca Mau. As it happens, these were precisely the southern areas that the Viet Minh and NLF used quite effectively in later years.

before conditions were ripe. Radical intellectuals realized very early that peasant grievances were not the same as those of the proletariat.[55] Members of the ICP working in the countryside in 1930–31 learned much more; yet doctrine failed to keep pace, leading some of them to criticize their peers for being "totally indifferent to the peasant masses."[56] In 1935 the ICP decided it had been wrong in 1930 to classify agricultural laborers as part of the proletariat and therefore ineligible to receive redistributed land in the bourgeois democratic revolution.[57] Subsequently, the ICP devoted considerable attention to poor peasants, tenants, and agricultural laborers alike, assisting them to convene meetings, to express their grievances publicly, and to form a wide variety of "mutual-aid associations" (*hoi tuong te*). By 1937 it was not uncommon to see peasant spokesmen addressing working-class and intelligentsia audiences rather than the reverse, as had always been the case.[58]

Members of the ICP and Trotskyists divided most sharply on the issue of the Vietnamese bourgeoisie. Committed to the idea of a bourgeois democratic revolution, the ICP could hardly call for the immediate overthrow of the bourgeoisie. Perhaps the closest it came was in 1932, when it angrily lumped the native bourgeoisie together with landlords and notables as "executioners" on behalf of the imperialists, massacring Vietnamese workers, peasants, and soldiers. The next year, however, a ranking Comintern analyst suggested that the ICP could win over that part of the native bourgeoisie which suffered from the import of goods from France.[59] In 1935, in line with the startling new policy enunciated at the Seventh Comintern Congress, it became imperative for the ICP to reach out to all except the most "reactionary" elements in Indochina. The objective was a broad united front of both Frenchmen and Vietnamese prepared to work for "democracy" and against "fascism."

Not much occurred until the May 1936 election victory in France of the Popular Front jolted everyone in Indochina. Rather surprisingly, the Trotskyists went along with ICP plans to give Constitutionalist Party leaders prominence in the

---

55. For example, Nguyen An Ninh, *Hai Ba Trung* (Saigon, 1928), pp. 21–32, is a dramatic recreation of peasants describing problems of conscription, indebtedness, heavy taxes, mandarin duplicity, and summary justice.

56. AOM (Aix) Résident Supérieur au Tonkin, series F-50, 2 Feb. 1931 letter from an unidentified cadre to the ICP's northern region committee. A colonial official has underlined this particular passage. AOM (Aix) G.G. series, F-7F4, vol. 2, item 6, contains an early (15 Apr. 1930) Communist Party flyer devoted entirely to peasant grievances in one district.

57. CMCD-7, p. 55.

58. Five out of nineteen speakers at a large Saigon meeting organized by the ICP on 28 November 1937, for example, appear to have represented peasant organizations in various delta provinces. Nguyen Van Kinh, *Chung Quanh cuoc Suu Tap Dan Nguyen va cuoc Meeting tai Rap Thanh Xuong* [Concerning the Collection of Popular Aspirations at the Meeting at Thanh Xuong Theater] (Saigon, 1937). See also CMCD-7, pp. 71–72.

59. Huynh Kim Khanh, "Vietnamese Communism," pp. 236–40.

Indochinese Congress. However, once the southern bourgeoisie recovered from the shock of having a Socialist prime minister and minister of colonies in Paris and ascertained that colonial policy was not going to change dramatically, they began backing away from the Indochinese Congress and all other radical schemes. Conditions were quite different in Tonkin, where tighter government controls forced the ICP to proceed more cautiously, but where it also succeeded in linking up with a number of bourgeois and petit bourgeois elements. Together they developed the private *quoc ngu* literacy program (see chapter 4), expanded cultural activities, endeavored to provide free professional services for the poor, and tested the limits of legal political activity. United front strategy for Tonkin and northern Annam was in large measure coordinated via the Hanoi editorial offices of *Le Travail*, manned by a remarkable team of ICP intellectuals and sympathizers.[60]

The ICP front with the bourgeoisie in Tonkin and northern Annam was successful partly because it had almost no left opposition to worry about, partly because the bourgeoisie was much smaller and had no political party of its own like the Constitutionalist Party in Cochinchina. Nevertheless, all was not smooth sailing. The Second International was equally active, mainly via French Socialist Party members residing in Hanoi. In 1938 the ICP managed to infiltrate several of its members to the newly established Socialist Party branch, one of whom, Phan Thanh (1908–39), proved extraordinarily effective in publicly criticizing the French authorities for failing to institute reforms. His untimely death in April 1939 was cause for a large public funeral reminiscent of that given for Phan Chu Trinh in 1926.[61]

Cooperation with the bourgeoisie inevitably meant political compromise. How far the ICP was willing to go was evident in the July 1939 election to fill Phan Thanh's seat in the Annam Chamber of Representatives. Dang Thai Mai, the Democratic Front candidate and a covert ICP member, had pamphlets distributed which extolled his background in both Western and traditional Chinese and Vietnamese studies, criticized his opponent for not being proficient in *quoc ngu* or

---

60. Begun in September 1936, *Le Travail* was frankly modeled on *La Lutte*, minus all but one Trotskyist (Huynh Van Phuong). Shut down in April 1937, its role was taken up by *Rassemblement* and other papers in succession. Court cases followed each closure, with freedom of the press serving as an important intelligentsia rallying point regardless of political tendency. From April to October 1938 the ICP also was able to sponsor an influential *quoc-ngu* weekly, *Tin Tuc* [News]. Books and pamphlets were published under the *Dan Chung* [People] label. Tran Huy Lieu, *Mat Tran Dan Chu Dong Duong* [The Indochinese Democratic Front] (Hanoi, 1960).

61. The impact of Phan Thanh's death reached Quang Nam, where he was an elected delegate to the Annam Chamber of Representatives, and Saigon, where he was remembered for contributing articles to a number of French-language papers. See Nguyen Son Tra, *Ve Phan Thanh* [About Phan Thanh] (Tourane [Da Nang], 1939); and *Dan Chung* 65 (6 May 1939) and 66 (13 May 1939).

The editorial committee of *Tin Tuc* [News], a popular front journal published in Hanoi in 1938. Standing from left to right on the first step are Tran Huy Lieu, Van Tan, and Truong Chinh. Courtesy of the Revolutionary Museum, Hanoi.

written French, and portrayed "upright" village officials as ignoring pressures from mandarin superiors to vote against him. The pamphlet concluded by recounting a dream in which Phan Thanh had come back and indicated that Dang Thai Mai was the best candidate.[62] Dang Thai Mai won the election, but one month later the Democratic Front was smashed by the colonial authorities.

Meanwhile, in Cochinchina, the ICP was getting the worst of the bargain from both sides. After 1937 only a handful of the southern bourgeoisie supported the popular-front concept. Yet the ICP continued to operate on the assumption that the majority of the bourgeoisie was "progressive" and could be wooed away from the "reactionary" minority. This left it increasingly vulnerable to Trotskyist criticism, a fact that became embarassingly obvious in the Colonial Council election of April 1939, when the Trotskyist slate trounced both the bourgeois Constitutionalist Party and the ICP. Internal criticism and self-criticism quickly turned into a press debate between Party leaders—perhaps the only time the ICP allowed this to happen. Three different strategies toward the native bourgeoisie were ar-

62. Cuong Truc and Cong Tam, *Ai Xung Dang?* [Who Is Worthy?] (Hanoi, 1939).

Cover of *The Gioi* [World], the youth magazine of the Indochinese Communist Party in Hanoi, 1938–39. Young people around the world march behind a placard demanding "Freedom, Peace, and Happiness." Courtesy of the Bibliothèque Nationale, Paris.

gued vigorously. Nguyen Van Tao believed that it was essential to smash (*danh do*) the Constitutionalists.[63] Le Hong Phong retorted that it was not necessary to smash any native class or political party, but only the imperialists and their lackeys.[64] Finally, after labeling those positions "left" and "right" deviations respectively, Nguyen Van Cu (1912–41) tried hard to define a middle strategy which involved attacking most of the Constitutionalist leaders without mercy, but also continuing serious efforts to attract away their bourgeois followers.[65] Apparently, no internal consensus was reached prior to the French crackdown in September; this was probably one of the main reasons why the southern branch of the ICP exhibited schismatic tendencies for some years thereafter.

63. *Dong Phuong Tap Chi* 6.

64. *Dan Chung* 67 (23 May 1939), 68 (31 May 1939), and 69 (13 June 1939). Le Hong Phong wrote under the pseudonym of Tri Binh.

65. Tri Cuong (Nguyen Van Cu), *Tu Chi Trich* [Self-Criticism] (Hanoi, 1939). The author states that *Dan Chung* refused to print his essay—a startling response when one considers that he was general secretary of the ICP. He was captured by the Sûreté in June 1940 and executed 24 May 1941.

In retrospect, it is remarkable, given existing policy constraints, how much the ICP was able to accomplish during the years 1936–39. Under Comintern guidelines it was not able to demand either national independence or sweeping social changes within the colonial framework. If the ICP simply did what French Popular Front leaders wished, it risked being discredited from both the patriotic and social revolutionary angles. As it was, this period saw a quiet resurgence of monarchist nationalism among Vietnamese landlords and officials, some looking to Bao Dai in Hue, others eyeing the pretender, Prince Cuong De, in Tokyo. Monarchist or republican, Vietnamese nationalism might receive sufficient support from Japanese or French sources to pose a grave threat to the Indochinese Democratic Front in general and the ICP in particular.[66] On the other side of the equation, most economic indices for 1936–39 remained below the level of 1929–30, causing continuing difficulty for workers and peasants in Vietnam.[67] The ICP had to avoid being blamed for the failures of the French Popular Front, particularly given the high hopes that had been aroused in the minds of many impoverished Vietnamese.

Basically, the ICP worked from the premise that the best defense is a good offense. It took the glowing rhetoric of the French Popular Front and thrust it in the face of colonial administrators, *colons,* and native landlords, demanding practical implementation. In this respect, the tactical alliance with the Trotskyists was a considerable asset, demonstrating to the Vietnamese public that the ICP was no passive creature of the Popular Front, much less the governor-general. When the alliance was broken in mid-1937, the ICP continued to attack the French government on a wide front. Among other things, it demanded that metropolitan labor laws be applied in Indochina, that the head tax and the salt and liquor monopolies be eliminated, that the sale of opium be banned, that land rents be reduced and corvée terminated, that full civil liberties be granted, that tariffs be readjusted to the advantage of the colony, and that privileges granted to the Bank of Indochina be removed.[68]

Perhaps more important than catchall grievance lists, however, was the visible readiness of ICP members to endure government harassment and punishment. Although operating conditions were undoubtedly more favorable during this pe-

66. Van Dinh [Vo Nguyen Giap], *Con Duong Chinh,* pp. 8–10, argued that German assistance to a "most reactionary" Arab independence movement in Palestine and Japanese support for Sakdalist and Islamic anticolonialist groups in the Philippines ought to be clear warning of what the fascists had in mind vis-à-vis Prince Cuong De's group and the Cao Dai in Indochina.

67. Hémery, *Révolutionnaires vietnamiens,* pp. 224–31, 340–43.

68. This is only a fraction of the demands put forth in 1937–38. Generally, the lists were designed so that almost everyone could find something of direct value to himself. The fact that some demands implicitly contradicted others was in the nature of popular-front politics of that time. CMCD-7, pp. 62–103. Cuu Kim Son and Van Hue, *Chi Em Phai Lam Gi?* (Hanoi, 1938), pp. 18–23, has demands relating to Vietnamese women in particular.

riod than ever before, people continued to be threatened, beaten up, detained, fined heavily or imprisoned for their political activities. The fact that the ICP at this time encouraged survivors of colonial prisons to publish their memoirs (which, among other things, indicted individual functionaries still employed under the Popular Front) spoke volumes too.[69]

On foreign affairs, as distinct from internal colonial developments, the ICP had much less room for maneuver. For example, ICP members felt the need to repeat in print each of Stalin's rationalizations for degrading, condemning, and executing his former comrades.[70] Vietnamese Trotskyists indicted Stalin for perverting the revolution and converting the Soviet Union into his personal fiefdom; as early as 1937 they predicted that Stalin would ally with Hitler were the latter amenable.[71] ICP members seem to have been unaware of the Soviet Union's decision in mid-1938 to abandon the Spanish Republic. Only in late January 1939 were readers informed that the news from Barcelona was grim.[72] Generally speaking, the ICP continued faithfully to uphold the popular-front concept long after it had been gutted politically in France, forsaken in Spain, and subjected to critical reappraisal by Stalin. Like almost everyone else in the world, ICP members were stunned by the Molotov-Ribbentrop non-aggression pact in late August. They had no time to discuss it before France declared war and the authorities began to repress all left-wing activity in the colony.[73]

Fortunately for the ICP, it had begun to take an increasing interest in events to the north as distinct from those in Europe. Indeed, as Japanese armies swept southward after the July 1937 Marco Polo bridge incident, Vietnamese of varying political tendencies started asking themselves how long it might be before an entirely new situation presented itself in Indochina. Almost all published accounts resolutely supported the Chinese cause, colonial censors not permitting pro-Japanese sentiments to be expressed overtly.[74] The majority gave first praise

69. Son Tra, in the preface to Le Van Hien, *Nguc Kontum* (Tourane [Da Nang], 1938) (see discussion in chapter 7), specifically draws the French government's attention to the colonial brutalities described and demands a total amnesty for political prisoners.

70. Thanh Huong, *Trotsky va Phan Cach Mang* [Trotsky and Counterrevolution] (Saigon, 1937). Nguyen Van Tan, *Su That ve Vu An Moscou* [The Truth about the Moscow Trials] (Saigon, 1937). See also *Dan Chung* 37 (14 Dec. 1938).

71. *Vu An Moscou* [The Moscow Trials] (Saigon, 1937). *Phai Staline va Lien Bang Soviet* [The Stalinist Clique and the Soviet Union] (Hanoi, 1938). *Tia Sang* (Saigon) 37 (8 May 1939).

72. *Dan Chung* 47 (24 Jan. 1939).

73. *L'Effort Indochinois* (Hanoi) 156 (20 Oct. 1939) contains details on the government's suspension of newspapers, dissolution of organizations, and initial arrest of hundreds of Trotskyists and ICP and Democratic Front members.

74. The Bibliothèque Nationale collection contains at least eleven *quoc ngu* titles on the first two years of the Sino-Vietnamese War. Earliest is an ICP account based probably on French Communist Party sources: *Tau Nhat: Ai Duoc Ai Thua?* [China and Japan: Who Will Win, Who Will Lose?] (Hanoi, 14 Aug. 1937). The popularity (and commercial potential) of the topic is

to Chu Teh and the Chinese Red Army, while a few were obviously more sympathetic to the Kuomintang. Both sides, however, accepted the necessity of anti-communists and communists burying their dispute in the interests of building a truly nationwide anti-Japanese united front. Both also urged the Western powers to take a firm stand against Japanese aggression. Finally, both demanded that France formulate a realistic defense strategy for Indochina, to include arming a substantial portion of the native population.[75]

Meanwhile, Vietnamese Trotskyists were adamantly opposed to the concept of an anti-Japanese united front in either China or Indochina. As early as December 1936 Ho Huu Tuong condemned Wang Ming's proposal for a national united front against Japanese imperialism as a "repetition of the errors of 1925–1927."[76] Trotskyists subsequently devoted an entire booklet to the question, *Who Lost the Chinese Revolution?*[77] The answer, of course, was Stalin, who had ordered the Comintern and the CCP to help Chiang Kai-shek (representing both capitalists and landlords) to gain national power, then had stood by while Chiang destroyed his left-wing allies. Now, Chinese workers and peasants were being asked once again to unite with their class enemies, to defer legitimate revolutionary interests indefinitely, and to risk yet another tragic betrayal, all in the name of a "patriotic" struggle against the Japanese.

Trotskyists called on Vietnamese workers and peasants to learn from the sad experience in China and continue to struggle on a class basis. They predicted that French and Japanese imperialists would get into bed with each other, so that the best strategy was that of the Bolsheviks in World War I: non-participation on any side of the conflict and patient fostering of a worldwide revolution.[78] As one slogan declared: "Imperialism—democratic or fascist—is equally the enemy of the proletarian revolution." To this end, Trotskyists vigorously opposed French impositions on the Vietnamese public in the name of national defense, including additional taxes and troop levies.[79] This stance found definite public support, at

evident in Nguyen Manh Bong and Mai Dang De, *Nhat Hoa Xung Dot* [Japan and China at War] (Hanoi, 1938[?]).

75. For a poignant non-communist plea to the French to lead an anti-Japanese struggle, see Nguyen Vy, *Cai Hoa Nhat Ban* [The Japanese Peril] (Hanoi, 1938), and Nguyen Vy, *Ke Thu la Nhat Ban* [Japan Is the Enemy] (Hanoi, 1939).

76. See *La Lutte*, 17, 24, and 31 December 1936 for an exchange of views on this question precipitated by the Sian incident.

77. Nhi Nhi, *Ai Lam That Bai Cach Mang Tau?* (Saigon, 1938).

78. Here it is worth contrasting the Vietnamese Trotskyist position with that of China's Ch'en Tu-hsiu, who eventually argued that "anyone who does not actively fight Japan is a traitor." What he had in mind was a revolutionary struggle independent of the Kuomintang, unlike the Comintern-CCP united-front strategy. Richard C. Kagan, "The Chinese Trotskyist Movement and Ch'en Tu-hsiu: Culture, Revolution and Polity" (Ph.D. diss., Univ. of Pennsylvania, 1969), pp. 140–60.

79. *Tia Sang* 20 (15 Apr. 1939), 41 (13 May 1939), and 46 (19 May 1939); *Cong Luan*, 30 May 1939.

least in Cochinchina. Ironically, once the Molotov-Ribbentrop pact produced a new Comintern line, the ICP was constrained to take the same position for about eighteen months. In early 1941, however, apparently without external guidance, Ho Chi Minh led the shift back to organization of a specifically anti-fascist united front, a strategy which became acceptable to the Comintern the moment that Hitler attacked the Soviet Union in June.

In late 1945 the ICP lashed out mercilessly at the Trotskyists, killing a number of leaders and forcing others to flee the country. Already in 1937 the doctrinal justification for such action was evident. Although each side accused the other of trying to deceive the working class, the ICP went further, labeling Trotskyism worldwide as a nest of provocateurs and enemy agents. Almost in the same breath, however, an olive branch was held out. ICP writers urged Vietnamese Trotskyists to see the evil of their ways, redeem themselves, and thus possibly become eligible for resumption of the alliance.[80] By 1939 the ICP position had hardened. The earlier *La Lutte* cooperation was now declared to be a mistake, allowing Trotskyists a chance to build their reputations and thus deceive large numbers of people.[81] Trotskyists were more dangerous than bourgeois Constitutionalists, the ICP's secretary general averred.[82] According to Vo Nguyen Giap, Trotskyists usually began as unwitting provocateurs, not realizing how their actions served the enemy. In the Soviet Union, Spain, and China, however, events had demonstrated how easy it was for Trotskyists to cross the line to willing cooperation with the fascists. In Indochina, by opposing the Democratic Front, by refusing to take the Japanese threat seriously, by advocating a defeatist antiwar posture, Trotskyists were *objectively* in the fascist camp, together with the "Cuong De gang." It was essential, he concluded, to expose their counterrevolutionary character before they became full-fledged fascist stooges like Cuong De.[83]

Having mostly ignored clandestine operations and neglected to develop extensive rural contacts, almost every Trotskyist leader was swept up quickly by the Sûreté in late 1939. Although many were subsequently released, they found wartime conditions quite inimical to their type of struggle. Meanwhile, the ICP satisfied itself that the Trotskyists were indeed collaborating wittingly with the Vichy French and Japanese.[84] Nonetheless, it was probably the hectic events of August and early September 1945 that proved decisive. Immediately following announcement of the Japanese surrender, Trotskyists joined with royalist groups

---

80. Thanh Huong, *Trotsky va Phan Cach Mang*, pp. 73–78.
81. *Dan Chung*, 52 (7 Mar. 1939).
82. Tri Cuong, *Tu Chi Trich*, pp. 32–34.
83. Van Dinh, *Con Duong Chinh*, pp. 17–21.
84. Since very little research has been done on Trotskyist activities from September 1939 to early 1945, scholarly judgment on this question must be deferred.

and religious sects to take control of the administration of Saigon. When the Viet Minh shoved them out of power on 25 August, the Trotskyists began a popular campaign to oppose return of the French in any guise, Gaullists included. This quickly led to indiscriminate attacks on white persons, which in turn provided the justification for massive British, Japanese, and French counteraction.[85] As the Viet Minh tried unsuccessfully to cope with this crisis, southern ICP leaders decided on physical elimination of all Trotskyist leaders within reach.

The Viet Minh

On 6 June 1941—two weeks before Hitler attacked the Soviet Union—Ho Chi Minh sent an emotional "Letter from Abroad" to his countrymen, calling on them to recognize the importance of recent international developments and prepare to seize Vietnamese independence. Metropolitan France, defeated by Germany the previous year, was in no position to send assistance to the French colonialists. Japan, bogged down in China and "hampered" by the British and Americans, could not apply adequate strength to crush a Vietnamese national liberation movement. In short, historical conditions were more favorable than ever before.[86]

Ho Chi Minh was acutely aware that it was one thing to exhort people to struggle, quite another to mobilize them to seize and hold national power. Even assuming the most favorable external conditions, the ICP and its sympathizers might not be prepared; they might allow the opportune moment to slip by or, worse yet, see it put to use by opposing political interests. At the time Ho sent the "Letter," in fact, the Party organization was still in a shambles due to the French dragnet at the outset of war in Europe, and to two precipitous uprisings in late 1940.[87] French colonial forces had demonstrated the capacity to maintain order despite being cut off from the *métropole*. The Japanese, increasingly reliant on Indochina as a military staging area, were content to see the French continue to function as policemen and provisioners.

85. Nguyen Ky Nam, *Hoi Ky 1925-1964*, vol. 2 (Saigon, 1964), pp. 33–80, 87–91, 185–88, 216–47. Joseph Buttinger, *Vietnam: A Dragon Embattled* (New York: Praeger, 1967), pp. 311–37.

86. Ho Chi Minh, *Selected Writings* (Hanoi, 1977), pp. 44–46. This "Letter from Abroad" was sent from the Sino-Vietnamese border area and signed Nguyen Ai Quoc, perhaps the last time Ho used that name publicly.

87. These uprisings occurred in Bac Son near the Sino-Vietnamese border and in eight provinces of Cochinchina. The latter outbreak was especially debilitating, as the French employed aircraft, armored units, and artillery to destroy whole villages and kill thousands of people. Up to 8,000 people were detained and more than one hundred ICP cadres executed. The southern branch of the ICP would not pull itself together again until early 1945. Le Duc Ton, *Bac Son Khoi Nghia* [The Bac Son Uprising], 4th printing (Hanoi, 1946). CMCD-10, pp. 17–30. Discussion with Tran Van Giau, Ho Chi Minh City, 25 March 1980.

Ho Chi Minh's June 1941 "Letter" was equally significant for its unabashed patriotism. He asked his countrymen to harken back to their legendary Lac Hong forebearers, to emulate the thirteenth-century defeat of the Mongols, and to recall the heroism of Phan Dinh Phung, Hoang Hoa Tham and others who had sacrificed their lives fighting the French. Indeed, most of his message could have been written by Phan Boi Chau three decades prior. There was not a hint of class struggle, and no mention of proletarian internationalism. All Vietnamese who loved their country were urged simply to contribute whatever they had the most of, be it money, physical strength, or talent—rhetoric borrowed from Chinese patriotic propaganda of the period.

Ho Chi Minh made the Chinese precedent explicit by calling on Vietnamese to emulate the "dauntless spirit of the Chinese people" in mounting their own struggle for national salvation. Having spent two years in both Kuomintang and Communist zones prior to returning to Vietnam, he knew whereof he spoke. Perhaps more significant, however, was the ability of other Vietnamese to understand immediately what he was talking about, due to numerous ICP booklets and articles describing the anti-Japanese resistance in China that had been published legally prior to the French crackdown.[88] Concepts such as "national-salvation association," "total mass mobilization," "guerrilla war," and "protracted resistance" were already commonplace, at least among Vietnamese radicals. Because colonial security remained very tight until 1944 in most parts of the country, Ho Chi Minh and other top leaders were often forced to use these terms as code words, pending detailed exposition. Many local ICP cadres cut off from provincial or regional Party leaders simply responded to informal Viet Minh propaganda containing these code words. Once they were able to form new Party cells and front organizations on their own, it proved much easier to reestablish contact with higher echelons.[89] Only the southern branch of the ICP

88. Nguyen Van Tay, *Lam Sao cho Tau Thang Nhat?* [How Can China Beat Japan?] (My Tho, 1938). Nguyen Duc Thuy, trans., *Phong Phap Khang Nhat cua Hong Quan Tau* [The Chinese Red Army's Techniques for Resisting the Japanese] (Hanoi, 1938). Van Dinh [Vo Nguyen Giap], *Muon Hieu Ro Tinh Hinh Quan Su o Tau* [Understanding Clearly the Military Situation in China] (Hanoi, 1939). *Tin Tuc* 17 (13 July 1938), 26 (14 Aug. 1938), 29 (27 Aug. 1938). *Dan Chung* 15 (10 Sept. 1938), 16 (14 Sept. 1938), 17 (17 Sept. 1938), and 18 (21 Sept. 1938) serializes a translated interview with Mao Tse-Tung. Subsequent *Dan Chung* issues discuss Chinese Red Army strategy and the CCP's Sixth Congress. *Notre Voix* had regular articles on China in early 1939, including a series of "Letters from China" signed "P. C. Lin," probably an alias for Ho Chi Minh.

89. Truong Sinh, in Bui Cong Trung et al., *Nguoi Truoc Nga, Nguoi Sau Tien* (Hanoi, 1960), pp. 59–74, provides a very useful account of provincial-level ICP initiatives in central Vietnam, 1941–42. Truong Sinh recalls that the first detailed communication from the ICP Central Committee on Viet Minh strategy arrived in late November 1941. In June 1942 the Sûreté captured Truong Sinh and other leaders, which meant that the phoenix-like process had to begin all over again.

remained entirely out of touch with the Central Committee, a fact of some importance when events came to a head in early 1945.[90]

Ho Chi Minh's new organizational framework was the Viet Nam Doc Lap Dong Minh (Vietnam Independence League), or Viet Minh. It was designed to represent all social classes via a range of national-salvation associations, each of which would be guided from within by clandestine ICP members. In each village the various salvation associations (of peasants, youth, women, elders, etc.) would elect representatives to a Viet Minh village committee. Eventually, village groups would elect representatives to a district committee, and so on.[91] The emphasis within these groups was to be on investigating, planning, proselytizing, organizing and training for armed struggle, not immediate uprisings. The enemy could be attacked, but only in guerrilla fashion, thus striking a balance between locally initiated violence and minimum risk to the overall Viet Minh organization pending the opportune moment for a general uprising. Meanwhile, besides this technique of organizing a united front from below, Viet Minh leaders tried to work out a united front from above with existing groups which had either declared themselves against the Vichy French and the Japanese already or might be convinced to take such a position.

As suggested above, Ho Chi Minh set the tone of Viet Minh propaganda by giving Vietnamese resistance to foreign aggression a timeless quality above and beyond the historical dialectic. Traditional culture, particularly as represented in folksongs and folk poetry, was said to reflect a unique and essentially good Vietnamese national character. Contemporary politics was reinterpreted in terms of the vast majority who would surely uphold the just cause versus the handful of traitors who would stick with the foreign bandits. The world at large was said to be engaged in an epic life-or-death struggle between the forces of democracy and fascism. By allying with the former, Vietnamese patriots were both helping to defend that which was virtuous and insuring their country's independence, since it was certain that fascism would be vanquished and that a just world would emerge from the ashes.

Simultaneously, however, the ICP Central Committee was assessing reality from a very different angle and attempting to disseminate its conclusions secretly to Party members. Essentially, it used the theory of contradictions to explain both domestic and foreign developments. As might be expected, the three contradictions inside Indochina which attracted the most attention were those between colonial ruler and ruled, between landlords and poor peasants or agricultural

---

90. Discussion 25 March 1980 in Ho Chi Minh City with Tran Van Giau, head of the ICP's Southern Region Committee, 1943–45.

91. The principles of interlocking horizontal and vertical hierarchies had been explained in ICP legal publications during the Popular Front period. See, for example, Cuu Kim Son and Van Hue, *Chi Em Phai Lam Gi?* (Hanoi, 1938[?]), pp. 27–31.

laborers, and between capitalists and workers. Within these principal contradictions there were said to be numerous secondary contradictions, for example, those between progressive and reactionary colonial elements, between large and small landlords, or between French, Japanese, and Vietnamese capitalists. Sometimes contradictions were refined even further, as when Party Secretary General Truong Chinh distinguished those Vietnamese serving as prefects or district officials from those who worked as government clerks, interpreters, or teachers. The latter were more likely to respond favorably to revolutionary overtures, he concluded.[92]

Internal ICP analyses of this type were designed both to uncover contradictions previously neglected and, more importantly, to suggest how contradictions detrimental to the enemy could be heightened while those detrimental to the Party could be dealt with tactically according to the needs of the moment. Assessing the overall balance of forces became a deadly serious job, with an increasing premium on investigation and experience rather than ideological supposition. These secret assessments were then used as the basis for refining the Party's approach to separate classes, strata, and minority groups.[93] By "increasing friends and reducing enemies," one brought closer the day of revolutionary victory. Thus, Truong Chinh criticized a particular central Vietnam national-salvation association for advocating confiscation of Catholic Church properties and indiscriminate opposition to the royal family and mandarinate.[94] On the other hand, the ICP was constantly worried that its national united-front strategy would disappoint poor peasants and agricultural laborers. It instructed cadres to promise these groups concrete if limited gains at the time of national liberation, and sweeping land redistribution once independence was consolidated. Beyond that, Party cadres themselves were reassured that both the national revolution and the land revolution were simply steps on the path to a full-fledged socialist revolution.[95]

Probably the most sensitive contradiction that ICP members had to deal with until early 1945 was that between ethnic Vietnamese (*Kinh*) and the highland minority peoples (*Thuong*) living in the provinces between the Chinese frontier and the Red River delta. Ho Chi Minh was well aware that there was no love lost

---

92. "Chien Tranh Thai-Binh-Duong va Cach Mang Giai Phong Dan Toc o Dong Duong" [The Pacific War and the National Liberation Revolution in Indochina], in Truong Chinh, *Cach Mang Dan Toc Dan Chu Nhan Dan Viet-Nam*, vol. 1, p. 244. Originally prepared as a Party training document, dated 10–20 Jan. 1942.

93. It is instructive to compare earlier such formulations—for example, as contained in Ho Chi Minh's *Duong Kach Menh* (1925) or the "Political Theses of the ICP" (Oct. 1930)—with the "Decision of the National Congress of the ICP" (13–15 Aug. 1945).

94. Truong Chinh, "Chinh Sach Moi cua Dang" [The Party's New Policies], in *Cach Mang*, p. 206. Originally formulated 23–24 Sept. 1941.

95. Ibid., pp. 199–205.

on either side, and that his ringing exhortations about Vietnamese defeats of the Yüan, Ming or Ch'ing had little or no significance for minorities such as the Tay, Nung, Dao (Man), Thai, or Meo. But without the active involvement of some of them, his plan to create and defend one or more liberated zones in the mountains was doomed to failure. He seems to have begun working on the problem many years earlier: in 1935, for example, he made sure that one of the three Party representatives sent to the Comintern Congress in Moscow was a Tay minority member from Cao Bang province.[96] After establishing his cave headquarters in Cao Bang in early 1941, he took time to write a long poem extolling the province's people, scenic beauty, and cultural traditions. He also made a point of learning basic conversation patterns in several of the local languages, and taught minority participants in his literacy classes how to transcribe their own languages as well as Vietnamese.[97] Ho Chi Minh's lieutenants took pains to bring cadres of different ethnic backgrounds into sustained working relationships and to make sure that minority villagers saw that *Kinh* activists were not necessarily in command positions.[98]

At a more fundamental level, ICP cadres explained to highland peoples how participation in the revolution could enable them to stand up to the colonial tax collector, avoid corvée or conscription, demand lower prices from *(Kinh)* itinerant merchants, and defend themselves against roving bandits. Once several individuals in a village were sufficiently convinced, outside cadres generally retreated to the shadows, especially if they were ethnic Vietnamese. Progress was slow, particularly since colonial troops were quick to punish entire villages for the suspected actions of a few. Rather than see the enemy burn down houses and crops once again, Viet Minh participants often had to withdraw to the forest and survive on tubers and occasional small donations of grain and salt.[99] On at least one occasion, however, ICP cadres ordered highland villagers to burn everything themselves and retreat to the forest—a decision that another Party member charged with caring for these refugees still recalled with shame many years later.[100] The delicacy of the inter-ethnic alliance was further demonstrated when

---

96. This was Hoang Tu Huu. Another minority member from Cao Bang, Hoang Dinh Giong, attended the 1935 ICP Congress in Macao and was elected to the Central Committee. A third, Hoang Van Thu, took a prominent role in the northern Vietnam regional committee until his capture in August 1943. He was executed in May 1944. Phan Ngoc Lien, "Tim Hieu ve Cong Tac," NCLS 149 (Mar.-Apr. 1973), p. 20. LT-2, pp. 196-97.

97. Phan Ngoc Lien, "Tim Hieu ve Cong Tac," pp. 14, 21.

98. Nguyen Van Rang, in Le Thiet Hung et al., *Rung Yen The* (Hanoi, 1962), pp. 69-70.

99. Duong Thi An, *Nguon Vui Duy Nhat* (Hanoi, 1974), provides a vivid account of the struggle from the point of view of a female Nung member of the Viet Minh. Her husband, Chu Van Tan, gives us a more military description in *Ky Niem Cuu Quoc Quan* (Hanoi, 1971), translated by Mai Elliott as *Reminiscences on the Army for National Salvation* (Ithaca, N.Y.: SEAP, 1974).

100. Ha Thi Que, in Le Thiet Hung et al., *Rung Yen The*, pp. 91-95.

the Viet Minh leaders praised minority participants for their hunting, tracking, and shooting skills but sharply criticized some for lacking discipline and being too quick to resort to armed threats or executions.[101] Amidst these difficulties a Viet Minh apparatus did take shape, modest guerrilla operations were conducted, and an increasing number of activists from other provinces were able to enter the hills for political instruction and military training.[102]

The ICP applied the theory of contradictions equally to international affairs. Ho Chi Minh's declaration in 1941 that the Axis would certainly be defeated was considered something of a pipe dream by most Vietnamese intellectuals, which left them all the more impressed by his predictive powers when the war turned in favor of the Allies. Meanwhile, the ICP was constantly assessing relationships within the Axis and Allied camps. Tensions between the local Vichy French administration and the Japanese were recognized very early; and in February 1944 the Central Committee told cadres to start preparing for the inevitable overthrow of the former by the latter, who would then install native puppets.[103] When this happened a year later, the ICP leadership gained further credibility.

During the years 1941–45 the ICP was even more concerned to analyze relations among the Allies with an eye to avoiding pitfalls, obtaining concrete assistance, and obtaining recognition of the Viet Minh as the sole legitimate representative of Vietnamese democratic, anti-fascist forces. Most careful attention had to be given to the Nationalist Chinese armies stationed in Kwangsi and Yunnan, since the fortunes of war could send them marching into Tonkin at any moment. In December 1941 the ICP Central Committee admitted that those Chinese units might act more like foreign invaders than allies, in which case it would be necessary to attempt various forms of passive or guerrilla resistance. On the other hand, the Central Committee suggested, it might be possible to convince the Chinese to rely to some degree on the independent struggle capacity of the Indochinese peoples, thus enhancing the prospects of victory. Either way, it was most important that the Viet Minh be able to improve its position on the ground in Vietnam. If it remained weak, it was likely to be merely a tool in the hands of others. If it became strong, the Allies could not help but take it seriously.[104]

101. *Co Giai Phong* 3 (15 Feb. 1944), reprinted in Tran Huy Lieu, ed., *Ngon Co Giai Phong* [The Flag of Liberation] (Hanoi, 1955), pp. 108–11.

102. Le Hien Mai, in Chanh Thi et al., *Len Duong Thang Loi* (Hanoi, 1960), pp. 113–21, describes with considerable emotion the readiness of Dao villagers in August 1944 to share whatever meager amounts of corn and manioc they possessed with his group, which was in transit to Chu Van Tan's Bac Son-Vu Nhai base area.

103. *Co Giai Phong* 3 (15 Feb. 1944), reprinted in Truong Chinh, *Cach Mang*, pp. 263–70.

104. Truong Chinh, *Cach Mang*, pp. 228–36. It is also suggested that glorification of Vietnamese struggles against northern invaders, especially in legal publications in Hanoi and Saigon, was being encouraged by the Japanese and French authorities to reduce the threat of joint Sino-Vietnamese operations. No mention is made of simultaneous Viet Minh efforts to glorify the same

Had it not been for the need to assess Allied attitudes in general and Kuomintang intentions in particular, Ho Chi Minh would not have dropped his work in Cao Bang and returned to China in August 1942. Shortly after crossing the border, however, he was arrested and jailed; he was lucky to have avoided being executed or dying of maltreatment.[105] After about a year the Chinese authorities gave him access to current publications and allowed him to reestablish contact with Cao Bang. Although still under loose detention, Ho Chi Minh was subsequently encouraged to help reorganize the Vietnam Revolutionary League (Viet Nam Cach Menh Dong Minh Hoi), the émigré anticolonialist organization recognized by the Chinese government.[106] After he was finally released and had made his way back to ICP headquarters in September 1944, Ho Chi Minh quickly vetoed a Central Committee plan for a three-province armed uprising. Convinced that both Germany and Japan were going to be defeated in the not-too-distant future, he wanted more time to prepare for a much more favorable opportunity.[107]

During his two-year sojourn in south China, Ho Chi Minh had not neglected to gather information on the other Allies, especially the French Gaullists and the Americans (both of whom had missions in Kunming). The Gaullists, already looking beyond the end of the war, were adamantly opposed to Allied operational links with any Vietnamese anticolonial group. Instead, they concentrated on contacting French officers within the Vichy administration in Indochina, receiving additional covert pledges of support with each German or Japanese reversal on distant battlefields. This placed the ICP in yet another delicate position. Firmly committed to the Allied side from 1941, it was just beginning to reap some advantages by early 1944. Yet it could not ignore Free French pronouncements that appeared to exclude any idea of autonomy or self-government for postwar Vietnam. From February 1944, therefore, the ICP called for immediate active cooperation between Free French, Chinese, and "Indochinese revolutionary" forces to defeat the Vichy traitors and the Japanese.[108] Instead, after the June 1944 Normandy invasion, the Gaullists, with British assistance, proceeded to parachute agents, weapons, and equipment to an entirely separate French underground in Indochina. The ICP hardened its stance, accusing the Gaullists of rank

---

historical struggles, which points up the sensitivity of the question of Chinese armies entering Vietnam.

105. David Marr, ed., *Reflections from Captivity* (Athens, Ohio: Ohio Univ. Press, 1978), pp. 57–109. Translation by Huynh Sanh Thong.

106. King C. Chen, *Vietnam and China, 1938–1954* (Princeton: Princeton Univ. Press, 1969), pp. 55–85.

107. CMCD-10, pp. 161–63.

108. *Co Giai Phong* 3 (15 Feb. 1944), reprinted in CMCD-8, pp. 33–36, and in Truong Chinh, *Cach Mang*, pp. 271–73.

hypocrisy in preaching the liberation of France from the Nazis but continued French subjugation of other nationalities. "We want total liberty," a June Viet Minh pamphlet warned, adding that "the Allied powers do not have the right to put a yoke on other peoples."[109] Nonetheless, throughout 1944 the ICP retained contact with local Gaullist sympathizers via a clandestine French Communist Party group still surviving in Hanoi. In November the ICP requested that the Gaullists use their positions within the colonial administration to try to stop the Japanese from confiscating rice, obtain release of political prisoners, and provide weapons to the Viet Minh. The Gaullists flatly rejected the request for weapons and proved unable to prevent continuing rice confiscations, but they did manage to engineer the release of 150 political prisoners in Hanoi.[110]

Aware of American needs for strategic intelligence and assistance to downed airmen, Ho Chi Minh in early 1945 took advantage of a Viet Minh unit having rescued a pilot to escort him personally to south China. As a result, he was able to meet General Claire Chennault, commander of the Fourteenth Air Force, and to begin regular cooperation with the OSS.[111] The Japanese *coup de force* of March 1945 practically eradicated the Free French network in Indochina, which made the Viet Minh all the more important to Allied operations. In May the first OSS team was parachuted to Viet Minh headquarters; weapons, ammunition, radios, and medicine soon followed.[112] What counted most, however, was that the Viet Minh leadership was able to present to followers and to the Vietnamese people at large convincing new evidence of Allied support for its cause. When the Liberation Army marched into Hanoi in late August, the American officers and their flag were right together with the Vietnamese commanders and the red flag with yellow star. Although subsequent efforts to gain U.S. recognition of Vietnam's independence proved futile, the Viet Minh had already gotten a great deal from this transient relationship in terms of tangible expressions of Allied respect.[113] The Democratic Republic of Vietnam continued publicly to draw on this image

---

109. As quoted in Paul Isoart, *Le Phénomène National Vietnamien* (Paris: Librairie Général de Droit et de Jurisprudence, 1961), pp. 321–22. See also *Co Giai Phong* 6 (28 July 1944), reprinted in Truong Chinh, *Cach Mang*, pp. 287–89.

110. CMCD-10, pp. 83–84.

111. Charles Fenn, *Ho Chi Minh: A Biographical Introduction* (New York: Charles Scribner's Sons, 1973), pp. 72–76. The author was an OSS agent in Kunming at the time.

112. R. Harris Smith, *OSS: The Secret History of America's First Central Intelligence Agency* (Berkeley: Univ. of Calif. Press, 1972), pp. 320–34; Charles Fenn, op. cit., pp. 76–83.

113. Many intellectuals, for example, were impressed by the inaugural ceremony for the Vietnam-American Friendship Association in Hanoi in October 1945, with General Philip E. Gallagher representing the American side. *Congressional Record*, Study No. 2, 3 April 1972. See also Hoi Viet-My Than Huu (Vietnamese-American Friendship Association), *Dieu Le* [Bylaws] (Hanoi, 1945).

of wartime anti-fascist, anticolonial cooperation for several years after its leaders knew that the United States was assisting the French to regain control in Indochina.

The 9 March 1945 *coup de force* by the Japanese successfully eliminated the French colonial presence in about forty-eight hours and signalled the beginning of what can properly be termed revolution in Vietnam. The ICP Central Committee, gathered partly in anticipation of such an event, responded with alacrity and precision. Indeed, the directive issued at the conclusion of that meeting stands as one of the most remarkable internal documents ever prepared by the ICP.[114] First of all, although the Central Committee was sure the Japanese coup would not produce an independent government, it predicted that people in the towns and cities in particular would have to go through a period of euphoria before they appreciated that fact. This meant that the Viet Minh ought not to focus its efforts on seizing power immediately (a decision reinforced by the unreadiness of many local units and by grudging admiration for the continuing military strength of the Japanese despite defeats elsewhere); instead, stress was to be given to the patient formation of more armed propaganda teams, to introducing the Viet Minh flag and doctrine to the people, to linking the desperate struggle for food (in northern Vietnam) with objects of political struggle, and to persuading village leaders to form more self-defense and youth organizations. All of this effort was to lead to a general insurrection, "for example, when the Japanese Army surrenders to the Allies or when the Allies are decisively engaged in Indochina."[115] Great importance was attached to the Viet Minh being the prime force working with the Allies, and to Viet Minh representatives being able to greet Allied units as they entered each village. These were the standing instructions when word spread of Japan's unconditional surrender five months later.

The August 1945 Revolution was in the first instance a giant, spontaneous outpouring of emotion, and secondarily a well-organized Leninist seizure of power. Some small measure of the electric atmosphere can be gained from publications of the period. In early May 1945, for example, the Hanoi weekly tabloid *Trung Bac Chu Nhat* splashed a photograph of a large crowd carrying "Independent Vietnam" banners across its cover. Inside, writers declared that a new historical epoch had arrived, and proudly introduced each member of the Tran Trong Kim cabinet. At the same time, one article did report uncomfortably that while rice was being burned for fuel in southern Vietnam, tens of thousands of citizens were still starving in the north.[116] Six weeks later the same tabloid featured a

114. "Nhat Phap danh nhau va hanh dong cua ta" [The Franco-Japanese Fight and Our Actions], reprinted in CMCD-11, pp. 13–23.

115. Ibid., p. 16.

116. *Trung Bac Chu Nhat* (Hanoi) 243 (6 May 1945).

photo of Minister of Youth Phan Anh, looking for all the world like Benito Mussolini as he exhorted an audience of twenty thousand.[117] Two months later Phan Anh had allied himself with the Viet Minh, and *Trung Bac Chu Nhat* was describing with awe the mass demonstrations of 17 and 19 August. Subsequent covers had photographs of American Major Archimedes Patti talking earnestly with Viet Minh representatives, of a haggard Ho Chi Minh (he had almost died of malaria and dysentery in July), and of two well-armed, determined-looking female members of the Liberation Army.[118]

From September 1945, even though the Democratic Republic of Vietnam exercised powers of censorship in Hanoi, it still allowed a great deal to be printed which did not conform with ICP or Viet Minh policies. Most obvious were booklets and articles lauding the Vietnam Nationalist Party, a concession that ended in early 1946.[119] More surprising, however, was the diversity of thinking evident in publications prepared by Viet Minh–affiliated authors. Reports of the fighting that had broken out in southern Vietnam in September and October were sometimes so bitter and uncompromising as to jeopardize ICP efforts to negotiate a settlement with the French while simultaneously expanding the anticolonial united front.[120] From another angle entirely, ICP leaders must have winced painfully when they saw a Department of Mass Education pamphlet on democratic elections incorporate a vignette in which a beggar, believing herself ineligible to vote because she had "not contributed anything to the country," was informed that the fact of her raising a son who would be able to take care of someone else's buffalo was qualification enough.[121] Veterans of several decades of intense political and armed struggle must have wondered if they were in the same country as another author who claimed that, just as Germany had been strong because of Nietzsche and the Soviet Union because of Gorki, Vietnam now waited impatiently to be able to "inscribe the names of its heroic revolutionary writers."[122]

Nevertheless, if one steps back from the intoxicating tumult of 1945, it becomes clear how well situated the ICP was to translate spontaneous upheaval into

117. *Trung Bac Chu Nhat* 249 (17 June 1945).
118. *Trung Bac Chu Nhat* 259 (26 Aug. 1945), 260 (2 Sept. 1945), 261 (9 Sept. 1945), and 262 (16 Sept. 1945).
119. See, for example, Hy Sinh, *Song va Chet cua Nguyen Thai Hoc* [The Life and Death of Nguyen Thai Hoc] (Hanoi, 1945). Pham Tat Duc's 1927 essay, "Chieu Hon Nuoc" [Summoning the National Soul], was republished, as were several other Viet Nam Quoc Dan Dang works of that period.
120. Hoc Tu, *Nhung Ngay Dau cua Mat Tran Nam Bo* (Hanoi, 1945).
121. Binh Dan Hoc Vu, *Ngay Hoi Lon* (Hanoi[?], 1945).
122. Hoai Tan, *Trung Bo Khang Chien* (Hanoi, 1946). The author's comment is all the more striking for being sandwiched between vivid accounts of battles, executions, and efforts to fend off famine.

focused struggle. Prior to Japanese surrender the Viet Minh already possessed a secure mountain base area, a shadow government, a clandestine network extending across most of northern and north-central Vietnam, the mystique of being with the winning side in a worldwide confrontation, and a carefully designed revolutionary strategy. At the time of Japanese capitulation, the Viet Minh managed to take administrative control in most locations without bloodshed. The DRVN was founded and functioning before Kuomintang troops could arrive in Hanoi to push their own Vietnamese candidates, and before the British and the French Gaullists could preempt the situation in Saigon. Although there would be tortuous negotiations with the Chinese and armed reversals in the South, it was already apparent by late September that Ho Chi Minh's government enjoyed tremendous popularity, and that most villages were responding to official requests to form revolutionary councils, self-defense units, literacy classes, and welfare committees. This promising beginning made it possible for the government to levy taxes, expand the army, and establish a wide range of specialized institutions from weapons factories to counter-intelligence teams, from broadcasting stations to theatrical troupes. Recruitment and training of new Party members naturally proceeded apace.

As the French moved to reassert colonial authority, this entire apparatus swung into action to prevent them from succeeding. During this protracted resistance, which continued until 1954, the supreme objective was to tighten revolutionary solidarity while simultaneously loosening the enemy's grip. Individuals had to reconcile their instinct for self-preservation, their group loyalties, and their ideological premises. Hundreds of thousands of Viet Minh participants learned to live with fear, uncertainty, misinformation, and violence. They had to obey orders which they did not necessarily understand and convince others to do the same. Just as political prisoners had formerly been forced to cooperate because they were shackled in pairs, now all members of the Viet Minh were bound together as parts of a machine designed to destroy the enemy or his will to fight. If there was any intellectual rationale, it was "simultaneously to promote broad unity and struggle, to struggle in order to achieve unity."[123]

Out of the protracted resistance there arose a curious blend of existentialism and idealism. Hai Trieu, for example, argued that Marxism without praxis was like a pretty flower placed in a vase, admired for awhile, and then inevitably thrown into the trash. A person who studied Marx but did not implement his teachings was a capon, a castrated cock. Only through action could one see who was right and who wrong, who had ability and who did not. On the other hand, Hai Trieu believed that spirit could alter material conditions, that willpower

---

123. *Cuoc Van Dong Cach Mang Thang Tam o Hanoi*, p. 185.

A popular woodcut of Viet Minh recruits marching to the front, witnessed by relatives and village leaders. The caption says, "Defend the Peace." Courtesy of l'Ecole d'Extrême-Orient, Paris.

could alter history.[124] Hoai Thanh, idealist critic of Hai Trieu in the 1930s, described trying to write under battle conditions in the late 1940s, constantly moving, hiding, and helping. Out of this he learned that it was necessary first to "live correctly" (*song cho dung*); only then might one work out one's way of looking at things.[125] Nevertheless, Hoai Thanh's essays remained more idealist than materialist in content.

From the 1941 formation of the Viet Minh onward it is possible to delineate in Communist ideology two different threads, one patriotic and idealistic, the other adhering to principles of dialectical materialism. Thirty-four years of bitter anti-imperialist struggle served to highlight this contradiction, without, however, producing a synthesis. Violent changes occurred in Vietnam with such rapidity that theorists were not able to keep pace with life. Although 1975 was seen as a watershed, a time for fundamental reappraisal as well as celebration, the results have not been impressive. A certain smugness is partly responsible, together with some

124. Hai Trieu, "Luat Anh Huong Tro Lai cua Tinh Than qua Vat Chat va tac dong cua con nguoi trong qua trinh phat trien xa hoi," *Tim Hieu* 1-2 (Mar.–Apr. 1949), pp. 24–31.

125. Hoai Thanh, "Nhin lai cuoc tranh luan ve nghe thuat hoi 1935–1936" [Looking Back on the Polemic over Art, 1936–1936], *Nghien Cuu Van Hoc* 1-1960, pp. 36–56.

institutional hardening of the arteries. Above everything looms the weight of experience—decades of war and deprivation that did not teach people how to build an economy suited to the world of the 1980s. New problems have arisen, most notably the confrontation with China. New answers will be required. As the last representatives of the intelligentsia of 1920–45 fade from the scene, perhaps they can convey to their successors the excitement of those days long ago, when any idea was worth studying and debating in the interest of a truly free and independent Vietnam.

10. Conclusion

Between that day in 1925, when several hundred spectators heard a French judge sentence Phan Boi Chau to life imprisonment, and the day in 1945, when a huge crowd listened to Ho Chi Minh proclaim independence, Vietnam underwent a profound transformation. In the mid-1920s, the colonial government had reason to believe that it had found a viable formula for the long-term, peaceful exploitation of Indochina. Only a smattering of Vietnamese dared to disagree openly. The vast majority accepted that change would have to come either by French fiat or by heavenly intervention, not by the actions of ordinary subjects.

Twenty years later, conditions were dramatically different. The French had been forced to drown several Vietnamese uprisings in blood. They had seen the colonial economy completely disrupted. They had been humiliated by the Germans in Europe and incarcerated by the Japanese in Indochina. Even to begin to reassert sovereignty in Indochina, the French were forced to go hat in hand to the Americans, British, and Chinese. Determined to regain pride in themselves, preoccupied by intra-Allied diplomacy, they failed to take accurate measure of Ho Chi Minh, of the new Democratic Republic of Vietnam, or—most importantly—of the political and social revolution sweeping the country. General Leclerc sensed a difficult struggle when he ordered his armored columns to push Vietnamese forces out of Saigon in October 1945. He had no inkling, however, that the end of the road lay at Dien Bien Phu, the ultimate French humiliation. Vietnamese had proven themselves energetic citizens rather than passive subjects.

Neither the August 1945 Revolution nor Dien Bien Phu can be understood without reference to prior changes in social structure and intellectual outlook. The traditional Vietnamese elite had become a pathetic shadow of its former self. Rural life had been altered fundamentally by the decline of the subsistence farmer, the spread of landlordism, the gutting of customary welfare palliatives, and the necessity for ever more family members to seek employment far beyond village boundaries. More than ever before, the tax system took from the poor and gave to the rich.

In place of informal village schools and the classical examination system stood a bewildering variety of French and Franco-Vietnamese educational programs.

413

Fewer than ten percent of the population was able to read in any language, yet this did not prevent a vigorous *quoc ngu* publishing effort from getting under way by the late 1920s. Surprisingly, even workers and peasants gained access to the printed word. Pham Quynh had reason to be worried when he overheard rickshaw pullers discussing the Phan Boi Chau trial on the basis of press reports. Chanh Thi, the disgruntled teenage peasant in search of a job, became a Communist Party member in part due to his being able to read about the Nghe-Tinh soviets in a heavily censored Hue newspaper. And, like most other literate Vietnamese, he transmitted his discoveries orally to a wider circle of compatriots.

At the heart of the literate constituency was the intelligentsia, perhaps 10,000 in number. Looking at photographs of these self-conscious young men and women in white linen suits and starched frocks it is easy to dismiss the entire group as Westernized misfits. Perusing French-language publications they still appear as rather faddish, over-eager students of Left Bank ideological currents. Only when one reads the profusion of Vietnamese-language materials can they be seen to be grappling with real problems which affected not just themselves but their less-educated countrymen as well. The act of writing in Vietnamese forced members of the intelligentsia to go beyond simple imitation, to experiment culturally, to overcome conceptual problems never dreamt of by their Western mentors. It also linked them to the spoken language, and hence to the intricate world of the Vietnamese village. By the early 1940s, many intellectuals were convinced that the future of Vietnam lay not in the cities but among the 95 percent of the population living in the countryside. The Viet Minh offered intellectuals a timely vehicle for working with peasants, whether as propaganda cadres, military officers, or literacy instructors.

Although the Vietnamese intelligentsia was fascinated by new ideas, eager to expose them to critical debate, to test them in varying contexts, it never defined itself primarily in cerebral terms or allowed a mood of detached scholasticism to prevail. Understanding reality was not enough. One also needed to discover the means to alter reality. In the process of ascertaining what is, one was never to lose sight of what ought to be.

Ideology was seen to provide the essential connection between objective analysis and ethical vision. Confucianism had fulfilled this function until defeat and colonization at the hands of the French rendered its world view unconvincing. At best it survived as a set of moral platitudes. Buddhism offered a subtle alternative to Confucianism, yet it was extremely difficult to reconcile with growing intellectual commitment to science and progress. Social Darwinism appeared to explain a great deal about the contemporary world, to the point where Vietnamese became convinced that they must struggle ruthlessly in order to escape extinction. At the individual and intragroup levels, nonetheless, very few were prepared to concede that might makes right. They continued to believe that evil conduct brings retribution, and that any true ideology had to defend right and attack wrong.

Marxism possessed scientific credentials equal to Social Darwinism plus a firm moral stance. It was also more timely, reaching Vietnamese intellectuals in the wake of the Russian Revolution and the Great Depression. Even conservatives could be found employing Marxist periodization and social categories. Many flocked to Marxism as a new religion, to the point of participating heatedly in international sectarian disputes. Still others focused on Leninist organizational theory and practice. By the early 1940s, whatever their political affiliations, writers were far more concerned with relating foreign models to specific Vietnamese conditions than with proving their global philosophical credentials. For Marxists, the crucial problem was to relate Vietnamese history and culture to group decisions about revolutionary strategy and tactics.

The colonial repression of September 1939 made most intelligentsia activities of the Popular Front period illegal. As had been the case a decade earlier, Vietnamese intellectuals were forced to choose between clamming up, modifying their public positions, or going underground; this time, however, the psychological shock was less profound and the individual readjustments more coherent. Also, the presence of Japanese troops in Indochina and of Allied forces in Kwangsi and Yunnan raised anticolonial stakes to the highest point in fifty years. Members of the Indochinese Communist Party, the Vietnam Nationalist Party, the Dai Viet, Cao Dai, and Hoa Hao each sensed that their moment in history had arrived. The Vichy French, appreciating their vulnerability, offered significant new educational and employment opportunities to those Vietnamese willing to eschew anticolonialism. These wartime developments, combined with the inevitable effects of age, growing family responsibilities, and personality differences, led to the demise of the intelligentsia in the early 1940s.

In 1941 the Indochinese Communist Party was in complete disarray, its members dead, incarcerated, demoralized, or surviving precariously in the forests and swamps. Organizationally it appeared to possess less potential than any of the other groups mentioned above. Yet, only four years later the ICP had devised and implemented a plan to seize power, establish a government, sustain popular enthusiasm, and mobilize millions of people to undertake a wide variety of onerous, often dangerous tasks. Subsequently the ICP was able to stymie all efforts by rival forces, foreign or domestic, to reverse these momentous historical events.

Fortune favored the ICP in several respects. Most notably, the Tokyo-Vichy détente seriously weakened those Vietnamese groups which looked to either the Japanese or the French for political advancement. By the same token, it allowed the ICP to mount violent attacks against French colonial rule without being accused of unfaithfulness to the Allied cause. Communist parties in Malaya, Indonesia, and the Philippines were not so lucky. Important, too, was that Ho Chi

Minh returned to Vietnam after thirty years, bringing with him impeccable credentials as an international revolutionary, unrivaled knowledge of world affairs, and a first-hand assessment of national united-front efforts in China.

Neither good fortune nor wise leadership would have counted for much, however, without the ideological transformations that preceded the formation of the Viet Minh and helped the ICP to take the historical initiative. Members of the intelligentsia had long before rejected the mood of bewilderment and pessimism which had characterized their elders. Instead, they possessed an infectious spirit of optimism and cultural pride. From an earlier naïve acceptance of all things Western, they moved on to critical investigation and attempts at selective acculturation. Intelligentsia concepts of struggle and progress reached Vietnamese villagers in the 1930s, leading some to look at current conditions in a very different light. The fact that the colonial economy was in turmoil and rural society severely disrupted facilitated this process. When Vietnamese intellectuals and peasants came together in 1945 to uphold national independence and create a new society, there remained significant areas of misunderstanding and disagreement. Yet, there was sufficient consensus to mobilize millions to defeat the French.

. Except for Ho Chi Minh, all ranking ICP leaders of the early 1940s had been members of the new intelligentsia. Many took prominent roles in the animated debates of the 1930s and drew heavily on the rhetoric of the Popular Front period in persuading people to join the Viet Minh. They defended the rights of the poor, encouraged women to participate in political struggle, stressed the importance of mass literacy, promised democratic freedoms, and portrayed the contemporary world in terms of a decisive confrontation between good and evil. To these themes were now added selective glorification of the Vietnamese past, praise of particular Vietnamese customs, and the claim that nothing could stand in the way of Vietnamese willpower asserted collectively.

The August 1945 Revolution was the sort of mass voluntarist surge of power that anticolonialists had dreamt of for decades. Even today, participants become excited as they recall the mood and events of 1945. For those who were in their teens or early twenties, it represented the formative experience of their lives, fostering a deep sense of solidarity and readiness to sacrifice; older Vietnamese saw the August Revolution as justification for previous agonies, capping three generations of struggle against unbelievable odds. Nothing that occurred subsequently, not even Dien Bien Phu or the rout of Republic of Vietnam forces in 1975, managed to capture the popular imagination in this way.

Being an occurrence of truly epic proportions, the August Revolution has continued to loom over Vietnam in much the same way as did the 1789 Revolution in France or the 1917 Revolution in Russia. Thirty-five years later, all Vietnamese remain to some degree prisoners of 1945. Top echelons of the party, the government, and the army are still occupied by men who engineered the Viet Minh success. Now in their sixties and seventies, they will be replaced soon by men (and perhaps women) of the generation of 1945, who obeyed Viet Minh leaders so enthusiastically, survived the terrible ordeals that followed, and are now in their fifties. Still younger generations, including those not yet born in 1945, are urged constantly to emulate the spirit of those days, to revere their revolutionary elders and do nothing to offend them.

If there was one idea on which almost all intelligentsia members of the 1930s could agree it was the historical dialectic. The only unchanging reality was that everything changed. "Natural law" (*luat thien nhien*), employed by conservatives to convince women to stay at home or to persuade young people to obey their elders, was debunked by the intelligentsia at every opportunity. Nonetheless, the more that Vietnamese intellectuals turned their attention to mass mobilization, the more they allowed timeless interpretations to slip into their writings. The historical dialectic might explain what is. It might even point to a bright future. However, it could not motivate most individuals to subordinate themselves willingly to a group and to risk their lives and property without hesitation. For that, one needed idealism.

Intellectuals within the ICP were not slow to perceive this problem. Their solution was to appropriate a broad range of idealistic images and arguments for use in convincing the Vietnamese masses, while retaining the dialectic for use within the Party. Thus, while World War II was being interpreted publicly in the manner of a vast morality play, internal ICP documents relied on the theory of contradictions to analyze not only the primary Allied-Axis confrontation but also tensions within the Allied camp, the Japanese-Vichy entente, and the revolutionary or counterrevolutionary potential of each indigenous social class and stratum. Theoretical justification for this "outer-inner" bifurcation lay with the concept of a two-stage revolution. During the "national democratic" stage almost anything was acceptable if it served the objective of seizing, consolidating, and defending state power. During the later "socialist" stage, on the other hand, the ICP would patiently instruct the general public on the merits of dialectical materialism. No ICP theorist imagined that the "national democratic" phase would last at least thirty years, leaving the Party with a serious ideological dilemma.

At the Fourth Communist Party Congress in December 1976, Pham Van Xo, an old Vietnamese revolutionary, summarized that event by contrasting it with the First Party Congress, held in Macao in 1935. In the latter case, he had been one of only ten representatives of a "people without a country, forced to assemble secretly in a location far from the Fatherland."[1] In 1976, he pointed out happily, the Congress could boast more than one thousand representatives, "meeting busily in Hanoi, capital of a unified and free Vietnam."[2] This same sense of

1. *Quan Doi Nhan Dan* (Hanoi), 19 Dec. 1976.
2. Ibid.

accomplishment led one Party Central Committee member to tell a Western correspondent, "Now nothing more can happen. The problems we have to face now are trifles compared to those of the past."[3] The National Assembly of the Socialist Republic of Vietnam went so far as to declare that Ho Chi Minh's cause was "everlasting, like our mountains and rivers," and his thought an "eternal beacon" for the nation in its future advances.[4]

Although such statements make good public-relations copy, they provide little help for those Vietnamese attempting to deal with the many new challenges of today. Conflict with China cannot be resolved in the same manner as earlier conflicts with France and the United States. Neither political rhetoric nor administrative fiat will overcome fundamental domestic problems relating to technological innovation, work incentives, capital accumulation, quality control, and efficiencies of scale. The roots of economic success are qualitatively different from the roots of victory in war. Ultimately, "building socialism" is an open-ended process, not a finite struggle that can be declared completed on a particular date, as was the case in 1954 and in 1975.

Vietnamese intellectuals today are certainly mindful of the need to explore and test new approaches to reality. They debate issues vigorously among themselves, try hard to keep in touch with developments overseas, give opinions to those officials willing to listen, and manage to convey some provocative findings to the public via the state-controlled media. Even the Communist Party's daily newspaper, *Nhan Dan* [The People], can occasionally be found wrestling with conceptual contradictions facing the current leadership. An October 1979 editorial, for example, warned against "worshipping spiritual motives and pursuing voluntarism."[5] On the other hand, it reaffirmed spirit as the key to victory in war, and declared that "A society in which all relations stem from the seeking of immediate interests and even personal financial gain is dull, without vitality, and without a future."[6] In recent years different interpretations have also been given to upholding "red" political orthodoxy versus accumulating technical expertise— a continuation of the controversy over "virtue" (*duc*) versus "talent" (*tai*).

Unlike the intelligentsia of the 1920s and 1930s, which often denounced all orthodoxies, today's intellectuals in Hanoi or Saigon must accept that Marxism-Leninism as interpreted by the Vietnam Communist Party is in command. This has not prevented them from pursuing certain lines of inquiry which, if substan-

3. Tiziano Terzani, *Giai Phong! The Fall and Liberation of Saigon* (New York: St. Martin's Press, 1976), p. 294.

4. Summary statement of the First Session of the reunified SRVN National Assembly, Hanoi, 3 July 1976. Reprinted in "Viet Nam News Bulletin," Embassy of the SRVN, Canberra, Australia, 20 July 1976, p. 3.

5. *Nhan Dan* (Hanoi), 23 Oct. 1979.

6. Ibid.

tiated, serve to challenge pet ideological premises. The research of Vietnamese economists, for example, has controverted and eventually helped to alter the Party's line on industrial versus agricultural investment. Economists provoked intense discussion, too, with their proposals for entering into a range of contractual relationships with the capitalist world. Thousands of young Vietnamese returning from study abroad have brought back ideas about music, art, literature, and the overall boundaries of intellectual exploration which some political leaders—including a few among the former intelligentsia—consider quite offensive. Whether a chasm emerges between politicians and intellectuals, as has often happened elsewhere, or whether communication can somehow be sustained, will become clear in the 1980s.

As in the past, Vietnamese intellectuals are conscious of the dialectic between analysis and propaganda. They recognize that claims to be able to divorce scholarly concerns from political beliefs are at best a self-deception, at worst a sly obfuscation. On the other hand, they understand that when ideology is formulated with little or no regard for ongoing scientific investigations, then the scholar is no different from the party official, and society is more apt to make time-consuming, wasteful mistakes. This clearly happened in southern Vietnam after the 1975 victory, when the new persons in authority made a number of important decisions without adequate consultation or reflection. Although subsequent events have forced reassessments, many programs continue to exhibit a rough trial-and-error character, as if the Communist leadership and the southern populace were still experiencing difficulties in basic political communication. Vietnamese social scientists from Hanoi have been slow to get to the roots of this problem, and few southern social scientists are trusted sufficiently to be able to participate in sensitive policy-related discussions.

Vietnamese Marxist-Leninists do not deny that they face serious problems both foreign and domestic. They also admit to having made major policy errors in recent years. Some of the fault is ascribed to "Maoist tendencies" within the Vietnam Communist Party. Perhaps this will prove to be merely a convenient whipping-boy in times of bitter confrontation with China. However, because Maoism is defined as a corruption of Marxism-Leninism characterized by chauvinism, idealism, and voluntarism, it seems that any rigorous discussion will have to open up questions specific to the history of the Vietnamese revolution, not merely those having to do with China.

How deep the criticism will go is uncertain. Elderly Party members surviving from the 1930s have no hesitation in discussing fundamental issues, partly out of sheer intellectual enjoyment, but also because they are confident that nothing is so formidable as to prevent history from continuing to move in their direction. For example, Tran Van Giau pointed out to me how the Party had overcome several crises of at least equal magnitude to the present one: the fierce colonial repressions of 1931 and 1940; the French military offensives of 1946–47; and the events of the late 1950s, when land reforms in the North and U.S.–Diem attacks in the South produced considerable distress.[7] Younger Party members might well have added 1969, when American pacification programs appeared to be succeeding in the South, or 1972, when U.S. bombers threatened to make a wasteland of the North. None of these past crises can teach new generations how to deal with the future, however.

It may be that the contradiction is more institutional than ideological, involving a large post-revolutionary bureaucracy that becomes more conservative with each succeeding year. In that case one can indeed predict increasing alienation among Vietnamese intellectuals, as the gap between the real and the ideal shows no signs of narrowing. With a well-defined tradition of political action, however, Vietnamese intellectuals are not likely to retreat permanently to private contemplation or to the circulation of a few extra-legal manuscripts. As for the bureaucracy, it may be forced eventually to choose between its ambitious programs for national development—many of which presuppose the involvement of enthusiastic, well-informed intellectuals—and the preservation of state orthodoxy.

Despite obvious historical differences, perhaps we all have something to learn from Vietnamese intellectuals of half a century ago. Individuals like Nguyen An Ninh, Tran Huy Lieu, or Phan Van Hum possessed both boundless curiosity and firm moral commitments. Neither their knowledge nor their principles were subject to strict external control. No tradition was so sacred as to be above debate. No intellectual felt fulfilled by simple contemplation or idle discussion; the purpose of thinking was to learn how, when, and where to act. There was no single court before which every action could be judged, but rather a variety of courts, to include History, Fate, Science, the People, the State, the Party, and one's family, friends, and peers. An intellectual was most effective when existing simultaneously as a part of society and outside of it, able both to be deeply involved and to "leap out of his shadow" to assess reality dispassionately. Albert Einstein was considered the outstanding example of this capacity.

Significantly, the Vietnam Communist Party continues to place Einstein at the top of its intellectual pyramid. His life is the object of a school textbook, and his kindly face can be found on Vietnamese postage stamps. A new generation of Vietnamese physical scientists and mathematicians are given the sort of attention Americans reserve for media personalities. Only time will tell if the Party is willing to permit such individuals to express iconoclastic political opinions in public, or whether that side of Einstein's character is declared inappropriate to a socialist society.

7. Personal discussion with Tran Van Giau in Ho Chi Minh City, 1 April 1980.

GLOSSARY

Complete Vietnamese readings, including diacritical marks, are provided here for all names and terms introduced in the main text and for those mentioned in the footnotes, apart from source listings. The arrangement is alphabetical, but not in standard Vietnamese fashion (i.e., broken down by diacritical markings, multiple-letter initial consonants, etc.), since this might be too confusing to some readers. Only one non-English initial consonant demands differentiation in the alphabet here: Đ (in lower case, đ), which follows D.

Ái	bẩm	ca
ái quốc	bán khai	ca dao
âm-dương	Bàn Thờ Tổ Quốc	Cà Mau
an	Băng Tâm nữ sĩ	cá nhân chủ nghĩa
An Nam	Bảo Đại	các bạn
An Nam Tạp Chí	bạo dạn	cải lương
An Toàn Khu	Bảo Định Giang	cần
anh chị em	Bảo Tâm	Cần Thơ
anh đồng chí	Bến Thủy	Cần Vương
áo dài	Bến Tre	Cảnh
	Bích Vân	cạnh tranh sinh tồn
	biến hóa	Cao Bá Quát
	biết ơn Nhà Nước	Cao Bằng
bà	bình đẳng	Cao Chánh
Ba Tơ	bình quyền	Cao Đài
bác	Bố Cái Đại Vương	Cao Hải Để
Bác Hồ	bộ-đội	Cao Lãnh
Bặc Liêu	bộ phận	Cao Thị Ngọc Môn
Bắc Ninh	bồi	Cao Văn Chánh
Bắc Sơn	Bùi Công Trừng	Cát Thành
Bạch Đằng	Bùi Quang Chiêu	cầu đồng
Bạch Thái Bưởi	Bùi Thị Xuân	cha

421

chấn hưng

Chánh Thi

cháu

Châu Đốc

Châu Văn Liêm

Chế Lan Viên

chèo

chị em bình dân

chi hội

chí khí

chí sĩ yêu nước

chính

chính nghĩa

Chinh Phụ Ngâm

Chợ Lớn

chú

chữ Chệt

Chu Lăng Vân

chủ nghĩa anh hùng
    cách mạng

Chu Văn Tấn

cô

cố

Có biết chữ kháng
    chiến mới thắng
    lợi

con

Côn Sơn

công

công bình

công dân

công dân giáo dục

công tâm

công truyền

công ty

cụ

cu-li

Cung Oan Ngâm Khúc

Cường Để

Cường Học Thư Xã

Cựu Kim Sơn

dạ

dân

dân khí

dân tộc

Dân Trí Thư Xã

danh dự

danh nhân

Dao

dị chủng

Dịch Kinh

Diệp Văn Kỳ

dốc sức phù lợi

dung

Dương Bá Trạc

Dương Kinh Quốc

Dương Quảng Hàm

Dương Tự Quán

Đà Nẵng

đại đồng

Đại Học

Đại Nam

Đại Pháp

Đại Việt

Đạm Phương

đảng ngụy

Đăng Thai Mai

Đặng Thái Thân

Đặng Thái Thuyến

Đặng Trần Côn

Đặng Văn Bảy

đánh đổ

đánh giặc với nhau

đạo

Đạo

đạo đức

đạo đức cách mạng

Đào Duy Anh

Đạo Người

Đào Trinh Nhất

Đạo Trời

đấu tranh

Đề Thám

Đi học là yêu nước

Điện Biên Phủ

đỉnh

định mệnh

Đinh Tiên Hoàng

Đỗ Đức Khôi

Đỗ Hữu Phương

Đỗ Nhuận

Đỗ Quý Tấn

đoàn kết

Đoàn Như Khuê

Đoàn Thanh Niên Dân
    Chủ

Đoàn Thị Điểm

Đoạn Tuyệt

Đôi Bạn

đồng bào

đồng chí

Đông Dương Tạp Chí

Đồng Hới

Đồng Khánh
Đông Kinh Nghĩa Thục
Đông Pháp Thời Báo
đồng tâm
Đông Tây
Đồng Tháp Mười
Đồng Xuân
đức
Đức Chúa Trời
đức dục
Đức Thượng Đế
Đuốc Nhà Nam
đường lối
Đường Thị Ân

em

giạ
Gia Định Báo
Gia Huấn Ca
Gia Long
gia phả
giặc
giặc dốt
giặc đói
giặc xâm
giải phóng
giới trí thức
giới trí thức mới
Gò Công
gọi hồn

Hà Đông
Hà Huy Tập

hạ lưu
Hà Thị Quế
Hà Tĩnh
Hải Dương
Hải Thượng Lãn Ông
Hải Triều
Hàm Nghi
hắn
Hàn Thuyên
Hán Việt
hạnh
hát bội
hiện đại hóa
hiếu
họ
Hồ Biểu Chánh
Hồ Chí Minh
Hồ Duy Kiên
Hồ Hữu Tường
Hồ Xuân Hương
hòa
Hoa Bằng
hòa giải
Hòa Hảo
hòa hợp
Hỏa Lò
Hoa Quân Nhập Việt
Hoa Tiên
Hoài Thanh
Hoàn Kiếm
hoàn toàn bác ái
Hoàng Diệu
Hoàng Đạo
Hoàng Đình Giong
Hoàng Hoa Thám
Hoàng Ngọc Phách

Hoàng Quốc Việt
Hoàng Tăng Bí
Hoàng Thiếu Sơn
Hoàng Thị Nga
Hoàng Thượng
Hoàng Thượng ngự-giá
   Bắc Kỳ, nay đã hồi
   loan
Hoàng Tích Chu
Hoàng Trọng Cu-Li
Hoàng Trọng Phu
Hoàng Tú Hưu
Hoàng Văn Thụ
học ăn, học nói, học
   gói, học mở
học hành
học hội
hỏi
Hội An
Hội Chợ Phụ Nữ
Hội Liên Hiệp Phụ Nữ
   Việt Nam
Hội Truyền Bá Học
   Quốc Ngữ
hội tương tế
Hội Văn Hóa Cứu Quốc
Hòn Gay
Hồng Bàng
Hồng Đức
hợp quần
Huế
Hùng Vương
Hưng Yên
Hữu Thanh
Huy Cận
húy tên

Huy Thông
Huỳnh Ngọc Nhuận
Huỳnh Phú Sổ
Huỳnh Thúc Kháng
Huỳnh Tịnh Của

ích
ích lợi

kẻ
kết hợp
Khải Định
Khái Hưng
khinh nhờn
khoa học
khoa học chủ nghĩa
Khoa Học Tạp Chỉ
khởi nghĩa
kịch nói
kiệm
kiêng tên
kiếp
Kiều
Kiều Nguyệt Nga
kim chỉ nam
Kim Đồng
Kinh
Ký Viện

Lạc Hồng
Lam Sơn
Lãng Bạc
Lặng Sơn
lão thành

Lê
lễ
Lê Dư
Lê Duẩn
Lê Đức Thọ
Lê Hoàn
Lê Hồng Phong
Lê Hồng Sơn
Lê Hữu Trác
Lê Lợi
lễ nghĩa
Lê Thánh Tông
Lê Thước
lễ tiến hóa tự nhiên
Lê Văn Duyệt
Lê Văn Hiến
Lê Văn Kháng
Lê Văn Khôi
Lê Văn Lương
lệnh
liêm
liên đoàn
lô gích
loạn
lợi
lợi dụng
Long Xuyên
luân lý
luật thiên nhiên
Lục Đầu Giang
Lục Vân Tiên
Lương Đức Thiệp
Lương Ngọc Quyến
lương tri
Lương Văn Can
Lưu Hữu Phước
Lưu Trọng Lư

Lý
lý
Lý Tế Xuyên
Lý Thái Tổ
Lý Thường Kiệt
lý trí
Lý Tự Trọng
lý tưởng

Mán
mạnh được yếu thua
Manh Manh
mất gốc
mất nước
Mặt Trận Thống Nhất
   Của Phụ Nữ Đông
   Dương
Mẫu Quốc
mày
mày tao
mẹ quốc-dân
mê tín
mệnh lệnh
mệnh trời
Mèo
Minh Mạng
Mọi
mù-u
Mường
Mỹ Tho

Năm Châu
Nam Đàn
Nam Định
Nam Hương

Nam Kỳ

nam nữ bình đẳng

nam nữ bình quyền

Nam Phong

Nam Phong Tạp Chí

Nam Tiến

Nàng Sơn

Nảy Công Dân Ơi

ngã

Nghệ An

Nghệ-Tỉnh

nghĩa

Nghĩa Lộ

nghĩa lợi

nghĩa vụ

Ngọ Báo

Ngô Đỉnh Diệm

Ngô Đỉnh Nhu

Ngô Đức Kế

Ngô Gia Tự

Ngô Giáp Đậu

Ngô Quyền

Ngô Tất Tố

Ngô Văn Hoà

Ngọc Hoàng Thượng Đế

ngôn

ngũ luân

người

người ngoài

người nhà quê

người văn minh quân
     tử

ngụy

Nguyễn

Nguyễn Ái Quốc

Nguyễn An Khương

Nguyễn An Ninh

Nguyễn Ánh

Nguyễn Bá Học

Nguyễn Bá Trác

Nguyễn Công Hoan

Nguyễn Du

Nguyễn Đỉnh Chiểu

Nguyễn Đỉnh Thi

Nguyễn Đôn

Nguyễn Đức Nhuận

Nguyễn Hảo Vĩnh

Nguyễn Huệ

Nguyễn Hữu Bài

Nguyễn Hữu Bồi

Nguyễn Huy Tưởng

Nguyễn Khắc Hiếu

Nguyễn Khoa Diệu Hồng

Nguyễn Khoa Tùng

Nguyễn Khoa Văn

Nguyễn Khuyến

Nguyễn Nghiêm

Nguyễn Phan Long

Nguyễn Phong Sắc

Nguyễn Thái Học

Nguyễn Thị Chỉnh

Nguyễn Thị Định

Nguyễn Thị Hưng

Nguyễn Thị Kiêm

Nguyễn Thị Kim Anh

Nguyễn Thị Minh Khai

Nguyễn Thị Nghĩa

Nguyễn Thị Nguyệt

Nguyễn Thị Thập

Nguyễn Trãi

Nguyễn Triệu Luật

Nguyễn Trọng Thuật

Nguyễn Trưởng Tộ

Nguyễn Tường Lân

Nguyễn Tường Tam

Nguyễn Tuyết Hoa

Nguyễn Văn Bá

Nguyễn Văn Cừ

Nguyễn Văn Ngọc

Nguyễn Văn Tạo

Nguyễn Văn Tố

Nguyễn Văn Tường

Nguyễn Văn Vĩnh

Nhà

Nha Bình Dân Học Vụ

Nhà Nước

nhà quê

nhạc

nhân

Nhân Chi

Nhân Dân

nhân sanh quan

Nhất Linh

Nhị Độ Mai

nho

Nho Giáo

nhu

nó

nôm

Nữ Công Học Hội

Nữ Giới Chung

Nữ Lưu Thơ Quán

nữ quyền

nữ sư

Nùng

nước

ông

ông bà

ông thần

Ông Vua Việt Nam đi
  chơi Bắc Kỳ, nay
  đã về Kinh rồi

Pác Bó

phá hoại

Phạm Công Cúc Hoa

Phạm Duy Tốn

Phạm Hồng Thái

Phạm Hùng

Phạm Huy Thông

Phạm Kiệt

Phạm Như Hồ

Phạm Quỳnh

Phạm Văn Điều

Phạm Văn Đồng

Phạm Văn Hảo

Phạm Văn Xô

Phan Anh

Phan Bội Châu

Phan Chu Trinh

phấn đấu

Phan Đình Long

Phan Đình Phùng

Phan Huy Ích

Phan Kế Bính

Phan Kế Toại

Phan Khôi

Phan Lan

Phấn Son Tô Điểm Sơn
  Hà, Làm Cho Rõ Mặt
  Đàn Bà Nước Nam

Phan Thanh

Phan Thị Bạch Vân

Phan Thị Nga

Phan Trần

Phan Văn Gia

Phan Văn Hùm

Phan Văn Trị

Phan Văn Trường

pháp

Pháp-Việt Đề Huề

phi chiến

phụ nữ chủ nghĩa

Phụ Nữ Tân Tiến

Phụ Nữ Tân Văn

Phụ Nữ Thời Đàm

Phụ Nữ Tùng San

Phú Thọ

Phùng Há

pin

Quả Dưa Đỏ

quá trình

Quắc

Quan Âm Thị Kính

Quả Dưa Đỏ

quá trình

Quắc

Quan Âm Thị Kính

quân giặc

Quan Hải Tùng Thư

quân-tử

Quảng Bình

Quảng Nam

Quảng Ngãi

Quang Trung

quê hương

Qui Nhơn

---

quốc âm

Quốc Âm Thi Tập

quốc-dân

quốc dân giáo dục

Quốc Học

quốc hồn

quốc ngữ

quốc tăng

quốc túy

quốc văn

quyền lợi

Rạch Giá

rau muống

rửa tội

ruộng dâu

ruộng lúa

sân khấu

Sĩ Nhiếp

sĩ-nông-công-thương

sĩ phu

sinh tồn

Sơn La

Sơn Trà

sống cho đúng

sự làm

sư phạm

sự thật

sum họp

Sương Nguyệt Anh

ta

Tạ Thu Thâu

tài
tài đức
tâm
Tâm Tâm Xã
tầm thường
tam tòng
tâm truyền
Tam Tự Kinh
Tản Đà
Tân Sơn Nhứt
tân trào
tân triều
Tân Việt Cách Mạng
    Đảng
Tày
Tây Sơn
Tết
Thạch Lam
Thạch Lan
Thạch Sanh
Thái
Thái Bình
Thái Sơn
Thần Chung
Thân Trọng Huề
thằng
thằng đỏ
Thăng Long
Thanh Hoá
Thanh Nghị
Thanh Niên Cộng Sản
    Đoàn
Thanh Niên Tiền Phong
Thất Sơn
thầy
thể dục
Thế Lữ

thể-dụng
thị dục
thi đua
thích hợp
thiên chức
thiên diễn
Thiên Mụ
Thiếu Sơn
thơ
Thơ Mới
thơ thuyền
thoát ly
thời cơ
thưa
thuận
Thuận Hoá
thực hành
Thực Nghiệp Dân Báo
Thượng
thượng lưu
Thúy Kiều
Tiền Hải
tiên sinh
Tiếng Dân
Tiếng Gọi Thanh Niên
tiếng mẹ đẻ
tiếng ta
tín
tin mê
tố
Tô Dân
Tố Quốc
Tố Tâm
tọa tỉnh quan thiên
tôi
Tôn Quang Phiệt
Tôn Thất Bình

Tôn Thất Thuyết
Tôn Thị Quế
Trần
Trần Bá Vinh
Trần Bạch Đằng
Trần Đức Sắc
Trần Hưng Đạo
Trần Hữu Độ
Trần Huy Liệu
Trần Khánh Dư
Trần Khánh Tuyết
Trần Phong Sắc
Trần Phú
Trần Tế Xương
Trần Thành Công
Trần Thị Như Mẫn
Trần Trọng Kim
Trần Văn Chương
Trần Văn Đôn
Trần Văn Giáp
Trần Văn Giàu
Trần Văn Tăng
Trần Văn Trà
trí
trí dục
tri giác
tri hành hợp nhất
Tri Tân
trí thức
trị yên
Triệu Thị Trinh
trinh
Trịnh
Trịnh Đình Rư
Trịnh Đình Thảo
Trời
trực giác

trung

Trưng

Trung Bắc Chủ Nhật

Trung Bắc Tân Văn

Trung Dung

Trung Lập Báo

Trung Nhị

trung quân

Trứng Rồng

trung thành

Trưng Trắc

Trường Chinh

Trương Quang Trọng

Trường Sinh

Trương Thị Mỹ

Trương Vĩnh Ký

trường hợp

Truyện Kiều

truyền thống

tư

từ bi

tự chủ

tự do

tự do bình đẳng

tứ đức

Tự Đức

Từ Hải

Tự Lực Văn Đoàn

Tú Mỡ

tư sản bản xứ

tú tài

tu thân

tu thân, tề gia, trị quốc, bình thiên hạ

tù treo

Tự Vựng

Tú Xương

tục ngữ

tuồng

tuồng cải lương

tùy thời

Văn Cao

Vân Đài

văn hoá

Văn Huệ

vận mệnh

văn minh

Văn Tân

Văn Tạo

Văn Tiến Dũng

vạn vật

Vỉ Chúa

vi trùng

Việt

Việt Điện U Linh

Việt Minh

Việt Nam

Việt Nam Cách Mệnh Đồng Minh Hội

Việt Nam Độc Lập Đảng

Việt Nam Độc Lập Đồng Minh

Việt-Nam Quang Phục Hội

Việt Nam Quốc Dân Đảng

Việt-Nam Sử Lược

Việt Nam Thanh Niên Cách Mệnh Đồng Chí Hội

Việt Trì

Vinh

Vĩnh Thủy

võ

Võ Nguyên Giáp

vô sản hoá

Võ Tánh

vô vi

vong gia thất thổ

Vòng ốc

Vũ Đình Hoè

Vũ Nhai

Vũ Như Lâm

Vũ Trọng Phụng

vua tôi

xe đạp

xe máy

Xuân Diệu

Xuân Thủy

ý chí

ỷ lại

yên

Yên Thế

SELECTED BIBLIOGRAPHY

In preparing this book it was necessary first to gain a superficial impression about a great deal of writing, then to narrow the field relentlessly so as to subject a smaller number of sources to rigorous analysis. This bibliography focuses on that inner core of books and articles, with annotations designed to assist individuals wanting to embark on their own reading adventures. Although the slant is inevitably toward intellectual developments during the period 1920–1945 in Vietnam, students of other topics, for example, Vietnamese political, social, and cultural history, should find many items of interest to them as well. Researchers in pursuit of very specific data are urged to consult the relevant text footnotes for additional titles and to utilize the various research aids mentioned below.

Authors are listed according to the name by which they are best known historically, be it their given name, their pen name, or a revolutionary pseudonym. Occasionally a second name is appended to facilitate identification in reference guides and library catalogues. Where a book has been prepared by a joint research committee, I list it under the name of the most prominent author, the others being signalled with an "et al." If a translation is available, however imperfect, the publication is listed in the Western-language section, with an appropriate reference to the original Vietnamese source.

Research Aids

The Bibliothèque Nationale's publication in Paris in 1980 of the *Catalogue du Fonds Indochinois de la Bibliothèque Nationale* (Vol. 1: Livres vietnamiens imprimés en *quoc ngu* 1922–1954), edited by Mme. Christiane Rageau, heralded the beginning of a new era of research on modern Vietnam. Available in microfiche, the *Catalogue* will enable scholars to plot a sensible study program in advance; it will also greatly simplify the problem of locating specific titles in a large and diffuse collection. As the *Catalogue* is only organized alphabetically by author (and by title for anonymous publications), researchers will still need to be quite familiar with the historical period to avoid making too many random requests. A subject catalogue is planned.

Periodicals of the French colonial period are housed separately in the Versailles annex of the Bibliothèque Nationale. Many overseas research libraries have purchased positive microfilms of the more important titles, courtesy of the Association pour la Conservation et la Réproduction Photographique de la Presse (Paris). As no bibliography of articles exists, scholars must work their own way through each periodical. The only exception is the monthly *Nam Phong* [Southern Ethos], for which one may consult Nguyen Khac Xuyen, *Muc Luc Phan Tich Tap Chi "Nam Phong" 1917-1934* [Index to Contents of the Journal *Nam Phong*, 1917-1934] (Saigon: Trung tam hoc lieu, 1968), which is organized by author and subject. Also useful is Pham Thi Ngoan, "Introduction au *Nam Phong* (1917-1934)," *Bulletin de la Société des Etudes Indochinoises*, vol. 48, nos. 2-3 (1973), pp. 167-502. Huynh Van Tong, "Histoire de la presse vietnamienne des origines à 1930," 2 vols., University of Paris, Thèse de doctorat de IIIe cycle, 1971, should be read prior to seeking periodical sources. A revised published version is Huynh Van Tong, *Lich Su Bao Chi Viet Nam tu Khoi thuy den 1930* [A History of the Vietnamese Press from Its Origins to 1930], Saigon: Tri Dang, 1973. Unfortunately, no similar study exists for the period after 1930. The closest is Daniel Hémery, "Journalisme révolutionnaire et système de la presse au Vietnam dans les années 1930," *Les Cahiers du Cursa* (Amiens), no. 8 (1978), pp. 55-85.

Articles appearing in *Van Su Dia* (1954-59) and *Nghien Cuu Lich Su* (1959-73) are cataloged according to author in Nguyen Dong Chi et al., editors, *Tong Muc Luc va Sach Dan Tap San "Van Su Dia" va Tap Chi "Nghien Cuu Lich Su" 1954-1973* [A General Catalog and Guide to the *Journal of Literature, History, and Geography* and the *Journal of Historical Research*, 1954-73] (Hanoi: Vien Su Hoc, 1976). Annotations further explain the contents of each article, and there is an excellent subject index.

Although archival sources were not as important to this study as published books and periodicals, many other researchers will find them absolutely essential. The Institut d'Etude du Vietnam Contemporain in Paris has prepared a *Guide Pratique de Recherche sur le Viet Nam en France*. Volume 1 (1972) introduces the reader to a wide range of archives, libraries, and museums; volume 2 (1976) updates information about the Archives d'Outre-mer, most notably the materials of the former Gouvernement Général de l'Indochine, now located in Aix-en-Provence. Michael Cotter, *Vietnam: A Guide to Reference Sources* (Boston: G. K. Hall, 1977), contains about 1,400 citations in Vietnamese, French, and English, organized by subject and cross-indexed by both author and title. It should be used in conjunction with Paul Boudet and Rémy Bourgeois, *Bibliographie de l'Indochine Française*, 4 volumes (Paris: Maisonneuve, 1929-1967), together with Cecil C. Hobbs et al., compilers, *Indochina: A Bibliography of the Land and People* (Washington: Library of Congress, 1950). Giok Po Oey et al., compilers, *Southeast Asia Catalog*, 7 volumes

(Boston: G. K. Hall, 1976), provides access to the many Vietnamese and Western-language publications housed in the Cornell University Library.

Three language dictionaries were of particular value to me in trying to fathom the nuances of Vietnamese. Dao Duy Anh, *Han Viet Tu Dien* [Chinese-Vietnamese Dictionary], originally published in two volumes in Hue in 1932 and 1936, remains unsurpassed in erudition. I relied on the third printing (Saigon: Truong Thi, 1957). Van Tan et al., compilers, *Tu Dien Tieng Viet* [Vietnamese Dictionary] (Hanoi: Khoa Hoc Xa Hoi, 1969), is an essential supplement to Dao Duy Anh's dictionary, as the latter is devoid of non-Chinese derived words. A revised edition of *Tu Dien Tieng Viet* was published in 1977. Nguyen Dinh Hoa, *Vietnamese-English Dictionary* (Saigon: Binh Minh, 1959), although imperfect, has the merit for my purposes of having been compiled before Americanisms flooded the Vietnamese language south of the seventeenth parallel.

No general encyclopedia exists for students of modern Vietnam. Trinh Van Thanh, compiler, *Thanh Ngu Dien Tich Danh Nhan Tu Dien* [Dictionary of Proverbs, Literary Expressions, and Personages], 2 vols. (Saigon: Trinh Van Thanh, 1966), is poorly researched and erratic in coverage. Newcomers to Vietnam studies will find Danny J. Whitfield's *Historical and Cultural Dictionary of Vietnam* (Metuchen, N.J.: Scarecrow Press, 1976), of value. M. Ro-Den-Tan and P. I-U-Din, editors, *Tu Dien Triet Hoc* [Philosophical Dictionary], 3rd ed. (Hanoi: Su That, 1976), is a translation from French of a Soviet work published in 1955. While topics such as Aristotelian logic and dialectical materialism are treated in loving detail, no entries exist for Confucianism, Buddhism, or Taoism. One of the handiest Vietnamese references of all is Tran Van Giap et al., *Luoc Truyen cac Tac Gia Viet Nam* [Biographical Outlines of Vietnamese Authors], 2 volumes (Hanoi: Su Hoc and Khoa Hoc Xa Hoi, 1962 and 1972). Volume 2 introduces 117 authors writing in *quoc ngu* and French from the late nineteenth century to 1945, but unfortunately excludes anyone still alive in 1970.

Western-Language Sources

Brocheux, Pierre. "Crise économique et société en Indochine française." *Revue Française d'Histoire d'Outre-mer* 232–33 (1976): 655–667. Outlines the impact of the Great Depression.

———. "L'implantation du mouvement communiste en Indochine française: le cas du Nghe-Tinh (1930–1931)." *Revue d'Histoire Moderne et Contemporaine* XXIV (Jan.–Mar. 1977): 49–74. Uses AOM sources to approach key socio-economic questions.

———. "Le prolétariat des plantations d'hévéas au Vietnam méridional: aspects sociaux et politiques (1927–1937)." *Le Mouvement Social* 90 (Jan.–Mar. 1975): 58–86.

Chesneaux, Jean, and Boudarel, Georges. "Le *Kim Van Kieu* et l'esprit public vietnamien aux XIXe et XXe siècles." In Maurice Durand, ed., *Mélanges sur Nguyen Du*. Paris: Ecole Française d'Extrême Orient, 1966.

Chesneaux, Jean; Boudarel, Georges; and Hémery, Daniel, ed. *Tradition et Révolution au Vietnam*. Paris: Editions Anthropos, 1971. Eighteen essays by recognized scholars and historical figures. The contributions of Pierre Brocheux, Phan Thanh Son, and Nguyen Tran Huan are particularly worthy.

Chu Van Tan. *Reminiscences on the Army for National Salvation*. Translated and annotated by Mai Elliott. Ithaca, N.Y.: Cornell Southeast Asia Program, 1974. Annotated translation by Mai Elliott of *Ky Niem Cuu Quoc Quan*. Hanoi: Quan Doi Nhan Dan, 1971.

Cong Huyen Ton Nu Thi Nha Trang. "The Traditional Roles of Women as Reflected in Oral and Written Vietnamese Literature." Ph.D. dissertation, University of California, Berkeley, 1973. Special attention is given to three texts: *Gia Huan Ca, Truyen Kieu* and *Luc Van Tien*.

Cook, Megan E. *The Constitutionalist Party of Cochinchina, 1930–1942: The Years of Decline*. Melbourne: Monash Centre of Southeast Asian Studies, 1977. Should be read in conjunction with Ralph Smith's article on Constitutionalists, listed below.

De Francis, John. *Colonialism and Language Policy in Viet-Nam*. The Hague: Mouton, 1977. A rather diffuse treatment of an important subject.

Duiker, William J. *The Rise of Nationalism in Vietnam, 1900–1941*. Ithaca, N.Y.: Cornell University Press, 1976. Provides a useful political chronology, yet fails to analyze Vietnamese nationalism.

Durand, Maurice, and Nguyen Tran Huan, *Introduction à la Littérature Vietnamienne*. Paris: G. P. Maisonneuve et Larose, 1969. An abundance of names, titles, and excerpts, but very little historical context.

Fall, Bernard B., ed. *Ho Chi Minh on Revolution*. New York: Praeger, 1967. More accessible than Ho Chi Minh's *Selected Works*, from which Fall has taken his own selection and provided a cogent biographical introduction.

Gouvernement Général de l'Indochine. *Notes périodiques sur l'activité des associations antifrançaises, 1930*. 5 vols. AOM (Aix), series F-7F4. Carbon copies of Governor-General Pasquier's detailed reports to the minister of colonies, together with almost one hundred annexed documents, including original Vietnamese pamphlets and leaflets confiscated by the authorities.

———. *Les manuels scolaires et les publications pédagogiques de la Direction Générale de l'Instruction Publique*. Hanoi: Imprimerie d'Extrême Orient, 1931.

———. "Rapport sur le fonctionnement de la Direction de l'Instruction Publique pendant l'année scolaire 1938–39." AOM (Paris), NF 2226.

Hémery, Daniel. "Aux origines des guerres d'indépendance vietnamiennes: pouvoir colonial et phénomène communiste en Indochine avant la Seconde Guerre Mondiale." *Le Mouvement Social* 101 (Oct.–Dec.1977): 3–35. Details French policy options and choices in the 1930s.

———. "Du patriotisme au marxisme: l'immigration vietnamienne en France de 1926 à 1930." *Le Mouvement Social* 90 (Jan.–Mar. 1975): 3–54.

————. *Révolutionnaires Vietnamiens et Pouvoir Colonial en Indochine: communistes, trotskystes, nationalistes à Saigon de 1932 à 1937.* Paris: Maspéro, 1975. Gives meticulous attention to the *La Lutte* alliance, the Indochinese Congress, and militant strikes in both urban and rural sectors of Cochinchina. Favorably reviewed by Tran Van Giau, in NCLS 166 (Jan.–Feb. 1976): 88–92, 95.

Ho Chi Minh. *Selected Works.* 4 vols. Hanoi: FLPH, 1960–62. Vols. 1 and 2 contain translations of most but not all of Ho Chi Minh's pre-1941 writings.

————[Nguyen Ai Quoc]. *Truyen va Ky* (Contes et Récits). Hanoi: Van Hoc, 1974. Contains both original French and *quoc ngu* translations by Pham Huy Thong of six articles, 1922–25.

Hoai Thanh et al. *Days With Ho Chi Minh.* Hanoi: FLPH, 1962. This is a translation of *Bac Ho, Hoi Ky* (Hanoi: Van Hoc, 1960), a collection of individual reminiscences.

Hoang Ngoc Thanh. "The Social and Political Development of Vietnam as Seen through the Modern Novel." Ph.D. dissertation, University of Hawaii, 1968. Valuable for its synopses of hundreds of works of fiction, but lacks theoretical framework.

Hoang Quoc Viet et al. *A Heroic People: Memoirs From the Revolution.* Hanoi: FLPH, 2nd ed. 1965. Translated from *Nhan Dan Ta Rat Anh Hung.* Hanoi: Van Hoc, 1960.

Huynh Kim Khanh. "The Vietnamese August Revolution Reinterpreted." *Journal of Asian Studies* XXX, 4 (Aug. 1971): 761–82.

————. "Vietnamese Communism: The Pre-Power Phase (1925–1945)." Ph.D. dissertation, University of California, Berkeley, 1972. Critically reviewed by Tran Van Giau, in NCLS 162 (May–June 1975): 65–77.

Huynh Sanh Thong, ed. and trans. *The Heritage of Vietnamese Poetry.* New Haven: Yale University Press, 1979. A selection of pre-twentieth-century poetry, well annotated and indexed.

Kelly, Gail P. "Colonial Schools in Vietnam: Policy and Practice." In Phillip G. Altbach and Gail P. Kelly, eds., *Education and Colonialism.* New York: Longman, 1978.

————. "Franco-Vietnamese Schools, 1918–1938." Ph.D. dissertation, University of Wisconsin, 1975. Strong on French policies and attitudes, weak on Vietnamese responses.

Langlois, Walter G. *André Malraux: The Indochina Adventure.* New York: Praeger, 1966. Colonial politics in Saigon, 1924–26, from the perspective of a soon-to-be-famous French author.

Le Van Luong. "Ready to Face the Guillotine." In *Saigon from the Beginning to 1945.* Hanoi: FLPH, Vietnamese Studies no. 45, 1976. Translated from Pham Hung et al., *Tren Duong Cach Mang* (Hanoi: Pho Thong, 1960).

McAlister, John T., and Mus, Paul. *The Vietnamese and Their Revolution.* New York: Harper, 1970. A provocative set of essays, with no attempt at documentary substantiation.

Mai Thi Tu and Le Thi Nham Tuyet. *Women in Viet Nam.* Hanoi: FLPH, 1978. Large segments are translated from Le Thi Nham Tuyet, *Phu Nu Viet Nam qua cac Thoi Dai* (Hanoi: Khoa Hoc Xa Hoi, 1973).

Marr, David G., ed. *Reflections from Captivity*. Athens, Ohio: Ohio University Press, 1978. Translations of Phan Boi Chau, *Nguc Trung Thu*, and Ho Chi Minh, *Nhat Ky Trong Tu*.

———. *Vietnamese Anticolonialism, 1885–1925*. Berkeley: University of California Press, 1971. Reviewed by Nguyen Cong Binh, in NCLS 144 (May–June 1972): 43–53.

Murray, Martin. *The Development of Capitalism in Colonial Indochina (1870–1940)*. Berkeley: University of California Press, 1980. This massive 600-page analysis has opened a whole range of economic issues for discussion.

Ngo Tat To. *When the Light Is Out*. Hanoi: FLPH, 1960. Translation by Pham Nhu Oanh of the influential novel *Tat Den*, first published in 1939.

Ngo Vinh Long. "The Indochinese Communist Party and Peasant Rebellion in Central Vietnam, 1930–1931." *Bulletin of Concerned Asian Scholars* 10, 4 (1978): 15–34.

———. "Peasant Revolutionary Struggles in Vietnam in the 1930s." Ph.D. dissertation, Harvard University, 1978. Filled with significant data which deserve more critical analysis.

———and Nguyen Hoi Chan. *Vietnamese Women in Society and Revolution*. Vol. 1: The French Colonial Period. Cambridge, Mass.: Vietnam Resource Center, 1974. A thoughtful introductory essay plus ten translated excerpts from short stories of the period.

Nguyen Cong Hoan. *Impasse*. Hanoi: FLPH, 1963. Translation of *Buoc Duong Cung*, a searing fictional treatment of colonial rural conditions, first published in 1938.

Nguyen Du. *The Tale of Kieu*. New York: Random House, 1973. Translation by Huynh Sanh Thong of *Truyen Kieu*, the early nineteenth-century epic poem which has remained a source of both controversy and inspiration.

Nguyen Khac Vien. *Tradition and Revolution in Vietnam*. Berkeley: Indochina Resource Center, 1974. Translations of seven French-language essays by the most prominent interpreter of contemporary Vietnam to the West. See, especially, "Confucianism and Marxism."

Nguyen Khac Vien and Huu Ngoc, ed. *Anthologie de la Littérature Vietnamienne*. 4 vols. Hanoi: FLPH, 1972–1977. Volume 3 covers the period 1858–1945, almost one hundred authors being represented.

Nguyen Khac Vien et al. *Viet Nam: A Historical Sketch*. Hanoi: FLPH, 1974. A Vietnamese Marxist summary, ignoring the thousand years of Chinese rule but devoting 229 pages to the twentieth century.

Nguyen Khanh Toan et al. *Vietnamese and Teaching in Vietnamese in D.R.V.N. Universities*. Hanoi: FLPH, 2nd ed., 1969. Partial translation of *Tieng Viet va Day Dai Hoc Bang Tieng Viet* (Hanoi: Khoa Hoc Xa Hoi, 1967).

Oliver, Victor L. *Cao Dai Spiritism: A Study of Religion in Vietnamese Society*. Leiden: E. J. Brill, 1976. Less useful than Werner dissertation, cited below.

Osborne, Milton E. "Continuity and Motivation in the Vietnamese Revolution: New Light from the 1930s." *Pacific Affairs* 47, 1 (Spring 1974): 37–55. Focuses primarily on the Nghe-Tinh confrontation, 1930–1931.

Pham Hung. "In the Death Cell." In *Saigon from the Beginning to 1945*. Hanoi: FLPH, Vietnamese Studies no. 45, 1976. Translated from Pham Hung, et al., *Tren Duong Cach Mang* (Hanoi: Pho Thong, 1960).

Pham Quynh. *Essais Franco-annamites*. Hue: Bui Huy Tin, 1937. Mostly taken from *Nam Phong* articles of the 1920s. See also his *Nouveaux Essais Franco-annamites*, published the following year.

Pham Van Dong et al. *Our President Ho Chi Minh*. Hanoi: FLPH, 1970. Includes a series of exploratory essays leading eventually, one hopes, to a full-scale biography.

Porter, Daniel Gareth. "Imperialism and Social Structure in Twentieth Century Vietnam." Ph.D. dissertation, Cornell University, 1976. Particularly useful on the Cochinchinese bourgeoisie after 1939.

———. "Proletariat and Peasantry in Early Vietnamese Communism." *Asian Thought and Society* vol. 1, no. 3 (Dec. 1976), pp. 333–46. Initial attempts (1925–30) to relate Marxist-Leninist social categories to Vietnamese conditions discussed.

Robequain, Charles. *The Economic Development of French Indochina*. London: Oxford University Press, 1944. Can still be read fruitfully in conjunction with Martin Murray's study, cited above.

Smith, Ralph B. "Bui Quang Chieu and the Constitutionalist Party in French Cochinchina, 1917–30." *Modern Asian Studies* 3, 2 (1969): 131–50.

———. "The Japanese Period in Indochina and the Coup of 9 March 1945." *Journal of Southeast Asian Studies* IX, 2 (Sept. 1978): 268–301. Includes Tokyo data seized by American occupation forces after World War II.

———. "The Vietnamese Elite of French Cochin China, 1943." *Modern Asian Studies* 6, 4 (1972): 459–82. Discussion of top collaborator careers, based largely on *Souverains et Notabilités d'Indochine* (Hanoi: Gouvernement Général de l'Indochine, 1943).

———. "The Work of the Provisional Government of Vietnam, August–December 1945." *Modern Asian Studies* 12, 4 (1978): 571–609. Effective use of a limited number of sources, especially the weekly official gazette.

Thompson, Virginia. *French Indochina*. London: Allen and Unwin, 1937. Colonial policy and performance thoughtfully assessed.

Truong Chinh and Vo Nguyen Giap. *The Peasant Question*. Ithaca, N.Y.: Cornell Southeast Asia Program, 1974. Translation by Christine P. White of *Van De Dan Cay* (Hanoi: Su That, 2nd ed., 1959). Originally published in two volumes under the pseudonyms Qua Ninh and Van Dinh (Hanoi: Dan Chung, 1937 and 1938).

Vella, Walter F., ed. *Aspects of Vietnamese History*. Honolulu: University of Hawaii Asian Studies, 1973. See, in particular, the essays on the 1920s by William Frederick and Milton Osborne.

Vietnam, Democratic Republic of. *History of the August Revolution*. Hanoi: FLPH, 1972. Translated from *Cach Mang Thang Tam 1945*. Hanoi: Su That, n.d.

———. *Struggle Against Illiteracy in Viet Nam*. Hanoi: FLPH, 1959. Demonstrates the relevance of literacy campaigns in accomplishing political, social, and military objectives, 1945–56.

Vo Nguyen Giap. *Unforgettable Days*. Hanoi: FLPH, 1975. Translation of *Nhung Nam Thang Khong The Nao Quen*. 2 vols. (Hanoi: Quan Doi Nhan Dan, 1970 and 1975). The first volume has also been translated and annotated by Mai Elliott: *Unforgettable Months and Years* (Ithaca, N.Y.: Cornell Southeast Asia Program, 1975). The author focuses on top-level policymaking, 1945–46.

Werner, Jayne S. "The Cao Dai: The Politics of a Vietnamese Syncretic Religious Movement." Ph.D. dissertation, Cornell University, 1976. Clear description of a complex phenomenon.

Woodside, Alexander B. *Community and Revolution in Modern Vietnam*. Boston: Houghton Mifflin, 1976. A complex book, particularly rewarding for its sociocultural insights. Woodside sees less historical transformation that I do. He also argues that the primary Vietnamese quest was for an organized national community; whereas I suggest that the search for a new world view came first, at least for the intelligentsia in the 1920s and 1930s.

—————. "The Development of Social Organizations in Vietnamese Cities in the Late Colonial Period." *Pacific Affairs* XLIV, 1 (Spring 1971): 39–64.

X. N. *Luttons contre l'Analphabétisme qui paralyse notre peuple*. Hanoi: An Thinh, 1937. One of the earliest detailed proposals to form a private society to combat the "disease" of illiteracy.

Vietnamese-Language Sources

Citation numbers are provided for those sources housed in the Fonds Indochinois of the Bibliothèque Nationale (Paris).

An Khe. "Quoc Tuy va Van Minh" [The National Essence and Civilization]. NP 78 (Dec. 1923): 453–58. A Confucian literatus discusses the decline of morality and the relationship between ideals and action.

Bao Dinh Giang. "Khi Hat Giong da Gieo Xuong" [When the Seeds Were Sown]. In Chanh Thi et al., *Len Duong Thang Loi* [On the Road to Victory]. Hanoi: Van Hoc, 1960. Attitudes in the author's home village in Dong Thap Muoi, before and after 1945.

Bui Cong Trung. "Ban qua ve Nghe Thuat" [A Discussion of Art]. In HT-5: 475–79. Originally published in *Tao Dan* 6 (1939). Criticizes romantics for ignoring the historical dialectic.

—————. "Tu Long Yeu Nuoc Chan Chinh toi da di den Chu Nghia Cong San" [My Passage from Genuine Patriotism to Communism]. In Bui Cong Trung et al., *Nguoi Truoc Nga Nguoi Sau Tien* [The Front Rank Falls, the Rear Advances] (Hanoi: Van Hoc, 1960). Memoirs of an overseas student, 1924–30. A description of his subsequent trial and Con Son prison experience is to be found in Chanh Thi et al., *Len Duong Thang Loi* [On the Road to Victory] (Hanoi: Van Hoc, 1960).

Bui Huy Hue. *Cong Dan Tu Tri* [Citizen's Self-Edification]. 2 vols. Hanoi: Legrand, 1939. 2nd- and 3rd-year primary textbook written by a teacher at the Pierre Pasquier private school in Hanoi. [16° Indochin. Pièce 136 and 8° Indochin. Pièce 4195]

Bui Quang Chieu. *Ngo Lai 20 Nam Chanh Tri Hoat Dong* [Looking Back on Twenty Years of Political Activity]. Saigon: Duc Luu Phuong, 1936. A Constitutionalist election pamphlet. Many other articles by this author are to be found in the thrice-weekly *Tribune Indigène* (1917–25) and *Tribune Indochinoise* (1926–41). [8° Indochin. Pièce 2891]

Bui The My. *The Gioi Bat Binh* [A World of Inequality]. Saigon: Than Chung Tong Tho, 1928. Vaguely Buddhist condemnation of Social Darwinism and appeal for peace and equality. [8° Indochin. Pièce 888]

Bui Vo Lo. *Xa Hoi Van Dong* [Social Mobilization]. Saigon: Bao Ton, 1937. A noncommunist but loosely Marxist analysis, with a definite anti-peasant orientation. [16° Indochin. Pièce 455]

Cao Hai De. *Tu Tuong Xa Hoi* [Social Thought]. Ben Tre: Bui Van Nhan, 1933. Demonstrates the influence of Marxism, albeit crude, even among bourgeois writers. [8° Indochin. Pièce 2448]

Cao Van Chanh [Thach Lan]. "Luan Ly va Kinh Te" [Morality and Economics]. PNTV 36 (9 Jan. 1930): 5–6. A classic appeal to break the link between ethics and politics, in the name of national survival.

Chanh Thi. "Roi Ba Duoc Vao Dang" [And Then Your Father Was Admitted to the Party]. In Chanh Thi et al., *Len Duong Thang Loi* [On the Road to Victory] (Hanoi: Van Hoc, 1960). A poor but literate peasant's transition from juvenile delinquent to Communist Party member, 1930–32.

Che Lan Vien. "Lam cho tieng noi trong sang, giau va phat trien" [Making the Spoken Language Clear, Rich and Expansive]. TCVH 3–1966: 28–32. A thoughtful positing of the contradiction between timelessness and development in language theory, by a well-known poet.

Cuu Kim Son [Van Tan] and Van Hue [Pham Van Hao]. *Chi Em Phai Lam Gi?* [Sisters, What Is to Be Done?] Hanoi: Dan Chung, 1938. Organizational methods, short-term demands, and longer-term socialist objectives. Cuu Kim Son was later better known as Van Tan, assistant editor of the journal *Nghien Cuu Lich Su* [Historical Research] from 1962 to 1976. Van Hue was Pham Van Hao, until 1975 director of the Revolutionary Museum in Hanoi. [16° Indochin. 307]

―――. *Doi Chi Em* [Sister's Life]. Hanoi: Dan Chung, 1938. Introduction by Truong Chinh [Qua Ninh]. Discusses sociocultural institutions in Vietnam inhibiting or oppressing women, together with proposals for change. [8° Indochin. Pièce 4058]

Dat Si Tu. *Van De Phu Nu Giai Phong* [The Women's Liberation Question]. Saigon: Tan Thanh Nien Hoc Xa, 1932. A male response to female debate in the periodicals *Trung Lap* and *Phu Nu Tan Van* leaning to support of the "progressive" side led by Phan Thi Bach Van. [8° Indochin. Pièce 1933]

Diep Van Ky. *Che Do Bao Gioi Nam Ky Nam Muoi Sau Nam Nay* [The South Vietnam Press System for These Fifty-Six Years]. Saigon: Bao Ton, 1928. An insider's view of the colonial publishing business. [16° Indochin. 259]

Duong Ba Trac. *Tieng Goi Dan* [A Call from the Rostrum]. Hanoi: Nghiem Ham An Quan, 1925. A widely read appeal from a reformist literatus, urging the elite to halt moral decline and take an active role as "intermediaries" with the French, leading to eventual independence. [8° Indochin. 324]

Dam Phuong. *Phu Nu Du Gia Dinh* [Women's Role in the Family]. 2 vols. Saigon: Bao Ton, 1929. The head of the Hue Women's Work-Study Association suggests modest reforms. [8° Pièce 898]

Dang Kim Giang. "Truong Quan Chinh trong Nha Tu Son La" [A Military-Political School Inside Son La Prison]. In Bui Cong Trung et al., *Nguoi Truoc Nga Nguoi Sau Tien* [The Front Rank Falls, the Rear Advances] (Hanoi: Van Hoc, 1960). Describes clandestine Communist Party training classes in jail during World War II.

Dang Ngoc Tot, Duong Duc Hien, and Nguyen Dinh Thi. *Suc Song cua Dan Viet Nam* [The Living Strength of the Vietnamese People]. Hanoi: Lua Hong, 1944. Although expressing widely divergent philosophies, these three came together as student leaders at the University of Hanoi during World War II and subsequently participated prominently in the Viet Minh. A slightly modified version of Nguyen Dinh Thi's essay on mass struggle capacities as mirrored in Vietnamese folk literature is available in HT-5, pp. 517–30. [16° Indochin. 1234)

Dang Thai Mai. "Ban ve Nguyen Tac Sang Tac" [On the Principles of Creativity]. HT-5: 486–89. A call for intelligentsia social responsibility by a covert Communist Party member.

———. ed. *Van Tho Cach Mang Viet Nam Dau The Ky XX* [Vietnam's Revolutionary Prose and Poetry in the Early Twentieth Century]. Hanoi: Van Hoc, 1964.

Dang Van Bay. *Nam Nu Binh Quyen* [Equal Rights for Both Sexes]. Saigon: Tam Thanh, 1928. A male schoolteacher tries to define a moderate position. [8° Indochin. 1387]

Dao Duy Anh. *Dan Toc* [Peoplehood]. Hue: Tieng Dan, 1929. As with most other studies in the Quan Hai Tung Thu series, the author presents new ideas in a simple yet compelling style. He draws a sharp distinction between peoplehood and statehood: the former is "natural" and "legitimate"; the latter is based on force and class differentiation, hence deserving of eventual elimination. [8° Indochin. 861]

———. *Khao Luan Ve 'Kim Van Kieu'* [An Examination of the 'Tale of Kieu']. Hue: Quan Hai Tung Thu, 1943. A convincing defense of the artistic and linguistic value of Ngyuen Du's epic poem, based on the author's high school teaching notes. [16° Indochin. 1317]

———[Ve Thach]. *Khong Giao Phe Binh Tieu Luan* [A Critique of Confucianism]. Hue: Quan Hai Tung Thu, 1938. Although the author stresses the outdated character of Confucian ideology, he obviously believes that it remains influential enough to deserve methodical attack. [16° Indochin. 294].

———. *Viet Nam Van Hoa Su Cuong* [An Outline History of Vietnamese Culture]. Hue: Quan Hai Tung Thu, 1938. Republished Saigon: Bon Phuong, 1951. One of the best works of scholarship produced by the Vietnamese intelligentsia. [8° Indochin. 2478]

Dao Trinh Nhat. *Dong Kinh Nghia Thuc* [The Eastern Capital Free School]. Hanoi: Mai Linh, 1937. A prominent journalist revives interest in turn-of-the-century literati efforts. [16° Indochin. 267].

Do Duc Vuong. "May Thuyet ve Luan Ly" [Some Theories on Morality]. *Bulletin de la Société d'enseignement mutuel du Tonkin* XVI (Jul.–Dec. 1936), offprint. A deft review of Western moral philosophies, with a concluding preference for Kant. [8° Indochin. Pièce 3043]

Do Thi Bich Lien. *Binh Dang* [Equality]. Phu Ly: Viet Dan, 1938. A good example of radical intellectual effort outside the main cities. [16° Indochin. Pièce 746]

Duong Thi An. *Nguon Vui Duy Nhat* [The Sole Source of Joy]. Hanoi: Phu Nu, 1974. The wife of General Chu Van Tan narrates her activities among minority women, 1941–45.

Grossin, Pierre. *Dan Que Nen Biet* [What Rural People Should Know]. 3rd printing, Hanoi: Vien Dong An Quan, 1928. Translated by Nguyen Van Nghi, a district mandarin. An attempt to tell Vietnamese villagers both what the government expected of them and how they might get ahead in life. [8° Indochin. 413]

Ha Thi Que. "Rung Yen The" [The Yen The Forest]. In Le Thiet Hung et al., *Rung Yen The*. Hanoi: Quan Doi Nhan Dan, 1962. Early 1945 Viet Minh activities in the hills as described by a key female participant.

Hai Trieu [Nguyen Khoa Van]. "Nghe Thuat vi Nghe Thuat hay Nghe Thuat vi Nhan Sinh" [Art for Art's Sake or Art for Life's Sake]. In HT-5: 467–74. Originally published in *Doi Moi*, 1935. The first coherent Vietnamese Marxist counterattack on the prevailing attitude of "Art for art's sake" among literary critics. Hai Trieu's attempt to define "realism" in literature is in HT-5, pp 463–67.

———. "Luat Anh Huong Tro Lai cua Tinh Than qua Vat Chat va tac dong cua con nguoi trong qua trinh phat trien xa hoi" [The Law of Reverse Influence of Spirit on Matter and the Impact of Man on the Process of Social Development]. *Tim Hieu* 1–2 (Mar.–Apr. 1949): 24–31. Demonstrates the strong idealist and voluntarist tendencies of many Vietnamese Marxists.

———. *Van Si va Xa Hoi* [Writers and Society]. Hanoi: Dong Tay, 1937. The importance of literary figures involving themselves directly in political struggle, with case studies of Gorki, Rolland, and Barbusse. [16° Indochin. Pièce 446]

Ho Chi Minh. *Nhung Loi Keu Goi cua Ho Chu Tich* [The Appeals and Exhortations of President Ho]. 4 vols. 2nd printing. Hanoi: Su That, 1958. Volume 1 contains almost two hundred pronouncements, 1941–49.

———. *Tuyen Tap* [Selected Works]. Hanoi: Su That, 1960. The Vietnam Communist Party is currently compiling the "Complete Works" of Ho Chi Minh for publication.

Ho Huu Tuong. *41 Nam Lam Bao* [Forty-One Years as a Journalist]. Saigon: Tri Dang, 1972. Disjointed but useful memoirs of a former Trotskyist.

Hoa Bang [Hoang Thuc Tram]. *Quang Trung Nguyen Hue: Anh Hung Dan Toc* [Quang Trung Nguyen Hue: National Hero]. Hanoi: Bon Phuong, 1958. First published in 1944, this is a serious discussion of the Tay Son movement of the late eighteenth century, most notably of the leader, Nguyen Hue, who defeated the Chinese and took the imperial name of Quang Trung. [8° Indochin. 2733]

Hoai Tan. *Trung Bo Khang Chien* [The Armed Resistance in Central Vietnam]. Hanoi: Quoc Te, 1946. Vivid reporting of anticolonial efforts, Sept.–Dec. 1945. [16° Indochin. 501]

Hoai Thanh. "Nhin lai cuoc tranh luan ve Nghe Thuat hoi 1935–1936" [Looking Back on the Polemic over Art, 1935–1936]. *Nghien Cuu Van Hoc* 1–1960: 36–56. In the form of a self-criticism.

Hoai Thanh, Le Trang Kieu, and Luu Trong Lu. *Van Chuong va Hanh Dong* [Literature and Action]. Hanoi: Phuong Dong, 1936. A key defense of the idealist and art-above-politics positions. [16° Indochin. 133]

Hoang Dao. *Muoi Dieu Tam Niem* [Ten Points to Ponder]. Saigon: Khai Tri, 1964. Originally published in Hanoi: Doi Nay, 1939. A forceful (if sometimes fuzzy) philosophical declaration by a member of the Tu Luc Van Doan.

Hoang Quoc Viet and Tran Huu Duc. *Dap Len Dau Thu* [Hitting the Enemy's Head]. Hanoi: Thanh Nien, 1971. Young communists in court confrontations and being tortured, 1930–41.

Hoang Van Dao. *Viet Nam Quoc Dan Dang* [The Vietnam Nationalist Party]. Saigon: Nguyen Hoa Hiep, 1965. One participant contributes a loose history.

Hoc Tu. *Nhung Ngay Dau cua Mat Tran Nam Bo* [First Days on the South Vietnam Battlefront]. Hanoi: Tranh Dau, 1945. Considerable detail about the crucial confrontations of Sept.–Oct. 1945 in and around Saigon. [16° Indochin. 1233]

Hoi Truyen Ba Hoc Quoc Ngu (Association for the Dissemination of *Quoc Ngu* Study). *May dieu can thiet cac Thay day giup Hoi nen biet* [Important Things Teachers Helping the Association Need to Know]. Hanoi: Imprimerie du Pacifique, 1940. Guide for volunteer literacy instructors. [16° Indochin. Pièce 1342]

Hong Phong. *Chanh Tri Kinh Te Hoc Chi Nam* [A Guide to Political Economy]. Saigon: Dai Chung Tho Cuoc, 1937. A discussion of historical determinism, social classes, poverty, the Soviet Union, the Great Depression, fascism, and a communist future without classes or oppression. The author may be Le Hong Phong, who did liaison work between the Comintern and the ICP in the 1930s. [16° Indochin. Pièce 438]

Huynh Thuc Khang. *Tu Truyen* [Autobiography]. Hue: Anh Minh, 1963. Should be read before tackling the author's influential Hue newspaper *Tieng Dan* [Voice of the People], published from 1927 to 1943.

Huynh Van Nghe. "Ra Mat Tran" [Out to the Front]. In Le Thiet Hung et al., *Rung Yen The* [Yen The Forest]. Hanoi: Quan Doi Nhan Dan, 1962. The excitement and chaos of late September 1945 Cochinchina relived.

Huynh Van Tong. *Lich Su Bao Chi Viet-Nam to Khoi Thuy den 1930* [History of the Vietnamese Press from Its Beginnings to 1930]. Saigon: Tri Dang, 1973.

Le Cuong Phung [Tung Lam]. *Phan Boi Chau Ngay Nay* [Phan Boi Chau Today]. Saigon: Xua Nay, 1926. Based on interviews with Phan Boi Chau after his parole to Hue. Phan's difficulty in finding a new role for himself is quite evident. [8° Indochin. Pièce 185]

Le Du [So Cuong]. "Lich Su Doi Tay Son" [History of the Tay Son Period]. NP 97 (July 1925): 11–28. Possibly the first call in the legal press for rehabilitation of the late eighteenth-century Tay Son movement and dynasty.

Le Sy Thang. "Ho Chu Tich va su nghiep truyen ba chu nghia Mac-le-nin vao Viet-

Nam" [President Ho and the Task of Spreading Marxism-Leninism to Vietnam]. NCLS 144 (May–June 1972): 12–23, 35; and 145 (July–Aug. 1972): 50–61. Amidst the hero worship one can also obtain information about Ho Chi Minh's early activities, as well as his viewpoint on key philosophical issues.

Le Thanh. *Cuoc Phong Van Cac Nha Van* [Interviews with Writers]. Hanoi: Doi Moi, 1942. Valuable insights on Tran Trong Kim, Nguyen Van To, Dao Duy Anh and five other authors. [8° Indochin. 129]

Le Thi Nham Tuyet. *Phu Nu Viet Nam qua cac Thoi Dai* [Vietnamese Women across the Ages]. Hanoi: Khoa Hoc Xa Hoi, 1973. Much important ethnographic data relating to traditional conditions and attitudes, but weak on the colonial period and open to challenge on women's achievements since independence.

Le Van Hien. *Nguc Kontum* [Kontum Jail]. Tourane [Da Nang]: Tu Tuong Moi, 1938. Second edition published Hanoi: Hoi Nha Van, 1958. French translation serialized in *Le Travail*, 1938. A shocking account of conditions for a prison work gang in the central Vietnam mountains. [8° Indochin. 2512]

Luong Duc Thiep. *Duy Vat Su Quan* [Historical Materialism]. Hanoi: Han Thuyen, 1945. Marxist dialectics according to a non-ICP writer. [16° Indochin. 450]

———. *Xa Hoi Viet-Nam* [Vietnamese Society]. Saigon: Hoa Tien, 1971. Originally published in Hanoi, 1944. Excellent social history, perhaps second only to Dao Duy Anh, *Viet Nam Van Hoa Su Cuong*, in conceptual scope. [16° Indochin. 399]

Luong Van Can [On Nhu]. *Au Hoc Tung Dam* [Stories for Children to Study]. Hanoi: Luong Ngoc Hien, 1929. A well-known participant in the Dong Kinh Nghia Thuc movement (1907–1908) tries to communicate ethics to a new generation, with curious but significant results. [8° Indochin. 895]

Luu Dong. *Buoc Dau Theo Dang* [First Step in Following the Party]. Hanoi: Thanh Nien, 1961. Frank recollections of an ICP member who drifted from Hanoi high school through clandestine activities to jail in 1939–41.

Moc Khue. *Ba Muoi Nam Van Hoc* [Thirty Years of Literature]. Hanoi: Tan Viet, 1942. An early survey of recent exciting developments in Vietnamese journalism, poetry, fiction, drama, historiography, critical essays, and translations. [8° Indochin. 2999]

Ngo Duc Ke, ed. *Phan Tay Ho Di Thao Van Tap* [Phan Chu Trinh Posthumous Anthology]. vol. 1. Hanoi: Luong Van Can, 1926. Introduction by Phan Boi Chau. [8° Indochin. 3047]

Ngo Quang Chau. *Luan ve Tieng Nam* [An Essay on the Vietnamese Language]. Hanoi: Doi Moi, 1941. Attacks those who moan about the poverty of the Vietnamese language, and argues for more coining of words from Vietnamese rather than adopting foreign neologisms. [16° Indochin. 826]

Ngo Tat To. *Phe Binh "Nho Giao" cua Tran Trong Kim* [A Critique of Tran Trong Kim's *Confucianism*]. Hanoi: Mai Linh, 1938. Especially critical of Tran Trong Kim's inability or refusal to distinguish Confucian texts of various historical periods (e.g., the "new text" versus "old text" controversy in China), instead giving readers a spurious timeless interpretation. [16° Indochin. 426]

Ngo Tat To and Nguyen Duc Tinh. *Lao Tu* [Lao-tzu]. Hanoi: Mai Linh, 1942. The authors try too hard to Westernize ancient Chinese thought, thus presumably making it more legitimate. [16° Indochin. 784]

Ngo Van Hoa and Duong Kinh Quoc. *Giai Cap Cong Nhan Viet Nam Nhung Nam Truoc Khi Thanh Lap Dang* [The Vietnamese Working Class in the Years Before Formation of the Party]. Hanoi: Khoa Hoc Xa Hoi, 1978. Particularly useful for its discussion of links between town and countryside.

Nguyen An Ninh. *Cao vong cua bon Thanh Nien An-Nam* [The Aspirations of Annamite Youth]. Saigon: Xua Nay, 1924. Translation for general distribution of an address, 15 Oct. 1923, that announced the arrival of the Vietnamese young intelligentsia as a coherent force, ready to challenge anyone in the name of truth, justice, and progress. Original French version in *La Cloche fêlée* 5 (7 Jan. 1924) and 6 (14 Jan. 1924). [8° Indochin. 274]

―――. *Hai Ba Trung* [The Trung Sisters]. Saigon: Bao Ton, 1928. A presentation of current political options, thinly disguised as a *tuong* drama about anticolonial struggle in the first century A.D. [8° Indochin. 760]

―――. *Phe Binh Phat Giao* [A Critique of Buddhism]. Saigon, 1937. Places Buddhism in historical context and argues that its message is outmoded.

―――. *Ton Giao* [Religion]. Saigon: Diep Van Ky, 1932. Discusses the historical and psychological reasons for religious faith, asserts that such faith is no longer so necessary, yet falters when describing the modern alternative. [8° Indochin. 1746]

Nguyen Ba Hoc. "Loi Khuyen Hoc Tro" [Words of Encouragement to Pupils]. NP 24 (June 1919): 472–80; 25 (July 1919): 61–65; and 26 (Aug. 1919): 142–45. The essence of morality according to a prominent literatus, organized in 32 categories.

―――. "May dieu yeu luoc ve Kinh Te Hoc" [A Summary of Economics]. NP 45 (Mar. 1921): 200–206; and 46 (Apr. 1921): 290–95. A heroic attempt to borrow Western economic expertise but avoid the philosophical implications.

Nguyen Ban. *Cuu Nan Kinh Te Khung Hoang* [Rescue from Economic Depression]. Hanoi: Van Thuong, 1935. Especially useful for its 20-page "Honor Roll of Meritorious Builders of the Indochina Economy." [8° Indochin. 2236]

Nguyen Bang. *Quyen Cong Dan trong Chinh the Cong Hao Dan Chu* [A Citizen's Rights in a Democratic Republic]. Hanoi: Tan Viet, 1945. A classic bourgeois presentation (although DRVN publication clearance was obtained). [16° Indochin. 1139]

Nguyen Duy Thanh. "Y cua toi ve Tieng Viet-Nam" [My Ideas on the Vietnamese Language]. PNTV 119 (18 Feb. 1932): 5–10. An electrical engineer in France condemns those who prefer coining words from French or Chinese rather than spoken Vietnamese.

Nguyen Dinh Thi. "Suc song cua Dan Viet-Nam trong Ca Dao va Co Tich" [The Life Strength of the Vietnamese People as Seen in Folk Songs and Folktales]. HT-5: 517–30. Originally a 1944 speech published together with those of Dang Ngoc Tot, and Duong Duc Hien (q.v.). One of the first public attempts to implement the ICP's 1943 "Theses on Vietnamese Culture." The author argues a timeless Vietnamese spirit of struggle, optimism, and faith in one's own kind.

Nguyen Gy. *Long Nguyen Vong cua Quoc Dan Viet Nam* [The Basic Aspirations of the Vietnamese Populace]. Hanoi: Moderne, 1933. Phrased as respectful suggestions to King Bao Dai upon the latter's return from education in France. [8° Indochin. Pièce 2649]

Nguyen Khac Dam. *Nhung Thu Doan Boc Lot cua Tu Ban Phap o Viet-Nam* [The Exploitative Activities of French Capital in Vietnam]. Hanoi: Van Su Dia, 1957. Colonial economic operations described in a Marxist framework. The limits on Vietnamese capital are also stressed.

Nguyen Khanh Toan. "Ho Chu Tich: Nguoi Cha, Nguoi Thay vi dai cua Dan Toc, vi lanh dao thien tai doi doi kinh yeu cach mang Viet-Nam" [President Ho: Father, Great Teacher of His People, Forever Beloved, Supremely Capable Leader of the Vietnamese Revolution]. NCLS 168 (May–June 1976): 1–7. Although a pointed attack on those who see Ho Chi Minh as a traditional sage or argue a link between Confucianism and Marxism-Leninism, the title of this article expresses well the contradictions contained therein.

Nguyen Khoa Toan. *Sach Cong Dan Giao Duc* [Citizen's Education Book]. 3rd printing. Hue: Mirador, 1940. An example of the new approach to morality instruction introduced in the late 1930s. [8° Indochin. 2461]

Nguyen Tao. *Chung Toi Vuot Nguc* [We Escape from Prison]. Hanoi: Van Hoc, 1977. Vivid memoir of jail and multiple escapes, 1931–34.

Nguyen Thi Kim Anh. *Van De Phu Nu* [The Question of Women]. Cho Lon: Than Dan Tho Xa, 1938. Mostly a synopsis of foreign Marxist formulations, but the last section treats Vietnamese conditions directly. [8° Indochin. 2489]

Nguyen Trieu Luat. "Tam Ly Hoc" [Psychology]. Serially published in NP 89 (Nov. 1924) through 108 (Aug. 1926). The discussions of perception in NP 102 and 103 and of "determinism versus voluntarism" in NP 108 are of particular interest.

Nguyen Van Cu [Tri Cuong]. *Tu Chi Trich* [Self-Criticism]. Hanoi: Dan Chung, 1939. The ICP secretary general bluntly reveals the difficulties of building a united front in Cochinchina. [16° Indochin. Pièce 155]

Nguyen Van Kinh. *Chung Quanh cuoc Suu Tap Dan Nguyen va cuoc Meeting tai Rap Thanh Xuong* [Concerning the Collection of Popular Aspirations and the Meeting at Thanh Xuong Theater]. Saigon: Le Peuple, 1937. Detailed record of a large meeting organized by the ICP on 28 Nov. 1937. [16° Indochin. Pièce 546]

Nguyen Van Ngoc, comp. *Tuc Ngu Phong Dao* [Proverbs and Folk Songs]. 2 vols. Saigon: Mac Lam, 1967. First published in Hanoi: Le Van Tan, 1928.

Nguyen Van Tay. *Lam sao cho Tau Thang Nhat?* [How Can China Beat Japan?] My Tho: Dong Phuong Thu Xa, 1938. An ICP description of united-front developments in China, with a concluding section pointing out the relevance for Indochina. [8° Indochin. Pièce 3072]

Nguyen Van Trung. *Chu Dich "Nam Phong"* [The Main Objective of *Nam Phong*]. Saigon: Dai Hoc Su Pham, 1972. Systematic criticism of previous non-communist interpretations that ignore or downgrade the political purpose of this seminal journal.

———. *Truong Hop Pham Quynh* [The Case of Pham Quynh]. Saigon: Nam Son, 1975. A thoughtful assessment of the editor of *Nam Phong*, 1917–32.

Nguyen Van Vinh [Tan Nam Tu]. *Thuc Tinh Dong Bao* [Awakening Sentiments of Countrymen]. Saigon: Xua Nay, 1926. An older intellectual condemns new intelligentsia members who ignore him. [8° Indochin. 262]

Nguyen Vy. *Cai Hoa Nhat Ban* [The Japanese Peril]. Hanoi: Bao Ngoc, 1938. An antifascist but non-communist plea to the French to help the Vietnamese prepare a credible defense. [8° Indochin. 2419]

———. *Ke Thu la Nhat Ban* [Japan Is the Enemy]. Hanoi: Thanh Nien Tung Thu, 1939. One year of French inaction had caused the author to become more bitter. [8° Indochin. 2183]

Nguyet Tu. *Chi Minh Khai* [Sister Nguyen Thi Minh Khai]. Hanoi: Phu Nu, 1976. Although partly fictional, the author apparently relies on a number of interviews with people who knew this highest-ranking female member of the ICP in the 1930s.

Nhan Chi. *Chi Em Lao Kho voi Xa Hoi* [Working Women and Society]. Thanh Hoa: Le Hien Vu, 1938. Begins with the women's question, but quickly shifts to Marxist economic analysis and the rationale for a proletarian party. [16° Indochin. Pièce 552]

Nhat Linh [Nguyen Tuong Tam]. *Doan Tuyet* [Breaking Off]. Hanoi: Doi Nay, 1936. Perhaps the best-known fictional attack on the traditional Vietnamese family system. [4° Indochin. 38]

Nhi Nhi. *Ai lam That Bai Cach Mang Tau?* [Who Caused the Defeat of the Chinese Revolution?]. Saigon: Tia Sang, 1938. A trenchant Trotskyist warning not to rely on Comintern direction, based on the 1925–1927 debacle in China. [8° Indochin. Pièce 3078]

Nhon, K. B. *Gia Dinh Dam Am va Hanh Phuc* [A Cozy and Happy Family]. Saigon: Viet Nam, 1936. Traditional partriarchy defended, but with modest reforms in ancestral ceremonies and forms of greeting. [8° Indochin. Pièce 2930]

Ninh Viet Giao, ed. and comp. *Hat Phuong Vai: Dan Ca Nghe-Tinh* [Cloth-Weaving Songs: Folk Songs of Nghe An and Ha Tinh]. Hanoi: Van Hoa, 1961. Meticulous description of a particular type of folk song demonstrating the traditional interaction between village scholars and their unlettered neighbors.

Pham Kiet. *Tu Nui Rung Ba To* [From the Ba To Highland Forests]. 4th printing. Hanoi: Quan Doi Nhan Dan, 1977. Tells how ICP detainees take advantage of the March 1946 Japanese *coup de force* to seize power in Quang Ngai province. See also Phan Kiet's shorter memoir in Le Thieu Hung et al., *Rung Yen The*. Hanoi: Quan Doi Nhan Dan, 1962.

Pham Quynh. "May Nhoi Noi Dau" [Some Opening Remarks]. NP 1 (July 1917): 1–7. An important editorial prospectus, carefully cleared with the colonial authorities.

———. "Phap Du Hanh Trinh Nhat Ky" [Diary of a Voyage to France]. Serially published in NP 58 (Apr. 1922) through NP 100 (Oct.–Nov. 1925). Revised version published as *Ba Thang o Paris* [Three Months in Paris] (Hanoi: Imprimerie Tonkinoise, 1927).

———. *Thuong Chi Van Tap* [The Writings of Thuong Chi]. 5 vols. Saigon: Bo Quoc Gia Giao Duc, 1962. First published in Hanoi: Dac Lo Thu Xa, 1943–45. Thuong Chi was one of the Pham Quynh's pen names. [16° Indochin. 612]

————. "Truyen Kieu" [The Tale of Kieu]. NP 30 (Dec. 1919): 480–500. The essay that tried to link Vietnam's most popular poem with the psychology of collaboration, thus sparking a long and bitter debate.

Pham Tat Dac. *Chieu Hon Nuoc* [Summoning the Soul of the Nation]. Hanoi: Bao Ngoc, 1945. As an 18-year-old student, the author had been jailed for distributing this patriotic tract. [16° Indochin. Pièce 833]

Pham Van Dieu. *Bien Chung Duy Vat Luan* [An Essay on Dialectical Materialism]. 2nd printing. Saigon: Van Hoa Tho Xa, 1937. [16° Indochin. Pièce 389]

Pham Van Dong. "Giu gin su trong sang cua tieng Viet" [Preserving the Brilliance of the Vietnamese Language]. TCVH 3–1966: 1–5, 93. Keynote address to a conference on this topic.

Pham Van Hao. "Lam bao bi mat" [Producing Clandestine Newspapers]. In Chanh Thi et al., *Len Duong Thang Loi* [On the Road to Victory]. Hanoi: Van Hoc, 1960. From the most primitive gelatin techniques of 1930 to taking over commercial plants in Hanoi during the August 1945 Revolution.

Phan Boi Chau. *Loi hoi cac ban Thanh Nien* [Questions for Young People]. Saigon: Xua Nay, 1928. Modeled on a Catholic catechism, stressing the patriot responsibilities of youth. [8° Indochin. Pièce 690]

————. *Nu Quoc Dan Tu Tri* [Female Citizen's Self-Instruction]. 2nd ed. Hue: Nu Cong Hoc Hoi, 1927. [8° Indochin. Pièce 121]

————. *Phap Viet De Hue Chinh Kien Thu* [Some Views on Franco-Vietnamese Collaboration]. 3rd ed. Hanoi: Tan Dan Thu Quan, 1926. Includes the original Chinese version and a *quoc ngu* translation of Phan Boi Chau's most controversial work, written in China in 1919 primarily as a warning about the growing Japanese threat to all of Asia including Vietnam, but used effectively thereafter to demonstrate that Phan had abandoned militant opposition to French rule. [8° Indochin. Pièce 6]

————. *To Thong Cao Toan Quoc* [A Communique to the Entire Country]. Hue: Dac Lap, 1926. Original Chinese plus *quoc ngu* and French translations. A first, not very successful effort at public expression after parole to Hue. Another edition titled *Loi Tuyen Cao Quoc Dan* (Hanoi: Tan Dan Thu Quan, 1926), has appended a blunt letter of advice to Phan from a group of Nghe An citizens. [8° Indochin. Pièce 286 and 8° Indochin. Pièce 114]

————. *Van De Phu Nu* [The Question of Women]. Saigon: Duy Tan Thu Xa, 1929. Probably Phan's most effective essay after being captured in Shanghai in 1925. First offering a picture of women's rights sundered by patriarchal despots, he then suggests various ways by which women can regain control of their own destinies. [8° Indochin. Pièce 910]

Phan Chu Trinh. *Bai dien thuyet Dao Duc, Luan Ly Dong Tay* [A Public Address on the Ethics and Morality of East and West]. Saigon: Xua Nay, 1926. This plus the following entry reveal Phan Chu Trinh's intense desire to provide the new intelligentsia a world view allowing for both continuity and change. [8° Indochin. Pièce 295]

————. "Bai dien thuyet ve Quan Tri Chu Nghia van Dan Tri Chu Nghia" [A Public Address on Monarchism and Democracy], in Tran Huy Lieu [Nam Kieu], ed., *Tieu*

Su Ong Phan Chau Trinh [A Biography of Phan Chu Trinh] (Saigon: Dong Phap Thoi Bao, 1926), pp. 68–86. Both speeches are also reprinted in The Nguyen, *Phan Chu Trinh* (Saigon: Tan Viet, 1956), pp. 101–164.

———. *That Dieu Thu* [Seven-Point Letter]. Chinese original sent to King Khai Dinh in 1922 as a condemnation of his behavior. A *quoc ngu* translation appears in Tran Huy Lieu, ed., *Tieu Su Ong Phan Chau Trinh* [A Biography of Phan Chu Trinh] (Saigon: Dong Phap Thoi Bao, 1926), pp. 25–43. Also available as *Thu That Dieu* (Hue: Anh Minh, 1958), and as "That Dieu Tran" in NCLS 66 (Sept. 1964), pp. 15–21, 31.

Phan Dinh Long. *Cay Kim Chi Nam* [The Compass Needle]. Saigon: Dan Tri Tho Xa, 1928. Although sharply critical of French policies, the author accepts French protection and cautions Vietnamese youth against violence. [8° Indochin. Pièce 788]

Phan Ke Binh and Le Van Phuc. *Nam Hai Di Nhan Liet Truyen* [Stories of Outstanding Heroes of the South Seas]. 5th printing. Hanoi: Tonkinoise, 1930. Used in preparation for baccalaureate examinations. The original text, published by Phan Ke Binh alone about 1912, was revised by Le Van Phuc to suit 1920s conditions. [8° Indochin. 1333]

Phan Khoi. "Doc cuon *Nho Giao* cua Ong Tran Trong Kim" [Reading Tran Trong Kim's *Confucianism*]. PNTV 54 (29 May 1930), pp. 11–15. The start of a polemic that can be followed in PNTV 60, 63, 64, 71, 72 and 74. Tran Trong Kim's replies are also appendixed to later editions of his *Nho Giao*.

———. "Su dung chu Tau trong tieng Viet Nam" (Using Chinese Words in the Vietnamese Language). PNTV 121 (3 Mar. 1932), pp. 5–7. The problems of word coinage summarized, and a solution proposed.

———. "Van de phu nu giai phong voi nhan sanh quan" [The Women's Liberation Question in Relation to One's Philosophy of Life]. PNTV 158 (7 July 1932), pp. 5–7; and 160 (21 July 1932), pp. 5–8. The author's stress on attitudinal transformation was sharply rebutted by Nguyen Thi Chinh in PNTV 162 (4 Aug. 1932), pp. 9–11, who instead demanded changes in the mode of production.

Phan Ngoc Lien. "Tim Hieu ve cong tac Van Dong, Giao Duc Quan Chung cua Ho Chu Tich trong thoi gian Nguoi o Pac-Bo" [Investigating President Ho's Mass Mobilization and Education Efforts While at Pac Bo]. NCLS 149 (Mar.–Apr. 1973), pp. 13–21, 30. An insight on the training program instituted by Ho Chi Minh upon his return from overseas in early 1941.

Phan Quan. "Biet kho lam de: hoc thuyet cua Ton Van" [To Know Is Difficult, to Act Is Easy: Sun Yat-sen's Thesis]. *Thanh Nghi* 28 (1 Jan. 1943), pp. 2–4. The theory and practice question cogently raised.

Phan Van Hum. *Bien Chung Phap Pho Thong* [The Dialectic Popularized]. Cho Lon: Do Phuong Que, 1936. Vietnam's best Trotskyist writer at work, relying heavily on Engel's *Anti-Dühring*, but incorporating many of his own pithy examples. Praxis receives special emphasis. [16° Indochin. 195]

———. *Ngoi Tu Kham Lon* [Sitting in Saigon Central Prison]. Saigon: Dan Toc, 1957. First serialized in *Than Chung*, January 1929, then republished as a book in Saigon: Bao Ton, 1929. A powerful instant memoir.

———. *Vuong Duong Minh* [Wang Yang-ming]. Hanoi: Triet Hoc Tan Viet, 1944. Based largely on compendiums published in China in the 1930s. Phan sees Wang's "unity of knowledge and action" as having major significance for contemporary Vietnam. [16° Indochin. 629]

Phan Van Truong. *Viec Giao Duc Hoc Van trong Dan Toc Annam* [Educational Efforts among the Annamite People]. Saigon: Xua Nay, 1925. Public address in Saigon, 17 March 1925. An impassioned call to build *quoc ngu* competence rather than accepting the existing French or Franco-Vietnamese programs. [8° Indochin. Pièce 229]

Quoc Thuy. *Van De Dan Toc* [The National Question]. Hanoi: Dai Chung, 1946. Essay signed 16 Sept. 1945. A clear de-emphasis of internal class struggle. [16° Indochin. Pièce 1467]

Sieu Hai. *Hoa Chien Tranh voi Van De Phong Thu Dong Duong* [The Peril of War and the Problem of Defending Indochina]. Vinh: Tu Sach Tien Bo, 1938. One of several pointed Popular Front proposals for colonial reforms that would give Vietnamese some reasons to resist the Japanese. [16° Indochin. Pièce 614]

[Nguyen] Son Tra. *Giai Cap la Gi?* [What Is a Class?]. Tourane [Da Nang]: Tu Tuong Moi, 1938. The author led an energetic radical education program in central Vietnam during the Popular Front period. [16° Indochin. Pièce 615]

Tan Da [Nguyen Khac Hieu]. *Tan Da Van Van* [Tan Da's Poetry]. 2 vols. Hanoi: Huong Son, 1952. First published in 1941–43. The author provided something of a bridge between turn-of-the-century poets like Tu Xuong and Nguyen Khuyen and the "New Poetry" (Tho Moi) movement of the 1930s. [16° Indochin. 1795]

Thai Phi. *Mot Nen Giao Duc Viet Nam Moi* [An Educational Foundation for a New Vietnam]. 4th printing. Hanoi: Doi Moi, 1943. Written in early 1941, this essay demonstrates how Vichy French ideology could be combined with Confucianism to both denigrate the existing educational system and buttress elitist "reform" proposals. [16° Indochin. 579]

Than Trong Hue. "Con duong Tien Bo cua Nuoc ta" [Our Country's Progressive Path]. NP 8 (Feb. 1918), pp. 61–64; and NP 9 (Mar. 1918), pp. 125–31. A prominent Hue mandarin chides people for not being more disciplined in the face of modern challenges.

Thanh Huong. *Trotsky va Phan Cach Mang* [Trotsky and Counterrevolution]. Saigon: Tien Phong Thu Xa, 1937. Bitterly attacks local Trotskyists for their "proletariat-above-all" approach, which leads to isolation and repression. [16° Indochin. 187]

Thich, J. M. *Van De Cong San* [The Communist Question]. Qui Nhon: Imprimerie de Quinhon, 1927. The Bolshevik peril as described by a Vietnamese Catholic priest. [8° Indochin. 251]

Thien Chieu. *Tai sao toi da cam on Dao Phat?* [Why Did I Thank Buddhism?] My Tho: Nam Cuong, 1936. A former Buddhist priest reaffirms his commitment to compassion, equality, and freedom, but argues that all religions, Buddhism included, have diverted people from achieving these goals. [16° Indochin. Pièce 722]

Thuc Nghiep Dan Bao. Tap An Phan Boi Chau [Phan Boi Chau Trial Proceedings].

Hanoi: Thuc Nghiep, 1925. Compilation of relevant articles in the 25–27 November 1925 issues of this daily newspaper. [8° Indochin. Pièce 327]

———. *Nhung Tin Tuc va Du Luan ve Ong Phan Boi Chau* [News and Public Opinion about Phan Boi Chau]. Hanoi: Thuc Nghiep, 1926. A sequel to the previous title. [8° Indochin. Pièce 163]

Ton Thi Que. *Chi Mot Con Duong* [Only One Road]. Nghe An: Ban Nghien Cuu Lich Su Dang, 1972. Memoirs of a female provincial-level ICP activist, particularly useful for the period 1925–35.

Tran Dan Tien. *Nhung Mau Chuyen ve Doi Hoat Dong cua Ho Chu Tich* [Various Anecdotes on Chairman Ho's Life Activities]. 4th printing. Hanoi: Van Hoc, 1960.

Tran Dinh Nam. *Tri Khon* [Intelligence]. Hue: Quan Hai Tung Thu, 1928. An introduction to Western psychology. [8° Indochin. Pièce 545]

Tran Do. "Nhung Mau Truyen . . . Sung" (Some Anecdotes on . . . Guns). In Chanh Thi et al., *Len Duong Thang Loi* [On the Road to Victory]. Hanoi: Van Hoc, 1960. A member of the security detachment for the ICP Central Committee in 1944–45 recalls the mystique of weaponry.

Tran Hoc Hai et al. *Vo San Hoa* [Proletarianization]. Hanoi: Thanh Nien, 1972. Memoirs of the late 1920s.

Tran Huu Do. *Bien Chung Phap* [Dialectics]. Saigon: Bao Ton, 1936. Down-to-earth explanation of Hegel by a Confucian-educated medical practitioner who joined the ICP. [16° Indochin. Pièce 310]

———. *De Quoc Chu Nghia* [Imperialism]. Saigon: Tan Van Hoa Tong Tho, 1937. Collation of translations and condensations of materials from the Third Internationale or the French Communist Party. [16° Indochin. 181]

———. *Hon Doc Lap* [The Independent Soul]. Saigon: Tu Do Tong Tho, 1926. The need to reassert the Vietnamese national spirit and to persevere against all obstacles. [8° Indochin. 192]

———. *Tieng Chuong Truy Hon* [The Bell Which Summons Souls]. Saigon: Tu Do Tong Tho, 1926. Discusses six forms of political passivity, together with three aspects of the Vietnamese world view that must be totally altered. [8° Indochin. Pièce 15]

———. *To Co Mat Quyen Tu Do* [The Causes of Our Loss of Freedom]. Saigon: Tu Do Tong Tho, 1926. A Social Darwinian critique of Vietnamese weaknesses. [8° Indochin. 417]

Tran Huu Ta. "Doc Hoi Ky Cach Mang, Nghi ve Ve Dep cua nguoi Chien Si Cong San Viet-Nam" [Reading Revolutionary Memoirs and Thinking of the Splendid Appearance of Vietnamese Communist Militants]. TCVH 2–1977, pp. 17–28. Reflections on the 82 Communist Party memoirs of the period 1930–45 published as of 1976.

Tran Huy Lieu. *Mot Bau Tam Su* [Gourdful of Confidences]. Saigon: Nam Dong Thu Xa, 1927. An emotional essay on Vietnam's plight, by one of the leading young journalists of the day. Draws many ideas from Liang Ch'i-ch'ao, but puts them in a different context. [8° Indochin. Pièce 61]

———. *Nghia Lo Khoi Nghia* [The Nghia Lo Uprising]. Hanoi: Hoi Van Hoa Cuu

Quoc, 1946. Self-critical description of a March 1945 prison breakout that was drowned in blood.

——. [Nam Kieu]. *Tieu Su Ong Phan Chau Trinh* [A Biography of Phan Chu Trinh]. Saigon: Dong Phap Thoi Bao, 1926. Two hundred pages of life story, public lecture reprints, funeral observances, and historical assessments.

——, comp. *Viec Phan Boi Chau* [The Phan Boi Chau Affair]. Saigon: Xua Nay, 1926. The November 1925 trial and subsequent demonstrations as reported in *Dong Phap Thoi Bao* [Indochina-France Times]. [8° Indochin. Pièce 294]

—— et al. *Cach Mang Can Dai Viet-Nam* [Vietnam's Modern Revolution]. 12 vols. Hanoi: Van Su Dia, 1955–1958. Vols. 4–12 deal with the period 1920–45.

Tran Thi Nhu Man. "Gia Dinh va Xa Hoi" [The Family and Society]. *Phu Nu Tung San,* no. 1 (May 1929), pp. 1–35. Draws inspiration from the theories of Lewis Morgan and Emile Durkheim. [8° Indochin. 837]

Tran Trong Kim. *Mot Con Gio Bui* [A Puff of Dust]. Saigon: Vinh Son, 1969. An autobiography written in 1949, of value mainly for the period 1943–45.

——. *Nho Giao* [Confucianism]. 2 vols. 4th printing. Saigon: Tan Viet, 1962. Originally published in 1929–1930. Reviewed critically by Phan Khoi in PNTV 54 (29 May 1930), pp. 11–15, precipitating an important polemic. A more favorable review by Pham Quynh (Thuong Chi) is to be found in NP 149 (April 1930), pp. 307–10. Later criticized by Ngo Tat To and Dao Duy Anh (qq.v.).

——. *Quan Niem ve cuoc Nhan Sinh* [Concepts of Human Life]. Hanoi: Trung Bac Tan Van, 1936. Reprint of a public lecture in Nam Dinh, 18 Jan. 1936. Taoist, Buddhist, Confucian, and scientific conceptions all discussed, the author ultimately opting for a "live-and-let-live" attitude. [8° Indochin. Pièce 2670]

——. *Viet Nam Su Luoc* [Outline History of Vietnam]. Saigon: Tan Viet, 1958. First published in Hanoi in 1928. An influential work, often extracted for use in school texts. The author's approach is similar to that of traditional court historians, and he avoids the colonial period. [16° Indochin. 1003]

—— et al. *Luan Ly Giao Khoa Thu* [Textbook on Morality]. 3 vols. (for the three primary grades), 6th printing. Hanoi: Nha Hoc Chinh Dong Phap, 1933. First published 1925. [8° Indochin. 232, 8° Indochin. 1940, and 8° Indochin. 1956]

Tran Tu Binh. *Phu Rieng Do* [Red Phu Rieng]. 2nd printing. Hanoi: Lao Dong, 1971. Memoir of survival and struggle on a Cochinchina rubber plantation, 1927–30.

Tran Van Giau. *Giai Cap Cong Nhan Viet Nam* [The Vietnamese Working Class], 3 vols. Hanoi: Vien Su Hoc, 1963.

——. *Su Phat Trien cua Tu Tuong o Viet-Nam tu The Ky XIX den Cach Mang Thang Tam* [The Development of Ideas in Vietnam from the Nineteenth Century to the August Revolution]. 3 vols. Hanoi: Khoa Hoc Xa Hoi, 1973 and 1975. The best intellectual history of Vietnam to be published in any language. Vol. 1, which delineates nineteenth-century "feudal consciousness" and its failure to deal with epic historical challenges, was reviewed by Hoang Tuan Pho in NCLS 161 (Mar.–Apr. 1975), pp. 69–74, and by Phong Hien in *Vietnam Courier,* nos. 42, 43, and 44. Under the rubric of "bourgeois consciousness," vol. 2 treats the period 1900–30; it is most valuable for its 200-page discussion of religious movements. Vol. 3, on "proletarian consciousness," is completed but not yet published.

Tran Van Tang. "Qua Khu va Hien Tai" [Past and Present]. NP 106 (June 1926), pp. 413–33. A coherent counterattack on Darwinism and scientism, as well as a defense of the link between ethics and politics.

Trinh Dinh Ru (Ngau Tri). *Nu Sinh Doc Ban* [Co-ed Reader]. Haiphong: Nguyen Kinh, 1926. A third-year primary school text with many patriotic overtones. [8° Indochin. 465]

Trung Bac Tan Van. *Viec Phan Boi Chau tai Hoi Dong De Hinh* [The Phan Boi Chau Affair at the Criminal Court Session]. Hanoi: Vinh Thanh, 1925. An extensive record of the 23 Nov. 1925 trial. [8° Indochin. Pièce 326]

Truong Chinh. *Cach Mang Dan Toc Dan Chu Nhan Dan Viet-Nam* [The Vietnamese People's Democratic National Revolution]. 2 vols. Hanoi: Su That, 1975. Selected writings of a key ICP leader. Vol. 1 includes some of his clandestine newspaper articles, 1941–45.

―――. *Chu Nghia Mac va Van Hoa Viet-Nam* [Marxism and Vietnamese Culture]. 2nd printing. Hanoi: Su That, 1974. Originally presented at a conference of cultural cadres, July 1948.

―――. "May nguyen tac lon cua cuoc van dong Van Hoa Viet Nam moi luc nay" [Major Principles for Activating the New Vietnamese Culture]. HT-5; pp. 480–85. An expansion of the 1943 "Cultural Theses," written in Sept. 1944 and published in *Tien Phong*, no. 2 (1945).

Truong Sinh. "Len Duong Thang Loi" [On the Road to Victory]. In Chanh Thi et al., *Len Duong Thang Loi*. Hanoi: Van Hoc, 1960. The author's two contributions in Bui Cong Trung et al., *Nguoi Truoc Nga, Nguoi Sau Tien* (Hanoi: Van Hoc, 1960) combine with this piece to give an excellent view of ICP activities in Quang Tri province.

Truong Thi My and Nguyen Thi Hung. *Niem Tin Khong Bao Gio Tat* [Feelings of Trust Never Extinguished]. Hanoi: Phu Nu, 1967. Two female ICP cadres recall events climaxing in the August 1945 Revolution.

Van Tao. *Chu Nghia Anh Hung Cach Mang Viet Nam* [Vietnamese Revolutionary Heroism]. Hanoi: Khoa Hoc Xa Hoi, 1972. An attempt to blend tradition and revolution, nation and class—with the Party naturally infallible on all matters.

Van Tien Dung. "Di tim Lien Lac" [Trying to Establish Contact]. In Chanh Thi et al., *Len Duong Thang Loi*. Hanoi: Van Hoc, 1960. Under suspicion as a double agent, the author built his own local clandestine network until being cleared by the ICP Central Committee in March 1943. The memoir is continued in Le Thiet Hung et al., *Rung Yen The* (Hanoi: Quan Doi Nhan Dan, 1962).

Viet Minh (Vietnam Independence League). Binh Dan Hoc Vu (Department of Mass Education). *Ngay Hoi Lon* [A Great Festival Day]. Hanoi: Dan Chung, Dec. 1945. A didactic story about villagers voting in a democratic election. [16° Indochin. Pièce 1614]

Viet Minh. Tong Bo (General Office). *Bac Son Khoi Nghia* [The Bac Son Uprising]. 4th printing. Hanoi: Tu Sach Cuu Quoc, 1946. Events of late 1940 along the Sino-Vietnamese frontier described and assessed. One source ascribes this essay to Le Duc Ton. [16° Indochin. Pièce 1570]

Viet Nam, Cong Hoa Xa Hoi Chu Nghia (Socialist Republic of Vietnam). *Suoi Reo* [Bubbling Spring]. Son La: Ty Thong Tin Van Hoa, 1977. Poems from Son La prison, including those of Le Duc Tho, Xuan Thuy, and Tran Huy Lieu.

Viet Nam, Dang Lao Dong (Vietnam Workers' Party). *Cach Mang Thang Muoi va Cach Mang Viet Nam* [The October Revolution and the Vietnamese Revolution]. Hanoi: Su That, 1967. Valuable for its reprints of Vietnamese materials 1924–44 relating to the Soviet Union.

———. *Cuoc Van Dong Cach Mang Thang Tam o Ha-Noi* [Activating the August Revolution in Hanoi]. Hanoi: Ban Nghien Cuu Lich Su Dang Thanh Uy Ha-noi, 1970. Devoid of personalities, but very helpful in understanding general attitudes, organizations, and tactics.

———. *Ngon Co Giai Phong* [The Flag of Liberation]. Hanoi: Su That, 1955. First published in 1946. Reprints of *Co Giai Phong* and *Tap Chi Cong San* articles, 1942–1945.

———. *Nhung Su Kien Lich Su Dang* [Historical Facts about the Party]. Vol. 1 (1920–45). Hanoi: Su That, 1976. Large quantity of information organized chronologically, with very little analysis.

———. *So Thao Lich Su Tinh Dang Bo Nghe An* [Preliminary History of the Nghe An Provincial Party Branch]. Vinh: Dang Bo Nghe An, 1967. Discusses the Party's ups and downs not only in terms of external pressures but also internal differences.

———. *Ve Su Lanh Dao Cua Dang tren Mat Tran Tu Tuong va Van Hoa 1930–1945* [The Party's Leadership on the Ideological and Cultural Front, 1930–45]. Hanoi: Su That, 1960. Excerpts and reprints of scores of relevant documents and articles.

Viet Nam, Hoi Van Hoa Cuu Quoc (Vietnam National Salvation Cultural Association). *Quyen va Bon Phan lam Dan* [The Rights and Responsibilities of a Citizen]. Hanoi: Hoi Van Hoa Cuu Quoc, 1945. Early Viet Minh civics primer. [16° Indochin. Pièce 1131]

Vo Ba Phan. *Van Dong Giai Phong Dan Toc* [Activating National Liberation]. Saigon: Tan Van Hoa Tong Tho, 1937. A Marxist analysis, but probably not under ICP direction. [16° Indochin. 193]

Vo Nguyen Giap [Van Dinh]. *Con Duong Chinh: Van De Dan Toc Giai Phong o Dong Duong* [The Main and Proper Road: The Question of National Liberation in Indochina]. Hanoi: Dan Chung, 1939. A vigorous attack on Japanese fascists and Vietnamese Trotskyists, with the clear suggestion of armed struggle. [8° Indochin, Pièce 2517]

———. *Muon hieu ro tinh hinh Quan Su o Tau* [Understanding Clearly the Military Situation in China]. Hanoi: Dan Chung, 1939. Description and some analysis, probably based mainly on a careful reading of current news reports. [16° Indochin. Pièce 694]

Vu Dinh Hoe. *Nhung Phuong Phap Giao Duc o cac nuoc va Van de Cai Cach Giao*

Duc [Education Methods in Various Countries and the Question of Educational Reform]. Hanoi: Thanh Nghi Tung Thu, May 1945. Compare with Thai Phi essay, cited above. [8° Indochin. 2669]

Vu Dinh Lien, Nguyen Trac, et al., ed. *Hop Tuyen Tho Van Viet Nam* [A Collection of Vietnamese Poetry and Prose]. 6 vols. Hanoi: Van Hoa, 1963. Vol. 4 (1858–1930) and vol. 5 (1930–45) are particularly relevant.

Vu Huy Phuc. "Vai net ve phong trao thanh toan nan mu chu o Viet Nam" [Some Comments on the Movement to Wipe out Illiteracy in Vietnam]. NCLS 30 (Sept. 1961), pp. 33–42. First-hand account, especially useful for its description of Department of Mass Education activities.

Vu Trong Phung. *Giong To* [The Tempest]. Saigon: Khai Tri, 1966. First published in Hanoi, 1937. The prime example of naturalist fiction.

X. X. "Triet Hoc voi Cuoc Doi" [Philosophy and Life]. Serialized intermittently in PNTV 198 (4 May 1933) through 226 (30 Nov. 1933). A popular introduction, beginning with Aristotle and Confucius, ending with Hegel and Marx. Possibly written by Ho Huu Tuong.

Xuan Dieu. "Su trong Sang cua tieng Viet trong tho" [The Brilliance of Vietnamese as Seen in Poetry]. TCVH 3–1966, pp. 9–20, 27. A poet reviews *nom* and *quoc ngu* poetry from Nguyen Trai to the 1930s.

Xuan Thuy. "Suoi Reo Nam Ay" [The Bubbling Spring in That Year]. In Chanh Thi et al., *Len Duong Thang Loi*. Hanoi: Van Hoc, 1960. Clandestine newspaper efforts in Son La prison, 1941–43.

INDEX

Designer: Nancy Guinn
Compositor: Computer Typesetting Services, Inc.
Printer: Thomson-Shore
Binder: Thomson-Shore
Text: 10/12 Caledonia
Display: Caledonia